ARTIFICIAL INTELLIGENCE PLANNING SYSTEMS
Proceedings of the First International Conference

Edited by James Hendler

June 15–17, 1992
College Park, Maryland

Sponsored by
AMERICAN ASSOCIATION FOR ARTIFICIAL INTELLIGENCE
DEFENSE ADVANCED RESEARCH PROJECTS AGENCY
UNIVERSITY OF MARYLAND INSTITUTE FOR ADVANCED COMPUTER STUDIES

Sponsoring Editor: Michael B. Morgan
Production Manager: Yonie Overton
Production Editor: Carol Leyba
Cover Designer: Victoria Ann Philp
Additional Composition/Pasteup: Technically Speaking Publications

Morgan Kaufmann Publishers, Inc.

Editorial Office:
2929 Campus Drive, Suite 260
San Mateo, California 94403

96 95 94 93 92   5 4 3 2 1

Library of Congress Cataloging-in-Publication Data

Artificial intelligence planning systems: proceedings of the first
    international conference, June 15-17, 1992, College Park, Maryland /
    edited by James Hendler ; sponsored by American Association for
    Artificial Intelligence, Defense Advanced Research Projects Agency,
    University of Maryland Institute for Advanced Computer Studies.
        p. cm.
    Includes bibliographical references and index.
    ISBN 1-55860-250-X
    1. Artificial intelligence—Congresses. 2. Planning—Data
processing—Congresses. I. Hendler, James A. II. American
Association for Artificial Intelligence. III. United States.
Defense Advanced Research Projects Agency. IV. University of
Maryland, College Park. Institute for Advanced Computer Studies.
Q334.A777 1992
006.3'3—dc   92-13636
                                                         CIP

Organization of the 1st International Conference on AI Planning Systems

Conference Chair

Drew McDermott, Yale University

Program Chair

James Hendler, University of Maryland

Program Committee

P. Agre, *UC San Diego*
J. Allen, *Rochester University*
P. Bonasso, *MITRE Corp.*
T. Dean, *Brown University*
M. Drummond, *Nasa Ames Research Center*
M. Georgeff, *Australian AI Institute*
M. Ginsberg, *Stanford University*
K. Hammond, *University of Chicago*
S. Hanks, *University of Washington*
J. Hertzberg, *GMD, Germany*
S. Kambhampati, *Arizona State Univ.*
P. Langley, *Nasa Ames Research Center*
A. Lansky, *Nasa Ames Research Center*
D. Nau, *University of Maryland*
E. Pednault, *Bell Laboratories*
M. Pollack, *University of Pittsburgh*
A. Segre, *Cornell University*
R. Simmons, *Carnegie-Mellon University*
S. Steel, *University of Essex, UK*
L. Stein, *Massachusetts Institute of Technology*
K. Sycara, *Carnegie-Mellon University*
A. Tate, *AIAI, Edinburgh Univ., UK*
M. Zweben, *Nasa Ames Research Center*

Foreign Chair

W.E. Hillier, *IEE, UK*

Acknowledgements

We would like to thank the following people for their help in the organization and running of this conference:

Conference Organization
Larry Davis
Nancy Parker
Johanna Weinstein
Dawn Vance

Additional Reviewers
John Benoit
R. Peter Bonasso
Christopher Elsæsser
Kutluhan Erol
Gerd Große
Hans Werner Güesgen
Alexander Horz
François Félix Ingrand
Paul Lehner
T. Richard MacMillan
Ambujashka Mahanti
James Reggia
Josef Shneeberger
Stephen J. Smith

Artwork
Rebecca Neimark
Lee Spector

Funding
American Association for Artificial Intelligence
Defense Advanced Research Projects Agency

Table of Contents

Posters

Foreword: Planning the Planning Conference

James Hendler
Program Chair
Computer Science Dept.
University of Maryland
College Park, MD 20742

Drew McDermott
Conference Chair
Computer Science Department
Yale University
New Haven, CT 06520

If you're looking for a domain for a new planning system that requires a huge amount of domain knowledge, an ability to react to unexpected events, powerful error handling mechanisms, and significant multiple-agent reasoning, then have we got a suggestion for you: Let it be the chair of the next AI Planning Systems conference!

Seriously though, it is our great pleasure to welcome you to the Proceedings of the 1st International Conference on AI Planning Systems. This conference has been several years in the making, and has involved a large number of people in the planning community, the University of Maryland Institute for Advanced Computer Studies (UMIACS), the American Association for Artificial Intelligence (AAAI), the UK's Institute of Electrical Engineers (IEE), and the Defense Advanced Research Projects Agency (DARPA).

This conference was conceived prior to the DARPA workshop on Innovative Approaches to Planning, Scheduling, and Control held in November, 1990. An ad hoc steering committee was formed to brainstorm on the plans for the conference, and a questionnaire was circulated to attendees at the DARPA workshop soliciting feedback. We received a large number of comments, suggestions, and criticisms, and the format of the current conference was developed based on this feedback. A proposal was put together, organizational support was provided by UMIACS, funding was provided by the AAAI and DARPA, the UK's IEE provided help in publicizing the conference in Europe and thus this conference became a reality.

We hope you will be pleased with the result. We have attempted to bring together a diverse group of people representing many approaches to the design and evaluation of planning systems. Although the choice of papers and posters was made solely on technical merit, the diversity of those which were finally accepted was a pleasant surprise. You will see results including interesting practical algorithms for achieving efficiency in planning, formal results on the completeness and complexity of planning algorithms in simple domains, the integration of planning theory with robot programming, cognitive approaches to planning, and many others.

In addition, we have tried to arrange a set of invited talks and panels that will both examine the role planning research plays in the larger AI picture and examine ways in which the community can evaluate our own products. The invited talks aim to represent a spectrum of views, with Earl Sacerdoti reflecting on the past (and current presence) of AI planning research, Nort Fowler reflecting on the present needs of DARPA and other "consumers" of planning technology, and James Allen discussing one view of the future of the field. Panels are aimed at exploring how to evaluate current systems and where the future of the field lies.

A great many people have put significant time and effort into the design and organization of this meeting. We hope you will agree that it was well worth the trouble.

Papers

Declarative Goals in Reactive Plans[*]

Michael Beetz and Drew McDermott
Yale University, Department of Computer Science
P.O. Box 2158, Yale Station
New Haven, CT 06520
beetz@cs.yale.edu, mcdermott@cs.yale.edu

Abstract

Classical planning started with goals and produced plans. To do something similar in a reactive framework, it is necessary to treat the achievement or maintenance of a goal as specifying a default behavior, while at the same time being able to deploy tools to generate more complex plans. These tools rely on representing the relations between goals and plan patterns that achieve them. An important component of the representation is a set of fast, local methods for making probabilistic estimations of the quality of proposed plans, including their *robustness, completeness,* and *efficiency.*

1 Introduction

A *reactive plan* is a program that specifies how an agent is to react to its environment. There is currently no widely accepted theory of how to generate reactive plans, or even if it makes sense for an agent to have an explicit plan when there are a lot of events for it to react to quickly. If things are happening too fast for the agent to compare the expected consequences of alternative courses of action, then it will have no option but to react with whatever behavior presents itself. When there is a little more breathing room, the agent can make such comparisons, but must still generate the alternative plans and compare them as fast as possible. Under such time pressure, it is unlikely that it will be possible to generate complex reactive plans from first principles. Instead, most plans will be made up of large canned segments retrieved from a library, pasted together, and debugged [Fir87, McD90, SD87].

The traditional way of giving a problem to a planner is to give it a list of propositions to be made true, such as "There should be at least three boxes in Room

101," or "Every blue block that is now in the kitchen should be in the living room." We will call this specifying *goals* to the planner instead of specifying *jobs*, such as "Find the white box in Room 202 and take it to Room 101." The jobs formulation is, in a way, more general, because a goal G can be thought of as a job "Achieve G." However, a goal $G_1 \wedge G_2$ cannot in general be decomposed into two such jobs, because of the requirement that both conjuncts be true in the end. Furthermore, thinking of problems as sets of goals has certain advantages, notably that it decouples the problem specification from the solution method.

Although goals are traditional, we run into trouble when we attempt to adopt the traditional techniques for generating plans to achieve them. These methods typically start from a description of a set of *operators* with propositional consequences (for example, addlists and deletelists). An operator is relevant to a goal if it adds propositions involving the predicates mentioned in the goal. A plan is typically found by proposing an operator to solve part of the goal, then embedding that operator in a plan for the rest of the goal [McD91b]. Unfortunately, the choice of operators and embeddings is not obvious, so we quickly get an intractable search problem [Cha87].

The best approach we see to reactive goal decomposition is to assume that for every goal G there is a default plan for the job (achieve G). If there is no time to think, this is the plan that gets executed. When there is more time, the planner can look for better plans. Methods for improving plans are represented as transformation rules and indexed by the patterns of plans they apply to. At the heart of our planner (called XFRM) [McD90] is a global technique for plan generation based on a *projector* and a *transformer*. The projector is used to predict what will happen when the current overall plan is executed. The outcome of a projector is a timeline and a set of "bugs". If bugs are anticipated, then the transformer tries to eliminate them by trying standard repairs indexed off the bugs. A typical bug in a plan for the goal $\forall x(P(x) \supset Q(x))$ might be "Some x with property P gets property Q

---

[*]The work reported here was supported by DARPA through ONR under contract N00014-91-J-1577.

and then loses it." A repair might be "Find and include a plan for preventing objects from losing property Q."

We distinguish between *global* and *local* methods for evaluating these plans. Global methods are so called because they consider the plan as a whole in the context of the current model of the environment. They are expensive because there may be several possible transformations which the planner has to search among. Local methods ask more constrained questions about the particular goal being planned for. An example of such a question for the goal $\forall x(P(x) \supset Q(x))$ is "How many objects have property P?" The answers to such questions determine which plans to select. As we will attempt to show in this paper, we can hope to use local methods to address some fairly sophisticated issues in selection of alternative plans under uncertainty and with respect to different optimality criteria.

XFRM searches through a space of complete and executable plans. The search space is defined by the set of transformation rules that are applied by the planner. XFRM moves through the search space by finding bugs in the current plan (for instance, a subplan that needs to be improved or debugged), determining the set of applicable transformation rules, and applying the one that is ranked best with respect to the local estimation methods.

The paper is organized into two main sections. Section 2 describes and discusses the representation used in the XFRM system, and section 3 describes the planning algorithms that operate on those representations.

2   Problems and Representations

XFRM could be used as a planning framework for a variety of domains. Currently we use it for errand planning in a simulated world of discrete locations. Some of the locations are rooms with doors which can be locked. At each location there are several objects. Objects have "categories" that are basically shape labels (block, pyramid, ...). One category, box, is special in that other types of objects can be put into boxes. Some objects move autonomously, and there may exist other agents that move objects around. The planner controls an agent that can look for objects with simple visual properties, reach out one of its hands to the positions of those objects, grasp, and thereby pick an object up. It can also lock and unlock rooms. If rooms are unlocked objects may appear in and disappear from them. The planner has a partial model of its environment, it knows about the location of rooms, but in general does not know what they contain. Expectations about how many objects of some sort are in a room are given by prior probability distributions and updated based on the observations of the robot. Sometimes the agent will be told to look for any object matching a description; other times it will be told to

find a particular object, but as far as it is concerned this can only mean: Find a unique object that resembles the target object and is in the right vicinity.

2.1   RPL - A Reactive Plan Language

It would be possible for the planner to feed low-level commands to the effectors directly, but we assume that it is usually better to think through a larger set of commands, a *plan*, and hand it off to the *plan interpreter* for execution. The plan is actually a program that can control the behavior of the agent completely without further intervention by the planner. These plans are written in RPL (Reactive Plan Language). Space does not allow a complete description of RPL (but see [McD91a]). Here we want to discuss extensions to RPL to support planning for declarative goals.

```
(achieve-for-all (λ (x) (and (category x block)
                             (color x blue)
                             (in x kitchen)))
                 (λ (x) (in x livingroom)))
```

Figure 1: RPL code for the task *"get all the blue blocks in the kitchen to the livingroom."*

RPL is a Lisp-like language, which, unlike classical plan languages, provides constructs for sequencing, conditionals, loops, local variables, and subroutines. Plans can explicitly fail if they detect a situation that they can't handle. Several high-level concepts (interrupts, monitors) are provided that can be used to synchronize parallel actions, to make plans reactive, etc. To add declarative goals, we simply augment our existing language with constructs like (achieve P) and (maintain P), or (prevent P), where P is a property of the world.

Constraints on the language come from both the plan interpreter and the planning system. From the point of view of the plan interpreter, it is important that the language be expressive enough to describe all sorts of complex problem-solving behaviors that the robot needs to perform. From the planner's point of view, it is important that the language describe plans transparently enough to allow the planner to reason about them. Fortunately, goals are comparatively easy to reason about. After projecting a plan to achieve a goal, the planner needs only check whether the goal is projected to be true; and similarly for plans to keep a fact true or false.

2.2   Representing Knowledge about RPL Constructs

It's no use having a plan step of the form (achieve P) unless the system actually knows what to do to make P true. This is especially true in a reactive system, which cannot tolerate nonexecutable plan fragments. Hence associated with P must be a *default* achieve *method* that can always be executed (and will, in benign circumstances actually cause P to become true.) But there must be other information associated with this action. We bundle this information into RPL *construct descriptions, predicate descriptions,* and *heuristic transformation rules.* For example, there will be a RPL construct definition matching (achieve (in x loc)), and specifying, to begin with, that the canned plan (deliver x loc) is the appropriate default method. Further information about the behavior of in assertions is found in the predicate description for in.

RPL construct description achieve-for-all	
syntax	(achieve-for-all (λ (?x) ?desc) (λ (?y) ?goal))
postcond	$\forall x \exists t. \ start \leq t \wedge t \leq end$ $\wedge \ holds(\sigma(?x \leftarrow x)(?desc)\ t)$ $\rightarrow holds(\sigma(?y \leftarrow x)(?goal)\ end)$
execution	achieve-for-all.default
generation	{ach-all.1 ach-all.2 ach-all.3}
debugging	{achieve-for-all.debug}
scheduler	achieve-for-all.scheduler

Figure 2: Representation structure for the representation of the RPL command achieve-for-all in XFRM. ?v denotes a pattern variable with name v. $\sigma(exp_1 \leftarrow exp_2)exp$ is the expression that results from the substitution of exp_2 for all occurrences of exp_1 in exp.

We start by discussing RPL construct descriptions, using the achieve-for-all construct as an example. The syntactic structure of the achieve-for-all statement is (achieve-for-all d g). The first argument of the achieve-for-all statement is a description specifying a set of objects. The second argument is a description that has to be achieved for each object in the set. The intention of the RPL construct achieve-for-all is that all objects which satisfied the property d at a time instant between the begin and end of the achieve-for-all task have to satisfy the property g at the end of the task. (An instance of achieve-for-all might have been supplied by the user, or itself be the output of a transformation of a quantified goal.)

The RPL construct description for the achieve-for-all statement is shown in figure 2. An RPL construct description specifies the postconditions that must be achieved for the action to be successful. In addition, it contains a default method that is used by the plan interpreter to reduce the expression, a set of heuristic transformation rules which can be applied to optimize and debug the expression, and a scheduler for controlling rule interpretation.

Postconditions are formalized in a temporal logic. The postcondition of achieve-for-all states that any object satisfying the description ?desc at an arbitrary time instant t between the beginning and the end of the achieve-for-all task must satisfy ?goal at the end of the task. A postcondition of an achieve-for-all expression is computed by matching the expression against the pattern in the syntax slot and instantiating the pattern in the postcond slot using the bindings obtained by the match. The postcondition is used by the planner as a query that, given a simulation of a plan, checks whether or not the task has been carried out successfully. The generation slot lists heuristic transformation rules that can be used to generate better candidate plans by transforming the RPL construct. The transformation rules in the generation slot suggest different implementations or improvements that may be advantageous under different circumstances. The different implementations resulting from the application of the transformation rules ach-all.1, ach-all.2, and ach-all.3 to the task in figure 1 are listed in figure 8. A default transformation is stored in the slot execution of each nonprimitive RPL construct and can be applied by the plan interpreter if the RPL construct is to be executed reactively. A default transformation is always applicable and should be, in general, the most reliable and robust method for the performance of the RPL construct in isolation. The debugging slot contains transformation rules for debugging plans when failures are detected during execution and simulation. The scheduler is a function that returns an ordered list of pairs for a given amount of computation time, where the first element in each pair is a transformation rule and the second element is a bound on the time resources assigned for checking the applicability of this rule. The task of the scheduler is to divide the available time resources so that the biggest gains in terms of plan quality can be expected [DB88]. Scheduling is often necessary because transformations that produce better plans require more computation time. Currently, the scheduling functions have to be provided by the programmer.

It would be nice if we had theorems that stated the conditions under which one RPL expression is semantically equivalent to, or a specialization of, another RPL expression. We could then use such a theory to generate transformation rules that would preserve the meaning of a plan while improving its efficiency [BP86]. A transformation rule is said to be *correct* if, for all cases for which its applicability condition holds, a plan matching its *input schema* is semantically equivalent to the one matching its *output schema.* Unfortunately, correct transformation rules are of little practical use for robot planning. The information available in robot planning problems is often uncertain and cannot be formalized as premises or facts which are necessary for proving applicability conditions. Even if we could prove the applicability conditions in principle, those proofs would typically be computationally intractable and could certainly not be derived under real-time constraints.

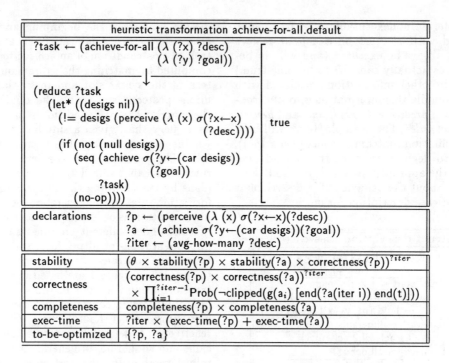

Figure 3: Default transformation rule for the RPL command achieve-for-all

XFRM uses heuristic transformation rules (HTRs) instead of correct transformation rules. HTRs allow a planning system to generate plan hypotheses efficiently using heuristic and associational reasoning. Candidate plans are flexibly generated based on given preferences (e.g., a preference for efficiency over robustness), and expectations about the environment. The use of decision-theoretic methods for choosing between alternative tasks is discussed in [HH90]. Since plan hypotheses are generated based on heuristics they have to be tested (by projection) before being passed to the plan interpreter.

HTRs provide useful plans soon and may continue to improve them [DB88]. HTRs may also have application conditions that are not strong enough to guarantee the maintenance of semantic equivalences of plans. The plan resulting from a transformation might be related to the original plan in several ways. It might be more or less likely to fail, slower or faster, or more or less likely to achieve the top-level task. Different heuristic variants of a correct transformation rule differ in their effects on the robustness, runtime efficiency, or degree of correctness of the resulting plan. Consequently, the planner has to decide quickly which of the rules to choose in order to transform a given piece of code. We are implementing local methods which estimate the quality of a plan under uncertainty and apply decision techniques to choose the most promising transformation.

XFRM evaluates a plan in terms of three qualities, *robustness*, *efficiency*, and *completeness*. The ability of the plan to allow the plan interpreter to recover from execution errors and achieve the postconditions is called the *robustness* of the plan. From a practical point of view, it is useful to separate robustness into *stability* and *correctness*. Stability is the likelihood that the execution of the plan does not result in an error state (explicit failure) from which the system cannot recover without further planning. Correctness is the likelihood that the postcondition of an expression will hold once the expression is executed. The robustness of a RPL expression as the product of its stability and correctness.

The robustness of a plan can be increased by constructing alternative courses of actions such that the plan interpreter can choose between them at runtime, depending on the situations the robot finds itself in [DB90]. Reasoning about disjunctive plans, however, is often very expensive in terms of computational resources. Therefore, the planner should focus on relatively few alternatives and generate others only when necessary, i.e., when none of the alternative ways incorporated in its current plan succeeds. The plan quality *completeness* characterizes this trade-off, representing the likelihood that the planner might find alternative plans which succeed and achieve their postconditions, once the current plan failed. *Execution time* is a third aspect of plan quality, which is estimated based on the estimations for the execution times of the subplans. Often plans which require less execution time should be preferred by the planner.

Figure 3 shows the default transformation rule for the achieve-for-all statement. A representation structure for a heuristic transformation rule consists of two major components: a representation of the transformation performed and methods for estimating the quality of the plan resulting from the plan transformation. In the output plan schema, the perceive expression returns a set of objects d for which $((\lambda\ (?x)\ ?desc)\ d)$ holds. If the set of objects returned by the perception subtask is nonempty, the task for achieving the goal for the first object in desigs is initiated. In the case of a successful achievement, achieve-for-all is recursively called until no object with the property ?desc can be found.

The planner controls the application of transformation rules based on local estimates for the robustness, completeness, and efficiency of the resulting plan. Our claim is that such estimates can be obtained based on the semantics of the plan language, the use of subexpressions, and statistical information. We will support this claim by sketching how we can obtain an estimate of the stability of a plan created by the transformation rule achieve-for-all.default.

The subtasks of the output plan schema are ?p, ?g, and ?task. (See Figure 3.) The semantics of the let* expression implies that the let* expression fails if a subtask for binding local variables or its body fails. Since the output plan schema does not contain code for error recovery, if one of its subtasks fails, then it will do so as well. However, we cannot simply multiply the stabilities of the subtasks because the subtasks interact in various ways and those interactions have to be reflected in the estimation method. These interactions imply that ?g almost certainly fails if ?p returns an object that can't be found later. Other interactions might occur due to the effects of ?p and ?g. Often it is a reasonable assumption that execution errors are equally distributed over the iterations. The programmer provides $(\theta \times stability(?p) \times correctness(?p) \times stability(?a))^{?iter}$ as a mathematical model of the stability of the resulting plan that reflects the considerations above. In this estimation method, θ is an *a priori* estimation of the impact of these interactions on the plan stability. θ can be estimated based on simulations of plans matching the output plan schema. The number of iterations has to be estimated given prior information about the number of objects satisfying $(\lambda\ (?x)\ ?desc)$.

The process of specifying estimation methods for a class of plans is heuristic and error prone. Therefore estimation methods should be tested by generating instances of output plan schemata, simulating them in different environments, evaluating the simulations, and comparing the results with the predictions made by the estimation methods. A powerful method for the revision of estimation methods is their specialization for different types of tasks, like delivery and stacking tasks. Whereas it is reasonable to assume that execution errors in delivery tasks are equally distributed over the number of iterations, stacking operations become less and less robust as stacks grow higher. Other important revision methods include parameter adjustment and the change of mathematical models.

2.3 Representation of Domain Knowledge

In order to project a plan, XFRM must make use of statistical knowledge about the distributions of events and states in the environment. For example, it might know that there are typically between four and twenty blocks in the kitchen. About half of them are usually blue; the rest are red and yellow (equally distributed). If another transportation robot is around, blocks stay in a room, on average, about 40 minutes. In addition to statistical information, knowledge about the domain physics is necessary. Two examples are that every object is, at any instant of time, in exactly one room and that the robot can only perceive objects which are in the same room.

Predicate Description IN	
syntax	(in ?ob ?rm)
pr-density-fct	(category ?ob block) $\rightarrow$ ((((?rm = kitchen) 0.5) ((?rm = livingroom) 0.3) ((?rm = bathroom) 0.2)) (category ?ob robot) $\rightarrow$ (...)
avg-lifetime	(avg-lifetime (in ?ob ?rm) ?t) $\leftarrow$ ((category ?ob block) $\wedge$?t=40min) $\vee$ ((category ?ob robot) $\wedge$?t=2min)
features	functional, perception-constraining
achieve	achieve.in
perceive	perceive.in
prevent	prevent.in
maintain	maintain.in

Figure 4: Representation structure for the predicate "in" in XFRM.

Because propositions are ultimately composed of atomic formulas, it is natural to organize knowledge around predicates. *Predicate descriptions* link predicates to methods for achieving, perceiving, maintaining, and preventing a certain aspect of the world with the predicate formalizing that aspect, along with the statistical information we discussed in the last paragraph. Figure 4 shows the predicate description of the predicate in. Information about typical situations in the environment can be inferred from the probability density functions (slot pr-density-fct) which specify the likelihood of aspects of the environment. Information

RPL construct description	achieve.in
syntax	(achieve (in ?ob ?rm))
postcondition	holds((in ?ob ?rm) end)
execution	in-achieve.default
generation	{ach-in.1 ach-in.2}
debugging	{ach-in-dbg.1 ach-in-dbg.2}
scheduler	achieve-in.scheduler

Figure 5: RPL description for achievement tasks concerning the predicate in.

heuristic transformation	in-achieve.default
(achieve (in ?ob ?rm)) ↓ (deliver ?ob ?rm)	true
stability	0.98
correctness	0.99
completeness	0.8
exec-time	5min

Figure 6: Default transformation for achievement tasks concerning the predicate in.

about the occurrence of events in the environment are stored in the form of average lifetimes of predicates. The slot **features** specifies that the predicate in is a functional predicate, i.e. at any time an object is in exactly one room. It also specifies that the predicate is perception constraining. The slots **achieve**, **perceive**, **prevent**, and **maintain** are references to RPL construct descriptions. The RPL construct description for achieving that an object will be in a certain room is shown in figure 5 and the corresponding default rule in figure 6.

3   Planning Algorithm

The planning system is designed according to the GENERATE-TEST-DEBUG (GTD) control strategy [SD87] and consists of a PLAN HYPOTHESIZER, a PLAN TESTER, and a PLAN DEBUGGER. The PLAN HYPOTHESIZER proposes plans that are promising under heuristic evaluation. The quality of promising plan hypotheses is evaluated globally by the PLAN TESTER in order to check whether the hypotheses are still promising when the context of the plan and task interactions are considered. Finally, the PLAN DEBUGGER transforms plans in order to avoid possible problems detected by the PLAN TESTER.

3.1   Generation of Plan Hypotheses

The PLAN HYPOTHESIZER transforms plans heuristically based on their syntactic structure, replacing *goal steps* — tasks defined in terms of achieving or maintaining goals — with plans that are expected to do better than the defaults. The plans resulting from transformation of a single goal step are rated using local statistical methods. When a promising version of the entire plan has been found, it is globally tested and debugged, as we will describe.

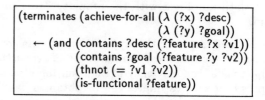

Figure 7: Procedure for proving the termination of an achieve-for-all expression

The basic algorithm for generating plan hypotheses is straightforward. The PLAN HYPOTHESIZER keeps a list of goal steps that need to be planned, and successively applies the knowledge stored in the RPL construct description for each. First the default transformation of the construct description is applied, and the quality of the default plan estimated and saved as a standard to compare later versions against. These other versions are generated by trying transformation rules in an order determined by the scheduler. Running a transformation rule consists of matching its input plan schema against the goal step, checking its applicability condition, and computing the quality of the resulting expression. When the hypothesizer runs out of time or rules, it returns the best version of the plan found so far.

Applicability conditions are checked by a collection of fast special-purpose decision procedures for termination proofs, probabilistic decision rules, and other categories of proofs useful for, and common in, plan transformation. An example of such a decision procedure is the PROLOG-like procedure **terminates** (see figure 7), which checks whether a given achieve-for-all goal step terminates. The top-level task in figure 1 terminates because any block that has been delivered to the living room cannot be in the kitchen anymore and thus, the number of blue blocks in the kitchen is decreasing. This standard type of termination proof is captured in **terminates** by having it check whether there is a feature ?feature common to all objects matching ?desc which is functional and provably changed by achieving ?goal. The information about whether a feature is functional, i.e. whether it can only have one value at a time, is contained in the slot **features** of predicate descriptions.

```
(let ((desigs                                          IMP₁
        (perceive (λ (?x) (and (category ?x block)
                               (color ?x blue)
                               (in ?x kitchen))))))
  (if desigs
      (seq (achieve '(in ,(car desigs) living-room))
           (achieve-for-all — —)
      (no-op)))
```

```
(let (desigs                                           IMP₂
      (loop
        (!= desigs
            (perceive (λ (?x) (and (category ?x block)
                                   (color ?x blue)
                                   (in ?x kitchen)))))
        while (not (null desigs))
        (achieve '(in ,(car desigs) living-room))))
```

```
(let ((desigs                                          IMP₃
        (perceive (λ (?x)
                     (and (category ?x block)
                          (color ?x blue)
                          (in ?x kitchen))))))
  (loop
    while (not (null desigs))
    (achieve '(in ,(car desigs) living-room))
    (!= desigs (cdr desigs)))))
```

Figure 8: Different implementations for the task *"get all the blue blocks in the kitchen to the livingroom."*

Running the default transformation and the **generator** transformation rules of the RPL construct description of **achieve-for-all** the PLAN HYPOTHESIZER proposes three different hypotheses for the implementation of the top-level task (see figure 8). The first implementation, proposed by the transformation rule **ach-for-all.default**, is a recursive solution; the robot senses the kitchen and perceives the blue blocks in the kitchen. The transformation rules in the predicate description of **in** specifies that the robot has to go into the kitchen in order to perceive objects in the kitchen. If the set of perceived blue blocks is not empty, the robot gets a blue block into the livingroom and calls the **achieve-for-all** task recursively. The second implementation performs a loop consisting of the perception and achievement steps instead of calling (**achieve-for-all** — —) recursively. In the third solution, descriptors for all the blue blocks in the kitchen are computed in advance and then for each of these descriptors the achievement task is executed. The **perceive** expression returns an effective designator for each blue block in the kitchen. A designator [McD90] is a data structure which carries the information necessary to resense and manipulate a perceived object. In particular, the designators contain the location of the objects. Thus the robot knows

that it has to go into the the kitchen to get the blue blocks it is supposed to deliver.

The **achieve** task fails if the robot cannot grasp the block it has to get into the livingroom. This happens if the block has moved since it was perceived. In the first and second plan versions, this is unlikely to happen, because the robot grasps a block immediately after it has been perceived. In the third version, all the objects are perceived in advance. In a stable world, getting this knowledge once and for all would save having to do repeated visual scans, and would allow for scheduling block deliveries. The difference between the first and the second implementation is that the first implementation delays the decision how to perform the **achieve-for-all** task. It gives the planner time to generate a better plan for (**achieve-for-all** — —) while the robot is already delivering the first blue block. On the other hand, the second implementation does not have to be further planned, which frees planning resources for the optimization of other subtasks.

The expected utility of the plan is the weighted sum of estimations for its stability, correctness, execution time, and completeness. One can change the planner's preferences between aspects of plan quality by changing the weights of the aspects. IMP₂, which is proposed by transformation rule **ach-for-all.1**, is preferred over IMP₃ if the average lifetime of the location of a block is comparatively low and/or the weight assigned to the robustness of a plan is higher than the weight assigned to the runtime efficiency. IMP₁, the plan hypothesis generated by the default transformation, can be returned by the PLAN HYPOTHESIZER if the generation of plan hypotheses has been interrupted before a better hypothesis was generated.

3.2 Test of Plan Hypotheses

The plan proposed by the PLAN HYPOTHESIZER is passed to the PLAN TESTER. The PLAN TESTER is a query component on top of a temporal projection module. It gets a plan hypothesis as its input and generates a set of projections[1], which enable it to estimate the stability, correctness, and execution time of the plan hypothesis. In addition, it computes the postconditions that have not been achieved and the tasks that failed.

The PLAN TESTER samples projections of the current plan hypothesis until it is interrupted or it runs out of time. It performs the following loop: (1) generate a random initial situation according to the probability density functions in the relevant predicate descriptions; (2) project the plan hypothesis for the initial situation. (During the projection, events in the environment are generated randomly according to the average lifetime defined for predicate descriptions.) (3)

---

[1] Subsequently, we use the terms projection and simulation interchangably.

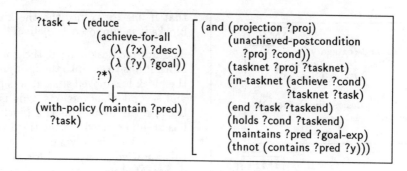

Figure 9: Debug transformation rule for the RPL command achieve-for-all

analyze the projection by checking whether a goal step failed, whether the postcondition was achieved, and how long the simulated execution took.

3.3 Debugging Plan Hypotheses

The PLAN DEBUGGER gets a set of projections of the current plan hypothesis as its input and produces a debugged plan by running the transformation rules in the **debug** slots of the relevant RPL construct descriptions (see [Sim88] for a theory of plan debugging). The debugged version of the plan is passed to the plan tester for further testing. The TEST-DEBUG cycle terminates when the PLAN TESTER module cannot find any more bugs in the hypothesis. Figure 9 shows a debug rule for the **achieve-for-all** construct. The rule makes use of built-in predicates on task networks, timelines and projections. For instance, the

query
```
(prolog '(and (projection ?proj)
              (unachieved-postcondition ?proj ?cond)))
```

succeeds if one of the projections in the current planning cycle did not achieve its postcondition. In this case the query returns a list of bindings, where ?proj is bound to the projection in which the plan could not achieve its postcondition and ?cond is bound to the condition which could not be achieved.

The applicability condition of the debug transformation in figure 9 checks first whether there is an unachieved postcondition ?cond, then tests whether the robot has tried to achieve the postcondition, i.e., whether (achieve ?cond) is in the tasknet. Suppose OB318 is an object in the initial state of the projection ?proj that satisfied (λ (x) (and (category x block) (color x blue) (in x kitchen))) for some time during the task simulation. If the task (achieve (in OB318 livingroom)) is not in the task network the robot has not recognized that OB318 satisfies the description and the perception task needs to be debugged. Next **holds** checks whether (in OB318 livingroom) holds at the end of (achieve (in OB318 livingroom)). If not, (achieve ?cond) needs to be debugged. Otherwise after the goal is achieved it is invalidated by another event after it has been achieved. In this case we compute a predicate that maintains

the goal and which is itself easy to maintain. Let us assume that the database contains the fact (maintains (locked ?rm) (in ?x ?rm)). This fact formalizes that no object can appear in, and disappear from, a locked room. The query (maintains ?pred (in OB318 livingroom)) would succeed and bind ?pred to (locked livingroom). The debug transformation would return

```
(with-policy (maintain '(locked livingroom))
             ?task)
```
where ?task is bound to the current plan. Note, that in order to debug the plan we apply the debug rules of the original abstract task. This is possible because RPL plans contain explicit representations of the transformations performed (**reduce** statement).

4 Related Work

A planning system for robots that solve complex tasks in realistic and changing environments has to provide solutions for several problems. First, it has to deal explicitly with the uncertainty that arises from the unpredictability of, and the incomplete information regarding, the environment in which the robot is operating [Han90]. It has to change the set of tasks it currently pursues according to user requests, information acquired, and given preference criteria. The robot planner has to treat planning time as a limited resource; i.e., it has to return plans for any allocation of computation time and has to reason about whether the expected gains from further planning will outweigh the costs of spending more planning time [DB88, BD89]. Finally, the planner has to be able to synthesize plans that implement any problem-solving behavior necessary to solve complex tasks in its environment—not just sequences of primitive robot actions [McD91c].

Various systems address different problems in the generation and revision of reactive plans. Representative approaches are the subsumption architecture [Bro86], situated automata [Ros85, RP86], GAPPS [Kae88], the Entropy Reduction Engine (ERE) [Dru89, DB90], and the Procedural Reasoning System (PRS) [GL87, RG91].

In the subsumption architecture [Bro86, Bro91] and situated automata [Ros85] approach, sensor data are mapped into decisions about which actions to enable and disable. The state information stored in these approaches is minimal and as a consequence all possible situations have to be associated with appropriate actions. While these approaches are characterized by fast response time to environmental events they are unable to deal with multiple and varying goals in a sophisticated manner.

GAPPS [Kae88] allows for the specification of reactive plans in terms of declarative tasks. Given declarative tasks (goals) of the form do(?a), achieve(?g), or maintain(?p), and a set of goal reduction rules, the system compiles the tasks into a synchronous digital circuit that achieves the tasks. Goals and plans in GAPPS are implicit in the compiled circuit. Rather than synthesizing executable plans from abstract specifications XFRM improves plans during their execution and therefore has to represent goals and reactive plans in an explicit way. These explicit representations allow XFRM to revise and specialize reactive plans if the robot acquires more information about the environment or if it changes its preferences, for instance, when it changes from a slow and robust execution mode to a fast and less reliable one.

ERE contains a synthetic projection algorithm [DB90]. Given declarative tasks and a probabilistic causal theory of the robot actions, ERE attempts to find a directed acyclic graph of situation control rules that maximizes the probability of successful task performance. ERE and XFRM share a number of similarities: they use probabilistic anytime algorithms for projecting plans and improving their robustness. In contrast, XFRM computes plans that are represented in RPL, a more complex plan representation language. As in GAPPS, toplevel tasks in ERE cannot be revised at execution time.

PRS [GL87] decides on actions and their order based on a database of current beliefs, a set of goals (desires), a set of intentions (goals the planner is committed to) and a set of plans specifying how to achieve goals and how to react to the environment. The PRS interpreter selects appropriate plans based on the set of goals and current beliefs, adds the plans to the set of intentions and executes them. PRS and XFRM explicitly represent goals and plans and reason about them. The difference is that XFRM provides a variety of planning methods for plan hypothesis generation, plan simulation, plan debugging, etc., and a control structure for them. PRS does not make a commitment to planning techniques and leaves it to the programmer to implement them when needed.

Describing the quality of reactive plans in terms of their robustness (probability of complete goal satisfaction), the estimated execution time, and their completeness, is a limited model of plan utility. We have restricted ourselves to these aspects, because so far these are the ones that can be checked by the plan simulator. A thorough discussion of more expressive utility models for plans, including resources other than time, partial goal satisfaction, etc., can be found in [HH90]. The problem of making decisions based on weak evidence arises in the evaluation of plans by sampling simulations. [MA91] discusses an approach in which these problems can be represented and solved.

5 Conclusion

In this paper we have described a representation scheme and the basic planning algorithms for handling declarative goals in a reactive planner. The planner is implemented and able to compute the different plans listed in this paper. Several features of the planner make it attractive for robot planning. The planning algorithm is time-dependent and proposes executable plans for any allocation of computation time. The approach is compatible with a general transformational framework (although it has not yet been embedded in such an overarching system). And, finally, decisions are controlled by explicitly modelled probabilities and utilities.

The paper describes what knowledge is necessary for this category of planners and how to represent and index it. This research, however, is still in an early stage and a lot remains to be done before we will have a practical system for achieving goals in a reactive system. The most critical issue in this framework is the derivation of the probabilities and utilities that govern the heuristic transformation rules. Currently these are supplied by hand, but we hope to be able to automatically estimate them by running projections, and by experience with the "real" simulated world.

Acknowledgements. We would like to thank Sean Engelson, Greg Hager, Steve Hanks, Anand Rangarajan, and the reviewers for valuable comments on an earlier version of this paper.

References

[BD89]   M. Boddy and T. Dean. Solving time-dependent planning problems. In *Proc. of the 11th IJCAI*, pages 979–984, Detroit, MI, 1989.

[BP86]   M. Broy and P. Pepper. Program development as a formal activity. In C. Rich and R. C. Waters, editors, *Artificial Intelligence and Software Engineering*, pages 123–131. 1986.

[Bro86]   R. A. Brooks. A robust layered control system for a mobile robot. *IEEE Journal of Robotics and Automation*, 2(1), 1986.

[Bro91]   R. A. Brooks. Intelligence without representation. *Artificial Intelligence*, 47:139–159, 1991.

[Cha87]   D. Chapman. Planning for conjunctive goals. *Artificial Intelligence*, 32:333–377, 1987.

[DB88]   T. Dean and M. Boddy. An analysis of time-dependent planning. In *Proc. of AAAI-88*, pages 49–54, St. Paul, MN, 1988.

[DB90]   M. Drummond and J. Bresina. Anytime synthetic projection: Maximizing the probability of goal satisfaction. In *Proc. of AAAI-90*, pages 138–144, Boston, MA, 1990.

[Dru89]   M. Drummond. Situated control rules. In R. J. Brachman, H. J. Levesque, and R. Reiter, editors, *KR'89: Proc. of the First International Conference on Principles of Knowledge Representation and Reasoning*, pages 103–113. Kaufmann, San Mateo, CA, 1989.

[Fir87]   J. Firby. An investigation into reactive planning in complex domains. In *Proc. of AAAI-87*, pages 202–206, Seattle, WA, 1987.

[GL87]   M. P. Georgeff and A. L. Lansky. Reactive reasoning and planning. In *Proc. of AAAI-87*, pages 677–682, Seattle, WA, 1987.

[Han90]   S. Hanks. *Projecting Plans for Uncertain Worlds*. Technical report 756, Yale University, Department of Computer Science, 1990.

[HH90]   P. Haddawy and S. Hanks. Issues in decision-theoretic planning: Symbolic goals and utilities. In K. Sycara, editor, *Proceedings of the Workshop on Innovative Approaches to Planning, Scheduling and Control*, pages 48–58, 1990.

[Kae88]   L. P. Kaelbling. Goals as parallel program specifications. In *Proc. of AAAI-88*, pages 60–65, St. Paul, MN, 1988.

[MA91]   N. Martins and J. Allen. A language for planning with statistics. In B. D'Ambrosio, P. Smets, and P. Bonissone, editors, *Proc. of the 7th Conference on Uncertainty in Artificial Intelligence*, pages 220–227, San Mateo, CA, 1991. Kaufmann.

[McD90]   D. McDermott. Planning reactive behavior: A progress report. In K. Sycara, editor, *Innovative Approaches to Planning, Scheduling and Control*, pages 450–458, San Mateo, CA, 1990. Kaufmann.

[McD91a] D. McDermott. A reactive plan language. Technical report 864, Yale University, Department of Computer Science, 1991.

[McD91b] D. McDermott. Regression planning. *International Journal of Intelligent Systems*, 6:357–416, 1991.

[McD91c] D. McDermott. Robot planning. Technical report 861, Yale University, Department of Computer Science, 1991.

[RG91]   A. S. Rao and M. P. Georgeff. Modeling rational agents within a BDI-architecture. In J. Allen, R. Fikes, and E. Sandewall, editors, *Principles of Knowledge Representation and Reasoning: Proc. of the Second International Conference (KR'91)*, pages 473–484. Kaufmann, San Mateo, CA, 1991.

[Ros85]   S. J. Rosenschein. Formal theories of knowledge in AI and robotics. *New Generation Computing*, 3:345–357, 1985.

[RP86]   S. J. Rosenschein and L. Pack Kaelbling. The synthesis of digital machines with provable epistemic properties. In *Proc. of the 1986 Conference on Theoretical Aspects of Reasoning about Knowledge*, pages 83–98, Monterey, CA, 1986.

[SD87]   R. Simmons and R. Davis. Generate, test and debug: Combining associational rules and causal models. In *Proc. of the 10th IJCAI*, pages 1071–1078, Milan, Italy, 1987.

[Sim88]   R. Simmons. A theory of debugging plans and interpretations. In *Proc. of AAAI-88*, pages 94–99, St. Paul, MN, 1988.

An Analysis of Search Techniques for a Totally-Ordered Nonlinear Planner *

Jim Blythe
Computer Science Dept.
Carnegie Mellon University
Pittsburgh, PA 15213
blythe@cs.cmu.edu

Manuela Veloso
Computer Science Dept.
Carnegie Mellon University
Pittsburgh, PA 15213
veloso@cs.cmu.edu

Abstract

In this paper we present several domain-independent search optimizations and heuristics that have been developed in a totally-ordered nonlinear planner in PRODIGY. We also describe the extension of the system into a full hierarchical planner with the ability to search among the different levels of abstraction. We analyze and illustrate the performance of the system with its different search capabilities in a few domains.

1 Introduction

The PRODIGY architecture is designed to be both a unified testbed for different learning methods and a general purpose planner to solve interesting problems in complex task domains. Since the beginning of the PRODIGY research project [Minton et al., 1989], we have been focusing our attention on both the aspects of machine learning and planning, as we believe that this integration is necessary in the presence of complex domains. In this paper we focus on PRODIGY's planning algorithm. We present some recent developments in PRODIGY's planner, as an efficient totally-ordered nonlinear hierarchical planner. We first briefly situate our approach with respect to the related research and also historically within the project.

Nonlinear planning was developed to deal with problems like Sussman's anomaly, which could not be solved optimally by linear planners such as STRIPS [Fikes and Nilsson, 1971, Sussman, 1975]. Least-commitment planners handle this anomaly by deferring decisions while building the plan [Sacerdoti, 1975,

Tate, 1977a, Wilkins, 1989]. These planners typically reason about a partially-ordered plan as opposed to a totally-ordered one. Typically, such plans have been referred to as *nonlinear* plans. However, the essence of the *nonlinearity* is not in the fact that the plan is partially ordered, but in the fact that a plan need not be a linear concatenation of complete subplans, each for a goal presumed independent of all others [Rich and Knight, 1991, Veloso, 1989, Regnier and Fade, 1992]. It is in this sense that we refer to our planner as totally-ordered and nonlinear.

The initial planner of PRODIGY [Minton et al., 1989] is linear and cannot therefore interleave subplans for different interacting goals. Its search procedure follows a *casual-commitment* approach, in which the planner, at choice points, commits to a particular alternative, generating the planning steps and testing their consequences, while searching for a solution. Background knowledge, whether hand-coded expertise, learned control rules or heuristic evaluation functions, guides the efficient exploration of the most promising parts of the search space. Provably incorrect alternatives are eliminated and heuristically preferred ones are explored first.

Later we developed a nonlinear planner, NOLIMIT [Veloso, 1989], that follows the same causal committment approach as the linear one does, but can also fully interleave goals at the different search levels. The plans generated are nonlinear, as they cannot be decomposed into a linear sequence of complete subplans for interacting conjunctive goals. The search space in a nonlinear planner is, by nature, much larger than in a linear planner. Efficiency becomes a major concern.

There have been a few recent attempts to analyze the advantages and disadvantages of totally-ordered versus partially-ordered nonlinear planning [Minton et al., 1991, Barrett et al., 1991]. In this paper we are not presenting a comparison between the two paradigms. It is well known that both algorithms in the general case are either exponential or NP-complete [Chapman, 1987].

We recently reimplemented and extended this nonlinear planner, focusing on developing efficient matching techniques [Wang, 1992], and an efficient hierarchical search

---

*This research was sponsored by the Avionics Laboratory, Wright Research and Development Center, Aeronautical Systems Division (AFSC), U. S. Air Force, Wright-Patterson AFB, OH 45433-6543 under Contract F33615-90-C-1465, Arpa Order No. 7597. The views and conclusions contained in this document are those of the authors and should not be interpreted as representing the official policies, either expressed or implied, of the U.S. Government.

algorithm [Blythe, 1992]. In this paper we analyze some efficient search techniques and present empirical results for the complete nonlinear planner in our latest version of the system, PRODIGY4.0.

We have been increasingly aware [Veloso et al., 1990] that scaling up a planner to deal with complex domains requires at least the following capabilities:

- An adequate representation for the specification of the domain.

- A baseline planner with an efficient default search strategy.

- The ability to analyze the domain and automatically extract different levels of abstraction among its predicates.

- An efficient and complete planner that can organize its search hierarchically using different abstraction levels.

- Learning methods, capable of analyzing and introspecting the problem solving performance, compiling experience to guide the planner in subsequent problems.

We want to preserve, and where needed extend, PRODIGY's ability to cope with these requirements. In fact PRODIGY provides a rich action representation language coupled with an expressive control language [Blythe et al., 1992]. The operators are represented by preconditions and effects. The preconditions are expressed in a typed first order predicate logic. They can contain conjunctions, disjunctions, negations, and both existential and universal quantifiers with typed variables. In addition, the operators can contain conditional effects, which depend on the state in which the operator is applied. (Chapman showed that extending a least-commitment planner — but *not* a casual-commitment planner — to reason about conditional effects is NP-hard [Chapman, 1987].) These language constructs are important for representing complex and interesting domains. The control language allows the problem solver to represent and learn control information about the various problem-solving decisions, such as selecting which goal or subgoal to address next, which operator to apply, what bindings to select for the operator or where to backtrack in case of failure. In PRODIGY, there is a clear division between the declarative domain knowledge (operators and inferences rules) and the more procedural control knowledge. This simplifies both the initial specification of a domain and the automatic learning of the control knowledge.

On the other hand, PRODIGY's planner produces a complete search tree, encapsulating all decisions – right ones and wrong ones – as well as the final solution. This information is used by each learning component in different ways: to extract control rules via EBL [Minton, 1988], to build derivational traces (cases) by the derivational analogy engine [Veloso and Carbonell, 1992], to analyze key decisions by a knowledge acquisition interface [Joseph, 1989], or to formulate focused experiments [Carbonell and Gil, 1990]. The axiomatized domain knowledge is also used to learn

abstraction layers [Knoblock, 1991], and statically generate control rules [Etzioni, 1990].

Although we do not present an analysis supporting our planning algorithm, we provide in this paper empirical evidence that PRODIGY's planner can handle complicated problems efficiently. In fact the paper only illustrates a small sample of the large variety of tasks that PRODIGY4.0 can effectively solve.

This paper is organized as follows. In the next section we describe the search algorithm used in PRODIGY4.0, explaining how the search space is elaborated as well as some of the heuristics and search reduction techniques used to make the system more efficient. The following section describes the integration of abstraction in PRODIGY4.0. This is done in a flexible way, so as to allow the system complete freedom to move between the different abstraction levels in the search. Finally, we present and discuss preliminary results with PRODIGY4.0 in a number of domains.

2   Search in PRODIGY4.0

The philosophy of the PRODIGY project is that a simple domain-independent planner can be combined with learning methods for acquiring control knowledge within a domain to provide sophisticated domain-independent planning [Minton, 1988, Etzioni, 1990, Veloso, 1992]. While PRODIGY4.0 still subscribes to this approach, a number of domain-independent search optimizations and heuristics have been added in order to improve the base-line performance of the system. It is intended that these will be used in conjunction with domain-dependent knowledge expressed as control rules [Minton, 1988, Etzioni, 1990] or other forms of learned control guidance, such as past problem-solving episodes stored as derivational cases [Veloso, 1992].

In this section we outline the search space explored by PRODIGY4.0 and present the search reduction techniques and heuristics that are used. For the purposes of this discussion, we view search reduction techniques, for example dependency-directed backtracking, as removing parts of the search space, while heuristics direct the attention of the searcher. Neither class can guarantee to reduce the amount of work needed to reach a solution.

Both dependency-directed backtracking and the heuristics used in PRODIGY4.0 are customized to its search algorithm, which we now briefly describe. By default, PRODIGY performs a depth-first, means-ends analysis in the state space to construct a plan. However, control rules can be used to switch attention to different points of the search tree as well as to determine local choices. Thus control rules can produce best-first or breadth-first search, for example.

PRODIGY4.0 uses four different types of nodes in its search tree, corresponding to the different decisions that are made.

- *Goal nodes* record the choice to work on a specific goal from the set of currently active goals in the system.

1. Initialize search tree T and the list O of open nodes to consist of one node r, an applied-op node recording the applications of inference rules on the initial state. Set $G(r)$ to the set of top-level goals.

2. Choose a node n from O to expand.

3. If n is a goal node, choose an operator to achieve n and make a child operator node reflecting this decision point.

4. If n is an operator node, choose a set of bindings for the operator and make a child binding node b. Add the preconditions of the instantiated operator to $G(b)$.

5. If n is a binding or applied-op node, choose either one goal from the set $G(n)$ of current goals or the nearest ancestor binding node that has not been applied on this branch of the search tree.

6. If n has no possible expansions that have not been explored, remove it from O. This is referred to as *closing* the node n.

7. Goto step 2.

Figure 1: A simplified version of the search algorithm.

- *Operator nodes* represent the choice to use a specific operator to achieve the goal currently being worked on.

- *Binding nodes* represent a set of bindings chosen to instantiate the variables of the current operator.

- *application nodes* represent the decision to apply an instantiated operator whose preconditions are true. The application nodes in a path through the search tree from the root to a leaf correspond to the partial plan that the path represents — a complete plan if the leaf node satisfies the goal description.

A simplified version of the basic search algorithm used by PRODIGY4.0 is shown in figure 1. It can be found in more detail in [Blythe et al., 1992]. $G(n)$, the goal set at node n, is by default calculated as the goal set of n's parent in the search tree, but augmented in step 4.

2.1 Search Reduction Techniques

PRODIGY4.0 uses three different kinds of search reduction techniques: checking for infinite loops, dependency-directed backtracking and a variant of look-ahead [Haralick and Elliot, 1980].

Two kinds of infinite loops are detected during search: *state loops*, where a sequence of operators has resulted in the same state, and *goal loops*, where through a chain of subgoals the system repeats the goal it is trying to solve. These two loops lie in different networks, which are maintained simultaneously. State loops are found by looking at the order in which operators are applied, recorded in PRODIGY's search tree, while goal loops are found by looking at the

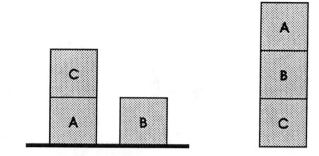

Figure 2: The initial and goal state descriptions for Sussman's Anomaly

subgoal tree. These are different because PRODIGY4.0 interleave subgoals from different higher-level goals.

The main effect of *dependency-directed backtracking* in PRODIGY4.0 is to remove binding nodes from consideration when a necessary subgoal introduced by the node is later found to be unachievable. To illustrate this and some of the techniques described later, we will use the blocksworld domain, and in particular Sussman's anomaly [Sussman, 1975]. The empirical results presented in section 4 include more realistic planning domains. The representation of the blocksworld for this paper uses the predicates on, ontable, clear, holding and armempty, and the four operators unstack, stack, pickup and putdown. Figure 2 shows a diagram of the starting and goal states for Sussman's anomaly. Figure 3 shows part of the goal tree that PRODIGY4.0 expands for this problem. Note that the goal tree is not the same as PRODIGY's search tree, in which a plan is represented by a linear path.

When PRODIGY4.0 solves this problem, it begins with the goal (on A B), subgoaling as shown in the figure on (holding A) and then on (clear A). Among the operators considered for achieving the last goal is <unstack B A>, leading to a subgoal (on B A), which is unachievable because the only operator for it, stack, causes a goal loop with (clear A). Dependency-directed backtracking at this point leads the system to close the binding node for <unstack B A> from the search tree, because it introduced this unachievable subgoal. Brute-force search would result in keeping this node in PRODIGY's search space in order to expand the path where the system switches attention to the goal (on B C) at this point, having now committed to using the unstack operator to achieve (clear A), although this can never work.

In this example the subgoal was unachievable because of a goal loop. Subgoals are also unachievable if no satisfactory bindings can be found for any relevant operator. We note in passing that it is not necessary at run time in PRODIGY to consider the case where there are no relevant operators for a subgoal. A pre-processing stage automatically detects such goals, and includes the necessary tests to avoid them in the matching stage as bindings are computed [Wang, 1992]. These predicates are called *static predicates*

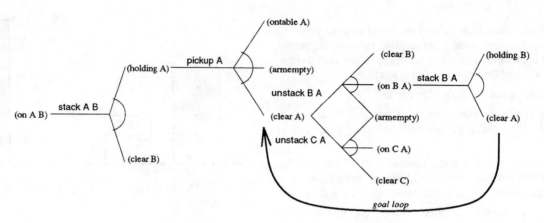

Figure 3: Part of the goal tree for Sussman's Anomaly

in PRODIGY, and are analogous in function to filters in Non-lin [Tate, 1977b].

One instance of *look-ahead* in PRODIGY4.0 is to eliminate fruitless operator nodes. Once an operator is chosen, a set of bindings is chosen to instantiate the operator. However, an analysis of the possible bindings made by regressing the goal through the operator and examining the weakest preconditions [Waldinger, 1977] may show that no good set of bindings can be found. When this happens, PRODIGY4.0 will remove the operator node from the search space without generating any of the binding nodes. Binding nodes represent are the most expensive portion of the search algorithm, the matching stage [Wang, 1992].

PRODIGY4.0 also uses lookahead to check for goal loops. Consider when the system is first trying to solve (clear A) in our example. Although it is not shown in the trace, the system actually first considers the operators put-down and stack to achieve (clear A), since it has no control knowledge to lead it to <unstack C A> at this point. Both of these operators are rejected before considering bindings, however. The weakest preconditions for stack to achieve (clear A) include (holding A), which would create a goal loop with the goal node above (clear A) in figure 3.

The savings in terms of the reduction in the search space produced by look-ahead as currently used in PRODIGY4.0 depend on the number of binding nodes that would otherwise be created, which is roughly exponential in the number of variables in the operator.

2.2   Search Heuristics

The search heuristics currently in use in PRODIGY4.0 take the form of orderings on lists of choices at a decision point, analogous to preference control rules. One heuristic is to prefer bindings with a minimum number of unsolved preconditions derived from considerations of conspiracy numbers for and/or trees [Elkan, 1989], [Blythe, 1992]. Another heuristic is to prefer goals with a maximum "abstraction level", which makes use of automatically generated

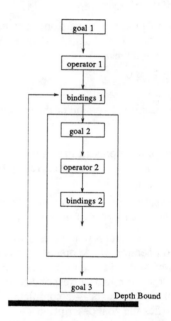

Figure 4: Possible incompleteness of dependency-directed backtracking in the presence of other control parameters.

information expressed as an abstraction hierarchy (see the next section) without explicitly using different abstraction spaces in the planning process.

2.3   Limits to the scope of search optimizations and heuristics

We now note some of the potential interactions between the search techniques described in this section and the control rules that also direct the search in PRODIGY4.0.

The search techniques listed here only use knowledge about PRODIGY's search algorithm, not domain-dependent knowledge. While such techniques will be very generally applicable, care has to be taken when using them in the presence of domain-dependent control knowledge to ensure that they do not combine to produce poor decisions.

Figure 4 illustrates this point. Suppose that the planner is attempting to achieve "goal 1", represented by the uppermost box in the figure, and that in doing so it chooses the expand the bindings node "bindings 1", which requires solving the conjunction of goals 2 and 3. Suppose that the planner works on goal 2 for a while, indicated by the surrounding box, and then turns attention to goal 3. At this point the planner hits a depth bound that has been imposed on the search, and fails. If dependency-directed backtracking was used in this case, the system would close the node for "bindings 1", since it requires a goal that failed. However, if an alternative plan could have achieved goal 2 in fewer nodes, then goal 3 may be solvable in some search tree rooted under "bindings 1". Thus in this case naive application of these techniques can destroy the completeness of the planner. Similar interactions can take place with control rules using information about the state of the search tree.

Of course, the use of a depth bound may destroy completeness single-handedly if it set too low, and in general the use of control rules that select or reject among the choices can have this effect. While this paper does not address the issue of maintaining completeness in the presence of control knowledge, it is worth mentioning that the issue is there.

3   Integration of abstraction in prodigy4.0

PRODIGY4.0 includes a mechanism for generating abstraction hierarchies automatically, and can incorporate different abstraction levels within the same search tree. The method for generating and plannig with abstraction hierarchies was developed by Knoblock [Knoblock, 1991] for PRODIGY's linear planner, although we have extended this. In particular, subgoals of goals at one abstraction level can be interleaved at the lower level, a feature which is necessary to preserve the completeness of PRODIGY4.0.

Hierarchical planning is a relatively widely-used technique for dealing with the complexity of fine detail in planning ([Sacerdoti, 1974], [Tenenberg, 1990], [Knoblock, 1991]), as well as having uses for limiting the effects of uncertainty in planning. In its most common form, a successive set of simplifications of the problem is generated. Then plans are made in the simplest version of the problem and progressively refined until the full problem is solved in the most detailed or *ground space*. If the hierarchy of versions of the planning problem is well chosen, this technique can lead to significant improvements in planning efficiency.

In   work   by   Knoblock   and   others   ([Knoblock et al., 1991],[Yang and Tenenberg, 1990]), some properties of abstraction hierarchies were identified that would allow hierarchical planners to be complete and correct, and enable efficient backtracking. The *monotonicity property*, which holds for all abstraction spaces, says that the existence of a solution in the ground space implies that there exists a solution in the more abstract space that can be refined to the ground level solution without undoing any of the domain features established in the abstract plan.

Min Unsolved	Dep-directed backtracking			
Preconditions	On		Off	
On	107	4.7	107	4.7
Off	128	5.6	128	5.6

Table 1: Different combinations of search techniques with abstraction.

This property can be used to constrain the refinement of an abstract plan.

The hierarchical planner implemented in the earlier version of PRODIGY makes use of a ground-space planner as a subroutine, which is called recursively on each subproblem at the different abstraction levels. Knoblock shows that this hierarchical planner is correct, but that it is only complete for the class of planning problems that is *linearizable* — in other words where every conjunctive set of goals that arises during problem solving can be solved in the order the goals appear in the abstraction hierarchy. The mechanism for planning with abstraction in PRODIGY4.0 maintains completeness by allowing steps needed to refine a plan to be inserted anywhere in the plan. This extension to the refinement method retains the *monotonicity property* and thus allows for efficient backtracking between abstraction levels.

In PRODIGY4.0, each node in the search tree has an abstraction level, and the single search tree represents plans at all levels once planning is completed. This allows for more flexible control of planning with abstraction than the previous approach, where the planner is called as a subroutine by the abstraction module. Control rules can be written to decide at a given node in the search whether to continue searching at the current abstraction level or move to a different one.

4   Empirical Results

The results in this section show preliminary results for the effects of the search optimizations and speedups and of the abstraction techniques described in the previous sections. PRODIGY4.0 has been applied to a number of domains, including a transportation domain which models moving packages by airplane and truck across the country, and a reduced version of a process planning domain [?].

In each of these domains, we have written a set of control rules that allow most problems to be solved efficiently. For the results in this section, however, they were not used. We found that the hierarchical planner was sometimes able to run comparably to the domain with control rules, but was not usually within an order of magnitude of this speed. Various improvements are possible, however, as there are a number of places in the algorithm for generating abstractions where domain knowledge and domain-independent heuristics can be brought to bear [Knoblock, 1991].

Min Unsolved	Dep-directed backtracking			
Preconditions	On		Off	
On	65	1.3	65	1.4
Off	69	1.3	797	12.2

Table 2: Sussman's anomaly with no use of abstraction.

Perhaps as could have been expected, abstraction showed typically a larger margin of improvement over planning in the ground space for more complex scenarios than for simpler ones. In various versions of the transportation domain without control rules, we only compared different combinations of the search reduction techniques and heuristics while using abstraction, because times for the ground space planner were so much greater. Table 1 is such an example, where we have used abstraction and various combinations of dependency-directed backtracking (along the row, labelled "D") and the heuristic to prefer fewer unsolved preconditions. In each cell we have the total number of nodes in the search tree, generated in all levels of the hierarchy, and the CPU time in seconds. This problem involved the routing of three packages in the transportation domain. Here, dependency directed backtracking has no bearing, and minimizing preconditions very little.

By contrast, table 2 shows the same combinations of techniques for the Sussman's anomaly problem mentioned in section 2.1, without the use of abstraction. In fact, the literals of the blocksworld do not exhibit sufficient structure to create an abstraction hierarchy using the reduced model method. The use of at least one of the two search techniques reduces the search by an order of magnitude in this case.

5   Conclusions and some future directions

In this paper we briefly described the nonlinear planning algorithm we use in PRODIGY. We discussed its philosophy in the context of an architecture for learning and planning.

We presented different search optimization techniques that improved the efficiency of the base planner as well as the hierarchical planning algorithm we developed. All of them were general in nature, and have been applied to a number of domains. We showed some results that illustrated the trade-offs among the different techniques used.

One advantage of this more flexible control of abstract planning is to allow a time-critical planner to flesh out the complete plan only at the most abstract levels and to progressively refine only the first step from each more abstract level. This would allow the planner to quickly arrive at a plausible first action to take, although it may not be guaranteed to succeed, and then to continue to expand the search space more thoroughly as time allowed. In this way abstraction hierarchies can provide a simple form of "anytime algorithm" for computing at least the first step of a plan ([Dean and Boddy, 1988], [Elkan, 1990]). We see this aspect as well as the potential for reasoning about plan quality

in a simplified, abstract domain as very interesting lines of future work.

The current default version of the algorithm returns with the first successful plan found, although it is possible to allow the system to produce more than one plan. Eventually we would like PRODIGY to consider the quality of the plan it produces, and to search for the best plan that can be found within given resource bounds. The search for a better plan, as opposed to simply one that satisfies the goals, will increase the size of the search space, however. One promising way to focus the search for better plans might be to first look for the best plans at more abstract levels of the system, and then to refine the better plans in the search for a best plan at the less abstract levels.

The PRODIGY system is freely available to research groups. We encourage interested parties to contact the Prodigy Project at the authors' address, or to send electronic mail to prodigy@cs.cmu.edu.

Acknowledgements

The design of PRODIGY4.0 was, and still is, a joint effort, for which the authors acknowledge the whole PRODIGY research team, but very much in particular Craig Knoblock, Xuemei Wang, Alicia Pérez, Dan Kahn, Yolanda Gil, Robert Joseph, Oren Etzioni, and William Reilly. The initial design was developed by Jim Blythe, Xuemei Wang, and Dan Kahn. We specially thank Craig Knoblock for his work on abstraction and for the many helpful discussions on the development of PRODIGY4.0's hierarchical planning strategy. Yolanda Gil provided some very helpful comments on an earlier draft of this paper. Last, but not least, the authors acknowledge Steven Minton, Jaime Carbonell, Craig Knoblock, and Dan Kuokka for starting the PRODIGYproject, in particular Steven Minton for PRODIGY2.0, and Daniel Borrajo for a major part of No-LIMIT's implementation. It was our past experience with PRODIGY2.0 and NOLIMIT that definitely drove our design and implementation of PRODIGY4.0.

References

[Barrett et al., 1991] Barrett, A., Soderland, S., and Weld, D. (1991). The effect of step-order representations on planning. Technical Report 91-05-06, Department of Computer Science and Engineering, University of Washington.

[Blythe, 1992] Blythe, J. (1992). Search techniques for PRODIGY4.0. Technical report, School of Computer Science, Carnegie Mellon University. forthcoming.

[Blythe et al., 1992] Blythe, J., Etzioni, O., Gil, Y., Joseph, R., Pérez, A., Reilly, S., Veloso, M., and Wang, X. (1992). Prodigy4.0: The manual and tutorial. Technical report, School of Computer Science, Carnegie Mellon University.

[Carbonell and Gil, 1990] Carbonell, J. G. and Gil, Y. (1990). Learning by experimentation: The operator refinement method. In Michalski, R. S. and Kodratoff, Y., editors, *Machine Learning: An Artificial Intelligence Approach, Volume III*. Morgan Kaufmann, Palo Alto, CA.

[Chapman, 1987] Chapman, D. (1987). Planning for conjunctive goals. *Artificial Intelligence*, 32:333–378.

[Dean and Boddy, 1988] Dean, T. and Boddy, M. (1988). An analysis of time-dependent planning problems. In *National Conference on Artificial Intelligence*.

[Elkan, 1989] Elkan, C. (1989). Conspiracy numbers and caching for searching and/or trees and theorem proving. In *International Joint Conference on Artificial Intelligence*.

[Elkan, 1990] Elkan, C. (1990). Incremental, approximate planning. In *National Conference on Artificial Intelligence*.

[Etzioni, 1990] Etzioni, O. (1990). *A Structural Theory of Explanation-Based Learning*. PhD thesis, School of Computer Science, Carnegie Mellon University. Available as technical report CMU-CS-90-185.

[Fikes and Nilsson, 1971] Fikes, R. E. and Nilsson, N. J. (1971). Strips: A new approach to the application of theorem proving to problem solving. *Artificial Intelligence*, 2:189–208.

[Haralick and Elliot, 1980] Haralick, R. M. and Elliot, G. L. (1980). Increasing tree search efficiency for constraint satisfaction problems. *Artificial Intelligence*, 14:263–313.

[Joseph, 1989] Joseph, R. L. (1989). Graphical knowledge acquisition. In *Proceedings of the 4th Knowledge Acquisition For Knowledge-Based Systems Workshop*, Banff, Canada.

[Knoblock, 1991] Knoblock, C. A. (1991). *Automatically Generating Abstractions for Problem Solving*. PhD thesis, School of Computer Science, Carnegie Mellon University, Pittsburgh, PA. forthcoming.

[Knoblock et al., 1991] Knoblock, C. A., Tenenberg, J. D., and Yang, Q. (1991). Characterizing abstraction hierarchies for planning. In *National Conference on Artificial Intelligence*.

[Minton, 1988] Minton, S. (1988). *Learning Effective Search Control Knowledge: An Explanation-Based Approach*. PhD thesis, Computer Science Department, Carnegie Mellon University.

[Minton et al., 1991] Minton, S., Bresina, J., and Drummond, M. (1991). Commitment strategies in planning: A comparative analysis. In *Proceedings of IJCAI-91*, pages 259–265.

[Minton et al., 1989] Minton, S., Knoblock, C. A., Kuokka, D. R., Gil, Y., Joseph, R. L., and Carbonell, J. G. (1989). PRODIGY 2.0: The manual and tutorial. Technical Report CMU-CS-89-146, School of Computer Science, Carnegie Mellon University.

[Regnier and Fade, 1992] Regnier, P. and Fade, B. (1992). Integrating linear planning and parallel execution of actions. In *IEEE, Robotics and Automation*.

[Rich and Knight, 1991] Rich, E. and Knight, K. (1991). *Artificial Intelligence*. McGraw-Hill, inc.

[Sacerdoti, 1974] Sacerdoti, E. D. (1974). Planning in a hierarchy of abstraction spaces. *Artificial Intelligence*, 5:115–135.

[Sacerdoti, 1975] Sacerdoti, E. D. (1975). The nonlinear nature of plans. In *Proceedings of IJCAI-75*, pages 206–213.

[Sussman, 1975] Sussman, G. J. (1975). *A Computer Model of Skill Acquisition*. American Elsevier, New York. Also available as technical report AI-TR-297, Artificial Intelligence Laboratory, MIT, 1975.

[Tate, 1977a] Tate, A. (1977a). Generating project networks. In *Proceedings of the Fifth International Joint Conference on Artificial Intelligence*, pages 888–900.

[Tate, 1977b] Tate, A. (1977b). Generating project networks. In *International Joint Conference on Artificial Intelligence*.

[Tenenberg, 1990] Tenenberg, J. (1990). Some representative article. *Artificial Intelligence*.

[Veloso, 1989] Veloso, M. M. (1989). Nonlinear problem solving using intelligent casual-commitment. Technical Report CMU-CS-89-210, School of Computer Science, Carnegie Mellon University.

[Veloso, 1992] Veloso, M. M. (1992). *Analogical Reasoning in General Problem Solving - Automatic Case Generation, Storage, and Replay*. PhD thesis, School of Computer Science, Carnegie Mellon University, Pittsburgh, PA. In preparation.

[Veloso and Carbonell, 1992] Veloso, M. M. and Carbonell, J. G. (1992). Derivational analogy in PRODIGY: Automating case acquisition, storage, and utilization. In *Machine Learning*. (in press).

[Veloso et al., 1990] Veloso, M. M., Carbonell, J. G., and Knoblock, C. A. (1990). Nonlinear planning in complex domains using a casual-commitment approach. In *Preprints of the AAAI-90 Workshop on Planning in Complex Domains*, MIT, MA.

[Waldinger, 1977] Waldinger, R. (1977). Achieving several goals simultaneously. *Machine Intelligence 8*.

[Wang, 1992] Wang, M. (1992). Matching in PRODIGY. Technical report, School of Computer Science, Carnegie Mellon University. forthcoming.

[Wilkins, 1989] Wilkins, D. E. (1989). Can AI planners solve practical problems? Technical Note 468R, SRI International.

[Yang and Tenenberg, 1990] Yang, Q. and Tenenberg, J. D. (1990). Abtweak, abstracting a nonlinear, least commitment planner. In *National Conference on Artificial Intelligence*.

Complexity Results for Extended Planning

Tom Bylander
Laboratory for Artificial Intelligence Research
Department of Computer and Information Science
The Ohio State University
Columbus, Ohio 43210 USA
byland@cis.ohio-state.edu

Abstract

I analyze the computational complexity of extended propositional STRIPS planning, i.e., propositional STRIPS planning augmented with a propositional domain theory for inferring additional effects. The difficulties of formalizing the extended STRIPS assumption are finessed by requiring a preference ordering of all literals; roughly, if two literals are true of the previous state, and if it is inconsistent to assert both in the next state, then the ordering indicates which literal remains true. My primary result is that planning with definite Horn domain theories is PSPACE-complete even if operators are limited to zero preconditions and one postcondition. I also analyze the complexity of planning with Krom theories. These results in combination with previous analyses are not encouraging for domain-independent planning.

1   INTRODUCTION

The STRIPS assumption requires that all effects of an operator be explicitly represented (Waldinger, 1977). Although long considered to be excessively restrictive, the tradeoff between relaxing this assumption and computational complexity (the expressiveness-tractability tradeoff (Levesque and Brachman, 1985)) has not been explored. No doubt one reason why this tradeoff has not been analyzed is because of the difficulties of formalizing the extended STRIPS assumption (Georgeff, 1987).

In this paper, I present *extended propositional STRIPS planning*, which finesses the underlying difficulties, but does not fully resolve them. First, I define a domain theory to be a set of propositional formulas such that all states must be consistent with the domain theory. Second, I require a preference ordering of all the literals so that, roughly, if two literals are true of the previous state, and if it is inconsistent to assert both in the next state, then the ordering specifies which literal remains true. With respect to the framework of Ginsberg and Smith (1988), each state corresponds to a "partial world" with the domain theory

as "protected" formulas, and the next state corresponds to a "possible world."

This definition is intended for theoretical analysis, rather than programming convenience. Although it would be tedious to encode knowledge propositionally, complexity results for extended propositional STRIPS planning will still apply to other planning problems and formalisms based on polynomial-time reducibility.

Other aspects of this planning model that might be considered undesirable include: the requirement to enumerate all ground formulas (hard to generalize to first-order planning), the model preference ordering induced by the ordering of literals, the sidestepping of any contentious issues involving causality, etc. Nevertheless, my definition leads to unambiguous results from applying operators and capitalizes on the familiar idea of preference ordering.

I have demonstrated the following results:

> Extended propositional STRIPS planning with propositional definite-Horn domain-theories is PSPACE-complete[1] even if operators are restricted to zero preconditions and one positive (non-negated) postcondition.

> With propositional Krom domain theories, it is PSPACE-complete even if operators are restricted to two positive preconditions and one positive postcondition.

> With Krom theories, it is NP-complete if operators are restricted to one precondition, even if operators are restricted to one positive precondition and one positive postcondition.

> With Krom theories, it is polynomial if operators are restricted to 1 precondition and a limited number of goals, or if operators are restricted to no preconditions.

---

[1] PSPACE is the set of problems solvable using an amount of space that is a polynomial of the size of the input. PSPACE-complete problems are the hardest problems in PSPACE. Although not proven, it is assumed that PSPACE-complete problems are harder than NP-complete problems, which in turn are harder than polynomial problems.

"Simple" propositional STRIPS planning (i.e., with no domain theories) is polynomial for each of the above restrictions.

Clearly, extremely severe restrictions on both the operators and the domain theory are required to guarantee tractability or even NP-completeness. In an extended discussion at the end of the paper, I shall argue that these results do not favor reactive systems over deliberative planning because they apply equally to any system that attempts to achieve goals by performing actions. Also, these results strongly suggest that there are no universally-applicable domain-independent properties that lead to tractable planning.

First, I discuss previous complexity results for simple propositional planning. Then, I define extended propositional STRIPS planning, relate it to previous approaches, and present some examples. Next, I describe and demonstrate the results. Finally, I discuss some of the implications.

2 PREVIOUS COMPLEXITY RESULTS

In (Bylander, 1991), I analyzed the complexity of propositional STRIPS planning without domain theories.[2] The updated results of that paper are illustrated in Figure 1. Each box in the figure describes restrictions on the number and type of pre- and postconditions, and its location indicates the complexity of answering the question of whether there is a plan that transforms the initial state into a goal state. For example, the following box:

```
2 + preconds
2 postconds.
```

specifies the restriction that each operator must have two or fewer preconditions, all of which must be positive, and must have 2 or fewer postconditions; for this problem, determining whether a solution plan exists is PSPACE-complete. The "*" denotes no numeric limits.

There are many negative (intractability) results, but there are also a few interesting restrictions that guarantee polynomial planning. In particular, the blocks-world problem can be reformulated into a subproblem of the "*+ preconds., 1 postcond." problem (Bylander, 1991).

---

[2] See (Erol et al., 1991) for an in-depth analysis of first-order STRIPS planning as well as additional results for propositional planning. Also see (Bäckström and Klein, 1991) for a polynomial planning problem in which multi-valued variables are used instead of literals, see (Bacchus and Yang, 1991) for tractable tests that determine when certain hierarchical planning problems have solutions, and see (Gupta and Nau, 1991) and (Chenoweth, 1991) for proofs that optimal blocks-world planning is NP-hard. All of these analyses rely on the STRIPS assumption, although it should be mentioned that Erol et al. also consider functions in postconditions.

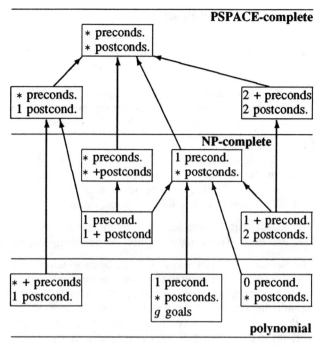

Figure 1: Previous Complexity Results for Simple Propositional STRIPS Planning

3 EXTENDED PLANNING

However, my previous results are based on the STRIPS assumption. In this section, I define a more general version of propositional STRIPS planning. Much of the notation is borrowed from (Dean and Boddy, 1988). After the definition, related work and examples are discussed.

3.1 DEFINITIONS

An instance of *extended propositional STRIPS planning* is specified by a tuple $\langle \mathcal{P}, \Sigma, \mathcal{O}, \mathcal{D}, \mathcal{I}, \mathcal{G} \rangle$, where:

$\mathcal{P}$ is a finite set of letters, called the *conditions*;

Σ is a set of propositional formulas, called the *domain theory*, that only uses letters from $\mathcal{P}$;

$\mathcal{O}$ is a finite set of *operators*, where each operator has the form $\langle \varphi, \eta, \alpha, \delta \rangle$:

$\varphi \subseteq \mathcal{P}$ is a set of *positive preconditions*;

$\eta \subseteq \mathcal{P}$ is a set of *negative preconditions*;

$\alpha \subseteq \mathcal{P}$ is a set of *positive postconditions* (add list);

$\delta \subseteq \mathcal{P}$ is a set of *negative postconditions* (delete list); and

$\Sigma \cup \varphi \cup \{\overline{p} \mid p \in \eta\}$ and $\Sigma \cup \alpha \cup \{\overline{p} \mid p \in \delta\}$ are consistent.

$\mathcal{D}$, called the *default preference ordering*, is a total ordering of all positive and negative conditions, i.e., the literals;

$\mathcal{I} \subseteq \mathcal{P}$ is the *initial state*, where $\Sigma \cup \mathcal{I} \cup \{\overline{p} \mid p \in \mathcal{P} \setminus \mathcal{I}\}$ is consistent; and

$\mathcal{G} = \langle \mathcal{M}, \mathcal{N} \rangle$ is the *goal*:

$\mathcal{M} \subseteq \mathcal{P}$ is a set of *positive goals*;

$\mathcal{N} \subseteq \mathcal{P}$ is a set of *negative goals*; and

$\Sigma \cup \mathcal{M} \cup \{\overline{p} \mid p \in \mathcal{N}\}$ is consistent.

$\mathcal{P}$ is the set of conditions that are relevant. A *state* is specified by a subset $S \subseteq \mathcal{P}$, indicating that $p \in \mathcal{P}$ is true in that state if and only if $p \in S$. A state S is *possible* if it is consistent with the domain theory Σ, i.e., if $\Sigma \cup S \cup \{\overline{p} \mid p \in \mathcal{P} \setminus S\}$ is consistent.

$\mathcal{O}$ is the set of operators that can change one state to another. The definition of an operator must be consistent with Σ; otherwise, impossible states can occur.

The initial state $\mathcal{I}$ specifies what conditions are initially true and false. The initial state must be possible.

The default preference ordering $\mathcal{D}$ specifies which literals that are true before applying an operator are preferred to be true after applying an operator. The idea is that by default literals true of the previous state are true of the next state. However, if conflicts occur, i.e., inconsistency with the domain theory Σ, then $\mathcal{D}$ indicates which default is preferred. A precise definition is given below.

$\mathcal{G}$ specifies the goals, i.e., $S \subseteq \mathcal{P}$ is a *goal state* if $\mathcal{M} \subseteq S$ and $S \cap \mathcal{N} = \emptyset$.

The consistency requirements simplify further definitions. Of course, determining whether a set of formulas is consistent can also be a hard problem. However, I shall only be considering tractable types of domain theories (definite Horn and Krom).

A finite sequence of operators $(o_1, o_2, \ldots, o_n)$ is a *solution* if $Result(\mathcal{I}, (o_1, o_2, \ldots, o_n))$ is a goal state, where $Result$ is defined as follows:

$$Result(S, (\ )) = S$$
$$Result(S, (o)) = \begin{cases} Extend(S, \Sigma, \alpha, \delta, \mathcal{D}) \\ \quad \text{if } \varphi \subseteq S \wedge S \cap \eta = \emptyset \\ S \quad \text{otherwise} \end{cases}$$
$$Result(S, (o_1, o_2, \ldots, o_n)) = Result(Result(S, (o_1)), (o_2, \ldots, o_n))$$

In essence, any operator can be applied to a state, but only has an effect if its preconditions are satisfied. An operator can appear multiple times in a sequence of operators. If its preconditions are satisfied, the next state is determined by the *Extend* function, which is defined as follows:

$$Extend(S, \Sigma, S_1, S_2, (\ )) = S_1$$
$$Extend(S, \Sigma, S_1, S_2, (p, l_1, \ldots, l_n)) =$$
$$\begin{cases} Extend(S, \Sigma, S_1 \cup \{p\}, S_2, (l_1, \ldots, l_n)) \\ \quad \text{if } p \in S \text{ and} \\ \quad \Sigma \cup S_1 \cup \{p\} \cup \{\overline{q} \mid q \in S_2\} \text{ is consistent} \\ Extend(S, \Sigma, S_1, S_2 \cup \{p\}, (l_1, \ldots, l_n)) \\ \quad \text{if } p \in S \text{ and} \\ \quad \Sigma \cup S_1 \cup \{\overline{q} \mid q \in S_2\} \models \overline{p} \\ Extend(S, \Sigma, S_1, S_2, (l_1, \ldots, l_n)) \\ \quad \text{if } p \notin S \end{cases}$$

$$Extend(S, \Sigma, S_1, S_2, (\overline{p}, l_1, \ldots, l_n)) =$$
$$\begin{cases} Extend(S, \Sigma, S_1, S_2 \cup \{p\}, (l_1, \ldots, l_n)) \\ \quad \text{if } p \notin S \text{ and} \\ \quad \Sigma \cup S_1 \cup \{\overline{p}\} \cup \{\overline{q} \mid q \in S_2\} \text{ is consistent} \\ Extend(S, \Sigma, S_1 \cup \{p\}, S_2, (l_1, \ldots, l_n)) \\ \quad \text{if } p \notin S \text{ and} \\ \quad \Sigma \cup S_1 \cup \{\overline{q} \mid q \in S_2\} \models p \\ Extend(S, \Sigma, S_1, S_2, (l_1, \ldots, l_n)) \\ \quad \text{if } p \in S \end{cases}$$

If an operator is applied to a state S, and its preconditions are true, then $Extend(S, \Sigma, \alpha, \delta, \mathcal{D})$ uses the default preference ordering $\mathcal{D}$ to decide whether literals true of the previous state S are true in the next state. If a literal l is true in the previous state S and is consistent with the domain theory, the effects of the operator, and previously assigned literals, then the l is assigned true in the next state; else if l is true in the previous state S, and the domain theory, the effects of the operator, and previously assigned literals imply the negation of l, then l is assigned false in the next state; else the decision is postponed.

The *Extend* function has the following properties. Given a possible state, *Extend* results in a possible state. Also, *Extend* makes a minimal set of changes from the previous state, i.e., the explicit effects of the operator plus sufficient changes to make the next state possible.

3.2   RELATED WORK

Extended propositional STRIPS planning is closely related to Ginsberg and Smith's (1988) possible worlds approach to reasoning about actions. A possible state S corresponds to a "partial world" W (a set of first-order formulas) in their approach. Each partial world would also include the domain theory Σ as "protected" formulas. The postconditions of an operator o corresponds to the consequences C of an action in their approach. They define a "possible world" as a maximal subset of $W \cup C$ that includes C, the protected formulas, and is consistent. The possible state resulting from the default preference ordering corresponds to a single possible world,[3] ignoring all other possible worlds. Ginsberg and Smith briefly discuss "prioritizing facts" in a manner similar to the default preference ordering so that a single possible world is preferred, but in their formalization, the resulting partial world is taken to be the intersection of all possible worlds.

Other approaches have dealt with the problem of determining the resulting state in a variety of ways. In TMM (Dean and McDermott, 1987), when a set of time tokens conflict with a new time token, all the time tokens in the set are constrained to end before or begin after the new one. This conservative approach would possibly create

---

[3] A minor(?) difference is that the formulas left out of a possible world are not negated in that possible world, while in a possible state, every condition is either true or false. To me, it looks like Ginsberg and Smith's definitions could be easily modified to take this into account.

more constraints than necessary to eliminate the contradiction. The plan net approach of Drummond (1987) requires a "reconciliation set selection function" to choose among alternative ways to resolve inconsistency, but does not specify any constraints on its definition. Of course, in the situation calculus, this is where the infamous frame problem appears (Hayes, 1973).

This problem can be recast as preferring one model over another, as in Shoham's preference logics (Shoham, 1988). Note that it is easy to map a possible state to its model. The result of the *Extend* function can then be formalized as follows:

Let S be a possible state, and M, its corresponding model. Let o be an operator whose preconditions are satisfied by S. Let S_1 and S_2 (with respective models M_1 and M_2) be two possible states consistent with o's postconditions. Let $\mathcal{D} = \{l_1, l_2, \ldots, l_n\}$ be a default preference ordering. Then $M_1 \sqsubseteq M_2$ (M_2 is preferred over M_1) if there exists an l_i such that:

for all l_j, $j < i$, $M_1 \models l_j$ if and only if $M_2 \models l_j$
$M \models l_i$, $M_1 \not\models l_i$, and $M_2 \models l_i$; or
$M \not\models l_i$, $M_1 \models l_i$, and $M_2 \not\models l_i$.

Of course, the fact that *Extend* can be formalized in terms of model preference ordering does not make it reasonable. Doyle and Wellman (1991) point out that any model preference ordering that is based on local ordering criteria (e.g., the default preference ordering) and that prefers one model over all others (e.g., the *Extend* function) generally violates some principle of rational reasoning. In this case, extended propositional STRIPS planning violates the nondictatorship principle that no local criterion dominates all other criteria. For example, if l_1 is true of the previous state, is consistent with the postconditions and domain theory, and is first in the default preference ordering, then any possible state with l_1 true will be preferred as the next state over any possible state with l_1 false. Thus, Doyle and Wellman's result suggests that extended propositional STRIPS planning is unreasonable for many domains, but it also implies that either ambiguity must be tolerated (as in Ginsberg and Smith's possible world approach) or some other principle must be violated. Whatever alternative is chosen, it would be folly to expect much improvement in computational complexity.

3.3 EXAMPLES

I illustrate extended propositional STRIPS planning with a blocks-world example, the cup and saucer example, and the STRIPS robot planning example.

3.3.1 Blocks-World Example

In the Sussman anomaly, there are three blocks A, B, and C. Initially C is on A, A is on the table, and B is on the table. The goal is to have A on B and B on C. Only one block at a time can be moved. The conditions, initial

state, and goals can be represented as follows:

$$\mathcal{P} = \{on\text{-}A\text{-}B, \ on\text{-}A\text{-}C, \ on\text{-}B\text{-}A,$$
$$on\text{-}B\text{-}C, \ on\text{-}C\text{-}A, \ on\text{-}C\text{-}B,$$
$$on\text{-}A\text{-}table, \ on\text{-}B\text{-}table, \ on\text{-}C\text{-}table,$$
$$clear\text{-}A, \ clear\text{-}B, \ clear\text{-}C\}$$
$$\mathcal{I} = \{clear\text{-}C, \ on\text{-}C\text{-}A, \ on\text{-}A\text{-}table,$$
$$clear\text{-}B, \ on\text{-}B\text{-}table\}$$
$$\mathcal{M} = \{on\text{-}A\text{-}B, \ on\text{-}B\text{-}C\}$$
$$\mathcal{N} = \{\}$$

The operators to stack and unstack blocks can be represented as:[4]

$$clear\text{-}A \wedge clear\text{-}B \Rightarrow on\text{-}A\text{-}B$$
$$clear\text{-}A \wedge clear\text{-}C \Rightarrow on\text{-}A\text{-}C$$
$$clear\text{-}B \wedge clear\text{-}A \Rightarrow on\text{-}B\text{-}A$$
$$clear\text{-}B \wedge clear\text{-}C \Rightarrow on\text{-}B\text{-}C$$
$$clear\text{-}C \wedge clear\text{-}A \Rightarrow on\text{-}C\text{-}A$$
$$clear\text{-}C \wedge clear\text{-}B \Rightarrow on\text{-}C\text{-}B$$
$$clear\text{-}A \Rightarrow on\text{-}A\text{-}table$$
$$clear\text{-}B \Rightarrow on\text{-}B\text{-}table$$
$$clear\text{-}C \Rightarrow on\text{-}C\text{-}table$$

That is, if two blocks are clear, then stacking the first block on the second has the "direct" effect of the first block being on top of the second. If a block is clear, then unstacking the block has the "direct" effect of the block being on the table.

The other effects of these operators can be inferred from domain knowledge. Some effects can be inferred from the direct effects, e.g., if A is on B, then A cannot be on C or on the table. These are encoded in the domain theory Σ, which includes the following:

$$on\text{-}A\text{-}B \vee on\text{-}A\text{-}C \vee on\text{-}A\text{-}table$$
$$on\text{-}B\text{-}A \vee on\text{-}B\text{-}C \vee on\text{-}B\text{-}table$$
$$on\text{-}C\text{-}A \vee on\text{-}C\text{-}B \vee on\text{-}C\text{-}table$$
$$on\text{-}B\text{-}A \vee on\text{-}C\text{-}A \vee clear\text{-}A$$
$$on\text{-}A\text{-}B \vee on\text{-}C\text{-}B \vee clear\text{-}B$$
$$on\text{-}A\text{-}C \vee on\text{-}B\text{-}C \vee clear\text{-}C$$
$$\overline{on\text{-}A\text{-}B} \vee \overline{on\text{-}A\text{-}C}$$
$$\overline{on\text{-}A\text{-}B} \vee \overline{on\text{-}A\text{-}table}$$
$$\overline{on\text{-}A\text{-}C} \vee \overline{on\text{-}A\text{-}table}$$
$$\overline{on\text{-}B\text{-}A} \vee \overline{on\text{-}C\text{-}A}$$
$$\overline{on\text{-}B\text{-}A} \vee \overline{clear\text{-}A}$$
$$\overline{on\text{-}C\text{-}A} \vee \overline{clear\text{-}A}$$
$$\ldots$$

Other effects depend on what was true in the previous state, e.g., if A was on C and is now on B, then C is now clear. From the effect of the operator, it can only be inferred that either C is now clear or that B is now

---

[4] The notation $\mathcal{F}_1 \Rightarrow \mathcal{F}_2$ shall be used for operators, where $\mathcal{F}_1$ and $\mathcal{F}_2$ are conjunctions of literals. The positive and negative preconditions are respectively the positive and negative literals of $\mathcal{F}_1$. The positive and negative postconditions are respectively the positive and negative literals of $\mathcal{F}_2$.

on C. However in the blocks-world, no *on* condition can indirectly become true after applying an operator, i.e., by default, false *on* conditions stay false. This domain knowledge can be encoded in the default preference ordering $\mathcal{D}$ by ordering negative *on* conditions before all others, as follows:

$$\mathcal{D} = (\overline{on\text{-}A\text{-}B}, \ \overline{on\text{-}A\text{-}C}, \ \overline{on\text{-}A\text{-}table}, \ \ldots,$$
$$on\text{-}A\text{-}B, \ on\text{-}A\text{-}C, \ on\text{-}A\text{-}table, \ \ldots,$$
$$\overline{clear\text{-}A}, \ \overline{clear\text{-}B}, \ \overline{clear\text{-}C},$$
$$clear\text{-}A, \ clear\text{-}B, \ clear\text{-}C)$$

As it happens, the ordering for the other conditions does not matter. Once negative *on* conditions are propagated from the previous state to the next state, all other changes are unambiguously implied by the domain theory.

Given the initial state of the Sussman anomaly, suppose that the operator to stack B on C is chosen:

$$clear\text{-}B \wedge clear\text{-}C \Rightarrow on\text{-}B\text{-}C$$

Given the direct effect *on-B-C*, the *Extend* function would be used to determine additional effects. Because negative *on* conditions are first in the default preference ordering $\mathcal{D}$, any negative *on* conditions true in the initial state and consistent with the operator's effect are determined to be true in the new state. Of course, $\overline{on\text{-}B\text{-}C}$ is not consistent with *on-B-C*, but the following literals are:

$$\overline{on\text{-}A\text{-}B}, \ \overline{on\text{-}A\text{-}C}, \ \overline{on\text{-}B\text{-}A}, \ \overline{on\text{-}C\text{-}B}, \ \overline{on\text{-}C\text{-}table}$$

Positive *on* conditions are next in $\mathcal{D}$. *on-B-table* is not consistent with *on-B-C* and $\overline{on\text{-}B\text{-}C} \vee \overline{on\text{-}B\text{-}table}$ and so $\overline{on\text{-}B\text{-}table}$ is inferred. The other positive *on* conditions—*on-C-A* and *on-A-table*—remain true.

Negative *clear* conditions are next in $\mathcal{D}$. Only $\overline{clear\text{-}A}$ is true of the initial state. It is also consistent with the effect of the operator, the indirect effects inferred so far, and the domain theory, so it is true of the new state.

Positive *clear* conditions are the last literals in $\mathcal{D}$. *clear-B* is consistent with the effects and the domain theory. *clear-C* is inconsistent with *on-B-C* and $\overline{on\text{-}B\text{-}C} \vee \overline{clear\text{-}C}$, so $\overline{clear\text{-}C}$ is inferred.

3.3.2 Cup and Saucer Example

In the cup and saucer example, two interesting cases are: if the cup is on the saucer, which is at location A, then (1) moving the saucer from location A to location B moves the cup, but (2) moving the cup does not move the saucer. In the first case, the *on-cup-saucer* condition remains true of the next state, but *loc-cup-A* does not. In the second case, *loc-saucer-A* remains true, but *on-cup-saucer* does not. Thus, it appears that no ordering of *on* and *loc* conditions will work.

Part of the answer is to order *on-saucer-A* before *on-cup-saucer*, followed by any location conditions, and

to include the following in the domain theory:

$$on\text{-}saucer\text{-}A \rightarrow loc\text{-}saucer\text{-}A$$
$$on\text{-}cup\text{-}saucer \wedge loc\text{-}saucer\text{-}A \rightarrow loc\text{-}cup\text{-}A$$
$$on\text{-}cup\text{-}saucer \wedge loc\text{-}saucer\text{-}B \rightarrow loc\text{-}cup\text{-}B$$
$$\overline{loc\text{-}saucer\text{-}A} \vee \overline{loc\text{-}saucer\text{-}B}$$
$$\overline{loc\text{-}cup\text{-}A} \vee \overline{loc\text{-}cup\text{-}B}$$

The first case corresponds to applying the operator $\Rightarrow loc\text{-}saucer\text{-}B$. *on-saucer-A* conflicts with *loc-saucer-B*, and so $\overline{on\text{-}saucer\text{-}A}$ is inferred. *on-cup-saucer* does not conflict with anything and, furthermore, implies *loc-cup-B* and $\overline{loc\text{-}cup\text{-}B}$

The second case corresponds to applying the operator $\Rightarrow \ loc\text{-}cup\text{-}B$. *on-saucer-A* does not conflict with *loc-cup-B*, and so remains true. Now *on-cup-saucer* creates a conflict because it would imply $\overline{loc\text{-}cup\text{-}B}$, and so $\overline{on\text{-}cup\text{-}saucer}$ is inferred. Finally, *loc-saucer-A* creates no conflicts and, consequently, remains true.

In both cases, more domain theory is needed to infer *on-saucer-B* and *on-cup-B*, respectively. The encoding becomes more complicated if additional objects are introduced. In general, the *on* conditions in $\mathcal{D}$ should be ordered from bottom to top. This can be achieved by incorporating a coordinate system into the conditions.

3.3.3 STRIPS Robot Example

In the STRIPS robot example (Fikes and Nilsson, 1971), the following operator is presented:

$goto2(m)$: Robot goes next to item m.
Preconditions:
(ONFLOOR) $\wedge$
$\{(\exists x)[\text{INROOM(ROBOT},x) \wedge \text{INROOM}(m,x)] \vee$
$(\exists x)(\exists y)[\text{INROOM(ROBOT},x) \wedge$
$\qquad\qquad \text{CONNECTS}(m, x, y)]\}$
Delete list: ATROBOT($\$$),NEXTTO(ROBOT,$\$$)
  Add list: NEXTTO(ROBOT,m)

Naturally, for propositional planning, an operator must be defined for each possible substitution of the variables. This would be tedious programming, but does not prevent a polynomial-time reduction. A couple of example operators are:

ONFLOOR $\wedge$ INROOM-ROBOT-ROOM1 $\wedge$
INROOM-BOX1-ROOM1
$\Rightarrow$ NEXTTO-ROBOT-BOX1

ONFLOOR $\wedge$ INROOM-ROBOT-ROOM1 $\wedge$
CONNECTS-DOOR1-ROOM1-ROOM5
$\Rightarrow$ NEXTTO-ROBOT-DOOR1

Inferring the other effects can be achieved by including the following kinds of formulas in the domain theory:

$$\overline{\text{NEXTTO-ROBOT-BOX1}} \vee \overline{\text{ATROBOT-e}}$$
$$\overline{\text{NEXTTO-ROBOT-BOX1}} \vee \overline{\text{NEXTTO-ROBOT-BOX2}}$$

If each formula is a disjunction of two literals, no default preference ordering is necessary. For example, asserting NEXTTO-ROBOT-BOX1 unambiguously implies that ATROBOT-e and NEXTTO-ROBOT-BOX2 are false.

4 COMPLEXITY RESULTS

This section considers the computational complexity of extended propositional STRIPS planning assuming various restrictions on the domain theory and on operators. Let EPLANSAT be the decision problem of whether an instance of extended propositional STRIPS planning has a solution.

4.1 NO RESTRICTIONS

Theorem 1 *EPLANSAT is PSPACE-complete.*

Proof: The results in Figure 1 from (Bylander, 1991) correspond to the case where the domain theory Σ is the empty set. Hence, EPLANSAT under the restriction that $\Sigma = \emptyset$ is PSPACE-complete, which implies that EPLANSAT is PSPACE-hard.

EPLANSAT is in PSPACE because the size of a state is bounded by the number of conditions. That is, if there are n conditions and there is a solution, then the length of the smallest solution path must be less than 2^n. Any solution of length 2^n or larger must have "loops," i.e., there must be some state that it visits twice. Such loops can be removed, resulting in a solution of length less than 2^n. Hence, no more than 2^n nondeterministic choices are required. Because NPSPACE = PSPACE, EPLANSAT is also in PSPACE. Because it is also PSPACE-hard, EPLANSAT is PSPACE-complete. □

4.2 DEFINITE HORN DOMAIN THEORIES

A domain theory Σ is definite Horn if each formula in Σ is a definite Horn clause, i.e., a disjunction of literals containing exactly one positive literal.

Theorem 2 *EPLANSAT restricted to definite Horn domain theories and to operators with zero preconditions and one positive postcondition is PSPACE-complete.*

Proof: EPLANSAT restricted to $\Sigma = \emptyset$ and to operators with two positive preconditions and two postconditions is PSPACE-complete (Bylander, 1991). Each such operator can be converted into two operators each with zero preconditions and one positive postcondition in combination with adding conditions, adding definite Horn clauses to Σ, and imposing an appropriate preference ordering on literals.

Suppose there are m operators to convert. Suppose $p_{i1} \wedge p_{i2} \Rightarrow p_{i3} \wedge \overline{p_{i1}}$ is operator o_i to be converted (converting other kinds of operators will be similar).

Let $\Rightarrow pre_i$ be the first operator, let pre_i, in_i, $post_i$, and nil be new conditions, add the following definite Horn clauses to Σ:

$$\overline{pre_i} \vee \overline{p_{i1}} \vee \overline{p_{i2}} \vee in_i$$
$$\overline{pre_i} \vee \overline{pre_j} \vee nil \qquad i \neq j$$
$$\overline{pre_i} \vee \overline{in_j} \vee nil \qquad i \neq j$$
$$\overline{pre_i} \vee \overline{post_j} \vee nil \qquad 1 \leq j \leq m$$

and impose the following orderings in the default preference ordering $\mathcal{D}$:

$$\overline{nil} \prec l \qquad \text{for any other literal } l$$
$$p_{i1} \prec \overline{in_i}$$
$$p_{i2} \prec \overline{in_i}$$

If p_{i1} and p_{i2} are true and nil false, then the result of applying $\Rightarrow pre_i$ will be that pre_i and in_i are true, all other pre_j and in_j are false, and all $post_j$ are false. The orderings ensure that nil remains false, and p_{i1} and p_{i2} remain true.

Let $\Rightarrow post_i$ be the second operator, add the following definite Horn clauses to Σ:

$$\overline{post_i} \vee \overline{in_i} \vee p_{i3}$$
$$\overline{post_i} \vee \overline{in_i} \vee \overline{p_{i1}} \vee nil$$
$$\overline{post_i} \vee \overline{post_j} \vee nil \qquad i \neq j$$
$$\overline{post_i} \vee \overline{pre_j} \vee nil \qquad 1 \leq j \leq m$$

and impose the following orderings in the default preference ordering $\mathcal{D}$:

$$\overline{nil} \prec l \qquad \text{for any other literal } l$$
$$in_i \prec \overline{p_{i3}}$$
$$in_i \prec p_{i1}$$

If in_i is true and nil false, then the result of applying $\Rightarrow post_i$ will be that $post_i$ and p_{i3} are true, p_{i1} is false, all other $post_j$ are false, and all pre_j are false. The orderings ensure that nil remains false, and in_i remains true.

To have the effect of operator o_i, operator $\Rightarrow pre_i$ can be followed by $\Rightarrow post_i$. Also, any sequence of the converted operators will only have the effect of some sequence of original operators. Only a $\Rightarrow post_i$ operator can affect the original conditions, and then only if in_i is true, which is possible only if $\Rightarrow pre_i$ has been previously applied, if the preconditions of o_i are true, and if no intervening $\Rightarrow pre_j$ has deleted in_i.

Thus, starting with any initial state (new conditions initially false) and goals (new conditions not included), some sequence of the converted operators is a solution if and only if some sequence of the original operators is a solution. Thus, EPLANSAT restricted to definite Horn domain theories and to operators with zero preconditions and one positive postcondition is PSPACE-hard. Because EPLANSAT is PSPACE-complete, the restrictive problem is also PSPACE-complete. □

4.3 KROM DOMAIN THEORIES

A domain theory Σ is Krom if each formula in Σ is a Krom clause, i.e., a disjunction of two literals. Note that the default preference ordering does not matter because no "ambiguities" about indirect effects can occur for Krom domain theories.

Theorem 3 *For any $m \geq 0$ and $g \geq 1$, the following problems have the same complexity:*

1. *EPLANSAT with Krom domain theories, with operators restricted to m preconditions, and with g goals.*

2. *EPLANSAT with $\Sigma = \emptyset$, with operators restricted to m preconditions, and with g goals; and*

3. *EPLANSAT with Krom domain theories, with operators restricted to m positive preconditions and one positive postcondition, and with g goals;*

Proof: The first problem is clearly the most general of the three. Let o_i be an operator from some instance of the first problem, and let Σ be the instance's Krom domain theory.

Because Σ is Krom, the "indirect" effects of o_i will be exactly the same for any state satisfying o_i's preconditions. A new operator o_i' can be constructed that explicitly includes these effects in its postconditions. This can be done for every original operator, thus making Σ superfluous. Therefore, any instance of the first problem can be converted to an instance for the second problem.

For the third problem, a new operator o_i' can be constructed as follows. Suppose o_i has m preconditions. Let o_i' be the operator $pre_{i1} \wedge \ldots \wedge pre_{im} \Rightarrow post_i$, where $pre_{i1}, \ldots, pre_{im}$, and $post_i$ are new literals. Note that there are m positive preconditions, and that there is exactly one positive postcondition. If l_j is the jth precondition of o_i, then add $\overline{l_j} \vee pre_{ij}$ and $l_j \vee \overline{pre_{ij}}$ to Σ. Thus, for any possible state, o_i''s preconditions are satisfied exactly when o_i's preconditions are satisfied. If l is a postcondition of o_i, then add $\overline{post_i} \vee l$ to Σ. This ensures that the effects of o_i' include the effects of o_i. Also, add $\overline{post_i} \vee \overline{post_j}$ for $i \neq j$ to Σ. This ensures that o_i' does not have any more effects than o_i, except for any changes to new literals.

Now if pre_{ij} conditions are added as needed to the initial state of the instance of the first problem so that the initial state is possible, then a sequence of converted operators is a solution if and only if the corresponding sequence of original operators is a solution. $\square$

This theorem leads to the following corollaries derived from the results displayed in Figure 1. Figure 2 displays the new results.

Corollary 4 *EPLANSAT with Krom domain theories and with operators restricted to two positive preconditions and one positive postcondition is PSPACE-complete.*

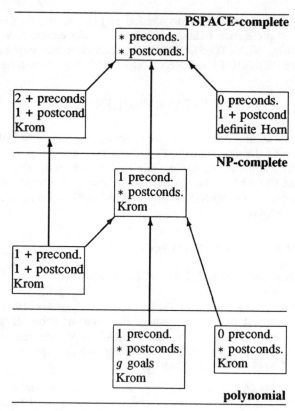

Figure 2: Complexity Results for Extended Propositional STRIPS Planning

Corollary 5 *EPLANSAT with Krom domain theories and with operators restricted to one precondition is NP-complete, even if operators are restricted to one positive precondition and one positive postcondition.*

Corollary 6 *EPLANSAT with Krom domain theories, with operators restricted to one precondition, and with no more than g goals is polynomial.*

Corollary 7 *EPLANSAT with Krom domain theories and with operators restricted to zero preconditions is polynomial.*

5 IMPLICATIONS

This and other analyses show that extremely severe restrictions on both the operators and the domain theory are required to guarantee tractability or even NP-completeness for planning problems. One must be careful, however, concerning the implications of these results.

Work on reactive systems is partly motivated by the complexity of planning. However, this motivation is misguided because the complexity arises from the properties of the problem, not from the properties of any particular algorithm that solves the problem. In other words, these results specify how hard it is to find a sequence of actions that accomplish a set of goals, but are completely neutral to how the sequence of actions are generated. Whether or not a system is reactive or deliberative, it is equally hard to achieve goals by performing actions. This in no way invalidates work on reactive systems, just that it must be put into the proper context.

Nevertheless, many successful planning systems attest to the fact that planning is indeed possible and practical for many domains. What then accounts for the large gap between the theoretical hardness of planning and its practical application? I believe that a large part of the answer is that the complexity analyses only consider properties of planning problems that are domain-independent, and so have some chance of being generally applicable. It seems clear by now that there is no such thing as a set of generally-applicable domain-independent properties that lead to tractable planning. A pessimistic view is that tractable planning domains are tractable for domain-dependent reasons, which in turn demand domain-dependent analyses and planning algorithms. More optimistically, it is possible that specific classes of planning domains might be tractable for similar reasons. In any case, the key issue is how much can domain-independent planning live up to its name.

Acknowledgments

This research has been supported in part by DARPA/AFOSR contract F49620-89-C-0110.

References

Allen, J., Hendler, J., and Tate, A., editors (1990). *Readings in Planning*. Morgan Kaufmann, San Mateo, California.

Bacchus, F. and Yang, Q. (1991). The downward refinement property. In *Proc. Twelfth Int. Joint Conf. on Artificial Intelligence*, pages 286–292, Sydney.

Bäckström, C. and Klein, I. (1991). Parallel non-binary planning in polynomial time. In *Proc. Twelfth Int. Joint Conf. on Artificial Intelligence*, pages 268–273, Sydney.

Bylander, T. (1991). Complexity results for planning. In *Proc. Twelfth Int. Joint Conf. on Artificial Intelligence*, pages 274–279, Sydney.

Chenoweth, S. V. (1991). On the NP-hardness of blocks world. In *Proc. Ninth National Conf. on Artificial Intelligence*, pages 623–628, Anaheim, California.

Dean, T. and Boddy, M. (1988). Reasoning about partially ordered events. *Artificial Intelligence*, 36(3):375–399.

Dean, T. L. and McDermott, D. V. (1987). Temporal data base management. *Artificial Intelligence*, 32(1):1–55. Also appears in (Allen et al., 1990).

Doyle, J. and Wellman, M. P. (1991). Impediments to universal preference-based default theories. *Artificial Intelligence*, 49:97–128.

Drummond, M. E. (1987). A representation of action and belief for automatic planning systems. In *Reasoning about Actions and Plans: Proc. of the 1986 Workshop*, pages 189–211, Timberline, Oregon.

Erol, K., Nau, D. S., and Subrahmanian, V. S. (1991). Complexity, decidability, and undecidability results for domain-independent planning. Technical report, Dept. of Computer Science, Univ. of Maryland, College Park, Maryland.

Fikes, R. E. and Nilsson, N. J. (1971). STRIPS: A new approach to the application of theorem proving to problem solving. *Artificial Intelligence*, 2(3/4):189–208. Also appears in (Allen et al., 1990).

Georgeff, M. P. (1987). Planning. *Annual Review of Computer Science*, 2:349–400. Also appears in (Allen et al., 1990).

Ginsberg, M. L. and Smith, D. E. (1988). Reasoning about actions I: A possible worlds approach. *Artificial Intelligence*, 35(2):165–195.

Gupta, N. and Nau, D. S. (1991). Complexity results for blocks-world planning. In *Proc. Ninth National Conf. on Artificial Intelligence*, pages 629–633, Anaheim, California.

Hayes, P. J. (1973). The frame problem and related problems in artificial intelligence. In Elithorn, A. and Jones, D., editors, *Artificial and Human Thinking*, pages 45–59. Jossey-Bass, San Francisco.

Levesque, H. J. and Brachman, R. J. (1985). A fundamental tradeoff in knowledge representation and reasoning. In Brachman, R. J. and Levesque, H. J., editors, *Readings in Knowledge Representation*, pages 42–70. Morgan Kaufmann, San Mateo, California.

Shoham, Y. (1988). *Reasoning about Change*. MIT Press, Cambridge, Massachusetts.

Waldinger, R. (1977). Achieving several goals simultaneously. In Elcock, E. and Michie, D., editors, *Machine Intelligence 8*, pages 94–136. Ellis Horwood, Edinburgh. Also appears in (Allen et al., 1990).

Abstract Probabilistic Modeling of Action

Lonnie Chrisman
School of Computer Science
Carnegie Mellon University
Pittsburgh, PA 15213
chrisman@cs.cmu.edu

Abstract

Action models used in planning systems must necessarily be abstractions of reality. It is therefore natural to include estimates of ignorance and uncertainty as part of an action model. The standard approach of assigning a unique probability distribution over possible outcomes fares poorly in the presence of abstraction because many unmodeled variables are not governed by pure random chance. A constructive interpretation of probability based on abstracted worlds is developed and suggests modeling constraints on the outcome distribution of an action rather than just a single outcome distribution. A belief function representation of upper and lower probabilities is adopted, and a closed-form projection rule is introduced and shown to be correct.

1 Introduction

Models of actions used in A.I. systems for planning and reasoning must necessarily be abstractions of reality. The real world is too complex and too intricate to model perfectly in complete detail. Whenever we model the effects of actions, we are forced to omit detail which could, in some situations, significantly influence the resulting outcome. It is natural, therefore, to include estimates of ignorance and uncertainty as part of an action model. Probabilistic models in various forms provide tools for expressing this uncertainty.

The most natural form for probabilistic models comes from the framework of Bayesian probability, where a conditional probability on outcomes for an action is specified as $P(o|s)$, where o is the outcome of executing the action from situation s. A number of examples of recent A.I. planning research have employed models of this form ([Drummond and Bresina, 1990],

[Kanazawa and Dean, 1989], [Hanks, 1990], [Chrisman and Simmons, 1991], [Christiansen and Goldberg, 1990]). Bayesian models provide a comfortable framework because the knowledge used (conditional probabilities) can be placed in correspondence with the causal structure of the system being modeled, and the probabilities can be easily interpreted. However, strict Bayesian models deal poorly with abstraction. This difficulty can be traced to the fundamental constructive interpretation of Bayesian probability [Shafer, 1981] that assumes unmodeled variables can always be compared to random chance processes. The next section demonstrates that this is a particularly bad assumption in a planning context. For example, unmodeled variables that influence outcome may depend upon previous actions an agent has taken, not upon random chance. Comparing action outcome to a random chance process is deceptive and can lead a planner to produce plans that work much differently in the real world than predicted. The correct way to address abstraction-related deficiencies in a Bayesian framework is to refine models to greater detail, an approach in direct conflict with the ubiquitous and often desirable demand to use abstract models.

This paper introduces an approach, designed to properly handle abstraction, for probabilistically modeling action. Section 3 introduces an alternative constructive interpretation of probability that adopts abstraction as fundamental. This suggests representing constraints on possible probability distributions over modeled variables rather than representing unique probability distributions. Section 4 introduces a model for action based on a belief function representation for lower probability. Finally, since projection is one of the most important uses of an action model, Section 5 presents a closed-form projection rule and two theorems demonstrating its correctness. The overall framework is a generalization of Bayesian probabilistic reasoning.

2   Abstraction Problems

Abstraction is the omission of detail. The presence of abstraction means that there will be some unmodeled factors that may influence the outcome of an action. Abstraction can arise in many different forms, all of which can be problematic to planning with strict Bayesian models which commit to complete specification of outcome probability distributions. The problems arise because many unmodeled variables are not governed by random chance. This section considers one specific form of abstraction, the omission of state variables, and presents an example to illustrate the problems.

I am considering the action of throwing a rock across a river, with the possible outcomes that the rock lands on the opposite shore or lands in the water. There are many factors that determine the outcome, including the rock's weight and coefficient of air friction, the wind velocity, my adrenaline level, the condition of my arm (warmed up, stretched out, injured, etc), my distance to the water's edge, and the quality of my footing. Many of these can be further refined to greater levels of detail, and many additional factors exist. Suppose, however, that some of this detail — for example, the quality of my footing — is omitted from my model for the throwing action. The Bayesian approach compensates for this missing information by adopting a probability distribution over the possible outcomes, reflecting in this case the expected frequencies that the rock will land in the water versus on the opposite shore. However, this distribution is not determined by the modeled variables alone. If I am wearing cleats on a grassy shore, the rock will be reasonably likely to clear the river, but when wearing flat bottom shoes on damp, moss-covered boulders, reaching the far side may be impossible. By committing to a single distribution, a Bayesian treatment does not admit ignorance (i.e., that there is any lack of knowledge about the actual outcome distribution). After accepting a Bayesian assessment that on any given throw consistent with the modeled situation, I will have a 15% chance of succeeding, I might happily produce a plan to repeatedly throw rocks until one lands on the far side. The model gives no indication that this may have no hope of ever succeeding. The problem here is that the quality of my footing is not governed by a random chance process, and modeling it as such is entirely misleading.

Unmodeled influences can be particularly bothersome for a planner when the agent's own decisions influence unmodeled variables. In this case, the outcome distribution really depends upon decisions made in the past, and different choices at those past decision points can result in different outcome distributions for the current action. My choice this morning to wear flat bottom shoes now affects the probability of getting a rock across the river. Just as some state variables will remain unmodeled, influences between actions will also go unmodeled. As a planner explores alternative projection paths, the distribution on effects of the same action in what appears to be identical situations (given the modeled variables) may be different. Pretending to know the distribution simply leads to the construction of plans that don't work as expected when actually executed in the real world.

3   Abstraction-Based Interpretation

The problems with Bayesian action models stem from implicit assumptions arising from the Bayesian interpretation of probability. Glenn Shafer [Shafer, 1981] has eloquently argued for a constructive view of probability. In the constructive view, the meaning of probability in any given formalism "amounts to comparing one's evidence to a scale of canonical examples, and a constructive theory of probability judgement must supply ... the scale of canonical examples." Random chance provides the canonical example for the Bayesian interpretation. If a variable does behave according to random chance, it is said to be aleatory. But as the previous section demonstrated, when abstraction is invoked in planning contexts, many variables might not be aleatory. In this section a different constructive view of probability is arrived at by accepting the abstracted grand aleatory world as the canonical example. Essentially, abstraction is assumed as a fundamental starting point for the development of this view, rather than random chance alone as in the Bayesian case.

Action models or state descriptions include certain (modeled) variables and necessarily omit others (unmodeled variables). A Bayesian model assumes that a fixed, stationary probability distribution exists over the set of modeled variables. Implicitly, this amounts to assuming that all unmodeled variables are aleatory, so that the modeled distribution is obtained from $P(mv) = \sum_{uv} P(mv|uv)P(uv)$, where mv are modeled values and uv are unmodeled values. To drop this assumption and obtain a new constructive interpretation for probability, assume that there is some (possibly infinite) set of unmodeled (non-aleatory) variables, such that if these were to be concatenated with our modeled variables, a fixed, stationary distribution would result. This entire collection of variables describes a grand aleatory world. Essentially, if we did have a complete model with no abstraction, then we would be able to model action outcomes with a probability distribution. When we consider only the modeled variables, assigning values to some of these variables does not imply that a unique probability distribution exists over the unassigned modeled variables because some unmodeled variables are non-aleatory. By considering all possible assignments to unmodeled variables, what we do get is a set of constraints defining a (possibly infinite) set of probability distributions over the unassigned modeled variables. This set of distributions properly describes the belief afforded to an abstract description.

In the example from the previous section, foothold quality is a non-aleatory unmodeled variable. Even though it (and other variables) are unmodeled, what we may know is that even in the best of all situations, we cannot possibly have more than a 30% probability of actually getting a rock across the river. As far as we know, the actual probability might be 30%, but it may also be 18%, 5% or even 0% (totally impossible). This can simply be expressed as $P(oppositeShore) \leq 0.3$. The use of constraints on probability distributions, rather than precisely specified distributions, provides one method for probabilistically modeling action outcomes, despite the problems introduced by abstraction. Because foothold quality cannot be compared to random chance, it is wrong to assume a single probability of success in this example. To handle examples such as this, strict Bayesian modeling would require the model itself to be refined all the way to a grand aleatory world — a process which could require infinite detail and contradicts the necessity (and our desire) to use abstract models.

Sets of probability functions are commonly referred to as lower probability distributions and can be traced back to [Good, 1962]. They have been studied mathematically by many people, but I have not seen the above constructive interpretation given previously. Usually, lower probability work assumes that an underlying distribution exists; conversely, the above interpretation does not assume a distribution to exist over the modeled space. Like some mathematical treatments of non-measurable sets, [Halpern and Fagin, 1990] do not assume that an underlying distribution exists, but they do not provide the scale of canonical examples necessary to qualify the formalism as a full constructive interpretation of probability.

4   Modeling Action

The previous section argued that abstract probabilistic models should utilize sets of distributions rather than always committing to exactly specified distributions. To apply this idea, it necessary to select a mechanism for representing sets of distributions. Since the number of such sets is uncountably infinite, the choice of representation scheme will necessarily limit the possible distributions that can be represented. [Fagin and Halpern, 1989], [Wasserman, 1990], and [Kyburg, 1987] have all advanced the use of belief function representations for conveniently representing convex[1] lower probability functions, and [Lemmer and Kyburg, 1991] proves that most of the important convex sets can be represented by belief functions. While it is easy to construct non-convex belief sets, the usefulness for planning or decision making of mechanisms which are general enough to represent non-convex sets of probabilities is dubious, so a belief function representation is adopted here. This framework is most similar to [Fagin and Halpern, 1989].

A belief function can be viewed as a type of data structure, much like a list is a type of data structure. As such, it is a useful mechanism both for representing lower probability, as it is used here, and for representing evidential support, as in the Dempster-Shafer theory [Shafer, 1976]. However, the semantics of what is represented differs in these two cases and should not be confused. For example, Dempster's rule of combination gives perfectly reasonable results when it is used to combine evidence, but it does not make sense to apply it to a lower probability interpretation such as the one advanced in this paper. The reader wishing to understand the difference between the representation of evidence and lower probability should read [Halpern and Fagin, 1990] and [Shafer, 1976]. For the purposes of the current discussion, the reader should just be aware that the Dempster-Shafer theory of evidence is not being utilized here, even though the same syntactic machinery is employed to represent belief in both cases.

A belief about the state of the world is modeled using a "marginal" belief function. This belief function simply specifies constraints on the possible probability distributions, thus characterizing the agent's beliefs about the state of the world. Let Ω_{pre} delimit a mutually exclusive and exhaustive propositional space of possible situations before an action's execution, called a *prestate frame of discernment*, and let Ω_{post} delimit a *poststate* (after the action's execution) *frame of discernment*. A prestate belief is represented internally by the mass-assignment $m_{pre} : 2^{\Omega_{pre}} \to [0,1]$ such that

$$\sum_{B \subseteq \Omega_{pre}} m_{pre}(B) = 1, \qquad m_{pre}(\emptyset) = 0$$

Usually only a few sets, called focal elements, will have non-zero mass-assignments. The mass-assignment specifies a set of constraints on the possible probability distributions describing the current state. For a set $B \subseteq \Omega_{pre}$, $m_{pre}(B)$ is the amount of probability mass that is constrained to the situations in B, but which may be freely allocated in any way between the

---

[1]A lower probability distribution is convex if any weighted average of any two consistent probability distributions is also consistent with the lower probability distribution.

situations in B. To simplify the notation, we will informally drop the subscripts and write $m(B)$ when it is clear that the set B refers to a prestate (B="before"). Belief and plausibility functions are defined as

$$Bel(B) = \sum_{C \subseteq B} m(C) \qquad (1)$$

$$Pls(B) = \sum_{C \cap B \neq \emptyset} m(C) \qquad (2)$$

The belief $Bel(B)$ is the total amount of probability mass that is trapped within B, and the plausibility $Pls(B)$ is the total amount of probability mass that is allowed in B. Each of the three functions m, Bel, and Pls uniquely determine the other two. For example, $Bel(B) = 1 - Pls(\bar{B})$ and m can be obtained from Bel using [Shafer, 1976]

$$m(B) = \sum_{C \subseteq B} (-1)^{|B-C|} Bel(C) \qquad (3)$$

A probability assignment $P : \Omega_{pre} \rightarrow [0,1]$ is said to be *consistent* with Bel when $Bel(B) \leq \sum_{b \in B} P(b)$ for all $B \subseteq \Omega_{pre}$. The set of all consistent probability assignments is denoted by $\mathcal{P}$. It is well known [Shafer, 1976] that $Bel(B)$ and $Pls(B)$ are lower and upper bounds respectively on the probability of B:

$$Bel(B) = \inf_{P \in \mathcal{P}} \sum_{b \in B} P(b)$$

$$Pls(B) = \sup_{P \in \mathcal{P}} \sum_{b \in B} P(b)$$

The relationship between a belief function and a particular consistent Bayesian distribution can be given by specifying how the mass assignment $m(B)$ for each set B is reallocated amongst the basic elements of B. This mapping, called an *allocation mapping function*, simply demonstrates how a given consistent probability distribution satisfies the constraints specified by a belief function on the possible distributions. The allocation mapping function is characterized by the following lemma. The proof appears in the Appendix.

Lemma 1 *A probability distribution P is consistent with belief function Bel if and only if there exists an allocation mapping function $f : 2^\Omega \times \Omega \rightarrow [0,1]$ such that the following conditions hold:*

1. $\sum_{B \subseteq \Omega} f(B,b) = P(b) \qquad \forall b \in \Omega$

2. $\sum_{b \in \Omega} f(B,b) = \sum_{b \in B} f(B,b) = m(B) \qquad \forall B \subseteq \Omega$

3. $f(B,b) \geq 0$, for all $B \subseteq \Omega$, $b \in \Omega$

4. $f(B,b) = 0$ if $b \notin B$

The effects of actions are modeled using basic conditional belief functions, $Bel_{post|b} : 2^{\Omega_{post}} \rightarrow [0,1]$. To simplify notation, we write $Bel(A|b)$ when it is clear that A refers to a poststate (A="after"). This is the belief assigned to the poststate situation A given that the prestate situation is exactly b, where $b \in \Omega_{pre}$. $Bel(A|b)$ is represented internally by $m(A|b)$ such that

$$Bel(A|b) = \sum_{C \subseteq A} m(C|b) \qquad (4)$$

Belief functions are generalizations of probability distributions. When only single element sets are assigned mass (i.e., $m_{pre}(B) = 0$ when B has more than one element), then Bel_{pre} represents an exact probability distribution and is called a Bayesian belief function. $Bel_{post|b}$ can similarly represent an exact conditional probability distribution. At the other extreme, when absolutely no information about the prestate is available, the vacuous belief function, where $m_{pre}(\Omega_{pre}) = 1$, can be used to represent a state of total ignorance. In between, the various assignments represent constraints on the possible probability distributions.

An action is modeled by associating one basic conditional belief function with each B_i, where $\{B_1, B_2, ..., B_m\}$ form a set partition on Ω_{pre}. An action model is given as

$$\forall b \in B_1, \qquad Bel_{pre|b}(\cdot) = Bel_1(\cdot)$$
$$\forall b \in B_2, \qquad Bel_{pre|b}(\cdot) = Bel_2(\cdot)$$
$$\vdots$$
$$\forall b \in B_m, \qquad Bel_{pre|b}(\cdot) = Bel_m(\cdot)$$

Each line of the action model represents one context-dependent outcome, where B_i is the precondition specifying the context. A finer partition granularity corresponds to greater knowledge about which distinctions influence the outcome, and finer distinctions usually lead to more precise outcome specifications. Each belief function, Bel_i, is represented internally by explicitly specifying the corresponding mass assignments. As with a prestate description, we say a conditional probability assignment, $P(a|b)$, is consistent with an action model $Bel(A|b)$ when $Bel(A|b) \leq \sum_{a \in A} P(a|b)$ for all $A \subseteq \Omega_{post}$ and $b \in \Omega_{pre}$. The set of all consistent distributions is denoted by $\mathcal{P}_{post|b}$.

As a simple example of modeling rock throwing, take the possible prestates to be $\Omega_{pre} = \{light, heavy\}$. While this leaves out many important state variables, it also abstracts in another way by representing a quantitative variable (weight) qualitatively. The precise weight of the rock is important for determining the probability of success, but this precision is abstracted away by adopting only the qualitative distinctions of *light* and *heavy*. If it were the case that of all the light rocks I typically pick up, the actual weight obeyed some fixed distribution, then a single probability distribution would also be sufficient for expressing the outcome probabilities in the abstracted model. This is unlikely to be the case, however, because the distribution of weight depends upon such things as the choice of decision procedure that I used in selecting which rock to pick up. Therefore, as was also the case with omitted variables, a single distribution may not suffice for summarizing the outcome distribution of an action when a quantitative variable is abstracted into a qualitative one. Therefore, a belief function is used to express the abstract action model. Take the possible poststates to be $\Omega_{post} = \{oppositeShore, inWater\}$. An action description might look like:

if $b \in \{light\}$: $\quad m(\{oppositeShore\}|b) = .15$

$\qquad\qquad\qquad m(\{inWater\}|b) = .7$

$\qquad\qquad\qquad m(\Omega_{post}|b) = .15$

if $b \in \{heavy\}$: $\quad m(\{inWater\}|b) = .8$

$\qquad\qquad\qquad m(\Omega_{post}|b) = .2$

The action model specifies that the probability of getting a light rock to the other side is between 15% and 30%, while the probability of throwing a heavy rock that far is less than 20% but may be impossible. Compare this to a Bayesian model that predicts that exactly 15% of the heavy rocks will land on the far side. Not only does the Bayesian model assert more precision than is actually warranted, it also gives no indication that the outcome may actually be impossible — information that could be critical to a planner.

5 Projection

Projection is the process of predicting the effects of an action's execution given an action model and prestate description. Projection is one of the primary uses for an action model, and is utilized directly by some planners ([Drummond and Bresina, 1990], [Hanks, 1990]). In this section, a closed-form projection operation for belief function representations is introduced, and two theorems prove its correctness. The method is a generalization of Bayesian projection, performed in a Bayesian framework using Jeffrey's rule:

$$P(a) = \sum_{b \in \Omega_{pre}} P(a|b)P(b) \qquad (5)$$

Given an action model as in the previous section, $Bel(A|b)$, and a belief about the prestate, $Bel(B)$, the projection operation derives a belief function, $Bel(A|Bel_{pre})$, that represents the belief about the poststate situation resulting from the action's execution. We will also make use of one additional condi-

tional belief function, $Bel(A|B)$, given by

$$Bel(A|B) = \min_{b \in B} Bel(A|b) = \min_{b \in B} \sum_{C \subseteq A} m(C|b)$$

$Bel(A|B)$ is almost the same as Halpern and Fagin's conditional belief functions; however, there are several subtle, but important differences too detailed to cover here. $Bel(A|B)$ is not considered to be the action model — it is only a function that is computed from the given model $m(A|b)$. Notice that there are four different belief functions involved here. In each of the four cases, mass-assignments $m(A|b)$, $m(B)$, $m(A|Bel_{pre})$, and $m(A|B)$ represent belief functions in memory (see (3) and (4)).

Lemma 2 *If $P_{post|b}$ is consistent with $Bel_{post|b}$, then for all $b \in B$*

$$Bel(A|B) \leq P(A|b) = \sum_{a \in A} P(a|b)$$

Proof:

$$Bel(A|B) = \min_{b' \in B} Bel(A|b') \leq \quad Bel(A|b) \; \forall b \in B$$
$$\leq \quad P(A|b)$$

$\square$

The projection, represented by $m_{post|Bel_{pre}} : 2^{\Omega_{post}} \to [0, 1]$, characterizes the belief about the state after the action is executed and is given by:

$$m(A|Bel_{pre}) = \sum_{B \subseteq \Omega_{pre}} m(A|B)m(B) \qquad (6)$$

The corresponding belief function can equivalently be written as

$$Bel(A|Bel_{pre}) = \sum_{C \subseteq A} m(C|Bel_{pre})$$
$$= \sum_{B \subseteq \Omega_{pre}} Bel(A|B)m(B) \quad (7)$$

This post-state belief is really a marginal belief function, but Bel_{pre} is included in the notation to avoid confusion. Note the similarity between (6), (7), and the Bayesian projection rule (5). Just as the action model and prestate belief functions can be interpreted as representing constraints over the possible probability distributions, $Bel(A|Bel_{pre})$ also represents distribution constraints. We say a projected probability distribution, P, is consistent with a projected belief function, $Bel(A|Bel_{pre})$ if $Bel(A|Bel_{pre}) \leq \sum_{a \in A} P(a)$ for all $A \subseteq \Omega_{post}$. The set of all consistent projected probability distributions is denoted $\mathcal{P}_{post|Bel_{pre}}$. The following theorem establishes the completeness of the projection procedure.

Theorem 1 *Let P represent a Bayesian projection obtained by (5) from a Bayesian action model $P_{post|b}$ and a Bayesian prestate belief P_{pre}, both of which are consistent with $Bel_{post|b}$ and Bel_{pre} respectively. Then P is consistent with the projected belief function $Bel(A|Bel_{pre})$. Formally*

$$\left\{ \begin{array}{l} P : \quad P(a) = \sum_{b\in\Omega_{pre}} P(a|b)P(b), \\ P_{post|b} \in \mathcal{P}_{post|b}, P_{pre} \in \mathcal{P}_{pre} \end{array} \right\} \subseteq \mathcal{P}_{post|Bel_{pre}}$$

Proof: Assume P_{pre} and $P_{post|b}$ are consistent with Bel_{pre} and $Bel_{post|b}$ respectively. Applying Equation (7) and Lemmas 1(2), 2, 1(4), and 1(1) (in that order) yields:

$$\begin{aligned} Bel(A|Bel_{pre}) &= \sum_{B\subseteq\Omega_{pre}} Bel(A|B)m(B) \\ &= \sum_{B\subseteq\Omega_{pre}} Bel(A|B)\sum_{b\in B} f(B,b) \\ &\leq \sum_{B\subseteq\Omega_{pre}}\sum_{b\in B} P(A|b)f(B,b) \\ &= \sum_{B\subseteq\Omega_{pre}}\sum_{b\in\Omega_{pre}} P(A|b)f(B,b) \\ &= \sum_{b\in\Omega_{pre}} P(A|b)P(b) = P(A) \end{aligned}$$

Therefore, by definition, P is consistent with $Bel(A|Bel_B)$. $\square$

This theorem verifies that the projection will not jump to conclusions that are not justified by the available information since valid poststate distributions will not be left out. However, this by itself is not a particularly strong guarantee. For example, the vacuous projection which always produces a poststate belief of total ignorance (i.e., $m(\Omega_{post}|Bel_{pre}) = 1$) also has this property. It is therefore of interest to explore whether the converse to Theorem 1 holds, i.e., whether $\mathcal{P}_{post|Bel_{pre}} \subseteq \{P : ...\}$. This would imply that $Bel(A|Bel_{pre})$ is the true convex projection. Unfortunately the converse does not hold. In fact, the true lower probability projection is not necessarily representable by a belief function, even if the prestate and the action model are represented by belief functions. This is demonstrated in the following example:

I am considering throwing a rock that is currently in my hand across the river. If it is a heavy rock, the odds are better than even that it'll land in the water. There is also at least a 20% chance that it lands on the opposite shore, and at least a 10% probability that I'll drop it without launching it at all. On the other hand, if it turns out to be light weight, the odds are better than even that it will land on the opposite shore, with absolutely no chance of accidentally dropping it and at least a 10% chance that it lands in the water. I

haven't the slightest idea whether the rock I am about to throw is light or heavy, but I do know it is one of the two.

If we set $\Omega_{pre} = \{light, heavy\}$, $\Omega_{post} = \{inWater, oppositeShore, dropped\}$, the prestate belief is given by $m(\Omega_{pre}) = 1$, and the action is modeled by:

```
if b ∈ {heavy}:    m({inWater}|b) = .5
                   m({oppositeShore}|b) = .2
                   m({dropped}|b) = .1
                   m(Ω_post|b) = .2
if b ∈ {light}:    m({inWater}|b) = .1
                   m({oppositeShore}|b) = .5
                   m({inWater, oppositeShore}|b) = .4
```

Applying the projection rule yields the following poststate mass-assignment:

$$\begin{aligned} m(\{inWater\}|Bel_{pre}) &= .1 \\ m(\{oppositeShore\}|Bel_{pre}) &= .2 \\ m(\{inWater, oppositeShore\}|Bel_{pre}) &= .4 \\ m(\{oppositeShore, dropped\}|Bel_{pre}) &= .1 \\ m(\Omega_{post}|Bel_{pre}) &= .2 \end{aligned}$$

This assignment coincides with intuition since the resulting Bel and Pls correctly bound the possible probability distributions. For example, the solution indicates that there is a 10% belief and 70% plausibility that the rock lands in the water. In a grand aleatory world for this situation, it may be the case that there is a 40% probability that the rock is light, a 30% chance that a light rock lands in the water, and a 60% chance that a heavy rock lands in the water. Notice that these are consistent with the problem. If this is the case, then the actual probability of landing in the water is 48%, which is clearly between the projected bounds of 10% and 70%. However, despite the intuitive appeal, the probability distribution

$$\begin{aligned} P(inWater) &= .1 \\ P(dropped) &= .3 \\ P(oppositeShore) &= .6 \end{aligned}$$

is also consistent with the projected belief function, yet it cannot be generated by any consistent Bayesian prestate-action model pair. In fact, the true poststate of this example cannot be exactly represented with a belief function.

One method for handling the above example exactly would be to adopt a representation scheme that is even more general than belief functions — for example, a scheme capable of representing certain non-convex sets of distributions. At this point, however, it is unclear how the additional generality could be of any use in the context of planning and decision making. Therefore, we keep the belief function based projection, even though a small amount of information is lost. Given that the representation is limited to belief functions, the following theorem shows that the projection rule is the best projection operation possible.

Theorem 2 *Let $A \subseteq \Omega_{post}$ be any set in Ω_{post}. There exists a consistent Bayesian prestate–action model pair, P_{pre} and $P_{post|b}$, such that*

$$P(A) = \sum_{b \in \Omega_{pre}} P_{post|b}(A|b) P_{pre}(b) = Bel(A|Bel_{pre})$$

Proof: Introduce the ordering $b_1, b_2, ..., b_n$ for all $b_i \in \Omega_{pre}$ such that $Bel(A|b_1) \leq Bel(A|b_2) \leq ... \leq Bel(A|b_n)$. Let $B_i = \{b_{i+1}, b_{i+2}, ..., b_n\}$, $B_n = \emptyset$. Then rewriting the sum in (7):

$$Bel(A|Bel_{pre}) = \sum_{i=1}^{n} \sum_{B \subseteq B_i} Bel(A|\{b_i\} \cup B) m(\{b_i\} \cup B)$$

$$= \sum_{i=1}^{n} Bel(A|b_i) \sum_{B \subseteq B_i} m(\{b_i\} \cup B)$$

$$= \sum_{i=1}^{n} P(A|b_i) P(b_i) = P(A)$$

where $P(A|b_i)$ was selected as equal to $Bel(A|b_i)$, and $P(b_i)$ was chosen by reallocating each mass $m(B)$ to the smallest element $b_i \in B$ as determined by the introduced ordering. $\square$

The theorem implies that if the projected poststate belief function is tightened in any way, then valid Bayesian poststate distributions will be left out. Theorem 1 implies that if it were weakened in any way, impossible distributions would be let in. Therefore, the projection rule is the best one can hope for if one is not willing to use more complex representations. Geometrically, the projection rule finds the convex hull of the possible poststate probability distributions.

6   Levels of Abstraction

It is usually possible to model a system at many different levels of detail. As more detail is left unmodeled, it is said that the model is at a greater level of abstraction. Increasing the level of abstraction of an action model decreases the precision at which predictions into the future can be made using the model.

The effects of abstracting too much can be easily spotted in a lower probability representation where ignorance is explicitly represented. For example, if an abstract model omits the most important variables in a given problem, after projecting through only a few consecutive actions, the agent may be left with the vacuous poststate belief (i.e., complete ignorance). In general, the distance into the future at which an agent can usefully make predictions (even statistical predictions) is limited by the level of abstraction of its models.

There is a distinct difference between how the lower probability approach handles the case of overly abstract models from how the Bayesian approach treats this case. If a Bayesian model is projected into the future to a point where unmodeled, non-aleatory variables significantly influence the final poststate, the Bayesian model still makes a precise statistical claim about the final poststate distribution without any explicit indication that the stated distribution lacks accuracy. If the actual outcome frequencies are measured, they are likely to be quite different from the predicted distribution (one example of this discrepancy actually occurring appears in [Christiansen and Goldberg, 1990]). On the other hand, the lower probability approach gives very loose bounds in this case, effectively admitting that it doesn't know precisely what to expect. It is important to realize that the actual accuracy is equivalent in the two cases, being determined not by the formalism, but by the level of abstraction in the models. The primary difference here between the formalisms is whether or not the level of precision is explicitly indicated. This also suggests that the extra information encoded by a belief function may be extremely valuable to any system that automatically adjusts its own level of abstraction during reasoning.

7   Conclusion

Current techniques for using probabilistic models for planning are weak and applicable only to fairly small or well behaved problems. Despite the development of Bayesian networks [Pearl, 1988] for concisely representing probability distributions, the ability to attack probabilistic planning problems with extremely large state spaces, the type typically of interest to A.I. researchers, will require the ability to properly handle abstract probabilistic models. The constructive framework presented here addresses these concerns. Conditional independence statements can still be asserted and used in the lower probability framework, for example, to address concerns related to the frame problem (cf. [Wellman, 1990]). However, the framework may also offer significant advantages for inference networks, since it may potentially allow "almost statistically independent" influences to be abstracted away, a feature which could be used to greatly reduce the number of predecessors of a node when it is more important to obtain a quick answer than it is to obtain a precise answer. This is one of the many interesting areas for future research.

One of my own research interests is closed-loop planning, where the planner considers, at planning time, whether or not to commit resources to obtain additional information at execution time [Chrisman and Simmons, 1991]. Not observing a state variable turns out to be a lot like abstracting a model. Since the unobserved state variable can usually be affected by the agent's own behavior, unobserved variables are not aleatory. The current framework arose out of an effort to deal with unobserved variables efficiently without having to continue reasoning about unobserved details as the strict Bayesian tools demand. Along with the projection rule, a closed-form conditioning rule, a generalization of Bayes' rule, has also been developed with similar associated theorems, thus allowing observations to be incorporated into the agent's belief about the state of the world (see also [Fagin and Halpern, 1989], [Wasserman, 1990]).

The most important area for future research is the development of effective probabilistic planning algorithms that use these abstract action models. Given the projection rule presented here, it should be fairly easy to adapt temporal projection algorithms ([Drummond and Bresina, 1990], [Hanks, 1990]) to the new representations. Additionally, the introduction of the extra representational power may contribute important capabilities that could significantly extend the state of the art of temporal projection algorithms. For example, Hank's algorithm bundles outcomes in order to obtain small projection graphs. The generalized probability representation may additionally allow action choices to be bundled as well. The result would be a form of least-commitment probabilistic temporal projection.

Models used by planners will always be abstractions of reality. Probability provides an important tool for representing uncertainty, but because many unmodeled influences are not governed by random chance, simply assuming a unique probability distribution over the possible action outcomes may work poorly. The new framework advocates representing constraints on outcome probability distributions rather than just single probability distributions. The extra representational power may be valuable for capturing ill-behaved and poorly understood actions while avoiding the misleading appearance of having more knowledge about the projected effects of an action than is actually the case.

Acknowledgements

I thank Sebastian Thrun for taking the time to examine my proofs (any remaining mistakes are my own), and to Reid Simmons, Sebastian Thrun, Rich Goodwin, and anonymous reviewers for comments on earlier drafts of the paper. The research was sponsored by NASA under contract number NAGW-1175. The views and conclusions contained in this paper are my own and should not be interpreted as representing the official policies, either expressed or implied, of NASA or the U.S. government.

References

[Chrisman and Simmons, 1991] Lonnie Chrisman and Reid Simmons. Sensible planning: Focusing perceptual attention. In *Ninth National Conference on Artificial Intelligence*, July 1991.

[Christiansen and Goldberg, 1990] Alan D. Christiansen and Kenneth Y. Goldberg. Robotic manipulation planning with stochastic actions. In *DARPA Workshop on Innovative Approaches to Planning, Scheduling, and Control*, San Diego, CA, November 1990.

[Drummond and Bresina, 1990] Mark Drummond and John Bresina. Anytime synthetic projection: Maximizing the probability of goal satisfaction. In *Eight National Conference on Artificial Intelligence*, July 1990.

[Fagin and Halpern, 1989] Ronald Fagin and Joseph Y. Halpern. A new approach to updating beliefs. Technical Report RJ 7222, IBM, May 1989.

[Good, 1962] I. J. Good. Subjective probability as the measure of a non-measurable set. In Nagel, Suppes, and Tarski, editors, *Logic, Methodology, and Philosophy of Science*, pages 319–329. Stanford University Press, 1962.

[Halpern and Fagin, 1990] Joseph Y. Halpern and Ronald Fagin. Two views of belief: Belief as generalized probability and belief as evidence. In *Eighth National Conference on Artificial Intelligence*, July 1990. A long version appears as IBM-TR-RJ-7221, 12/18/89.

[Hanks, 1990] Steve Hanks. Practical temporal projection. In *Eighth National Conference on Artificial Intelligence*, July 1990.

[Kanazawa and Dean, 1989] Keiji Kanazawa and Thomas Dean. A model for projection and action. In *Eleventh International Joint Conference on Artificial Intelligence*, August 1989.

[Kyburg, 1987] Henry E. Kyburg, Jr. Bayesian and non-bayesian evidential updating. *Artificial Intelligence*, 31:271–293, 1987.

[Lemmer and Kyburg, 1991] John F. Lemmer and Henry E. Kyburg, Jr. Conditions for the existence of belief functions corresponding to intervals of belief. In *Ninth National Conference on Artificial Intelligence*, July 1991.

[Pearl, 1988] Judea Pearl. *Probabilistic Reasoning in Intelligent Systems: Networks of Plausible Inference*. Morgan Kaufmann, San Mateo, CA, 1988.

[Shafer, 1976] Glenn Shafer. *A Mathematical Theory of Evidence*. Princeton University Press, 1976.

[Shafer, 1981] Glenn Shafer. Constructive probability. *Synthese*, 48:1–60, 1981.

[Wasserman, 1990] Larry A. Wasserman. Prior envelopes based on belief functions. *Annals of Statistics*, 18:454–464, 1990.

[Wellman, 1990] Michael P. Wellman. The STRIPS assumption for planning under uncertainty. In *Proceedings Eighth National Conference on Artificial Intelligence*, July 1990.

Appendix: Proof of Lemma 1

Proof: First, assume the conditions hold for some f. Then

$$
\begin{aligned}
Bel(B) &= \sum_{C \subseteq B} m(C) = \sum_{C \subseteq B} \sum_{b \in C} f(C,b) \\
&= \sum_{b \in B} \sum_{C:b \in C, C \subseteq B} f(C,b) \\
&\leq \sum_{b \in B} \sum_{C \subseteq \Omega} f(C,b) = \sum_{b \in B} P(b)
\end{aligned}
$$

Therefore, P is consistent with Bel.

For the other direction, assume P is consistent with Bel. Pick a set $B \subseteq \Omega$ and an element $b \in B$ and change the belief function by transferring mass in the amount of $f(B,b)$ from B to $\{b\}$, where

$$ f(B,b) = \min m(B), \min_{C \subseteq \Omega} \{P(C) - Bel(C) : B \not\subseteq C, b \in C\} $$

Repeatedly apply the transfer for every pair of $B \subseteq \Omega$ and $b \in B$, at each step modifying Bel by the shift in mass and using the modified belief to evaluate $f(B,b)$ for successive pairs. Take $f(B,b) = 0$ for all $b \notin B$. Notice from (1) that the only sets C for which the transfer will alter $Bel(C)$ are the sets where $B \not\subseteq C$ and $b \in C$. For these sets, the minimization ensures that the new $Bel(C)$ continues to be less than or equal to $P(C)$. Therefore, P will continue to be consistent with Bel after each mass transfer.

Next, it is shown that all the mass will eventually be transferred to single element subsets, therefore exactly specifying the probability distribution P. After all the mass has been transferred, suppose there is a set with more than one element where $m(B) > 0$. Then for each $b \in B$, there is a set $C_b : B \not\subseteq C_b \wedge b \in C_b$ such that $Bel(C_b) = P(C_b)$. But these sets $\{C_b | b \in B\}$ totally account for all the mass in $\hat{C} = \bigcup_{b \in B} C_b$. However, $m(B)$ also contributes to the belief of $\hat{C}$, so that

if $m(B) > 0$, then the mass in $\hat{C}$ is overaccounted for, i.e., $Bel(\hat{C}) > P(\hat{C})$. This contradicts the fact that P is consistent; therefore, $m(B)$ must be zero for all B with more than one element. The resulting Bel is a Bayesian belief function, and the total amount of mass assigned to $m(\{b\})$ is $\sum_{B \subseteq \Omega} f(B,b)$, thus proving condition 1. Since all the mass is transferred out of B to the elements $b \in B$, condition 2 is proved. The third and fourth conditions follow directly from the specification of $f(B,b)$ above. $\square$

Semantics for tasks that can be interrupted or abandoned

Ernest Davis
Courant Institute
New York, New York
(212) 998-3123
DAVISE@CS.NYU.EDU

Abstract

It is often desirable to allow a robot in a dynamic, uncontrolled environment to interrupt or abandon some task that engages it. To facilitate this, it is helpful to include in the language of plans such control structure as "Carry out task T1 until condition Q becomes true," or "Proceed with the execution of task T1 whenever it does not interfere with task T2." To define such control structures formally, it is necessary to define what it means to begin carrying out a task, independently of whether the task is completed. This paper presents a formal semantics for a language of plans that includes these control structures, together with concurrency and partial specification. Such a semantics will support the formal verification of plans of this kind.

1 SEMANTICS FOR ALGOL-LIKE PLANNING LANGUAGES

A plan can be viewed as a program that controls the actions of an autonomous agent (McDermott 1991a). Pursuing this analogy, it is natural to use successful existing programming languages as models for the general structure of a planning language. In particular, if the ALGOL family of languages is chosen as a model, then plans will be compound statements, formed by recursively applying predefined control-structure operators to primitive statements.[1] Some of the basic control structure operators that arise naturally in planning are familiar elements of programming languages, such as sequencing, conditional, loops, and concurrency; others, including those introduced in this paper, are not. Such planning languages have been used in planners such as HACKER (Sussman 1975), RAP (Firby 1989), RPL (McDermott 1991b), and considered in theoretical studies such as (Manna and Waldinger 1987) and (Moore 1985). Primitive statements can be either *physical*, such as "puton(A,B)" or *computational*, such as "$X := X + 1$."

As the number of control structures and the complexity of the language increases, it becomes increasingly more desirable to have a precise definition of the meaning of plans in the language. A common form for such a definition is in terms of *behavioral conditions:* necessary and sufficient conditions for a particular physical behavior of the robot in a particular dynamic environment to constitute an execution of a given plan.[2] That is to say, if you are told that a robot is going to execute plan P, and then you observe the robot's physical behavior and all relevant aspects of his environment, then the semantics of the planning language should define the answer to the question, "Could the robot's behavior be considered an execution of plan P?" Of course, it may possible for two different plans to generate the same behavior in a given circumstance, so the question "Does the robot have plan P in mind?" is not answerable.

Following the ALGOL analogy, we may assume that all relevant aspects of the physical behavior correspond to executions of primitive physical statements, and that the control structures and computational primitive statement serve to determine which primitives are executed and when they are executed. We can therefore refine the previous paragraph, and say that a semantics for the planning language is the set of conditions under which a particular chronology of primitive actions constitutes an execution of a plan. If the robot can execute concurrent primitive actions, then there may be a set of primitive actions being executed at any given time.

---

[1] In this paper, the word "statement" is used by analogy to programming languages. In the formalism discussed in this paper, these are not sentences, but terms. In a modal language, though, they could be sentences.

[2] By way of comparison, the definition of the semantics of a programming languages often consists of a specification of what value a program returns, or what function it computes.

Our purpose in this paper is to define the semantics of the control structures: how control structures are used to structure the execution of physical primitives. For simplicity, we will ignore computational primitives. To do any reasoning about plans, there also has to be a theory specifying the physics of the external world and the physical relations between the external world and the robot's actions and perceptions. This body of knowledge is dependent on the physical microworld being considered, and on the physical properties of the robot. In the full version of this paper (in preparation), where we give a full formal verification of a plan, such a theory is developed for a very simple microworld.

A major objective is designing such a language of plans is to facilitate the construction of plans by a hierarchical task-reduction planner. The task reduction paradigm for planning assumes that the planning process consists largely of three types of operations: finding reductions of subtasks to "canned" routines in a plan library; combining these routines under an overall control structure; and performing a relatively small amount of "criticism" to create positive interactions and eliminate negative interactions. For this purpose, it is critical to have an appropriate and powerful collection of control structures. Such a design seems at least intuitively plausible: for example, the actions performed in preparing a dinner consisting of several dishes are very largely, though not entirely, the union of those actions performed for each dish separately. A well-designed planning language is one in which the partial plans can generally be combined to a complete plan using a small number of operators and modifications.

2   INTERRUPTING AND SUSPENDING SUBTASKS

In defining plans for a robot that operates within uncontrolled environments, it is often useful to allow a supertask to interrupt or abandon subtasks when certain specified conditions are detected. Such control structures are not generally found in standard programming languages, though some have been used in robotic programming languages such as OWL [Donner, 87]. We give three examples of such plans: (In the pseudo-code below, actual control structure primitives are printed in lower-case Roman. Names of procedures (sub-plans) are in block capitals. Text in italics is informal, English descriptions of actions or plans.)

Example 1: Crossing a lightly-trafficked street.

AVOID-CARS =
whenever(*car coming*,
   hold_valve(*wheels, move or stay out of the way*))

CROSS-STREET =
monitor(*on far side of street*,

hold_valve(*wheels, move forward*))

SAFE-CROSS-STREET =
interrupt_for(AVOID-CARS,CROSS-STREET).

The subplan AVOID-CARS is a general policy to avoid cars by moving out of their way when they are approaching. The subplan CROSS-STREET is a simple plan to cross a street by moving forward until the street is crossed. Both of these subplans requires exclusive control of the wheels. This control is called a valve[3] in our planning language. The plan SAFE-CROSS-STREET states that CROSS-STREET should be carried out, being interrupted by AVOID-CARS whenever that conflicts.

The control structure primitives above are defined as follows:

- whenever(Q, P) – At any moment when fluent Q is true, proceed with executing P.
- monitor(Q, P) — Continue doing P until fluent Q is true, then abandon P.
- hold_valve(V, P) — Mark act P as requiring exclusive access to valve (resource) V.
- interrupt_for$(P1, P2)$ — Carry out statement $P2$ interrupting it when necessary for $P1$. That is, if possible, carry out both $P1$ and $P2$ concurrently. When they conflict by simultaneously demanding the same valve, then $P2$ is suspended until $P1$ releases the valve. When $P2$ is complete, the overall task is also complete.

The full version of this paper shows a formal verification of this plan. A sketch is given in section 7.

Example 2: Salesman plan. The salesman begins by giving his pitch. If the customer asks a question, the salesman answers the question and then continues with the pitch. If the customer indicates a willingness to buy, either at the end of the pitch or in the middle of the pitch, the salesman immediately presents the contract for signature. When he is done, he packs up and leaves.

SALES-PITCH =
hold_valve(*mouth, Give sales pitch.*)

ANSWER-QUESTION =
whenever(*customer has asked a question*,
         hold_valve(*mouth, answer question*)).

SIGN = *Present contract for signature.*

GO-AWAY = *Pack up and go.*

---

[3]The terminology of "valves" is from (McDermott 1991b).

SALESMAN =
sequence(interrupt_for(ANSWER-QUESTION,
              monitor(*customer is willing to buy*,
                   SALES-PITCH)),
        cond(*customer is willing to buy*, SIGN),
        GO-AWAY).

Here "monitor", "whenever", "hold_valve," and "interrupt_for" are as in example 1. "Sequence" and "cond" are the usual sequencing and conditional operators from regular programming or planning languages.

Example 3: Conversation over an ice-cream cone. The agent must repeatedly eat bites of ice cream cone and make appropriate remarks, being sure not to talk with his mouth full, not to stop mid-sentence to eat more, and not to drop the cone.

BITE-OF-CONE =
hold_valve(*mouth*,
              sequence(*take bite of cone, swallow*)).

CONSUME-CONE =
sequence(*grasp cone*,
        concurrent(monitor(*no cone left*,
                       hold onto cone),
              while(*some cone left*,
                   BITE-OF-CONE))).

REMARK = hold_valve(*mouth, make a remark*)

CONVERSE =
whenever(*appropriate to say something*, REMARK).

CONVERSE-OVER-CONE =
concurrent(CONSUME-CONE, CONVERSE)

This introduces two more primitives. "While(Q, P)" is a conventional iterative while loop, with Q as an initial continuation condition. "Concurrent($P1, P2$)" executes $P1$ and $P2$ concurrently. If one statement holds a valve and the other demands the same valve, then the second must wait for the first to complete.

3   THE SEMANTICS OF CONTINUING A TASK

The central problem addressed in this paper is how to define a formal semantics, as discussed in section 1, for a language containing control structures like those in section 2. This is difficult because the techniques generally used to define semantics for standard control like sequence, conditional, and loop, cannot be extended to deal with control structures like "monitor" and "interrupt_for" which cause their component statements to be abandoned or interrupted. Standard control structures have the property that, if the interpreter starts to execute a substatement P, it completes the execution

of P. Therefore, it is possible to define their semantics by recursively defining the criteria under which a statement is run to completion. For example, the statement "sequence($P1, P2$)" is executed in interval I if $P1$ is executed in full in $I1$ and $P2$ is executed in $I2$ and I is the join of $I1$ with $I2$. The statement "if($Q, P1, P2$)" is executed in interval I if either Q is true at the start of I and $P1$ is executed during I or Q is not true at the start of I and $P2$ is executed during I. Loops may be defined analogously.

However, this approach is clearly inadequate for the control structures discussed above. Let $P1$ be the statement "monitor($Q, P2$)". We cannot define what it means for $P1$ to be completed in terms of what it means for $P2$ to be completed, for $P2$ may not be completed. We can only define what it means to carry out $P1$ if we know it means to *begin* $P2$.[4] Similarly, to interpret a task like "interrupt_for($P1, P2$)" it is necessary to specify what it means to *resume* $P2$ at an arbitrary point. To interpret the task "sequence($P1, P2$)" it is necessary to specify what it means to *complete* $P1$.

Thus, let P be a statement of the form "$\mathcal{C}(P_1 \ldots P_k)$", where $\mathcal{C}$ is a control structure operator and $P_1 \ldots P_k$ are substatements. The core of the definition of the control operator $\mathcal{C}$ is the relation between set of primitive actions involved in executing each of P_1 through P_k in a given situation S and those involved in executing P in S. The semantics must also describe constraints among the times when the superstatement and each substatement are begun, suspended, resumed, abandoned, and completed. The top-level plan is unique in that it must be executed in full, without interruption.

Indeterminate (partially specified) plans can be easily be incorporated within this semantics, simply by making the relation between the statement form and the behaviors that execute it a partial relation rather than a functional dependence. We use the operator "one_of($P1 \ldots Pk$)", which is executed by executing any one of the substatements $P1 \ldots Pk$. More generally, if PP is a set of statements then "one_of(PP)" is executed by executing a statement in PP. For example, "one_of($\{$ pick_up(X) | red(X) $\wedge$ block(X)$\}$)" means "Pick up some red block."

This approach also solves a problem that can arise with the semantics of indeterminate plans, if the semantics of statements is defined solely in terms of ways that the statements can be completed. Consider, for example, an agent who wishes to mail a letter, and consider the

---

[4]It may be suggested that using a branching-time ontology, we can define beginning a task in terms of completing the task: Statement P begins to execute over interval I if P is completed in an interval extending I on some branch of the time structure. But this will not work in general. In particular, it may be impossible to complete P.

following two plans:

> P1: sequence(put letter in envelope, seal envelope, put envelope in mailbox)
>
> P2: unordered(put letter in envelope, seal envelope, put envelope in mailbox)

where P2 is the indeterminate plan to do the actions in arbitrary order. Intuitively, P1 should be correct, while P2 should be incorrect. But if we define the semantics of P2 as "the timelines in which P2 occurs," the two plans are in fact identical, since the only timelines in which P2 occurs are those in which P1 occurs. Our new semantics avoids this by defining what it means to begin a plan, independently of completing it. We may say that P2 is incorrect, precisely because there are ways to begin P2 in which it cannot be completed. ([Davis, 90] gives another, clumsier, solution.)

A disadvantage of our view of plans is that it narrows the range of partial plans that can be described. In particular, "Achieve G" can no longer be viewed as a reasonable substep of a plan, since it is not well defined what it means to begin or continue work on achieving G. Similarly, partial descriptions of plans in terms the set of intervals over which they occurs must in general be excluded, since it is not clear what it means to "begin" such a plan (McDermott 1982), (Morgenstern 1987). However, within a fixed task reduction system, it is possible to get around this by defining "achieve G" just to be the indeterminate execution of one of its known reductions.

4   EMBEDDING IN CONTINUOUS TIME

In order to give a smooth theoretical connection between the robot's plans, the robot's actions, and the physics of the external world, it is desirable to use a continuous theory of time rather than a discrete theory. The question then arises: Should we view the plan interpreter as operating continuously or as operating at discrete moments? Consider, for example, executing a statement like "Carry out P until Q becomes true." Should we assume that P is abandoned instantaneously when Q becomes true, or that there may be some small delay between the time when Q becomes true and the time when the agent reacts to it?

It turns out that the second approach is not only more realistic, but also easier to define coherently.[5] In this approach, the semantics of the plan interpreter views the interpreter as "making decisions" at a sequence of discrete instants of time. The plan interpreter wakes up instantaneously, figures out what the plan says to do now, tells the effectors to do that, and then goes back to sleep for a while. The effectors continue doing

what they were told to do until the plan interpreter wakes up again and tells them what to do next.

Clearly, the interpreter had better not go to sleep for very long. Also, it is undesirable to have the correctness of a plan depend on any very strong assumptions about the frequency of the waking moments, such as an assumption that the waking moments are evenly spaced. Therefore, we define an execution of a plan with time delay Δ as an execution in which there is never more than Δ delay between the waking moments of the plan interpreter.[6] A plan is correct, relative to parameter Δ if every execution with delay Δ is correct. In particular, if $\Gamma < \Delta$ than any execution with delay Γ is also an execution with delay Δ, so that, if P is correct with delay Γ, it is also correct with delay Δ. (To avoid the problem of "infinite loops in finite time" (Davis 1992) we also assume that, in any given execution, there is a minimum delay between waking moments.)

The semantics can thus be viewed as a specification for an interpreter that translates a high-level languages into a low-level language that generates commands for primitive actions every machine cycle. Its structure thus resembles Kaelbling's (1988) work on the compilation of GAPPS, a high-level robotics language, into REX, a low-level language that describes the dependence of the output of a robot controller on its input in each cycle. The actual languages involved are quite different, however. Plans in GAPPS are primarily specifications of goals to be achieved or maintained, while our language is an imperative language describing actions to be carried out. At the other end, REX is designed to be implemented directly in hardware, while our low-level action description is designed to support reasoning about action at any chosen level of primitives.

Also, it should be noted that our intent is to define a semantics, not to specify an implementation. As long as the output actions fall within the specifications, it does not matter how the computations are implemented. For example, they could be implemented using tasks that run asynchronously and communicate via interrupts.

5   PRIMITIVE ACTIONS

It is important that the planning language allow the greatest possible flexibility in the choice of primitives. For example, it would be overly restrictive to require that all actions be characterized in terms of state changes, or that all actions be characterized in terms of the motions and forces of the effectors.

We consider three types of primitive actions:

---

[5] I am particularly indebted to Drew McDermott for helping me reach this conclusion.

[6] An alternative approach is to use a non-standard model of the reals, and take Δ to be infinitesimal (Davis 1984).

- **Instant acts:** Acts that can be executed within a single time delay, no matter how short this is taken to be. Examples: Computational acts such as setting a variable. Changing discrete states, such as flipping a switch.

- **Extended acts:** Acts that can be continued for arbitrary lengths of time. These are "liquid events" in Shoham's (1988) terminology. These must be placed within the scope of some interrupting control structure to bring them to an end. Examples: Rotate in place. Go forward. Exert a pressure of 3 Newtons with the hand.

- **Finite Acts:** These are acts that require a finite length of time to execute, but are "primitive" in the sense that the planner has no access into their internal structure. The command to execute them is shipped off to a black box: an effector control unit, or a separate module, or even a lower-level planner. It is assumed that the black box knows what it means to "begin", "continue", "interrupt", "resume", and "complete" such an act, and can report to the plan interpreter when the act has been completed. Examples: Eat and swallow a bite of ice-cream cone. Make a remark. Grasp a block.

6   FORMAL SEMANTICS

Having made the design decisions above, the development of the formal semantics is reasonably straightforward. The full version of this paper presents a complete formal account of the semantics; here we give a summary. We use sorted first-order logic. Time is taken to be continuous and forward branching (McDermott 1982); that is, each branch in the time line is isomorphic to the real line. The following sorts of entities are used: situations, fluents, events, statements, tasks, actions, valves; sets of statements, tasks, and actions; and domain-specific sorts, such as spatial sorts or physical objects.

A *statement* is a piece of code. A *task* is a particular execution of a statement. Thus in the code

for i := 1 to 100 do
    begin print(i); print(i) end

there are two statements of the form "print(i)". If this loop is executed once, each of these statements will give rise to one hundred different tasks.

The planning language contains the control structures discussed above: sequence($P1, P2 \ldots Pk$); if($Q, P1, P2$); while(Q, P); concurrent($P1 \ldots Pk$); whenever(Q, P); monitor(Q, P); hold_valve(V, P); interrupt_for($P1, P2$); and one_of(PP).

The core of the semantics is the set of rules that relate a task's starting time, its completion, and the primitive actions that execute it in a situation, to those of its subtasks. We present a sampling of these rules below. The key non-logical symbols here are the following: (Throughout this section, the sort of variables is indicated by their first letter. T means task; S means situation; Q means fluent; V means valve; Z means a set of tasks.)

- start(T) — Function. The situation in which T starts.

- completed(T, S) — Predicate. Task T has been completed by or before time S. If T is abandoned, then this is never true.

- end(T) — Function. The situation in which T ends. Defined only if T is completed.

- active(T, S) — Predicate. Task T is started but not completed in situation S. This includes interrupted tasks.

- steps(T, S) — Function. The set of primitive actions to be executed for task T in situation S. S must be a moment when the interpreter is "awake".

Base of the recursion: Primitive acts.

primitive(T) $\land$ active(T, S) $\Rightarrow$ steps(T, S) = { T }.
(The execution of the primitive action T has the single step T.)

extended_prim(T) $\Rightarrow$ ¬completed(T, S).
(An extended primitive act never completes. The completion of an instant act is defined relative to the execution of the overall plan. The completion of a finite act is domain-specific.)

Recursive definition of the control structures.

T=sequence($T1, T2$) $\Rightarrow$
[[active($T1, S$) $\Leftrightarrow$ active(T, S) $\land$ ¬completed($T1, S$)] $\land$
[active($T2, S$) $\Leftrightarrow$ active(T, S) $\land$ completed($T1, S$)] $\land$
[completed(T, S) $\Leftrightarrow$ completed($T2, S$)] $\land$
[active($T1, S$) $\Rightarrow$ steps(T, S)=steps($T1, S$)] $\land$
[active($T2, S$) $\Rightarrow$ steps(T, S)=steps($T2, S$)]]

(Executing sequence($T1, T2$) involves first executing $T1$, and then if and when that completes, executing $T2$. The steps for the supertask are the same as those of the active subtask.)

T = cond($Q, T1, T2$) $\Rightarrow$
[holds(start(T),Q) $\land$ steps(T, S) = steps($T1, S$) $\land$
start(T) = start($T1$) $\land$ end(T)=end($T1$)] $\lor$
[¬holds(start(T),Q) $\land$ steps(T, S) = steps($T2, S$) $\land$
start(T) = start($T2$) $\land$ end(T)=end($T2$)]

(Executing cond($Q, T1, T2$) involves executing $T1$ if Q is true at the beginning of the task, and executing $T2$ if Q is false.)

T=monitor$(Q, T1) \Rightarrow$
$[[$active$(T1, S) \Leftrightarrow$ active$(T, S)] \wedge$
$[$completed$(T, S) \Leftrightarrow$
$[$completed$(T1, S) \vee$
$\exists_{S1} S1 \leq S \wedge$holds$(Q, S1)]] \wedge$
steps(T, S)=steps$(T1, S)]$.

(The steps for monitor$(Q, T1)$ are the same as those for $T1$. The monitor is complete either when Q becomes true or when $T1$ is complete.)

T=whenever$(Q, T1) \Rightarrow$
$[[$active$(T1, S) \Leftrightarrow$ active$(T, S)] \wedge$
$[$completed$(T, S) \Leftrightarrow$ completed$(T1, S)] \wedge$
$[$holds$(Q, S) \Rightarrow$ steps$(T, S) =$ steps$(T1, S)] \wedge$
$[\neg$holds$(Q, S) \Rightarrow$
steps$(T, S)=\{$ suspend$(P) \mid P \in$steps$(T1, S)$]] }.

(The subtask $T1$ of T=whenever$(Q, T1)$ is active when T is active. The steps for T are the same as for $T1$ when Q is true. The steps of $T1$ are all suspended when Q is false.)

T=one_of$(Z) \Leftrightarrow T \in Z$.
(The task "one_of(Z)", where Z is a set of tasks, is just one of the tasks contained in Z.)

T=hold_valve$(V, T1) \Rightarrow$
$[[$active$(T1, S) \Leftrightarrow$ active$(T, S)] \wedge$
$[$completed$(T, S) \Leftrightarrow$ completed$(T1, S)] \wedge$
$[$active$(T, S) \Rightarrow$
steps$(T, S) =$ steps$(T1, S) \cup \{$ maintain_valve$(V) \}]]$.

(hold_valve(V, T) is defined as executing T while maintaining a hold on valve V. maintain_valve(V) is defined as an extended primitive action.)

T=interrupt_for$(T1, T2) \Rightarrow$
$[[$active$(T, S) \Leftrightarrow$ active$(T2, S)] \wedge$
$[$completed$(T, S) \Leftrightarrow$ completed$(T2, S)] \wedge$
$[$start$(T1, S) =$ start$(T, S)] \wedge$
$[$active$(T1, S) \Rightarrow$ active$(T, S)] \wedge$
$[$active$(T, S) \Rightarrow [$active$(T1, S) \vee$ completed$(T1, S)]]$
$[[\exists_V$ maintain_valve$(V) \in$
steps$(T1, S) \cap$ steps$(T2, S)] \Rightarrow$
steps$(T, S) =$ steps$(T1, S) \cup$
$\{$ suspend$(T) \mid T \in$steps$(T2, S) \}] \wedge$
$[[\neg\exists_V$ maintain_valve$(V) \in$
steps$(T1, S) \cap$ steps$(T2, S)] \Rightarrow$
steps$(T, S) =$ steps$(T1, S) \cup$ steps$(T2, S)]]$.

(In interrupt_for$(T1, T2)$, if $T1$ and $T2$ have conflicting claims to a valve, then execute $T1$ and suspend all the actions in $T2$. Otherwise, carry out both $T1$ and $T2$.)

7 FORMAL VERIFICATION OF A PLAN (SKETCH)

The full version of this paper contains a verification of the plan SAFE-CROSS-STREET; that is, a proof that, if traffic is sufficiently light, oncoming cars can be seen far enough ahead, and the cycle time is sufficiently small, then a robot executing SAFE-CROSS-STREET will succeed in reaching the far side of the street without being hit by a car. We consider a simple microworld in which the road runs parallel to the x-axis from $y = 0$ to $y =$road_width; where cars run in the positive x direction with maximum speed max_car_speed; and where the robot can move in any direction with maximum speed max_robot_speed. The cars have width car_width and length car_length; their position is specified by the coordinate of their front point. The plan is then formally defined as follows:

First we define a parameter "danger_distance" which is a distance within which a car presents a threat to the robot. (We include a margin of safety of a factor of 3.)

danger_distance =
$3 \cdot$ car_width $\cdot$ max_car_speed / max_robot_speed

For our sample verification, we make the benign assumption that at any time there is only one car within the danger distance. We define the fluent "oncoming_car" to be that car within the danger distance, if any.

oncoming_car =
$\lambda(S) \iota(C) [$car$(C) \wedge$
$-$danger_distance $<$ x_coor$(C, S) \leq$ car_length$]$

Here $\lambda(S)\phi(S)$ constructs a fluent (a function over time.) The notation $\iota(X)\alpha(X)$ denotes some X satisfying α, if there exists any such; otherwise, it denotes $\perp$.

Now we can define the primitive actions used in example 1.

AVOID-CARS =
whenever(oncoming_car $\neq \perp$
  hold_valve(wheels,
    let(D=y_coor(oncoming_car) $-$ y_coor(robot),
      cond($[D >$ car_width $/2$, move(0)]
        $[$car_width$/2 \geq D > 0$,
          move$(-$max_robot_speed $\cdot \hat{y})]$,
        $[0 \geq D-$car_width$/2$,
          move(max_robot_speed $\cdot \hat{y})]$,
        $[-$car_width$/2 \geq D$, move(0)]$)))))

Here "let" binds a variable, and "cond" gives a set of test-action pairs, as in LISP. They can be formally defined as syntactic sugar for longer expressions in standard predicate calculus.

CROSS-STREET =
monitor(y_coor(robot) $\geq$ road_width,
            hold_valve(wheels,
                        move(max_robot_speed $\cdot$ $\hat{y}$)))

SAFE-CROSS-STREET =
interrupt_for(AVOID-CARS,CROSS-STREET)

It should be noted that this verification cannot be carried out by simply simulating the execution of the plan, since the motion of the cars is not specified in advance. Also, there is a strong relation between the form of the proof and the form of the plan. For example, a key lemma has the form, "If traffic is light enough, then a robot executing the plan 'interrupt_for(AVOID_CARS,P)' will not be hit by a car, whatever P happens to be." There is reason to hope, therefore, that knowledge useful for plan construction can be associated with these canned subplans.

8   FUTURE WORK

The major next step is to extend the planning language. Useful features include the ability to impose constraints between tasks; the definition of local variables; and the definition of "shut-down" and "resumption" procedures to be executed when a task is interrupted and resumed.

Also, it would be desirable to have subplans "pass up" constraints rather than actions. For example, our plan in the previous section has the undesirable feature that the robot stands still even if the oncoming car is passing behind him. (A tighter definition of "oncoming car" can reduce this problem, but not eliminate it.) A better language would allow AVOID-CARS to issue the constraint that the robot may not move backward, if there is an oncoming car behind him, and may not move forward if there is an oncoming car in front of him. The higher-level task SAFE-CROSS-STREET could then see that the constraint not to move backward is, in fact, consistent with CROSS-STREET, so CROSS-STREET does not have to be interrupted for that case. The semantics for such a language might work by having each task denote a set of options, each option being a set of concurrent primitive actions. The interpreter would choose one option to execute, and then perform all the actions in that option. Thus, AVOID-CARS would denote the set of all options that keep the robot out of the way of the car. The major problem here is to find a suitable set of control structure operators, that allow these sets of options from different subtasks to be combined in a reasonable way.

Another issue for future study is the definition of knowledge preconditions for this planning languages. In our example, we would like to express the fact that the plan AVOID-CARS is feasible if the robot can see cars at a distance of danger_distance, and is infeasible

if it cannot. (Davis 1988) presents a theory that allows such constraints on perception to be stated and to be related to knowledge. It still remains to define the connection between knowledge and plan feasibility for this kind of planning language. Such a definition could bridge the gap between the epistemic theory for a low-level robotic language defined in (Rosenschein and Kaelbling 1986), and the epistemic theories of high-level planning languages defined in (Moore 1985) and (Morgenstern 1987). In particular, there is reason to hope that the specific rules for the knowledge preconditions of control structures, which are given as axioms by Moore and by Morgenstern, can, in this alternative semantics, be proven as theorems from the general rule: "Agent A knows enough to execute plan P if he knows that in each situation S he will know the steps of P in S."

Acknowledgements

This research was supported by NSF grant #IRI-9001447. Many thanks to Drew McDermott for helpful discussions.

References

E. Davis (1984). "A High Level Real-Time Programming Language." NYU Tech. Rep., #145.

E. Davis (1988). "Inferring Ignorance from the Locality of Visual Perception." *AAAI-88*, 786-790.

E. Davis (1990). *Representations of Commonsense Knowledge*, Morgan Kaufmann, San Mateo, CA.

E. Davis (1992) "Infinite Loops in Finite Time: Some Observations." NYU Tech. Rep. #599.

M. Donner (1987). *Real-Time Control of Walking.* Birkhauser Pubs, Boston.

J. Firby (1989). *Adaptive Execution in Complex Dynamic Worlds*, Yale Research Report #672.

L. Kaelbling (1988). "Goals as parallel program specifications." *Proc. AAAI-88.*

Z. Manna and R. Waldinger (1987). "A Theory of Plans." In M. Georgeff and A. Lansky (eds.) *Reasoning about Actions and Plans: Proc. 1986 Workshop, Timberline, Oregon.* Morgan Kaufmann, San Mateo, CA.

D. McDermott (1982). "A Temporal Logic for Reasoning about Processes and Plans." *Cognitive Science,* vol. 6, pp. 101-155.

D. McDermott (1991a). "Robot Planning." Yale Research Report #861.

D. McDermott (1991b). "A Reactive Plan Language." Yale Research Report #864.

R. Moore (1985). "A Formal Theory of Knowledge

and Action." In J. Hobbs and R. Moore (eds.) *Formal Theories of the Commonsense World.* ALBEX Pubs., Norwood, NJ.

L. Morgenstern (1987). "Knowledge Preconditions for Actions and Plans." *Proc. ICJAI-87.*

S. Rosenschein and L. Kaelbling (1986). "The Synthesis of Digital Machines with Provable Epistemic Properties." In J. Halpern (ed.) *Proc. First Symposium on Theoretical Aspects of Reasoning about Knowledge.* Morgan Kaufmannm, San Mateo, CA.

G. Sussman (1975). *A Computational Model of Skill Acquisition.* American Elsevier, New York.

Acquiring Search Heuristics Automatically for Constraint-based Planning and Scheduling

David S. Day
The MITRE Corporation
Burlington Road
Bedford, MA 01730
Email: Day@linus.mitre.org

Abstract

Many naturally occurring planning problems can be usefully represented as constraint satisfaction problems for which a variety of general purpose algorithms are available. However, to date the ability to improve planning performance with experience has been largely limited to learning constraints to prune the search space or other value-ordering heuristics whose applicability is restricted to completely identical constraint networks. In this research we show how value-ordering heuristics can be formed using a language that allows for their application across very different problem instances. This language is formed incrementally on the basis of the variables seen in the course of solving different problems. The mechanism we have developed begins by inducing problem-specific constraints, and then generating successively more general versions of these constraints by replacing references to specific variables with terms selected from the variable description hierarchy. This hierarchy is constructed using Fisher's *incremental conceptual clustering* technique, modified to handle recursively defined, structured objects. Eventually, supervised learning can be used to help assess the utilities of the induced heuristics.

1 Introduction

This paper describes a constraint satisfaction problem (CSP) solving system for generating plans in which automatically constructed categories of variables are used to improve planning performance across different problem instances. We show that the induced categories provide a set of terms in which generalized value-ordering heuristics can be expressed and so made useful across many different problem instances of a domain. These ideas have been implemented in a system called ARC. The knowledge transfer abilities of this system argue strongly for the general utility of augmenting the initial formulation of a problem with induced representations that reflect regularities discovered in the training set. We think that the technique described here is of some immediate practical utility in many different application areas—we are concentrating on the area of transportation planning and scheduling. The existing implementation provides a vehicle for empirically examining a number of issues surrounding the application of representation learning techniques to large-scale planning problems.

2 Background

Constraint satisfaction is a general approach to problem solving in which a problem is cast as a set of variables and a set of constraints that express required relationships of values assigned to those variables. A valid solution consists of a set of assignments of values to all variables in the problem such that all of the constraints are satisfied. In standard tree-search approaches to solving these problems, each un-assigned variable is selected iteratively and assigned a value from among its domain of values that satisfies all of the incident constraints until all variables have assignments. If all of the values for a given variable cause constraint violations, then backtracking over previous variable assignments is invoked. The search complexity for a given problem can be controlled by varying aspects of the search process: the order in which variables are selected, and the order in which values for individual variables are selected. In this paper we concentrate on automatically obtaining value ordering heuristics.

It is possible to learn to avoid some inappropriate assignments of values to variables (that is, those that lead to backtracking) for a given CSP formulation [4, 2]. This can be done by using dependency directed backtracking as an opportunity for forming constraints that in the future exclude the variable assignments for the set of variables that "caused" the backtracking. With a very limited amount of computation it is possible to form a constraint that rules out a set of assignments that is much smaller than the complete set of variable assignments prior to backtracking; this smaller set of variable assignments is more likely to be useful in pruning other parts of the search. With larger amounts of analysis the number of involved variable assignments can be reduced further, which will result in constraints with greater likelihood of being used later. Dechter [4] refers to these as *shallow* and *deep* learning, respectively.

The main weakness with this type of learning is that there is no transfer to other closely related constraint satisfaction problems. The induced constraints that prune the search space can only be used for problems that involve the identical constraint network—although under all possible value and variable orderings and particular variable instantiations. To remove this limitation we have adopted a mechanism whereby these constraints are transformed into "soft" (weighted) constraints whose effect on subsequent problems is to modify the order in which candidate values are assigned to variables but *not* to rule out those (sets of) variable assignments completely.

However, this is not enough to enable the heuristic knowledge to be usefully employed in subsequent problems, because it is not clear to which variables these induced constraints should apply. Strictly speaking, the "identity" of a variable within a CSP is the sum of its intrinsic characteristics (e.g., what values are in its domain) and its connections to other variables in the constraint network via constraints. This means that there can be no variable in one constraint network that is strictly identical to a variable in another constraint network unless the networks are completely isomorphic. How, then, can we know on which variables to apply the value-ordering heuristics obtained from earlier learning?

The approach we have taken to address this problem is to incrementally construct a classification hierarchy of variables using conceptual clustering techniques [7, 8]. Every CSP variable encountered by the system (which will include a specification of its local graph structure) is used as a training instance in the incremental conceptual clustering algorithm. The desired result of this process is a classification hierarchy whose internal nodes represent important classes of variables in the domain of variables seen by the learning system. In solving new CSP problems (selected, we assume, from a domain of related CSP problems) the similarity of variables to those seen in previous problems can be gauged by classifying the new variables in the growing variable hierarchy, and so knowledge gleaned about one variable can be associated with other similar variables.

3   Learning about Variables

We want to learn terms for describing variables such that generalized value-ordering constraints can be composed using these terms. The terms will have intensional semantics (the probabilistic concept description stored at the node itself) derived on the basis of its extensional semantics (the set of variable instances that fall under the internal node of the hierarchy) and will be related to other terms through clear subsumption relationships. These properties of the new terms will prove useful in applying acquired heuristics to novel planning problems.

The system we have constructed to study these ideas is called ARC. In figure 1 is the network for a very simple CSP; we will use this example to illustrate the mechanisms introduced in this research.[1] Our first question is: What is it that uniquely distinguishes the variable var1 in this problem? If we ignore the name "var1" that it happens to be assigned in this problem, this variable is defined by the fact that its domain of candidate values is ":alphabet" (a predefined value type that implicitly specifies the Lisp symbols W, X, Y and Z for the purposes of this example), that the current value assigned to this variable is :no-value (i.e., no value has yet been assigned to it), and that the value of the variable is constrained to be lexicographically "less than" the value assigned to var2. It is features of the latter type—how a variable is connected to other variables via constraints—that pose some difficulty for standard conceptual clustering algorithms, since these variables are themselves defined in terms of their connections with this (and other) variables.

Our approach to getting around this recursive nature of a variable's identity is to generate a "flattened" attribute-value specification of each variable in which the network structure local to a variable is captured to some path depth. For example, the structure defining variable var1 is specified in the "flat" representation in figure 2 (with a depth cutoff at 2). In this example we assume that variables var2 and var3 have already been assigned the values W and X respectively. The attributes of this variable description are not simply symbols, however, but contain structure indicating the constraint relationships from which this attribute was derived. In order to decide how to match up attributes between two variables represented in this manner (or between a variable and a probabilistic variable concept descriptor) we have adopted the approach taken by Fisher, *et. al.* [8], namely, to use a greedy graph-matching algorithm that has relatively good perfor-

---

[1] We have avoided the use of constraints on integer- and real-valued variables because there are many specialized constraint propagation techniques used in ARC (taken from the constraint processing literature) that are not germain to the present discussion and tend to obscure the learning mechanisms being discussed here.

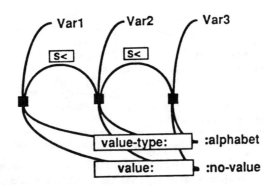

Figure 1:

A very simple constraint satisfaction problem (Problem-1). The constraint predicate "s<" means lexicographically prior, and takes Lisp symbols as its arguments. One solution to this problem, therefore, is simply var1=W, var2=X and var3=Y.

mance characteristics ($O(n^2)$), but is not guaranteed always to find the best match.[2] This step is performed immediately prior to invoking the conceptual clustering algorithm proper (involving the object to be classified and the root node of the hierarchy). During the clustering algorithm proper the mapping from object features to class features has already been decided, and so this internal structure is ignored.

The numbers following a constraint indicator (as in s<-1) are used to uniquely identify constraint instances, and are generated by the system itself. In this case, the s indicates that this is a "structured" attribute, that is, an attribute derived from a constraint connecting this variable to some other variable in the network. The type of constraint connecting this and some other variable is a "less-than" (<) constraint. Taken together, the attribute/value pair "(s< value-type): :alphabet" indicates that the variable var-1 has the property of being connected to some other unnamed variable via a less-than (<) constraint and the value-type of this other variable is :alphabet. In those cases where there are multiple instances of structure indicators (e.g., (s<-1 s>-3 value-type)), this indicates the connections of the neighboring variable to still other variables (and so on, recursively).

In this network, all of the constraints on variables are of unique types, but it is possible that there might be, for example, two s< constraints on one variable, so the numerical identifier appended to the contraint-name (s<-1) uniquely identifies distinct constraint instances. This is important when attempting to compare the (local) graph structures of two variables represented in

this fashion.[3] Note also that in this alternate description of var1 (in figure 2) there is nowhere any mention of any variable by name, since in this description the identity of a variable is the totality of its local characteristics and the characteristics of the variables to which it is connected.

It is these types of representations of variables that are used to incrementally generate a classification hierarchy of variable types. The iterative conceptual clustering algorithm we use is derived from CLASSIT [8]. In this algorithm each successive object to be classified (each training instance) is added to the hierarchy by first adding it to the root, and then deciding which of several modifications to the level of nodes directly below should be performed based on an evaluation metric of the possible partitionings at that level. The evaluation metric is derived from the notion of *category utility* [9]. For reasons of space we will not describe this well-known conceptual clustering algorithm here.

For the very few variables in Problem-1 the hierarchy of probabilistic variable categories is not particularly useful or interesting (it has one root node, with the three variables indexed underneath it). However, suppose we were later presented with a problem like that depicted in figure 3. Representing these in the manner discussed above and adding them incrementally to the existing variable hierarchy results in the variable description hierarchy shown in figure 4. From this small example it is clear that important similarities among variables across these two problems have been captured in the resulting hierarchy. For example, variables var1 and var4 are both constrained to be lexicograph-

---

[2]Other researchers have addressed this problem, and we imagine refining our current approach in the future. See [10, 12, 13, 1].

[3]It is possible that two constraints on a variable could both lead to the same constraining variable. This special case would not cause our more general treatment of constraint identification to introduce any problems.

```
                            var1
        ATTRIBUTES                        VALUES
        value-type: ................ :alphabet
        value: .................... :no-value
        (s<-1 value-type): ......... :alphabet
        (s<-1 value): ............. W
        (s<-1 s>-3 value-type): .... :alphabet
        (s<-1 s>-3 value): ......... :no-value
        (s<-1 s<-4 value-type): .... :alphabet
        (s<-1 s<-4 value): ......... X
```

Figure 2:
The attribute-value representation of var1 from Problem-1. The attributes themselves contain structure mimicking the paths from this variable to all those variables related to it via constraints, up to depth 2 (in this particular case).

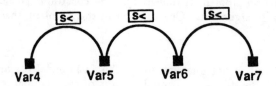

Figure 3:
Another very simple CSP (Problem-2). (Left out are the shared features of these variables as shown in figure 1.)

ically less than variables which are themselves similar to each other, and the internal node node-22 captures this regularity in the form of a probabilistic concept. As the numbers and variety of objects (variables) in the training set grows, we can expect that the fidelity with which certain classes of variables are captured will similarly increase.

4 Generalized Constraints

It is this new and continually evolving terminological hierarchy that allows us in a natural way to construct generalizations of the heuristic value-ordering constraints formed on the basis of individual problem instances. For example, ARC induced three constraints in the course of solving Problem-1. Two constraints exclude from var3 the values W and X, respectively, and the third constraint excludes from var2 the value W. The predicates of these constraints have the following form: (exclude var3 W), where W, X and Y refer to the LISP symbols.[4]

Whenever, in the course of problem solving, ARC generates a constraint to avoid backtracking in the future, the system now also attempts to generate suc-

cessive generalizations of these constraints over the variable classification hierarchy available to it at the time. This is done by replacing the variable terms in the induced constraints with successively more general characterizations of the variables available in the hierarchy. In the case of Problem-1 the generalization hierarchy is trivially small—there is only one more general term, node-17. The two generalized constraints created during the processing of Problem-1, therefore, are (exclude node-17 X) and (exclude node-17 Y).

Of course both of these are over-generalizations. They are allowed because they will not rule out solutions, only the order in which candidate solutions are generated. This is not to say that all possible generalizations should be kept around, for there is some cost associated with maintaining (and evaluating) these constraints. The degree to which a constraint is an accurate generalization can be approximated using the intensional properties of the induced terms.[5] At the time generalized constraints are being produced, each successive generalization is tested as to the relative

[4]The constraints induced from these simple problems happen to involve only one variable, but more complex problems generally result in the formation of constraints with variable assignment restrictions of many variables.

[5]It is perhaps better to say that the probabilistic concept description at each internal node is quasi-intensional, since determining the class membership of an object in this system cannot be based solely on the information at a single node but implicitly requires comparing the measures of similarity of all the competing classes at a single level in the hierarchy.

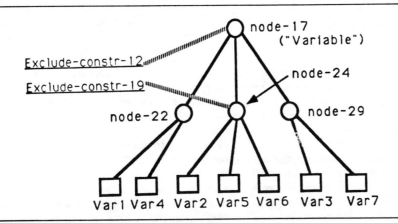

Figure 4:
The variable classification/descriptor hierarchy available after being presented with Problem-2. (For illustrative purposes the generalized constraints indexed off of this hierarchy include those created after *solving* both Problem-1 and Problem-2.)

number of problem instances indexed under the nodes that satisfy the constraint. If this number is below some percentage (currently set arbitrarily at 20%), then the generalized constraint is not made, and no attempt is made to construct more general versions of this same constraint (at that time). In this way, as the size of the variable hierarchy grows, the amount of over-generalization is controlled.

Consider now that we are presented with Problem-2 (as depicted in figure 3) after having already seen and solved Problem-1. While it is different from Problem-1, Problem-2 clearly has strong similarities to that of Problem-1. Incrementally modifying the variable classification hierarchy so that the variables in Problem-2 are classified along with those previously seen in Problem-1 results in the hierarchy of probabilistic concepts shown in figure 4. Having classified the variables in this new problem, ARC can apply all of the value-ordering constraints above a variable in the hierarchy to that variable. In this case, the two generalized constraints are indexed at node-17, which means that every variable in Problem-2 will inherit these value-ordering constraints. (The generalized constraint indexed on node-24 is a result of continued constraint formation during the problem solving for Problem-2, and so is available for only a portion of the problem solving activity.) As the system's base of experience increases, the appropriateness of the value-ordering heuristics on node-17 will be refined by being moved to lower-level, internal nodes of the hierarchy, and thereby having its applicability restricted.

The worst-case search space for Problem-1 is initially 22. After having induced constraints, solving this exact same problem can be solved by searching only 10 nodes. The worst-case search space for Problem-2 is 54, but applying the heuristics learned in Problem-1 to

Problem-2 (and without learning any new constraints during this problem solving) the search space is reduced to 42. If we allow the induction of constraints *during* the problem solving for Problem-2 the search space can be reduced further to 34. Of course, these data do not in any way constitute a rigorous analysis of the costs and benefits of this approach, a process which we are just now beginning. Nonetheless, they seem to indicate that with this technique there is the potential for powerful transfer effects across problems within some restricted domain of related problem instances.

To reiterate how all of the machinery described above works together, we present below the modified constraint satisfaction algorithm used in ARC in abbreviated form. There are two significant parameters used in the algorithm which we have already mentioned: one is the path depth used in capturing the network structure local to a variable, and the other is the degree a generalized constraint must be satisfied by the variable instances indexed under it in the variable type hierarchy.

(1) Select a variable. If none are available, then exit (we are done). (2) Add the selected variable to the variable classification hierarchy. (3) Add to this variable the weighted, generalized constraints inherited from concept nodes "above" the variable in the classification hierarchy. (4) Select a value for the variable, respecting the ordering imposed on candidate values by problem-specific and "inherited" constraints. If there is no candidate value available to select, then we have exhausted this variable, requiring that we backtrack (see below). (5) Check constraints. If the selected value is unacceptable, go to 4; otherwise, go to 1.

Whenever backtracking is forced upon the problem solver, ARC carries out the steps described below before conducting dependency-directed backtracking.

(1) Discover the conflict set of variable assignments. (The conflict set consists of those variable assignments that together have "caused" the current variable to be exhausted. **(2)** Form a weighted constraint which causes the variable assignments in the conflict set to be generated after others. **(3)** Replace variable instances in the constraint predicate with abstractions from the variable type hierarchy, and test the applicability of this (generalized) constraint against the probabilistic concept representations of variables by testing against the relative frequency of prohibited values stored in those clusters. This test is efficient, since it saves one from having to actively test all (or some significant random subpopulation) of the instances indexed under this abstract variable node. **(4)** If the newly formed generalized constraint is satisfied by some significant percentage of variable instance bindings, index the constraint under all of the applicable variable class nodes, and go to 4 again to attempt further generalization; otherwise, go to 5. **(5)** Jump to the most recently set variable in the conflict set (as is normal for standard dependency-directed backtracking).

5   Discussion

We have presented the ideas on which ARC is based in the context of quite trivial problems in order to simplify the figures and associated explanations. The catalyst for these ideas, however, has been the extremely large size of transportation planning and scheduling problems faced by the United States Transportation Command (TRANSCOM). In these problems there are thousands to hundreds of thousands of "movement requirements" that specify allotments of cargo and passengers that must be delivered within certain time requirements to some set of locations. It was the size and complexity of these resource allocation problems that led us to investigate opportunities for incremental performance improvements.[6] Another important simplification we made here was to discuss only tree-search methods for constraint satisfaction problem solving. However, the amount of knowledge available about a desired transportation plan is sufficient to make *approximation plus local search* a viable search technique [11], and ARC allows one to use this technique. Including a discussion of this (and other) control strategies here would have needlessly complicated the exposition.

Indeed, there is a host of global control strategies for constraint satisfaction that we have ignored here, for we believe most of them are independent of (and can be used in conjunction with) the mechanisms for in-

cremental performance improvement made available in ARC. Recently there has been some work reported on learning the conditions under which some global search strategies are preferable to others [5].

The transportation domain should prove fruitful for carrying out the extensive empirical analyses that we anticipate. One of the most important of these has to do with assessing the absolute costs of maintaining and evaluating these extra constraints, which we hope eventually to incorporate into a supervised learning component of ARC. A related concern has to do with the cost of maintaining in memory the huge number of variables that will be encountered in the course of both many different problem instances, and the potentially very large initial size of any single problem instance in this domain. This issue has been studied by others in other domains [8, 6], and we believe a judicious use of a *cutoff* parameter can manage this problem. The cutoff parameter specifies a lower limit on similarity between objects and categories (or individual objects) in the hierarchy; objects that are too similar to already stored concepts/individuals are used to update concept statistics, but are not retained within the concept hierarchy.

The very size of these tasks leads us to believe that another potential problem exhibited by incremental learning algorithms will be largely avoided. The hill-climbing nature of the incremental clustering algorithm used in ARC is such that initial "mis-steps" in constructing the term hierarchy are overcome with the analysis of subsequent training instances. This sensitivity to presentation order can cause problems when the training set is small and/or sparse. But with the training sets we expect to encounter in real world planning and scheduling, these initial over generalizations ought to be corrected relatively quickly.

Finally, we note that the form of constraints induced by ARC is completely general, and does not take advantage of any knowledge that might be available about the relationships among values for particular types of variables. For example, the domain for some variables might be specified as restricted to a certain type, where there is *a priori* knowledge of the hierarchical relations among the different values of that type. Instead of creating generalized constraints by climbing the *variable description* hierarchy, we might be able to profitably generalize along the variable *value* dimension as well [3]. For variables with numerical domains, these generalizations will take the form of ranges (as in CLASSIT). We imagine that under some circumstances inequality constraints on numerical variables might also be able to be induced.

Acknowledgements

This research was supported by Air Force/Rome Laboratory contract no. F19628-89-C-0001. A slightly mod-

---

[6]ARC incorporates a number of mechanisms (that we cannot describe here) to make it easy for the system designer to specify resources and their particular properties, and in other ways to set up very large transportation planning problems.

ified version of this paper was presented at the International Machine Learning Workshop, Northwestern University, 1991.

Alexander Yeh was a major contributor to the implementation of ARC. Alex Yeh, Rich Piazza and Marc Villain made valuable comments on earlier drafts. I have enjoyed many lively discussions on related topics with Dennis Connolly.

References

[1] John A. Allen and Kevin Thompson. Probabilistic concept formation in relational domains. In L. A. Birnbaum and G. C. Collins, editors, *Proceedings of the Eighth International Workshop on Machine Learning*, Northwestern University, Evanston, Illinois, 1991.

[2] Maurice Bruynooghe and Luis M. Pereira. Deduction revision by intelligent backtracking. In J. A. Campbell, editor, *Implementation of Prolog*, pages 194–215. Ellis Harwood, 1984.

[3] Dennis Connolly, Steve Coley, Phyllis Koton, Stuart McAlpin, Alice Mulvehill, and Marc Villain. Learning representation by integrating case-based and inductive learning. Technical report, The MITRE Corporation, 1991.

[4] Rena Dechter. Learning while searching in constraint-satisfaction problems. In *Proceedings of the Fifth National Conference on Artificial Intelligence*, pages 178–183. American Association for Artificial Intelligence, Morgan Kaufman, 1986.

[5] Megan Eskey and Monte Zweben. Learning search control for constraint-based scheduling. In *Proceedings of the Ninth National Conference on Artificial Intelligence*, pages 908–915, Boston, Massachusetts, 1990.

[6] Douglas Fisher, Jungsoon Yoo, and Hua Yang. Case-based and abstraction-based reasoning. In *Working Notes, AAAI Spring Symposium on Case-Based Reasoning*, Stanford University, Palo Alto, CA, 1990.

[7] Douglas H. Fisher. Knowledge acquisition via incremental conceptual clustering. *Machine Learning*, 2:139–172, 1987.

[8] J. H. Gennari, P. Langley, and D. Fisher. Models of incremental concept formation. *Artificial Intelligence*, 40(1):11–62, 1989.

[9] M. A. Gluck and J. E. Corter. Information, uncertainty and the utility of categories. In *Proceedings of the Seventh Annual Conference of the Cognitive Science Society*. Lawrence Erlbaum Associates, 1985.

[10] R. Levinson. *A Self-organizing retrieval system for graphs*. PhD thesis, University of Texas, Austin, Texas, 1985.

[11] Steven Minton, Mark D. Johnston, Andrew B. Philips, and Philip Laird. Solving large-scale constraint satisfaction and scheduling problems using a heuristic repair method. In *Proceedings of the Ninth National Conference on Artificial Intelligence*, pages 17–24, Boston, Massachusetts, 1990.

[12] Jakub Segen. Graph clustering and model learning by data compression. In *Proceedings of the Workshop on Machine Learning*, pages 93–98, 1990.

[13] Kevin Thompson and Pat Langley. Incremental concept formation with composite objects. In *Workshop on Machine Learning*, pages 371–374, 1989.

PLAN RECOGNITION
IN
UNDERSTANDING INSTRUCTIONS

Barbara Di Eugenio   **Bonnie Webber**

Department of Computer and Information Science
University of Pennsylvania
Philadelphia, PA
E-mail: {dieugeni@linc, bonnie@central}.cis.upenn.edu

Abstract

Plan recognition is generally understood as the process of inferring the higher level goals that an action is meant to achieve. In this paper, we will discuss such inferences in the context of understanding and executing Natural Language instructions and show that they follow from the partial nature of Natural Language descriptions: borrowing the term from Lewis [1979], we collectively call them *accommodation*. Accommodation can be seen as a type of plan recognition: we will compare accommodation with other kinds of inferences that have been studied in the plan recognition literature – in particular by Kautz [1990] and Pollack [1986].

1 Introduction

It is widely held that understanding and executing Natural Language instructions involves steps of both planning and plan recognition – see [Alterman *et al.*, 1991], [Cohen and Levesque, 1990], [Vere and Bickmore, 1990]. [1]

One definition of plan recognition, due to Kautz [1990], is as follows: *One is given a fragmented, impoverished description of the actions performed by one or more agents, and expected to infer a rich, highly interrelated description. The new description fills out details of the setting, and relates the actions of the agents in the scenario to their goals and future actions.*

Kautz applied this definition to inferring an agent's goals from observing his actions. However, instruc-

tions too can be considered as an impoverished description, from which the observer – the hearer or reader – is meant to infer a *rich, highly interrelated description*: in fact, following [Pollack, 1990], we assume that the description we obtain from instructions is a plan to act *seen as a complex mental attitude, one comprising a structured collection of beliefs and intentions*. In this paper, we will describe inferences that we have found necessary to infer such a description of behavior from instructions: we will call them collectively *accommodation*. We will show that there is not just one type of inference needed for accommodation but several – two of which we will discuss here.

We will discuss accommodation starting with the definition given by Lewis [1979], modifying it as required by understanding instructions, and relating it to plan recognition. Apart from differences in the inference processes, what is special to accommodation as plan recognition is that accommodation takes seriously the linguistic nature of its objects, which are the action *descriptions* contained in the instructions. Instead, the objects of much of plan recognition work are rigid structures that don't capture the richness and the underspecificity of a corresponding Natural Language action description. The significance of this can be seen by considering the following pair:

Ex. 1 *a) Flex your legs and arms.*
  b) Flex your legs and arms
    10 times twice a day for a month.

In a null context, not much can be inferred in 1.a about the higher goals that performing such a physical action can achieve. In 1.b, inferring a goal like *exercising* seems much more plausible, and is possible because of the linguistic structure of the described action, which adds to it a sense of iteration. The point we would like to make is that in general plan recognition systems,

---

[1] For a different point of view on instruction understanding see [Chapman, 1991].

even those that deal with Natural Language phenomena – such as [Lambert and Carberry, 1991], [Litman and Allen, 1990], [Pollack, 1986] – have not been concerned with the fact that adding modifiers to an action description can actually change the description itself – for example, its aspectual class – so that different inferences are warranted.

Another important point is that NL instructions rarely describe an action in all of its possible aspects, so that often a richer description of the action itself may need to be inferred besides the goal that the action achieves – we will discuss such inferences in sect. 2.2.

Finally, certain objects, exactly because they are intrinsically linguistic, have been rarely studied in a plan recognition context. This is the case for *negatives* - specifying *not* to do something. It clearly does not make sense to do *general* plan recognition based on what the agent is not doing, as there are too many such things. It does make sense, though, to do plan recognition on what the agent is *told* not to do because it is further evidence of what the instructor has in mind, and rules out some choices the agent could make as regards *how* to achieve a goal α – see sect. 2.3.

2   Accommodation

2.1   Lewis on accommodation

The term *accommodation* was introduced by Lewis [1979] to refer to the process by which *conversational score does tend to evolve in such a way as is required in order to make whatever occurs count as correct play*, where by *conversational score* Lewis means the state of the conversation, described by various components.

Lewis uses the concept of accommodation to deal with such phenomena as presuppositions and definite reference. He also talks about planning, albeit briefly:

> Much as some things said in ordinary conversation require suitable presuppositions, so some things that we say in the course of planning require, for their acceptability, that the plan contains some suitable provisions. If we say "Then you drive the getaway car up to the side gate", that is acceptable only if the plan includes provision for a getaway car. That might or might not have been part of the plan already. *If not, it may become part of the plan just because it is required by what we said.* [2]

Lewis's plan accommodation thus refers to a global process of making room for (relatively) new things in the plan if they are not already there. Thomason [1990] takes accommodation to be an even more general phenomenon, that *consists in acting to remove*

---

obstacles to the achievement of desires or goals that we attribute to others.

We will discuss more *local* processes of accommodation, that allow an agent to understand instructions that don't exactly mirror his knowledge. In our opinion, the fundamental concept that comes to play during accommodation of an action α described in an instruction is the *purpose* to achieve which α has to be performed.

Lewis doesn't mention the mechanism by which accommodation happens, but notice that his example is set in the context of a plan for *stealing plutonium from a nuclear plant*; a subgoal of this plan is *escape safely*, and it is the presence of this subgoal that makes it possible to readily perform the accommodation necessary to account for the *getaway car*.

Also notice that mentioning the function of the car, *getaway*, is crucial to the accommodation process: if the instruction to be accommodated had been *Then you drive the car up to the side gate*, it would have been much harder to find its place in the global plan, if no car had been mentioned so far.

In conclusion: accommodation is not a blind process. It happens because there is something that justifies it, and this *something* is the *purpose* to achieve which the action to be accommodated has to be performed.

In the following sections, we will illustrate this point by means of two kinds of Natural Language constructions that give rise to different kinds of accommodation: *purpose clauses*, that explicitly encode the purpose that the action described in the main clause achieves, and *negative imperatives*, the understanding of which also requires the notion of *goal*. In each case, we will also discuss the kind of accommodation involved.

Before turning to the accommodation inferences that arise in the context of these two syntactic constructions, it is necessary to spend a few words on the relations between actions that we use in our representation. [Pollack, 1986] proposes that relations between actions should crucially include *generation* and *enablement*: her motivations stem from philosophical and planning issues. To her motivations, we add the evidence that derives from the analysis of naturally occurring data presented in [Di Eugenio, 1992], namely, that the relation between the actions described in the matrix and purpose clauses, respectively, is in fact mainly generation, and less frequently enablement.

Generation has been extensively studied in the literature, first in philosophy [Goldman, 1970] and then in planning [Allen, 1984], [Pollack, 1986], [Balkanski, 1990].
Informally, if action α generates action β, we can say that β is executed **by** executing α. An example is *The agent turns on the light* **by** *flipping the switch*.

Without going into too many details, we can say that an action α generates another action β iff:

1. α and β are simultaneous;

2. α is not part of doing β (as in the case of *playing a C note* as part of *playing a C triad* on a piano);

3. when α occurs, a set of conditions $\mathcal{C}$ hold, such that the joint occurrence of α and $\mathcal{C}$ imply the occurrence of β. For example in the *turning on the light* example, $\mathcal{C}$ may include that the wire, the switch and the bulb are working.

Enablement. Following first [Pollack, 1986] and then [Balkanski, 1990], enablement can be defined as holding between two actions α and β if and only if an occurrence of α brings about a set of conditions that are necessary (but not necessarily sufficient) for the subsequent performance of β.

An example is *buying ingredients* enables *preparing the dish*: buying ingredients brings about a condition that is necessary for the dish preparation action to be executable [Balkanski, 1990].

We will now turn to discussing purpose clauses, negative imperatives and their relations to accommodation.

2.2 Purpose clauses and accommodation

A *purpose clause* is an infinitival clause that explicitly encodes the goal that an action achieves [3] - for example,

Ex. 2 *Cut the square in half to create two triangles.*

Here the action α described in the matrix sentence, *cut the square in half*, is underspecified in that there are an infinite number of ways of cutting a square in half, including along an axis and along a diagonal. However, an agent with basic knowledge about the world won't have any difficulty in executing this instruction correctly, because the goal β *to create two triangles* unambiguously specifies how to perform the cutting action, namely, along one of the two diagonals. [4] Notice that the relation between *cut the square in half along the diagonal* and *create two triangles* is *generation*.

---

[3]In the syntactic literature, the term *purpose clause* refers to a particular type of infinitival *to* clauses, which are adjoined to NPs. In contrast, the infinitival clauses we have concentrated on are adjoined to a matrix clause, and are termed *rational clauses* in syntax; in fact the *purpose clauses* discussed in this paper belong to a particular subclass of such clauses, subject-gap rational clauses. For a syntactic account of rational and purpose clauses and their differences, see [Jones, 1985], [Hegarty, 1990].

[4]We won't deal here with the additional issue of choosing the diagonal along which to cut.

The process of accommodation invoked here yields a more specific action α_1 which achieves the goal specified by the purpose clause, as shown in Fig. 1 - β represents a goal, α the action to accommodate, solid lines relations between goals and actions, i.e. *generation* or *enablement*, and dotted lines IS-A links.

If we apply the inference schema shown in Fig. 1 to Ex. 2, we obtain $\beta = create\ two\ triangles$, $\alpha = cut\ the\ square\ in\ half$, $\alpha_1 = cut\ the\ square\ in\ half\ along\ the\ diagonal$.

In this case the only object that needs to be accommodated is α. However, it may happen that also the goal β needs to be accommodated with respect to the structure of the intentions that H has built so far. In such cases, accommodation must be hierarchical, with the goal β accommodated first, then the action α. In fact, during accommodation of the goal β, β may be further specified and become β': α will have then to be accommodated with respect to β', not to β. This is also consistent with the communication function of purpose clauses: the speaker uses them to tell the hearer that s/he should adopt the intention of achieving the goal β, and that α contributes to achieving β - see [Di Eugenio, 1992].

A second kind of accommodation allows us to find the conditions under which the current instruction makes sense. Consider

Ex. 3 *Go into the other room to get the urn of coffee.*

This instruction only makes sense if the urn is in the other room, or if, when the agent gets into the other room, he or she will come to know how to get the urn. These conditions can be worked out by relating the effects of *go* to what the performance of *get* requires. Schematically, one could represent this kind of inference as in Fig. 2 - β stands for goal, α for the instruction to accommodate, A_k for the actions belonging to the plan to achieve β, $\mathcal{C}$ for the necessary assumptions. An instantiation of this general schema for Ex. 3 is shown in Fig. 3.

It may happen that the two kinds of accommodation need to be combined. In this case, we would need to find the conditions under which an instruction α makes sense in the context of a certain goal; we may then discover that the relevant action is not α, but a more specific α_1, as in Fig. 4. In this case, it may be necessary to check whether α_1 remains compatible with the higher goal(s).

These examples show that the function of goals is not only to give the agent a reason for performing an action. In particular, Ex. 2 above shows that the goal constrains the interpretation of the action to be executed. For further evidence, consider the contrast between a) and b) in the following example:

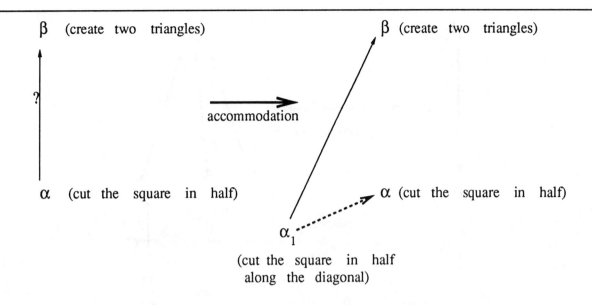

Figure 1: Schematic Depiction of the First Kind of Accommodation

Ex. 4 *a) Place a plank between two ladders.*
b) Place a plank between two ladders
to create a simple scaffold.

In both a) and b), the action to be executed is *place a plank between two ladders*. However, 4.a would be correctly interpreted by placing the plank *anywhere* between the two ladders: this shows that in b) the agent must be inferring the proper position for the plank from the expressed goal *"to create a simple scaffold"*. This shows that the goal *to create a simple scaffold* isn't simply used to tell H why he should *place a plank between two ladders*, but also to help him identify the action to be executed.

2.3 Negative imperatives and accommodation

While goals aren't always given in instructions, they may still be required for instructions to be correctly understood. This is true of negative imperatives.

As we said in the introduction, negatives are intrinsically linguistic objects: what the agent is *told* not to do is further evidence of what the instructor has in mind, and rules out some choices the agent may make in order to achieve a goal α.

One notable exception to ignoring negatives is [Vere and Bickmore, 1990]: there, negative imperatives are taken to be global constraints on the activities the agent can perform. However, by looking at naturally occurring negative imperatives, we realized that there seem to be two basic classes of negative imperatives, that give rise to different kinds of inferences:

DONT imperatives, *Don't do* α. They are characterized by the negative auxiliary *don't*. They appear to be used when S thinks that H is likely to adopt the intention to perform α, and wants to prevent H from adopting it - see Exs. 6 and 7 below.

Neg-TC imperatives, *"Do β. Take care not to do α".* They are formed by verbs such as *take care, be sure* and the like - *TC verbs* for short - followed by a negative infinitival complement, such as *"not to ..."*. They appear to be used when S wants H to perform a certain β and thinks that H may adopt the intention of performing it in an undesirable way, or that H may NOT adopt the intention of preventing an undesirable consequence of β - α describes such an undesirable feature. For example, in

Ex. 5 *When nailing the panels,* **be careful not to mar the surfaces.**

nail the panels is β, the action to be performed, *mar the surfaces* is α, a possible side-effect of β.

Here we will focus on *DONT* imperatives. Notice however that the inferences the hearer has to perform to understand a *neg-TC* imperative are different from those needed to understand a *DONT* imperative: *neg-TC* imperatives pattern like purpose clauses, in that the action β to be performed is constrained by the undesirable feature α described by the *neg-TC* imperative. For further discussion, see [Di Eugenio, 1992].

DONT imperatives may appear not to require any particular kind of inference, as they could be simply

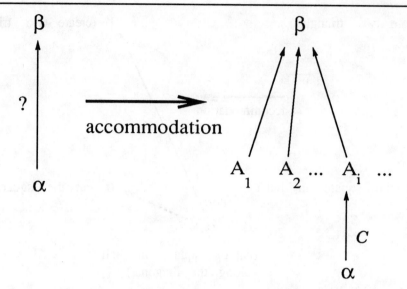

Figure 2: Schematic Depiction of the Second Kind of Accommodation

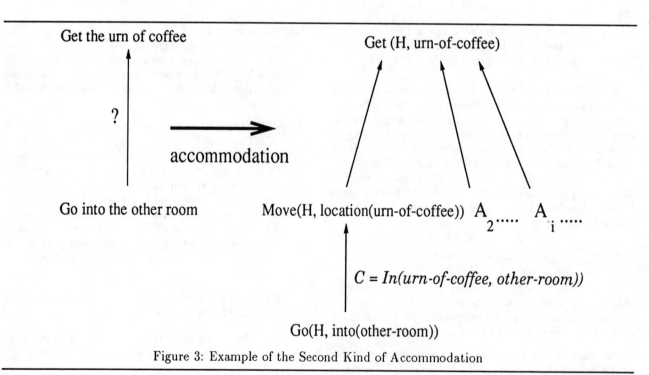

Figure 3: Example of the Second Kind of Accommodation

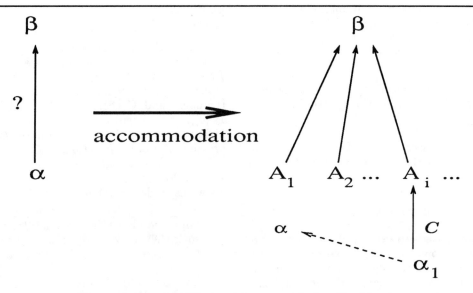

Figure 4: The two Kinds of Accommodation Combined

mapped into an intention that H should not adopt. This is certainly true for

Ex. 6 *In case of fire, do not use elevator.*

However, the intention not to be adopted may be related to other goals that H has to achieve and to the ways in which s/he is supposed to achieve them. Consider:

Ex. 7 *Caring for the floor. A good paste wax - not a water-based wax - will give added protection to the wood. Buff about twice a year; wax about once a year. Excessive waxing can cause wax to build up, detracting from the floor appearance.*
Dust-mop or vacuum your parquet floor as you would carpeting. **Do not scrub or wet-mop the parquet.** *Use a damp cloth to remove fresh food spills.*

The goal to be achieved is *cleaning the parquet*. This is not stated explicitly, but requires a step of plan recognition. This step uses the fact that the whole paragraph is under the heading *Caring for the floor*. *Waxing* is one aspect of floor care. *Dust-mopping* and *vacuuming* are not used in *waxing* floors, but in *cleaning* floors, which is taken to be an aspect of floor care subsequently discussed.

The fact that *scrub* and *wet-mop* are (undesirable) alternatives with respect to *dust-mop* and *vacuum* can be easily inferred by using plan recognition techniques similar to Kautz's, as we will describe in the next section.

3   Related work

The issues discussed in this paper relate to different fields of investigation, such as linguistic theories, formal theories of action, and work in plan recognition. We will in particular compare our approach to plan recognition work, but we will first spend a few words on the former two areas of investigation.

3.1   Linguistic theories

As mentioned above, purpose clauses have received attention in syntactic literature – see for example [Jones, 1985], [Hegarty, 1990]. Negation has also been extensively studied in syntactic literature – the interested reader can refer to the bibliography of [Horn, 1989].

As far as we know, very little attention has been paid to purpose clauses in the semantics literature: in [1990], Jackendoff briefly analyzes expressions of *purpose, goal, or rationale, normally encoded as an infinitival, in order to-phrase, or for-phrase.* He represents them by means of a subordinating function FOR, which has as an argument the adjunct clause; in turn, FOR plus its argument is a restrictive modifier of the main clause. However, Jackendoff's semantic decomposition doesn't go beyond the construction of the logical form of a sentence, and he doesn't pursue the issue of what the relation between the actions described in the matrix and adjunct really is.

Negation has instead been extensively studied: [Horn, 1989] presents a (semantic) history of negation that starts with Aristotle. However, semanticists are interested in issues such as the entailments of a negated sentence, the interaction of negation and quantifiers, or issues relative to implicatures. Hamblin in his book about imperatives [1987] does deal with negative imperatives, however he doesn't seem to address the complex relations between actions we have been talking about here.

Our conclusion is that, even if negation, but not purpose clauses, has been object of linguistic investigation, nobody has really dealt with the issues we raised here: the effects that such imperatives have on the hearer, and the inferences that the hearer has to perform in order to derive the description of the action to execute.

3.2   Formal theories of action

Actions and goals have been extensively studied in formal theories of action: as an example of those, we will discuss [Cohen and Levesque, 1990]. Cohen and Levesque provide a formal characterization of goals and intentions, and they characterize the communicative effect that an utterance in a particular syntactic mode has on the hearer. With regard to imperatives, they say

> After speaker S's imperative to addressee H to do action a if H does not think that S was insincere about his wanting H to do a - ... - then H believes that S wants H to do a.

However, they don't address at all the issues of how the description of the action a is extracted from the imperative, and that a may be subject to further computations.

In a more recent paper [1991], Cohen and Levesque go into some details on how an agent comes to intend to do an action to achieve a goal, and they use an action representation language built *inductively out of primitive events, and complex expressions created by action-forming operators for sequential, repetitive, concurrent, disjunctive, and contextual actions.* This is evidence for the fact that they consider event descriptions to be primitive, namely, that they are not interested in the internal structure of such "primitive" events; besides, they still don't address at all the issue of computing which action an instruction really describes.

We think that their work only addresses one facet of the problem: in [Di Eugenio, 1992] a first attempt is made to link such a theory to the issue of inferring more constrained descriptions of actions as described in this paper.

3.3   Plan recognition

As we stated in the introduction, most accommodation inferences are different from the implementations of plan recognition that are found in the literature - in particular those investigated by Kautz [1990] and by Pollack [1986].

Moreover, the point of view that the actions described in the input have to be considered as *linguistic objects* is at the basis of our efforts. While others have looked at plan recognition in a linguistic setting (e.g. [Lambert and Carberry, 1991], [Litman and Allen, 1990]), their linguistic considerations concern recognizing which speech-acts a certain utterance is an expression of, not what actions it describes. Taking the point of view that the inference processes have to deal, at least down to a certain level, with linguistic objects allows us to deal with the two following facts:

1. linguistic objects are partial descriptions and as such they may need further refinement in order to understand their relationship to goals;

2. linguistic objects are equally relevant whether they specify what to do and how to do it, or what *not* to do and / or how *not* to do it.

3.4   Kautz

Kautz in [1990] uses an *is-a* hierarchy and a *part-of* hierarchy to infer what plans a certain event can be part of; he then uses the goals he discovers to constrain the search for the plan of which the next event is part of. Suppose he starts with an event description ϵ; he may then deduce that ϵ can be part of the plans to achieve e.g. G_1 or G_2 - this is represented by a graph. A second event description ω is in turn part of plans to achieve G_1 or G_3. Finally, by merging the two graphs, Kautz obtains a description of what plans both ϵ and ω may be part of - in this case the one achieving G_1.

The difference between accommodation and Kautz's inferences is that the former doesn't assume an exact description of the action to be performed, while Kautz's event descriptions exactly match those included in his two hierarchies. Moreover, the inferences derived from purpose clauses use a known goal to compute the more refined actions needed to satisfy the goal. Kautz goes the other way, as he exploits known and complete descriptions of events to infer higher and unknown goals. The treatment of certain kinds of negative imperatives is instead similar to Kautz's inferences: going back to Ex. 7, that *cleaning the parquet* is the goal common to *dust-mop, vacuum, scrub, wet-mop* can be inferred by means of inference processes very similar to Kautz's. In fact, we would first infer that *dust-mop* and *vacuum* both generate *clean parquet floor*; then we would infer that *scrub* and *wet-mop* also generate *clean parquet floor*. At this point, the two graphs are unifiable, although the information should be maintained that these actions are in alternative one to the other, with the former two being admissible, and the latter two not admissible, alternatives.

3.5   Pollack

Pollack in [1986; 1990] is concerned with finding the relation between a known goal β and a known action α. The relation is a complex one, that is embedded in what Pollack calls *explanatory plan*, or *E-plan*. An E-plan is composed of the beliefs that the inferring agent R has about the beliefs and intentions of the agent A with respect to actions and to relations between actions. Crucially, relations between actions are expressed in terms of *conditional generation*: among the beliefs that R attributes to A, the ones relevant here have as object the following conjunct

$$\mathrm{CGEN}(\gamma, \delta, \mathcal{C}) \land \mathrm{HOLDS}(\mathcal{C}, t_2)$$

Namely, R believes that A believes that there is a conditional generation relation – CGEN – holding between γ and δ, and that the corresponding conditions $\mathcal{C}$ hold at the execution time t_2, so that the generation relation can go through. Given that generation is a transitive relation, if R manages to build a chain of beliefs that links α and β, then R can attribute the corresponding E-plan to A. By exploiting these notions, R is able to detect invalidities in A's plan: A may believe that a $\mathcal{C}$ pertaining to a certain CGEN relation holds, while R knows it doesn't, and R can point this out. Moreover, R can point out some other action γ' such that the generation chain going from α through γ' generates β.

The conditions on the generation relation may seem similar to the assumptions whose computation we propose as the second type of accommodation – see Figs. 2 and 3. However, conditions on generation are known a priori, as they are an inherent part of the definition of conditional generation between two actions. More than with conditions relative to generation relations, we are concerned with the expectations that the hearer develops after having been given an instruction, expectations necessary to make sense of the instructions themselves – such as the assumption *urn in the other room*. In particular, notice that in Ex. 3 *go into the other room* may successfully contribute to *getting the urn of coffee* even if there is no urn in the other room – if for example in the other room there is a note saying how to get the urn of coffee. The assumption *urn in the other room* is simply an expectation that the hearer comes to have as a consequence of the accommodation process, not a condition that has to hold for the relation between the two actions to hold.

4   Implementation of inferences

This work on understanding instructions is being done in the context of the *Animation from Natural Language (AnimNL)* project at the University of Pennsylvania.

Over the years, Penn's Graphics Laboratory has developed an extensive model-based animation system.

The system embodies anthropometric, kinematic and dynamic models, so that agents of different builds and strengths can be animated to perform tasks such as *grasp, look at, stand up, sit down* etc.

Given such model-based animation, it makes sense to envision a system where agents are given goals to achieve, or instructions to perform. Such a system could be used, among other things, to instruct human agents on how to perform a task, or as an aid to designers, e.g. to check that the product is designed correctly for maintenance and repair. Given the wide variety of possible users and applications for such a system, the most suitable and flexible language for interacting with the animated agent is Natural Language [Badler *et al.*, 1990].

The types of accommodation we discussed in this paper are being implemented, using a lexicon and an action library whose primitives are Jackendoff-type Conceptual Structures [Jackendoff, 1990]. Action types so represented are organized into a virtual lattice in the CLASSIC language [Brachman *et al.*, 1990]. Algorithms use this knowledge to build the structure of the agent's intentions, called a *plan graph*, which is further elaborated until sufficient to drive a simulation and produce animation [Badler *et al.*, 1990; Levison, 1991; Webber *et al.*, 1991].

We show in [Di Eugenio and White, 1991] that employing the semantic primitives that Jackendoff proposes facilitates certain inferences. We represent the actions in our action library by means of Jackendoff's primitives, and we show how primitives such as PATH and PLACE are useful to compute the assumptions necessary to make sense of Ex. 3. Informally, if a component of the body of *GETting an object j from l to m* is that the agent goes to PLACE$_1$ - where j is, and *Go into the other room* is analyzed as *going to* PLACE$_2$ - *the other room*, the relation between the two actions can go through by equating PLACE$_1$ and PLACE$_2$, which is equivalent to making the assumption that the urn is in the other room.

On the other hand, a CLASSIC type system is useful because it provides a virtual lattice, and so it is able to deal with concepts it has not yet seen. Consider Ex. 2: presumably the system has knowledge about γ = *cutting a square in half along the diagonal*, and the fact that this action generates β = *create two triangles*. However, α = *cut the square in half* is underspecified: the system recognizes α as an ancestor of γ and, by means of its position in the lattice and of the goal β, can assume that the action to be performed is actually γ.

Further details on the action representation, the inference processes, and the plan graph can be found in [Di Eugenio, 1992] and [Di Eugenio and White, 1991].

5   Summary

In this paper, we have shown that Natural Language instructions motivate some inference processes that can be seen as a local type of accommodation. The processes of accommodation we have described can be considered as a subtype of plan recognition, using the broad definition of plan recognition given by Kautz. However, accommodation differs from the work done so far in taking seriously the linguistic nature of its objects:

1. linguistic objects are partial descriptions and as such they may need further refinement in order to understand their relationship to goals;

2. linguistic objects are equally relevant whether they specify what to do and how to do it, or what *not* to do and / or how *not* to do it.

Acknowledgements

Thanks to the members of the AnimNL group, in particular to Mike White, for useful discussions. The first author is supported by DARPA grant no. N0014-90-J-1863 and ARO grant no. DAALO3-89-C0031PR1.

References

[Allen, 1984] James Allen. Towards a general theory of action and time. *Artificial Intelligence*, 23:123–154, 1984.

[Alterman *et al.*, 1991] Richard Alterman, Roland Zito-Wolf, and Tamitha Carpenter. *Interaction, Comprehension, and Instruction Usage*. Technical Report CS-91-161, Dept. of Computer Science, Center for Complex Systems, Brandeis University, 1991.

[Badler *et al.*, 1990] Norman Badler, Bonnie Webber, Jeff Esakov, and Jugal Kalita. Animation from instructions. In Badler, Barsky, and Zeltzer, editors, *Making them Move*, MIT Press, 1990.

[Balkanski, 1990] Cecile Balkanski. *Modelling act-type relations in collaborative activity*. Technical Report TR-23-90, Center for Research in Computing Technology, Harvard University, 1990.

[Brachman *et al.*, 1990] Ronald Brachman, Deborah McGuinness, Peter Patel Schneider, Lori Alperin Resnick, and Alexander Borgida. Living with CLASSIC: when and how to use a KL-ONE-like language. In J. Sowa, editor, *Principles of Semantic Networks*, Morgan Kaufmann Publishers, Inc., 1990.

[Chapman, 1991] David Chapman. *Vision, Instruction and Action*. Cambridge: MIT Press, 1991.

[Cohen and Levesque, 1990] Philip Cohen and Hector Levesque. Rational Interaction as the Basis for Communication. In J. Morgan, P. Cohen, and M. Pollack, editors, *Intentions in Communication*, MIT Press, 1990.

[Cohen and Levesque, 1991] Philip Cohen and Hector Levesque. Teamwork. 1991. Manuscript.

[Di Eugenio, 1992] Barbara Di Eugenio. *Goals and Actions in Natural Language Instructions*. Technical Report MS-CIS-92-07, University of Pennsylvania, 1992.

[Di Eugenio and White, 1991] Barbara Di Eugenio and Michael White. On the Interpretation of Natural Language Instructions. 1991. Submitted to COLING 92.

[Goldman, 1970] Alvin Goldman. *A Theory of Human Action*. Princeton University Press, 1970.

[Hamblin, 1987] Charles Hamblin. *Imperatives*. Basil Blackwell, 1987.

[Hegarty, 1990] Michael Hegarty. Secondary Predication and Null Operators in English. 1990. Manuscript.

[Horn, 1989] Laurence Horn. *A Natural History of Negation*. The University of Chicago Press, 1989.

[Jackendoff, 1990] Ray Jackendoff. *Semantic Structures. Current Studies in Linguistics Series*, The MIT Press, 1990.

[Jones, 1985] Charles Jones. Agent, patient, and control into purpose clauses. In *Chicago Linguistic Society, 21*, 1985.

[Kautz, 1990] Henry Kautz. A circumscriptive theory of plan recognition. In J. Morgan, P. Cohen, and M. Pollack, editors, *Intentions in Communication*, MIT Press, 1990.

[Lambert and Carberry, 1991] Lynn Lambert and Sandra Carberry. A tripartite plan-based model of dialogue. In *Proceedings of the 29th Annual Meeting of the ACL*, pages 47–54, 1991.

[Levison, 1991] Libby Levison. *Action Composition for the Animation of Natural Language Instructions*. Technical Report MS-CIS-91-28, University of Pennsylvania, 1991.

[Lewis, 1979] David Lewis. Scorekeeping in a language game. *Journal of Philosophical Language*, 8:339–359, 1979.

[Litman and Allen, 1990] Diane Litman and James Allen. Discourse processing and commonsense plans. In J. Morgan, P. Cohen, and M. Pollack, editors, *Intentions in Communication*, MIT Press, 1990.

[Pollack, 1986] Martha Pollack. *Inferring domain plans in question-answering*. PhD thesis, University of Pennsylvania, 1986.

[Pollack, 1990] Martha Pollack. Plans as complex mental attitudes. In J. Morgan, P. Cohen, and

M. Pollack, editors, *Intentions in Communication*, MIT Press, 1990.

[Thomason, 1990] Richmond Thomason. Accommodation, Meaning, and Implicature: Interdisciplinary Foundations for Pragmatics. In J. Morgan, P. Cohen, and M. Pollack, editors, *Intentions in Communication*, MIT Press, 1990.

[Vere and Bickmore, 1990] Steven Vere and Timothy Bickmore. A basic agent. *Computational Intelligence*, 6:41–60, 1990.

[Webber *et al.*, 1991] Bonnie Webber, Norman Badler, Barbara Di Eugenio, Libby Levison, and Michael White. Instructing Animated Agents. In *Proc. US-Japan Workshop on Integrated Systems in Multi-Media Environments. Las Cruces, NM*, 1991.

Building Symbolic Primitives with Continuous Control Routines

R. James Firby
Artificial Intelligence Laboratory
Computer Science Department
University of Chicago
1100 East 58th Street
Chicago, IL 60637

Abstract

This paper is about the interface between continuous and symbolic robot control. We advocate describing continuous actions and their related sensing strategies as *situation specific activities*, which can be manipulated by a symbolic reactive planner. The approach addresses the issues involved in turning symbolic actions into continuous activities, and using task specific sensing routines to support those activities. Situation specific activities help preserve the convenient fiction of "primitive actions" for use in planning without requiring that they all be programmed into the control system in advance. We demonstrate the utility of this architecture with an object tracking example. A control system is presented that can be reconfigured by a the RAP reactive executor to achieve different tasks. We show how this system allows us to build interchangeable tracking activities that use different sensing/action feedback loops in different situations.

1 Introduction

Traditional AI planning research depends on the convenient fiction of discrete "primitive actions". Plans consist of sequences of primitive actions and planners search through state spaces defined by primitive actions. Everyone knows that primitive actions cannot actually be realized, real actions are continuous and overlap and blend into one another, but the fiction seems to work in many situations. However, the one situation in which it doesn't work is in the control of real robots.

Consider the problem of a general purpose mobile robot following a person through a crowded room. The robot must track the person while moving smoothly through an area containing both other people and fixed obstacles like desks and chairs. It must speed up and slow down to stay near the person it is following and it must not hit other objects or people moving about the room.

What would the primitive actions be in this situation? One could argue that the robot execute a plan that consists of many primitive steps of the form "move forward 1cm" and "turn 2 degrees". However, such a plan cannot be built in advance because the path of the person being followed is not known. To keep up, the robot's planner would have to be able to assess the situation and build a new plan very quickly and very often. A more parsimonious description of person following comes from the ideas of behavior-based control.

Controllers for continuous processes are particularly good at managing actions that rely on the use of real time feedback, involve smooth motion over extended time, or require the coordination of multiple concurrent behaviors. Following a person might include: tracking by continuously pointing a video camera at the person and processing the image to give the direction to move, using that direction as feedback to steer the robot toward the person, and using sonar to monitor for nearby obstacles that need to be avoided.

This paper addresses the problem of preserving the fiction of primitive actions for planning purposes while actually controlling a robot using multiple concurrent behaviors. The goal is an integrated architecture for both planning and control. The approach taken to achieve this goal is to extend the RAP reactive execution system [4, 5] to interface with a behavior-based control system.

2 Background

The overall integrated architecture under investigation is shown schematically in Figure 1. This architecture (originally proposed in [5]) consists of three layers: A planning layer which produces sketchy plans for goals as they come in, the RAP execution system to fill in the

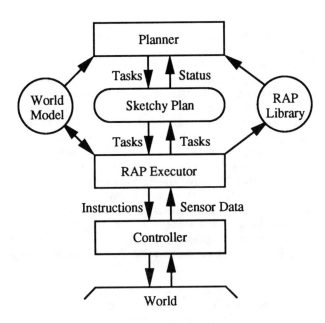

Figure 1: An Integrated Agent Architecture

details of the sketchy plan at run time, and a control system to actually carry out actions in the world.

The key component of this architecture, in terms of this discussion, is the RAP execution system which serves as a bridge between the planner and the control system. The control system requires detailed instructions but typically the planner can only create relatively vague plans due to uncertain and incomplete information about the future. The RAP system expands vague plan steps into detailed instructions at run time by choosing a method for the next step, appropriate to the current situation, from a preexisting library. Waiting until run time allows direct rather than predicted knowledge of the situation and much of the uncertainty and incompleteness plaguing the planner will disappear. However, some uncertainty will always remain and incorrect methods will sometimes be chosen. The RAP system copes with these problems by checking to make sure that each method achieves its intended goal and, if it doesn't, choosing another method and trying again.

The role of the RAP system within this architecture can be seen in two different ways. On the one hand, the RAP system is a reactive system which can accomplish quite complex goals on its own given appropriate methods in the library and enough time to muddle through. On the other hand, the RAP system can be viewed as supplying the planner with abstract "primitive actions". Once a task (*i.e.*, a plan step) is given to the RAP system, the system will work on it tenaciously, trying different methods and coping with whatever difficulties arise, until either the task is accomplished or every possible method has been tried. Thus, each task given to the RAP system, no matter how detailed or

how vague, can be treated by the planner as a primitive action because the the RAP system attempts to guarantee success if the task is possible or fail predictably if not. This use of RAPs as planning operators is discussed in more detail in [8].

Even when the RAP system is seen as preserving the fiction of abstract discrete primitives for planning purposes, there remains the difficulty of preserving the fiction of primitive actions for the RAP system itself. Eventually the hierarchy of RAP task methods bottoms out in steps for the control system to execute. The problem is to make these steps look discrete even though the control system operates continuously.

2.1   Behavioral Control

The most successful examples of robot control systems in the AI literature are organized around the idea of behaviors. Behavior based systems draw much from classical control theory but go on to make the observation that behavior which appears complex on the surface often arises from simple, interacting processes. Rather than generate a single control function that maps all inputs into all outputs, these systems are broken down into relatively independent processes that monitor a subset of inputs and produce a specific result. The results are then combined to drive the outputs in a coherent fashion. This modularization gives the control system more structure and makes it easier to build and understand [6, 11, 2].

Behavior based control systems have been very successful on quite sophisticated robots. Brooks has made particular progress using his subsumption architecture [3]. In subsumption, each behavior is described by a finite automaton and the overall behavior of the system arises from the interaction of the automata with the environment and each other. Typical behaviors in a mobile robot might be "move away from obstacles", "move forward", and "turn towards the light". The more complex task of "move toward a light without hitting anything" is achieved by running these simple behaviors together.

This architecture has been used by Horswill to build a robot which follows arbitrary moving objects [9] and by Mataric to build a robot that does navigation and learning in hallways [10]. Gat has used a similar notion of interacting simple behaviors to construct a robot that gathers up small toys [7] and Soldo uses interacting simple behaviors to navigate robustly in office hallways [13].

2.2   A Flexible Control System

Behavioral control systems represent a single control program designed to be more responsive to the environment than can easily be managed by a symbolic planner. However, the trade-off is that all of the goals,

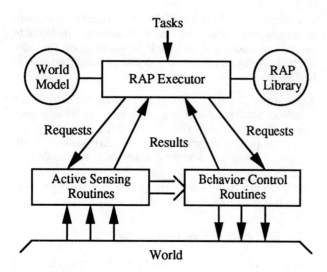

Figure 2: An Integrated Agent Architecture

and combinations of goals, that a robot is to achieve must be programmed into its control system in advance. In a complex world, building all goals into the robot ahead of time, limits it to simple sets of tasks.

One way to extend the applicability of such a control system is to program in a set of primitive actions that the planner could use to achieve many different goals. Unfortunately, when the world is very complex, and the planner can distinguish many different situations, there must be a huge number of primitive actions. For example, a different action is needed to follow a person, to travel down a hallway to the end, and to move down a hallway to the second door on the right. Each of these actions is a simple movement command but each uses different sensor feedback and has different termination condition to be monitored. This explosion of primitive actions either requires a large underlying control system or again limits the robot to a restricted set of tasks.

Our goal is to construct a control system that is able to exhibit a multitude of different primitive actions while remaining relatively small. Our approach is to build a behavior-based control system that can be "reprogrammed" by the RAP execution system. Allowing the control system to be reconfigured allows the same behaviors to be used in many different ways without having to encode them all in advance.

3   Situation Specific Robot Control

The system we are building to interface the RAP system with continuous control is illustrated in Figure 2. This part of the architecture consists of three main components: the RAP system, a collection of active sensing routines, and a collection of behavioral control routines.

The active sensing and behavioral routines make up the real-time control system. Drawing on ideas from behavioral control, the control system is split into relatively independent sensing and action routines that can be activated, deactivated, and reconfigured individually. By carefully choosing the order in which routines are enabled and disabled, the planner can produce behavior sets with stable properties that extend over a period of time. For example, enabling collision avoidance behaviors, a visual tracking routine, and a routine to move the robot in the direction of the tracked feature, the planner can produce a state in which the robot follows a person without bumping into anything. This state will last indefinitely without further intervention as long as the tracked feature stays in view and the path toward it stays reasonably clear.

By shifting between stable sets of active routines, the RAP system breaks the continuous world of control into discrete activities designed to achieve individual goals. Each activity can be treated as a discrete entity that produce a predictable action over a period of time in which the setup of the control system does not change. Activities take the place of primitive actions and the word *activity* will be used to mean both a meaningful primitive goal that can be achieved in the world and the set of active control routines that together achieve that goal.

While activities emulate primitive actions, the RAP system does not generate activities; it generates instructions to enable, disable, and reconfigure routines. Thus, activities are conceptual primitive actions that must be turned into control instructions by the RAP system. The ability to choose the control instructions to implement an activity at run time allows the control system to be used very flexibly. Routines can be mixed and matched as needed to produce the same behavior in different situations or different behaviors in the same situation.

3.1   Situation Specific Activities

The goal in writing the RAPs for an activity is to create methods that configure the control system to predictably achieve a particular goal in a specific situation. Once activated, the routines making up the activity will run continuously as feedback control loops without intervention. The trick is to define configurations that *reliably* move the robot through a task in an uncertain, dynamic environment.

Sometimes defining a situation specific activity is easy because the desired goal requires only a single routine. Usually, however, the activities useful in plans will be much more complex than a single hardware invocation and will require a whole set of routines for their definition. Following a person requires a routine to move the robot in the right direction, another to direct the robot away from obstacles, and yet another to keep the robot from getting too close or too far away from the person being followed. Executing "follow person" as a single action means invoking all of these routines together. Once activated, their interaction with each other and the world will have the *emergent* property of satisfying the desired goal.

3.2   Finite Situation Specific Activities

Selecting the routines necessary to achieve a goal is not enough to define a useful activity. A critical feature of the tasks juggled by the RAP system is that they are discrete and finite. Each action must have a well-defined beginning and end. A situation specific activity has a clear beginning: when it is invoked. However, typically the routines that make up an activity will run happily forever.

When the purpose of an activity is emergent, there is no clear sign that it has been achieved. Moving forward, avoiding obstacles, and staying a constant distance from the wall might have the effect of moving the robot down a hall, but when is that action complete? Completion may mean many things: having traveled a specific distance, having reached the end of the hall, or having passed three doorways. Regardless of which of these goals is desired, noticing that it has been achieved requires monitoring states in the world beyond those needed just to carry it out. These additional monitoring activities must be included in any activity designed to implement a discrete action.

Activities that define actions must not just signal completion; they must also reliably signal when they fail. The real world is filled with uncertainty and real sensors are not 100% accurate. As a result, configurations of routines will not always achieve the goals that they were intended to achieve. This is particularly true when the desired goal is emergent. For example, suppose a robot is executing a set of routines designed to move it down a hall 10 ft. What happens if the hallway is only 5 ft. long? Presumably the robot will eventually come to a halt under the direction of its obstacle avoidance routines but its completion monitor will not yet be satisfied because it hasn't moved 10 ft. At that point something should happen or the robot will just sit there forever, secure in the fact that its active routines are moving it down the hall, not realizing that they have been stymied by the context the robot unwittingly finds itself in.

The solution to this problem is to augment the routines implementing the action with additional routines to monitor for failure states as well as for success states. This procedure is mandatory for every activity that is to define a reliable symbolic action. In the hallway, this may involve something simple like signaling that the robot has been stationary for 10 seconds, or something more complicated like signaling that the robot is moving back and forth to go around the obstacle making up the end of the hall but is making no measurable progress. The important point is that the activity must *always* signal that it is wedged. Only with such assurances can the planner and RAP system trust that their planned actions will interact with the world in a sensible fashion.

3.3   Activities and Sensing

Notice that the routines selected by the RAP system to instantiate an activity include not just action routines but sensing routines as well. Authors of control systems for real robots routinely make the claim that their systems work because sensing is restricted to precisely those features of the world that are relevant to the task at hand [9, 13]. Underlying this claim is the realization that processing all available sensor data is both too slow to support control and unnecessary in most cases. Sensing strategies must be specialized to the particular needs of the control routines that use them.

The sensing and action routines within an activity are coupled together via the attributes of objects and situations in the world. For example, the direction to an object can be used by routines designed to approach the object, to avoid the object, and to point in the object's direction. As long as the direction is known, these activities can proceed. It is the direction attribute that has a functional use in the routines, not the object itself or the way that the attribute is extracted.

There will often be many different active sensing routines for extracting the same functional attribute from the world. This allows the RAP system substantial leeway to instantiate activities in different ways under different circumstances. For example, tracking the location of an obstacle might be done using color, shape, or motion, depending on what is most reliable in the specific context. When selecting a tracking strategy, the RAP system uses its knowledge of the obstacle to focus the interpretation of visual data (*i.e.*, color, motion, shape) down to just that which is necessary to reliably keep track of the object's relevant functional attribute (*i.e.*, position).

In [1] Agre and Chapman describe attributes of the world like the direction to an object as functional-indexical references. The RAP system's choice of an active sensing routine to extract an attribute from the world is precisely the generation of a functional-indexical designation for that attribute. The sensing routine operationalizes exactly what is needed to reliably refer to and use an abstract symbolic property of the world. A person being followed becomes "the-direction-I-am-tracking" and the follow activity uses "the-direction-I-am-tracking" as its reference.

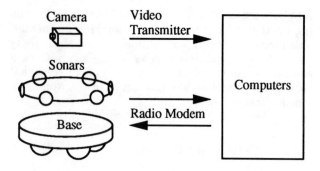

Figure 3: The University of Chicago Robot

4   An Example: Object Following

To illustrate the ideas outlined above, consider part of the initial reconfigurable control system we have implemented on the mobile robot at the University of Chicago AI Lab. The robot is a small mobile robot configured as shown in Figure 3. The round base can turn in place and is topped by a ring of 6 sonars and a color video camera mounted on a pan/tilt head.

The control system is implemented on an off-board computer that receives a steady stream of sonar range readings and pan/tilt positions and asynchronously replies with new heading, speed, and pan/tilt commands. The video image from the robot is also processed off-board using DataCube boards and an attached computer that can be configured to carry out different visual processing tasks at different times. The control system and vision processing computers are connected so that the results of one are always available to the other.

4.1   The Control System

Four types of building block are used in the control system design: attribute trackers, action generators, constraint generators, and resolvers. Attribute trackers process sensor data to produce a continuous quantity, or attribute, that corresponds to some property of the world needed as feedback to an action generator, such as direction to some target, or the relative position of some location. Attribute trackers translate features of the world into a limited number of meaningful attributes relative to the robot.

Action generators process robot relative attributes to produce desired control actions. Action generators correspond to the simple behaviors that the system can actually carry out in the world, such as turning to face in a direction, moving toward a location, or reaching out to touch a nearby point. The control actions generated are desired set-points for actual hardware actions like rotation and translation velocities.

A typical activity is constructed by choosing attribute trackers to process the features of the world impor-

tant to the activity and action generators to move the robot appropriately with respect to those attributes. This idea is similar in flavor to the reflexive control plans described by Payton [12]. Reflexive control plans pair virtual sensors with reflexive behaviors to produce activities that control robot actuators. However, we place a stronger constraint on the overall system by allowing only one action generator to be actively requesting each hardware action during an activity. For example, if the robot is to follow a person by using a "track person" attribute to give a relative direction for a "move in direction" action generator, no other action generator can be active that would also request changes to the robot's rotation and translation velocities. Similarly, no other attribute tracker can be active that would require the same visual sensor processing resources. These restrictions simplify the arbitration of conflicting desired control actions.

Constraint generators are similar to action generators except that they generator constraints on hardware control actions rather than requesting particular set-points. Constraints take the form of intervals that a control action must either obey or avoid. Constraint generators are used to implement minor behavior modifications on the primary action generator. For example, a rotation velocity constraint generator might prevent the robot from turning left and hurting its arm if there is an object being tracked very close on the left.

Each hardware action has a resolver that takes the desired control input from the active action generator and any constraints on that desire from active constraint generators and produces a final control action. The constraint resolution process is typically quite simple with the resolver choosing the control action closest to that desired without violating any constraints.

4.1.1   Motion Control

Some of the simple sonar-based motion control attribute trackers and constraint generators are shown schematically in Figure 4. The first attribute tracker produces the relative direction of the most open area visible by the sonars and the second produces the relative direction to the nearest object detected by the sonars. The two speed constraint generators can be used to keep the robot from hitting things and the heading constraint generator keeps the robot from hurting its arm by turning when obstacles are too close.

The final output for the robot's speed and heading are generated by resolvers that take as input a desired setting and any number of constraints as shown in Figure 5. The two simple actions shown can be used to turn the robot to face in a given tracked direction, or move the robot in a given tracked direction. The move and turn actions cannot be enabled together as both

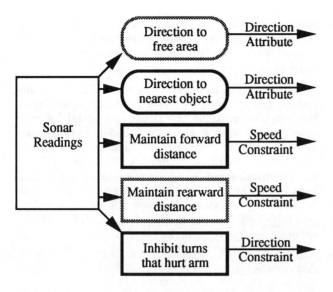

Figure 4: Sonar-Based Attribute and Constraint Routines

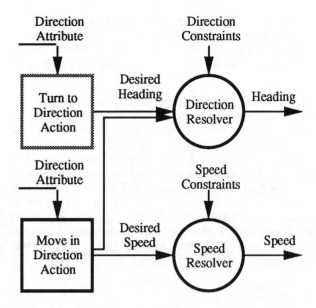

Figure 5: Simple Action Generators and Resolvers

actions turn the robot.

The sonar based direction routines can be used quite flexibly by altering their activity and parameters. For example, suppose the `direction-to-nearest-object` attribute tracker is active and its output is connected to the move action as the desired direction. The robot will now continually move towards the nearest object assuming that the constraints allow it. By changing the settings on the `maintain-forward-distance` constraint generator, the robot can be configured to stay some distance away from the nearest object, move up to touch it, or even push on it.

4.1.2   Active Vision Routines

The vision system consists of two tracking routines. Each controls the pointing of the robot's pan-tilt head and is also an attribute tracker producing a relative direction. The first routine is based on the color histogram object recognition work done by Swain [14]. An object, or person, is represented by a static histogram of its surface colors and it can be recognized when encountered again by matching that histogram against its current colors. When tracking an object, the current video image is searched until an area that matches the object's histogram is found. The robot's pan/tilt head is then moved to center that area in the image and the direction of the pan/tilt head is the direction attribute generated. The second routine does a vary similar thing but searches the image for areas of motion as defined by image subtraction.

These two active vision routines are direction attribute trackers so they can be configured to supply the desired direction to same the move and turn action generators discussed above. Such a configuration connects the active vision routines to the sonar-based speed and direction controls. As a result, the robot can be configured to follow someone just as it can be configured to approach the nearest object. The only change necessary is to disable the `direction-to-nearest-object` attribute tracker and enable either the color histogram or motion tracking direction attribute in its place.

4.1.3   Interface to the RAP System

The vocabulary of instructions that the control system presents to the RAP system is:

> Activate/Deactivate `free-area` tracker
> Activate/Deactivate `nearest-object` tracker
> Activate/Deactivate color histogram tracker
> Activate/Deactivate motion tracker
> Activate/Deactivate `move` generator
> Activate/Deactivate `turn` generator
> Set `maintain-forward-distance` distance window
> Set `maintain-rearward-distance` distance window
> Set color histogram to track

In addition to receiving instructions, the control system can generate signals to the RAP system. In particular, each active attribute tracker, action generator, constraint generator, and resolver can signal that it met some goal, or failed in some way. For example, the color histogram tracker signals if the histogram moves out of its field of view (*i.e.*, it looses track of its target), the maintain forward distance constraint generator signals when it is at its buffer distance, and the speed and heading resolvers signal when their constraints rule out all possible action or are inconsistent. This allows these routines to be used as monitors for the completion or failure of activities they take part in.

A typical RAP defining an activity will package several methods that generate different sets of these instructions as primitive subgoals in different situations. For example, the RAP for (follow ?x) might have one method that enables tracking ?x using a color histogram if ?x has distinctive colors and another that enables tacking ?x via motion if there are no other moving objects around. It is the ability to represent many such methods for the same primitive activity that moves the idea of primitive action out of the control system and increases the flexibility of the system as a whole.

5   Summary

This paper describes an architecture in which discrete, symbolic RAP methods can be used to configure a continuous behavior-based control system. The two central concepts within this architecture are:

1. Activities form a useful abstraction for discussing and representing primitive actions.
2. Activities can be implemented in a control system as instructions to enable, disable, and configure a fixed set of sensing and action routines.

Activities are the convenient fiction of primitive actions overlaid on the continuous control system. Hence, activities represent primitive actions to both the RAP and the higher level planning systems. However, the fact that activities look like primitive actions for planning purposes does not change the fact that they are simply subgoals within the RAP expansion hierarchy. As specific situations arise in the world, the RAP system must assemble customized sets of routines to carry out desired activities.

The actual outputs from the RAP system are not primitive actions in the usual sense but instructions to configure the control system's routines. By carefully choosing appropriate instructions, the RAP system can place the control system into stable states that achieve emergent goals in the world. By reprogramming the control system at run time, a small control system can be used to generate a large number of different, discrete actions.

5.1   Future Work

The interface between symbolic and continuous control described in this paper shows how the fiction of discrete actions can be preserved for use in planning. However, the construction of a content theory remains, as yet, undone. If the architecture is to support general purpose behavior, it must support the activities that make up the "primitive" components of general purpose behavior.

We will continue to expand the vocabulary of sensing and action routines available for building activities. We will also continue to expand the activities available for achieving goals. Our belief is that, because activities rely on sensing and action routines coupled together via functional attributes, the process of building activities everyday tasks in the real world will highlight the behaviors and indexical-functionals necessary for everyday activity. We hope the result will be a generally useful, robot independent way of describing ordinary, everyday behavior.

Acknowledgements

The author would like to thank Mike Swain for helpful discussion and comments on the ideas presented in this paper. He would also like to thank Mike Swain, Mark Stricker, and Tom McDougal for the work they put into the implementation of the control system routines and activities described.

References

[1] Philip E. Agre and David Chapman. Pengi: An implementation of a theory of activity. In *Sixth National Conference on Artificial Intelligence*, Seattle, WA, July 1987. AAAI.

[2] Ronald C. Arkin. Motor schema based navigation for a mobile robot: An approach to programming by behavior. In *International Conference on Robotics and Automation*, Raleigh, NC, March 1987. IEEE.

[3] Rodney A. Brooks. A robust layered control system for a mobile robot. *IEEE Journal of Robotics and Automation*, RA-2(1), March 1986.

[4] R. James Firby. An investigation into reactive planning in complex domains. In *Sixth National Conference on Artificial Intelligence*, Seattle, WA, July 1987. AAAI.

[5] R. James Firby. Adaptive execution in complex dynamic worlds. Technical Report YALEU/CSD/RR #672, Computer Science Department, Yale University, January 1989.

[6] Erann Gat. Bdl: A language for programming reactive robotic control systems. Jet Propulsion Laboratory, 1990.

[7] Erann Gat and David P. Miller. Modular, low-computation robot control for object acquisition and retrieval. Jet Propulsion Laboratory, 1990.

[8] Steven John Hanks. Projecting plans for uncertain worlds. Technical Report YALEU/CSD/RR

#756, Computer Science Department, Yale University, January 1990.

[9] Ian Douglas Horswill and Rodney Allen Brooks. Situated vision in a dynamic world: Chasing objects. In *Seventh National Conference on Artificial Intelligence*, St. Paul, MN, August 1988. AAAI.

[10] Maja J. Mataric. *A Model for Distributed Mobile Robot Environment Learning and Navigation.* PhD thesis, Department of Electrical Engineering and Computer Science, MIT, 1990.

[11] David Payton. Exploiting plans as resources for action. In *Workshop on Innovative Approaches to Planning, Scheduling, and Control*, San Diego, CA, November 1990. DARPA.

[12] D.W. Payton. An architecture for reflexive autonomous vehicle control. In *International Conference on Robotics and Automation*, San Francisco, CA, 1986. IEEE.

[13] Monnett Hanvey Soldo. Fusion without representation. In *Vol. 1198 Sensor Fusion II: Human and Machine Strategies*, Philadelphia, PA, November 1989. SPIE.

[14] Michael J. Swain. Color indexing. Technical Report 360, Department of Computer Science, University of Rochester, 1990.

Rational Handling of Multiple Goals for Mobile Robots

Richard Goodwin and **Reid Simmons**
School of Computer Science
Carnegie Mellon University
Pittsburgh, Pennsylvania 15213-3890

Abstract

The mobile robot planning domain is dynamic, with goals becoming active asynchronously. In order to successfully operate in this environment, a robot must be able to interrupt and reformulate its plans of action on-the-fly. This paper investigates a method for incorporating the accomplishment of a new goal into a partially executed plan. A decision theoretic approach using net present value as the decision criterion serves as the basis for doing dynamic goal ordering. The appropriateness of net present value over benefit-cost ratio is argued. The approach has been implemented on a robot operating in an office setting. Examples from this domain are used to show the advantages of the approach with respect to fixed priority and heuristic based approaches.

1 Introduction

This paper examines a method for handling multiple active goals in mobile robots. Specifically, the focus is on asynchronous goal activation and on how to incorporate the accomplishment of a newly active goal into a partially executed plan. A utility based decision theoretic approach is adopted for investigating the tradeoffs that must be made.

The applicability of decision theory to problems in artificial intelligence and planning in particular has long been recognized [Horvitz et al., 1988]. Feldman and Sproull, in their analysis of planning for the hungry monkey problem, use utility based decision theory to evaluate plans taking into account uncertainty and risk [Feldman and Sproull, 1977]. More recent work has focused on deciding when to refine plans [Boddy and Dean, 1989]. The work presented here differs from these in that it focuses on plan evaluation when all goals are not initially known and the plan must be reformulated as goals become active. In such cases, the time dependent utility of goal satisfaction, as well as the time distribution of utilities and resource use, must be taken into account.

Given a utility based framework, one must choose an appropriate decision criterion. In this paper two such criteria are analyzed: net present value and benefit-cost ratio. While both measures take into account the time distribution of utilities, net present value is shown to have some advantages over benefit-cost ratio when dealing with non-independent goals with discrete resource requirements. Plan evaluation based on net present value has been incorporated into a planning system that can interrupt an executing plan and dynamically order goals. The planning system has been applied to two mobile robot domains. The Ambler [Simmons and Krotkov, 1991], a prototype planetary exploration robot designed to carry out scientific missions, has been used as a model for a number of simulations. A Hero 2000 robot, used to perform a number of tasks in our lab, has been used as a vehicle for implementing the ideas. This paper examines a number of examples from the Hero domain to show the advantage of using a decision theoretic approach over heuristic based methods and fixed priority schemes.

2 Utility Based Rationality

Modern decision theory is concerned with making rational choices between alternatives [Raiffa, 1968] [Schoemaker, 1980] [Sinn, 1983] [Dawes, 1988]. Rational is taken to mean choosing the course of action that maximizes the expected value of some desired quantity, such as utility. Decision theory provides mechanisms for dealing with uncertainty and the cost of acquiring information. For this reason, it is being increasingly used for planning in real-world domains [Wellman, 1988] [Boddy and Dean, 1989] [Hansson et al., 1990] [Chrisman and Simmons, 1991].

There are two requirements for formulating a planning problem in terms of decision theory. A method is needed to assign benefits or utilities to the accomplishment of each goal and costs or negative utilities to the consumption of each resource. Secondly, a decision criterion is needed to assess the relative merit of alternative plans.

The assignment of utilities is highly dependent on the set of tasks being considered and the desired behaviour. The exact magnitude of the utility values assigned is not as significant as the relative magnitudes which should reflect the relative priority of the goals.

A number of possible decision criteria have been suggested in the literature [Sassone and Schaffer, 1979]. Much of the body of work done on the development and analysis of the different criteria has focused on its applicability to economic domains [Simon, 1982]. The insights resulting from this work can be adapted to the mobile robot domain. Two commonly used criteria are examined below with comments on their appropriateness.

2.1 Benefit-Cost Ratio

The benefit-cost ratio is the sum of the present value of the benefits divided by the sum of the present value of the costs. The present value of a cost or benefit is the actual value discounted, by a fixed discount rate (d), for how long in the future it will occur.

$$\frac{B}{C} = \frac{\sum_{t=0}^{n} \frac{B_t}{(1+d)^i}}{\sum_{t=0}^{n} \frac{C_t}{(1+d)^i}} \ or \ \frac{\int_0^n \frac{B_t}{(1+d)^i} dt}{\int_0^n \frac{C_t}{(1+d)^i} dt} \qquad (1)$$

d discount rate
B_t Benefit at time t
C_t Cost at time t

Using the present value of the costs and benefits takes into account their time distribution. Discounting future utilities creates a preference for benefits that accrue sooner and costs that occur further in the future. For example, given the choice between two plans that achieve the same benefit for the same initial cost, the one that returns the benefit sooner is preferred.

Taking the ratio of the present values of the benefits and the costs gives a measure of the rate of return. Alternatives that incur less cost to produce the same net benefit will be preferred. In economics, investments are selected by ranking the investment opportunities in order of decreasing benefit-cost ratio and accepting investment opportunities until the available resources are exhausted or the rate of return falls below the cost of capital. This greedy optimization algorithm allows the opportunities to be considered independently and leads to a very efficient decision procedure that is linear in the number of opportunities. [Etzioni, 1989], in the design of an autonomous agent, uses the algorithm as a basis for the agent's decision control loop.

As [Etzioni, 1989] points out though, there are problems when the opportunities require a discrete amount of each resource and resources are limited. In such cases, the problem can be shown to be intractable by a reduction from the knapsack problem [Garey and Johnson, 1979]. In practice, use of the greedy algorithm does lead to problems. Imagine a situation in which an exploration robot has located two adjacent items of interest. One item has a higher value than the other, but also consumes proportionately more resources to extract. Further suppose that there were not enough re-

sources to take both samples — exactly one must be chosen. The greedy algorithm can fail in this case by selecting the option that gives the higher rate of return, but a lower net return.

A modified version of the greedy algorithm can be used in which the greedy solution is compared to a solution consisting solely of the item with the maximum net return, and the better of the two solutions selected. This modified algorithm can be shown to be within a factor of two of optimal [Garey and Johnson, 1979]. In the above sample selection example, the modified greedy algorithm correctly chooses the option with the highest net return. Suppose, however, that the situation was changed so that there were enough resources to sample both but that the item with the lower rate of return was degrading over time. The modified greedy algorithm would not be able to generate the optimal plan to first sample the low rate of return item and then to sample the high rate of return item. The algorithm fails because the opportunities are not independent. In general, considering opportunities in isolation is insufficient and combinations must be evaluated when selecting a plan.

Another difficultly with using the benefit-cost ratio is that it is dependent on the exact definition of costs and benefits. Suppose there are two methods a robot can use to traverse a room: one that is fast and uses little energy, but is noisy, and a second method that is quiet, but takes longer and uses more energy. Should the negative utility of disturbing others in the room with the noisy traversal be counted as a cost or as a negative benefit? Clearly, the way in which such external effects are treated will affect the ratio, and hence the robot's decisions.

2.2 Net Present Value

The net present value of a sequence of costs and benefits is the net of the present value of each negative utility/cost or positive utility/benefit. This is the most widely used metric in cost-benefit analysis and is generally considered superior to other metrics [Sassone and Schaffer, 1979]. In contrast to the benefit-cost ratio criterion, net present value chooses to maximize the net return rather than the rate of return.

$$Utility: \ U_t = B_t - C_t$$

$$NPV = \sum_{t=0}^{n} \frac{U_t}{(1+d)^t} \ or \ \int_0^n \frac{U_t}{(1+d)^t} dt \qquad (2)$$

As with benefit-cost ratio, the use of present values creates a preference for benefits that accrue sooner and costs that occur later. Resource investments are chosen by generating all feasible combinations of opportunities and selecting the one with the highest net present value. Even in the case where the investment options are not independent (as in the second version of the sampling example above) this method prefers the option that maximizes the net return.

Net present value treats negative benefits and costs equivalently. There is no need to make arbitrary distinctions.

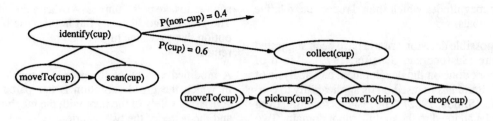

Figure 1: **Cup Collection Plan.**

Summing the costs and benefits does mean, however, that they must be normalized to the same scale. In economics this is done by expressing quantities in equivalent dollar values. For the robot domain, quantities can be normalized to their equivalent value in terms of a specific resource or benefit such as time, battery charge or samples taken.

The net present value method does not exhibit a preference for options that conserve resources. No distinction is made between two options that have the same net return but incur different costs. Conserving resources is desirable to the extent that it allows the unused portion to be used for other purposes. The benefit-cost ratio naturally prefers plans that incur less cost to produce the same net benefit since it is a measure of the rate of return. When using net present value, the opportunity cost of consuming a resource has to be taken into account. In a situation where net present value does not distinguish between two options, the one with the lower cost should be preferred.

Adopting the use of net present value leads directly to the intractable problem of having to generate and evaluate a combinatorial number of alternatives. Some method must be used to reduce the number of alternatives that have to be considered. The approach taken in this work has been to generate only a subset of the possible combinations and to do this incrementally as new opportunities become available. Details of the method used are given in the following section on the planning framework.

2.3 Discount Rate

While discounting future values accounts for the time preferences of costs and benefits, the choice of a discount rate is highly problematic. The discount rate reflects a willingness to trade present benefits for future costs. A low discount rate results in decisions that focus on long term impacts; a high discount rate results in greedy decisions. The discount rate incorporates assumptions about risk aversion and the predictability of the environment. For example, using a higher discount rate decreases risk by reducing dependence on the accuracy of predictions about the future since shorter plans with more current benefits are preferred. It would be desirable to adjust the discount rate as the model of the environment was refined and confidence in its accuracy increased.

3 Planning Framework

We have developed a planning framework that is geared towards handling asynchronous activation of goals involving robot motion and manipulation. A set of abstract actions is used to construct linear, conditional plans which are refined for execution by means of hierarchical decomposition of the abstract actions. Associated with each abstract action is the information needed to determine if and how the action can be interrupted. This information is used by a plan generator to create a set of plans that merge the handling of a newly active goal into the existing plan. The plan with the highest estimated net present value is selected for execution.

The conditional plan to achieve a set of active goals is represented as a tree of abstract actions. Figure 1 shows a simplified version of the plan for putting a potential cup in the bin. The plan consists of two abstract actions: one to determine if the object is a cup and the second to put it in the bin if it is. There is a branch in the plan for each possible outcome of an abstract action and associated with each branch is the probability of the corresponding outcome. These probabilities are used to weight the value of each branch when calculating the net present value of a plan.

Executing actions requires use of the robot's resources, such as grippers. As in the O-PLAN plan representation [Currie and Tate, 1985] each abstract operation specifies the resources that it requires. Resource information allows the planner to efficiently interrupt an action. For example, if the *collect(cup)* action in Figure 1 were interrupted to handle a recharge goal, the robot would not need to put the cup down since recharging does not require the gripper resource. Abstract actions may need to include "phantom" sub-actions [Secerdoti, 1977] to establish any required state since conditions may be clobbered between abstract actions. In the cup collection plan of Figure 1, both abstract actions include the *moveTo(cup)* sub-action. The second moveTo is a "phantom" action since it will not actually be executed if the plan is not interrupted.

Generating a plan for a set of goals is, in general, an intractable problem [Chapman, 1987]. The use of the linearity assumption that goals can be satisfied one at a time allows the planner to decompose the problem and generate a plan efficiently. Even with this linearity assumption, there is still a combinatorial number of possible goal orderings that could be considered when trying to optimize the plan. In order to avoid considering all possible orderings, the plan generator creates only a subset of the alternatives that is linear in the size of the original plan. New plans are created by inserting the plan for the new goal immediately, if the current action can be interrupted, or after that action otherwise and after each subsequent abstract action.

The decision not to consider goal reordering or interleaving is based on the assumption of a benign world and a near optimal original ordering for the actions. It is similar to the strategy used in intention-based planning where the planner makes a commitment to its existing plan and filters out options that are inconsistent with this commitment [Bratman et al., 1988]. Unlike Bratman et al.'s IRMA architecture, our current planner does not have a mechanism to override its commitment to its current plan. Whether limiting the planner to examining only a subset of possible goal orderings is rational depends on whether the opportunity cost of not considering other possible orderings is offset by the savings in computation time [Doyle, 1988].

The plan generator can also include domain-specific methods for generating plans. For the Hero domain, a method was added for inserting a new goal when the currently executing action involves carrying an object from one location to another. An *on-the-way* plan is created in which the robot immediately starts achieving the new goal, but drops any objects it is carrying at the point on the new path that is closest to its intended destination.

4 Hero Robot Domain

The Hero 2000 robot operates in an office setting performing a number of tasks [Simmons et al., 1990]. These include delivering printer output, taking objects from one workstation to another, and finding cups on the floor and putting them in a bin. The robot must also maintain its battery charge in order to be able to perform these tasks. The robot has a single manipulator and can carry only one object at a time.

Plan interruption, generation and selection using a net present value decision criterion has been incorporated into the software used to control the Hero 2000 robot. The Task Control Architecture [Simmons et al., 1990], an operating system for robot's, is used as a basis for the implementation. It provides the mechanisms needed to schedule and control multiple goals and actions and to monitor the environment.

Direct experimentation with the Hero robot is time consuming. In order to investigate a larger variety of examples and a larger range of parameter values, a system for simulating the robot, using the planning framework described above, was created with the Maple symbolic math system [Char, 1987]. The simulation software is domain independent. It is targeted to a particular domain by specifying action models, expected time and outcome probabilities as well as the utility of accomplishing each goal.

The characteristics of the Hero domain were determined empirically. Euclidean distance and average speed are used to estimate travel times. A discount rate of 0.2% per second was chosen which results in discounting utilities six minutes in the future by 1/2. The six minute time frame is sufficient for the robot to complete one or two tasks, reflecting the robots effective planning horizon.

The utility of having the robot accomplish one of its goals depends on its value to the people in the office in terms of the amount of time it saves them. Time saved, or not saved, was used as a basis for normalizing costs and benefits. The utility values used are the normalized sums of the costs and benefits for satisfying each goal. The time dependent nature of the goals was also taken into account. Delivering printer output and carrying objects from one workstation to another must be done in a timely fashion since people are waiting. The utility of both these activities is represented by a function that is initially almost flat, but that decreases to near zero after a delay. The height of the function represents the intrinsic value of accomplishing the goal and the cut off represents the acceptable delay (Eqs 3 and 4). Cup collection is of general benefit, but since no one is waiting for it, it is time insensitive and of relatively low importance (Eq 5). Charging after a low battery indication is not directly beneficial to anyone, but is necessary for the robot to operate. If the robot delays recharging too long and runs out of charge, someone will be required to intervene. For this reason, recharging is characterized by a function containing a negative exponential component, making the utility prohibitively negative after an initial delay. This delay represents the time before the robot would start to lose power (Eq 6).

Hero utility functions (delay in seconds)

$$Utility(printer, delay) = \frac{100}{1 + e^{\frac{delay - 200}{10}}} \quad (3)$$

$$Utility(delivery, delay) = \frac{200}{1 + e^{\frac{delay - 200}{10}}} \quad (4)$$

$$Utility(collectCup, delay) = 10 \quad (5)$$

$$Utility(recharge, delay) = -e^{delay - 200} \quad (6)$$

The following three examples illustrate the usefulness of the methods described.

4.1 Cup Collection Example

Suppose the robot is attending to a low utility goal when a new high utility request is received. The decision to be made is whether to continue with the current plan or suspend it until the new high utility goal is accomplished. In this example, the robot has an initial plan to collect a cup and receives a new request to deliver printer output. The room layout for the example is given in Figure 3. Objects are placed in the room in such a way that the cup and the bin

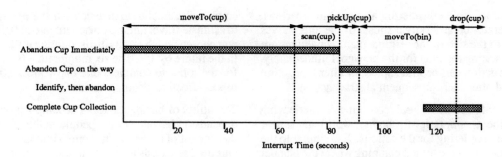

Figure 2: **Best Goal Ordering versus Interrupt Time, Cup Collection**

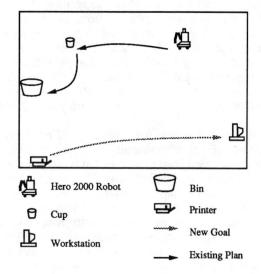

Figure 3: **Cup Collection Example.**

goal is accomplished. The utility of accomplishing each goal is determined by substituting the corresponding goal delay time into the appropriate utility equation (Eqs 3 – 6). The discount interval for a goal is the amount of time over which the utility of each goal must be discounted in order to find its present value. This will be different from the delay time if some time has elapsed since the request time, as in the case with the cup collection goal. The utility values and the discount intervals are used in formula (2) to determine the net present value of each plan.

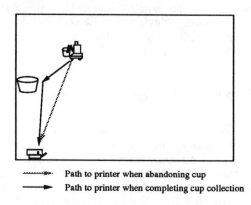

Figure 4: **Printer Path Difference.**

are only short detours on the way to the printer from the initial robot location.

Figure 2 shows how the preferred plan varies as a function of the new goal's activation time. This graph was produced by running the simulation with different interrupt times for the new printer delivery goal. The graph shows that before the robot has picked up the cup, it will suspend cup collection in favour of the printer request. Once the cup is picked up, it will be dropped off on the way to the printer, unless the robot is sufficiently close to the bin to make putting the cup in the bin worthwhile. The distance at which it becomes worthwhile to complete the cup collection is affected by the relative utilities of cup collection and printer output delivery, by the discount rate, by the cost of re-acquiring the cup, and by the relative positions of the robot, the bin and the printer. Abandoning the cup collection task incurs an extra cost to retrieve the cup since the robot must put it down in order to deliver the output. The relative positions are significant since moving towards the bin may move the robot towards or away from the printer.

The time line in Figure 5 describes the "Abandon Cup Collection" plan. The time delay for each goal is the time interval between when the request is received and when the

The tradeoff that is being made can be seen more clearly by considering the differences in the paths the robot would take to get to the printer. Figure 4 shows the two paths: one that goes directly to the printer and one that goes by way of the bin. The direct path will always be shorter, but as the robot approaches the bin, the difference becomes arbitrarily small. The corresponding added delay in deferring the printer goal approaches zero, as does the corresponding opportunity cost. The point at which this opportunity cost equals the opportunity cost associated with deferring the cup collection goal corresponds to the point at which the preferred plan switches from abandoning the cup to completing the cup collection. In Figure 2, the point at which the "complete cup collection" plan becomes the preferred plan occurs when the robot is about 4.5 feet from the bin.

The example illustrates the advantage of this method over fixed priority schemes. If a fixed priority scheme were

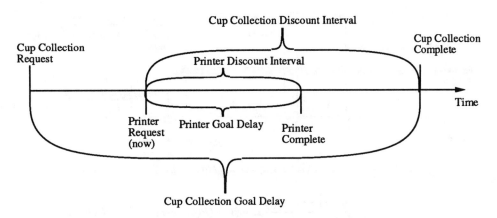

Figure 5: **Time line for Abandoning Cup Collection.**

used, as was done in the original Hero system, it could result in situations where the robot drops the cup beside the bin rather than expend the extra few seconds needed to drop it in the bin. This would get the printer output delivered a few seconds earlier, but it requires the robot to expend a significantly greater amount of time to return, re-acquire the cup and finish the task.

This example also serves to show some of the limitations of heuristic-based approaches. As stated above, the distance at which the cup collection should be completed depends on a number of factors. For a heuristic method to take these factors into account would require either a large number of simple heuristics [Feldman and Sproull, 1977] or a few heuristics that essentially embody the same calculations used in our method.

4.2 Delivery Example

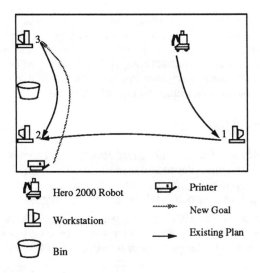

Figure 6: **Delivery Example.**

By properly ordering the achievement of goals, the robot can take advantage of the opportunities derived from the spatial relationships between goals. This result follows naturally from the utility-based approach. Consider the situation shown in Figure 6. The robot is making a sequence of deliveries, one from workstation 1 to workstation 2 and a second from workstation 3 to workstation 2. If a printer request arrives for workstation 3 then the robot can reduce its amount of travel by picking up the output on the way to workstation 3.

Figure 7 shows how the preferred strategy changes with the new goal activation time. Inserting the printer output request between the two deliveries reduces the total amount of travel needed by taking advantage of the fact that the printer request ends at the location where the second delivery begins. Note that the robot will initially go back to the printer even after starting towards workstation 3 to do the second delivery. It is advantageous to do so as long as the robot has not moved too far away from the printer.

A priority based scheme, if used in this example, would not be able to take advantage of the spatial relationships between the goals. The printer request would always be serviced last since it has the lowest utility. A heuristic-based approach could be used to suggest ordering goals such that the destination of one was the start of the next. However, this would not take into account situations as in the example where workstation 2 is only near the printer and not at the same location.

4.3 Contingency Example

In the course of working with the Hero Robot, an informal experiment was run to see how people handle the same tasks as the robot. It was observed that sometimes people would elect to "recharge" rather than go collect a cup, even though they had sufficient battery charge. Invariably, the reason given was that they wanted to have enough charge in reserve to be able to handle a possible printer or delivery request.

The techniques described in this paper can be applied to model this type of contingency planning. The situation in the experiment was modeled as a choice between two

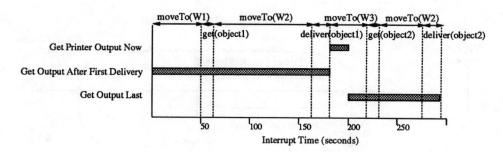

Figure 7: **Best Goal Ordering versus Interrupt Time, Deliveries**

$$NPV_1 = \int_0^T \frac{P(printer) * Plan_1'(t)}{(1+d)^t} dt + (1 - (P(printer) * T)) * NPV(Plan_1) \tag{7}$$

plans: plan₁, to collect the cup first, and plan₂, to recharge first. These plans were evaluated taking the possibility of a printer request into account. It was assumed that there was a constant probability $P(printer)$ of a printer request arriving in any minute, (the possibility that two or more requests would arrive was ignored). Let $Plan_1'(t)$ be the net present value at time t of the plan that would be selected if plan₁1 were used and a printer request arrived at time t. Multiplying $Plan_1'(t)$ by the probability that a request will arrive at time t and discounting it back to time zero gives the current net present value weighted by its probability. Integrating gives the total net present value. (See equation 7) A similar calculation gives the result for the plan₂.

Using the utility values selected for the domain and a 20% probability of a printer request arriving from workstation 3 in any minute results in a preference for the plan that recharges. If the possibility of a printer request is not taken into account, the other plan is preferred. Obtaining this result using full numerical integration in Maple is computationally expensive requiring a few minutes of elapsed time on a sparc II workstation. The example does serve to suggest, however, that the approach may be applicable using a more efficient implementation and further approximations.

5   Conclusions

This paper has presented some initial results on rational planning for mobile robots. The examples presented show that a mobile robot can take advantage of opportunities as they arise if it can interrupt and reformulate its plan of action. A decision theoretic approach to plan reformulation is more general than heuristic based methods and produces more rational results than do fixed priority schemes. The use of a net present value decision criterion for the mobile robot domain has some advantages over a benefit-cost ratio criterion when dealing with limited resources and non-independent alternatives.

Decision criteria using present values of utilities are highly sensitive to the discount rate. Choosing a discount rate is still a matter of experimentation. Further work is needed to determine how the characteristics of the domain should be taken into account when selecting a discount rate. One possibility is to have the robot adjust its discount rate as it refines its time and probability estimates.

The planning framework chosen has a number of limitations. Using the linearity assumption and considering only a limited number of plans serve to reduce the amount of computation needed. These are fundamental limitations, however, and they could be removed with a corresponding increase in computation time. The question to be studied is when it is advantageous to do so.

A decision theoretic approach to plan evaluation is useful when dynamically reordering multiple active goals. Coupled with the use of net present value and consideration of opportunity costs, it provides the basis for effective operation of a mobile robot.

Acknowledgments

We wish to express our thanks to Long-Ji Lin and Lonnie Chrisman for their work on the initial design and implementation of the Hero robot system. This research is supported by NASA under contract NAGW-1175 and in part by a Natural Sciences and Engineering Research Council of Canada 1967 Science and Engineering Scholarship.

References

[Boddy and Dean, 1989] Mark Boddy and Thomas Dean. Solving time-dependent planning problems. In *IJCAI-89 Proceedings of the Eleventh International Joint Conference on Artificial Intelligence*. AAAI, August 1989.

[Bratman et al., 1988] M. E. Bratman, D. J. Isreal, and M. E. Pollack. Plans and resource-bounded practical reasoning. *Computational Intelligence*, 4(4), 1988.

[Chapman, 1987] D. Chapman. Planning for conjunctive goals. *Artificial Intelligence*, 32, 1987.

[Char, 1987] Bruce W. Char. A tutorial introduction to maple. Technical Report CS-85-56, University of Waterloo, 1987.

[Chrisman and Simmons, 1991] Lonnie Chrisman and ,Reid Simmons. Senseful planning: Focusing perceptual attention. In *Proceedings, Ninth National Conference on Artificial Intelligence*. AAAI, July 1991.

[Currie and Tate, 1985] K. Currie and A. Tate. O-plan-control in the open planning architecture. *Expert Systems*, 1985.

[Dawes, 1988] Robyn M. Dawes. *Rational Choice in an Uncertain World*. Harcourt Brace Jovanovich, Toronto, 1988.

[Doyle, 1988] Jon Doyle. Artificial intelligence and rational self-government. Technical Report CMU-CS-88-124, Carnegie Mellon University, March 1988.

[Etzioni, 1989] Oren Etzioni. Tractable decision-analytic control. In *Proceedings, First International Conference on Principles of Knowledge Representation and Reasoning*, May 1989.

[Feldman and Sproull, 1977] Jerome A. Feldman and Robert F. Sproull. Decision theory and artificial intelligence ii: The hungry monkey. *Cognitive Science*, 1, 1977.

[Garey and Johnson, 1979] Michael R. Garey and David S. Johnson. *Computers and Intractability*. W. H. Freeman and Company, 1979.

[Hansson et al., 1990] Othar Hansson, Andrew Mayer, and Stuart Russell. Decision theoretic planning in bps. In *Proceedings of the AAAI Symposium on Planning*. AAAI, 1990.

[Horvitz et al., 1988] Eric J. Horvitz, John S. Breese, and Max Henrion. Decision theory in expert systems and artificial intelligence. *International Journal of Approximate Reasoning*, 2, 1988.

[Raiffa, 1968] Howard Raiffa. *Decision Analysis Introductory Lectures on Choices under Uncertainty*. Addison-Wesley, Reading Mass., 1968.

[Sassone and Schaffer, 1979] Peter G. Sassone and William A. Schaffer. *Cost-Benefit Analysis A Handbook*. Academic Press Inc, 1979.

[Schoemaker, 1980] Paul J. H. Schoemaker. *Experiments on Decisions Under Risk: The Expected Utility Hypothesis*. Kluwer Nijhoff, 1980.

[Secerdoti, 1977] Earl Secerdoti. *A Structure for Plans and Behavior*. American Elsevier, New York, NY, 1977.

[Simmons and Krotkov, 1991] Reid Simmons and Eric Krotkov. An integrated walking system for the Ambler planetary rover. In *Proc. IEEE International Conference on Robotics and Automation*, pages 2086–2091, Sacramento, CA, April 1991.

[Simmons et al., 1990] Reid Simmons, Long Ji Lin, and Chris Fedor. Autonomous task control for mobile robots. In *Proc. IEEE Symposium on Intelligent Control*, Philadelphia, PA, September 1990.

[Simon, 1982] Herbert A. Simon. *Theories of Decision-Making in Economics and Behavioral Science*, pages 287–317. The MIT Press, 1982.

[Sinn, 1983] Hans-Werner Sinn. *Economic Decisions Under Uncertainty*. North-Holland, 1983.

[Wellman, 1988] Michael P. Wellman. Formulation of tradeoffs in planning under uncertainty. Technical Report MIT/LCS/TR-427, MIT, August 1988.

A Framework of Simplifications in Learning to Plan

Jonathan Gratch and Gerald DeJong
Beckman Institute for Advanced Studies,University of Illinois
405 N. Mathews, Urbana, IL 61801
e–mail: gratch.cs.uiuc.edu

Abstract

Learning shows great promise to extend the generality and effectiveness of planning techniques. Research in this area has generated an impressive battery of techniques and a growing body of empirical successes. Unfortunately the formal properties of these systems are not well understood. This is highlighted by a growing corpus of demonstrations where learning actually *degrades* planning performance. In this paper we view learning to plan as a search problem. We argue that the complexity of this search precludes a general solution and can only be approached by making simplifying assumptions. We discuss the frequently unarticulated commitments which underly current learning approaches. From these we assemble a framework of simplifications which a learning planner can draw upon. These simplifications improve learning efficiency but not without tradeoffs.

1   INTRODUCTION

If planning is to have widespread benefit, we must provide planning approaches which apply to a variety of situations. Careful analysis has highlighted the challenges to domain independent planning (e.g. [Chapman87]). The performance of such domain–independent planners will probably compare poorly to their domain–specific counterparts in complex tasks. Learning provides a means for capturing such information. Through learning we can adapt general techniques to exploit the idiosyncrasies of particular domains and problem distributions. Thus, it may serve as a powerful tool for enhancing the usefulness of planning.

Before learning techniques can receive wide attention from the planning community, the conditions under which learning is advantageous must be clearly articulated. The appropriateness of a learning approach depends on its expected benefit and generality. An ideal technique would produce optimal planners and have wide applicability. Unfortunately this standard of performance is rarely possible in practice. A minimal requirement is that learning not hurt performance. In either case the learning process should be tractable.

A surprising observation is that most published learning techniques do not even ensure the minimal requirement. There is growing evidence that learning can degrade planning performance [Etzioni90a, Gratch91a, Minton85, Subramanian90]. Part of the difficulty lies in the unarticulated simplifications adopted by these techniques.

In this paper we will develop a view of learning as search through a space of possible planners. We compare alternative learning strategies using this common perspective. We argue that the complexity of the general task of improving a planner must be approached by imposing simplifications. Learning techniques frequently embody unarticulated commitments to address this complexity. We discuss these commitments and assemble them into a framework of simplifications which a learning planner can draw upon. These simplifications improve learning efficiency but not without tradeoffs. In some cases these tradeoffs result in less than optimal behavior. In others, they lead to planners which grow worse through learning. By articulating these commitments in an explicit framework we can better understand their motivation and ramifications for planning.

2   ADEQUATE LEARNING

Before proceeding we must clarify what is expected from a learning system. A learning system should take a particular planning system operating within a particular domain and tailor it to more effectively solve problems. This can be viewed as a transformational process where a series of transformations are applied to the original problem solver (see [Gratch90, Greiner92]). A planner may be transformed by the addition of control knowledge. Different forms of control knowledge include macro–operators [Braverman88a, Laird86, Markovitch89], control rules [Etzioni90a, Minton88, Mitchell83], and static board evaluation functions [Utgoff91]. Alternatively, a learning system may modify the domain theory. Such transformations could be truth (accuracy) preserving (as in conjunct reordering or deletion of redundancy [Smith85], or non–truth preserving (as in theory revision tasks [Richards91, Towell90]). Several non–learning techniques can also be viewed from this perspective. For example several reactive planning systems transform a causal theory into a set of reactive rules [Drummond90, Schoppers87]. Automatic abstraction systems can also be viewed as transformational processes [Knoblock90].

The transformations available to a learner define its *vocabulary of transformations*. These are essentially learning operators and collectively they define a *transformation space*. For instance, acquiring a macro–operator can be viewed as transforming the initial system (the original planner) into a new system (the planner operating with the macro–operator). In [Drummond90], the addition of a reactive rule transforms one subset of the universal plan into another. In [Minton88], a planner's search control strategy is transformed by the addition or deletion of a control rule. A learning technique must explore this space for a sequence of transformations which results in a better planner.

First, we discuss the notion of the *adequacy* of a learning system. Given an initial planner, P_{old}, a learning system is *minimally adequate* if it: 1) halts without making any changes, or 2) applies a sequence of transformations which yields a new planner P_{new} which is preferred to P_{old} (i.e. if it does anything, it produces a better planner). One learning system is *more adequate* than another if it always produces preferred planners. A learning system which identifies any most preferred planner in the transformation space (there may be more than one) is *optimal*. To make this notion concrete we must define a preference function over planners.

There are many ways to assign preferences. Here we view preference in terms of a numeric *utility function* which ranks planners in the transform space according to an intuitive notion of preferences. In particular, we will consider the case where a utility value can be assigned to a planner's behavior on any problem. The utility of a planner is then defined with respect to a particular problem distribution as the sum of problem utilities weighted by the probability of each problem. The flexibility of such a definition is highlighted in [Greiner92]. This covers the obvious measures of effectiveness. For example, if we are interested in minimizing problem solving cost, utility increases as the cost to solve problems decreases. The utility of the planner is then:

$$UTILITY(planner_i) = -\sum_{prob \in Distribution} Cost(planner_i, prob) \times Pr(prob)$$

Note that with this definition, higher utility does not entail that the planning time of any particular problem is reduced. Rather, the expected cost of solving any representative sample of problems is less.

Utility is a preference function which ranks different planners. It is also useful to discuss the utility of individual transformations. The *incremental utility* of a transformation is defined as the change in utility that results from applying the transformation to a particular planner (i.e., adopting a control rule, a macro–operator, a set of reactive rules,

etc.).[1] In other words, this is the difference between the utility of a planner and the utility of a planner augmented by the transformation. This definition implies that the incremental utility of a transformation depends on (is conditional on) the planner to which it is applied. We denote this as: ΔUTILITY(Transformation|Planner). Applying a transformation with positive incremental utility results in a more effective planner.

A learning system need not explicitly compute utility values to identify preferred planners, but it must act (at least approximately) as if it does. In fact many learning systems do not explicitly evaluate utility. For example, many speed–up learning systems incorporate *operationality criteria* to determine which transformations to adopt (e.g. [Braverman88a, Letovsky90, Mitchell83]). This can be viewed as a binary approximation to incremental utility — transformations which satisfy the operationality criteria are expected to exhibit positive incremental utility, while those rejected by the criteria are expected to exhibit negative incremental utility.

3 CHALLENGES AND DIRECTIONS

A learning system must explore the transformation space to identify preferred planners. This task can be decomposed into three basic components:

* A search component which explores transformations,

* A utility estimation component which determines which transformations to incorporate into the final planner,

* An observation component which provides information about the task environment and the performance of the planner to the other two components.

The search space is determined by which transformations are proposed by the learning system and what combinations of transformations are sanctioned. Typically, transformations are proposed in response to problem–solving successes or impasses. Incremental utility might be estimated by combining information from multiple problems drawn from the distribution. The observation component must extract from examples the particular information required to propose and evaluate transformations.

Before proceeding, it is important to emphasize that the choice of utility function can have dramatic impact on the requirements of these three components. For example, consider a degenerate utility function which assigns constant utility to any transformed planner. With respect to this utility function, any transformation sequence has zero incremental utility. A search component which is informed of this consequence can safely collapse the transformation

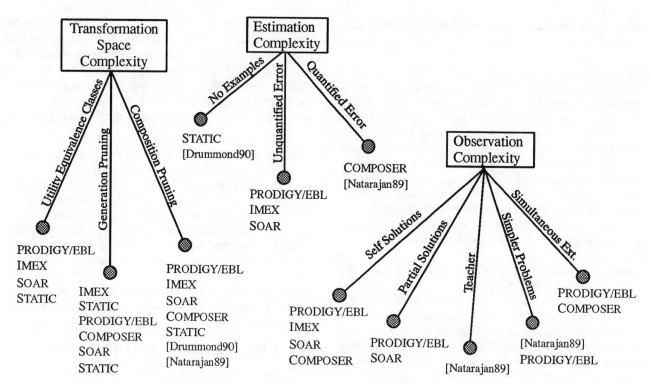

Figure 1: Framework of simplifications

space to a single node. More realistically, the utility function will determine the information requirements of the search and estimation components. For example, if the utility function is based solely on planning cost, the observation component must extract information about the impact transformations have on planning cost. Obtaining this information may entail problem solving, but will not require the execution of the resulting plans. In contrast, a utility function based on the quality of solutions may require plan generation *and* execution–time monitoring.

There are three challenges to adequate learning: 1) the space of possible transformations may be large, 2) many planning episodes may be necessary to reliably estimate incremental utility of a transformation, and 3) it may be expensive to extract the necessary information from a planning episode. Taken together, these difficulties suggest there there does not exist a general solution to the problem of adequate learning. Nevertheless, there are a number of published techniques which claim to work well. We resolve these apparent contradictions by illustrating how learning techniques adopt simplifications to address each challenge.

Simplifications are rarely explicitly noted in these works. It is often difficult to determine the precise simplifications an algorithm embodies. Our framework present concise and obvious simplifications to each challenge. We believe it is sufficient to cover the majority of learning approaches, but is not intended as exhaustive. We then argue how different techniques are best viewed as approximating these commitments. Figure 1 summarizes the framework, which is organized into approaches for each of the three basic challenges.

The subsequent discussion mirrors the organization of the framework.

3.1 TRANSFORMATION SPACE COMPLEXITY

Even if incremental utility values are known, the task of efficiently identifying an advantageous sequence of transformations is challenging. A learning system must explore a potentially large space of transformation sequences. This space is infinite if the transformation vocabulary is unbounded or if the same transformation can be applied an unbounded number of times. Even with a finite vocabulary and restricting each transformation to at most one application, the complexity is still daunting: for n transformations there are $O(n!)$ distinguishable sequences (any planner may be the result of up to n ordered transformations). Depending on the vocabulary of transformations and utility function, each of these alternative planners can have different utility.

3.1.1 Utility Equivalence Classes

The complexity of the transformation space must be reduced. In the utility based view of learning there is a notion analogous to the VC–dimension in classification learning [Blumer89]. Not all of transformation sequences will necessarily produce planners with distinguishable utility. For example, depending on the vocabulary of transformations, the order in which transformations are adopted may be irrelevant to the utility of the final planner. In this circumstance, any of the $m!$ permutations of a set of m transformations. would yield planners with equivalent utility if applied to the initial planner. These permutations form a *utility equivalence class*. The notion of equivalence class also applies to incremental utility. The incremental utility of a transformation is conditional on the transformations which have already been applied. If we again assume that utility is independent of transformation order, it is clear that many conditional utilities are equivalent. For example, given the transformations, T_1, T_2, and T_3, the incremental utility of T_1 given T_2T_3 is equal to the incremental utility of T_1 given T_3T_2.

If utility equivalence classes can be identified, they can be exploited in two ways to reduce search. First, the learning system can narrow the search such that only one member of each equivalence class is considered. In the case of order independence, only one ordering of transformations must be considered. Secondly, if a utility value is known for one member of an equivalence class it is known for all members of that class, thus reducing the number of distinct utility computations which are required. If a system has computed the utility of T_1 given T_2T_3, it "knows" the utility of T_1 given T_3T_2.

We are not aware a learning system which explicitly uses a utility equivalence class. However, many learning systems can be viewed as using *approximate* utility equivalence classes. The members of an approximate utility equivalence class would have utility values which are roughly equivalent. The consequence of this simplification depends on the accuracy of the approximation and how it is used. If the equivalence classes are used to narrow the search, the approach amounts to a heuristic pruning strategy. Some transformation sequences — which may benefit the system — are made inaccessible in the interest of increased efficiency. If the utility of one member of a equivalence class is approximated by the utility of another member, the adequacy of the learning system may suffer. This second point will be elaborated shortly.

Many learning systems adopt a particular simplification which is best viewed as exploiting an approximate utility equivalence class. The simplification is to treat the incremental utility of a transformation as *independent* of other transformations. This means that the incremental utility of a transformation is the same regardless of what other transformations have been adopted. Formally, let Σ be the vocabulary of transformations. Then:

$$\forall T \in \Sigma, \ \forall C_1, C_2 \in \text{Powerset}(\Sigma - T):$$
$$\Delta \text{UTILITY}(T|C_1) = \Delta \text{UTILITY}(T|C_2)$$

Using these equivalence classes a learning system can dramatically reduce the complexity of the search. The simplification allows a local decision procedure for adopting transformations. Each transformation can be evaluated without regard for the current context of adopted transformations. If the transformation is beneficial, it can be adopted, otherwise it should be discarded. If there are n transformations in the vocabulary, the complexity of search is reduced to $O(n)$. The use of this simplification is clearest in systems which determine incremental utility from many examples. For example, PRODIGY/EBL [Minton88] determines incremental utility estimates from multiple observations. For a given transformation, each observation may be derived from a different context, but all of the values are combined into a single context–independent measure. This averaging across contexts is only appropriate if independence approximately holds.

Ignoring interactions leads to adequate learning under certain sufficient conditions. If the transformations are in fact independent, a learning system can in $O(n)$ identify the planner with *optimal* utility. If this condition cannot be guaranteed, weaker conditions are sufficient to display at least minimal adequacy. A learning system can act *as if* transformations are independent as long as negative interactions are not overwhelming. An example of an overwhelming negative interaction would be the case where, individually, two transformations benefit the planner but, collectively, they hurt performance.

Many learning systems do not explicitly consider interactions (including STATIC [Etzioni90a], PRODIGY/EBL, RECEBG [Letovsky90], IMEX [Braverman88a], and PEBL [Eskey90]). Ma and Wilkins illustrate a similar situation for knowledge–base revision systems [Wilkins89]. Systems which do not adopt this simplification include PALO [Greiner92], COMPOSER [Gratch91b], and [Leckie91].

Unfortunately, accounts of systems which ignore interactions do not characterize when this simplification is appropriate. Furthermore, it is becoming clear that the transformations utilized by these systems do interact. In [Gratch90] and [Gratch91a] we demonstrate macro operators and control rules can produce harmful interactions. The later article discusses a simple domain which exhibits strong negative interactions. When tested on this domain, the utility analysis technique of PRODIGY/EBL and the nonrecursive hypothesis of STATIC generate planners an order of magnitude *worse* than the initial planner. These results show that independence can produce inadequate performance. They also highlight why more emphasis must be placed on highlighting and providing sufficient conditions for the simplifications which underlay learning techniques.

3.1.2 Generation Pruning

Most learning systems do not attempt to identify the optimal sequence of transformations (an exception is [Greiner91]). Instead, these systems simply seek a transformed planner which exhibits higher utility than the initial planner. Without an optimality requirement, systems are free to employ powerful pruning techniques to reduce the space of alternatives, although frequently these techniques are not articulated by the designer of the learning system. One way to reduce the complexity is to reduce the number of transformations which must be entertained. Most transformation vocabularies define a vast space of possible transformations. For example, a system using macro–operators might consider macros built from any legal sequence of operators in the domain. Most learning systems only consider a tiny fraction of the legal transformations.

We say a system employs *generation pruning* if it restricts the class of transformations which are actively considered. A common approach is *event driven learning*. Under this strategy, transformations are only proposed in response to planning events such as success or failure which are observed in the course of problem solving. For example SOAR [Laird86] only learns new chunks in response to planning impasses. STRIPS [Fikes72] only acquires new macro-operators from successful plans. Even given a single planning event, there may be many transformations which could be proposed. This complexity is frequently handled by a heuristic selection criterion called an *operationality criterion* [Mitchell86]. For example, Braverman and Russell describe the vast number of macro-operators which could be acquired from a single planning success [Braverman88b] and they propose a criterion for choosing one macro-operator from among these possibilities. Etzioni's *nonrecursive hypothesis* can also be viewed as a generation pruning strategy [Etzioni90a]. His criterion states that a control rule should only be considered if it is based on a nonrecursive explanation.

These simplifications reduce the effective number of transformations which are considered by the learning system. The consequences of a generation pruning strategy depends on the effectiveness of its heuristic.

3.1.3 Composition Pruning

In addition to restricting the class of available transformations, many learning systems restrict how transformations are composed. For example, a common simplification is to avoid multiple applications of the same transformation. Acquiring a macro-operator may help the planner, but adding the same macro-operator again and again will degrade performance. If the vocabulary contains n transformations where n is finite, this simplification prunes an infinite transformation space into one of size $O(n!)$.

For many transformation vocabularies, the previous pruning strategy does not effect the potential adequacy of learning. However, many simplifications are clearly heuristic. For example, even when transformations are not order independent, many techniques only consider a single permutation of the transformation sequence. In some cases the order is resolved in a particular way. In the case of macro-operators, Shavlik suggests an ordering scheme: order the library of macro-operators such that each newly learned macro-operators is placed before the original domain theory but after previously learned macro-operators [Shavlik88]. Thus the organization of macro-operators is determined by the order in which the transformations were applied and the learning system cannot alter this order. Minton's PRODIGY/EBL system arbitrarily maintains control rules in the order they were learned [Minton88 p. 79]. In both cases the

authors acknowledge that different ordering schemes would result in different planning behavior.

Restricting the search to a particular ordering rules out many alternatives. When the best ordering can be determined without search, this simplification can be adopted without cost. Without such guarantees, the system may not find preferred planners when they exist. Thus it may preclude optimality or otherwise lower the adequacy of the learning system. On the other hand, a system utilizing this simplification retains minimal adequacy: it does not enable the adoption of transformation sequences which otherwise would have been rejected. Some systems which ignore alternative permutations are IMEX [Braverman88a], COMPOSER [Gratch91b], STATIC [Etzioni90a], BAGGER [Shavlik88], and PRODIGY/EBL [Minton88].

Another powerful simplification is to adopt a heuristic search technique like hill-climbing or beam search. For example, COMPOSER and PALO employ hill-climbing search to restrict the space of alternatives. The anytime synthetic projection algorithm of Drummond and Bresina is another hill-climbing approach [Drummond90] where a set of situated control rules is incrementally generated such that each new control rule increases the probability of goal satisfaction. A greedy technique can climb the gradient of incremental utility values, picking the transformation with highest incremental utility with respect to the previously selected transformation. Hill-climbing reduces the complexity. However, as in other pruning techniques efficiency is gained at the cost of reduced learning opportunities. A hill-climbing technique which is stuck at a local maximum may produce a planner which is less adequate than what a more comprehensive learner would produce.

3.2 ESTIMATION COMPLEXITY

The utility of a transformation depends on information which is frequently unavailable such as the distribution of future problems. The natural approach is to estimate utility from training examples. The simplest approach is estimation by brute force. If there is a known finite set of problems of interest, the planning system might attempt them all, observing its behavior. After applying a transform, the planner could be rerun on the set. The difference between the runs is, by definition, the incremental utility of the transformation. This procedure identifies a single incremental utility value and the process must be repeated for each utility determination. As the set of problems may be large, unavailable, or infinite, and there may be many transformations from which to choose from, this approach is clearly impractical.

3.2.1 Learning Without Examples

Some learning approaches employ syntactic criteria to identify transformations with positive incremental utility. As we noted in Section 3.1, operationality criteria were originally introduced to constrain which transformations are generated. The idea was broadened, however, into a criterion for estimating utility as well [Braverman88a,

Hirsh88, Letovsky90]. These learning systems adopt transformations if and only if they satisfy the constraints of some operationality criterion. In this sense, operationality can be seen as a two–valued approximation of incremental utility. Proposed criteria avoid the need for examples as they are based on syntactic properties of transformations. For example, EBG introduced an operationality criterion for macro–operators. The user supplies a set of predicate names which are "easily evaluated." Learned macro–operators are constrained to have preconditions drawn from this set [Mitchell86]. The STATIC [Etzioni90a] and RECEBG [Letovsky90] systems utilize criteria based on the concept of recursive unwindings.

A potential problem with these approaches is that they do not account for distribution information. As utility is defined with respect to a particular distribution of problems, a distribution–ignorant criterion is only sanctioned if it identifies transformations which reduce the problem solving cost of all possible problems (otherwise there exist distributions for which the criterion is incorrect). This is similar to the notion of *dominance* in [Wellman90]. If this property can be demonstrated, a transformation will yield an improved planner independent of the problem distribution. Such transformations do exist. For example, a planner can only benefit from deleting an unsatisfiable or redundant operator.[2] The STATIC system — which "learns" without training examples — is grounded in the claim that its set of transformations will increase utility independent of distribution [Etzioni90b p. 134]. Etzioni illustrates some domains where STATIC's criterion leads to performance improvements, but negative results appear in [Gratch91a]. Similar conflicting results exist for other operationality criteria [Minton85, Subramanian90]. One interpretation of these criteria is that they produce heuristic estimates — they do not guarantee accurate estimates for every distribution, but they are sufficiently close on "typical" distribution. Unfortunately it is quite difficult to characterize the distributions which are acceptable to these techniques.

3.2.2 Unquantified Error

The empirical approach views utility as a random variable. Incremental utility values on individual problems represent data points; utility is estimated as the mean of a sample of problems. This approach yields a learning system which is probabilistically adequate. PRODIGY/EBL was perhaps the first system to average incremental utility values across many training problems. The simplification imposed by this technique is to forbid reasoning about the accuracy of utility estimates. The average of a sample is only an approximation to the true average. A transformation which is estimated to be good may in fact have negative utility. The likelihood of a large discrepancy may be minimized by drawing more examples, but techniques which do not reason about

the confidence of their estimates have no way of assessing if sufficient examples have been taken. Approaches which adopt the simplification of *unquantified error* require the user to determine the number of training examples. If this number is insufficient, the learning approach may not be minimally adequate.

3.2.3 Quantified Error

More recent approaches have provided bounds on the probability of mistakes. Greiner and Cohen [Greiner92] introduce a method based on Chernoff bounds. This distribution–free approach adopts transformations after drawing enough examples to ensure (with high probability) that the transformation will improve performance. The guarantee is gained at the cost of many training examples, but Greiner and Cohen show how (under weak assumptions) to achieve an arbitrary level of confidence with a number of examples polynomial in the error level. Another distribution–free approach is embodied in the COMPOSER system [Gratch91b]. COMPOSER's statistical technique is based on the Central Limit Theorem which states that simple transformation of the sample mean of any distribution is normally distributed as the sample size grows without bound [Hogg78 p. 193]. For any *finite* sample the mean will only approximate the normal distribution but given a sufficiently large sample this approximation can be quite close. This provides somewhat weaker guarantees than Chernoff bounds and is thus a simplification, but typically requires far fewer examples (see [Gratch92] for a comparison).

3.3 OBSERVATION COMPLEXITY

Learning techniques must provide the information necessary to generate transformations and to estimate their incremental utility. The previous section illustrated that distribution information can be approximated by combining information from multiple examples drawn randomly from the distribution. In this section we focus on the information which must be extracted from each example, and the complexity of this process. As was mentioned in the beginning of this section, the type of information necessary is determined by the particulars of the utility function. A utility function based on planning cost requires information on how a transformation affects the resource usage patterns of the planner. A utility function based on solution quality requires first that a solution be generated, and second that information about quality be assessed. In many cases the problem of determining such information is non–trivial.

We will focus on the situation where utility is a function of planning cost. In this case the incremental utility of a transformation for a particular problem is the difference in cost between a planner not using the transformation and a planner using it. The simplest way to obtain this information is to solve the problem twice, once with the transformation incorporated into the planner, and once without the transformation. If the learning system is evaluating m transformations, the problem must be solved $m+1$ times (once without any transformation and once for each of the m alternatives).

---

[2]An operator is redundant if its removal does not impact the completeness of the planner.

Planning is undecidable in general. Thus it is desirable to develop observation techniques which do not rely on complete and repeated solutions. Unfortunately, given the vocabulary of transformations which are currently in use, some observation of planning behavior appears necessary. This is further reinforced by the fact that many learning techniques require a trace of planning behavior simply to generate these transformations.

To make these difficulties concrete, we introduce an example using control rules as the vocabulary of transformations. Control rules are condition–action rules which recommend particular planning decisions when their preconditions are satisfied. Minton illustrates that the incremental utility of a particular control rule is influenced by three factors: the savings afforded by the rule when its preconditions are satisfied, how often the preconditions succeed, and the cost of evaluating the preconditions [Minton88]. Each of these factors depend intimately on the characteristics of the planner's search space for each problem.

Figure 2 illustrates the planning search space for a particular problem (the problem and corresponding statistics are based on an actual problem solved by PRODIGY/EBL). The initial planner must expand nine search nodes before finding a solution. The planner backtracks twice after reaching dead–ends at nodes four and six. The cost of expanding each node appears to the right of each node (PRODIGY/EBL implements a utility function based on planning *time* so cost is represented by milliseconds). The total cost is 1350. We consider the introduction of one transformation (control rule). This transformation avoids the two backtracking events, leading the planner directly from node two to node seven. The transformation avoids the cost of generating the dead–end nodes (a savings of 1050), but the preconditions must be evaluated for each planning alternative. This cost is represented by the numbers beside each link in the planning space (a cost of 905). In this example the savings exceeds the cost so the transformation has positive incremental utility.

Ideally, the observation component should report that, for this example, the incremental utility is forty–five. It would be exceedingly difficult to surmise this information without a detailed and annotated representation of the planning trace associated with this problem. For this reason, PRODIGY/EBL requires an annotated problem solving trace to extract information about incremental utility. As PRODIGY/EBL is an explanation–based learning technique, it also requires traces for its generation component. These requirements are shared by most learning techniques, including [DeJong86, Drummond90, Gratch91b, Laird86, Leckie91, Mitchell83, Mitchell86, Natarajan89, Tadepalli91]. Given the need for a planning trace, the question is how is such a trace efficiently generated, given that its generation as a side–effect of planning, is not tractable in general.

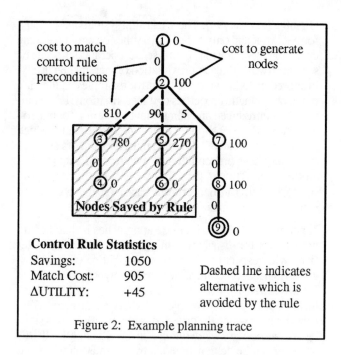

Control Rule Statistics
Savings: 1050
Match Cost: 905
ΔUTILITY: +45

Dashed line indicates alternative which is avoided by the rule

Figure 2: Example planning trace

3.3.1   Learning From Self–solutions

Many learning techniques employ the currently transformed planner to generate a planning trace. As the system is generating its own information, we refer to this process as *learning from self–solutions*. This approach equates observation complexity with the complexity of the initial planner in the domain of interest. If this approach is to be feasible, this complexity must be sufficiently small. While this condition is rarely articulated, it is implicit in a wide range of learning techniques [Braverman88a, Gratch91b, Greiner92, Laird86, Leckie91, Minton88, Mitchell83, Ruby91]. One might ask why we need to learn at all if problem solving is already feasible. However, in many circumstances this is quite reasonable. For instance, in situations where large numbers of problems must be solved, small increases in efficiency can result in huge savings.

A common approach to making planing efficient is through the use of resource bounds. This can have interesting ramifications for learning systems which estimate incremental utility. Consider a situation where the initial planner is so inefficient that it cannot begin to solve problems within the allowed resources. In Figure 2 this might correspond to the case where search is terminated after node 2. Hill–climbing techniques like COMPOSER and PALO can be rendered ineffective if no single transformation is sufficient to enable solutions to be found. In this case any single transformation yields another planner which takes as much time to not find a solution (i.e. ΔUTILITY = 0). The possibility that the transformed planner is in some sense closer to findings solutions is not captured by the definition of incremental utility. A technique which could entertain sets of transformations would not face this problem.

3.3.2 Learning From Partial Solutions

The simplest approach to learning from self–solutions is to solve the problem $m+1$ times and compare the difference between transformed and untransformed planners. However, as planning can be expensive, we may not have the resources to completely solve each problem. Considerable savings could result if the system can learn from partial solution attempts. Two obvious ways to generate partial solutions would be to terminate problem solving after the first sign of inefficiency (e.g. when backtracking occurs) or by giving the planner fewer resources during learning than are normally used.

Several learning techniques utilize information from partial solution attempts when they *generate* transformations. For example, SOAR interleaves generation and planning by proposing transformations after each planning impasse. In fact, most failure–driven learning techniques should be able to generate transformations in response to partial planning traces. Some "learning from success" techniques will be hampered by partial solutions as they rely on a solution of the top–level goal for their transformations. Macro–operator systems are an example of such a technique.

Several techniques provide the means to extract incremental utility information from partial solution traces. A key example is PRODIGY/EBL which maintains statistics about planner and control rule behavior at each node in the solution trace. Referring back to Figure 2, we can see that if the planner terminates after the first backtracking event, there is some information about the incremental utility of the transformation. Unfortunately, evaluating the incremental utility from partial solutions can be problematic. This is because the effects of transformations may not be homogeneous over the solution space. This is clearly illustrated in the example. Simply looking at the first backtracking event, the transformation appears to have negative incremental utility (ΔUTILITY = 780 – 810 = –30), while a complete analysis would reveal that the transformation has positive incremental utility for this problem. Extracting utility information from partial solution traces will only be effective if incremental utility is relatively homogeneous for the transformations in use. This sufficient condition may prove difficult to demonstrate. It it does not hold, the increase in observation efficiency is gained at the cost of estimation accuracy which in turn can violate minimal adequacy.

3.3.3 Learning From a Teacher

An alternative to self–solutions is to require a teacher to provide the appropriate data. This places the observation complexity in the hands of the teacher. The teacher, through its superior knowledge, presumably can elicit the information with reasonable cost. For example, Korf demonstrates that when domains are *serially decomposable,* a system can generate a polynomial–time problem solver by learning a body of control knowledge called a macro–table, but the observation component relies on exponential search [Korf85]. Ta-

depalli[introduced a variant of this system with polynomial observation cost [Tadepalli91]. Tadepalli's learning system requires a teacher which knows the macro–table we wish to learn. This teacher then provides the learning system with solutions generated according to the table. In this case the teacher can be tractably simulated by a planner using the macro–table. Natarajan discusses an approach to learning control rules which also relies on a teacher. In this case the teacher must provide the system with optimal solution paths [Natarajan89]. The availability of a teacher can greatly simplify the observation complexity. Unfortunately, as the necessary information is a function of the utility function and the vocabulary of transformations, it may be difficult to provide an adequate teacher.

3.3.4 Learning From Simpler Problems

An intriguing alternative is to learn to solve intractable problems by training on simpler, tractable problems. This is analogous to classroom learning were a carefully selected set of "text book" problems leads to sophisticated problem solving ability. Minton informally adopts this approach in his evaluation of PRODIGY/EBL [Minton88 pp. 137–138]. In these experiments the training set is biased such that problem difficulty is gradually increased as learning proceeds. It this way, it is conjectured, PRODIGY/EBL learns much as a person, proceeding to complicated problems as the simpler ones are mastered. As compelling as this analogy seems, there are several reasons to be cautious. This idea shares the potential drawbacks of learning from partial information. The incremental utility of transformations varies across different problems. If the incremental utility of a transformation varies systematically with problem difficulty, a multi–example estimate of incremental utility will be compromised. Such an approach amounts to making an assumption that incremental utility is relatively insensitive to problem difficulty — a transformation which is effective for difficult problems is equally effective for simple problems, and vice versa. Under certain circumstances, however, such biasing can prove effective. Natarajan demonstrates some sufficient conditions under which this type of learning is possible [Natarajan89].

3.3.5 Simultaneous Extraction

The previous discussion highlighted a number of approaches toward reducing the cost of extracting information from a single problem. In the beginning of the section it was suggested that estimating the incremental utility of m transformations might require $m+1$ solutions. Many learning approaches implement observation procedures which enable the the extraction of utility values for multiple transformations from a single solution trace. We refer to such an approach as *simultaneous extraction.* PRODIGY/EBL, COMPOSER, SYLLOG [Markovitch89], and PALO [Greiner92] perform simultaneous extraction. For example, COMPOSER, a control rule learning system, produces annotated traces like the one in Figure 2. This trace contains information about every transformation currently under evaluation. This information includes which search path each rule avoids and its precondition match cost. This information, along with the cost of each node in the graph is sufficient to produce a utility value for each transformation. This avoids m solution attempts, however there is some overhead in generating the necessary annotated information, making the actual savings: $m \times$ original_cost − overhead. PALO introduces another technique for simultaneous extraction. From each example PALO generates an upper and lower bound on incremental utility for each transformation. The disadvantage of this approach is that bounds are weaker information than a single incremental utility value. Thus more examples may be required to reach the same level of confidence as if the problem was solved $m+1$ times.

Simultaneous extraction is intended to reduce the cost of extracting information. However, it is possible that such techniques might compromise the veracity of the utility values. For simultaneous extraction to maintain accuracy, it must be the case that the incremental utility value determined for one transformation is not influenced by whatever other transformations are being determined. This condition does not always hold. For example, PRODIGY/EBL gathers statistics for control rules as other rules are learned and forgotten. These shifting conditions influence the estimates. In [Gratch91a] we illustrate a domain where these influences lead to learning behavior which is not minimally adequate.

4   VALIDATING SIMPLIFICATIONS

It may be difficult to determine *a priori* whether a simplification is valid in a the context of a particular domain. A powerful technique is to validate the simplification empirically. The simplification is adopted but its effects in the context of problem solving are monitored for a time. The collected data can be interpreted as evidence for or against the simplification's validity in the monitored context.

Consider, for example, simultaneous extraction. This simplification can disrupt the adequacy of learning if the perceived incremental utility value of one transformation is influenced by presence of other transformations being estimated. It may be difficult to prove this cannot occur, but the possibility can be assessed empirically. For a particular learning system one can run a sensitivity analysis which compares how utility values change as different transformations are simultaneously estimated. The experiment might be as follows: Consider transformation A as the list of transformations being evaluated. Solve problem P1 and record the incremental utility value. Consider transformations A and B as the list of transformations being evaluated. Solve problem P1 again and record the incremental utility value for A, noting any difference with the previous value. By repeating this with several transformations and several problems one can gather evidence about the veracity of the simultaneous extraction technique.

Such an experiment amounts to validating the assumptions which underly a learning technique. Ideally we would like

an analytic justification for each simplification, however this can be quite difficult. Short of this, experiments like the one described can raise confidence in the heuristic adequacy of a system as well as highlight areas of potential difficulty. Furthermore it can focus research onto aspects of learning systems, rather than treating each program as a single large heuristic.

5   CONCLUSIONS

Learning shows great promise to extend the generality and effectiveness of planning techniques. But if learning is to be useful, we must explicitly characterize the properties of these systems. This article introduces the notion of adequacy to assess the merits of learning techniques. Surprisingly, many learning systems are not even minimally adequate; they may degrade planning performance.

The complexity of learning makes unconstrained techniques infeasible. But the task can be approached by introducing one or more simplifications. We presented a framework of simplifications which makes explicit the commitments adopted by many learning techniques. In many cases these simplifications are not justified with the result that these systems are not even minimally adequate. This highlights the need for explicit justifications in future research.

Acknowledgements

This research is supported by the National Science Foundation, grant NSF IRI 87–19766. We thank Nick Lewins, Dan Oblinger, Russ Greiner, and David Page for many interesting comments and discussions. We extend special appreciation to Steve Minton who provided us with his PRODIGY/EBL system. This work grew out of our first hand experience with his system. The comments of Jim Hendler and the two anonymous reviewers are also gratefully acknowledged. Thanks to Melinda Gervasio and Nick Lewins for commenting on a draft on very short notice.

References

[Blumer89] A. Blumer, A. Ehrenfeucht, D. Haussler and M. K. Warmuth, "Learnability and the Vapnik–Chervonenkis Dimension," *Journal of the ACM 36*, 4 (1989).

[Braverman88a] M. S. Braverman and S. J. Russell, "IMEX: Overcoming intractability in explanation based learning," *AAAI88*, St. Paul, MN, 1988, pp. 575–579.

[Braverman88b] M. S. Braverman and S. J. Russell, "Boundaries of Operationality," *ML88*, Ann Arbor, MI, June 1988, pp. 221–234.

[Chapman87] D. Chapman, "Planning for Conjunctive Goals," *Artificial Intelligence 32*, 3 (1987), pp. 333–378.

[DeJong86] G. F. DeJong and R. J. Mooney, "Explanation–Based Learning: An Alternative View," *Machine Learning 1*, 2 (April 1986), pp. 145–176.

[Drummond90] M. Drummond and J. Bresina, "Anytime Synthetic Projection: Maximizing the Probability of Goal Satisfaction," *AAAI90*, Boston, MA, pp. 138–144.

[Eskey90] M. Eskey and M. Zweben, "Learning Search COntrol for Constraint–Based Scheduling," *AAAI90*, Boston, MA, August 1990, pp. 908–915.

[Etzioni90a] O. Etzioni, "A Structural Theory of Search Control," Ph.D. Thesis, Department of Computer Science, Carnegie–Mellon University, Pittsburgh, PA 1990.

[Etzioni90b] O. Etzioni, "Why Prodigy/EBL Works," *AAAI90*, Boston, MA, August 1990, pp. 916–922.

[Fikes72] R. E. Fikes, P. E. Hart and N. J. Nilsson, "Learning and Executing Generalized Robot Plans," *Artificial Intelligence 3*, 4 (1972), pp. 251–288.

[Gratch90] J. Gratch and G. DeJong, "A Framework for Evaluating Search Control Strategies," *Proceedings of the Workshop on Innovative Approaches to Planning, Scheduling and Control*, San Diego, CA, 1990.

[Gratch91a] J. Gratch and G. DeJong, "A Hybrid Approach to Guaranteed Effective Control Strategies," *ML91*, Evanston, IL, June 1991.

[Gratch91b] J. M. Gratch and G. F. DeJong, "On comparing operationality and utility," TR UIUCDCS–R–91–1713, University of Illinois, Urbana, IL, 1991.

[Gratch92] J. Gratch and G. DeJong, "COMPOSER: A Probabilistic Solution to the Utility Problem in Speed–up Learning," *AAAI92*, San Jose, CA, July 1992.

[Greiner91] R. Greiner and P. Orponen, "Probably Approximately Optimal Derivation Strategies," *KR91*.

[Greiner92] R. Greiner and W. W. Cohen, "Probabilistic Hill–Climbing," *Proceedings of Computational Learning Theory and 'Natural' Learning Systems*, 1992.

[Hirsh88] H. Hirsh, "Reasoning about Operationality for Explanation–Based Learning," *ML88*, Ann Arbor, MI, June 1988, pp. 214–220.

[Hogg78] R. V. Hogg and A. T. Craig, *Introduction to Mathematical Statistics*, Macmillan Publishing Co., Inc., London, 1978.

[Knoblock90] C. Knoblock, "Learning Abstraction Hierarchies for Problem Solving," *AAAI90*, Boston, MA, 1990.

[Korf85] R. E. Korf, "Macro–Operators: A Weak Method for Learning," *Artificial Intelligence 26*, (1985), pp. 35–77.

[Laird86] J. E. Laird, P. S. Rosenbloom and A. Newell, *Universal Subgoaling and Chunking: The Automatic Generation and Learning of Goal Hierarchies*, Kluwer Academic Publishers, Hingham, MA, 1986.

[Leckie91] C. Leckie and I. Zukerman, "Learning Search Control Rules for Planning: An Inductive Approach," *ML91*, Evanston, IL, June 1991, pp. 422–426.

[Letovsky90] S. Letovsky, "Operationality Criteria for Recursive Predicates," *AAAI90*, Boston, MA, pp. 936–941.

[Markovitch89] S. Markovitch and P. D. Scott, "Utilization Filtering: a method for reducing the inherent harmfulness of deductively learned knowledge," *IJCAI89*, De-troit, MI, August 1989, pp. 738–743.

[Minton85] S. Minton, "Selectively Generalizing Plans for Problem–Solving," *AAAI85*, Los Angeles, pp. 596–599.

[Minton88] S. N. Minton, "Learning Effective Search Control Knowledge: An Explanation–Based Approach," Ph.D. Thesis, Department of Computer Science, Carnegie–Mellon University, Pittsburgh, PA, March 1988.

[Mitchell83] T. M. Mitchell, P. E. Utgoff and R. Banerji, "Learning by Experimentation: Acquiring and Refining Problem–solving Heuristics,"in *Machine Learning: An Artificial Intelligence Approach*, R. S. Michalski, J. G. Carbonell, T. M. Mitchell (ed.), Tioga Publishing Company, Palo Alto, CA, 1983, pp. 163–190.

[Mitchell86] T. M. Mitchell, R. Keller and S. Kedar–Cabelli, "Explanation–Based Generalization: A Unifying View," *Machine Learning 1*, 1 (January 1986).

[Natarajan89] B. K. Natarajan, "On Learning from Exercises," *COLT89*, Santa Cruz, CA, JULY 1989, pp. 72–87.

[Richards91] B. L. Richards and R. J. Mooney, "First–order theory revision," *ML91*, Evanston, IL, June 1991.

[Ruby91] D. Ruby and D. Kibler, "SteppingStone: an empirical and analytical evaluation," *AAAI91*, Anaheim, CA, July 1991, pp. 527–532.

[Schoppers87] M. J. Schoppers, "Universal Plans for Reactive Robots in Unpredictable Environments," *IJCAI89*, Milan, Italy, August 1987, pp. 1039–1046.

[Shavlik88] J. W. Shavlik, "Generalizing the Structure of Explanations in Explanation–Based Learning," Ph.D. Thesis, Department of Computer Science, University of Illinois, Urbana, IL, January 1988.

[Smith85] D. E. Smith and M. R. Genesereth, "Ordering Conjunctive Queries," *Artificial Intelligence 26*, 2 1985.

[Subramanian90] D. Subramanian and R. Feldman, "The Utility of EBL in Recursive Domain Theories," *AAAI90*, Boston, MA, August 1990, pp. 942–949.

[Tadepalli91] P. Tadepalli, "Learning with Inscrutable Theories," *ML91*, Evanston, IL, June 1991, pp. 544–548.

[Towell90] G. G. Towell, J. W. Shavlik and M. O. Noordewier, "Refinement of approximate domain theories by knowledge–base neural networks," *AAAI90*, Boston, MA, August 1990, pp. 861–866.

[Utgoff91] P. E. Utgoff and J. A. Clouse, "Two kinds of training information for evaluation function learning," *AAAI91*, Anaheim, CA, July 1991, pp. 596–600.

[Wellman90] M. Wellman, *Formulation of Tradeoffs in Planning Under Uncertainty*, Pitman & Morgan Kaufmann, 1990

[Wilkins89] D. C. Wilkins and Y. Ma, "Sociopathic knowledge bases: correct knowledge can be harmful even given unlimited computation," TR UIUCDCS–R–89–1538, Department of Computer Science, University of Illinois, Urbana, IL, 1989.

Decision-Theoretic Recursive Modeling and the Coordinated Attack Problem

Piotr J. Gmytrasiewicz and Edmund H. Durfee
Department of Electrical Engineering and Computer Science
University of Michigan
Ann Arbor, Michigan 48109

Abstract

In our decision-theoretic recursive modeling approach, interacting autonomous agents view their own decision making as an attempt to solve a multiperson game they play with other agents. To predict the actions of others, agents model the decision making of other agents (solving their own games), which in turn is based on their models of other agents, and so on. Considering the changes in the recursive hierarchy of models due to communication, we can compute corresponding changes to the utilities the agents can expect in their interactions. The utility of a message can be defined in terms of this change, and agents can choose to communicate only messages of the highest utilities. In this paper, we illustrate the power of our methodology by applying it to the coordinated attack problem, discussed by others using different methodology. We show how autonomous agents using our method are able to coordinate their attacks and defeat the enemy. This result contrasts with results of other work that has used a logic-based approach to decision making about actions.

Introduction

A central issue in distributed artificial intelligence (DAI) and multiagent planning systems is how to get autonomous intelligent agents, each of whom may have its own preferences and view points, to model each other and coordinate their activities for their mutual benefit. Following our previous work [Gmytrasiewicz et al., 1991a; Gmytrasiewicz et al., 1991b], this paper briefly summarizes a recursive method that agents can use to model each other in order to estimate expected utilities more completely in multiagent situations, and thus to make rational and coordinated decisions about physical and communicative actions. We illustrate this method using the example of the coordinated attack problem [Halpern and Moses, 1984].

[0]This research was supported, in part, by the Department of Energy under contract DG-FG-86NE37969, by the National Science Foundation under grant IRI-9015423, and by Presidential Young Investigator award IRI-9158473.

The novelty of our approach, when compared to more traditional methods, lies in designing agents that choose to execute physical and communicative actions because they are expected to bring the best payoff, as opposed to executing only provably sound actions, as in logic-based approaches [Doyle, 1990]. The difference between these methodologies is particularly visible when they are applied to the coordinated attack problem, discussed using logic-based methods by Halpern and Moses [Halpern and Moses, 1984]. Halpern and Moses developed a definition of common knowledge, which they postulated was essential for reaching agreements and coordinating action in problems like the coordinated attack. They also showed that the state of common knowledge is not attainable in practical distributed systems. This negative result cannot be circumvented on rigorous ground, and in order for coordination to be possible in practical distributed environments, a "leap of faith" on the part of the participants is required, called the "eager protocol". An eager protocol, moreover, works only if the communication between the agents involved is guaranteed, i.e. the messages are guaranteed to reach their destinations in finite time. If communication is not guaranteed, Halpern and Moses used the concept of "likely" common knowledge—a concept that seems to step outside of the requirements of logical soundness.

Our solution to the coordinated attack problem uses decision-theoretic principles for selecting actions, including communication acts. As we show, even if the communication channels used are not guaranteed to deliver messages, the agents are often able to undertake coordinated actions. We are able to include in our calculation the reliability of the communication channel, expressed as a probability, p_c, that a message sent will be delivered, and from our calculations can derive minimal values for channel reliability that still permit coordination, depending on the parameters of the problem.

In the following sections we first briefly review our Recursive Modeling Method (see [Gmytrasiewicz et al., 1991b] for more details), and then explain its application in calculating the value of messages (following

[Gmytrasiewicz *et al.*, 1991a]). We apply our method to the coordinated attack problem, highlighting the advantages and shortcomings of our approach, concluding with a brief discussion of future directions.

The Recursive Modeling Method (RMM)

This section follows quite closely our exposition of the Recursive Modeling Method in [Gmytrasiewicz *et al.*, 1991b]. RMM is intended to include all the information an agent might have about the other agents and can be viewed essentially as an extension of case analysis [Luce and Raiffa, 1957] to situations in which other players' payoffs and alternatives are uncertain. This technique attempts to put oneself in the shoes of the other player(s) and to guess what he (they) will prefer to do. Our approach thus follows, and extends to deeper levels of recursion, the main idea of a hypergame method [Bennett and Huxham, 1982; Vane and Lehner, 1990]. Our principal contribution is a complete and rigorous formalism that, unlike similar work [Cohen and Levesque, 1990; Rosenschein, 1988], directly relates the recursive levels of the agents' knowledge to the utilities of their actions and thus to the intentions of rational agents [Dennett, 1986].

Before we introduce the general form of RMM, consider the example in Figure 1. We assume for simplicity, each agent can only achieve one goal, so agent R1 has formed 3 alternative, high-level plans: achieve G1, achieve G2, or do something (including nothing) else (G1, G2 and S for short). Depending on R2's actions, R1 can compute the payoffs corresponding to each of these plans as the difference between the sum of the worth of all of the achieved goals and cost of performing only its own plan, which can be represented as a matrix (top of the hierarchy in Figure 2). The expected utility of R1's alternative plans naturally depend on what R2 chooses to do. R1 can assume that R2 will maximize its own payoff [Dennett, 1986]. The payoff matrix of R2, as modeled by R1, is depicted on the second level of the hierarchy in Figure 2. The modeling can continue, and thus, R1 can model R2, and R2's model of R1, and R2's model of R1's model of R2, and so on, as depicted in Figure 2. Let us note that due to the fact that in the scenario described the agents have full knowledge about the situation, and about the other agent's view of this situation, the recursive models contain no uncertainty, which could be represented as a branching of the hierarchy, as in [Gmytrasiewicz *et al.*, 1991b].

R1 builds and uses this hierarchy to help guess what R2 will do, summarizing its knowledge as a probability distribution $p_{R2}^{R1} = (p_{G1}, p_{G2}, p_S)$ indicating the probability of R2 taking action G1, G2, and S, which we call an *intentional* distribution. Regularities in the hierarchy in Figure 2 allow us to solve the hierarchy within a finite number of recursive levels. In this case, when developed down to an even number of levels, our algorithm computes R2's option G2 as the preferred one.

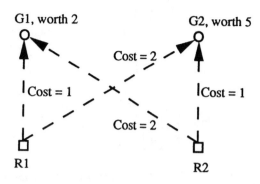

Figure 1: Example Scenario of Interacting Agents

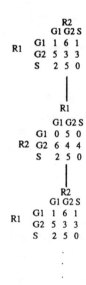

Figure 2: Example of the Recursive Hierarchy

However, when developed down to an odd number of levels, options G1 and S are equally preferred by R2. As we detail in [Gmytrasiewicz *et al.*, 1991b], when the hierarchy oscillates like this, a probabilistic mixture of the alternative results above should be regarded as a solution. Hence, in this case: $p_{R2}^{R1} = (0.25, 0.5, 0.25)$. Based on this solution, R1 can estimate the expected utilities of its options G1, G2 and S as 3.5, 3.5 and 3, respectively. R1 is thus indifferent between G1 and G2 and cannot expect a payoff of more than 3.5 in this interaction.

We now temporarily step back from this example and introduce the more general formulation of RMM. It includes the possibility of uncertainty in how agents' view other agents, as in [Gmytrasiewicz *et al.*, 1991b]. Let us assume that R1 is interacting with $(N-1)$ other

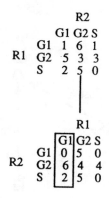

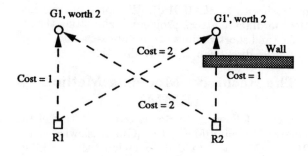

Figure 4: Variation of the Example Scenario

Figure 3: Recursive Hierarchy After a Received Intentional Message

truncate the hierarchy (Figure 3), assuming that R2 will believe R1's commitment to the stated intention. R1 believes that R2, after receiving M_1, will conclude that its option to pursue G2 will pay off the most. Thus, R1 forms a new probability distribution over R2's moves, $p_{M_1} = (0, 1, 0)$. R1 has committed itself to G1, but now R1 computes the expected utility of executing this plan as 6. According to Equation (4), therefore, the utility of message M_1 is $U(M_1) = U_{p_{M_1}}(G1) - U_p(G1 \lor G2) = 6 - 3.5 = 2.5$.

The above analysis assumes that R2 is guaranteed to receive M_1. Unfortunately, communication channels are seldom so reliable. We can formalize this risk by assuming that the communication channel will correctly deliver a message with probability p_c, where $0 \le p_c \le 1$. From R1's perspective: with probability p_c, M_1 will be received, in which case the probability distribution over R2's actions is $(0, 1, 0)$ as we just derived; and with probability $(1 - p_c)$, M_1 will not be received, so the probability distribution over R2's actions is the same as with no communication at all: $(0.25, 0.5, 0.25)$. Combining these we get:

$$p_c(0, 1, 0) + (1 - p_c)(0.25, 0.5, 0.25) =$$
$$= (0.25 - 0.25p_c, 0.5 + 0.5p_c, 0.25 - 0.25p_c).$$

Because R1 is committed to pursuing G1, it computes the expected utility of this action to be $U_{p_{M_1}}(G1) = 3.5 + 2.5p_c$, so the utility of M1 is: $U(M_1) = 2.5p_c$.

Modeling Messages

Modeling messages contain information about the modeling probabilities p_{Pi}^{R1}, p_{Ai}^{R1}, and p_{Wi}^{R1} in Equation 2, and update the hearer's and the speaker's model of the multiagent world. Consider, for example, what would happen in a variation of our original scenario. In this variation (Figure 4), instead of G2, we have G1', so that both agents will regard both goals as equally valuable. Also, there is a wall that probably obstructs R2's view of G1'.

The recursive hierarchy R1 will build for this scenario is depicted in Figure 5, where p_{W2}^{R1} represents the probability that R1 assigns to R2's seeing G1', which we assume to be low (0.01) because of the wall. R1 also assumes that, if R2 does see G1', it knows that R1 sees it too. As the progressively deeper levels of the left branch are analyzed, the solution quickly converges on R2's best option being S. The analysis of the right branch shows that the best option of R2, if it sees G1', is to pursue it. The resulting probability distribution over R2's moves is then $p = (0, 0.01, 0.99)$, which results in G1 being R1's best choice, with its expected utility of 1.02.

Intentional messages will not help in this case: R1's committing itself to G1 results in the same expected utility (because that is what R1 believes R2 will expect R1 to do, anyway); R1's commitment to G1' gives $p_{M_{G1'}} = (0.5, 0, 0.5)$ over R2's options, which results in an expected utility of G1' of 1; and R1's commitment to S results in an expected utility of 1.01. Thus, none of these messages can better the expected utility of 1.02 gained without communication.

However, on inspecting R1's payoff matrix, it is clear that R1's action of G1 will be better if R1 can increase the chances of R2 pursuing G1'. This requires that R1 increase the probability of the right branch of the model. A simple way to do this is for R1 to send R2 message M_2 stating that goal G1' is behind the wall. If, for the time being, we assume that communication channels never lose messages, then R1 models R2's response by changing p_{W2}^{R1} to 1, and $p_{W2}^{R1,R2,R1}$ to 1, and so on. Due to message M_2, the hierarchy has only one branch all the way down. Computing utilities, R1's best option is still G1, but now it expects R2 to pursue G1'. R1's action thus now has an expected utility of 3 rather than 1.02, so $U(M_2) = 1.98$.

Considering that communication channels are not perfect, let us see how the probability of communication p_c factors into these calculations. Combining the weighted intentional probabilities for R2, we get:

$$p_{M2} = p_c(0, 1, 0) + (1 - p_c)(0, 0.01, 0.99) =$$
$$= (0, 0.01 + 0.99p_c, 0.99 - 0.99p_c)$$

which gives an expected utility for G1 (still R1's best

agents, R2–RN. The utility of R1's m-th alternative action can be evaluated as:

$$u_m^{R1} = \sum_k \cdots \sum_l \{p_{R2-k}^{R1} \cdots p_{RN-l}^{R1} u_{m,k,\ldots,l}^{R1}\} \quad (1)$$

where p_{Ri-k}^{R1} represents the probability R1 assigns to Ri's choosing to act on the k-th element of Ri's set of options; as mentioned before, we will refer to these as intentional probabilities. $u_{m,k,\ldots,l}^{R1}$ is R1's payoff (utility) as an element of the N-dimensional game matrix.

R1 can estimate the intentional probabilities p_{Ri-k}^{R1} by guessing how the game looks from Ri's point of view. R1 models each Ri using probability distributions p_{Pi}^{R1}, p_{Ai}^{R1}, and p_{Wi}^{R1}, which we call modeling probabilities. p_{Pi}^{R1} summarizes R1's knowledge about Ri's preferences (goals it will value). p_{Ai}^{R1} summarizes R1's knowledge about Ri's abilities (goals it can pursue), given its preferences. p_{Wi}^{R1} summarizes R1's knowledge about Ri's world model, given its abilities. In every case of Ri having various preferences, abilities and world models, R1 assumes that Ri is rational and considers the probability that the k-th element of Ri's set of options is of the highest utility to Ri. The modeling probabilities can then be used to compute the intentional probabilities p_{Ri-k}^{R1}, as the following probabilistic mixture:

$$p_{Ri-k}^{R1} = \sum_{Pi} \sum_{Ai} \sum_{Wi} \{p_{Pi}^{R1} p_{Ai}^{R1} p_{Wi}^{R1} \times$$
$$Prob(Max_{k'}(u_{k'}^{R1,Ri}) = u_k^{R1,Ri})\} \quad (2)$$
$$(3)$$

where $u_{k'}^{R1,Ri}$ is the utility R1 estimates that Ri will assign to its option k', and is computed as:

$$u_{k'}^{R1,Ri} = \sum_r \cdots \sum_s \{p_{R1-r}^{R1,Ri} \cdots p_{RN-s}^{R1,Ri} u_{k',r,\ldots,s}^{R1,Ri}\} \quad (4)$$

Utilities $u_{k',r,\ldots,s}^{R1,Ri}$, are how R1 sees Ri's payoffs in the N-dimensional game matrix. The probabilities R1 thinks Ri assigns to agent Rn acting on its o-th option, $p_{Rn-o}^{R1,Ri}$, can in turn be expressed in terms of $p_{Rv-w}^{R1,Ri,Rn}$ and $u_{o',w,\ldots}^{R1,Ri,Rn}$ and so on.

RMM generaly needs not generate many levels of recursion (4 or 5, typically) before it converges on a consistent set of probability distributions over other agents' moves [Gmytrasiewicz et al., 1991b]. As in our example, if this set contains multiple distributions, a probabilistic mixture of them is used. Even so, RMM can be computationally intensive [Gmytrasiewicz, 1991]. We have investigated a number of heuristics that can be used to overcome its complexity, and methods that can be used to estimate the expected cost of running RMM on one hand, and the upper bound of benefits of doing so, on the other hand. These techniques, on which we do not elaborate further here, provide guidelines to using RMM when large numbers of agents are involved in time-critical situations.

The Utility of Communication Using RMM

We treat decisions about communication just like decisions about any other actions, and thus employ decision-theoretic techniques to select the action with the highest expected utility [Gmytrasiewicz et al., 1991c]. For communication actions, the agents use their nested models to predict the impact of messages on the expected utilities of alternative actions, and then send the highest utility message—the message that causes the greatest gain in the expected utility of the agent's action.

For example, using a hierarchy such as that in Figure 2, an agent computes a probability distribution p over the actions of the other agent, indicating the likelihood of another agent taking each of those actions (we drop the superscript and subscript for now). The initial agent can thus compute its best action, which we denote as X, as the action with the highest expected utility $U_p(X)$.

If the initial agent sends a message M to the other agent, it expects the message to cause the receiving agent to modify its hierarchy, and thus cause the probability distribution over its actions to change to p_M. This new distribution, in turn, can affect the expected utilities of the initial agent's actions, such that the action Y that it will now take (which may or may not be the same as X) has an expected utility of $U_{p_M}(Y)$. The utility of a message, M, is defined as the difference between the expected utility of the preferred action before M was sent and the expected utility of the agent's chosen action after the message was sent:

$$U(M) = U_{p_M}(Y) - U_p(X). \quad (5)$$

We broadly classify messages into types, depending on how they will impact a recipient and sender. In this paper we investigate two types—intentional and modeling messages.

Intentional Messages

An intentional message corresponds to an agent committing to an action, and informing other agents about it, i.e. it contains information about the intentional probabilities $p_{R1-r}^{R1,Ri}$ in Equation 3. If we assume that agents must meet their commitments, then a recipient can use this message to predict exactly what the sender will do. In modeling the recipient, therefore, the sender can truncate the recursion because it knows exactly how it will be modeled by the recipient.

For example, consider the scenario in Figure 1 and the hierarchy in Figure 2. As discussed before, R1's two options, G1 and G2, both have an expected utility of 3.5. Can R1 use communication to increase the quality of interaction and better its payoff?

The answer, in this case, is yes. Suppose that R1 considers transmitting an intentional message M_1 to R2 declaring its intention to pursue G1. R1 can thus

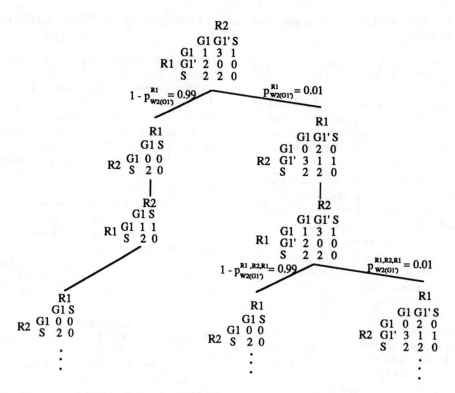

Figure 5: Recursive Hierarchy for Scenario Variation

choice) as $U_{G1} = 1.02 + 1.98p_c$, for a message utility of $U(M_2) = 1.98p_c$. In other words, sending the message is always to R1's benefit, unless $p_c = 0$. And if $p_c = 1$, the message allows R1 to maximize its expected utility.

Finally, consider how R1's model changes if R2 acknowledges receiving M_2, as depicted in Figure 6. Even after an acknowledgment, the model still includes uncertainty associated with R2 not knowing whether R1 received the acknowledgment. Because R1 now knows that R2 knows about G1', p_c no longer enters into the probability mixture R1 has of R2's actions (because R2's only rational action given that it now knows about G1' is to pursue G1'). G1 is still R1's best choice, but now has an expected utility of 3, meaning that the utility of the acknowledgment message is equal to $1.98(1 - p_c)$. Additional acknowledgment messages have no influence on R1's expected utility in this case because, once it knows that R2 has received the message, it knows that R2 should pursue G1' regardless of deeper uncertainties about knowledge about knowledge.

Decision-Theoretic Solution to the Coordinated Attack Problem

The coordinated attack problem has been discussed in an influential paper by Halpern and Moses [Halpern and Moses, 1984], which analyzed ways in which messages change the state of knowledge in a distributed system. Key concepts in the paper are those of E^k

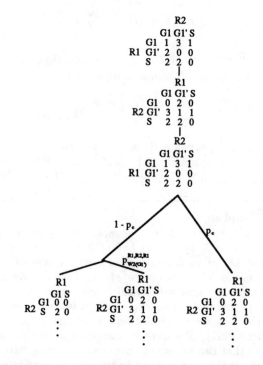

Figure 6: Recursive Hierarchy after M2 was Acknowledged

knowledge and common knowledge. A group of N agents is said to possess E^k knowledge of the fact p

if everybody in the group knows p, everybody knows that everybody knows p, and so on down to the level k. Common knowledge is then defined as E^k knowledge when $k = \infty$. Further, it is postulated that, in a distributed environment, the parties have to have common knowledge about the terms of an agreement for the agreement to actually exist, and for the agents to undertake a coordinated action.

Let us consider a variation of the coordinated attack problem to illustrate these concepts and the results contained in [Halpern and Moses, 1984]. Imagine two divisions of an army camped on two hilltops overlooking a common valley. In the valley awaits the enemy. It is clear that if both divisions attack simultaneously they will win the battle, whereas if only one attacks it will be defeated. The divisions do not initially have plans to launch an attack on the enemy and the commanding general of the first division wishes to coordinate a simultaneous attack (at some propitious time the next day). Neither general will decide to attack unless they reach agreement that they will both attack. The generals can only communicate by means of a messenger. Normally, it takes the messenger one hour to get from one encampment to the other. However, it is possible that he will get lost in the dark or, worse yet, captured by the enemy. Fortunately, on this particular night, everything goes smoothly. How long will it take them to reach agreement?

Halpern and Moses show that the coordinated attack problem is unsolvable on rigorous logical grounds, because the generals will never achieve common knowledge, and so will not agree to attack the next day. The same kind of reasoning can be used to show that the attack will actually never take place! To see the reason for this result, consider the messenger successfully reaching its destination carrying the message "Let's attack at dawn" from general **I** to general **II**. **II** then knows the message, but since **I** does not know that **II** knows (the messenger might have been captured), general **II** sends the messenger back with an acknowledgment. **I** gets the acknowledgment, but realizes that **II** does not know that, and another acknowledgment is needed. Therefore, each time the messenger completes the journey the parties that received him deepen their knowledge about the other's knowledge one level down, but, of course, are hopelessly far away from the infinite depth required for common knowledge.

There is something counterintuitive in the analysis above—we, in our every day life, do seem to reach what we think are agreements, despite imperfect communication media, and actually are able to execute coordinated actions. It also seems that the surer we are that the message will reach its destination, the less need there is for an acknowledgment, and the acknowledgment of the acknowledgment, and so on. In what follows we will attempt to critique some of the features of the above analysis and present our own solution that does not suffer from these problems.

First, let us look at the assumption that the generals in question perform an act that requires coordination to succeed only if the agreement, i.e. common knowledge, has been reached. Note that this assumption can lead to irrational behavior and that the fact that the actions of the opponent are not known with certainty does not by itself mean that any action should, or should not, be undertaken. Clearly, for any finite payoffs involved in the action's bringing the desired result or not, just a high enough probability of its succeeding should always be enough to make it a worthwhile choice. Our basic claim here is that it is more realistic, and in the end more beneficial, to treat decision makers as being rational in the decision-theoretic sense, as *homo economicus*, as opposed to treating them in orthodox logical terms in which they perform only actions that are "sound", i.e. are guaranteed to result in the desired outcome (*homo logicus*).

Second, let us look closely at the message that the generals are supposed to have exchanged in the original example. What information is it attempting to convey? Remember that neither general will attack unless he is sure that the other will attack. What could, then, "Let's attack at dawn" mean? It surely can not express that the sender actually believes that both generals will attack at dawn. It also can not mean that the sender himself will attack at dawn. The most reasonable interpretation seems to be something along the lines of "I will attack at dawn if I am sure that you will attack at the same time". The acknowledgment of the reception of this message could then contain something like "Got your message, I will also attack if I am sure you will". From this angle it becomes clear that the further acknowledgments exchanged cannot convince either generals and cannot make them do anything but to exchange more messages.

We will now describe how our approach would deal with the problem of coordinated attack. As we mentioned, the autonomous agents we have in mind do not do things that are logically sound, i.e. are guaranteed to work as intended; instead, they chose an option of the highest expected utility. Let us denote the utility of winning the battle with the enemy in the valley as W, and the utility of not attacking the enemy as N. Further denote the utility associated with a loss of the generals' own division as L and the loss of the other allied division as l. We postulate the ordering $W > N > l > L$, with the utility N less than or equal to zero.

Let us now make the following **Opportunity Assumption:** There is a time, t_0, such that if the generals do not attack at t_0, they will not have the opportunity to attack at all.[1] Under this assumption one can construct payoff matrices using the payoffs defined above. The payoff matrix describing the decision situ-

---

[1]That t_0 has the unique feature of being the last possible time to attack makes it a focal point [Kraus and Rosenschein, 1992].

ation that general **I** finds himself in is:

$$
\begin{array}{c}
\text{II} \\
\begin{array}{ccc}
 & \text{A} & \text{notA} \\
\text{I} \quad \text{A} & W & L \\
\text{notA} & l & N
\end{array}
\end{array}
$$

where A stands for attacking the enemy at t_0, and notA stands for not attacking at t_0. General **I** has no problem with modeling the decision making situation of general **II** with a similar matrix:

$$
\begin{array}{c}
\text{I} \\
\begin{array}{ccc}
 & \text{A} & \text{notA} \\
\text{II} \quad \text{A} & W & L \\
\text{notA} & l & N
\end{array}
\end{array}
$$

The generals can build the RMM hierarchy out of these matrices, which is simply a non-branching sequence of these alternating matrices. The result of solving this hierarchy is that the generals will chose to attack if $W + L > N + l$. Thus, if this inequality and the Opportunity Assumption both hold, communication is not necessary to arrive at the coordinated attack decision.

Let us now consider the case in which the Opportunity Assumption does not hold. In this case, communication between the generals in question is necessary to achieve coordination. Note that if either general, finding himself in the above situation, receives the message saying "I will attack at dawn" (or any other future moment in time) from the other general, the only rational choice for the receiving general is undoubtedly to attack at dawn and get the payoff of W. Let us now consider general **I** sending the message "I will attack at dawn" and estimating the probability that it will be delivered before dawn to be p_c. The expected utility for general **I** of attacking at dawn after having sent this message is then $p_c * W + (1 - p_c) * L$, and the expected utility of not attacking is $p_c * l + (1 - p_c) * N$. This means that general **I** will attack after having sent this message when $p_c * W + (1-p_c) * L > p_c * l + (1-p_c) * N$. The value of this message, calculated using Equation 4, is $p_c * W + (1 - p_c) * L - N$. Of course, the general would compute the utility of the message and make sure that it is positive before actually sending it. This also implies that it will pay for him to fulfill the promise contained in the message and actually attack at dawn.

Pursuing the matter further, one may ask what happens if the value of the message, $p_c * W + (1-p_c) * L - N$, is negative. In this case, it does not pay to declare an attack for either of the generals. This case corresponds to the generals facing a difficult military operation without a channel of communication that is reliable enough to get the job done. In particular, in order to be able to converge on a coordinated action, the agents require a communication channel of reliability at least $p_c = (N - L)(W - L)$. Let us note that, as the value of L approaches $-\infty$, the reliability of the communication channel has to approach 100%. In this extreme case, the economic rationality demands complete certainty, corresponding to the logical provability postulated in [Halpern and Moses, 1984].

Discussion

Summarizing the results of the last section, we showed the power of the decision-theoretic approach when compared to the logic-based one described in [Halpern and Moses, 1984]. Our approach[*] allowed the agents to coordinate and synchronize their actions in spite of the imperfect communication channel. We have also shown how reliable the communication channel has to be for the coordination to be possible, depending on the losses and gains involved.

Let us be fair here and note that the power of our method comes with a price. We postulate that the generals' actions be chosen when they are *expected* to pay off most. That means that in some unfortunate circumstances it *may* happen that one of our generals will be the only one to attack at dawn, and may be dead by noon. This can be contrasted with a logic-driven approach according to which only the provably successful action can be undertaken. But that, of course, means that an intelligent agent might find *no* provably successful actions in its repertoire, which leaves it immobile on the hill top for ever. This case is particularly likely when agents have to deal with complex, uncertain circumstances or, in other words, the real world.

Our computations for message utility in the coordinated attack problem described above treat each of the messages in isolation. That is, we did not consider what happens to the utility of a successfully sent message that is interleaved with another message exchange. As an example of this, consider what happens to the utility of a message "I will attack at dawn" if the general that sent it receives immediately afterward the message: "I will attack at noon" from the other general. It seems intuitive that the utility of the original message, equal to $W - N$, should somehow be decreased by the second message. Our treatment to date does not account for this effect and extensions aimed at including it belong to future work.

We have not spent much time in this paper elaborating on ways in which the agents generate their alternative plans. In our current implementation of the Recursive Modeling Method, these plans are generated by a set of hierarchical planning routines, described in more detail in [Gmytrasiewicz *et al.*, 1991c]. These routines contain a number of heuristics that, as we found, make sense for the scenarios we have considered, but are not universally valid. For example, our agents consider only plans of actions that they are able to execute themselves; that heuristic neglects the fact that what was not a feasible plan for one agent may well turn out to be a feasible plan for two or more agents. In our future work we will attempt to fully address the issue of planning heuristics suitable for multiagent domains.

Acknowledgements

We would like to acknowledge the contributions made to this work by David Wehe, the members of the Michigan DIAG (distributed intelligent agents group), and the anonymous reviewers.

References

[Bennett and Huxham, 1982] P. G. Bennett and C. S. Huxham. Hypergames and what they do: A 'soft OR' approach. *Journal of Operational Research Society*, 33:41–50, 1982.

[Cohen and Levesque, 1990] P. R. Cohen and H. J. Levesque. Rational interaction as the basis for communication. In P. R. Cohen, J. Morgan, and M. E. Pollack, editors, *Intentions in Communication*. MIT Press, 1990.

[Dennett, 1986] D. Dennett. Intentional systems. In D. Dennett, editor, *Brainstorms*. MIT Press, 1986.

[Doyle, 1990] Jon Doyle. Rationality and its role in reasoning. In *Proceedings of the National Conference on Artificial Intelligence*, pages 1093–1100, August 1990.

[Gmytrasiewicz et al., 1991a] Piotr J. Gmytrasiewicz, Edmund H. Durfee, and David K. Wehe. The utility of communication in coordinating intelligent agents. In *Proceedings of the National Conference on Artificial Intelligence*, pages 166–172, July 1991.

[Gmytrasiewicz et al., 1991b] Piotr J. Gmytrasiewicz, Edmund H. Durfee, and David K. Wehe. A decision-theoretic approach to coordinating multiagent interactions. In *Proceedings of the Twelfth International Joint Conference on Artificial Intelligence*, August 1991.

[Gmytrasiewicz et al., 1991c] Piotr J. Gmytrasiewicz, Edmund H. Durfee, and David K. Wehe. Combining decision theory and hierarchical planning for a time-dependent robotic application. In *Proceedings of the Seventh IEEE Conference on AI Applications*, pages 282–288, February 1991.

[Gmytrasiewicz, 1991] Piotr Gmytrasiewicz. *A Decision-Theoretic Model of Coordination and Communication in Autonomous Systems*. PhD thesis, University of Michigan, December 1991.

[Halpern and Moses, 1984] Joseph Y. Halpern and Yoram Moses. Knowledge and common knowledge in a distributed environment. In *Third ACM Conference on Principles of Distributed Computing*, 1984.

[Kraus and Rosenschein, 1992] Sarit Kraus and Jeffrey S. Rosenschein. The role of representation in interaction: Discovering focal points among alternative solutions. In Y. Demazeau and Eric Werner, editors, *Decentralized AI*. Elsevier Science Publishers, New York, 1992.

[Luce and Raiffa, 1957] R. D. Luce and H. Raiffa. *Games and Decisions*. John Wiley and Sons, 1957.

[Rosenschein, 1988] Jeffrey S. Rosenschein. The role of knowledge in logic-based rational interactions. In *Proceedings of the Seventh Phoenix Conference on Computers and Communications*, pages 497–504, Scottsdale, AZ, February 1988.

[Vane and Lehner, 1990] R. R. Vane and P. E. Lehner. Hypergames and AI in automated adversarial planning. In *Proceedings of the 1990 DARPA Planning Workshop*, pages 198–206, November 1990.

Systematic Adaptation for Case-Based Planning

Steven Hanks & Daniel S. Weld*
Department of Computer Science and Engineering
University of Washington
Seattle, WA 98195
hanks@cs.washington.edu
weld@cs.washington.edu

Abstract

Research efforts in case-based reasoning have made advances in various problem domains, but general principles and domain-independent algorithms have been slower to emerge. We seek to explore the theoretical foundations of case-based planning, in particular to characterize the fundamental trade-offs that govern the process of plan adaptation. To do so we view the planning process as a search through a graph of partial plans: plan generation starts at the graph's root and adds constraints, plan adaptation starts at an arbitrary place in the graph and can either add or delete constraints.

This paper develops a domain-independent algorithm for case-based plan adaptation that is sound, complete, and systematic. Since our algorithm is sound, every plan it returns is guaranteed to achieve the goal. Since our algorithm is complete, it is guaranteed to find a plan if one exists, regardless of the initial plan returned from the library. Systematicity guarantees that our algorithm explores the space of partially specified, incomplete plans avoiding redundant or wasted effort. The algorithm provides an excellent vehicle for further study, particularly on issues involving the role of heuristic and problem-specific knowledge in the planning process. This paper describes the algorithm and its implementation in some detail, and presents experimental results that shed light on performance issues an implementation must confront.

1 Introduction

Case-based planning is an attractive reasoning paradigm for several reasons. First, cognitive studies have shown that human experts depend on a knowledge of past cases for good problem-solving performance. Second, computational complexity arguments show that reasoning from first principles requires time exponential in the size of the problem. Case-based reasoning systems may avoid this problem by solving a smaller problem: that of adapting a previous solution to the current task. Intuition tells us that most new problem-solving situations closely resemble old situations, therefore there is a clear advantage to using past successes to solve new problems.

Case-based planners typically accomplish their task in three phases. *Retrieval* takes the problem's initial and goal conditions and finds in the plan library a plan that has worked under circumstances similar to those posed by the the current problem. The retrieval phase may also involve some superficial modification of the library plan to make it applicable to the current problem. *Adaptation* modifies the retrieved plan, *e.g.* by adding and removing steps, by changing step orders or variable bindings, until the resulting plan achieves the input goal. *Storage* may generalize the newly created plan and store it as a new case in the library. This paper is concerned mainly with the adaptation phase.

1.1 Motivation

Previous work in case-based reasoning has been mainly oriented toward specific domains. Although the work has produced promising prototypes and considerable insight into the difficult issues and structure of the paradigm, general principles and domain-independent algorithms have been slow to emerge. And without a precise foundation of basic algorithms, it is difficult for researchers to evaluate each other's work and to apply these insights to new domains.

Our intent is to provide a domain-independent and rigorous foundation for the study of case-based planning, much as the classical planners have done for generative planning. In fact our framework is based on SNLP [Barrett *et al.* 1991], a lifted version of McAllester and Rosenblitt's [1991] formulation of classical nonlinear

---

*Author's names listed alphabetically.

constraint-posting planning. SNLP is a simplified version of Chapman's [1987] TWEAK which descended in turn from Tate's [1977] NONLIN.

1.2 Overview

In this paper we present the SPA[1] system—an algorithm for plan adaptation that is sound, complete, and systematic—along with a description of that algorithm's implementation. Soundness means that the output plan is guaranteed to satisfy the goal, completeness means that the planner will always find a plan if one exists (regardless of the library plan provided by the retriever), and systematicity means that the algorithm explores the space of adaptations nonredundantly (in short, it will never consider an adaptation more than once).

Systematicity is the most tricky property to attain, and for two reasons: first, the adapter operates in a space of abstract, or incomplete, plans[2]. Each incomplete plan can expand into an exponential number of completions; systematicity requires that the adaptation algorithm never consider two incomplete plans that share even one completion, while completeness requires that every potential completion be considered. Second, plan adaptation requires a combination of retracting previous planning decisions (choice and ordering of plan steps, binding of variables within the operator schemas), as well as making new decisions. Systematicity requires that a decision, once retracted, never be considered again. Achieving this property without incurring a tremendous amount of bookkeeping overhead is a triumph of our algorithm.

We view the general planning problem as a search through a directed graph of incomplete plans (Figure 1): the graph's root represents the null plan and its leaves represent complete plans. Generative planning algorithms start at the root of the graph and search for a leaf node. They move down the graph by successively refining (constraining) the plan. The retrieval phase of a case-based planner, on the other hand, returns an arbitrary node in the graph, and the adapter begins searching from that point. It must be able to search down the graph like a generative planner but also must be able to search backward through the graph by retracting constraints, producing more abstract plans. A complete and systematic adaptation algorithm must be able to search every node in the graph, but without considering any node more than once.

We have implemented our algorithm in Common Lisp on UNIX workstations and tested it in both the blocks world and a more sophisticated transportation scheduling domain. Experimental studies compare

our algorithm to a similar effort, [Kambhampati and Hendler 1992]. Initial results on our unoptimized prototype shows a systematic speedup from plan re-use in certain controlled cases, but the results are very sensitive to the domain and problem specifications. Subsequent analysis explains this phenomenon and identifies several issues important in the design of any similar planner.

2 Definitions

This section will describe a plan's components and provide a precise definition of the planning problem.

Our planner uses a simplification of the STRIPS action representation [Fikes and Nilsson 1971] identical to that used by [Chapman 1987] and [McAllester and Rosenblitt 1991], and we accordingly begin by defining propositions, operator schemas, and plan steps, as well as the constraints the planner can place on them.

• A *binding constraint* is of the form (obj = obj) or (obj <> obj), where obj is either a variable or a constant. Explicit binding constraints involving two constants are either uninteresting or illegal, since we implicitly enforce the additional constraints that (K = K) and (K1 <> K2) when K1 is distinct from K2. We also assume that (?X = ?X) for all variables ?X.

• A *proposition* is a function-free atom in some logical language. Propositions can contain variables, and two propositions can be unified. Unification produces a set of binding constraints or a failure indicator. Substitution applies to a proposition and a set of binding constraints, and produces a new proposition.

• An *operator schema* consists of a unique *name*, three lists of propositions—*precond*, *add* and *delete*—and a set of binding constraints that restrict the objects that variables in its propositions can be bound to.

• A *step* is an instance of an operator schema inserted into a plan. We will notate steps S_i where S is the operator's name and i is an index unique to the step within the plan. Note that i does not refer to the step's execution order, rather to the order that it was *added* to the plan.

• Steps can be ordered within a plan using *ordering constraints* of the form $i < j$, where i and j are step indices. The term *constraints* will refer to ordering or binding constraints.

• A *link* is a triple consisting of a producing step index, a consuming step index, and a proposition, notated $i \xrightarrow{P} j$ or equivalently $S_i \xrightarrow{P} S_j$. A link records a dependency within a plan.

• A *plan* consists of a set of steps, a set of links, a set of orderings, and a set of binding constraints. A plan must contain an initial step I_0 and a goal step G_1,

[1] Systematic Plan Adapter

[2] An incomplete plan's steps may be partially ordered, its steps may contain unbound variables, or additional steps may by required to achieve the goal.

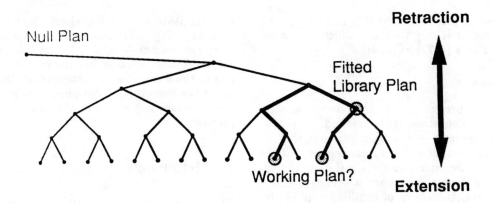

Figure 1: Plan extension and retraction as search in a space of incomplete plans

orderings $0 < i$ for all $i \neq 0$, and orderings $i < 1$ for all $i \neq 1$. The initial step asserts the initial world state for a planning problem and the goal step's precondition set corresponds to the desired world state.

• A *null plan* contains *only* steps I_0 and G_1, no links, no binding constraints, and the single ordering $0 < 1$.

• We can compute from a plan a set of *open conditions* and *threatened links*. The former represents a step precondition that has no supporting link, and is notated $\xrightarrow{P} i$. The latter is a pair $\prec i \xrightarrow{P} j, S_k \succ$ where S_k may be ordered between S_i and S_j, and S_K either possibly adds or possibly deletes P[3].

• A plan is *complete* just in case it has no open conditions and no threatened links.

• Two plans $\mathcal{P}_1$ and $\mathcal{P}_2$ are *isomorphic* just in case

  1. there is a 1:1 mapping from steps in $\mathcal{P}_1$ and $\mathcal{P}_2$ such that corresponding steps have identical names (take the correspondence to be $S_1, S_2, \ldots S_n$ to $R_1, R_2, \ldots R_n$),

  2. $S_i \xrightarrow{P} S_j \in \mathcal{P}_1$ iff $R_i \xrightarrow{P} R_j \in \mathcal{P}_2$,

  3. $S_i < S_j \in \mathcal{P}_1$ iff $R_i < R_j \in \mathcal{P}_2$, and

  4. $\mathcal{P}_1$ and $\mathcal{P}_2$ have identical binding constraints.

This definition implies that two isomorphic plans have the same open conditions and threatened links as well. Note that two plans may have corresponding steps and identical orderings and *not* be isomorphic, however, since they may differ on one or more causal links.

Referring ahead to Figure 2, each node in the graph represents a plan. The graph's root is the null plan, and each leaf represents a complete plan. A directed arc represents the addition of constraints (links, orderings, and binding constraints). Planning consists of

searching this graph for a leaf node. Generative planning starts at the root and adds constraints; adaptive planning starts at an arbitrary node and either adds or deletes constraints.

Having set up the formal notion of a plan, we will proceed to describe our algorithm and its implementation in terms of the three phases of case-based planning: retrieval and fitting, adaptation, and storage.

3 Retrieval and Fitting

The retrieval phase takes as input the problem's initial and goal conditions (each a set of propositions), tries to find a good match between these and one of the library plans, then may perform some superficial modifications on the library plan before returning it.

We have not studied the retrieval problem in any depth (see [Hammond 1989] for example), and in the longer paper we describe the simple match-and-fit algorithm we implemented. Here we note briefly what the adapter requires from the retriever.

The retriever must return a *plan* structure, and one whose initial step adds the problem's initial conditions and whose goal step requires the problem's goal conditions.

Furthermore, the plan must correspond to a plan that SPA could itself have generated. For example, whenever SPA adds a step S to a plan, that step is always the producer in a causal link, and is ordered before the consumer of that link. If the fitting phase ever deletes a link (say because the link's consumer proposition was in the library plan's goal condition but not in the input problem's) it must also delete the producing step, provided that step is not a producer for another link.

The SPA algorithm may not be complete if it begins with a partial plan it could not have generated itself. We return to this issue in Section 5.

---

[3]Note that a threat can be not only a step that may make P false, but also a step that redundantly makes P true.

4   Adaptation

Plan adaptation modifies the retrieved plan, trying to eliminate all open conditions and threats. It can do so in two ways: *extension* (which adds new steps and constraints) and *retraction* (which removes steps and constraints).

4.1   Extension

Extension adds constraints or causal links (and thus, sometimes new steps) to the plan. We extend plans in the same manner as [McAllester and Rosenblitt 1991]. Viewing extension as an operation that takes as input an incomplete plan $\mathcal{P}$ and generates 0 or more children which are more constrained than $\mathcal{P}$, we do the following:

1. Choose nondeterministically a condition to resolve, from among $\mathcal{P}$'s open and threat conditions.

2. Given such a choice, return *all possible* resolutions of the condition:

   - If the choice is an open precondition $\xrightarrow{P} j$ then $\mathcal{P}$'s children are all plans that can be constructed by adding a link $k \xrightarrow{P} j$, an ordering $k < j$, and appropriate variable-binding constraints, where S_k is either an existing step or a newly created step that possibly adds P and can consistently be ordered prior to j.

   - Otherwise, if the choice is a threat $\prec i \xrightarrow{P} j$, $S_k \succ$ then the plan's children are all plans that can be consistently constructed by adding ordering constraints of the form $k < i$ and $j < k$, or by adding variable-binding constraints that force all propositions in S_k's add and delete list *not* to codesignate with P.

We take extension to be a function that takes a partial plan as input and returns its extended children as output:

```
FUNCTION ExtendPlan(PLAN p): SET-OF PLAN
  ResolveCondition(ChooseCondition(p), p);
```

where **Choosecondition** makes the nondeterministic choice of what to extend, and **ResolveCondition** returns the set of incomplete plans generated by adding a new causal link or resolving a threat as shown below:

```
FUNCTION ResolveCondition(CONDITION c, PLAN p):
                               SET-OF PLAN
  IF OpenCondition?(c) THEN
    RETURN ResolveOpen(c,p)
     ELSE IF ThreatCondition?(c) THEN
       RETURN ResolveThreat(c,p)
         ELSE ERROR;
```

Here **ResolveOpen** and **ResolveThreat** apply all possible methods of constraining away the open condition or threat. Details of these routines appear in [Hanks and Weld 1991]. Figure 2 shows the extension operation in plan space: a call to **ExtendPlan** generates a node's descendents in the graph of partial plans.

4.2   Retraction

Retraction, conversely, chooses some part of the plan's structure to delete; the deleted part has to correspond to some part of the plan originally added by **ExtendPlan** when the plan was generated. This can be one of two things:

1. Resolving an open condition adds a link, an ordering, and possibly a step as well. The corresponding retraction chooses a link, deletes it, and if the producing step no longer participates in any links, deletes the step along with its ordering and variable binding constraints.

2. Resolving a threat condition adds either an ordering constraint or a set of variable-binding constraints. The corresponding retraction deletes that ordering or that set of variable-binding constraints.

To do the retraction the plan's variable-binding constraints must therefore be indexed to indicate why they were added to the plan. [Hanks and Weld 1991] discusses this machinery in more detail.

Once a constraint is retracted the planner must also consider *other* ways to establish the condition just deleted. The retraction algorithm can call **Extendplan** to re-establish the condition, but has to be careful not to consider the extension that corresponds to the condition it just retracted. In addition to considering establishing the same condition in different ways, the algorithm also has to consider retracting *other* constraints in the plan. Referring to Figure 3, we see that the retraction function takes a partial plan p and returns its *parent* and its *siblings* in plan space:

```
FUNCTION RetractPlan(PLAN p):
              <PLAN, SET-OF PLAN>
  c := ChooseCondition(p);
  parent := RetractCondition(c, p);
  siblings := ResolveCondition(c, p);
  LOOP FOR sib IN siblings
    IF PlanIsomorphic?(sib, p)
       THEN Delete!(sib, siblings)
  RETURN <parent, siblings>;
```

4.3   Adaptation

Now we can view the adaptation process as a function that takes as input a partial plan returned by the adapter, and manages a queue of operations to perform on the graph. Each queue entry consists of a

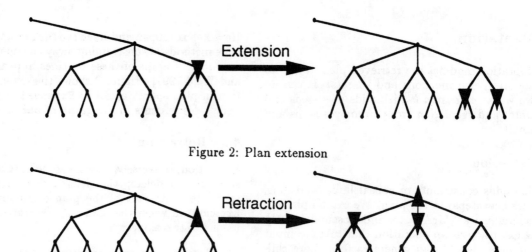

Figure 2: Plan extension

Figure 3: Plan retraction

partial plan and an operation extend (DOWN) or retract (UP) to perform on that plan. The application supplies a ranking function that determines which queue entry to process next (see Section 6).

```
FUNCTION AdaptPlan(PLAN p-init): PLAN
  q := InitQueue();
  Enqueue!(<p-init, UP>, q);
  Enqueue!(<p-init, DOWN>, q);
  LOOP
    IF Empty?(q) THEN RETURN FAILURE
      ELSE
        <p,dir> := Dequeue!(q);
        IF Complete?(p) THEN RETURN p
          ELSE
            IF (dir = DOWN) THEN
              FOR np IN ExtendPlan(p) DO
                Enqueue!(<np, DOWN>, q);
                ELSE
                  IF (dir = UP) THEN
                    <parent, children> :=
                        RetractPlan(p)
                    Enqueue!(<parent, UP>, q);
                    FOR child IN children DO
                      Enqueue!(<child, DOWN>, q);
```

Note that the initial plan (the one returned by the retrieval mechanism) is queued both for retraction *and* for extension. After that, if a node is queued for extension then its children are extended too. If a node is queued for retraction, its *parent* is queued for further retraction whereas its *siblings* are queued for extension. These operations are pictured in Figures 2 and 3 respectively.

Next we sketch the proofs that this algorithm searches the entire space of plans and does so without searching any part of the graph more than once.

5   Formal Properties

[Hanks and Weld 1991] demonstrates that the SPA algorithm is sound, complete, and (with one minor qualification) systematic. Here we will just explain the properties and outline their proofs.

Since our adaptation algorithm is built around the representation and algorithm in [McAllester and Rosenblitt 1991] (hereafter called MCAR), we first demonstrate in the longer paper that our algorithm's behavior when it extends plans only (that is, when the queue is initialized with a DOWN-tagged entry) is identical to [McAllester and Rosenblitt 1991]'s generative algorithm.

5.1   Soundness

A planning algorithm is sound if any plan it returns actually solves the input planning problem. This property follows directly from the soundness of MCAR: it depends on properties of a complete plan, and not on the way that plan is found. Our algorithm defines a plan and a completed plan in the same way that MCAR does, and therefore SPA is sound as well.

5.2   Completeness

Completeness consists of two claims:

1. that every solution to the planning problem is realized in the graph as a leaf node, and

2. that the search algorithm will eventually visit every leaf node in the graph.

The first condition once again does not depend on the way the graph is searched, therefore it is true of SPA because it is true of MCAR. The second condition is less clear, however: MCAR makes sure it covers the entire graph by starting at the root and expanding the graph downward in a systematic fashion, whereas SPA starts at an arbitrary point in the graph and traverses it in both directions.

We demonstrate completeness by an inductive argument, essentially showing that SPA, starting at the initial library plan $\mathcal{P}_L$, will eventually retract its way back to the null plan $\mathcal{P}_\emptyset$, and in doing so will search completely every child of every subgraph it generates along the way.

Completeness relies on two additional factors. First of all, the algorithm's search strategy must guarantee that it will eventually reach any node in the graph, given enough time. (That is, it cannot spend an infinite amount of time searching any node's child before searching its other children.) MCAR ensures this property by using iterative deepening breadth-first search. We assume that the application-supplied search-control function has this property.

Second, although we can guarantee that SPA will eventually retract every choice in its input plan, it is not necessarily the case that the resulting plan will indeed be the null plan (the plan consisting only of initial and goal steps I and G, and the single ordering I<G). This property depends on the algorithms employed by the plan generation and fitting phases: they cannot leave any superfluous steps or constraints in the plan, otherwise SPA may not retract them, and will not eventually arrive at the null plan.

Fortunately, it is easy to modify the RetractPlan function to achieve completeness with any library retrieval and fitting strategy. We do so by adding to the algorithm another retraction option that deletes superfluous steps—steps other than the initial and goal steps that neither produce a causal link nor threaten one [Hanks and Weld 1991].

5.3 Systematicity

Systematicity, like completeness, consists of two claims. The first is formal: that the plan graph is a tree—in other words, that the policy of generating a node's children by making a nondeterministic but fixed choice of a condition (open or threat) to resolve, then applying all possible ways to resolve that condition, means that any two distinct plan nodes represent non-isomorphic plans. The second claim is that the strategy for searching the graph never visits a plan node more than once.

The first claim applies just to the formal definition of the plan graph, so the systematicity of MCAR suffices to prove the systematicity of SPA. We verify the second claim in the longer paper (1) by equating "visiting" a node with Adaptplan's dequeueing the corresponding partial plan, (2) by noting that unless a

Prblm	Goal Stack	Init. Config.	
3BS1	I J K	(ON J K)	
4BS1	I J K L	(ON J L)	
5BS1	I J K L LL	(ON I L)	
6BS1	I J K L JJ LL	(ON J L)	(ON JJ LL)
6BSEZ	K L M N O P	(ON N P)	
7BS1	I J K L JJ LL II	(ON J L)	(ON JJ LL)
8BS1	I J K L M N O P	(ON J L)	(ON N P)

(All blocks are initially on the table and clear, except those explicitly noted.)

Figure 4: Problem configurations for xBS1 Problems

partial plan is queued both UP and DOWN it will never be queued more than once, and (3) by showing that the only plan that is queued both UP and DOWN is the initial plan $\mathcal{P}_L$. Therefore SPA is systematic except that it may consider its initial plan twice.

6 Empirical Study

We tested the SPA implementation using experiments from the PRIAR adaptation system, described in [Kambhampati and Hendler 1992]. PRIAR, like SPA, is based on the idea that a generative planning algorithm can be used to adapt library plans, provided that (1) the planner keeps some record of the reasons for its choices, and (2) the planner can retract as well as make those choices. PRIAR also uses a STRIPS-like action representation.

The PRIAR experiments pose two general classes of block-stacking problems, named respectively xBS and xBS1. x is an integer (ranging from 3 to 12) designating the number of blocks involved in that problem. The first class, e.g. 3BS, involve an initial state in which all the blocks are on the table and clear. Problems in the second class, e.g. 5BS1, have some blocks stacked on others in their initial states. Figure 4 shows the initial configurations for all of the problems considered in this paper. The experiments then involved comparing the planner's performance on a problem when the plan was generated from scratch with its performance when the solution to a smaller problem was used as a library plan. A typical problem would thus be 6BS→8BS1: using the library plan for 6BS to solve the 8BS1 problem.

We tried to imitate PRIAR's representation language as closely as possible: both representations. have two predicates, ON and CLEARTOP, and two primitive operators, PUT-BLOCK-ON-BLOCK and PUT-BLOCK-ON-TABLE[4]. PRIAR uses a hierarchical

---

[4]The domain theory in [Kambhampati and Hendler 1992, Appendix B] also mentions pyramids and blocks, as well as various rules like nothing could be ON a pyramid. Since no pyramids figured in the experiments from

representation, including non-primitive operators expressing concepts like "to get A on B, first generate a plan to clear A, then generate a plan to clear B, then execute the (primitive) PUT-BLOCK-ON-BLOCK operator." SPA has only the two operator descriptions. The closest analogue in SPA to hierarchical domain-specific knowledge is the notion of search-control information: application-supplied functions that determine which node in the graph of partial plans to consider next, what operators to introduce, in what order, how preconditions are to be achieved, and so on.

There is no obvious correspondence between PRIAR's hierarchical plan representation and SPA's control knowledge, so the question immediately arose as to what control information we should provide in running the experiments. SPA uses control information in three places: to decide which library plan to adapt, to decide which queue entry (partial plan) to consider next, and to decide which part of the partial plan to work on next. Since our experiments specify the library plan, the first source of control information is irrelevant to this discussion.

The experiments reported in this paper use a fairly sophisticated evaluation function, one that is specific to the block-stacking task. It favors plans in which ON relationships lower in the desired stack of blocks are achieved earlier in the plan (thus implementing a policy of building stacks from the bottom up). In the longer paper we report on the failure of several other evaluation functions.

Figure 5 shows, as a baseline, the planner running as a generator only on selected problems[5]. For the BS problems we see a systematic degradation in performance with added blocks: adding a new block to the situation tends to increase planning time by a factor of about 2.25, a result of having to consider about 1.5 times as many nodes. The time spent per node increases with plan size too, by a constant factor of about 1.5, since the cost of generating new plans and rating the plan both increase with the plan's size.

Performance on the BS1 problems was less consistent, since it turned out to depend strongly on how the blocks were configured in the initial state. 3BS1 and 6BS1 were easy, for example, because an ON relationship in the goal state was present in the initial state, and could be preserved. 5BS1 was of intermediate difficulty in that the initial ON relationship was irrelevant to the goal state. Our planner could not solve 7BS1 because a goal ON form *did* appear in the initial state, but

had to be made false subsequently in order to achieve the goal.

Figure 6 now shows the result of refitting a smaller library plan to a larger input problem[6]. The BS experiments showed consistent results: increasing the size of the library problem decreased time to solution by a factor that varied between 1.2 and 1.9. This was mainly due to a similar decrease in the number of nodes considered. Time spent per node was higher than for solving 8BS from scratch, presumably because the library plan started with more links, steps, and orderings, all of which tend to make plan-generation and ranking more expensive. This overhead meant that unless the library plan was fairly close to the target plan, it was actually more expensive to do the refit. We will discuss the reason for this phenomenon below.

Solving 8BS1 using a smaller BS1 problem showed a less consistent trend, but the same qualitative message: using a larger library plan tended to decrease the amount of time spent in modification, but once again the break-even point was disturbingly high: 5BS1 or better was necessary for a refit to perform better than from-scratch planning. The problem 6BSEZ was designed to be as close to the target 8BS1 as possible: the two problems were identical except for the addition in 8BS1 of two blocks and a superfluous ON form in the initial condition. This particular refit actually worked quite well, at least comparatively, supporting the (fairly obvious) hypothesis that similarities in the initial conditions should lead to more efficient refitting.

Despite the trend which shows improvement as library problems get bigger, the absolute numbers are discouraging: surely we should get some substantial benefit for using 6BS as a template for 8BS, especially since an insignificant amount of time is spent in the initial retrieval and fitting phase. Yet Figure 6 shows that the 6BS→8BS refit takes almost as much time as generating the 8BS plan from scratch.

Intuition tells us that since going from 6BS to 8BS simply involves putting two more blocks on the stack, the amount of additional time spent in refitting should be roughly equal to the time spent in generating 3BS from scratch. Figure 7 sheds light on the nature of the problem: at each search iteration the planner decides to resolve either an open condition or a threatened link. SPA resolves eight open conditions in doing the 6BS→8BS refit, which is exactly the number it resolves when generating 3BS from scratch. But the refit also requires it to resolve 21 *threat* conditions, which is the same number required to generate *the original 8BS from scratch*. The problem, therefore, is that the refit reduces the number of new conditions to plan for, but gets bogged down in verifying that the new steps actually work.

---

their Chapter 8, we omitted them from our representation. PRIAR's representation also includes several domain axioms, *e.g.* one that defines CLEARTOP as the absence of one block ON another. SPA has no domain axioms, so we incorporated that information into the operator and problem definitions.

[5]Time is seconds elapsed. "# Plans" is the total number of partial plans generated.

---

[6]We present here only problems involving refits to the 8BS and 8BS1, but results were similar for other input plans.

Problem	Time	# Plans	sec/plan
3BS	6.5	25	0.3
4BS	21.1	41	0.5
7BS	236.8	107	2.2
8BS	428.4	135	3.2
12BS	2784.5	277	10.1
3BS1	2.13	14	0.2
4BS1	44.1	49	0.9
5BS1	92.8	67	1.4
6BS1	101.3	69	1.5
7BS1	incomplete		
8BS1	892.5	163	5.5
9BS1	1880.3	230	8.1

Figure 5: Generative planning

Problem		Time			# Plans	sec/plan
Target	Library	Retrieval	Adaptation	Total		
8BS	3BS	0.6	757.1	757.7	121	6.3
8BS	4BS	1.5	688.5	690.0	107	6.4
8BS	5BS	5.1	535.6	540.7	88	6.1
8BS	6BS	15.1	334.6	349.7	64	5.4
8BS	7BS	47.3	141.5	188.8	35	5.3
8BS	8BS	3.4	0.1	3.5	2	1.8
8BS1	3BS1	0.4	1371.5	1371.9	163	8.4
8BS1	4BS1	2.0	1030.0	1032.0	103	10.0
8BS1	5BS1	5.5	839.0	843.5	92	9.16
8BS1	6BS1	13.3	850.9	864.2	92	9.39
8BS1	6BSEZ	2.2	654.0	656.2	45	14.6
8BS1	8BS1	3.5	0.2	3.7	2	1.9
8BS1	6BS	15.2	1302.5	1317.7	109	12.1
8BS1	7BS	27.0	746.5	773.5	70	11.0
8BS1	8BS	3.5	454.3	457.8	46	9.9
8BS	6BS1	3.6	1028.7	1032.3	101	10.22
8BS	8BS1	6.3	918.5	924.8	56	16.3

Figure 6: Library refitting

Target	Library	Time	Total Nodes	Iterations	Open	Threat
8BS	(none)	428.4	135	50	28	21
8BS	6BS	334.6	64	30	8	21
3BS	(none)	6.5	25	10	8	1

Figure 7: Comparing queue statistics

We can therefore report mixed results from the experiments: we can establish a systematic speedup from using a library refit, but the absolute amount of the speedup is unacceptably slow, for reasons noted above. Also deserving attention in future work is the search's (in both generative and adaptive cases) sensitivity to the problem's initial condition, and also (reported in [Hanks and Weld 1991]) the results' dependence on the search-control function.

7   Related Work

We have already mentioned the work on PRIAR [Kambhampati and Hendler 1992] as close to our own, in particular its use of the generative planner to provide library plans and dependencies that can later be retracted. PRIAR and SPA also share the same STRIPS-like action representation. The main difference between the two approaches is the underlying planning algorithm: SPA uses a SNLP [Barrett *et al.* 1991], a lifted version of McAllester's [1991] simplified TWEAK algorithm [Chapman 1987]. PRIAR, on the other hand, uses a variant of the NONLIN hierarchical planner [Tate 1977].

As a result, PRIAR's plan representation and the algorithms that manipulate them are more complicated than those in SPA. There are three different types of validations (relationships between nodes in the plan graph), for example—filter condition, precondition, and phantom goal—as well as different "reduction levels" for the plan that represents a hierarchical decomposition of its structure, along with five different strategies for repairing validation failures. Contrast this representation with SPA's simple plan representation consisting of causal links and step-order constraints.

The fact that PRIAR is more complicated makes it harder to prove formal properties of the algorithm. [Kambhampati and Hendler 1992] prove a soundness result and argue informally for a property like completeness: "we claim that our framework covers all possible modifications for plans that are describable within the action representation described in this paper." (p. 39) It is not clear the exact relationship between this property and our completeness property, but PRIAR requires a large set of explicitly provided reduction schemata. PRIAR carries no guarantee of systematicity: there seems to be no guarantee that a combination of repairs would not cause it to consider the same plan more than once.

Although PRIAR is a more complicated system than SPA, it performs much better, both in absolute terms and in terms of the speedup it offers for plan reuse. The last numbers are particularly interesting, since they indicate that something in PRIAR's validation structure is preventing it from experiencing the overhead slowdown we noted in Section 6. We are currently attempting to analyze the nature of the performance difference and hope to incorporate those ideas into the SPA framework.

The work on adaptation for case-based planning has mainly been concerned with finding good strategies for applying adaptations; these strategies generally try to exploit the causal structure of the planning domain. CHEF [Hammond 1990], for example, confronts the problem of repairing a plan that has been showed by a simulator to have failed, and uses a memory structure called a TOP to select between possible repair strategies.

GORDIUS [Simmons 1988], though not strictly a case-based planner (it generates an initial solution to a problem by composing stored solutions to subproblems), uses transformational techniques to make the retrieved solution solve the input problem. GORDIUS uses a simulator to find bugs in the plan, the nature of which suggest repairs.

Both of these approaches start with a complete plan that fails to satisfy the goal, and use transformations to generate a new complete plan, which hopefully comes closer to satisfying it. In contrast with SPA, there is no notion of partial plan, and no explicit notion of retracting a commitment. Trying to unify the two approaches is an interesting topic for future research: SPA offers a clean framework in which to analyze transformational planning operations. Our preliminary investigation indicates that ten of CHEF's seventeen repair strategies are relevant given our assumption of the STRIPS action representation. Of these ten transformations, all but one can be mapped into a sequence of at most two SPA operations (e.g., a single retraction followed by a single extension). This suggests that CHEF's apparent success is due more to the power of its heuristic search than it is to the ability to "jump" long distances in plan space.

8   Conclusion

We have presented the SPA algorithm, which is based on the idea that the adaptation of library plans is really a process of appropriately retracting old planning constraints and adding new constraints to make the library plan skeleton solve the problem at hand.

The algorithm is clean, and has nice formal properties: soundness, completeness, and systematicity. It also makes clear the distinction between domain-independent algorithms and the application of domain-dependent control knowledge. As such it is an excellent vehicle for studying the problem of case-based planning.

Preliminary experiments indicate, however, that the simple model of locally retracting and adding constraints does not offer acceptably good performance.

The experiments in Section 6 seem to indicate that we need a better control mechanism than local retraction and addition of constraints guided by a simple search-control function. Providing a more effective control mechanism will lead us to try to incorporate adaptation methods used by existing case-based planners, which make better use of the domain's causal structure and allow better-informed manipulation of the plan graph.

We are currently using a modified version of SPA to perform plan revision during execution when sensor operations indicate that underlying assumptions about the state of the world have been violated. Future work also includes trying to implement within our framework CHEF's transformational repair strategies [Hammond 1990], investigate the use of hierarchical plan organization [Kambhampati and Hendler 1992], and also to extend the representation language beyond the present STRIPS operators.

Acknowledgements

This research was improved by discussions with Tony Barrett and Oren Etzioni. Ying Sun provided helpful comments on a draft of this paper. This work was funded in part by National Science Foundation Grants IRI-8902010, IRI-8957302, and IRI-9008670, by Office of Naval Research Grant 90-J-1904, and by a grant from the Xerox corporation.

References

[Barrett et al. 1991] A. Barrett, S. Soderland, and D. Weld. The Effect of Step-Order Representations on Planning. Technical Report 91-05-06, University of Washington, Department of Computer Science and Engineering, June 1991.

[Chapman 1987] D. Chapman. Planning for Conjunctive Goals. Artificial Intelligence, 32(3):333–377, July 1987.

[Fikes and Nilsson 1971] R. Fikes and N. Nilsson. STRIPS: A new Approach to the Application of Theorem Proving to Problem Solving. Artificial Intelligence, 2(3/4), 1971.

[Hammond 1989] Kristian Hammond. Case-Based Planning: Viewing Planning as a Memory Task. Academic Press, 1989.

[Hammond 1990] K. Hammond. Explaining and Repairing Plans That Fail. Artificial Intelligence, 45, 1990.

[Hanks and Weld 1991] Steven Hanks and Daniel S. Weld. Systematic adaptation for case-based planning: Algorithm description, formal properties, and empirical results. Technical Report 91-10-03, University of Washington, Department of Computer Science and Engineering, October 1991.

[Kambhampati and Hendler 1992] S. Kambhampati and J. Hendler. A Validation Structure Based Theory of Plan Modification and Reuse. Artificial Intelligence, to appear, 1992.

[McAllester and Rosenblitt 1991] D. McAllester and D. Rosenblitt. Systematic Nonlinear Planning. In Proceedings of AAAI-91, pages 634–639, July 1991.

[Simmons 1988] R. Simmons. A Theory of Debugging Plans and Interpretations. In Proceedings of AAAI-88, pages 94–99, August 1988.

[Tate 1977] A. Tate. Generating Project Networks. In Proceedings of IJCAI-77, pages 888–893, 1977.

Predicting and Explaining Success and Task Duration in the Phoenix Planner

David M. Hart
Experimental Knowledge Systems Laboratory
Department of Computer Science
University of Massachusetts
Amherst, MA 01003
dhart@cs.umass.edu

Paul R. Cohen
cohen@cs.umass.edu

Abstract

Phoenix is a multi-agent planning system that fights simulated forest-fires. In this paper we describe an experiment with Phoenix in which we uncover factors that affect the planner's behavior and test predictions about the planner's robustness against variations in some of these factors. We also introduce a technique—path analysis—for constructing and testing causal explanations of the planner's behavior.

1 INTRODUCTION

It is difficult to predict or even explain the behavior of any but the simplest AI programs. A program will solve one problem readily, but make a complete hash of an apparently similar problem. For example, our Phoenix planner, which fights simulated forest fires, will contain one fire in a matter of hours but fail to contain another under very similar conditions. We therefore hesitate to claim that the Phoenix planner "works." The claim would not be very informative, anyway: we would much rather be able to predict and explain Phoenix's behavior in a wide range of conditions (Cohen 1991). In this paper we describe an experiment with Phoenix in which we uncover factors that affect the planner's behavior and test predictions about the planner's robustness against variations in some factors. We also introduce a technique—path analysis—for constructing and testing causal explanations of the planner's behavior. Our results are specific to the Phoenix planner and will not necessarily generalize to other planners or environments, but our techniques are general and should enable others to derive comparable results for themselves.

In overview, Section 2 introduces the Phoenix planner; Section 3 describes an experiment in which we identify factors that probably influence the planner's behavior; and Section 4 discusses results and one sense in which the

planner works "as designed." But these results leave much unexplained: although Section 4 identifies some factors that affect the success and the duration of firefighting episodes, it does not explain how these factors interact. Section 5 shows how correlations among the factors that affect behavior can be decomposed to test causal models that include these factors.

2 PHOENIX OVERVIEW

Phoenix is a multi-agent planning system that fights simulated forest-fires. The simulation uses terrain, elevation, and feature data from Yellowstone National Park and a model of fire spread from the National Wildlife Coordinating Group Fireline Handbook (National Wildlife Coordinating Group 1985). The spread of fires is influenced by wind and moisture conditions, changes in elevation and ground cover, and is impeded by natural and man-made boundaries such as rivers, roads, and fireline. The Fireline Handbook also prescribes many of the characteristics of our firefighting agents, such as rates of movement and effectiveness of various firefighting techniques. For example, the rate at which bulldozers dig fireline varies with the terrain. Phoenix is a real-time simulation environment—Phoenix agents must think and act as the fire spreads. Thus, if it takes too long to decide on a course of action, or if the environment changes while a decision is being made, a plan is likely to fail.

One Phoenix agent, the Fireboss, coordinates the firefighting activities of all field agents, such as bulldozers and watchtowers. The Fireboss is essentially a thinking agent,[1] using reports from field agents to form and maintain a global assessment of the world. Based on these reports (e.g., fire sightings, position updates, task

---

[1] Though it has the same architecture as other agents, it has few sensors or effectors and is immobile. For a detailed description of the Phoenix agent architecture and planning mechanisms see Cohen et al. 1989.

progress), it selects and instantiates fire-fighting plans and directs field agents in the execution of plan subtasks.

A new fire is typically spotted by a watchtower, which reports observed fire size and location to the Fireboss. With this information, the Fireboss selects an appropriate fire-fighting plan from its plan library. Typically these plans dispatch bulldozer agents to the fire to dig fireline. An important first step in each of the three plans in the experiment described below is to decide where fireline should be dug. The Fireboss projects the spread of the fire based on prevailing weather conditions, then considers the number of available bulldozers and the proximity of natural boundaries. It projects a bounding polygon of fireline to be dug and assigns segments to bulldozers based on a periodically updated assessment of which segments will be reached by the spreading fire soonest. Because there are usually many more segments than bulldozers, each bulldozer digs multiple segments. The Fireboss assigns segments to bulldozers one at a time, then waits for each bulldozer to report that it has completed its segment before assigning another. This ensures that segment assignment incorporates the most up-to-date information about overall progress and changes in the prevailing conditions.

Once a plan is set into motion, any number of problems might arise that require the Fireboss's intervention. The types of problems and mechanisms for handling them are described in Howe & Cohen 1990, but one is of particular interest here: As bulldozers build fireline, the Fireboss compares their progress to expected progress.[2] If their actual progress falls too far below expectations, a plan failure occurs, and (under the experiment scenario described here) a new plan is generated. The new plan uses the same bulldozers to fight the fire and exploits any fireline that has already been dug. We call this error recovery method *replanning*. Phoenix is built to be an adaptable planning system that can recover from plan failures (Howe & Cohen 1990). Although it has many failure-recovery methods, replanning is the focus of the experiment described in the next section.

3   IDENTIFYING THE FACTORS THAT AFFECT PERFORMANCE

We designed an experiment with two purposes. A *confirmatory* purpose was to test predictions that the planner's performance is sensitive to some environmental con-

ditions but not others.[3] In particular, we expected performance to degrade when we change a fundamental relationship between the planner and its environment—the amount of time the planner is allowed to think relative to the rate at which the environment changes—and not be sensitive to common dynamics in the environment such as weather, and particularly, wind speed. We tested two specific predictions: 1) that performance would not degrade or would degrade gracefully as wind speed increased; and 2) that the planner would not be robust to changes in the Fireboss's thinking speed due to a bottleneck problem described below. An *exploratory* purpose of the experiment was to identify the factors in the Fireboss architecture and Phoenix environment that most affected the planner's behavior, leading to the causal model developed in Section 5.

The Fireboss must select plans, instantiate them, dispatch agents and monitor their progress, and respond to plan failures as the fire burns. The rate at which the Fireboss thinks is determined by a parameter called the *Real Time Knob*. By adjusting the Real Time Knob we allow more or less simulation time to elapse per unit CPU time, effectively adjusting the speed at which the Fireboss thinks relative to the rate at which the environment changes.

The Fireboss services bulldozer requests for assignments, providing each bulldozer with a task directive for each new fireline segment it builds. The Fireboss can become a bottleneck when the arrival rate of bulldozer task requests is high or when its thinking speed is slowed by adjusting the Real Time Knob. This bottleneck sometimes causes the overall digging rate to fall below that required to complete the fireline polygon before the fire reaches it, which causes replanning (see Section 2). In the worst case, a Fireboss bottleneck can cause a thrashing effect in which plan failures occur repeatedly because the Fireboss can't assign bulldozers during replanning fast enough to keep the overall digging rate at effective levels. We designed our experiment to explore the effects of this bottleneck on system performance and to confirm our prediction that performance would vary in proportion to the manipulation of thinking speed. Because the current design of the Fireboss is not sensitive to changes in thinking speed, we expect it to take longer to fight fires and to fail more often to contain them as thinking speed slows.

In contrast, we expect Phoenix to be able to fight fires at different wind speeds. It might take longer and sacrifice more area burned at high wind speeds, but we expect this effect to be proportional as wind speed increases and we

---

[2] Expectations about progress are stored in *envelopes*. Envelopes represent the range of acceptable progress, given the knowledge used to construct the plan. If actual progress falls outside this range, and envelope *violation* occurs, invoking error recovery mechanisms (Cohen, Hart & St. Amant 1992, Hart, Anderson & Cohen 1990).

---

[3] The term "planner" here refers collectively to all Phoenix agents, as distinct from the Fireboss agent.

expect Phoenix to succeed equally often at a range of wind speeds, since it was designed to do so.

3.1 EXPERIMENT DESIGN

We created a straightforward fire fighting scenario that controlled for many of the variables known to affect the planner's performance. In each trial, one fire of a known initial size was set at the same location (an area with no natural boundaries) at the same time (relative to the start of the simulation). Four bulldozers were used to fight it. The wind's speed and direction were set initially and not varied during the trial. Thus, in each trial, the Fireboss receives the same fire report, chooses a fire-fighting plan, and dispatches the bulldozers to implement it. A trial ends when the bulldozers have successfully surrounded the fire or after 120 hours without success.

The experiment's first dependent variable then is Success, which is true if the fire is contained, and false otherwise. A second dependent variable is shutdown time (SD), the time at which the trial was stopped. For successful trials, shutdown time tells us how long it took to contain the fire.[4]

Two independent variables were wind speed (WS) and the setting of the Fireboss's Real Time Knob (RTK). A third variable, the first plan chosen by the Fireboss in a trial (FPLAN), varied randomly between trials. It was not expected to influence performance, but because it did, we treat it here as an independent variable.

WS: The settings of WS in the experiment were 3, 6, and 9 kilometers per hour. As wind speed increases, fire spreads more quickly in all directions, and most quickly downwind. The Fireboss compensates for higher values of wind speed by directing bulldozers to build fireline further from the fire.

RTK: The default setting of RTK for Phoenix agents allows them to execute 1 CPU second of Lisp code for every 5 minutes that elapses in the simulation. We varied the Fireboss's RTK setting in different trials (leaving the settings for all other agents at the default). We started at a ratio of 1 simulation-minute/cpu-second, a thinking speed 5 times as fast as the default, and varied the setting over values of 1, 3, 5, 7, 9, 11, and 15 simulation-minutes/cpu-second. These values range from 5 times the normal speed at a setting of 1 down to one-third the normal speed at 15. The values of RTK reported here are rescaled. The normal thinking speed (5) has been set to RTK=1, and the other settings are relative to normal. The scaled values (in order of increasing thinking speed) are .33, .45, .56, .71, 1, 1.67,

and 5. RTK was set at the start of each trial and held constant throughout.

FPLAN: The Fireboss randomly selects one of three plans as its first plan in each trial. The plans differ mainly in the way they project fire spread and decide where to dig fireline. SHELL is aggressive, assuming an optimistic combination of low fire spread and fast progress on the part of bulldozers. MODEL is conservative in its expectations, assuming a high rate of spread and a lower rate of progress. The third, MBIA, generally makes an assessment intermediate with respect to the others.[5] When replanning is necessary, the Fireboss again chooses randomly from among the same three plans.[6]

We adopted a basic factorial design, systematically varying the values of WS and RTK. Because we had not anticipated a significant effect of FPLAN, we allowed it to vary randomly.

4   RESULTS FOR SUCCESS RATE AND SHUTDOWN TIME

We collected data for 343 trials, of which 215 succeeded and 128 failed, for an overall success rate of 63%. Tables 1a-c break down successes and failures for each setting of the independent variables RTK, WS, and FPLAN. Column S in these tables is the number of Successes, F is the number of Failures, and Tot is the total number of trials. Certain trends emerge in these data that confirm our earlier predictions. For example, in Table 1a, the success rate improves steadily as the thinking speed of the Fireboss increases. However, other patterns are less clear, such as the differences for each setting of WS in Table 1b. How do we know if these values are significantly different? For a *categorical* dependent variable such as Success (which has only two possible values), a chi-square test (x^2) will determine whether the observed pattern is statistically significant.

Figures 1a-c show the success rates for each setting of each independent variable. The table categories Success and Failure are broken down further into those trials which did not replan and those that did.

---

[4] Several other dependent variables were measured, most notably Area Burned. However, using Area Burned to assess performance requires stricter experimental controls over such factors as choice of fire-fighting plan than were used here.

---

[5] The first plan of this variety developed in Phoenix was called Multiple-Bulldozer-Indirect-Attack, or MBIA, which signified a coordination of bulldozers working at some distance from the fire on fireline segments determined by the Fireboss's projections. SHELL is a variant of MBIA that builds a tighter shell of fireline, thus reducing the cost of forest burned. MODEL is another variant of MBIA that applies an analytical model of fire projection (Cohen 1990). It makes conservative projections at the default parameters used in this experiment.

[6] The same high-level plans can be used in the initial attack on a fire and on subsequent tries. When used in replanning, a plan is adapted to take advantage of any fireline that has already been dug near the fire. It is also based on updated conditions such as the current size and shape of the fire.

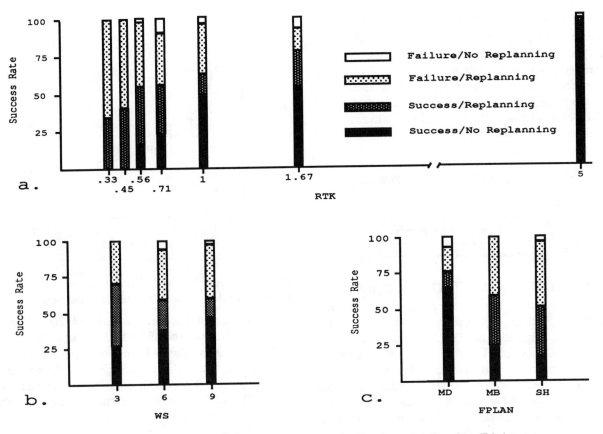

Figure 1: Successes by a) Real Time Knob, b) Wind Speed, and c) First Plan Tried

4.1 EFFECT OF INDEPENDENT VARIABLES ON SUCCESS

Table 1a shows successes by the independent variable RTK. A chi-square test on the Success-Failure x RTK contingency table in Table 1a is highly significant ($X^2(6) = 49.081$, $p < 0.001$), indicating that RTK strongly influences the relative frequency of successes and failures. At the fastest thinking speed for the Fireboss, RTK=5, the success rate is 98%, but at the slowest rate, RTK=.33, the success rate is only 33%. Figure 1a shows graphically that as RTK goes down (i.e., thinking speed decreases) the success rate declines. At RTK=1, the default setting, 63% of the trials were successful. Note how rapidly the *success of the initial plan* decreases—for RTK ≤ .45, no trial succeeds without replanning. However, the overall success rate declines more slowly as replanning is used to recover from the bottleneck effect described in Section 3. If we compare the rate of success without replanning to that with replanning in Figure 1a, we see that replanning buffers the Phoenix planner, allowing it to absorb the effect of changes in Fireboss RTK without failing. This effect is statistically highly significant.

Table 1a: Trials Partitioned by Real Time Knob.

RTK	S	F	Tot
.33	10	20	30
.45	14	19	33
.56	22	18	40
.71	54	42	96
1	27	16	43
1.67	38	11	49
5	50	2	52

Table 1b shows successes by wind speed. The small differences in success are marginal ($X^2(2) = 5.354$, $p < 0.069$), as we predicted in Section 3. Figure 1b shows a curious trend—as WS increases, the success rate for the first plan goes up, while the success rate in trials involving replanning diminishes. The increase in success rate for the first plan occurs because as WS increases, Phoenix overestimates the growth of the fire and plans a more conservative containing fireline.

Table 1b: Trials Partitioned by Wind Speed.

WS	S	F	Tot
3	85	35	120
6	67	50	117
9	63	43	106

Table 1c shows successes by first plan tried. Differences in success are highly significant ($X^2(2) = 16.183$, $p < 0.001$), which we had not expected when designing the experiment. As shown in Figure 1c, SHELL has a very low success rate without replanning, reflecting its aggressive character, while the conservative MODEL has an initial success rate of 65%. MBIA's initial success rate is slightly better than SHELL's (though the difference is not statistically significant).

Table 1c: Trials Partitioned by First Plan Tried.

FPLAN	S	F	Tot
shell	69	62	131
mbia	48	35	83
model	98	31	129

4.2 EFFECT OF RTK ON SHUTDOWN TIME

Figure 2 shows the effect of RTK on the dependent variable Shutdown time (SD). The interesting aspect of this behavior is the transition at RTK=1. SD increases gradually between RTK=5 and 1, and the 95% confidence intervals around the mean values overlap. Below 1, however, the slope changes markedly and the confidence intervals are almost disjoint from those for values above 1. This shift in slope and value range for SD suggests a threshold effect in Phoenix as the Fireboss's thinking speed is reduced below the normal setting of RTK. The cost of resources in Phoenix is proportional to the time spent fighting fires, so a threshold effect such as this represents a significant discontinuity in the cost function for resources used. For this reason we pursued the cause(s) of this discontinuity by modeling the effects of the independent variables on several key endogenous variables,[7] and through them on SD, with the intent of building a causal model of the influences on SD.

5 INFLUENCE OF ENDOGENOUS VARIABLES ON SHUTDOWN TIME

We measured about 40 endogenous variables in the experiment described above, but three are of particular interest in this analysis: the amount of fireline built by the bulldozers (FB), the number of fire-fighting plans tried by the Fireboss for a given trial (#PLANS), and the overall utilization of the Fireboss's thinking resources (OVUT).

---

[7] A variable is called endogenous if it is influenced by independent variables and influences, perhaps indirectly through other endogenous variables, dependent variables.

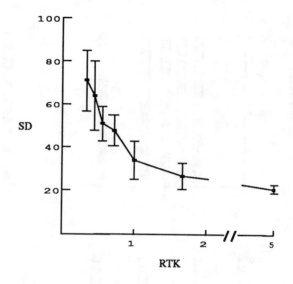

Figure 2: Mean Shutdown Time (in Hours) by Real Time Knob. Error Bars Show 95% Confidence Intervals.

FB: The value of this variable is the amount of fireline actually built at the end of the trial. FB sets a lower limit on SD, because bulldozers have a maximum rate at which they can dig. Thus, when the Fireboss is thinking at the fastest speed and servicing bulldozers with little wait time, SD will be primarily determined by how much fireline must be built.

#PLANS: When a trial ran to completion without replanning, #PLANS was set to 1. Each time the Fireboss replanned, #PLANS was incremented. #PLANS is an important indicator of the level of difficulty the planner has fighting a particular fire. It also directly affects FB. As described in Section 2, replanning involves projecting a new polygon for the bulldozers to dig. Typically the new polygon is larger than the previous one, because the fire has now spread to a point where the old one is too close to the fire. Thus, the amount of fireline to be dug tends to increase with the number of replanning episodes.

OVUT: This variable, overall utilization, is the ratio of the time the Fireboss spends thinking to the total duration of a trial. Thinking activities include monitoring the environment and agents' activities, deciding where fireline should be dug, and coordinating agents' tasks (Cohen et al. 1989). The Fireboss is sometimes idle, having done everything on its agenda, and so it waits until a message arrives from a field agent or enough time passes that another action becomes eligible. We expected to see OVUT increase as RTK decreases; that is, as the Fireboss's thinking speed slows down, it requires a greater and greater proportion of the time available to do the cognitive work required by the scenario. Replanning only adds to the Fireboss's cognitive workload.

5.1 REGRESSION ANALYSIS

Having identified these variables, we set about quantifying their effects using multiple regression.[8] We regressed SD on WS, RTK, FPLAN, OVUT, #PLANS and FB. These factors accounted for 76% of the variance in SD. Standardized beta coefficients are often cited as measures of the relative influence of factors; in Table 2a they tell us that FB has the largest influence on SD (beta = .759) , with RTK and OVUT following close behind. But if the beta's represent the strength of influence, they are surprising. OVUT has a negative influence on SD, which is counterintuitive and appears to contradict the positive correlation (.42) between them in Table 2b. WS and #PLANS have virtually no influence on SD, even though #PLANS is strongly correlated with SD (.718). And although WS is essentially uncorrelated with SD (-.053), it is correlated with FB (.363), which in turn is strongly correlated with SD (.755). Finally, WS and RTK are correlated in Table 2b (.282), which seems impossible given that they were varied systematically. In short, the regression analysis and the correlation matrix contain counterintuitive entries. We will see this is because regression is based on an implicit model, one that almost certainly does not correspond to the structure of Phoenix.

Table 2a: Regression For Y: SD on X's: WS, RTK, FPLAN, OVUT, #PLANS, FB

	B	Beta	t statistic of B
WS	-2.564	-0.261	-5.334 p < .001
RTK	-8.057	-0.580	-6.503 p < .001
FPLAN	.968	.035	.827 p < .283
OVUT	-.347	-.438	-4.879 p < .001
#PLANS	3.411	.115	1.742 p < .088
FB	.002	.759	11.641 p < .001

Table 2b: Correlation Coefficients

	WS	RTK	FPLAN	OVUT	#PLNS	FB
WS	1.000					
RTK	.282	1.000				
FPLAN	.117	.151	1.000			
OVUT	-.257	-.913	-.016	1.000		
#PLNS	-.183	-.409	-.432	.379	1.000	
FB	.363	-.249	-.088	.288	.658	1.000
SD	-.053	-.484	-.193	.420	.718	.755

---

[8] Multiple regression builds a linear model of the effects of any number of X variables on a *continuous* variable Y, which in this case is SD. It fits a hyperplane to the data in an n-dimensional space using the least-squares method, where n = the number of X variables + 1. One of the measures produced by multiple regression is R^2, which is the percentage of variance accounted for by the linear model.

5.2 PATH ANALYSIS

A technique called *path analysis* (Asher 1983, Li 1975) lets us view correlation coefficients of the variables in Table 2b as sums of hypothesized influences among factors. Consider the surprising result that wind speed (WS) is essentially uncorrelated with shut-down time (SD). We expected WS to have two possible effects on SD:

Effect 1. If WS increases then the fire burns faster, and this means more fireline must be built (i.e., FB increases), which will take longer. Therefore increasing WS should increase SD.

Effect 2. For high wind speeds, if a fire isn't contained relatively quickly, then it might not be contained at all. For example, if a fire has been burning for 60 hours or more, and WS = 3, then the probability of the fire being eventually contained is .375. But if WS = 6, the probability of eventually containing an old fire is only .2, and if WS = 9, the probability drops to .13. We measured SD for successful trials only, because, by definition, an unsuccessful trial is one that exceeds a specified SD without containing the fires. But successful containment of old fires is relatively unlikely at higher wind speeds, so as WS increases, we see fewer older fires contained, thus fewer high values of SD. This leads us to expect a negative correlation between WS and SD. Note that this correlation represents an effect of missing data, not a true negative causal relationship between WS and SD.

Path analysis enables us to test a model in which the correlation $r_{WS\,SD}$ is composed of Effect 1 and Effect 2, which cancel each other out. Consider, for example, the path diagram in Figure 3. It shows WS positively influencing the amount of fireline that gets built (FB), and FB positively influencing SD (we will shortly describe how the numbers are derived). This path, WS→FB→SD, corresponds to Effect 1, above, and is called an *indirect* effect of WS on SD, mediated by FB. At the same time, WS *directly* and negatively influences SD on the path WS→SD, corresponding to Effect 2. Figure 3 shows the strength of WS→SD is -.377. The rules of path analysis dictate that the strength of WS→FB→SD is the product of the strengths of the constituent links, WS→FB and FB→SD, that is, (.363)(.892) = .328. The estimate of the correlation between WS and SD, $\hat{r}_{WS\,SD}$, is obtained by summing the direct and indirect effects, that is, .328 – .377 = -0.53. This is the sum of all legal ways for WS to influence SD given the structure in Figure 3. For the model in Figure 3, $\hat{r}_{WS\,SD} = r_{WS\,SD}$, but this doesn't happen in general.

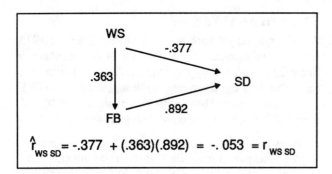

Figure 3: A Simple Path Diagram Showing Three
Variables and Their Influences.

Thus we decompose the correlation $r_{WS\,SD}$ into two additive effects: WS increases FB as expected and decreases SD (spuriously, as noted above) as expected, and these effects cancel.

Path analysis involves three steps:

1) Propose a *path model* (such as the one in Figure 3). The model represents causal influences with directed arrows (e.g., FB→SD) and correlations with undirected links (see Figure 4a).

2) Derive *path coefficients* (such as -.377, .363 and .892). The magnitude of a path coefficient is interpreted as a measure of causal influence.

3) Estimate the strength of the relationship between two factors (such as WS and SD) by multiplying path coefficients along paths between the factors and summing the products over all legal paths between the factors.

Step 3 is entirely algorithmic given some simple rules (described below) that define legal paths. Step 2 involves some judgment because some models allow multiple ways to derive one or more path coefficients. A model is a concise statement of hypothesized causal influences among factors, and the space of models grows combinatorially with the number of factors, so step 1, proposing a model, is apt to benefit from knowledge about the system we are modeling.[9]

All three steps will be clearer if we briefly describe the relationship between multiple linear regression and path analysis. They are basically the same thing: both derive path coefficients for a model. The difference is simply that one particular model is implicit in multiple regression. Consider an elaboration of Figure 3, in which we add the RTK as an additional causal influence on SD. Figure 4a shows the implicit model fit by multiple regression, and

Figure 4b shows a model that we think is a better representation of what is actually going on in Phoenix.

The regression model assumes that all predictor variables (WS, FB, RTK) are correlated, and assumes all directly influence the criterion variable (SD). Correlated variables are linked by undirected paths, which are labeled with the correlations. Table 2b presents the correlation matrix derived from our experiment. Multiple regression generates standard partial regression (beta) coefficients for each direct path between the predictor and criterion variables. These are -.291, .81 and -.2 in Figure 4a. Each represents a standardized measure of the influence of one predictor variable on the criterion variable with the effects of the other predictor variables held constant. The resulting regression equation in standard format is $\hat{SD}$ = .81 FB - .29 WS - .2 RTK. Because the regression coefficients are standardized they can be compared: a unit change in FB produces .81 units change in SD, whereas a unit change in WS produces -.29 units change in SD. FB is the stronger influence.

Figure 4a represents a decomposition of the correlations between SD and the other variables. The correlations can be reconstituted by summing the influences along paths just as we did in Figure 3. Path analysis has three rules for identifying paths:

1) No more than one undirected link can be part of a path (e.g., FB → RTK → SD is legal, but WS→FB→RTK→SD isn't)

2) A path cannot go through a node twice.

3) A path can go backward on a directed link, but not after it has gone forward on another link (e.g. FB ← WS → SD in Figure 4b is legal but #PLANS→FB←WS in Figure 5 isn't).

The strength of each multilink path is just the product of its constituent coefficients, so the strength of the path FB→RTK→SD in Figure 4a is (-.249)(-.2) = .0498. The estimated correlation between a predictor and a criterion variable is the sum of the strengths of the paths that connect them. Thus

$$\hat{r}_{FB\,SD} = .755 = \;\; .81 \qquad\qquad\quad\;\; \textit{direct FB→SD path}$$
$$+ \; (.363)\,(-.291) \qquad \textit{FB→WS→SD}$$
$$+ \; (-.249)\,(-.2) \qquad\;\; \textit{FB→RTK→SD}$$

So multiple regression follows the three steps of path analysis. First, propose a model, specifically, a model in

---

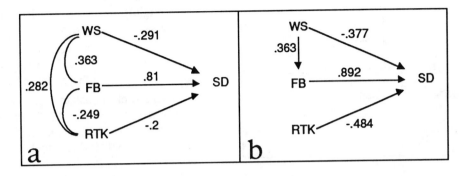

Figure 4: A Shows the Path Model Implicit in Multiple Regression. The Path Model in B
Better Captures the Relationships Among These Variables in Phoenix.

which all predictor variables are correlated and directly linked to the criterion. Second, estimate path coefficients, specifically, calculate standard partial regression coefficients for the direct paths between predictor and criterion variables, and label the undirected links with the appropriate correlations. Third, estimate the correlations between each predictor and criterion variable by identifying legal paths between them, calculating the strength of each path, and summing the path strengths. In multiple regression, the estimated correlations are always identical to the actual correlations.

Multiple regression is a fine way to decompose correlations into their component influences *if you believe that multiple regression's implicit causal model represents your system*. Multiple regression is just path analysis on this implicit model, so if you don't believe the model you can propose another and run path analysis on it. This is what we did in Figure 4b. We know that WS and RTK are independent because our experiment varied them independently in a factorial design. (The reason they are correlated is the sampling bias identified as effect 2, above.) So we want to test a model in which WS influences SD directly and through FB, and RTK influences SD directly. The only question is how to estimate the path coefficients. The basic rules, which yield the coefficients in Figure 4b, are:

1) If W and X are uncorrelated causes of the criterion variable Y, then the path coefficients ρ_{YX} and ρ_{YW} are just the correlation coefficients r_{YX} and r_{YW}, respectively.

2) If W and X are correlated causes of the criterion variable Y, then the path coefficients ρ_{YX} and ρ_{YW} are the standard partial regression coefficients $b'_{YX \cdot W}$ and $b'_{YW \cdot X}$, respectively, obtained from the regression of Y on X and W.

Is Figure 4b a better model than Figure 4a? We can answer the question in two ways. The statistical answer is that no model fits the data better, in terms of accounting

for variance in the criterion variable, than the regression model. But this is hardly surprising when you consider that the regression model assumes everything influences everything else. The system analyst's answer is that we don't want models in which everything influences everything else: we want models in which some links are left out, in which causal influences are localized, not dissipated through a network of correlations. Let's ask, then, what it means for one such model to be better than another. Again, the judgment depends on how well each accounts for the variance in the criterion variable and how accurately each estimates the correlations between variables, and, how well each represents what we surmise to be the causal structure of our system. Clearly, these criteria interact. We can imagine a model that fits the data well but cannot represent what we know to be the causal structure, but often we explore different plausible causal structures by seeing how well each fits the data.

The structure in Figure 5 represents one of our first guesses at the causal structure that relates WS, FPLAN and RTK to SD. We expected WS and FPLAN to each directly influence both #PLANS and FB, but neither to directly influence SD. We also expected RTK to influence #PLANS and SD directly. We thought #PLANS might influence FB and SD. We made these guesses based on regression analyses, the correlation matrix in Table 2b, some of the graphs shown earlier, and our general knowledge about how the Phoenix planner works.

After estimating the path coefficients as shown in Figure 5, we estimated the correlations $\hat{r}_{SDi}$ between SD and each variable i. The estimates and the actual correlations are as follows:

	WS	FPLAN	RTK	#PLANS	FB
$\hat{r}_{SDi}$	.118	-.197	-.533	.719	.778
r_{SDi}	-.053	-.193	-.484	.718	.755

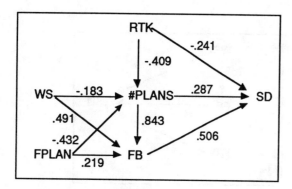

Figure 5: Path Model Relating Variables Influencing Shutdown Time.

Except for the disparity between the estimated and actual correlations between WS and SD, this model accounts pretty well for the actual correlations. At this point, we wanted to explain the influence of RTK on #PLANS. Why should decreasing RTK (slowing the Fireboss's thinking speed) increase the number of plans? One explanation is something like thrashing: There is always the possibility that the environment will change in such a way that a plan is no longer appropriate, but this is much more likely when the environment changes rapidly relative to planning effort (i.e., when RTK is decreased). Thus, decreasing RTK means the Fireboss will have to throw away plans before they make much progress, resulting in an increase in #PLANS. To test this we introduced another variable, OVUT, which measures the percentage of time in a trial that the Fireboss spends planning. We expected OVUT to decrease with RTK, supporting the thrashing explanation. Figure 6 shows a modification of Figure 5, with the path RTK→OVUT→#PLANS instead of RTK→#PLANS.

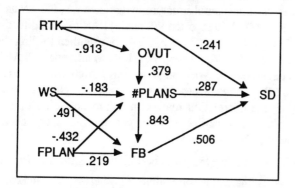

Figure 6: Adding the Endogenous Variable OVUT.

For this model, estimated correlations between SD and all the other variables are not appreciably different than they were for the model in Figure 5. But it appears that the variable OVUT does not add much to our understanding of thrashing, because it is completely determined by RTK.

Consider what happens when we derive path coefficients for a slightly different model (Figure 7). In this case, OVUT has almost no influence ($r_{OVUT\#PLANS} = .032$) on #PLANS. Recall, however, that this path coefficient is the standardized partial regression coefficient $b'_{OVUT\ \#PLANS \bullet RTK}$; that is, the effect of OVUT on #PLANS with RTK held constant. The fact that this number is nearly zero means that OVUT has no effect on #PLANS *when RTK is held constant*; in other words, the effect of OVUT on #PLANS is due entirely to RTK.

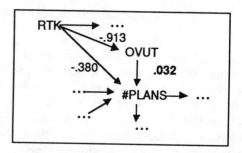

Figure 7: Showing the Effect of OVUT on #PLANS is Due Entirely to RTK.

6 CONCLUSION

We have presented results of an experiment with the Phoenix planner that confirm our predictions that its performance would be sensitive to some environmental conditions but not others. We have shown that the planner is not sensitive to variation in initial wind speed, a common environmental dynamic it faces. On the other hand, our results show that performance degrades as we change a fundamental relationship between the planner and its environment–the rate at which the Fireboss agent thinks. As we slowed the Fireboss's thinking speed in the experiment by decreasing RTK, performance degraded to the point where no plan succeeded on the first try. However, the planner was still able to succeed in many cases by replanning. While the success rate using replanning also degrades, replanning acts as a buffer, preventing the planner from failing catastrophically when it can't think fast enough to keep up with the environment. The data also show that replanning exerts a large influence on SD. We have presented a causal model, developed using path analysis, of the effects on SD of the various independent and endogenous variables we measured.

Replanning occurs when the environment doesn't match the Fireboss's expectations. In the current experiment, the rate at which the expectations became invalid was set by RTK. But the effect was indirect: Low RTK ensured that the Fireboss would be swamped (OVUT), which meant that bulldozers had to wait for instructions, which, in turn, increased the probability that they would not be able to carry out their instructions by their deadlines. This is what caused plans to fail. Environmental changes were only the instrument of the problem; RTK initiated it. But expectations, and thus plans, can also fail if the environment itself changes. We have yet to study whether replanning makes Phoenix robust against these changes, though our results with RTK suggest it does.

Acknowledgements

This research is supported by DARPA under contract #F49620-89-C-00113; by AFOSR under the Intelligent Real-time Problem Solving Initiative, contract #AFOSR-91-0067; by NSF under an Issues in Real-Time Computing grant, #CDA-8922572; and by Texas Instruments Corporation. Thanks go to David Westbrook for invaluable design and programming help, Mike Sutherland for his statistical expertise, Scott Anderson for insightful comments on an early draft, and the many members of EKSL who have contributed to Phoenix. We also wish to thank an anonymous reviewer for a thorough and constructive reading. The US Government is authorized to reproduce and distribute reprints for governmental purposes notwithstanding any copyright notation hereon.

References

Asher, H.B. 1983. *Causal Modeling.* Sage Publications.

Cohen, P.R., Hart, D.M. & St. Amant, R. 1992. Early warnings of plan failure, false positives, and envelopes: Experiments and a model. Dept of Computer Science, Technical Report #92-20, University of Massachusetts, Amherst.

Cohen, P.R. 1991. A survey of the Eighth National Conference on Artificial Intelligence: Pulling together or pulling apart? *AI Magazine* 12(1): 16-41.

Cohen, P.R. 1990. Designing and analyzing strategies for Phoenix from models. *Proc. of the Workshop on Innovative Approaches to Planning, Scheduling and Control.* Pp. 9-21.

Cohen, P.R., Greenberg, M.L., Hart, D.M. & Howe, A.E. 1989. Trial by fire: Understanding the design requirements for agents in complex environments. *AI Magazine* 10(3): 32-48.

Hart, D.M., Anderson, S.D. & Cohen, P.R. 1990. Envelopes as a vehicle for improving the efficiency of plan execution. *Proc. of the Workshop on Innovative Approaches to Planning, Scheduling, and Control.* Pp. 71-76.

Howe, A.E. & Cohen P.R., 1990. Responding to environmental change. *Proc. of the Workshop on Innovative Approaches to Planning, Scheduling, and Control.* Pp. 85-92.

Li, C.C. 1975. *Path Analysis–A Primer.* Boxwood Press.

National Wildlife Coordinating Group, Boise, Idaho. *NWCG Fireline Handbook.* November, 1985.

Pearl, J. & Verma, T.S. 1991. A theory of inferred causation. *Principles of Knowledge Representation and Reasoning: Proc. of the Second International Conference,* J. Allen, R. Fikes, & E. Sandewall (Eds.). Morgan Kaufman. Pp. 441-452.

Characterizing Multi-Contributor Causal Structures for Planning

Subbarao Kambhampati
Department of Computer Science and Engineering
Arizona State University
Tempe, AZ 85287-5406
email: rao@asuvax.asu.edu

Abstract

Explicit causal structure representations have been widely used in classical planning systems to guide a variety of aspects of planning, including plan generation, modification and generalization. For the most part, these representations were limited to single-contributor causal structures. Although widely used, single-contributor causal structures have several limitations in handling partially ordered and partially instantiated plans. The foremost among these is that they are incapable of exploiting redundancy in the plan. In this paper, we explore multi-contributor causal structures as a way of overcoming these limitations. We will provide a general formulation for multi-contributor causal links, and explore the properties of several special classes of this formulation. We will also discuss their applications in plan generation, modification and generalization.

1 Introduction

Representation and use of causal structure of the plans has been a long-standing theme in classical planning. Some of the specific (though similar) causal structure representations that have been proposed include *Protection intervals* [19, 20] [23], *goal structure* [21], *plan rationale* [24], *causal links* [12], and *validations* [9]. Such representations have been used extensively in plan generation to keep track of interactions and to systematize the search process [21][12]; in plan recognition to capture the plan rationale [14]; in replanning, plan modification and abstraction planning to justify individual planning decisions and to retract unjustified ones [9][5][25]; in plan debugging to characterize the plan failures [19][17]; and in plan generalization to explain plan correctness and use that explanation as a basis for generalization [10][2].

Most of the previous work modeled plan causal structures in terms of single-contributor causal links, which capture the dependencies between a consumer step requiring a prerequisite, and a *single* producer step which contributes that prerequisite. Such single contributor causal structures suffer from several disadvantages in capturing the causal structure of partially ordered partially instantiated plans. The biggest problem is their inability to deal with, and exploit redundant contributors. Consider, for example, the prerequisite R of the step *fin* in the plan MP shown in Figure 1 (the add and delete lists literals of each step are shown above the step with + and − signs, while the prerequisites of the step are in parentheses under the step). The steps $w0$, $s5$ and $w2$ can all independently provide R to *fin*. This type of redundancy in the causal structure of plan can be gainfully utilized to make interaction resolution more efficient during planning, as well as to facilitate more efficient plan modification and replanning strategies. Unfortunately however, we cannot do this in a planner using single-contributor causal structures. In the example above, a planner using single contributor causal links will have to commit to one of $w0$, $s5$ or $w2$ as the contributor.

Apart from failing to exploit the redundancy in the causal structure, such a premature commitment may also lead to unnecessary backtracking in the planning process (especially in planners that employ goal protection). Especially troublesome in this respect are planners such as [12][18][13] that widen the definition of protection violation to include both those nodes that intervene and delete the protected condition and those which intervene and merely reassert the protected condition. This stronger definition of un-threatened and un-usurped causal links is introduced to avoid redundancy in the planner's search process (i.e., to make sure that the planner will not visit two plans with overlapping completions). Our empirical studies with [18] in a variant of blocks world (that induces multiple redundant contributors for some pre-requisites) demonstrate that not only do such planners fail to exploit redundant contributors, but their performance actually *worsens* in the presence of redundant contributors [11][1].

A way of avoiding this overcommitment, while still keeping down the redundancy in the planner's search space (See Section 5), is to model causal links as depen-

---

[1]Note that use of abstraction techniques, such as precondition abstraction[16, 25] can mitigate this to some extent by postponing achievement of preconditions which are likely to have multiple contributors (and thus are easily achievable).

dencies between a prerequisite and several contributor nodes such that one of those contributor nodes is guaranteed to provide the prerequisite for every execution sequence of the plan.

Although the idea of multi-contributor causal links has been first introduced in Tate's NONLIN [21] (see Section 5), there has not been any systematic study of their properties. The primary goal of this paper is to develop a formal characterization of multi-contributor causal structures for planning. We will present a general formulation for multi-contributor causal links, and within that formulation explore several sub-classes with useful properties. We will then describe the advantages of using these causal structures in plan generation, modification and generalization. Specifically, we will describe a planning algorithm based on them, and will develop a justification framework based on multi-contributor causal structures that can form the basis for plan modification and generalization.

Guide to the paper: The rest of the paper is organized as follows: Section 1.1 introduces some preliminary terminology that is used throughout the rest of the paper. Section 2 provides the general formulation of multi-contributor causal links, and characterizes the correctness of a plan with respect to this formulation. Section 3 defines and explores a variety of special classes of of multi-contributor validation structures with useful properties. Section 4 discusses the applications of these causal structure representations in planning. Section 4.1 describes a planning algorithm that can exploit the multi-contributor causal structures described in preceding sections. Section 4.2 develops the notion of justifying individual planning decisions with respect to causal structure, which is useful in plan modification and generalization. Section 5 discusses the relations with past research, and Section 6 summarizes the paper and discusses some outstanding issues. Readers eager to understand the applications of multi-contributor causal structures before looking at the detailed formulations may want to go directly to Section 4.1 after Section 2 on their first reading.

1.1 Terminology

In this paper, we will be using the following terminology for partially ordered partially instantiated plans (widely referred to also as nonlinear plans): A partially ordered partially instantiated plan $\mathcal{P}$ is represented as a 3-tuple $\langle T, O, \Pi \rangle$, where: T is the set of actions in the plan, and O is a partial ordering relation over T, and Π is a set of codesignation (binding) and non-codesignation (prohibited bindings) constraints on the variables in $\mathcal{P}$. T contains two distinguished nodes t_I and t_G, where the effects of t_I and the preconditions of t_G correspond to the initial and final states of the plan, respectively. Actions are represented by instantiated STRIPS-style operators with *Add*, *Delete* and *Precondition* lists, all of which are conjunctions of functionless first order literals.

A partially ordered partially instantiated plan corresponds to a set of totally ordered totally instantiated execution sequences, called *completions*, each corresponding to a fully instantiated topological sort of the plan

that is consistent with the binding constraints Π and ordering constraints O. Such a plan is considered correct if and only if each of its completions is an executable STRIPS plan capable of transforming the world to a state where all the pre-requisites of t_G are satisfied. For plans involving strips type operators without conditional or deductive effects, the TWEAK truth criterion [1] provides a set of necessary and sufficient conditions under which every completion of a partially ordered partially instantiated plan will be correct in the above sense.

2 Formulating Multi-contributor causal links

In formulating multi-contributor validation structures we are faced with a choice as to how conservative our formulation should be. In particular, given a prerequisite p of a step w which needs contributors, we can be very conservative and decide to include those and only those contributors that are absolutely necessary to support p in all the completions of the plan. On the other hand, we can also be anti-conservative and include in our formulation any step which can *possibly* contribute the prerequisite p (i.e., the step does not follow w, and it has an effect that can possibly codesignate with p). Our formulation below strikes a middle ground:

Definition 1 (Causal Link/Protection Interval) *A causal link (or protection interval) of a plan $\mathcal{P}$ is a 3-tuple $\langle \mathcal{S}, p, w \rangle$ (or $\mathcal{S} \xrightarrow{p} w$ in McAllester's notation [12]) where (i) w is an individual step and $\mathcal{S}$ is a set of steps belonging to plan $\mathcal{P}$, (ii) w requires a condition p (iii) $\forall s \in \mathcal{S} \ \Box(s \prec w)$ and (iv) for each step $s \in \mathcal{S}$, there exists an effect $e \in \mathit{effects}(s)$ such that $\Box(e \approx p) \in \Pi$.*[2]

Definition 1.1 (Validation) *Corresponding to each causal link $\langle \mathcal{S}, p, w \rangle$, we associate the notion of a validation $\langle \mathcal{SE}, p, w \rangle$, where $\mathcal{SE}$ is a set of tuples: $\{ \langle s, e \rangle | s \in \mathcal{S}, e \in \mathit{effects}(s), \Box(e \approx p) \}$.*

Consider again the plan MP shown in Figure 1. From our definitions, $\langle \{w0, w2\}, R, fin \rangle$ is a causal link for this plan, and $\langle \{\langle w0, R \rangle, \langle w2, R \rangle\}, R, fin \rangle$ is the corresponding validation. Thus the only difference between a causal link and the validation is that the latter explicitly lists the effects of the individual contributors that actually supply the condition being supported by the causal link. In view of this tight correspondence,

---

[2] Note that requiring that all the contributors of a causal link must provide an effect that will necessarily codesignate with the condition being supported, is in general stronger than the constraints imposed by TWEAK truth criterion [1]. Consider, for example, the case of a plan where a step w needs a condition $P(v)$, $s1$ has an effect $P(x)$, s_2 has an effect $P(z)$, $s_1 \prec w$, $s_2 \prec w$, s_1 and s_2 are unordered w.r.t. to each other. We also have two other steps s_g and s_d such that $s_g \prec s_1$, $s_d \prec s_2$, and s_g negates $P(u)$, and s_d negates $P(y)$. Now, if we use a multi-contributor validation link to support $P(v)$ at w, then the weakest constraints we need are $[x \approx v \wedge z \approx v]$. This is stronger than what is required by the modal truth criterion for guaranteeing the truth of $P(u)$ at w, which is $[x \approx v \wedge z \approx v] \vee [x \approx v \wedge (y \not\approx v \vee z \approx v)] \vee [z \approx v \wedge (u \not\approx v \vee x \approx v)]$.

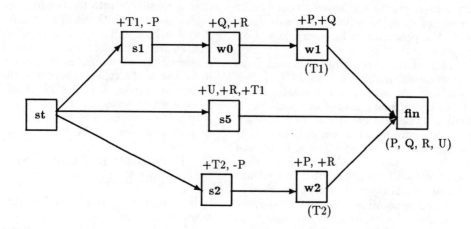

Figure 1: MP: A partially ordered plan

we will use the words **causal link, protection interval** and **validation** interchangeably in the rest of the paper.

Definition 2 (Violated Causal Links)
*A causal link $\langle S, p, w \rangle$ of a plan $\mathcal{P}$ is said to be violated if there are completions of $\mathcal{P}$ where none of the contributors of S can successfully provide the effect p to w, without some other step s' of the plan possibly intervening and **deleting** p. A causal link is said to hold if and only if it is not violated.*

From the definition, we have the following necessary and sufficient conditions to ensure that a validation is not violated:

Property 2.1 *A validation $\langle S, p, w \rangle$ is not violated if and only if $\forall s' \in \mathcal{P}$ s.t. $\neg q \in effects(s')$ and $\Diamond(q \approx p)$, either $w \prec s'$ or $\exists s \in S$ such that $s' \prec s$*

The above formulation explicitly admits the possibility that p is contributed by different members of S for different completions of the plan. This facilitates a more flexible way of accommodating plans that are correct by the *white-knight* clause of TWEAK truth criterion [1]. Consider, for example, the prerequisite P of step *fin* in the plan MP shown in Figure 1. Although both $w1$ and $w2$ provide P, neither of them can do it in all the completions of MP. The standard way of accommodating this type of situations within single-contributor causal structure representations is to utilize the white-knight declobbering clause, and to consider one of $w1$ and $w2$ as the node contributing P for *fin* and the other node as the white-knight. The choice here, of which node to refer to as the contributor and which to refer to as the white knight, is completely arbitrary. It hides the fact that $w1$ and $w2$ are in fact complementary contributors for different completions. Multi-contributor causal links obviate this problem. In particular, the causal link $\langle \{w1, w2\}, P, fin \rangle$ can support p for *fin* according to our formulation.

2.1 Causal Structure and Plan Correctness

Using the definitions above, we can now characterize the correctness of the plan with respect to a set of causal

$$
\begin{array}{ll}
\langle \{s1\}, T1, w1 \rangle & \langle \{s2\}, T2, w2 \rangle \\
\langle \{w1, w2\}, P, fin \rangle & \langle \{w0, w1\}, Q, fin \rangle \\
\langle \{w2, w0\}, R, fin \rangle & \langle \{s5\}, U, fin \rangle
\end{array}
$$

Figure 2: A multi-contributor validation structure for the plan MP

links in a straightforward fashion.

Definition 3 (Plan Correctness w.r.t. Validation Structure) *A plan $\mathcal{P}$ is said to be correct with respect to a set of causal links (validations) $\mathcal{V}$, if and only if (i) For each precondition p of each step w of the plan, there exists a causal link $\langle S, p', w \rangle \in \mathcal{V}$ such that $(p' \approx p) \in \Pi$ and (ii) None of the causal links of $\mathcal{V}$ are violated. The set $\mathcal{V}$ is called a causal structure or the validation structure for the plan $\mathcal{P}$.*

It can be easily be shown that if a partially ordered partially instantiated plan $\mathcal{P}$ is correct by the above definition, then every completion of it will constitute a executable solution for the corresponding planning problem. In particular, we can show that in any completion of the plan, corresponding to each prerequisite p of each step w, there will necessarily be a step s of the plan that provides the prerequisite p to w without any intervening steps of the plan denying it.[3] Figure 2 shows a set of valid (multi-contributor) causal links under which the plan MP shown in Figure 1 is correct. The converse of the above is however not necessarily true. In particular, a plan may be incorrect according to a validation structure $\mathcal{V}$ and may still be correct according to the modal truth criterion.

---

[3]To see this, consider a completion T' of the plan. Let v be the last step before w in T' such that v deletes p. By definition 3, there must be a causal link $\langle S, p', w \rangle$ in the plan such that $p' = p$. Further more, since the $\langle S, p', w \rangle$ is not violated, by definition 2 there must be a step $s \in S$ such that $v \prec s$. Thus, s can contribute p to w without any intervening nodes denying it.

3   Specializations of Multi-contributor causal structures

The formulation of multi-contributor validation structure developed in the previous section is too general in that it does not differentiate between causal links with irrelevant contributors (i.e., contributors which will always be superseded by other contributors), redundant contributors (i.e., contributors which can be removed without affecting the correctness of the plan), and irredundant contributors (i.e., contributors which cannot be removed without affecting the correctness of the plan). In the following we tighten this formulation by imposing some additional restrictions to derive special classes of multi-contributor causal structures with interesting properties.

3.1   Irredundant Validation Structures

The most stringent restriction on multi-contributor causal links would be to stipulate that every contributor in the causal link is *required* in some strong sense. This is captured by the notion of irredundant validation structures defined below:

Definition 4 (Irredundant Contributors) *A contributor s of an initially un-violated causal link $\langle S, p, w \rangle$ is said to be irredundant if removing s from S will violate the validation (according to Definition 2).*

Property 4.1 *Given a validation $\langle S, p, w \rangle$, a contributor $s \in S$ is irredundant if and only if either S is a singleton set, or there exists some step n in the plan such that: (i) $(n \prec s) \wedge (w \not\prec n)$ and (ii) $\neg d \in effects(n)$ such that $\Diamond(d \approx p)$ and (iii) $\forall s_i \in S$ if $(s_i \neq s)$ then $(n \not\prec s_i)$ (In other words, s is the only step in the plan capable of foiling the interaction caused by n.)*

Definition 4.1 (Irredundant Validation Structure) *A validation structure V is said to be irredundant for a plan P if and only if each contributor of every validation belonging to V is irredundant.*

Property 4.2 *If V is an irredundant validation structure for a plan P, then a validation $\langle S, p, w \rangle \in V$ will have multiple contributors (i.e. S is not a singleton) if and only if proving the truth of p at w in the plan P would require using the white-knight clause in TWEAK's truth criterion [1].*

Thus, *irredundancy* generalizes the single contributor validation structure (cf [9][12]) just enough to allow plans that have white-knight interactions. In particular, irredundant validation structures admit multiple contributors in causal links only when they are absolutely necessary. Since they *do not* admit any form of redundant contributors, a planning algorithm that constructs plans with irredundant validation structures can suffer from the some of the same drawbacks as the planner's using single contributor causal links in terms of premature commitment to contributors (see Section 1) [12].

3.2   Relevant Validation Structures

Next, we will look at the notion of *relevant validation structure* which is more general than irredundant validation structures — in that it allows redundant contributors, but more specific than the formulation in Section 2 as it stipulates that each contributor should be an effective contributor in at least one completion of the partially ordered plan. To define this formally, we need the notion of *effective contributor in a completion*:

Definition 5 (Effective Contributor in a completion) *Let CP be a completion of plan P. For every step w in P, and a precondition p of that step, p holds at w in the completion CP, if and only if there exists a step s such that s is the last step before w in CP which asserts p without any other step between s and w asserting or deleting p. If such a step s exists (and it is guaranteed to exist, if the plan P is correct) then that step is called the effective (or relevant) contributor of p to w in the completion CP.*

Definition 6 (Irrelevant Contributors) *A step s is said to be an irrelevant contributor of a validation $\langle S, p, w \rangle$ of a plan P if and only if $s \in S$ and s cannot be an effective contributor of p to w in any completion of the plan P.*

Property 6.1 *Given a validation $\langle S, p, w \rangle$, a step s belonging to S is an irrelevant contributor if there exists a step u in the plan P, such that $\Box(s \prec u \prec w)$ and either $e \in effects(u) \wedge \Box(e \approx p)$ or $\neg e \in effects(u) \wedge \Box(e \approx p)$ (i.e., u comes after s and either reasserts or deletes p).*

In the validation structure shown in Figure 2, $w0$ is an irrelevant contributor for the causal link $\langle \{w0, w1\}, Q, fin \rangle$. This is because $w1$ follows $w0$ in every completion of the plan and thus the latter can never be the last step to assert Q before fin in any completion of MP.

Definition 6.1 (Relevant Validation Structure) *If a plan P has a validation structure V such that no causal link in V has any irrelevant contributors, then V is said to be a relevant validation structure for P.*

Property 6.2 *All the contributors of a relevant validation are necessarily unordered with respect to each other*

This property can be derived as a corollary of property 6.1, by selecting the step u from S. The validation structure in Figure 2 is not a relevant validation structure for MP. However, it can be made relevant by removing $w0$ from the validation $\langle \{w0, w1\}, Q, fin \rangle$.

It can be easily seen that *irredundancy* of validation structure is a stronger condition than *relevance*. Consequently, the properties 6.1 and 6.2 also hold for irredundant validation structures.

3.3   Exhaustive Validation Structures

We will now look at a specialization of relevant validation structures called *exhaustive validation structures*. These have the useful property that for every prerequisite in the plan, the validation structure will account for every step in the plan that can possibly be a contributor of that prerequisite.

Definition 7 (Exhaustive Validation) *A valida-tion $\langle S, p, w \rangle$ of a plan $\mathcal{P}$ is said to be* **exhaustive** *if the validation is relevant, and for every completion $C\mathcal{P}$ of the plan $\mathcal{P}$, the effective contributor of p to w in $C\mathcal{P}$ belongs to S.*

From the definition, we have the following necessary and sufficient conditions for exhaustiveness of a validation.

Property 7.1 *A validation $\langle S, p, w \rangle$ of a plan $\mathcal{P}$ is exhaustive if and only if it is relevant, and $\forall n \in \mathcal{P}$, if n has an effect e such that $\Diamond(e \approx p)$, then it must* **either** *be the case that $n \in S$* **or** *it must be the case that $w \prec n$* **or** *it must be the case that $\exists s \in S$ such that $n \prec s$.*

In Figure 2, the validation $\langle \{w2, w0\}, R, fin \rangle$ is not a exhaustive validation since $s5$ also provides R to Fin and it is not included in the validation. (It can also be seen that except for this validation and $\langle \{s1\}, T1, w1 \rangle$, the rest of the validations are exhaustive).

Definition 7.1 (Exhaustive Validation Structure) *A validation structure $\mathcal{V}$ is said to be* exhaustive *with respect to a plan $\mathcal{P}$ if and only if all the causal links in $\mathcal{V}$ are exhaustive.*

Unlike irredundance and relevance, exhaustiveness imposes additional constraints on a plan. Given a plan $\mathcal{P}$, it is not always possible to find a exhaustive validation structure for $\mathcal{P}$ without adding additional constraints to it.[4] Consider the example of the validation $\langle \{w2, w0\}, R, fin \rangle$ in Figure 2. We can make this validation exhaustive by simply adding $s5$ as an additional contributor (making it $\langle \{w2, w0, s5\}, R, fin \rangle$). However, the validation $\langle \{s1\}, T1, w1 \rangle$ cannot be made exhaustive without also adding an ordering constraint $s5 \prec w1$ to MP. In other words, we cannot find a exhaustive validation structure for MP as it stands.

In spite of their restrictiveness, exhaustive validation structures are useful because of their uniqueness: A plan may have many different relevant or irredundant validation structures, but it can only have *at most one* exhaustive validation structure:

Property 7.2 *If $\mathcal{V}$ and $\mathcal{V}'$ are two exhaustive validation structures for a plan $\mathcal{P}$, then it must be the case that $\mathcal{V} = \mathcal{V}'$.*

An interesting corollary of this property is that in the single-contributor case, exhaustive validation structures can be used to define a equivalence class relation between nonlinear plans and their completions. In particular, given a validation structure $\mathcal{V}$, and a totally ordered totally instantiated plan $C\mathcal{P}$, we can uniquely determine the nonlinear abstraction of $C\mathcal{P}$ to which $\mathcal{V}$ is an exhaustive validation structure. This tight correspondence is used in McAllester's planner [12] to ensure the systematicity of the planning algorithm.

---

[4] For the special case of single contributor causal structures, the plans produced by NONLIN [21] do not in general have exhaustive validation structures, while those produced by McAllester's planner [12], and Minton et al's UA planner [13] have exhaustive validation structures.

4   Applications of Multi-contributor Causal Links

4.1   Planning with Multi-Contributor Causal Links

In this section, we will describe how multi-contributor validation structures described in the previous sections can be used in planning. In particular, we will provide a McAllester style planning algorithm [12] that is capable of generating plans with *relevant* and *exhaustive*[5] validation structures. One of the advantages of this algorithm is that it enables the planner to maintain multiple parallel contributors without committing to any one of them prematurely (thereby avoiding the limitations of the single-contributor validation structures, described in Section 1).

Before we describe the planning algorithm, we need to specify the notion of conflict/interaction used by the planner, and the termination condition for the planner. Since we want to maintain exhaustive (and thus relevant) validation structure, from property 7.1, we see that a validation $\langle S, p, w \rangle$ is threatened by any step $v \notin \mathcal{V}$ that either asserts or deletes p.[6] Thus, we define the notion of *threat* of a validation as follows:

Definition 8 (Threat for a Validation) *A step v is called a* threat *to a causal link $\langle S, p, w \rangle$ if v is a step other than w, and $v \notin S$ and either $q \in effects(v)$ or $\neg q \in effects(v)$ such that $\Diamond(q \approx p)$.*

Although this definition of threat is stronger than that used in most classical planners, we will see that the use of multi-contributor causal structures makes sure that it does not cause any excessive backtracking (as was the case in [12, 13]). Using this definition, we can now develop the termination condition for the planner. In particular, we define a complete plan as follows:

Definition 9 (Complete Plans) *A plan $\mathcal{P} : \langle T, O, \Pi \rangle$ is called* complete *with respect to a validation structure $\mathcal{V}$ if the following conditions hold*

- *If w is a step in $\mathcal{P}$, and w has a prerequisite p', then $\mathcal{V}$ contains some causal link of the form $\langle S, p, w \rangle$, such that $(p' \approx p) \in \Pi$.*

- *If $\mathcal{P}$ contains a causal link $\langle S, p, w \rangle$, and a step v that is a threat to the causal link $\langle S, p, w \rangle$, then O contains either $v \succ w$ or $v \prec s$ for some $s \in S$.*

- *For every causal link $\langle S, p, w \rangle \in \mathcal{V}$, the members of S are unordered with respect to each other.*

It can be easily seen that completeness is a specialization of the notion of correctness (definition 3). In particular, any plan that is complete by the above definition is also *correct* by definition 3, has a *relevant* validation structure by property 6.2, and has an *exhaustive* validation structure by definition 7.1.

The completeness condition should be seen as imposing a particular *bias* (c.f. [15]) on the search space of

---

[5] See Section 5 for a rationale for maintaining exhaustive validation structures

[6] Note that by Definition 2, a step asserting p will not violate the validation $\langle S, p, w \rangle$. Thus the notion of threat is stronger than that of violation.

The Procedure FindCompletion($\mathcal{P}$, $\mathcal{V}$, c)

1. If the partially ordered plan $\mathcal{P}$ is order inconsistent, or the total cost of the steps in $\mathcal{P}$ is greater than c, then fail.

2. If $\mathcal{P}$ is *complete* (by definition 9), then return $\langle \mathcal{P}, \mathcal{V} \rangle$.

3. *Threatened Causal Links:* If there is a causal link $\langle \mathcal{S}, p, w \rangle$ in $\mathcal{V}$ and a threat v to this link in the plan $\mathcal{P}$, such that $\mathcal{P}$ does not contain either $(v \succ w)$ or $(v \prec s)$ for some $s \in \mathcal{S}$, then nondeterministically return one of the following:

    (a) **FindCompletion**($\mathcal{P} + (w \prec v)$, **MakeRelevant**($\mathcal{V}, (w \prec v)$), c)

    (b) Non-deterministically choose some s from $\mathcal{S}$ and return
    FindCompletion($\mathcal{P} + (v \prec s)$, **MakeRelevant**($\mathcal{V}, (v \prec w)$), c)

    (c) If v adds p, then return
    FindCompletion($\mathcal{P} + (v \prec w)$, **MakeRelevant**($\mathcal{V} - \langle \mathcal{S}, p, w \rangle + \langle \mathcal{S} + v, p, w \rangle, (v \prec w)$), c)

4. There must now exist some open prerequisite (a step w and a prerequisite p of w, such that there is no causal link of the form $\langle \mathcal{S}, p, w \rangle$ in $\mathcal{V}$). In this case, nondeterministically do one of the following:

    (a) Let s be (nondeterministically) some step in $\mathcal{P}$ that adds p. Return the plan
    FindCompletion($\mathcal{P} + (s \prec w)$, **MakeRelevant**($\mathcal{V} + \langle \{s\}, p, w \rangle, (s \prec w)$), c)

    (b) Select (nondeterministically) an operator O_i from the allowed set of operations such that O_i adds p. Create a new step s in $\mathcal{P}$ corresponding to the operator O_i. Then return the plan
    FindCompletion($\mathcal{P} + \langle \{s\}, p, w \rangle + (s \prec w), c$)

The Procedure MakeRelevant($\mathcal{V}$, $(s_1 \prec s_2)$)

    foreach $\langle \mathcal{S}, p, w \rangle \in \mathcal{V}$ do
        If $prec(s_1) \cap \mathcal{S} \neq \emptyset$ and $\mathcal{S} \cap succ(s_2) \neq \emptyset$
            then $\mathcal{V} \leftarrow \mathcal{V} - \langle \mathcal{S}, p, w \rangle + \langle \mathcal{S} \setminus prec(s_1), p, w \rangle$
    od
    Return $\mathcal{V}$.

Figure 3: A procedure for generating ground plans with exhaustive and relevant (multi-contributor) causal structures

partially ordered plans defined by Chapman's truth criterion [1]. It is easy to show that this bias does not affect the completeness of the planner (in the sense that for every planning problem solvable by TWEAK, there exists a plan for that problem which satisfies the termination condition specified in definition 9).[7]

Figure 3 shows a McAllester style planning algorithm [12] that generates plans that are complete by this definition. To simplify discussion, we only show the procedure for generating ground partially ordered plans. The procedure for generating partially instantiated and partially ordered plans can be obtained in a straightforward fashion using the lifting transformation discussed in [12]. The important difference between our algorithm and the one proposed in [12] is that ours maintains multiple possible contributors for each prerequisite in a systematic fashion. Because of this, its treatment of unsafe causal links is different.

When the procedure finds an unsafe causal link $\langle \mathcal{S}, p, w \rangle$ (in Step 3), it has three choices: The threat can either be promoted to come after w (3(a)), or be demoted to come before *one* of the the steps in $\mathcal{S}$ (3(b)). In addition, if the threat is adding the prerequisite, then the procedure also has the choice of merging the threat

into the contributor set $\mathcal{S}$.[8] This is what is done in step 3(c). Although all the three choices are applicable to a threat that adds the prerequisite, it is obviously heuristically advantageous to prefer the alternative 3(c).

Finally, in step 4.a. when the procedure establishes an open prerequisite with the help of existing steps of the plan, it simply selects one of the possible contributors nondeterministically. The contributor set will grow appropriately at a later point, when threats are discovered and merged.[9]

Any time we introduce ordering constraints between two existing steps of the plan (as is done in steps 3(a), 3(b), 3(c) and 4(a)), it is possible to make some contributors of some causal links irrelevant, thereby affecting the relevance of the validation structure. We use the sub-routine called **MakeRelevant** to maintain the relevance of the plan validation structure all through the planning cycle.[10] This procedure takes the existing

---

[7] However, because of the restrictive nature of exhaustive validation structures, it is possible that there exist plans which are correct according to the TWEAK truth criterion, but do not satisfy the completeness criterion.

[8] By this stage in the procedure, we know that $\not\exists s \in \mathcal{S}$ s.t. $v \prec s$. From this it can easily be shown that no node in $\mathcal{S}$ necessarily follows v. Thus, v can be included in the contributor list, as v is the last such contributor

[9] In implementing this procedure, it is possible to reduce some of this later interaction resolution by setting $\mathcal{S}$ initially to the set of steps that are the last incoming contributors of p in each branch. (Such steps are called the critical PV nodes in NONLIN terminology [21]).

[10] An alternative to maintaining a relevant validation structure all through the planning cycle is to wait until a correct plan is generated and then check for irrelevant contrib-

causal structure and the newly introduced ordering relation as inputs, removes any irrelevant contributors from the causal links, and returns the resultant causal structure (which is guaranteed to be relevant with respect to the current plan). The algorithm uses the functions $prec(s)$ and $succ(s)$. The former comprises of s and all the nodes that necessarily precede s, while the latter comprises of s and all its the nodes that necessarily follow s. The idea behind this procedure is the following: When we add an ordering between two steps s_1 and s_2, we essentially have to be worried about the situation where we have a validation $\langle S, p, w \rangle$ such that S contains both s_1 or some of its predecessors, and s_2 or some of its successors. When this happens, the members of S are no longer unordered with respect to each other, and thus $\langle S, p, w \rangle$ will no longer be relevant. We can however make it relevant by removing s_1 and its predecessors from S.

Note that since the procedure removes only irrelevant contributors, for any step s that is removed from any validation $\langle S, p, w \rangle$, there will be a step $s' \in S$ such that $s \prec s'$. Further, the test at the beginning of step 3 in the procedure ignores any threat that necessarily precedes any of the current contributors of the validation. Thus, once a step has been removed from a causal link by **MakeRelevant**, it will *never be* reintroduced into that link in that branch of the search process (in other words, there will not be any looping behavior because of removal of irrelevant contributors).

When the procedure **FindCompletion** terminates successfully, it returns a plan $\mathcal{P}$ and a validation structure $\mathcal{V}$. It can be easily shown that $\mathcal{P}$ will be correct, and that $\mathcal{V}$ will be a relevant and exhaustive validation structure for $\mathcal{P}$. The advantage of this algorithm is that it exploits redundancy in the plan causal structure, and avoids excessive backtracking. At the same time, by maintaining exhaustive (and relevant) validation structures, it keeps the redundancy in the planner's search space low. We are currently conducting empirical experimentation with an implementation algorithm to characterize the computational benefits it can offer.

There is one other point to be noted about the treatment of unsafe causal links in algorithm in Figure 3. In step 3 of the algorithm, when the threat v is deleting the condition being supported by the causal link $\langle S, p, w \rangle$, one possibility is to see if there is a way of eliminating this interaction by *removing* some non-irredundant contributor from S (cf. [21]). If this is possible, then we can eliminate the interaction without putting any further constraints on the plan (see Section 5). Such a step, however, introduces two complications: (i) Allowing removal of contributors as a way of resolving interactions introduces *retraction* into the truth criterion of the planner. This is contrary to the philosophy of most first principles generative planners (such as TWEAK [1]) which have *monotonic refinement* truth criteria. (ii) Even if the planner were to allow retraction as a part of its truth criterion, retraction in general introduces

utors. However, this latter alternative can produce spurious interactions involving irrelevant contributors during planning and bog down the planner.

superfluous constraints into the plan, affecting its minimality. Failing to remove these superfluous constraints in turn can lead to loss of completeness[11]. To deal with this, we need a way of keeping track of the dependencies between the planning decisions. For both these reasons, in the algorithm shown in Figure 3, we avoided doing interaction resolution through retraction. We will however discuss how retraction can be accomplished without loss of completeness in the next section, where we will describe a validation-structure based justification framework that can be used for this purpose.

4.2   Justifying Plans with Multi-contributor Causal Structures

Causal structure representations have been shown to be very valuable in guiding plan modification [9][5], and generalization [10]. From a first principles perspective, the only augmentation that is needed to enable a generative planner to modify a given plan to solve a new problem, or to generalize a given plan by removing unnecessary constraints, is the ability to *retract* some constraints on the plan. Retracting decisions from a plan typically may introduce inconsistencies and/or superfluities into the plan which need to be handled appropriately.

Causal structures can help in this process by serving as a basis to justify individual planning constraints (steps, ordering constraints and binding constraints) of a plan. In particular, we can justify causal links in terms of the over all goals of the plan, and then justify the other constraints in the plan in terms of the causal links they support [9][25][4]. Such a justification structure allows the planner to locate parts of the plan that become superfluous whenever a particular retraction occurs.

When we allow multi-contributor causal structures, however, the mere fact that a step is supporting a validation does not necessarily mean that it is justified. This is because the step could be a redundant or irrelevant contributor of the validation and consequently removing it will not lead to incorrectness of the plan. In the following, we will develop a framework for justifying a plan in terms of a multi-contributor causal structure.

---

[11] Note however, that the removal of irrelevant contributors in the procedure **MakeRelevant** in Figure 3 **does not** introduce any superfluous constraints into the plan. To see why, consider the case where a step s_1 has just been removed from a causal link $\langle S, p, w \rangle$. Then it must have been the case that some node s_2 has just been added to S such that $s_1 \prec s_2$. The question we need to answer is whether there are any constraints that we imposed when making s_1 a contributor of p that we can remove now. Obviously, the constraint $s_1 \prec w$ cannot be removed since $s_1 \prec s_2 \prec w$. The only other constraints may have been some orderings imposed on the plan to allow s_1 to contribute p to w. Suppose, at the time we decided to have s_1 as a contributor, we had threat v such that v deletes p. Obviously, if it was the case that $s_1 \prec v \prec w$, then we could not have avoided that interaction anyway. The only other possibility is that v was unordered with respect to either s_1 or w. In either of these cases, v will still be a threat to the new validation, and thus any constraints added to the plan to deal with v will still remain justified.

We will start by justifying causal links in terms of plan correctness, and then go on to justify individual constraints in terms of the causal links.

Definition 10 (Causal Link Justification)
Given a plan $\mathcal{P}$ with a validation structure $\mathcal{V}$, a causal link $\langle \mathcal{S}, p, w \rangle \in \mathcal{V}$ is justified if and only if it ultimately supports a prerequisite of the goal step t_G. That is either $w = t_G$ and $\exists q \in prerequisites(t_G)$ such that $(q \approx p)$ or there exists another justified causal link $\langle \mathcal{S}', p', w' \rangle$ such that $w \in \mathcal{S}'$.

Definition 11 (Step Justification) *A step s of a plan $\mathcal{P}$ is said to be justified with respect to a relevant validation structure $\mathcal{V}$ if and only if there exists a validation $\langle \mathcal{S}, p, w \rangle \in \mathcal{V}$ such that $s \in \mathcal{S}$. In particular, the set of such validations for which s is a contributor is defined as its justification.*[12]

A step s is said to be strongly justified if s is an irredundant contributor for at least one validation.

A step s is said to be weakly justified if s is not strongly justified, and every co-contributor of s in any causal link that s participates in is strongly justified.

A justified step that is neither strongly justified nor weakly justified is said to be conditionally justified.

In the validation structure of Figure 2 for the plan MP, the steps $w1, w2, s1, s2$ and $s5$ are all strongly justified. But, the step $w0$ is not strongly justified since $w0$ is not a irredundant contributor with respect to any of the two validations in which it participates. Additionally since the co-contributors of $w0$ are all strongly justified, $w0$ is weakly justified.

The idea of conditional justification applies to steps that are redundant contributors to every causal link to which they contribute. No strongly justified steps can be removed from the plan without making the plan incorrect (by definition 3). All unjustified steps and weakly justified steps can be removed simultaneously without affecting the correctness of the plan (in the later case, some redundancy in the validation structure is eliminated). Any one conditionally justified step can be removed without affecting the correctness of the plan. Removing more than one conditionally justified step simultaneously can make the plan incorrect. This is because the step could be a redundant contributor of a causal link along with another step. Each contributor by itself can be removed without violating the causal link, but not both at the same time.

Similar justifications can also be developed for ordering constraints and binding constraints:

Definition 12 (Ordering justification) *An ordering relation $(s_1 \prec s_2) \in O$ of a plan $\mathcal{P} : \langle T, O, \Pi \rangle$ is said to be justified with respect to a validation structure $\mathcal{V}$ of the plan, if and only if one of the following conditions is true: (i) $\exists \langle \mathcal{S}, p, w \rangle \in \mathcal{V}$ such that $s_1 \in \mathcal{S} \wedge s_2 = w$ or (ii) $\exists \langle \mathcal{S}, p, w \rangle \in \mathcal{V}$ such that $s_1 = w$ and $\neg q \in effects(s_2)$ and $\Diamond(q \approx p)$ or (iii) $\exists \langle \mathcal{S}, p, w \rangle \in \mathcal{V}$ such that $s_2 \in \mathcal{S}$ and $\neg q \in effects(s_1)$ and $\Diamond(q \approx p)$. Additionally we say that the ordering*

---

[12]Note: For the special case of single-contributor validation structures, this definition reduces to that of of e-conditions of a step defined in [9][10].

relation $s_1 \prec s_2$ is strongly justified if it is either justified by one of the last two clauses, or if it justified by the first clause and s_1 is an irredundant contributor of $\langle \mathcal{S}, p, w \rangle$.

Definition 13 (Codesignation justification)
A codesignation constraint $(q \approx p) \in \Pi$ of a plan $\mathcal{P} : \langle T, O, \Pi \rangle$ is justified with respect to a validation structure $\mathcal{V}$ if and only if there exists a causal link $\langle \mathcal{S}, p, w \rangle \in \mathcal{V}$ such that $\exists s \in \mathcal{S}$ and $q \in effects(s)$ (i.e., the validation corresponding to the causal link $\langle \mathcal{S}, p, w \rangle$ (see Definition 1.1) is $\mathcal{SE}$ such that $\langle s, q \rangle \in \mathcal{SE}$).

Further, if s is an irredundant contributor of the validation $\langle \mathcal{S}, p, w \rangle$, then the codesignation constraint is said to be strongly justified.

Definition 13.1 (Separation justification) *A non-codesignation constraint $(q \not\approx p) \in \Pi$ of a plan $\mathcal{P} : \langle T, O, \Pi \rangle$ is justified with respect to a validation structure $\mathcal{V}$ if and only if there exists a causal link $\langle \mathcal{S}, p, w \rangle \in \mathcal{V}$, and a step u in the plan such that $\neg q \in effects(u)$, and $\forall s \in \mathcal{S} \Diamond (s \prec u \prec w)$.*

Additionally, every justified non-codesignation constraint is also said to be strongly justified.

Finally, using the justifications for individual constraints, we can now discuss the notion of justifying a plan with respect to a validation structure as follows:

Definition 14 (Justification of a plan w.r.t. to a validation structure) *A plan $\mathcal{P} : \langle T, O, \Pi \rangle$ is said to be justified with respect to a validation structure $\mathcal{V}$ if and only if every causal link in $\mathcal{V}$ is justified, and every step $s \in T$, every ordering constraint $o \in O$ and every binding constraint $c \in \Pi$ is justified with respect to $\mathcal{V}$.*

Additionally, it is said to be strongly justified w.r.t. $\mathcal{V}$ if all the steps, ordering constraints and binding constraints are strongly justified.

Justifications like these can be computed for each individual decision in polynomial time or can be maintained incrementally during planning and plan modification (*cf* [9]). These justifications can be used to *retract* superfluous constraints from the plan while preserving the correctness of the plan. In the following we describe two slightly different justification procedures with differing properties:

Justifying a Plan: Justifying a plan is an iterative process. Given a plan $\mathcal{P}$ and a causal structure $\mathcal{V}$, we construct the justified plan $\mathcal{P}'$ by removing all constraints of $\mathcal{P}$ that are unjustified with respect to $\mathcal{V}$. The resultant plan $\mathcal{P}'$ will still be correct with respect to $\mathcal{V}$. $\mathcal{V}$ may however contain some unjustified causal links with respect to $\mathcal{P}'$ as a result of this retraction. If this is the case, then we construct a new validation structure $\mathcal{V}'$ by removing all the unjustified causal links from $\mathcal{V}$. We then repeat the whole process for $\mathcal{P}'$ and $\mathcal{V}'$ (until $\mathcal{P}'$ is justified w.r.t. $\mathcal{V}'$ and vice versa).

Minimizing a Justified Plan: A justified plan is not necessarily the minimal such plan capable of achieving the goals of the problem. In particular, there may be weakly justified and conditionally justified constraints in the plan. We can minimize a justified plan further by removing such weakly justified constraints. However, every time a conditionally justified constraint is retracted, we need to update the justifications before retracting another one, since removal of one conditionally justified constraint can make another constraint strongly justified.

When justifying a plan, we attempt to keep the intent of the validation structure intact. If for example, the plan was designed to have redundant contributors for some prerequisite (either to increase robustness or ensure exhaustiveness), then justifying a plan will not thwart this intent. Minimization, on the other hand, cares only about the correctness of the plan. If V is a relevant and exhaustive validation structure for a plan P, and P' is the result of strongly justifying P with respect to V. Then V is not guaranteed to be a relevant or exhaustive validation structure for P'. Both these notions of justifications become equivalent in single contributor validation structures.

The justification framework described in this section can form the basis for plan modification [9] and plan generalization (cf. [10]) procedures, based on multi-contributor validation structures. It can also be used to support retraction of contributors as a way of resolving interactions during planning (as discussed at the end of Section 4.1).

5   Related Work

To our knowledge, NONLIN [21] and its successors are the only previous planners to have used multi-contributor causal links. NONLIN's GOST table, in conjunction with its Q&A procedure, was capable of maintaining multiple redundant contributors for each prerequisite in the plan. NONLIN's method of maintaining the multiple contributors was not complete, however. It would include multiple contributors only when it was achieving the prerequisite for the first time. In this case, it used its Q&A procedure (which is equivalent to TWEAK truth criterion for ground plans) to check for simple establishment. If Q&A returns more than one possible contributor (the so called critical PV-nodes in NONLIN terminology[13]), then all such nodes are included as contributors of the prerequisite. During subsequent planning, additional contributors of that prerequisite may be introduced into the plan, but NONLIN will not increment the contributor set unless there is negative interaction between the effects of some newly introduced node and one of the contributors of the pre-requisite. Thus, the validations in the GOST are not in general guaranteed to be either *relevant* or *exhaustive*.

During interaction resolution, NONLIN exploited the presence of multiple contributors – when a particular interaction clobbers the desired effect of one of the contributors for a prerequisite, NONLIN would check to see if there were other contributors that are unaffected. If so, NONLIN would simply delete the affected contributors from GOST and continue. The initial implementations

of NONLIN did not attempt to re-justify the plan after such a retraction. This may leave the plan with unjustified constraints (thereby affecting the minimality of the plan and the completeness of the planner). O-PLAN [3], a successor of NONLIN, has some provisions to rectify this [4]. The development of justification framework in Section 4.2 provides a systematic basis for doing this. O-PLAN also had a more generalized notion of protection intervals called "clouds" [22], which were designed to manage the contributors and terminators of aggregated sets of dependencies. Clouds also allowed O-PLAN to manage multiple contributors all through the planning, by actively keeping track of the "last incoming contributor" wavefront.

There are also some interesting relations between this paper and the recent work on systematic nonlinear planning algorithms. In contrast to traditional planning algorithms like NONLIN [21] and TWEAK [1], the planning algorithms described in [12] and [13][14] maintain exhaustive validation structures. As mentioned in Section 3.3, exhaustiveness property provides a tight correspondence between a nonlinear plan and its completions, which is used in these planners to avoid redundancy in the search space. As we pointed out in Section 3.3, maintaining exhaustive validation structures in general forces the planner to make additional (ordering and binding) commitments on the plan. Our empirical experimentation with a systematic planner ([12]) shows that this increased commitment leads to excessive backtracking on the average and thereby adversely affect the planners performance [11].

What we have here is a tradeoff between redundancy in the search space explored by the planner, and the amount of commitment the planner is making. Planners like TWEAK [1] have very low commitment, but may be searching in highly redundant search spaces. Planners like UA [13] and SNLP [12, 18] guarantee systematicity, but impose higher commitment and thus may lead to more backtracking. The tradeoff between non-redundancy in search space and least-commitment will depend to a large extent on the density of solutions in the domain [6]. In particular, if the domain is such that the planner is forced to go through most of its search space before finding a solution, a planner with low redundancy in its search space can be expected to do better than a fully least-committed planner such as TWEAK [1]. On the other hand, when the solution density is not very low, a planner which provides systematicity property through increased commitment may do worse than TWEAK.

The planning algorithm based on multi-contributor causal structures, described in Figure 3 strikes an interesting balance here. In particular, by using multi-contributor validation structures, our planner reduces amount of commitment, while still maintaining exhaustiveness. Compared to TWEAK [1], which does not maintain any type of causal structures, this algorithm still

---

[13]Critical PV-nodes are essentially the last nodes on each incoming branch which assert the condition, without it being asserted or deleted subsequently in that branch. Thus, none of the initial contributors are all irrelevant. However, subsequent planning may introduce ordering relations among them, making them irrelevant

[14]Although Minton et al's planner does not explicitly keep track of causal structures, the net effect of the *unambiguity restriction* used in their planner seems to be to provide exhaustiveness of causal structure.

does more commitment and higher backtracking. However, by maintaining exhaustive and relevant validation structures during planning, it also keeps down the redundancy in its search space.

6 Conclusion and Future Directions

Although widely used in classical planning, single-contributor causal structures have several disadvantages in dealing with partially ordered partially instantiated plans, which can be overcome by using multi-contributor causal structures. The primary contribution of this paper is a clear characterization of multi-contributor causal structures for classical planning. We provided a general formulation of multi-contributor causal links, and explored a variety of sub-classes of this formulation with interesting properties. We have also discussed applications of these formulations in plan generation, modification and generalization.

There are several issues that remain to be addressed regarding multi-contributor causal structures. Foremost among these is characterizing their effect on the planning performance. In Section 5, we suggested that the algorithm shown in 3 strikes the middle ground between planners such as TWEAK [1] which have very low commitment but have high redundancy in the search space, and planners such as SNLP [12] and UA [13] which have very high commitment but avoid redundancy in the search space. Our next task will be to implement the planning algorithm shown in Figure 3, and conduct empirical experimentation to test this conjecture.

Acknowledgements:

Thanks are due to Austin Tate, who read a draft of this paper and provided many valuable suggestions and pointers; to Mark Drummond who listened to some of these ideas in the early stages and provided useful feedback; to John Bresina, whose comments about validation structure based generalization of plans lead me to look into multi-contributor validation structures seriously in the first place; and to the anonymous reviewers of AAAI-92 and AIPS-92 for their helpful comments.

References

[1] D. Chapman. Planning for conjunctive goals. *Artificial Intelligence*, 32:333–377, 1987.

[2] S.A. Chien. An Explanation-Based Learning Approach to Incremental Planning. (Ph.D. Dissertation). Available as Technical Report UIUCDCS-R-90-1646, Dept. of Computer Science, University of Illinois, Urbana, IL, 1990.

[3] K. Currie and A. Tate. O-Plan: The Open Planning Architecture. *Artificial Intelligence*, 52:49-86.

[4] L. Daniels. Planning and operations research. In: *Artificial Intelligence: Tools, Techniques, and Applications* (T. O'Shea and M. Eisenstadt (Ed). Harper & Row, New York, 1984.

[5] S. Hanks and D. Weld. Systematic Adaptation for Case-Based Planning. Technical Report 91-10-03, Department of Computer Science and Engineering, University of Washington, Seattle, WA, 1991.

[6] P. Langley. Systematic and Nonsystematic search strategies. Submitted to AAAI-92.

[7] S. Kambhampati. Mapping and retrieval during plan reuse: A validation-structure based approach. In *Proceedings of 8th National Conference on Artificial Intelligence*, August 1990.

[8] S. Kambhampati. A theory of plan modification. In *Proceedings of 8th National Conference on Artificial Intelligence*, August 1990.

[9] S. Kambhampati and J.A. Hendler. A validation structure based theory of plan modification and reuse. *Artificial Intelligence (To appear)*. (Available as Technical Report STAN-CS-90-1312, Computer Science Department, Stanford University).

[10] S. Kambhampati and S.T. Kedar. Explanation-Based Generalization of Partially Ordered Plans. In *Proc. 9th AAAI*, 1991.

[11] S. Kambhampati. Characterizing Multi-Contributor Causal Structures for Planning. Technical Report, Dept. of Computer Science and Engineering, Arizona State University, Tempe, AZ 85287.

[12] D. McAllester and D. Rosenblitt. Systematic Nonlinear Planning. In *Proc. 9th AAAI*, 1991.

[13] S. Minton, J. Bresina and M. Drummond. Commitment Strategies in Planning: A Comparative Analysis. In *Proc. 12th IJCAI*, 1991.

[14] M.E. Pollack. A Model of Plan Inference that Distinguishes Between the Beliefs of Actors and Observers. In *Proceedings of the 1986 Workshop on Reasoning about Actions and Plans*, Morgan Kaufmann, Palo Alto, 1987.

[15] P.S. Rosenbloom, S. Lee and A. Unruh. Bias in Planning and Explanation-Based Learning. In *Machine Learning Methods for Planning and Scheduling*. S. Minton (Ed.). Morgan Kaufmann (*in press*)

[16] E. Sacerdoti. Planning in a Hierarchy of Abstraction Spaces. *Artificial Intelligence*, 5(2), 1975.

[17] R. Simmons. A Theory of Debugging. In *Proceedings of 7th AAAI*, St. Paul, MN, 1988.

[18] S. Soderland A. Barrett and D. Weld. The effect if step-order representations on planning. Technical Report 91-05-06, Department of Computer Science and Engineering, University of Washington, Seattle, WA, June 1991.

[19] G.J. Sussman. *A Computer Model of Skill Acquisition*. American Elsevier, New York, 1975

[20] A. Tate. Interacting Goals and Their Use. In *Proceedings of IJCAI-75*, pages 215-218, Tbilisi, USSR, 1975.

[21] A. Tate. Generating Project Networks. In *Proceedings of IJCAI-77*, pages 888–893, Boston, MA, 1977.

[22] A. Tate. Goal Structure, Holding Periods and "Clouds." In *Proceedings of 1986 Timberline workshop on Reasoning about Actions and Plans*, pages 267-277, Morgan Kaufmann, 1986.

[23] R. Waldinger. Achieving several goals simultaneously. In *Machine Intelligence 8*, Ellis Horwood Limited, Chichester, 1977.

[24] D. Wilkins Domain Independent Planning: Representation and Plan Generation. *Artificial Intelligence*, 22:3, 1984.

[25] Q. Yang and J.D. Tenenberg. ABTWEAK: Abstracting a nonlinear, least-commitment planner. In *Proceedings of 8th AAAI*, 1990.

An Analysis of ABSTRIPS

Craig A. Knoblock
University of Southern California
Information Sciences Institute
4676 Admiralty Way
Marina del Rey, CA 90292
knoblock@isi.edu

Abstract

ABSTRIPS [Sacerdoti, 1974] was the first system to automate the construction of abstraction hierarchies for planning. Despite the seminal nature of this work, the method AB-STRIPS uses to construct abstraction hierarchies is only described in vague terms, and there is no analysis of how the method works or when it will be effective. This paper fills this gap and presents a reconstruction and analysis of the algorithm used in AB-STRIPS. The analysis shows that the method for constructing abstractions implicitly assumes that the preconditions that are determined to be details will be independent. In those cases where the independence assumption fails to hold, ABSTRIPS can degrade the performance of the planner. The paper also compares the ABSTRIPS approach to generating abstractions to the one used in ALPINE [Knoblock, 1990] and describes how ALPINE avoids the problem that arises in ABSTRIPS.

1 Introduction

One approach to reducing search in planning is to exploit abstractions of a problem space to plan hierarchically. A problem is first solved in an abstract space and then refined at successively more detailed levels. The ABSTRIPS system [Sacerdoti, 1974] provided some of the earliest work on abstraction in planning. AB-STRIPS was built on top of the STRIPS planning system [Fikes and Nilsson, 1971] and would first construct an abstraction hierarchy for a problem space and then use the abstractions for hierarchical planning. Hierarchical planning was pioneered in GPS [Newell and Simon, 1972], but ABSTRIPS was the first system that automated the construction of abstraction hierarchies.

In ABSTRIPS, the abstraction spaces are constructed by assigning *criticalities*, numbers indicating relative difficulty, to the preconditions of each operator. The system uses these criticalities to plan abstractly. First, an abstract plan is found that satisfies only the preconditions of the operators with the highest criticality values. The abstract plan is then refined by considering the preconditions at the next level of criticality and inserting steps into the plan to achieve these preconditions. The process is repeated until the plan is expanded to the lowest level of criticality.

The work on ABSTRIPS is widely viewed as seminal work on abstraction in planning [Korf, 1987, Tenenberg, 1988]. Yet, to date there has been no detailed description or analysis of the method used in ABSTRIPS for constructing abstraction hierarchies. In addition, recent results presented in [Knoblock, 1991] indicate that the abstraction hierarchies generated by ABSTRIPS actually degrade performance rather than improve it when used in the PRODIGY problem solver [Minton *et al.*, 1989, Carbonell *et al.*, 1991]. This paper presents a detailed analysis of how ABSTRIPS works. It also explains the apparent contradiction in that the abstractions generated by ABSTRIPS worked well in the STRIPS system, yet produced poor performance when used in PRODIGY.

The remainder of this paper is organized as follows. The next section presents a rational reconstruction of the algorithm for generating abstractions and an analysis of how and when this approach will work. The third section presents an example problem that illustrates a shortcoming of the ABSTRIPS approach. The fourth section compares the approaches used in AB-STRIPS and ALPINE [Knoblock, 1990, Knoblock, 1991] for generating abstractions and shows how ALPINE avoids the problem that arises in ABSTRIPS. The fifth section presents experimental results that compare ABSTRIPS' abstractions to ALPINE's in the PRODIGY problem solver. The sixth section compares the criteria used for generating abstractions in ABSTRIPS to the criteria used in other systems, and the last section summarizes the findings presented in this paper. In addition, the Lisp code for the ABSTRIPS algorithm is included in Appendix A, and the definition of the STRIPS robot planning domain is provided in Appendix B.

An Analysis of ABSTRIPS 127

2 Algorithm and Analysis of ABSTRIPS

ABSTRIPS is given a definition of a problem space and a partial order of predicates, and it forms abstract problem spaces by assigning criticalities to the preconditions of the operators. According to [Sacerdoti, 1974], the criticalities are assigned as follows:

> A predetermined (partial) ordering of all the predicates used in describing the problem domain was used to specify an order for examining the literals of the precondition wffs of all the operators in the domain. First, all literals whose truth value could not be changed by an operator in the domain were assigned a maximum criticality value. Then, each remaining literal was examined in an order determined by the partial ordering. If a short plan could be found to achieve a literal from a state in which all previously processed literals were assumed to be true, then the literal in question was said to be a detail and was assigned a criticality equal to its rank in the partial ordering. If no such plan could be found, the literal was assigned a criticality greater than the highest rank in the partial order.

The crucial point left unspecified in the description of the algorithm is how the system determines whether a given precondition can be achieved by a short plan. To understand this point, I constructed a complete version of the algorithm that matches the description in the original paper and produces the same criticality assignments as those published on ABSTRIPS. The core of the algorithm is presented in Table 1 and the complete program is provided in Appendix A. The algorithm described below appears to be quite close to the original since it produces the same criticality assignments for the STRIPS domain, requires the same axioms that ABSTRIPS required to produce these criticalities, and is quite simple.

The algorithm presented in Table 1 assigns a criticality value to a precondition of an operator by attempting to prove that for any instantiation of the precondition, there exists a sequence of operators that will achieve the precondition. It is unclear what was meant by a short plan in the description above. The algorithm presented here considers a short plan to be any nonrecursive sequence of operators.

The function, `assign-precond-crit`, is given an operator and a precondition of that operator and assigns a criticality to that precondition. If the precondition cannot be changed by any operator it is *static* and is assigned a criticality of two plus the maximum value in the partial order. If it cannot show that a plan exists to achieve the precondition it is assigned a criticality

Table 1: Algorithm for Assigning Criticalities

```
function assign-precond-crit (precond,operator)
begin
if precond is static
then return(2 + maximum value in partial order)
else
  begin
  context ← context(precond,operator,[]);
  if not plan-exists(precond,context,operator)
  then return(1 + maximum value in partial order)
  else return(level of precond in partial order)
  end
end

function context (goal,operator,prev-context)
begin
new-context ← preconditions of operator higher
                than goal in the partial order;
derived-context ← conditions derived from axioms,
                goal, and new-context;
return(new-context ∪ derived-context
                ∪ prev-context)
end

function plan-exists (goal,context,stack)
begin
relevant-ops ← operators relevant to goal;
if there-exists op ∈ relevant-ops such-that
    begin
    preconds ← preconditions of op;
    and op ∉ stack;
        achievable(preconds,context,op,stack)
    end
then return(true)
else return(false)
end

function achievable (preconds,context,op,stack)
begin
if forall pre ∈ preconds
  begin
  new-context ← context(pre,op,context);
  new-stack ← push(op,stack);
  or pre ∈ context;
      plan-exists(pre,new-context,new-stack)
  end
then return(true)
else return(false)
end
```

of one plus the maximum value in the partial order. If a plan does exist, it is assigned a criticality equal to its level in the partial order.

Before determining whether a plan exists, the function `context` is called first to determine the context of the precondition. The context consists of the conditions that will hold at the time the precondition arises as a goal. These conditions consist of the other preconditions of the operator that are higher in the partial order than the precondition under consideration, any conditions that can be derived from these conditions using the axioms, and any previous context or conditions that held up to this point.

Given the context, the function `plan-exists` attempts to show that a plan will always exist for achieving the given precondition. It first determines the set of relevant operators for achieving the precondition and then tests each operator to see if its preconditions will be achievable in the given context. The algorithm avoids recursing infinitely by keeping a stack of the operators under consideration and failing whenever it encounters an operator that is already on the stack.

The function `achievable` determines whether a set of preconditions will be achievable in the given context. To do this, the function attempts to show that for each of the preconditions, the precondition either holds in the given context or a plan exists to achieve the precondition. In the later case, the function `plan-exists` is called recursively on the precondition, first updating the context and operator stack with the operator under consideration.

The essence of this approach is to determine whether a plan will always exist to achieve a given precondition. If such a plan exists, the precondition is considered a detail and can be separated from the more difficult aspects of the problem. Thus, the system *automatically* produces only a three-level abstraction hierarchy, with the static literals at the top of the hierarchy, the difficult to achieve literals next, and the details at the bottom. The user-defined partial order is then used to partition the details into separate levels.

For the problems tried in the ABSTRIPS paper this algorithm for generating abstractions appears to work very well. However, the algorithm assumes that the different preconditions or goal conditions will not interact with one another. This assumption arises because the algorithm only considers each of the preconditions independently. In practice, a plan for achieving a subgoal may interact with a plan for achieving another subgoal. Even in the STRIPS domain there are combinations of goal conditions where this type of interaction occurs. The effect of such an interaction is that a precondition that appeared to be achievable in the analysis, might not be achievable because the plan for achieving another goal could interact with it.

3   An Example Problem

Consider an example that illustrates the problem that can occur in ABSTRIPS when the independence assumption is violated. The problem is from the STRIPS robot planning domain [Fikes and Nilsson, 1971] and was selected from the randomly generated problems used in the experiments described later in this paper. This domain is defined in Appendix B.

The problem involves achieving the following conjunction of five goals:

```
(and (inroom a room1)
     (status door56 closed)
     (status door12 closed)
     (inroom robot room3)
     (inroom b room6)),
```

where the initial state for this problem is shown in Figure 1. The complete specification of this problem is included in Appendix D of [Knoblock, 1991].

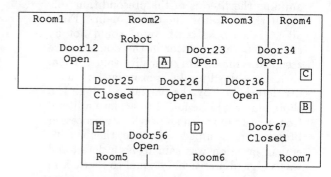

Figure 1: Initial State for the Example Problem

The criticality assignments generated by ABSTRIPS for this problem domain are specified in [Sacerdoti, 1974] and shown in Appendix B. ABSTRIPS assigns the static preconditions the highest criticality, 6. It assigns the preconditions that cannot be achieved by a short plan a criticality of 5. These preconditions include all of the `inroom` conditions and the `status` and `nextto` preconditions of the operators for opening and closing doors. The `status` and `nextto` preconditions of the remaining operators are shown to be details and are assigned criticalities that correspond to their values in the partial order given to ABSTRIPS, which is 2 for the `status` preconditions and 1 for the `nextto` preconditions.

Problem solving using this abstraction hierarchy proceeds as follows. Since ABSTRIPS only drops preconditions, all the top-level goals are considered in the abstract space. The system constructs an abstract plan to move box a into `room1`, closes the door to the room, and then moves the robot through the closed door in order to achieve the remaining goals. When the system is planning at this abstraction level it ignores all preconditions involving door status, so it does not notice that it will later have to open this door to make the plan work. When the plan is refined to the next level of detail, the steps are added to open the door before moving the robot through the door, deleting a condition that was achieved in the abstract space. At this point the problem solver would need to either backtrack or insert additional steps for closing the door again. The original ABSTRIPS system would not have even noticed that it had violated the precondition, and would simply produce an incorrect plan

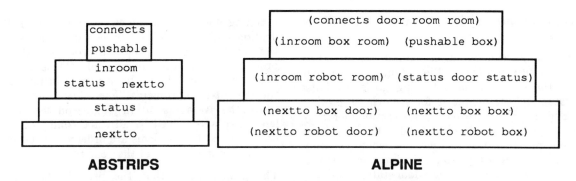

Figure 2: Abstraction Hierarchies Generated by ABSTRIPS and ALPINE

[Joslin and Roach, 1989, pg.100]. In the analysis used by ABSTRIPS, the door status appeared to be a detail, but during planning considerable time can be wasted before it finally backtracks to the correct point in the search space and corrects the mistake.

4   Comparison with ALPINE

The ALPINE system [Knoblock, 1990, Knoblock, 1991] completely automates the generation of abstraction hierarchies from the definition of a problem space. Each abstraction space in a hierarchy is formed by dropping literals (atomic formulas) from the original problem space, thus it abstracts the preconditions and effects of operators as well as the states and goals of a problem space. ALPINE forms abstraction hierarchies based on the *ordered monotonicity* property [Knoblock *et al.*, 1991], which requires that the truth value of a literal introduced at one level is not changed at a lower level. This property guarantees that the preconditions that are achieved in an abstract plan will not be deleted (clobbered) while refining that plan. To construct abstraction hierarchies with this property, ALPINE analyzes the preconditions and effects of the operators to determine potential interactions. If a plan for achieving literal C_1 can change the truth value of literal C_2, then literal C_1 cannot be in a lower abstraction level than literal C_2. The detailed algorithm is described in [Knoblock, 1991].

ALPINE's approach to generating abstractions differs from ABSTRIPS in several important ways. First, ALPINE forms abstractions based on the ordered monotonicity property, while ABSTRIPS forms abstractions by considering whether each precondition of each operator can be achieved by a short plan. Second, ALPINE completely automates the construction of the abstraction hierarchies using the definition of the problem space, while ABSTRIPS requires an initial partial order on the predicates to form the abstraction hierarchy. Third, ALPINE forms abstractions that are tailored to each problem, while ABSTRIPS constructs a single abstraction hierarchy for the entire domain. Fourth,

ALPINE forms *reduced models* where each level in the abstraction hierarchy is an abstraction of the original problem space, while ABSTRIPS forms *relaxed models* where only the preconditions are dropped.

The abstraction hierarchies generated by each system for the example problem are shown in Figure 2. As described earlier, ABSTRIPS uses the same four-level abstraction hierarchy for the entire problem domain. The most abstract space consists of all the static preconditions (the preconditions that cannot be changed), the second level consists of the preconditions that cannot be achieved by a short plan. This includes all of the **inroom** preconditions, and some of the **nextto** and **status** preconditions. The third level consists of the **status** preconditions that can be achieved by a short plan, and the fourth level contains the remaining **nextto** conditions that can also be achieved by a short plan.

The abstraction hierarchy built by ALPINE for this problem consists of the three-level abstraction hierarchy shown in Figure 2. (ALPINE builds finer-grained hierarchies by separating literals with the same predicate but different argument types.) The most abstract space consists of all the static literals and the (**inroom box room**) literals. The next level contains both the (**inroom robot room**) and the (**status door status**) literals. These two sets of literals are placed at the same level in order to satisfy the ordered monotonicity property since it may be necessary to get the robot into a particular room to open or close a door. Finally, the last level contains the **nextto** literals for both the robot and the boxes.

Using ALPINE's abstraction hierarchy to solve the example problem, a planner would first generate a plan for moving the boxes into the appropriate rooms. At the next level it would deal with the goals involving closing the doors and moving the robot. If it closed a door and then tried to move the robot through the door, it would immediately notice the interaction since these goals are considered at the same abstraction level. After producing a plan at the intermediate level it would refine this plan into the ground space by inserting the remaining details, which consists of the conditions involving `nextto`.

In constructing the abstraction hierarchy to solve this problem, ALPINE recognized the potential interaction between the operator for achieving goals involving door status and the operators for achieving the other top-level goals, and it created an abstraction hierarchy where door status is not considered a detail. Given a different problem, for example, one where the only goal is to get the robot into a particular room, ALPINE would recognize that in that case door status is a detail and place it at a lower abstraction level.

5   Experimental Results

To illustrate the difference between ALPINE's and AB-STRIPS's abstractions, the use of these abstractions are compared using the PRODIGY problem solver [Carbonell *et al.*, 1991] in the STRIPS domain. This is not a completely fair comparison because the abstraction hierarchies generated by ABSTRIPS were intended to be used by the STRIPS problem solver. STRIPS employed a best-first search instead of a depth-first search, so the problem of expanding an abstract plan that is then violated during the refinement of that plan would probably be less costly. Nevertheless, the comparison emphasizes the difference between the abstraction hierarchies generated by ALPINE and ABSTRIPS and demonstrates the problem with the approach used to generate abstractions in ABSTRIPS.

First consider the results on the example problem described earlier. Table 2 shows the CPU time (in seconds), nodes searched, and solution length for each configuration. ALPINE significantly reduces both the search and the solution length compared to PRODIGY. In contrast ABSTRIPS takes almost six times longer than PRODIGY, although it does produce a solution of the same length as ALPINE. Note that since ALPINE must construct an abstraction hierarchy for each problem, the CPU times reported for ALPINE throughout this paper include the time to construct an abstraction hierarchy.

Table 2: Performance on the Example Problem

System	Time	Nodes	Length
Prodigy	14.5	259	25
Prodigy + Alpine	10.2	114	19
Prodigy + Abstrips	83.0	1,631	19

The graphs in Figure 3 compare the solution times and solution lengths of PRODIGY without using abstraction, PRODIGY using the abstractions produced by ABSTRIPS, and PRODIGY using the abstractions produced by ALPINE. Each configuration was run on 200 randomly generated problems in the STRIPS robot

planning domain. PRODIGY was run in each configuration and given 600 CPU seconds to solve each of the problems. Out of the 200 problems, 197 of the problems were solvable in principle. The solution time graph in Figure 3 shows the average solution times for the 197 solvable problems. The solution length graph shows the average solution lengths on the 153 problems that were solved by all three configurations. In both graphs the problems are ordered by the shortest solution found by any of the configurations.

The graphs show that the use of ABSTRIPS' abstractions significantly degrades performance, while ALPINE's abstractions improve performance over the basic PRODIGY system. PRODIGY performs quite well on these problems even without abstraction. This is because the problem solver only needs to search a small portion of the search space since most mistakes can be undone by adding additional steps. Thus, on problem-solving time PRODIGY performed quite well, but it achieved this performance by trading solution quality. On the hardest set of problems, PRODIGY produces solutions that were on average fifty percent longer than ALPINE. In contrast, the use of ABSTRIPS' abstractions significantly increased the problem solving time, although they did improve the quality of the solutions. The reason for the poor performance using ABSTRIPS' abstractions is that the interactions between different subgoals in a problem generated many redundant choice points, which resulted in wasted effort in backtracking. In addition, the problems used in these experiments were much larger than the ones used in the original experiments and as a result these problems were much more likely to have interacting subproblems.

6   Related Work

The purpose of abstraction in planning is to solve the more difficult aspects of a problem first and then fill in the details. The general problem that arises in finding useful abstractions is determining which parts of a problem are details. ABSTRIPS defined the details to be those preconditions that are always achievable independent of the other subgoals in a problem. Thus the abstractions generated by ABSTRIPS consider the difficulty in achieving individual conditions, but do not take into account the potential interactions among different subgoals. This section compares the criterion used by ABSTRIPS for constructing abstractions to other closely related work.

PABLO [Christensen, 1991] is another system that generates abstractions for hierarchical planning. It uses a technique called *predicate relaxation* to determine the number of steps needed to achieve each predicate by partially evaluating the operators. This information is then used to focus the problem solver on the part of the problem that requires the greatest number of

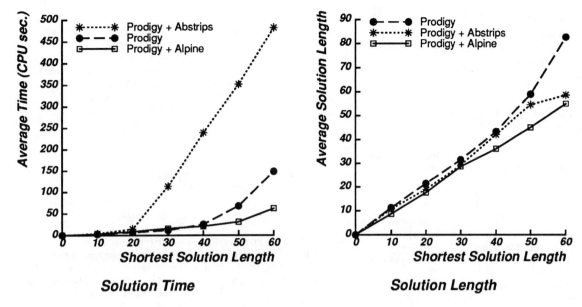

Figure 3: Comparison of the Average Solution Times and Average Solution Lengths

steps. The approach is quite similar to the one used by ABSTRIPS in that the abstractions are based on how many steps (in the worst case) it will take to achieve a given precondition instead of just whether or not a condition is always achievable. In is interesting to note that PABLO will suffer from exactly the same problem as ABSTRIPS because the predicate relaxation process does not consider interactions with plans for achieving other subgoals. Thus, due to interactions between subplans, it may believe that a subgoal is achievable when it is not, and it may underestimate the number of steps required to achieve a subgoal.

As described earlier in this paper, ALPINE forms abstractions based on the ordered monotonicity property. This property guarantees that any plan for achieving a condition ignored at an abstract level will not add or delete a literal in a more abstract space. In effect, the ordered monotonicity property partitions those conditions that interact with one another and orders the partitioned sets of conditions in a way that minimizes the interactions among them. While this property does consider the interactions between different goals, it does not guarantee that the conditions ignored at an abstract level will be achievable. However, neither AB-STRIPS or PABLO guarantee this property either since although they consider whether a individual precondition is achievable, they do not consider possible interactions that may preclude a solution.

Bacchus and Yang [1991] identified a stronger property called the *downward refinement property*, which states that if a problem is solvable then any abstract solution must have a refinement. Thus, if a solution to a problem exists, then the conditions ignored at the abstract level will be achievable. While clearly this is a desirable property, the problem is that this property can only be guaranteed in very restricted cases.

7   Conclusion

This paper presented a rational reconstruction of the algorithm used in ABSTRIPS for generating abstraction hierarchies. ABSTRIPS assigns criticalities to preconditions of operators by separating out those preconditions that can be shown to be always achievable. These preconditions are the details and achievement of them is delayed until the more difficult parts of the problem are solved. The flaw in this approach is that evaluating whether a precondition can be achieved is done in isolation from the rest of a problem. As shown in this paper, this can lead to performance that is worse than no abstraction at all when there are interactions between plans for achieving different subgoals. From this we can conclude that the problem spaces in which ABSTRIPS will be effective are those in which there are preconditions that can be shown to be achievable and those preconditions can be achieved independently.

The approach to generating abstractions in ABSTRIPS was compared to the approach in ALPINE. ALPINE produces abstraction hierarchies that have the ordered monotonicity property, which guarantees that the goals and subgoals that arise in the process of refining an abstract plan will not interact with the conditions already achieved in a more abstract level. Unlike ABSTRIPS, ALPINE considers all of the potential interactions in a problem space and avoids precisely the type of interactions that lead to poor performance in ABSTRIPS. As a result, ALPINE was able to improve the performance of PRODIGY, while ABSTRIPS degraded it.

A   Program for Assigning Criticalities

```lisp
; Top-level function for assigning criticalities.
(defun abstrips (&optional (ops *OPERATORS*))
  (load-operators ops)
  (calc-max-value-in-po)
  (assign-criticalities ops))


; Process each operator in the problem space.
(defun load-operators (ops)
  (cond ((null ops))
        (t (load-operator (caar ops)(cdar ops))
           (load-operators (cdr ops)))))

; Store preconds and effects on property list.
(defun load-operator (name body)
  (cond ((null body))
        (t (setf (get name (caar body))
                 (cadar body))
           (load-operator name (cdr body)))))

; Maximum value in the partial order.
(defun calc-max-value-in-po ()
  (setq *MAX-VALUE-IN-PO*
    (apply #'max (mapcar #'cdr *PARTIAL-ORDER*))))

; Assign criticalities to each operator.
(defun assign-criticalities (&optional
                               (ops *OPERATORS*))
  (cond ((null ops))
        (t (format t "~%~%~a" (caar ops))
           (assign-op-crits
            (caar ops)(preconds (caar ops)))
           (assign-criticalities (cdr ops)))))

; Assign criticalities to each precondition.
(defun assign-op-crits (op preconds)
  (cond ((null preconds))
        (t (format t "~%   ~a ~a"
                     (assign-precond-crit
                      (car preconds) op)
                     (car preconds))
           (assign-op-crits op (cdr preconds)))))

; Assigns criticality based on whether the
; precondition is static and whether or not a
; plan always exists to achieve the precondition.
(defun assign-precond-crit (precond operator)
  (cond ((static precond)
         (+ 2 *MAX-VALUE-IN-PO*))
        ((not (plan-exists
               precond
               (context precond
                        (preconds operator)
                        nil)
               (relevant-ops precond)
               (list operator)))
         (+ 1 *MAX-VALUE-IN-PO*))
        (t (level-in-po precond))))

; A plan exists to achieve a goal if the
; preconditions of any of the relevant operators
; are achievable.  Maintains a stack of operators
; under consideration to avoid looping.
```

```lisp
(defun plan-exists (goal context relevant-ops
                         op-stack)
  (cond ((null relevant-ops) nil)
        ((member (car relevant-ops) op-stack)
         (plan-exists goal context
                      (cdr relevant-ops)
                      op-stack))
        ((achievable (preconds
                      (car relevant-ops))
                     context
                     (car relevant-ops)
                     op-stack))
        (t (plan-exists goal context
                        (cdr relevant-ops)
                        op-stack))))

; A set of preconditions is achievable if each
; precondition is either true in the given context or
; it can be shown that a plan exists to achieve it.
(defun achievable (preconds context relevant-op
                            op-stack)
  (cond
    ((null preconds))
    ((or (member (car preconds) context
                 :test #'matches)
         (plan-exists
          (car preconds)
          (context (car preconds)
                   (preconds relevant-op)
                   context)
          (relevant-ops (car preconds))
          (cons relevant-op op-stack)))
     (achievable (cdr preconds) context
                 relevant-op op-stack))))

; Given both a goal and the preconditions of
; an operator that are relevant to achieving that
; goal, the context consists of all those preconditions
; that are higher in the partial order than the goal,
; the conditions that in turn can be derived from those
; preconditions, and the conditions in the previous
; context in which the goal arose.
(defun context (goal preconds prev-context)
  (let ((new-context (higher-in-po
                      (level-in-po goal)
                      preconds)))
    (append (derive-context goal new-context)
            new-context
            prev-context)))

; Level in the partial order of a given goal.
(defun level-in-po (cond)
  (cdr (assoc (car cond) *partial-order*)))

; Finds conditions higher in the partial order
; than the given criticality.
(defun higher-in-po (crit list)
  (cond ((null list) nil)
        ((<= (level-in-po (car list)) crit)
         (higher-in-po crit (cdr list)))
        (t (cons (car list)
                 (higher-in-po crit
                               (cdr list))))))
```

```
; The derived context consists of those conditions
; that can be derived from the negation of the
; goal (the negation of the goal must hold or it
; wouldn't be a goal) and from the given context.
(defun derive-context (goal context)
  (append (derive (list 'not goal))
          (derived-context context)))

; A condition can be derived from the context if
; it can be derived from an atomic formula in the
; context.
(defun derived-context (context)
  (cond ((null context) nil)
        (t (append (derive (car context))
                   (derived-context
                    (cdr context))))))

; Attempts to match a condition against the
; left-hand side of the axioms.  If it matches,
; the right-hand side of the axiom holds.
(defun derive (cond)
  (cdr (assoc cond *AXIOMS* :test #'matches)))

; A precondition is static if there are no
; operators relevant to achieving it.
(defun static (condition)
  (cond ((null (relevant-ops condition)))))

; An operator is relevant to achieving a goal if
; it is in the primary effects of the operator.
(defun relevant-ops (condition)
  (cdr (assoc condition *PRIMARY*
              :test #'matches)))

; Two literals match if the constants match
; and the variables can be bound appropriately.
; Note that no substitution list is maintained, so
; this function could incorrectly determine that
; two literal match.
(defun matches (cond1 cond2)
  (cond ((and (null cond1)(null cond2)))
        ((or (null cond1)(null cond2)) nil)
        ((listp (car cond1))
         (if (matches (car cond1)(car cond2))
             (matches (cdr cond1)(cdr cond2))))
        ((and (not (is-variable (car cond1)))
              (not (is-variable (car cond2)))
              (not (eq (car cond1)(car cond2))))
         nil)
        (t (matches (cdr cond1)(cdr cond2)))))

; Returns a list of preconditions of an operator.
(defun preconds (operator)
  (let ((preconds (get operator 'preconds)))
    (if (eq 'and (car preconds))
        (cdr preconds)
        preconds)))

; A variable begins with a '<'.
(defun is-variable (atm)
  (and (symbolp atm)
       (eql '#\< (char (symbol-name atm) 0))))
```

B   Strips Robot Planning Domain

```
; An equivalent version of this domain first
; appeared in [Sacerdoti 1974].

; Initial partial order of the predicates.
(defparameter *PARTIAL-ORDER*
  '((type . 4)(connects . 4)
    (locinroom . 4)(pushable . 4)
    (inroom . 3)
    (status . 2)
    (nextto . 1)))

; Axioms that state invariant properties of the
; domain.  The first axiom states that if something
; is pushable, then it is of type object.  The
; second axiom states that if a door is not open,
; then it is closed.
(defparameter *AXIOMS*
  '(((pushable <x>)(type <x> object))
    ((not (status <x> open))(status <x> closed))))

; Specifies which operators have a literal as
; a primary add.
(defparameter *PRIMARY*
  '(((nextto robot <object>) . (GOTO-BOX
                                GOTO-DOOR))
    ((at robot <loc> <loc>) . (GOTO-LOC))
    ((nextto <object> <object>) . (PUSH-BOX
                                   PUSH-TO-DOOR))
    ((at <object> <loc> <loc>) . (PUSH-TO-LOC))
    ((inroom robot <room>) . (GO-THRU-DOOR))
    ((inroom <object> <room>) . (PUSH-THRU-DOOR))
    ((status <door> open) . (OPEN-DOOR))
    ((status <door> closed) . (CLOSE-DOOR))))

; The operators are defined in the PRODIGY
; language [Minton et al, 1989], so the syntax
; differs slightly from the original.  The
; criticalities assigned by ABSTRIPS are
; shown in curly braces.
(defparameter *OPERATORS* '(

(GOTO-BOX
 (params (<bx>))
 (preconds
  (and (type <bx> object) ;{6}
       (inroom <bx> <rx>) ;{5}
       (inroom robot <rx>))) ;{5}
 (effects ((del (at robot <loc1> <loc2>))
           (del (nextto robot <obj1>))
           (add (nextto robot <bx>)))))

(GOTO-DOOR
 (params (<dx>))
 (preconds
  (and (type <dx> door) ;{6}
       (inroom robot <rx>) ;{5}
       (connects <dx> <rx> <ry>))) ;{6}
 (effects
  ((del (at robot <loc1> <loc2>))
   (del (nextto robot <obj1>))
   (add (nextto robot <dx>)))))
```

```
(GOTO-LOC
 (params (<x> <y>))
 (preconds
  (and (inroom robot <rx>) ;{5}
       (locinroom <x> <y> <rx>))) ;{6}
 (effects
  ((del (at robot <loc1> <loc2>))
   (del (nextto robot <obj1>))
   (add (at robot <x> <y>)))))

(PUSH-BOX
 (params (<bx> <by>))
 (preconds
  (and (type <by> object) ;{6}
       (pushable <bx>) ;{6}
       (nextto robot <bx>) ;{1}
       (inroom <bx> <rx>) ;{5}
       (inroom <by> <rx>) ;{5}
       (inroom robot <rx>))) ;{5}
 (effects
  ((del (at robot <loc1> <loc2>))
   (del (nextto robot <obj1>))
   (del (at <bx> <loc3> <loc4>))
   (del (nextto <bx> <obj2>))
   (del (nextto <obj3> <bx>))
   (add (nextto <by> <bx>))
   (add (nextto <bx> <by>))
   (add (nextto robot <bx>)))))

(PUSH-TO-DOOR
 (params (<bx> <dx>))
 (preconds
  (and (pushable <bx>) ;{6}
       (type <dx> door) ;{6}
       (nextto robot <bx>) ;{1}
       (inroom robot <rx>) ;{5}
       (inroom <bx> <rx>) ;{5}
       (connects <dx> <rx> <ry>))) ;{6}
 (effects
  ((del (at robot <loc1> <loc2>))
   (del (nextto robot <obj1>))
   (del (at <bx> <loc3> <loc4>))
   (del (nextto <bx> <obj2>))
   (del (nextto <obj3> <bx>))
   (add (nextto <bx> <dx>))
   (add (nextto robot <bx>)))))

(PUSH-TO-LOC
 (params (<bx> <x> <y>))
 (preconds
  (and (pushable <bx>) ;{6}
       (nextto robot <bx>) ;{1}
       (inroom robot <rx>) ;{5}
       (inroom <bx> <rx>) ;{5}
       (locinroom <x> <y> <rx>))) ;{6}
 (effects
  ((del (at robot <loc1> <loc2>))
   (del (nextto robot <obj1>))
   (del (at <bx> <loc3> <loc4>))
   (del (nextto <bx> <obj2>))
   (del (nextto <obj3> <bx>))
   (add (at <bx> <x> <y>))
   (add (nextto robot <bx>)))))

(GO-THRU-DOOR
 (params (<dx> <rx>))
 (preconds
  (and (type <dx> door) ;{6}
       (type <rx> room) ;{6}
       (status <dx> open) ;{2}
       (inroom robot <ry>) ;{5}
       (connects <dx> <ry> <rx>))) ;{6}
 (effects
  ((del (at robot <loc1> <loc2>))
   (del (nextto robot <obj1>))
   (del (inroom robot <ry>))
   (add (inroom robot <rx>)))))

(PUSH-THRU-DOOR
 (params (<bx> <dx> <rx>))
 (preconds
  (and (pushable <bx>) ;{6}
       (type <dx> door) ;{6}
       (type <rx> room) ;{6}
       (status <dx> open) ;{2}
       (nextto <bx> <dx>) ;{1}
       (nextto robot <bx>) ;{1}
       (inroom <bx> <ry>) ;{5}
       (inroom robot <ry>) ;{5}
       (connects <dx> <ry> <rx>))) ;{6}
 (effects
  ((del (at robot <loc1> <loc2>))
   (del (nextto robot <obj1>))
   (del (at <bx> <loc3> <loc4>))
   (del (nextto <bx> <obj2>))
   (del (nextto <obj3> <bx>))
   (del (inroom robot <ry>))
   (del (inroom <bx> <ry>))
   (add (inroom <bx> <rx>))
   (add (inroom robot <rx>))
   (add (nextto robot <bx>)))))

(OPEN-DOOR
 (params (<dx>))
 (preconds
  (and (type <dx> door) ;{6}
       (status <dx> closed) ;{5}
       (nextto robot <dx>))) ;{5}
 (effects
  ((del (status <dx> closed))
   (add (status <dx> open)))))

(CLOSE-DOOR
 (params (<dx>))
 (preconds
  (and (type <dx> door) ;{6}
       (status <dx> open) ;{5}
       (nextto robot <dx>))) ;{5}
 (effects
  ((del (status <dx> open))
   (add (status <dx> closed)))))
))
```

Acknowledgments

I would like to thank Yigal Arens, Oren Etzioni, Soowon Lee, Ramesh Patil, Paul Rosenbloom, and Tom Russ for their comments and suggestions on various drafts of this paper.

The research reported here was supported in part by an Air Force Laboratory Graduate Fellowship through the Human Resources Laboratory at Brooks AFB, in part by the Avionics Laboratory, Wright Research and Development Center, Aeronautical Systems Division (AFSC), U.S. Air Force, Wright-Patterson AFB, OH 45433-6543 under Contract F33615-90-C-1465, Arpa Order No. 7597, and in part by Rome Laboratory of the Air Force Systems Command and the Defense Advanced Research Projects Agency under contract no. F30602-91-C-0081. Views and conclusions contained in this report are the author's and should not be interpreted as representing the official opinion or policy of DARPA, HRL, AL, RL, the U.S. Government, or any person or agency connected with them.

References

[Bacchus and Yang, 1991] Fahiem Bacchus and Qiang Yang. The downward refinement property. In *Proceedings of the Twelfth International Joint Conference on Artificial Intelligence*, pages 286–292, Sydney, Australia, 1991.

[Carbonell *et al.*, 1991] Jaime G. Carbonell, Craig A. Knoblock, and Steven Minton. PRODIGY: An integrated architecture for planning and learning. In Kurt VanLehn, editor, *Architectures for Intelligence*, pages 241–278. Lawrence Erlbaum, Hillsdale, NJ, 1991. Available as Technical Report CMU-CS-89-189.

[Christensen, 1991] Jens Christensen. *Automatic Abstraction in Planning*. Ph.D. Thesis, Department of Computer Science, Stanford University, 1991.

[Fikes and Nilsson, 1971] Richard E. Fikes and Nils J. Nilsson. STRIPS: A new approach to the application of theorem proving to problem solving. *Artificial Intelligence*, 2:189–208, 1971.

[Joslin and Roach, 1989]
David Joslin and John Roach. A theoretical analysis of conjunctive-goal problems. *Artificial Intelligence*, 41(1):97–106, 1989.

[Knoblock *et al.*, 1991] Craig A. Knoblock, Josh D. Tenenberg, and Qiang Yang. Characterizing abstraction hierarchies for planning. In *Proceedings of the Ninth National Conference on Artificial Intelligence*, Anaheim, CA, 1991.

[Knoblock, 1990] Craig A. Knoblock. Learning abstraction hierarchies for problem solving. In *Proceedings of the Eighth National Conference on Artificial Intelligence*, pages 923–928, Boston, MA, 1990.

[Knoblock, 1991] Craig A. Knoblock. *Automatically Generating Abstractions for Problem Solving*. Ph.D. Thesis, School of Computer Science, Carnegie Mellon University, 1991. Available as Technical Report CMU-CS-91-120.

[Korf, 1987] Richard E. Korf. Planning as search: A quantitative approach. *Artificial Intelligence*, 33(1):65–88, 1987.

[Minton *et al.*, 1989] Steven Minton, Jaime G. Carbonell, Craig A. Knoblock, Daniel R. Kuokka, Oren Etzioni, and Yolanda Gil. Explanation-based learning: A problem solving perspective. *Artificial Intelligence*, 40(1-3):63–118, 1989.

[Newell and Simon, 1972] Allen Newell and Herbert A. Simon. *Human Problem Solving*. Prentice-Hall, Englewood Cliffs, NJ, 1972.

[Sacerdoti, 1974] Earl D. Sacerdoti. Planning in a hierarchy of abstraction spaces. *Artificial Intelligence*, 5(2):115–135, 1974.

[Tenenberg, 1988] Josh D. Tenenberg. *Abstraction in Planning*. Ph.D. Thesis, Computer Science Department, University of Rochester, 1988.

An Empirical Study of
Sensing and Defaulting in Planning

Kurt Krebsbach
Computer Science Dept.
University of Minnesota
4-192 EE/CSci Building
200 Union Street SE
Minneapolis, MN 55455
krebsbac@cs.umn.edu

Duane Olawsky
Math/CS Dept.
Macalester College
228A Olin Hall
1600 Grand Avenue
St. Paul, MN 55105
olawsky@macalstr.edu

Maria Gini
Computer Science Dept.
University of Minnesota
4-192 EE/CSci Building
200 Union Street SE
Minneapolis, MN 55455
gini@cs.umn.edu

Abstract

Traditional approaches to task planning assume that the planner has access to all of the world information needed to develop a complete, correct plan which can then be executed in its entirety by an agent. Since this assumption does not typically hold in realistic domains, we have implemented a planner which can plan to perform sensor operations to allow an agent to gather the information necessary to complete planning and achieve its goals in the face of missing or uncertain environmental information. Naturally this approach requires some execution to be interleaved with the planning process. In this paper we present the results of a systematic experimental study of this planner's performance under various conditions. The chief difficulty arises when the agent performs actions which interfere with or, in the worst case, preclude the possibility of the achievement of its later goals. We have found that by making intelligent decisions about goal ordering, what to sense, and when to sense it, the planner can significantly reduce the risk of committing to premature action. We have studied the problem both from the perspective of reversible and irreversible actions.

1 INTRODUCTION

The study described in this report constitutes part of an ongoing research project in the area of task planning under uncertainty. Traditional approaches to task planning assume that the planner has access to all of the world information needed to develop a complete, correct plan which can then be executed in its entirety by an agent. Of course, for most complex domains, having all of the necessary world information at plan time cannot be assumed. We have implemented a planner, BUMP, which is capable of interleaving planning and execution. BUMP is able to defer portions of the planning process which depend on unknown or uncertain information until the information in question can be obtained through sensors. In this case, BUMP inserts sensor operations directly into the plan which the agent executes to enable further planning.

Alternately, BUMP may choose to assume a default value for the uncertain information rather than plan to sense it. We call this distinction the defer/default question, and it has played a central role in guiding our recent research efforts.

Deferral and defaulting each have strengths and weaknesses. Deferral can be attractive with good sensors because it reduces planner uncertainty, however, sensing can become prohibitively expensive. In addition, satisfying preconditions for sensor operations can in itself be time-consuming, and as we will see, increases the probability of performing premature actions.

Defaulting can be risky, but it allows the planner to complete more of the plan before execution begins. This allows the planner to see further into the plan and detect problems which may lie beyond the horizon of the deferral point. As domain uncertainty increases however, further planning becomes increasingly arbitrary.

In general, it is difficult to know whether to defer and sense a given uncertain value or simply choose a default value and face the risks. Deciding on the best strategy for a given planning problem consists of computing the tradeoffs of various strategies, but as we will see, such a computation quickly becomes intractable for even a modest degree of uncertainty, suggesting the need for heuristic techniques.

2   PURPOSE OF STUDY

The experiments described here were designed to answer general questions about factors that influence the plan quality, and how to use those factors when deciding on planning strategies. In this section we discuss three types of planning strategies and three measures of plan quality. It is useful to think of the quality measures as functions to minimize or maximize, and the strategies as means to that end.

2.1   PLANNING FACTORS

We have identified the following as important factors of task planning with sensors. Our studies have shown that by intelligently controlling these factors, a planner can improve its performance, often dramatically. Thus, we define an *overall planning strategy* as a set of algorithms to determine each of the following parameters for a given problem instance.

Goal ordering: The initial goal ordering describes the order in which BUMP will attempt to construct portions of the plan to satisfy each goal. This ordering is fixed when planning commences and does not change. It is important to note however, that this order is not necessarily the order of execution. BUMP is fairly good at ordering and reordering actions to exploit helpful goal interactions and avoid harmful ones. Choosing an initial goal ordering to facilitate intelligent action reordering is one way to improve BUMP's performance. We found it advantageous to carefully order the planner's initial goals based on the amount and type of unknown information at the start of planning. Thus, we varied and examined goal orders to determine heuristics for a *goal ordering strategy*.

When to sense: A critical decision when interleaving planning and execution is *when* to switch from one to the other. In related research, Olawsky and Gini [1990] identified two general strategies to manage the transfer of control between the planning and execution modules (i.e., *control strategies*). In each strategy, if the planner discovers that it requires unknown information it inserts a sensor operation into the plan to obtain the information. It then plans to satisfy any preconditions of this sensor operation.

In the first strategy, known as Stop and Execute (SE), when the planner encounters a goal whose achievement depends on information it has planned to sense, control is transferred to the execution module. The sensor process and all processes ordered before it in the current partial plan are executed. Control then returns to the planner. In the second strategy, Continue Elsewhere (CE), goals whose achievement depends on information

to be sensed are deferred. Planning continues elsewhere. Only when all goals are either planned to completion or deferred does execution initially commence. Execution halts after each sensor operation to allow completion of a deferred goal. In general, CE allows much more planning, albeit less informed planning, to occur ahead of the first execution phase.

We believe these two strategies to be of particular interest because they seem to be the only truly *domain independent* control strategies which we have found useful. Any other strategies we have considered are not general-purpose, and are only useful under rather specific circumstances.

What to sense: Finally, there is the question of *which* uncertain quantities to sense and which to default. We will refer to this as the *deferral strategy*. Choosing a reasonable deferral strategy requires careful consideration of domain-specific factors such as default reliabilities, sensor reliabilities, planning costs, execution costs, and the cost of human intervention.

2.2   PLAN QUALITY CRITERIA

Before discussing the strategies above, we must be clear as to the objectives they are intended to serve. We call these objectives *plan quality criteria*, and we have identified and gathered data on a number of them, each of which could stand alone, or be used in conjunction with other criteria as a measure of plan quality.

Success Rate: For this measure of planner performance, we computed the *percentage of problems* in which BUMP was able to construct plans in which no processes needed to be undone as a result of being executed prematurely. One of the major challenges in interleaving planning and execution is to keep the robot from performing actions which may interfere with goals not yet considered. The most common example of this in our experiments occurred when the robot bolted closed a tool box only to discover that it contained a wrench (or bolt) needed to accomplish a later goal. Under this criterion we considered such plans failures, in effect assuming the agent was unable to recover from such premature action.

Execution Cost: For this criterion we measured the cost of all actions to be performed in the final plan when the planner is allowed to recover from premature action (i.e. undo and redo these actions). This provided us with some indication of *how* inefficient the inferior solutions were to previously unsuccessful problems. For these experiments, we simply counted each instantiated process (action) in the plan as having unit cost, although it would be trivial to assign varying costs to various types of actions.

Planning Cost: Finally, in some experiments we tracked the amount of planning work done by the planner. Since BUMP is an agenda-based planner, a reasonably accurate indication of planning work is the number of items it placed on its agenda.

When the quality criterion is the success rate, we assume there are no deadlines which must be met by the planner in order to succeed. In domains in which such deadlines are important, execution and planning cost should be used as quality criteria.

3   EXPERIMENTS IN THE TOOL BOX WORLD

Each experiment consisted of running BUMP on a carefully controlled set of problems. We attempted to select subsets of problems which were especially prone to premature action, and study BUMP's performance in solving each of them. In the near future we plan to conduct a study in which subsets are randomly constructed to examine BUMP's average case performance as well.

The experiments consisted of problems in the *tool box world*. In this world, the robot is in a room with n tool boxes, each containing wrenches and bolts of various sizes. The robot knows the initial locations of the wrenches and bolts. Bolts are identified by a unique name, and wrenches are identified by size. The robot has been instructed to close and bolt one or more tool boxes with particular bolts. To perform each bolting operation, the robot must use a wrench of a size that matches the bolt. A sensor is available that can classify bolts by their size (e.g., a number from 1 to 10). For simplicity, the bolt sizes are indicated along the same scale as the wrench sizes. We also assume the robot has a tool belt into which it can put an unlimited number of bolts and wrenches.[1]

The test set for our experiments varied slightly from one experiment to the next, but there are a number of characteristics shared by most of them. More detailed descriptions of the experiments can be found in [Krebsbach *et al.*, 1991]. The majority of the studies deal with a three-box world. These boxes are called S, T, and U, and they are to be bolted with bolts b_s, b_t and b_u, respectively. Each of these three bolts has a different size—b_s has size 4, b_t size 5, and b_u size 6. The bolts are initially in their respective boxes (e.g., b_s is in box S).[2] All of the tool boxes are initially

Table 1: Summary of Experiments for Success Rates, Execution Cost, and Planning Cost Criteria.

Exp	Boxes	Quality	Control Strategy	Goal Orders	Num of Unknowns
1	3	success	SE	all	all
2	3	success	CE	all	all
3	3	e-cost	SE	all	all
4	3	e-cost	CE	all	all
5	3	p-cost	SE	all	all
6	3	p-cost	CE	all	all
7	4	e-cost	SE	4	1
8	4	p-cost	SE	4	1
9	4	e-cost	SE	6	2
10	4	p-cost	SE	6	2

open. In all of the experiments described in this paper the robot begins at a neutral site (one unrelated to any work that it must do). Since the planner's goals are strongly associated with particular tool boxes, this assumption was meant to avoid any bias in our results.

Each experiment consists of hundreds or thousands of planner runs using systematically defined sets of initial conditions, goal orderings and planning strategies. The variables defining these test sets are the following:

Wrench Location: Each of the wrenches may initially be in any tool box. For three box experiments this implies 27 possible wrench placement scenarios.

Goal Ordering: We studied the effect of reordering the initial goals on the performance of the planner. For three box experiments, this involves 6 possible orderings.

Control Strategy: SE versus CE.

Defer/Default Decisions: The size of each bolt is either known or unknown at the start of the first planning phase. For three bolts there are 8 combinations.

Table 1 provides a short summary of the ten experiments conducted. Complete experimental data can be found in [Krebsbach *et al.*, 1991].

4   MAJOR RESULTS

In this section we will outline the major results of the experiments, and principles and heuristics we developed based on the results. The results of experiments

---

[1]We are not concerned here with the arm-empty conditions as used in typical definitions of the blocks world. Our main goal in defining this domain is to study how sensor use can be interleaved with planning.

[2]This causes the robot to see less of the world while solving its early goals since it need not go anywhere to

get a bolt. While this may at first appear to simplify the problem, in effect it tests the planner on a more difficult set of problems than it would by chance. The more places BUMP travels to to get bolts, the more of a chance it has to gather other information, quite possibly information it could use to make more informed action ordering decisions. This in turn would decrease BUMP's vulnerability to failures due to premature action.

Table 2: Experiment 1 (3 Box, Stop and Execute, Success Based).

	456	45-	4-6	-56	4--	-5-	--6	---
STU	100	63	63	100	37	63	63	37
TSU	100	63	100	63	63	37	63	37
TUS	100	63	100	63	63	37	63	37
SUT	100	63	63	100	37	63	63	37
UST	100	100	63	63	63	63	37	37
UTS	100	100	63	63	63	63	37	37
Avg	100	75	75	75	54	54	54	37

Table 3: Experiment 3 (3 Box, Stop and Execute, Execution Cost Based).

	456	45-	4-6	-56	4--	-5-	--6	---
STU	20.5	24.5	24.8	22.1	29.1	26.1	26.4	30.8
TSU	20.5	24.5	22.1	24.8	26.1	29.1	26.4	30.8
TUS	20.5	24.8	22.1	24.5	26.4	29.1	26.1	30.8
SUT	20.5	24.8	24.5	22.1	29.1	26.4	26.1	30.8
UST	20.5	22.1	24.5	24.8	26.1	26.4	29.1	30.8
UTS	20.5	22.1	24.8	24.5	26.4	26.1	29.1	30.8
Avg	20.5	23.8	23.8	23.8	27.2	27.2	27.2	30.8

1 and 3 are provided in Tables 2 and 3 respectively. In each table, the headings along the horizontal axis indicate which of the three bolt sizes are known in the order b_s, b_t, and b_u respectively. So, for instance, 4-6 indicates that bolt b_s is of size 4, bolt b_t is of unknown size, and bolt b_u is of size 6. Vertical lines separate columns into groups with the same number of unknowns. The labels along the vertical axis denote goal orderings. For example, an ordering of TSU means the initial goal involving box T was attempted first, followed in turn by the S and U goals.

One immediate observation from Tables 2 and 3 is that more unknown information means decreased success and increased cost. Certainly the planner will be more likely to perform premature actions with less a priori information. This general trend continued throughout all of the experiments.

4.1 CHOOSING A GOAL ORDERING

One of the major results of this study was that most sensing should come as early as possible in the plan. The disadvantage of potentially premature action caused by early sensing was, in most cases, outweighed by the advantage of constructing most of the plan with more information.

4.1.1 Ordering To Maximize Success

Consider Table 2, in particular, experiments STU 45- and STU --6. In the former, there is only one unknown, b_u. In the latter, there are two, b_s and b_t, how-

ever BUMP performs at the same 63% level for both. Also, average success rates in columns with the same number of unknowns are identical, however, the percentages in each column are distributed differently by goal ordering. For instance, in each column with one unknown there are two goal orderings which produce 100% success, and four which produce only 63% success, but the goal orderings are different in each column. Both of these behaviors are the result of a single underlying principle.

To understand this behavior, we consider an example more closely. Note that 100% success can be achieved in column 45- (of Table 2) by ordering the U-goal first (either as UST or UTS). We hypothesized that in cases where the size of b_u was unknown, it was crucial to BUMP's success to know the size of b_u early in the planning process. This could be accomplished by reordering goals so that the U-goal was attacked first. If this was not done, the goal involving b_u would be one of the last two BUMP would try to accomplish. Therefore, it would not sense the size of b_u until later, increasing the chances that achieving it would involve undoing some actions which had already been executed. Since planning and execution are interleaved, some execution is very likely to have been performed by the time BUMP encounters its later goals. If any of the executed actions involve bolting closed a box containing a needed wrench for b_u, the plan will no longer be successful.[3] Experiment 1 confirmed our suspicions that it is possible to improve average performance by controlling the goal ordering based on which information is missing for a given problem. The following heuristic describes the optimal ordering:

Success-Based Ordering Heuristic: When there are goals whose achievement depends only on known information, and other goals which depend on unknowns, order all goals involving unknowns before those involving only knowns.[4]

The same general principle applies to Continue Elsewhere.

---

[3]In general, more specialized strategies are probably necessary to avoid such problems. We have performed some experiments using a strategy called Sense Before Closing, in which all sensor processes are ordered before all closing operations. This solves the problem, but often introduces severe costs of its own. In the worst case, each tool box would have to be visited twice instead of once, so Sense Before Closing trades bolting/unbolting operation costs with transportation costs. Whether this is a good trade of course depends on the domain.

[4]This goal ordering heuristic depends critically on the assumption that the planner can identify connections between its top-level goals and the unknown domain propositions in the problem. In these experiments there is a one-to-one correspondence between goals and potential unknowns, so the issue is not addressed. Another related issue not addressed here is what should be done when goals rely on differing numbers of unknowns.

4.1.2   Ordering to Minimize Cost

Similar observations on goal ordering can be made when cost is the quality criterion. From Table 3 we can see that the highest cost occurs when a known goal is considered first. However, looking at the 4--column, cost is minimized when there is an unknown first and an unknown last.[5] The goal orderings TSU and UST are both examples of this. We compared the plans generated with the TSU and TUS goal orderings to determine the cause of this behavior. As shown in Table 2 there is no difference in the number of plans involving premature actions for these two goal orderings. The slight difference in cost results from the way in which SE breaks up the planning work into phases. With the TSU goal ordering, BUMP plans the entire S-goal as soon as it obtains the sensor reading for bolt b_t. In several problems this allows BUMP to do two things while it is at S: to get wrench 5 and to close box S. This allows it to complete its task with only one trip to box S. When the TUS ordering is used, BUMP does not plan the S-goal until it has already closed box T and sensed bolt b_u. If wrench 5 (the one needed to close box T) is in box S, the robot must make one trip to S to obtain wrench 5 and a second trip after sensing b_u to close box S. This extra goto operation accounts for the increased cost.

To better understand this behavior we conducted experiments 7 through 10 using 4 boxes (SE control strategy only). Complete results of these experiments are described in [Krebsbach *et al.*, 1991]. These results are summarized by the following heuristic:

Cost-Based Ordering Heuristic: When there are goals whose achievement depends only on known information, and other goals which depend on unknowns:

1. place one unknown in the first position,
2. place one in the final position (if possible),
3. place any other unknowns following the first one,
4. place all knowns in the remaining positions.

4.2   CHOOSING A CONTROL STRATEGY

We found the CE strategy to be more susceptible to small increases in uncertainty, performing better than SE with one unknown, usually worse with two, and markedly worse with three. CE's sensitivity to unknown information makes sense when one considers CE's main advantage and disadvantage. Its advantage is that it performs more planning prior to the first execution cycle. This reduces the risk of performing premature actions if there are few unknowns, because BUMP can see further into the plan and perform action reordering to avoid conflicts it wouldn't detect

with SE until it's too late. However, as uncertainty increases this further planning becomes less informed, and ordering decisions become more arbitrary, increasing the probability of performing premature actions which lead to failure or severe cost penalties. For instance, in the case of 3 unknowns, BUMP using CE was able to find successful plans in only 22% of the 3 box problems, as compared with 37% for SE.

5   A SUCCESS-BASED OVERALL STRATEGY

Let us now make a first attempt at our goal of finding a good overall planning strategy. In addition to the ordering heuristic we must have a method for selecting a control strategy and a deferral strategy. We will try to maximize success through our selection of a strategy. We will assume here that once a control strategy and a deferral strategy have been selected, the top-level goals are reordered to obtain the highest success rate for the given number of unknowns.

As we have shown, we can always improve success rates by having additional known information. Thus, if our default information were 100% reliable, it would always make sense to use it and obtain a 100% success rating (with either control strategy). Of course, default information is rarely, if ever, 100% reliable. (We define reliability of a value to be the probability that it is correct. No notion of amount of error or distance from the correct value is considered.) If incorrect default information is used, the robot will most likely encounter an execution time error. This will necessitate some sort of execution time error recovery, and the resulting execution will certainly be inefficient. We consider this a failure. So, the increased success with extra "known" information must be adjusted by the reliability of that information. A similar point can be made regarding sensor reliability.[6] The data in all of our experiments assume that all sensor readings are correct, and this is clearly fictional.

5.1   ANALYSIS

To make this discussion more concrete, let us analyze the expected success rates given the reliability of our default values and our sensors. Let r_1, r_2 and r_3 be the reliabilities of our three defaults, d_1, d_2 and d_3 and let s_1, s_2 and s_3 be the reliabilities of the associated sensor readings. Also, assume $r_1 \geq r_2 \geq r_3$. (d_1, d_2, and

---

[5]This ordering tied for best in the success-based case.

---

[6]Note that the relative reliability of defaulted information does not affect the optimal goal ordering from a success-based perspective, since BUMP will fail if any of the defaults are incorrect, regardless of when they are used. The same applies to the relative reliabilities of sensed information. To obtain an optimal goal ordering, it is only important that the success-based ordering heuristic be followed.

Table 4: Success-Based Strategies.

Take	$\sigma = 1.0$	$\sigma = 0.8$	$\sigma = 0.6$
d_1	$r_1 \geq 0.55$	$r_1 \geq 0.44$	$r_1 \geq .33$
d_1, d_2	$r_2 \geq 0.67$	$r_2 \geq 0.54$	$r_2 \geq .40$
d_1, d_2, d_3	—	$r_3 \geq 0.80$	$r_3 \geq .60$

d_3 are in no particular order relative to the planning process.) When a bolt size is known at the start of planning, this corresponds to a default reliability of 100%. Let q_0, q_1, q_2 and q_3 be the maximum potential success rates for cases with 0, 1, 2 and 3 unknowns respectively. From our experiments, these values are 1.0, 1.0, 0.67 (with CE), and 0.37 (with SE).

We can now calculate the expected success rate taking into account the default and sensor reliabilities. For example, the success rate when taking default d_1 and sensing the other unknowns is $r_1 s_2 s_3 q_2$. The best overall strategy in any particular instance of the three box problem can be found by computing the maximum of the following set of values:

$$\{r_1 r_2 r_3 q_0, r_1 r_2 s_3 q_1, r_1 s_2 r_3 q_1, s_1 r_2 r_3 q_1,$$

$$r_1 s_2 s_3 q_2, s_1 r_2 s_3 q_2, s_1 s_2 r_3 q_2, s_1 s_2 s_3 q_3\}$$

Once the maximum is found, the associated deferral strategy consists of the default/defer decisions indicated.

It is interesting to examine the default reliabilities required in the three box domain. For simplicity, assume that all sensor readings have the same reliability σ. Table 4 shows for various values of σ how reliable the defaults must be to make them worth taking. Looking at the column labeled $\sigma = 1.0$, we note that if the best default has reliability ≥ 0.55 it is better to take that default than to use a 100% reliable sensor. If $r_1 \geq r_2 \geq 0.67$, it is better to take two defaults. For more realistic values of σ, we see that the defaults need not be very reliable at all. This is due to the reduction in premature actions that can be avoided by having more knowledge early in the planning process.

6   A COST-BASED OVERALL STRATEGY

When the robot is able to detect at some point that a default value or a sensor reading was erroneous and then take corrective actions, it makes more sense to use cost as the quality criterion. As described earlier, cost can be measured either in terms of execution cost or planning effort. We will focus on execution cost since we believe this is generally the more significant aspect. A similar analysis could be developed for plan-

ning effort.[7]

6.1   ANALYSIS

The analysis in this case is a good deal more complicated since many more options come into play. For example, if a decision is made to try a default which later turns out incorrect, the robot could then try to recover by using a sensor. If the sensor reading also turns out to be incorrect, it might still be possible to recover with human intervention (presumably at a very high cost).[8]

As before, let r_i be the reliability of a default value and s_i the reliability of the sensor reading. In place of the success rates q_i that we used in our previous analysis, we need the average execution costs under various scenarios. We define the function C_i to return these costs when there are i unknowns. C_i takes i arguments where each argument is a sequence of one, two or three of the letters D, S and I. This sequence reflects which of the resources — default, sense and intervene — were used for the given unknown as well as the order in which they were tried. It is assumed that the last resource is always successful and that intervention is always successful. For example, DS means an incorrect default followed by a correct sensor operation. SDI means an incorrect sensor reading followed by an incorrect default value followed by successful human intervention. $C_1(SDI)$ would be the expected execution cost under this scenario when there is one unknown.

Given this information we can develop formulas for the expected costs of various attempted solutions. For example, with one unknown the expected cost of defaulting with sensing and intervention as backup actions is expressed by the following weighted sum:

$$r_1 C_1(D) + (1-r_1)s_1 C_1(DS) + (1-r_1)(1-s_1)C_1(DSI)$$

---

[7] The cost of recovering from incorrect information (sensed or defaulted) depends on the state of the environment when the false information is discovered. Thus, the optimal goal ordering from a cost-based perspective may be influenced by the relative reliabilities of the information in question. This is in contrast to our observations regarding optimal success-based goal ordering. We are currently investigating this question.

[8] Some other options that we do not consider in this analysis are

1. to try a different sensor, or

2. to continue trying the same sensor.

If the sensor is working at all (i.e., there is a non-zero probability of a correct reading), then with persistence the second option should eventually produce a correct reading. The probability of n readings all being incorrect goes to 0 as $n \to \infty$. This might also have a very high cost. The same analysis technique could be used to characterize the cost of both these options.

Table 5: Sample C_1 Values.

D	20	S	22
DS	30	SD	30
DI	40	SI	42
DSI	50	SDI	50
I	35		

Table 6: Expected Costs.

Strategy	$r_1 = 0.7$ $s_1 = 0.8$	$r_1 = 0.2$ $s_1 = 0.8$
default, sense, intervene	**24.2**	31.2
sense, default, intervene	24.8	26.8
sense, intervene	26.0	**26.0**
default, intervene	26.0	36.0
intervene	35.0	35.0

Assuming the C_1 values shown in Table 5 and the reliabilities $r_1 = 0.7$ and $s_1 = 0.8$ the expected cost is 24.2.

An alternative strategy would try sensing first followed by defaulting and then intervention. The weighted sum cost formula for this strategy is

$$s_1 C_1(S) + (1 - s_1) r_1 C_1(SD) + (1 - s_1)(1 - r_1) C_1(SDI)$$

There are three other strategies in which one or more of the resources is not tried. The expected costs are

no default: $s_1 C_1(S) + (1 - s_1) C_1(SI)$

no sensing: $r_1 C_1(D) + (1 - r_1) C_1(DI)$

neither default nor sense: $C_1(I)$

One of these strategies might be appropriate if sensing or defaulting is particularly unreliable and the cost of intervention is light.

Given the C_1 cost estimates and the reliabilities, we can calculate the optimal strategy for one unknown by evaluating the five above formulas and finding the minimum. The expected costs under the five strategies, assuming the costs in Table 5 and the reliabilities $r_1 = 0.7$ and $s_1 = 0.8$, are shown in the second column of Table 6. In this case, the best strategy is default, sense then intervene. If on the other hand the reliability of the default is 0.2 we get the costs shown in column 3. Here, the best strategy is to sense then intervene. Note that it is better in this case to ask immediately for intervention than to try a default and then request help if there is a problem. The default is not reliable enough to risk the extra cost associated with an incorrect guess and the cost of intervention is small.

Let us next consider the formulas for expected cost with two unknowns. One scenario would try both

defaults first, backed up by sensing and intervention. The resulting formula is

$$
\begin{aligned}
& r_1 r_2 C_2(D, D) + \\
& \quad (1 - r_1) r_2 s_1 C_2(DS, D) + \\
& \quad r_1 (1 - r_2) s_2 C_2(D, DS) + \\
& \quad (1 - r_1)(1 - r_2) s_1 s_2 C_2(DS, DS) + \\
& \quad (1 - r_1) r_2 (1 - s_1) C_2(DSI, D) + \\
& \quad r_1 (1 - r_2)(1 - s_2) C_2(D, DSI) + \\
& \quad (1 - r_1)(1 - r_2)(1 - s_1) s_2 C_2(DSI, DS) + \\
& \quad (1 - r_1)(1 - r_2) s_1 (1 - s_2) C_2(DS, DSI) + \\
& \quad (1 - r_1)(1 - r_2)(1 - s_1)(1 - s_2) C_2(DSI, DSI)
\end{aligned}
$$

This formula is certainly much more complicated than the formulas for one unknown. In fact the number of terms to be summed in a formula that considers all three resources — default, sense and request intervention — grows exponentially (3^n for n unknowns). The number of factors in the longest term is $2n + 1$. Thus, calculating the expected cost of just one scenario is $O(n3^n)$. Even the amount of cost data that must be collected grows exponentially in the number of unknowns. There are many other scenarios that must be evaluated and compared to this one to find the optimal strategy of sensing and defaulting.

Clearly, we cannot effectively calculate this optimal strategy unless the number of unknowns is quite small. Rather, we need heuristic techniques that will help us find an approximately optimal strategy. Finding such techniques will be a subject of our future research.

7 DISCUSSION

A well recognized problem with planning is the inability of most planners to deal with the inexactness and noise of the real world.

Several solutions have been proposed that range from eliminating planning altogether in favor of reactive planning [Brooks, 1986] or situated systems [Agre and Chapman, 1987, Kaelbling, 1988], to combining reactivity and planning [Georgeff and Lansky, 1987, Sanborn and Hendler, 1988], to interleaving planning with execution [McDermott, 1978, Durfee and Lesser, 1986, Chapman, 1991], to preplanning for every contingency [Schoppers, 1987], to verifying the executability of plans and adding sensing whenever needed to reduce the uncertainty [Brooks, 1982, Doyle et al., 1986].

Brooks [1982] verifies the feasibility of a plan in light of uncertainties and errors and decides when sensors are needed to reduce the amount of error. Doyle et al. [1986] use sensors to verify the execution of a plan. The sensor requests are generated after the plan has been produced by examining the preconditions and postconditions of each action in the plan. Domain dependent verification operators map assertions to perception requests and expectations. The entire process is done before executing the plan. Hager and Mintz

[1991] have more recently proposed methods for sensor planning based on probabilistic models of uncertainty.

Few have addressed the more specific problem we address. Our work has been inspired, among others, by the work of Turney and Segre [1989], who alternate between improvising and planning. Since sensing is assumed to be expensive, their system prefers actions with the fewest sensor requests first. The results obtained show the importance of good heuristics over sophisticated planning strategies. The quality of the heuristic improvisation strategy has the largest effect on the quality of the solution. This seems to suggest that it is more important to develop good heuristics than to develop a sophisticated planner.

The need to plan with incomplete information raises important theoretical issues. A number of authors have proposed decision theoretic approaches to planning and control. Horvitz et al. [1989] propose a general model for reasoning under scarce resources that is based on decision theory [Dean, 1990]. Chrisman and Simmons [1991] produce near optimal cost plans by using Markov Decision Processes to decide what to sense.

Drummond and Bresina [1990] propose an algorithm that maximizes the probability of satisfying a goal. More recent work of Minton et al. [1991] analyzes in a rigorous way a linear and a non-linear planner in terms of their overall efficiency, examining both search space complexity and time cost. Hsu [1990] proposes to plan with incomplete information by generating a "most general partial plan" without committing to any choice of actions not logically imposed by the information available at that point. She uses an anytime algorithm [Dean and Boddy, 1988] to choose the appropriate action on the current partial plan when the system has to act.

Acknowledgement

We would like to thank Mark Boddy for useful and influential discussions about topics in this paper, most notably issues of cost analysis and decision theory.

References

[Agre and Chapman, 1987] Philip Agre and David Chapman. Pengi: A theory of activity. In *Proc. of AAAI-87*, Washington, July 1987.

[Brooks, 1982] Rodney A. Brooks. Symbolic error analysis and robot planning. *International Journal of Robotics Research*, 1:29–69, 1982.

[Brooks, 1986] Rodney Brooks. A robust layered control system for a mobile robot. *IEEE Journal of Robotics and Automation*, RA-2(1):14–23, March 1986.

[Chapman, 1991] David Chapman. Combinatorics and action. In *Working Notes of the AAAI Fall Symposium on Sensory Aspects of Robotics Intelligence*, pages 26–30, 1991.

[Chrisman and Simmons, 1991] Lonnie Chrisman and Reid Simmons. Sensible planning: Focusing perceptual attention. In *Proc. of AAAI-91*, Los Angeles, CA, 1991.

[Dean and Boddy, 1988] Thomas Dean and Mark Boddy. An analysis of time-dependent planning. In *Proc. of AAAI-88*, St. Paul, MN, 1988.

[Dean, 1990] Thomas Dean. Planning under uncertainty and time pressure. In *Proceedings of the DARPA Workshop on Planning*, pages 390–395, San Diego, CA, November 1990.

[Doyle et al., 1986] Richard Doyle, David Atkinson, and Rajkumar Doshi. Generating perception requests and expectations to verify the execution of plans. In *Proc. of AAAI-86*, pages 202–206, Philadelphia, 1986.

[Drummond and Bresina, 1990] Mark Drummond and John Bresina. Anytime synthetic projection: maximizing the probability of goal satisfaction. In *Proceedings of the Eighth National Conference on Artificial Intelligence*, Boston, Mass, August 1990.

[Durfee and Lesser, 1986] Edmund H. Durfee and Victor R. Lesser. Incremental planning to control a blackboard-based problem solver. In *Proc. of AAAI-86*, Philadelphia, PA, 1986.

[Georgeff and Lansky, 1987] Michael P. Georgeff and Amy L. Lansky. Reactive reasoning and planning. In *Proceedings of the Sixth National Conference on Artificial Intelligence*, Seattle, WA, 1987.

[Hager and Mintz, 1991] G. Hager and M. Mintz. Computational methods for task-directed sensor data fusion and sensor planning. *International Journal of Robotics Research*, 10:285–313, 1991.

[Horvitz et al., 1989] Eric J. Horvitz, Gregory F. Cooper, and David E. Heckerman. Reflection and action under scarce resources: theoretical principles and empirical study. In *Proc. of IJCAI-89*, pages 1121–1127, Detroit, MI, August 1989.

[Hsu, 1990] Jane Yung-jen Hsu. Partial planning with incomplete information. In *Proceedings of the AAAI Spring Symposium on Planning in Uncertain, Unpredicatable, or Changing Environments*, 1990.

[Kaelbling, 1988] Leslie Pack Kaelbling. Goals as parallel program specifications. In *Proceedings of the Seventh National Conference on Artificial Intelligence*, pages 60–65, St. Paul, MN, August 1988.

[Krebsbach et al., 1991] Kurt Krebsbach, Duane Olawsky, and Maria Gini. Deferring task planning in the tool box world: Empirical results. Technical Report TR 91-60, University of Minnesota Department of Computer Science, Minneapolis, MN, 1991.

[McDermott, 1978] Drew McDermott. Planning and acting. *Cognitive Science*, 2:71–109, 1978.

[Minton et al., 1991] Steven Minton, John Bresina, and Mark Drummond. Commitment strategies in planning: a comparative analysis. In *Proceedings of the 12th International Joint Conference on Artificial Intelligence*, pages 259–265, Sydney, Australia, August 1991.

[Olawsky and Gini, 1990] Duane Olawsky and Maria Gini. Deferred planning and sensor use. In *Proceedings of the DARPA Workshop on Planning*, San Diego, CA, November 1990.

[Sanborn and Hendler, 1988] James Sanborn and James Hendler. A model of reaction for planning in dynamic environments. *Artificial Intelligence in Engineering*, 3(2):95–102, 1988.

[Schoppers, 1987] Marcel Schoppers. Universal plans for reactive robots in unpredictable environments. In *Proceedings of the Tenth International Joint Conference on Artificial Intelligence*, pages 1039–1046, Milan, Italy, August 1987.

[Turney and Segre, 1989] Jennifer Turney and Alberto Segre. A framework for learning in planning domains with uncertainty. Technical Report 89-1009, Department of Computer Science, Cornell University, Ithaca, NY 14853-7501, May 1989.

Systematic and Nonsystematic Search Strategies

Pat Langley

(Langley@ptolemy.arc.nasa.gov)
AI Research Branch (M/S 269-2)
NASA Ames Research Center
Moffett Field, CA 94035 USA

Abstract

In this paper we compare the relative costs of a systematic problem-solving method – depth-first search – and a nonsystematic method – iterative sampling. An average-case analysis reveals that, for a well-specified class of domains, depth-first search always requires less effort when there exists a single solution, and is generally superior on tasks with shallow solution paths and few solutions. In contrast, iterative sampling is superior on tasks with deep solution paths and many solutions. Depth-first search scales better to cases with high branching factors if the number of solutions remains the same, but random search scales better when the density of solutions remains constant. The search costs predicted by the analysis closely fit the costs observed in experiments with artificial search tasks. We also relate iterative sampling to other methods, including iterative broadening, which is based on similar intuitions.

1. Introduction

Most AI problem-solving systems employ systematic methods such as depth-first, breadth-first, and best-first search, which retain information about states they have considered to avoid duplication of effort. In contrast, humans are remarkably nonsystematic in their problem solving, using methods that may cover the same ground many times. Typically, researchers have assumed that such behavior resulted from limitations in human short-term memory, and that when such limits are not present, the systematic approach should always be preferred. However, in this paper we argue that this intuition is incorrect, and that there are situations in which nonsystematic methods are superior to systematic ones.

Our analysis will deal with a problem space that has a uniform branching factor b, and in which one or more solutions lie exactly at depth d. We also assume that information about success or failure is not available until one reaches level d. Finally, we assume that the search space is a tree rather than a directed graph, so

the node-branching and edge-branching factors (Korf, 1985) are equal. One simple problem of this type involves cracking a safe with b settings that requires d turns. One can also formulate some constraint satisfaction tasks (e.g., scheduling) in these terms.

At each branch point in the search tree, one must select from among b alternative children. We will use e to refer to the expected number of nodes one must try at each branch point before selecting a node that lies on a solution path, provided the path one has traversed so far also leads to a solution. In some domains, heuristics are available to bias this selection and reduce e to a reasonable level. For instance, a skilled safe cracker might occasionally hear a click that suggests a likely setting, significantly reducing her expected amount of search. In other domains, e may be low because many solutions exist. We will focus on this latter issue, although we will return briefly to the effects of heuristics in the final section.

2. Analysis of Two Search Algorithms

We will consider two algorithms that handle the class of problems described above. The first method, *depth-first search*, systematically explores each node and its associated subtree in turn, without duplicating any effort. However, one disadvantage of this strategy is that, having selected a node N, it does not return and consider N's siblings unless it has expanded the entire subtree below N and found no solution. Thus, a selection error high in the tree can lead to considerable unnecessary search.

We will call the second algorithm *iterative sampling*, though we will sometimes refer to *random* or *nonsystematic* search. At each branch point in the search, iterative sampling selects a node at random and then recurses until it reaches the depth limit. Thus, the method is similar to a greedy technique in that it selects a single option without backtracking, though it need not use an evaluation function. If the generated path does not lead to a solution, iterative sampling begins again at the initial state. The method continues in this fashion until it finds a path that solves the problem. Unlike depth-first search, the nonsystematic algorithm retains no memory of the states it has visited, so it can retrace entire paths. However, decisions made high in the tree cannot lock the method into a 'wild goose chase' as in the depth-first scheme, so it seems possible that iterative sampling may outperform the more systematic strategy.

2.1 Overall Cost of the Algorithms

In order to determine the relative cost of these algorithms, we will analyze their average-case behavior as a function of the branching factor b, the solution depth d, and the expected number of nodes e considered at each branch point before selecting the correct one, if it exists in the set of alternatives. Later we will ground e in other factors, but for now we assume it as a separate parameter of the domain and method. We will measure cost as the total number of nodes generated during search, assuming that, at each branch point, one generates all children before any are expanded themselves. We use this metric because it is biased in favor of the systematic strategy, which generates each node only once.

Let us first examine the behavior of depth-first search. Even if the algorithm selects the right node on its first attempt at each branch point, it will generate a total of bd nodes. In addition, recall that depth-first search expands the entire subtree below each node that it selects incorrectly. If the search has reached a node N at level j out of d, then there remain $d - j$ levels to explore, and the total number of nodes below (but not including) N is $\sum_{k=1}^{d-j} b^k$. If we let e_{dfs} be the expected number of nodes required for depth-first search to make the right selection at each branch point, then for each level j, on the average it will consider $(e_{dfs} - 1)\sum_{k=1}^{d-j} b^k$ nodes in following fruitless paths before it selects a good child. This recurs at each of d levels, giving

$$t_{dfs} = (e_{dfs} - 1)(\sum_{j=1}^{d-1} \sum_{k=1}^{d-j} b^k) + bd$$

as the expected number of nodes that depth-first search will generate before finding a solution. Furthermore, since $\sum_{k=1}^{d-j} b^k = (\frac{b}{b-1})(b^{d-j} - 1)$, we can factor $\frac{b}{b-1}$ out of the remaining summation, giving

$$t_{dfs} = (e_{dfs} - 1)(\frac{b}{b-1})(\sum_{j=1}^{d-1}(b^{d-j} - 1)) + bd \quad .$$

One can rewrite the summation in this expression as

$$(\sum_{j=1}^{d-1} b^{d-j}) - (\sum_{j=1}^{d-1} 1) = (\sum_{j=1}^{d-1} b^j) - (d-1)$$

$$= \frac{b^d - b}{b-1} - d + 1 = \frac{b^d - 1}{b-1} - d \quad .$$

Substituting this into the second expression for t_{dfs}, we have

$$t_{dfs} = (e_{dfs} - 1)(\frac{b}{b-1})(\frac{b^d - 1}{b-1} - d) + bd$$

$$= (e_{dfs} - 1) \cdot \frac{(b^{d+1} - db^2 + db - b)}{(b-1)^2} + bd$$

as the expected number of nodes the depth-first scheme will examine during its search. Note that e_{dfs} is much less significant than b in this expression.

The analysis for the iterative sampling algorithm is more straightforward. Let p be the probability of selecting a good node (one on a solution path) at a given branch point. We know that, if one is sampling with replacement, the expected number of attempts until one selects a good node is $1/p$. We refer to this expected value as e_{is} to distinguish it from that for depth-first search. The probability that the algorithm will solve the problem on any given pass is p^d, giving $1/p^d = e_{is}^d$ as the expected number of attempts before finding a solution. Finally, since there are exactly $b \cdot d$ nodes generated on each pass, we have $t_{is} = b \cdot d \cdot e_{is}^d$ as the expected number of nodes that iterative sampling will generate.

2.2 The Expected Number of Nodes

The above analysis referred to e, the expected number of nodes one must try at each branch point of the search tree before selecting one on a solution path. This number is simple to compute for problems with a single solution. For a systematic strategy like depth-first search, which samples states without replacement, we have $e_{dfs} = (b+1)/2$. In contrast, for a nonsystematic strategy that randomly samples states with replacement, we simply have $e_{is} = b$.

However, we are also concerned with problems that have multiple solutions, so that $e_{dfs} < (b+1)/2$ for the systematic case and $e_{is} < b$ for the nonsystematic one. Following Ginsberg and Harvey (1990), we will assume there exists some integer s such that, if a node lies on a solution path, exactly s of its b children also lie on a solution path. If a problem with branching factor b and depth d can be solved, then its initial state lies on such a path, and there will be exactly s^d solutions. These solutions will not be evenly distributed in the space, but will be 'clustered' near one another.

Because a nonsystematic strategy samples with replacement, the probability of selecting a good node is s/b on each pass. This gives $e_{is} = b/s$ as the expected number of nodes examined by iterative sampling at each branch point. This term can vary from b, for problems with a single solution, to 1, for problems in which all paths lead to a solution. Substituting for e_{is} in the earlier analysis gives $t_{is} = b \cdot d \cdot (\frac{b}{s})^d$ as the total number of nodes that we expect iterative sampling to generate before finding a solution.

Computing e_{dfs} for a systematic strategy is more complicated. Given a finite set of outcomes with values from 1 to n, the expected value is simply $\sum_{k=1}^{n} k p_k$. Since depth-first search samples without replacement, we know that it will never select more than $b - s + 1$ nodes at any branch point. If we let p_n be the probability of selecting a good node on the n_{th} attempt, then p_1 is simply s/b. However, to compute later terms we must multiply the probability of failure on the previous passes by the probability of success on the current one. Each time the algorithm fails to select a node on a solution path, there is one fewer child in competition. Thus, we have $(1-\frac{s}{b})(\frac{s}{b-1})$ for p_2, $(1-\frac{s}{b})(1-\frac{s}{b-1})(\frac{s}{b-2})$ for p_3, and so forth.

Multiplying these terms by the respective values of k, we get the general expression

$$
e_{dfs} = \frac{s}{b} + \sum_{k=2}^{b-s+1} \left[k \frac{s}{b-k+1} \prod_{j=0}^{k-2} (1 - \frac{s}{b-j}) \right]
$$

$$
= \frac{(b-s)}{(s+1)} + 1
$$

as the expected number of nodes examined by a systematic method at each branch point before finding one on a solution path. This reduces to $(b+1)/2$ in the case where $s = 1$ and there is a unique solution. Substituting for e_{dfs} in the earlier analysis gives

$$
t_{dfs} = \frac{(b-s)}{(s+1)} \cdot \frac{(b^{d+1} - db^2 + db - b)}{(b-1)^2} + bd
$$

as the total number of nodes that we expect depth-first search to generate before finding a solution.

3. Behavior of the Search Algorithms

The above analysis makes specific predictions about the amount of search required by the random and depth-first algorithms under various conditions. In particular, it predicts the effects of the branching factor, the solution depth, and the number of solutions. For any search task within the space analyzed, comparing t_{dfs} to t_{is} will let us predict the more efficient method. However, to gain better intuitions about the relative costs of the algorithms, we will examine their behavior across a range of settings for the three domain parameters.

Figure 1 (a) shows the predicted behavior of the two search algorithms for ten settings of the depth d when only one solution exists and when the branching factor b is two. The dependent measure is the number of nodes generated before finding a solution, presented in logarithmic scale to counter the exponential growth inherent in search.

The figure also shows experimental results obtained for the two methods using artificial search problems. We implemented versions of iterative sampling and

depth-first search that accepted parameters for the breadth b, depth d, and good children s, and that explored search trees with these characteristics. If a node selected by an algorithm lay along a solution path, then s out of b of its children also lay along solution paths. The nonsystematic method selected one child at random, whereas the depth-first technique ordered them randomly and considered each in turn.

Each experimental point in Figure 1 (a) represents an average of 1000 runs for one of the algorithms on a specific setting of the parameters b, d, and s. Note that the theoretical values typically fall within the 99% error bars that bound the observed means. The close fit between the predictions and observations lends confidence that the overall analysis is correct, though computational constraints limited our experimental runs to problems that involved under 300,000 nodes.

The basic results are somewhat discouraging. In the absence of multiple solutions, depth-first search always outperforms iterative sampling. The systematic nature of the former algorithm, which reduces the expected number of nodes one must consider at each branch point, more than compensates for the extra search it carries out when it strays down a useless path. At first glance, this suggests that our intuitions were incorrect, and that one should prefer systematic methods to nonsystematic ones.

However, the curves in Figure 1 (b) reveal a quite different story when multiple solutions are present. When the branching factor is four and two children at each branch point lead to solutions, we again find that iterative sampling requires more search than the depth-first scheme on problems in which the depth d is low. But as d increases, the difference between the two methods decreases, until their curves cross over each other near $d = 7$. Beyond this point, random search outperforms depth-first search, and its relative advantage increases with the depth. Recall that the curves present cost on a logarithmic scale; thus, for $d = 12$, the analysis predicts that depth-first search will take 20 times as long as iterative sampling. In the presence of sufficient numbers of solutions, nonsystematic search scales to longer solution paths much better than the systematic technique. The experimental points in the figure are consistent with these predictions.

The results change again when we hold the depth and solutions constant and vary the branching factor b. Figure 2 (a) shows that the systematic method initially fares slightly worse than the nonsystematic one, but as b increases, depth-first search pulls slightly ahead. When the depth is five and each good node has three good children, the crossover occurs when the branching factor is around ten. After this point, the depth-first algorithm requires less search than iterative sampling, and its advantage increases with the setting for b. Thus, the systematic method scales better to problems with higher branching factors than does it-

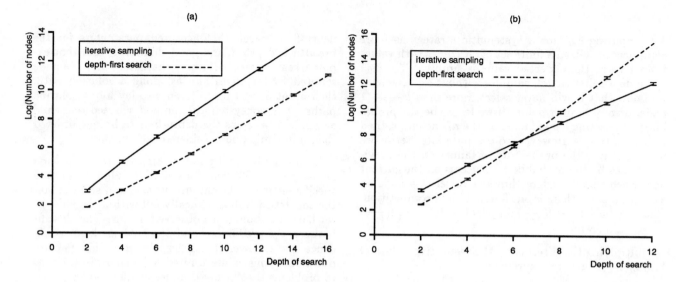

Figure 1: Nodes generated by depth-first search and iterative sampling for different depths d (a) when there is a unique solution and the branching factor b is two, and (b) when the number of good nodes s is two and the branching factor b is four. The lines represent theoretical behavior; the error bars indicate experimental results.

erative sampling, but the difference is small compared to other factors we have examined. In fact, the experimental points in the graph are so close that the difference is barely detectable. Interestingly, nearly indistinguishable behavior also occurred for a number of other settings for d and s that we examined.

Both crossovers occur in the presence of multiple solutions, but not when it is absent, suggesting that we examine the role of this factor more closely. Figure 2 (b) reveals the effect of varying s, the number of children on a solution path at each branch point, given a branching factor of six and a solution depth of five. For low settings of s, iterative sampling carries out substantially more search than the depth-first approach. However, this difference decreases as the number of solutions increases, and around $s = 3$ the curves intersect. Past this point, the nonsystematic method outperforms the systematic one, except in the degenerate case where $s = b$, where neither requires any search. Thus, iterative sampling benefits more from multiple solutions than does depth-first search, making the former more desirable in domains where they are present.

This result suggests an alternative treatment of the effect of the branching factor b. In some classes of domains, as one increases the branching factor, the number of solutions increases as well. To model this situation, we examined the effect when we varied b but held the depth d at four and held the ratio b/s at the constant two. Figure 3 (a) shows the curves that result. Under these conditions, we again find that iterative sampling starts off requiring more search than the depth-first organization, but that a crossover occurs near $b = 8$ or $s = 4$, and that after this point, the

the nonsystematic method outperforms the systematic one. Thus, iterative sampling scales to higher branching factors better than does depth-first search, provided that the number of good nodes at each branch point keeps pace, and thus the density of solutions remains constant. Whether there exist real-world tasks with this characteristic remains an open question.

In comparing depth-first search to their iterative broadening method, Ginsberg and Harvey (1990) examine behavior as the depth d becomes very large. In a similar manner, we can compare systematic and nonsystematic search in the 'large depth limit'. To determine the conditions under which iterative sampling will outperform depth-first search, we set $t_{is} < t_{dfs}$ and solve for s. As Ginsberg and Harvey note, one can simplify t_{dfs} for large d, giving us the inequality

$$b \cdot d \cdot \left(\frac{b}{s}\right)^d < \frac{(b-s)}{(s+1)} \cdot \frac{b^{d+1}}{(b-1)^2} \quad .$$

Dividing both sides of this expression by b^{d+1} produces

$$\frac{d}{s^d} < \frac{(b-s)}{(s+1)(b-1)^2} \quad ,$$

and taking both sides to the limit as d approaches infinity gives the inequality

$$0 < \frac{(b-s)}{(s+1)(b-1)^2} \quad ,$$

provided $s > 1$, since in this case the denominator s^d dominates the numerator d. Finally, adding to both sides and then dividing gives the relation

$$s < b \quad .$$

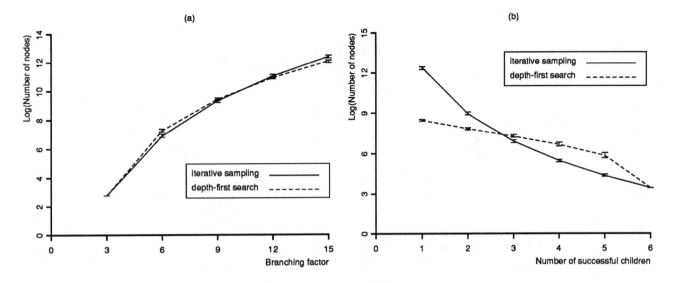

Figure 2: Predicted and observed search for the depth-first and iterative sampling algorithms (a) on different branching factors b when the number of good nodes s is three and the depth of the solution d is five, and (b) for different numbers of good nodes s when the branching factor b is six and the depth of the solution d is five.

In other words, in the large depth limit, iterative sampling requires less effort to find a solution than depth-first search whenever the number of good children s is greater than one and less than the branching factor b.

This result is similar to the one that Ginsberg and Harvey report for their iterative broadening method, which outperforms depth-first search for large depths whenever $s^d > 2(b-1)/(b-2)$. One conclusion they draw is that when $b > 3$, their method will be more efficient (for large d) even when there exist only three terminal goal nodes. However, this result follows from an extension of their analysis to nonintegral values of s between one and two. This range of values is crucial, since it seems unlikely that many real-world domains have 2^d or more solutions.

Our equations do not cover the nonintegral case for iterative sampling, but we have carried out experimental studies of this condition. Figure 3 (b) presents curves for systematic and nonsystematic search when $b = 2$ and the expected value of $s = 1.5$. In this experiment, half of the nodes along solution paths had one child that also led toward a solution ($s = 1$) and half had two such children ($s = 2$). In general, nonintegral s values can follow other distributions, but this one is analogous to that in Ginsberg and Harvey's analysis. As for integral values, the random method starts out worse than depth-first search, but eventually a crossover occurs, in this situation around $d = 10$. Additional experiments show that this effect recurs for other nonintegral s values.

Although our analysis has focused on a specific class of domains, we hoped that iterative sampling would have advantages in other search tasks as well. To this end, we compared the behavior of iterative sampling with that of depth-first search on the eight puzzle. One can reach nodes in the eight puzzle through many paths, which clearly violates our assumption about tree structure. In one experiment, we ran both algorithms on problems that could be solved in a minimum of four steps, but we varied the depth limit used to control backtracking and iteration. The idea here was that, lacking knowledge of minimal solution length, one might overestimate this factor. Under these conditions, we found that depth-first search carried out progressively more search as one increases the depth limit, whereas random search was nearly unaffected by the parameter. In this study, crossover occurred when the depth limit exceeded ten. However, in another experiment with the eight puzzle, we varied the length of the minimal solution path while setting the depth cutoff equal to this minimum. In this case, depth-first search consistently outperformed iterative sampling even for problems with 20 steps in their solutions.

In summary, depth-first search is clearly superior to iterative sampling in the absence of multiple solutions, but the case is much less clear cut when there exists more than one successful path. For tasks that involve shallow solution paths and few solutions, depth-first search remains the method of choice. However, the random algorithm scales better to domains that involve deep searches, and it receives greater benefits from multiple solutions. The situation with respect to the branching factor is even more complex. The systematic technique scales better to problems with high branching factors when the number of solutions remains constant, but the nonsystematic method scales better when the density of solutions remains the same.

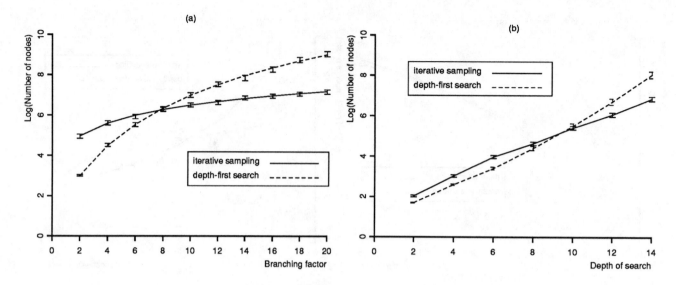

Figure 3: (a) Predicted and observed search for the depth-first and iterative sampling algorithms for different branching factors b when the depth of the solution d is four and the ratio b/s is two; and (b) the observed cost for depth-first search and iterative sampling when b is two and s is 1.5.

Thus, the preferred method depends on the characteristics of the problem-solving domain, but there exist clear cases where random search is more desirable.

4. Discussion

Our work is not the first on nonsystematic search, and we hope it will not be the last to explore the potential of this intriguing class of methods. Here we briefly review some related work and discuss open issues for future research.

4.1 Relation to Iterative Broadening

Our intuitions about the superiority of nonsystematic search over depth-first search are similar to Ginsberg and Harvey's (1990) arguments for the advantages of their *iterative broadening* technique. This method first carries out a depth-first search with a breadth limit of two. If this fails, it repeats the search with a breadth limit of three, and so on, until it finds a solution. As in iterative sampling, the iterative broadening method can repeat previous effort, but it does not get locked into expanding entire subtrees because of errors made early in its search. It differs from the iterative sampling algorithm in its systematic nature, but it also appears to benefit from situations in which multiple solutions are present.

Ginsberg and Harvey's analysis of iterative broadening lets one calculate its expected performance on particular search tasks. The results one obtains in this manner suggest that, like depth-first search, iterative broadening outperforms random search initially, but that as the depth increases, the nonsystematic approach fares better. The theoretical crossover point for iterative broadening and random search (around $d = 12$ for $b = 4$ and $s = 2$) occurs later than that for depth-first and random search, but otherwise the effects of solution depth are very similar, presumably because Ginsberg and Harvey's method sometimes expands entire breadth-limited subtrees.

Experiments with artificial search tasks are consistent with these predictions. Figure 4 (a) presents the results for $b = 4$ and $s = 2$, which suggest that the crossover does indeed occur near $d = 12$. Figure 4 (b) shows that similar curves occur in the nonintegral case when $b = 2$ and $s = 1.5$. However, other experiments indicate that iterative broadening is much less affected by higher branching factors than iterative sampling, and that it benefits from higher values of s as well as the nonsystematic approach. In summary, iterative broadening does not scale to large depths as well as does random search, but it outperforms iterative sampling on other dimensions and in general is much harder to beat than depth-first search.

4.2 Related Studies of Random Search

A number of researchers have reported methods that incorporate some notion of random search. For instance, Brassard and Bratley (1988) described a set of nonsystematic techniques that they called *Las Vegas* algorithms. One variant, which they applied to the eight queens puzzle, is almost identical to the iterative sampling algorithm. They reported experiments showing that their method outperforms depth-first search on the queens puzzle, but they did not systematically explore the effect of the branching factor, search depth, or number of solutions.

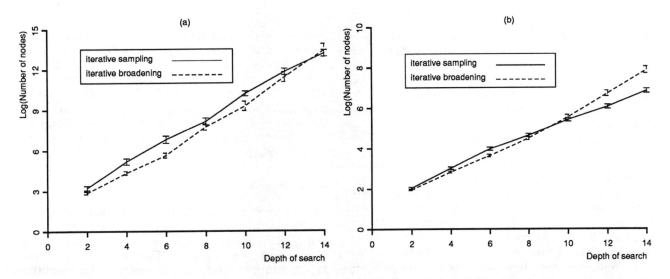

Figure 4: (a) Observed search for iterative broadening and iterative sampling for different depths d when the branching factor b is four and s is two; and (b) the observed search for the two algorithms when b is two and s is 1.5. These curves do not include theoretical costs.

On the other hand, unlike our analysis, Brassard and Bratley's treatment included separate costs for success and failure. This takes into account the chance that one will abandon a path before reaching the depth d, which seems quite possible in constraint satisfaction domains where one can detect illegal partial states. They also showed that a combination of systematic and nonsystematic search can outperform either method in isolation, at least in the queens domain. In closely related work, Minton, Johnston, Philips, and Laird (1990) have also collected experimental evidence that iterative sampling outperforms the depth-first approach on the queens task. Their explanation of this result hinged on the presence of multiple solutions that were clustered in the search space; this is analogous to our assumption that s is greater than one.

Janakiram, Agrawal, and Mehrotra (1988) have applied similar ideas to parallel search methods. They retained the idea of systematic depth-first search, but to minimize redundancy on parallel processors, they ordered children randomly at each choice point. For some classes of problems, they obtained speedup that was linear in the number of processors. More important from our perspective, they analyzed and experimenally studied a number of different problem types, including ones in which solutions were clustered and others in which they followed a uniform distribution. However, they did not examine nonsystematic methods like iterative sampling, despite their suitability for parallel processing.

4.3 Nonsystematic Search in Planning

Findings in the psychology of human planning and problem solving are also relevant to our work. For ex-

ample, De Groot (1965) has reported that chess players rely on *progressive deepening*, a search method in which they repeatedly return to the initial state. From this base position they explore a single path at ever greater depths, considering side branches only briefly before returning to the main path. Newell and Simon (1972) observed similar behavior in their subjects, and thus incorporated progressive deepening into their theory of human problem solving. There is no clear evidence that chess players use random selection, but they do favor an iterative greedy approach.

More recently, Jones (1989) has described EUREKA, a model of human problem solving that used a variant of iterative sampling to control a means-ends planner. The system probabilistically selected one state to expand at each branch point in its search, but if this path did not produce a solution by a prespecified depth, it returned to the initial state and began again from there. This continued until the model found a solution or gave up after a number of passes. EUREKA also used a heuristic to bias selection in favor of some states and incorporated a simple form of reinforcement learning that let it improve this selection process with experience.

Minton, Drummond, Bresina, and Philips (1992) have also used iterative sampling to generate plans. They examined interactions between the search strategy and the nature of the search space, finding the construction of partial order plans was more efficient than generation of total order plans when using depth-first search, but that this difference disappeared when using iterative sampling. From these experimental results, they concluded that solutions for their planning tasks (the blocks world) were clustered, lending plausibility to this assumption in our analysis. Although depth-first search outperformed iterative sampling for the problems that Minton et al. studied, they also found that a simple heuristic – preferring the partial plan with the fewest unmatched preconditions – completely reversed this result.

4.4 Directions for Future Work

Our analysis of nonsystematic search also makes a variety of assumptions and omissions that we should address in further research. In particular, our model assumes that the branching factor, depth of search, and number of good nodes at each branch point are constant. We should run experiments to examine the behavior of the algorithms when b, d, and s vary across nodes and branches. Hopefully, the analysis will remain a good predictor when using the average values of these parameters rather than constant ones. Our experimental study of nonintegral s values provides a reasonable start, but we must examine other forms of variation as well. We should also extend the analysis beyond trees to include search through graphs.

As we have noted, heuristics feature prominently in the work by Jones and by Minton et al., and we should examine their role more carefully in the future. Preliminary analyses suggest that, for certain definitions, iterative sampling benefits more from heuristic knowledge than does depth-first search. This hypothesis is consistent with Minton et al.'s results on planning tasks. Moreover, it makes intuitive sense in that heuristics reduce e, the expected number of nodes examined at each branch point, which has a greater effect on iterative sampling than on depth-first search. However, one can imagine different formulations of heuristic information, and an extended analysis should use one that reflects characteristics of actual heuristics.

Iterative sampling bears a strong similarity to reactive methods for interacting with the external environment, in that the latter select one of many actions and cannot backtrack. This connection suggests that nonsystematic planning methods may be easier to integrate with reactive executors, as Drummond (personal communication, 1992) has noted that the former generate the same probability distribution of behaviors as many reactive systems. The similarity of iterative sampling to reactive methods should also let one directly apply techniques for reinforcement learning to acquire heuristic knowledge from successful and unsuccessful iterations.

Despite the research issues that remain, the results to date demonstrate that, in some circumstances, nonsystematic methods like iterative sampling can solve problems much more efficiently than systematic techniques, including depth-first search and iterative broadening. Moreover, the nonsystematic approach appears to scale better on some dimensions of difficulty and seems better able to take advantage of multiple solutions. These results cast a different light on the nonsystematic nature of human problem solving, suggesting that this behavior is more adaptive than it appears. Future work should further clarify the conditions under which random search is desirable, examine the effect and acquisition of heuristic knowledge, and evaluate the approach on real-world problem-solving and planning tasks.

Acknowledgements

Thanks to S. Minton, G. Iba, P. Andreae, P. Laird, A. Philips, W. Iba, J. Allen, S. Ohlsson, R. Jones, and M. Drummond for discussions that refined many of the ideas in this paper. Thanks also to J. Allen, M. Ginsberg, R. Korf, and the reviewers for insightful comments on earlier drafts.

References

Brassard, G., & Bratley, P. (1988). *Algorithmics: Theory and practice*. Englewood Cliffs, NJ: Prentice Hall.

de Groot, A. D. (1965). *Thought and choice in chess*. The Hague: Mouton.

Ginsberg, M. L., & Harvey, W. D. (1990). Iterative broadening. *Proceedings of the Eighth National Conference on Artificial Intelligence* (pp. 216–220). Boston, MA: MIT Press.

Janakiram, V. K., Agrawal, D. P., & Mehrotra, R. (1988). A randomized parallel backtracking algorithm. *IEEE Transactions on Computers, 37*, 1665–1676.

Jones, R. (1989). *A model of retrieval in problem solving*. Dissertation, Department of Information & Computer Science, University of California, Irvine.

Korf, R. E. (1985). Depth-first iterative-deepening: An optimal admissible tree search. *Artificial Intelligence, 27*, 97–109.

Minton, S., Johnston, M. D., Philips, A. B., & Laird, P. (1991). Solving large-scale constraint satisfaction and scheduling problems using a heuristic repair method. *Proceedings of the Eighth National Conference on Artificial Intelligence* (pp. 17–24). Boston, MA: MIT Press.

Minton, S. N., Drummond, M. E., Bresina, J. L., & Philips, A. B. (1992). *Total order vs. partial order planning: Factors influencing performance*. Unpublished manuscript, Artificial Intelligence Research Branch, NASA Ames Research Center, Moffett Field, CA.

Newell, A., & Simon, H. A. (1972). *Human problem solving*. Englewood Cliffs, NJ: Prentice Hall.

A Practical Approach to Integrating Reaction and Deliberation

D. M. Lyons and A. J. Hendriks
Philips Laboratories
North American Philips Corporation
Briarcliff Manor NY 10510
dml@philabs.philips.com

Abstract

A robot system operating in an environment in which there is uncertainty and change needs to integrate the ability to react with the ability to plan ahead. In this paper, we present a novel approach to this integration for a practical robot problem, the *kitting robot*. In our approach, planning is cast as the ongoing adaptation of a reactive system, incrementally bringing its behavior into line with a set of goals. A method is presented whereby the planner can make iterative improvements to the reactor so that it eventually converges on the ideal reactor (a concept related to the universal plan) for its environment and set of planner goals. To balance this theoretical work, our current implementation on a Puma 560 robot is overviewed.

1 INTRODUCTION

We are interested in building robot planning systems that operate in real-world, commercial/industrial robotic applications. This means developing systems that can cope with uncertain and changing environments, not just in theory or in simulation, but also in practice. This constraint has led us to a novel approach to integrating reaction with planned and guaranteed behavior.

We take the kitting robot (Sellers & Nof 1989) as exemplary for our work. A kitting robot is a robot system that puts together assembly kits — trays containing all the necessary parts from which to build a specific product. Simpler and cheaper automation can construct the assemblies once they have been placed in the kits and routed appropriately. So rather than having to build a factory full of expensive, intelligent robots, a manufacturer can focus the intelligence and cost into a small number of kitting robots which feed the rest of the factory. The key characteristic of the kitting robot is not so much its ability to reason about assembly, but rather its ability to choose timely and effective actions to suit an uncertain and changing environment. To deal with events as they happen, the kitting robot needs to be capable of *real-time, reactive response*. On the other hand, to deal with changes in the environment (e.g., bursts of errors in parts, or failures of resources) or new goals issued by factory management, the kitting robot needs to be able *to plan ahead 'on the fly'*. Thus we need to integrate the versatility and robustness of the reactive systems described by Brooks (Brooks 1986) and others, with the *a-priori* deliberation of traditional planning systems. In addition, to be successful in a real-world commercial/industrial application, the kitting robot, like any other piece of machinery (or indeed any employee) needs to be capable of operating reliably within a set of specifications. Therefore, our objective is to build a system with a sufficiently formal basis that it is possible to give engineering guarantees about its behavior before it is put into operation. Our focus in this paper will be on the issue of integration of reaction and deliberation for such systems; in particular in the case of repetitive behavior such as robotic kitting.

In the next section, we look at some of the existing work on the problem of integrating reaction and deliberation from our perspective of the kitting robot problem. Section 3 presents an overview of our approach to this problem: we cast planning as the *on-going, incremental* adaptation of a separate and concurrent reactive system. Our need for guaranteed behavior leads to the following constraint: we insist that the planner only make adaptations to the reactive system when these adaptations are improvements. Section 4 presents the detailed description of how we represent reactors and reactor adaptation (Lyons et al 1991). In section 5, we discuss our approach to generating adaptations to meet this constraint. Central to this section is our definition of a *situation*: a unit with which to decompose problem spaces in a manner appropriate to reasoning about reactions. Section 5 overviews our testbed implementation.

2   INTEGRATING REACTION AND DELIBERATION

The classical definition of a planner is a program that generates a sequence of operations, the plan, which when applied, will take the world from its initial state to a goal state. A plan is first generated and then sent to an executor which carries out each of the actions. This approach becomes very fragile in a dynamic and changing environment (McDermott 1991, Lyons & Hendriks 1992). The concept of reactive systems, e.g., (Brooks 1986), (Agre & Chapman 1987), was introduced to address this problem. Such a system doesn't plan in the classical sense, but rather reacts directly to its environment. These systems are surprisingly robust and versatile, however, they do not support *a-priori* deliberation about action sequences. Our kitting robot application demands both reactive abilities and *a-priori* deliberation. This integration places constraints upon both the architecture of the planning and reacting system and also the plan representation.

2.1   ARCHITECTURE

Schoppers introduced the notion of *universal plans* to combat the fragility of classical planning in realistic environments (Schoppers 1989). A universal plan guarantees the eventual achievement of its goals, no matter what the initial state of the environment (cf. STRIPS triangle tables). Such plans are essential when a robot cannot accurately predict the current state of the environment. Unfortunately, for most realistic domains, universal plans tend to be very large and extremely complex. While constructing a universal plan may be an appropriate long-term objective for a planner, in practice we will need to settle for a short-term approximation to it.

In the field of robotics, the typical approach to integrating planning and reaction has been to 'piggy-back' a planner on top of a reactive scheduler/executor, e.g., SROMA (Xiadong & Beckey 1988) for robotic assembly, and (Fraichard & Laugier 1991) for robot motion planning. An abstract 'plan' is generated *a-priori* and then fed to a reactive scheduler or executor which is allowed to modify action ordering or introduce minor

deviations. We argue that the resultant system behavior is only partially reactive for the following reasons:

1. the generation and loading of entire plans is simply not feasible for most uncertain and changing environments, and

2. such a reactive scheduler/executor can only 'react' while it has been issued with a plan; a true reactive system needs to be able to act at *any* time.

Bresina & Drummond (Bresina & Drummond 1990, Drummond & Bresina 1990) describe an architecture, ERE, that integrates planning, scheduling and control. Their architecture consists of a *reactor*, that immediately responds to the environment, a *projector*, that expands possible futures and advises the reactor on appropriate ones, and a *reductor*, that provides search control to the projector. Bresina & Drummond emphasisize the *anytime* property of their architecture. However, ultimately this property results in their system taking arbitrary enabled actions. While this approach supports an elegant inductive description of reactor refinement, in an industrial/commercial application such a strategy can be disastrous. We need to emphasize timely, relevant actions over anytime arbitrary actions.

It is also interesting that the idea of planning by adapting a reactive system has some similarity to recent machine learning architectures, e.g., DYNA (Sutton 1990) . In such systems, the reactor is constructed by the trial and error learning of the regularities in the environment. Sutton demonstrated for a simple example task that such architectures can support a mutually enriching integration of learning, planning and reaction. For the present, we will not address learning issues in our work. Instead, we will here assume that although the environment is uncertain and changing, a correct and static description of that uncertainty and change is known.

2.2   PLAN REPRESENTATION

Controlling a real robot in a realistic environment puts great demands on the plan representation: the borderline between robot plan representation and robot programming language begins to blur (McDermott 1991). Conditional and iteration commands are necessary in the plan, as are commands to access and process sensor data and to set actuator signals. McDermott suggests an improved version of Firby's RAPS (Firby 1987) as an appropriately detailed plan/programming representation. A plan representation does have one additional requirement above those of a robot programming language:

it must be possible to predict and reason about the behavior that the plan causes the robot to exhibit. It is not yet clear that RAPS meets this requirement.

Lyons & Arbib (Lyons & Arbib 1989) developed a special model of computation for sensory-based robot programming. That work was begun by putting together a list of the computational characteristics of the robot programming domain. The principle among these were:

1. robot programming is inherently parallel and based on building hierarchical connections between sensors and actuators, and

2. the principle objective of a robot program is to have some effect on the external world.

The model developed was called $\mathcal{RS}$ (Robot Schemas), and had the following style: All actions, whether computational or physical, were cast as concurrent processes, and programs/plans were cast as networks of these processes. That paper provided a port automaton formalism for reasoning about the behavior of these networks. In (Lyons 1989, 1990) we extended the representation and formal analysis vocabulary of $\mathcal{RS}$ using the techniques of the process algebra field (Hoare 1985): We investigated representing and reasoning about interacting plans and world models build by composing processes together using a set of formally defined process composition operators. This process style has much in common with Nilsson's ASTRAL language (Nilsson 1988). A crucial point of similarity is that both models address the issue of 'communications' between actions *while* the actions are in progress. This capability is important in plans that interact with an uncertain world.

3   PLANNING AS ADAPTATION OF A REACTIVE SYSTEM

Our definition of planning is akin to that of Bresina & Drummond, and more recently, of McDermott (McDermott 1991): a planner is a system that continually modifies a concurrent and separate reactive system so that its behavior becomes more goal directed. We will refer to the reactive system as the *reactor* after the terminology established by Bresina & Drummond. Figure 1 illustrates our architecture. A reactor, a network of sensory-motor reactions, interacts directly with an uncertain and changing environment. The planner is a concurrent and separate system that monitors the reactor and its environment by issuing perception requests. These are distinct from the reactor's sensory actions. When, in the planner's view, the the reactor structure does not conform with the planner's goals,

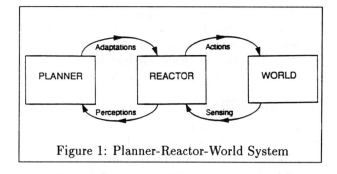

Figure 1: Planner-Reactor-World System

the planner issues adaptations, structural changes to the reactor, to bring reactor behavior back into line with the goals. Our focus in this paper will be on the interaction between planner and reactor; in particular, on the cumulative effect of planner modifications and on the necessity for the planner to be able to introduce perception actions potentially separate and distinct from reactor sensory actions.

3.1   REACTOR

The reactor contains a network of sensory-motor 'linkages' called reactions. In our framework, these reactions are sensory processes composed with effector (or action) processes in such a fashion that should the sensory process detect its triggering condition, then it will in turn trigger the effector process. The reactor has several key properties:

1. It can produce action at *any* time. Unlike a plan executor, a reactor can act independently of the planner; it is always actively inspecting the world, and will act should one of its reactions be triggered. A reactor should produce useful behavior even without a planner.

2. It is a *real-time* system. The central objective of the reactor is to produce the appropriate action at the appropriate time. To make this possible, all the 'knowledge' in a reactor is encoded into reactions and cross-connections between them, and annotated with time-constraints.

The reactor encapsulates what would typically be called the plan in more traditional approaches. By making it a completely separate system, we remove the delays involved when a general deliberation subsystem is always interposed between sensing and action. The reactor is also responsible for the default behavior of the system in the following sense: It is initialized with a number of generally useful behaviors already in place, for example, distinguishing objects from background, locally avoiding obstacles, and scanning its sensors around the environment. Note that our reactor differs from that proposed by Bresina & Drummond in that it does not, by default, contain all the action descriptions and their preconditions. The inclusion of these reactions is what leads to their reactor producing arbitrary enabled actions on occasion.

3.2 PLANNER

The planner is completely separate from, and concurrent with, the reactor. Rather than seeing the planner as a higher-level system that loads plans into an executor, we see the planner as a system that continually refines the reactor to produce appropriate behavior (Figure 1). The input to the planner includes: a model of the environment (EM) in which the planner is operating; a description of the reactor (R); and advice (G) from a user about objectives the reactor should achieve (e.g., in the kitting problem domain, geometric goals such as kit layouts) and constraints the reactor should obey in its behavior (e.g., batch mix or resource usage constraints).

The planner continually determines from R if the reactor's behavior in the current environment will indeed conform to the restrictions G. If the planner finds that the reactor will not obey the restrictions, it makes an incremental change to the reactor configuration to bring the reactor more into line with G. As indicated in Figure 1, there are two routes of interaction between planner and reactor.

1. Adaptations. The planner alters the structure of the reactor by specifying adaptations.

2. Perceptions. These are sensory data collected by the reactor to be sent to the planner.

An adaptation is essentially an instruction to delete part of the reactor structure or to add in some extra structure. The mechanism of adaptation is described in detail in the next section. Each individual adaptation should be small in effect and scope; large changes in reactor behavior only come about as the result of iterated adaptation. Large adaptations would be equivalent to downloading 'plans' to the reactor; something we need to avoid.

The knowledge needs of the planner and reactor are almost always different. The reactor uses sensory data to determine whether to fire its reactions. The planner needs sensory data to allow it to predict the future state of the environment. Thus, in addition to being able to adapt the reactor to contain new reactions, the planner needs to be able to insert its own sensory data collection processes. To distinguish between reactor and planner sensory data, we refer to any data collected by the reactor as sensory data, but sensory data collected to be sent to the planner will be referred to as perceptual data. Without any sensory data, the planner is detached from the environment. In contrast, systems with share a sensory data-base between the reactive and deliberative components force the latter to receive all and only all the sensory data that the reactive component accumulates. As a result, the deliberative component ends up with too much uninteresting data and, more seriously, missing data needed only by itself. The perceptual data needed will be strongly dependent on current goals, and will most likely change as those goals change.

4 MECHANISM OF ADAPTATION

The section reviews our progress in representing the reactor using the $\mathcal{RS}$ model. We begin with a short review of $\mathcal{RS}$ notation. For a more detailed motivation and description see (Lyons 1989,1990) .

4.1 $\mathcal{RS}$ NOTATION

Plans, actions and world models are all represented in $\mathcal{RS}$ as hierarchical networks of concurrent processes. A description of a process, or network of processes, is called a *schema*. For example, $\texttt{Joint}_v\langle x\rangle$ denotes a process that is an instance of the schema $\texttt{Joint}$ with one ingoing parameter v and one outcoming result x. Networks are built by composing processes together using several kinds of *process composition operators*. This allows processes to be ordered in various ways, including concurrent, conditional and iterative orderings. At the bottom of this hierarchy, every network must be composed from a set of atomic, pre-defined processes. The set of *basic schemas* defines what processes are atomic. The main composition operations are *sequential* $\texttt{A;B}$, *concurrent* $\texttt{(A,B)}$, *conditional* $\texttt{A:B}$ and *disabling* $\texttt{A\#B}$.

Sequential composition is used to enforce a strict ordering on operations. For example, ensuring that *part2* is always placed after *part1*: $\texttt{Place}_{part1}; \texttt{Place}_{part2}$.

Concurrent composition indicates that two or more processes should be carried out concurrently. This allows us to represent a lack of ordering between activities, e.g., $(\texttt{Place}_{part1}, \texttt{Place}_{part2})$, or parallel actions — actions which need to be done simultaneously, e.g., squeezing an object *obj* with two fingers $f1$ and $f2$: $(\texttt{ApplyForce}_{f1,obj}, \texttt{ApplyForce}_{f2,obj})$. A set of concurrent processes $\texttt{A}^i, i \in P$ is written $\left\|_{P}\texttt{A}^i\right.$.

Conditional composition allows the construction of networks whose behavior is conditional. The network of $T = P:Q$ behaves like $P;Q$ iff P terminates successfully. If P aborts, then Q is not carried out, and T aborts. For example, in $\text{LidOpen}_{box} : \text{Place}_{x,box}$ whether Place is carried out or not depends on whether LidOpen terminates successfully or not.

Disabling composition allows one process to terminate another. The network $T = A\#B$ behaves like (A,B) except that it terminates whenever either process terminates.

Finally, two non-atomic composition operations are defined in terms of these four: *synchronous recurrent* $A ::B = A : (B;A::B)$, and *asynchronous recurrent* $A ::B = A : (B,A::B)$. Synchronous recurrent composition is similar to *while-loop* iteration. Asynchronous recurrent composition does not iterate, but rather 'spawns' off a set of concurrent processes every time its 'condition' is satisfied.

It is important to represent how process networks evolve over time, as processes dynamically terminate or are created. This is captured by the evolves operator: We say that process A evolves into process B under condition Ω if A becomes equal to B when condition Ω occurs; we write this as $A \xrightarrow{\Omega} B$. Evolves is axiomatized from the definitions of the composition operators, e.g., $A;B \xrightarrow{\Omega A} B$.

4.2   REACTOR ADAPTATION

The reactor consists of a set of guarded sensory-action pairs (reactions) and a well-defined interface through which the planner can modify the reactor structure:

$$\text{REACTOR} = (\ \|E^i\#P^i\ ,\ \text{ADDPLAN}\langle k\rangle :: (E^k\#P^k)\ )\quad(1)$$

where

1. P^i is a reaction or reactor segment (as explained later).

2. E^i is a guard process by which (by the #-composition) P^i can be removed by the planner.

3. ADDPLAN is the interface through which the planner can add (by the ::-composition) new guarded reactions $E^m\#P^m$.

Reactions — hard-wired responses to sensory conditions — are specified in $\mathcal{RS}$ as compositions of sensory and motor processes. For example, a useful reaction for a kitting robot might be to notice anytime some instance of part $p1$ arrives in its buffer area and to acquire that object instance and move it into the workspace. This can be expressed as follows:

$$\text{Locate}_{p1}\langle obj\rangle :: \text{Place}_{obj,dest}$$

where Locate_m is a basic sensory process that inspects the world for an instance of part m and terminates when it finds one, producing a pointer to the instance in obj. Place then acquires and moves object instance obj to location $dest$. The recurrent composition '::' forces the network to be *continually* recreated.

A reactor does not contain/execute plans in the same sense that a classical plan executor/scheduler does, i.e., as a data structure that is manipulated or executed. Nonetheless, certain parts of the reactor structure can be identified as corresponding to the instructions necessary for a specific task or subtask; we call these parts *reactor segments*. They are represented in a *situation-labeled* form:

$$P^t = \ \|_{s\in sit(t)}\ \text{CheckSit}_s : \text{Reaction}_{t,s}\ \#\ I_{t,s}\quad(2)$$

as a concurrent set of reactions, each of which carries its own monitor process CheckSit to determine if the world and reactor present an appropriate situation with respect to task t for that reaction to be active. $sit(t)$ is the set of situations for task t for a particular world model. We postpone to the next section a more detailed description of our situation concept and how to get $sit(t)$. Every segment is 'guarded' by a condition monitor I that monitors the applicability conditions for the segment; should the monitor fail (I terminates), that segment is disabled (by the #-composition), and the planner is notified. Again, we postpone justifying this construct until the next section.

We can write down how the reactor is affected by the changes described in items 2 and 3 of eq. (1):

$$\begin{array}{ll}(R ,E^k\#P^k)\ \xrightarrow{Dk}\ & R\\ R\ \xrightarrow{Ak}\ & (R ,E^m\#P^m)\end{array}\quad(3)$$

where Dk is $E^k \longrightarrow \text{STOP}$
where Ak is $\text{ADDPLAN}(k) \longrightarrow \text{STOP}\ \&\ k = m$

That is Dk can be used to *delete* reactions, and Ak can be used to *add* reactions. Thus, we can express the process of reactor adaptation as follows

$$R \xrightarrow{\alpha} R'\quad(4)$$

where R' is the adapted reactor and α is some combination of Ak and Dk conditions. This adaptation mechanism describes the way in which the planner can modify the reactor to improve its behavior.

5   INCREMENTAL REACTOR RE-FINEMENT

In our framework, planning is a continual process of accepting goals from a user and perceptions from the reactor, and producing incremental adaptations to the reactor, when necessary. Since our problem domain requires carrying out repetitive tasks within an uncertain and possibly changing environment, the speedy construction of an initial working reactor as well as the incremental generation of reactor improvements are important.

This section first describes the ultimate objective of the planner, the *ideal reactor*. However, since it is very unlikely that a planner can generate this ideal reactor at once in a timely fashion, we describe our approach to initially restricting the planner's objective (by restricting the domain) so that it can produce an initial reactor more quickly. The subsequent incremental lifting of these restrictions then allows the planner to incrementally construct reactor improvements, while *at all times* maintaining a working reactor structure. Lastly, we examine in more detail the way the planner arrives at a reactor adaptation from a set of goals G, an environment model EM and a reactor model R_t.

5.1   THE IDEAL REACTOR

The ultimate objective of the planner is the construction of a reactor that achieves the goals G not only in the current environment, but because change is possible, in all environments that might occur, as indicated by the environment model. A reactor that fulfills this criterion is called an *ideal reactor*, and is similar in behavior to Schoppers universal plans.

For a given goal G and environment model EM, let the ideal reactor be modeled by the $\mathcal{RS}$ process R^*. Then, the behavior of this ideal reactor, operating in the environment, modeled by the process EM, is described by their *concurrent composition*, written as (R^*, EM). To analyze how their joint behavior evolves over time, we use the $\mathcal{RS}$ evolution operator. The behavior of the ideal reactor R^* operating in environment EM is characterized by the following evolution equation:

$$(R^* , EM) \longrightarrow (R^* , GEM) \tag{5}$$

That is, when the ideal reactor is run concurrently with a environment model process, the latter will always evolve to an environment in which the goal is satisfied GEM.

By this definition, the ideal reactor is the most robust reactor possible; however, it is unrealistic to suppose that a planner will always be able to generate the ideal reactor in one step for the following reasons:

1. it may not have sufficient time because of the time constraints within the reactor;

2. there may be too much uncertainty in the world model for the reactor to be constructed without doing some more sensing; or,

3. it may not be possible to build the ideal reactor because of resource and action constraints.

Thus, while the ideal reactor is an eventual target for the planner, in general it cannot be constructed all at once. It becomes important therefore to find a method that constructs the ideal reactor in 'useful' increments.

5.2   INCREMENTAL CONSTRUCTION OF THE IDEAL REACTOR

A natural constraint to make is that any change to the reactor should result in another working reactor which is capable of behavior at least as goalworthy as the the original reactor. To investigate this issue, we can restrict the ideal reactor definition above (5) with conditions:

$$(R, EM) \xrightarrow{\omega} (R, GEM) \tag{6}$$

Thus, as long as conditions ω hold, R behaves like the ideal reactor. We call this the ω-ideal reactor R^ω for environment EM and goals G.

In planner terms, ω is a set of assumptions under which R has been constructed. This suggests the following incremental plan construction strategy: ω is initially chosen to allow the planner to quickly produce a working reactor and then ω is gradually relaxed over time. We can rewrite the evolution of the reactor as:

$$R^{\omega 1} \xrightarrow{\alpha 1} R^{\omega 2} \xrightarrow{\alpha 2} R^{\omega 3} \xrightarrow{\alpha 3} \ldots \xrightarrow{\alpha n} R^* \\ for \ \omega 1 > \omega 2 > \omega 3 > \ldots > \emptyset \tag{7}$$

where the αi are the adaptation commands generated by the planner.

The assumption relaxation priorities are governed by the chosen ordering on ω. Using the likelihood of ω holding in the environment as the ordering criterion enables the planner to build reactor adaptations to abolish the least likely assumptions first. It will take care of increasingly more likely assumptions as it has time. Of course, at any point the reactor may be forced to deal with the fact that it's assumptions *do not hold* in the current environment. As it stands, eq. (6) claims nothing about the behavior of the reactor if the assumptions don't hold. In the case of failed assumptions, it is necessary that the reactor do nothing that would prohibit a future improved version of the reactor from operating successfully. Sometimes it is okay to simply disable the inappropriate behavior. But in other cases, it may be necessary to actually carry out some actions to prevent harmful side effects from the failed assumption. As of yet, we have not developed a general approach to this part of the problem; we describe our partial solution below.

To guard against failing assumptions, it is important that the ω-ideal reactor contain assumption condition monitors that 'protect' ω. For example, a reasonable assumption to make in the kitting robot problem is that the parts to be kitted will not move (on their own) once they have been delivered to the workcell. The planner can built a reactor $\mathtt{R}^{static}$ based on this assumption and over time would eventually adapt this reactor to deal with moving objects. In the interim, $\mathtt{R}^{static}$ need to include monitors that detect the violation of the static position assumption, i.e., that trigger when part positions change inexplicably. The triggering of an assumption monitor should force the planner to prematurely relax the violated assumption.

5.3 INCREMENTAL CONSTRUCTION OF THE ω-IDEAL REACTOR

For the same reasons that the ideal reactor can't be produced in one increment, it is unrealistic to believe that the ω-ideal reactor can be produced in one increment. Thus the planner needs to be able to incrementally adapt a reactor $\mathtt{R}$ to become $\mathtt{R}^{\omega}$.

Any reactor $\mathtt{R}$ can be seen as a part of the ideal reactor, since we can always choose a set of reactions that inhibit reactions in $\mathtt{R}$ not in $\mathtt{R}^{\omega}$ and add in reactions in $\mathtt{R}^{\omega}$ missing from $\mathtt{R}$. At every planner stage t, based on the environment model EM_t and current goals G_t, the planner generates what we call an *expectation*, E_t, an abstract description of the changes it expects to have to make to the reactor R_t to achieve G_t. It expresses the planner's confidence that it can achieve its goals. At every stage, therefore, the combination of the reactor model R_t and the expectation should be exactly the ω-ideal reactor, constraining the reactor adaptation ΔR_t to be an improvement (where ω is the current set of assumptions the planner is working with):

$$R_t + E_t^{\omega} = R_t^{\omega} = (R_t + \Delta R_t) + (E_t^{\omega} - \Delta E_t^{\omega}) \quad (8)$$

The process of incremental improvement of the reactor can now be seen as incremental reduction of the planner's expectation by some ΔE_t and corresponding improvement of the reactor by some corresponding ΔR_t, until when E_t is null, the current reactor is exactly the ideal reactor.

To reduce the expectation, the planner reasons within a problem solving context consisting of the rele-

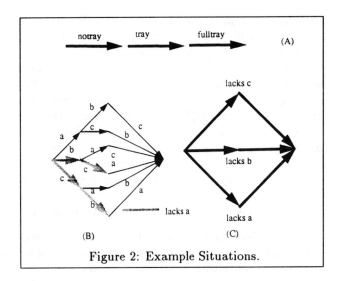

Figure 2: Example Situations.

vant parts of the Environment Model, the action repertoire and the assumptions ω. The outcome is a reactor adaptation ΔR_t, the reactions necessary to implement the expectation reduction ΔE_t. The manageable size of ΔE_t is constrained by the following factors:

1. The response time of the planner. This can come from the design specification of the planner, or from the temporal constraints on goals and actions in the plan.

2. The effects of uncertain knowledge on the plan; the planner may need to issue perception requests before more of the expectation can be reduced.

3. Resource use and mappings.

The planner maintains its expectation as the time-ordered set of *situations* that it needs to address in more detail. Formally, situations are equivalence relations on the state-space for a specific task in a specific environment. Multiple situations may be active at one time. For the reactor, a *situation* being *active* expresses the appropriateness of a particular set of reactions; those *associated with* that situation.

5.4 SITUATIONS

To illustrate the concept of a situation, take for example, a kitting robot assembling a tray with three independent parts a, b and c. There are multiple orders in which the parts can be placed into the tray, all of which lead to the situation in which the tray is full, and all of which are equivalent (Figure 2(B)). At one level of abstraction, the kitting task can be divided into three sequential situations: *notray*, in which the reactions that locate and transfer trays into the workspace are active; *tray,* in which the reactions to fill a tray are active; and, *fulltray,* in which the reactions to transfer a tray out of the workcell are active (Figure 2(A)). Situations can be nested hierarchically, though this nesting is not as straightforward as for states. The *fill-kit* situation can be decomposed into three concurrent situations (Figure 2(C)) *lacks-a, lacks-b* and *lacks-c*; where *lacks-a* means that the kit is still missing part *a*, and it enables the reactions which find and place part *a*. Any combination of these three situations may be active within *tray,* and that combination can change as parts are successfully placed.

Situations have the following useful characteristics:

1. They lend themselves to the use of reactions: Within a situation, the planner doesn't really care what path the reactor takes to achieve the goal. Thus, the actions in a situation can be handled by a set of reactions keyed to fire in that situation.

2. They facilitate incremental construction: The situation defines a unit of useful activity, so the planner can reduce its expectation in units of situations.

3. They facilitate relaxation of assumptions: The relaxation of an assumption will always result in either addition of one or more new situations, (reflecting the extra work needed in the absence of the assumption), or the addition of additional reflexes into a situation (if removal of the assumption can be covered by a generalized behavior within the same situation), or both.

5.5   PERCEPTION

In our framework, we have made a clear distinction between perception for planner purposes and sensing for reactor purposes. In addition to being able to adapt the reactor to contain new reactions, the planner can also adapt the reactor to contain its own sensory data collection processes.

The use of perception is a key part of the planning process, allowing a planner to "familiarize" itself with the environment, resolve uncertainties and prioritize its work by the state of affairs in the environment. We distinguish three types of perception:

1. Direct perceptions — these resolve uncertainties.

2. Situation monitors — these signal the occurrence of situations.

3. Assumption monitors — these signal the failure of an assumption.

Direct perceptions are perception processes that the planner inserts in the reactor to resolve uncertainties in its model of the environment. The other two types help the planner to focus and prioritize its remaining work to adapt the reactor. Situation monitors are perception processes inserted in the reactor to signal the planner that a situation has become active, in the case that that situation is still part of the planners expectation and thus needs to be worked out in detail. Finally, assumption monitors are perception processes inserted in the reactor to warn the planner that a particular assumption has failed and needs to be relaxed for the reactor to behave adequately again.

Thus through the use of perception, the planner can always work on relevant parts of problem first, be that reducing expectations to concrete reactor adaptations or relaxing assumptions to achieve more robust behavior. As a result, its planning process is focused on those adaptation needs that the current environment dictates.

6   TESTBED ENVIRONMENT

We have implemented a planner-reactor system for kitting robot experiments (figure 3).

6.1   HARDWARE

A Puma-560 robot is the basis of the kitting workcell. The original VAL-based controller is used to control the manipulator. The Puma carries a four-fingered, 2-DOF pneumatic gripper, equipped with finger force and position sensors. The workcell has two cameras: A global camera situated above the workcell, whose view covers the entire workspace, but consequentially doesn't yield much detail; and a local camera, embedded in the 'palm' of the gripper, whose view is determined by the position and pose of the gripper, and which can be used to get a close-up view of an object.

6.2   REACTOR

A subset of the $\mathcal{RS}$ model has been implemented as a robot programming language. The RS-L3 programming environment consists of a YACC/LEX-based parser and a real-time executor. The reactor is a set of RS-L3 process definition equations, as described in Section 4, which allow for incremental additional and deletion of reactor structure.

6.3   PLANNER

The planner uses Pelavin's Interval Temporal Logic (ITL) formalism to represent world models (Pelavin 1988). It maintains these models as sets of temporal

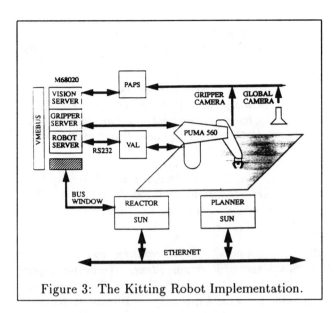

Figure 3: The Kitting Robot Implementation.

predicates and rules. Temporal relations between intervals of time are maintained in a network and new relations are enforced by constraint propagation (Allen 1983). Actions have executability condition and effect formulas. Once the executability conditions are satisfied, execution of the action will guarantee that the effects will occur in the world. The use of ITL as the basis for our planner enables us to specify and reason about communicating concurrent actions, since executability conditions can include conditions that must hold *while* the action is executing. The planner maintains the link with the reactor using asynchronous signal handling to catch incoming perceptions.

For more details of this testbed, see (Lyons & Hendriks 1991).

7   DISCUSSION

7.1   SUMMARY

This paper builds upon our reactor description in (Lyons et al 1991) and described the objectives and internal structure of the planner component. In particular, it took a closer look at the cumulative effects of planner adaptation actions. To support iterative improvement of the reactor, we introduced the concepts of planner *expectation*, the production of *perception processes* by the planner, and the use of *situations* as a modular unit. Our current implementation environment was briefly described.

7.2   COMPARISONS

Our approach is centered on the concept of having separate, but coupled, planner and reactor systems. It is possible to combine planning and action in a single

architecture, e.g., Robo-Soar (Laird 1990). While this has tremendous advantage in allowing for arbitrary interaction between planning and execution, it also has the disadvantage that it allows for arbitrary interference between execution and planning. For example, when an event that should be reacted to occurs, Robo-Soar loses its intermediate planning state in order to react to the event.

The most directly related work to ours is that of Bresina & Drummond . The principle differences with their work are: The $\mathcal{RS}$ model gives us a formal framework to explore the problems of iterative adaptation. Our planner and reactor are less tightly coupled than theirs (discrete adaptations and perceptions are the only channels of interaction), but *mutually* influence each other. Finally, we use a planner based on the concept of situations and reducing expectation to ensure that the reactor is always improved by planner adaptations.

7.3   FURTHER EFFORT

We believe that it is possible to construct a stronger theoretical treatment of the iterative effects of planner adaptation. In basic design, the planner-reactor falls into the class of what in adaptive control are called *self-tuning regulators*. $\mathcal{RS}$ provides us with a powerful discrete-event control representation: more concise than automaton or petri-net models, and yet with some mathematical tools (such as the evolves operator) available. A stronger theory will also help the issues of what constitutes a good base-line reactor and the observability of assumptions.

References

[1] P. Agre and D. Chapman. Pengi: an implementation of a theory of action. In *Proc. AAAI-87*, pages 123–154, Santa Cruz, CA, Oct. 1987.

[2] J.F. Allen. Towards a general theory of action and time. *Artificial Intell.*, 23(2):123–154, 1984.

[3] J. Bresina and M. Drummond. Integrating planning and reaction. In J. Hendler, editor, *AAAI Spring Workshop on Planning in Uncertain, Unpredictable or Changing Environments*, Stanford CA, Mar. 27–29 1990. Systems Research Center, Univ. of Maryland.

[4] R. Brooks. A robust layered control system for a mobile robot. *IEEE J. Rob. & Aut.*, RA-2(1):14–22, Mar. 1986.

[5] M. Drummond and J. Bresina. Anytime synthetic projection: maximizing the probability of

goal satisfaction. In *AAAI-90*, pages 138–144, Jul. 29th – Aug. 3rd 1990.

[6] R.J. Firby. An investigation into reactive planning in complex domains. In *Proceedings, AAAI-6*, pages pp. 202–206, 1987.

[7] Th. Fraichard and C. Laugier. On-line reactive planning for a non-holonomic mobile in a dynamic world. In *IEEE Int. Conf. Robotics & Automation*, pages 432–437, Sacramento, CA, Apr. 1991.

[8] C.A.R. Hoare. *Communicating Sequential Processes*. Prentice-Hall International Series in Computer Science, 1985.

[9] J. Laird. Integrating planning and execution in soar. In J. Hendler, editor, *AAAI Spring Symposium on Planning in uncertain and changing environments*, Stanford CA, Mar. 27–29 1990. Systems Research Center, Univ. of Maryland.

[10] D.M. Lyons. A Process-Based Approach to Task-Plan Representation. In *IEEE Int. Conf. Robotics & Automation*, Cincinatti, Ohio, May 1990.

[11] D.M. Lyons. A formal model for reactive robot plans. In *2nd International Conference on Computer Integrated Manufacturing*, RPI, Troy, NY, May 21–23 1990.

[12] D.M. Lyons and M.A. Arbib. A Formal Model of Computation for Sensory-Based Robotics. *IEEE Trans. on Robotics & Automation*, 5(3):280–293, June 1989.

[13] D.M. Lyons and A.J. Hendriks. Implementing an integrated approach to planning and reaction. In *SPIE Conference on Intelligent Robotic Systems; Algorithms and techniques*, Boston, MA, November 1991.

[14] D.M. Lyons and A.J. Hendriks. Reactive planning. In S.Shapiro Editor in chief, editor, *Encyclopedia of AI (2nd Ed.)*. John Wiley and Sons, 1992. Also: Philips TR-91-016 (public).

[15] D.M. Lyons, A.J. Hendriks, and S. Mehta. Achieving robustness by casting planning as adaptation of a reactive system. In *IEEE Int. Conf. Robotics & Automation*, Apr. 7–12th 1991.

[16] D.M. Lyons and I. Mandhyan. Fundamentals of $\mathcal{RS}$ - part II: Process composition. Technical Report TR-89-033, Philips Laboratories, 345 Scarborough Rd., Briarcliff Manor, NY 10510, Jun. 1989.

[17] D. McDermott. Robot planning. Technical Report YALEU/CSD/RR#861, Yale University, Aug. 1991.

[18] N.J. Nilsson. Action networks. In J. Weber, J. Tenenberg, and J. Allen, editors, *From Formal Systems to Practical Systems*, pages 21–52. Dept. of Computer Science, Univ. of Rochester, Oct. 27–29th 1988.

[19] R. Pelavin. *A Formal Approach to Planning With Concurrent Actions and External Events*. PhD thesis, Univ. of Rochester, Dept. of Computer SC., Rochester, NY, 1988.

[20] M. Schoppers. *Representation and Automatic Synthesis of Reaction Plans*. Technical report uiucdcs-r-89-1546 (phd thesis), Dept of Computer Science, University of Illinois at Urbana-Champaign, 1989.

[21] C.J. Sellers and S.Y. Nof. Performance analysis of robotic kitting systems. *Rob. & Comp. Integ. Manuf.*, 6(1):15–24, 1989.

[22] R. Sutton. First results with dyna. In J. Hendler, editor, *AAAI Spring Symposium on Planning in uncertain and changing environments*, Stanford CA, Mar. 27–29 1990. Systems Research Center, Univ. of Maryland.

[23] X. Xiaodong and G.A. Bekey. Sroma: An adaptive scheduler for robotic assembly systems. In *IEEE Int. Conf. Robotics & Automation*, pages 1282–1287, Philadelphia, PA, 1988.

Towards Structural Abstraction

Fritz Mädler
Hahn-Meitner-Institut (HMI)
Project SOLEIL - Department D/D1
Glienicker Strasse 100, W 1000 Berlin 39, F.R.G.
maedler@vax.hmi.dbp.de

Abstract

Abstraction techniques, as used by Sacerdoti and Wilkins, seem to have a domain-independent structural equivalent. Constellations of "needle's eyes" in the state graph may be conceived of as an extensional representation of an abstract operator whose intensional description can be accomplished by inductive learning. Thus, a complete and correct description of a cluster of planning problems is obtained which are decomposed in the operator expansion under preservation of optimality. We use the *Towers of Hanoi* example to illustrate our approach. Some formal results are added to point out the general nature of the method. - An intuitive, somewhat less formal predecessor of the needle's eye principle has been used in the SOLEIL prototype-system for process control. It may be regarded as a step towards a general method for planner-based acquisition of control knowledge that can be supported by inductive learning.

1 INTRODUCTION

Abstraction is a widely acknowledged technique for reducing search complexity. Sacerdoti's [1974] progressing from the planning system STRIPS to ABSTRIPS is the classic example of *state abstraction*. The precondition literals are assigned "criticality" values that partially order these literals according to their significance. At first only the most important predicates of the operator preconditions are required to hold. After the resulting abstract problem is solved, the preconditions are refined gradually. More generally, Wilkins [1988] defines hierarchical planning as a multi-level elimination of details in the representation, where each abstraction level has its own set of predicates with a specific fineness of detail, the granularity. Decreasing description accuracy allows larger sections of the state space to be embraced. It is assumed that at the highest abstraction level the search space is "thinned out" to such an extent that the abstract problem becomes tractable. Planning then means descending in this hierarchy; at each level missing details are supplemented, if necessary by backtracking across higher levels until a complete plan is found at the base level. Assumptions for the generation of "good" abstraction hierarchies are presented in [Knoblock, Tennenberg and Yang 1991].

In *operator abstraction* the operators are additionally equipped with a "plot" [Wilkins 1984], i.e. a subplan of (primitive or abstract) operators into which the abstract operator is to be expanded during planning. At each level the corresponding abstract solution is used to handle smaller subproblems at the next level down.

Both types of abstraction are hierarchical forms of problem decomposition that can produce a logarithmic reduction in search complexity: smart problem decomposition accomplishes that instead of the product one has to handle only the sum of the individual complexities arising from the search at the different levels [Minsky 1963], [Korf 1988]. Christensen's [1990] empirical evidence confirms that the size of the search space can be reduced from exponential to linear in the solution length. Knoblock [1990, 1991] identifies a set of sufficient assumptions for the proof of such a result, in his first paper for hierarchical planning, in the second for hierarchical problem solving.

In this paper we present a domain-independent method for optimality-preserving decomposition of problem clusters [Mädler 1991a]. "Needle's eye" constellations in the structure of the state space are conceived of as an extensional representation of abstract operators, whose pre- and postconditions can be given an intensional form by inductive learning. We call this approach *structural abstraction*, for reasons which will become clear in the next section.

Recently Horz [1992] suggested a new heuristic for criticality assignment in the context of nonlinear planning. In his method the criticality value assigned to a literal is inversely proportional to the number of operator instances producing this literal. In essence such an approach is based on a heuristic estimation of structural properties of the problem space and does not depend on the peculiarities of a specific planner. - Meyer-Fujara [1992] applies concepts from algebraic topology to introduce the notion of "obstacles" in the state space. States are grouped by an equivalence relation, if they belong to the same obstacle. Abstraction levels can then be distinguished by the size of the obstacles. In the sense that these two approaches relate precondition elimination to the structure of the problem space they are steps towards structural abstraction also.

The principle presented here is applied in a prototype system modelling parts of a plasma-deposition apparatus which is used to produce photovoltaic layers as needed for solar cells. During acquisition, control knowledge is ascertained for the subsequent generation of operation sequences used to control the device. It is a specific property of this application that it requires minimal length at least for certain sequences of actions. Therefore, needle's eyes are considered with respect to this optimality criterion, although interesting weaker formulations are feasible.

2   THE CENTRAL IDEA

The basic idea can be illustrated by the *Towers of Hanoi* problem with three disks $a < b < c$.

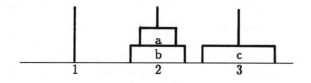

Figure 1: A State of the *Towers of Hanoi*

We adopt Nilsson's and McCarthy's representation [Nilsson 1971] and use the triple (CBA) to describe the state, with the values of the variables A, B, C indicating the number of the peg (1 or 3) on which the disks a, b and c are placed. If more than one disk is on the same peg, the disks are assumed to be ordered according to size. The triple (322), for example, represents the state shown in figure 1.

On the left of figure 2 (see next page) a section of the state space is shown in which the arcs represent the admissible state transitions. The right side of the triangle depicts the optimal solution to the problem of moving the complete pile of disks from peg 1 to peg 3, i.e. the solution to the problem ((111),(333)). In [Christensen 1990] and [Knoblock 1990, 1991] abstraction hierarchies are given that allow hierarchical planning of the optimal solution to this problem. In all three papers,

moving the largest disk c from peg 1 to peg 3 is part of the abstract solution at the highest level. Obviously, this corresponds to decomposing the problem into the subproblems ((111),(322)) and ((322),(333)).

In real-world applications, as, for instance, in plant control, it is not only single problems that must be solved. Plans need to be generated flexibly from varying initial states to different goals. Then needle's eyes (henceforth NEs)[1], such as (322) (or (122) as well), will gain importance, because they allow "economical" collective decomposition not only of a single problem but of problem clusters. Clearly, the problem ((112),(312)) can also be decomposed in state (322) in such a way that the concatenation of the optimal subplans will produce the optimal overall solution to the problem. On the other hand, this is not true, for instance, for problem ((133),(311)). On the right of the state space in figure 2 we find a maximal cluster (with respect to set inclusion) of problems that can all be decomposed in state (322) without losing the optimality of their solutions. To the right of the dashed line, for all problems with initial states above $\mathcal{N}_2$ and goal states below $\mathcal{N}_2$, the arrows in figure 2 indicate the optimal solutions to all of these problems.

The problem cluster chosen has one remarkable property: the set Z_{opt} of all states occurring in any of the optimal solutions is partially ordered as shown by these arrows. This partial order, henceforth denoted by $\prec$, opens up a general way of generating optimality-preserving operator abstractions from subgraphs of the state space.

2.1   THE EXTENSIONAL FORM OF THE OPERATOR

In order to generate an abstract operator from the structural constellation at node (322) of our example we introduce a predicate P_S to describe the initial set $S := \{Start | Start \in Z_{opt}, Start \prec (322)\}$ and a predicate P_G to describe the goal set $G := \{Goal | Goal \in Z_{opt}, (322) \preceq Goal\}$. Then the following operator decomposes every problem $(Start, Goal)$ with $Start \in S$ and $Goal \in G$ into the subproblems $(Start, (322))$ and $((322), Goal)$:

$$
\begin{array}{lcl}
\text{decompose\_at\_}\mathcal{N}_2 & : & \\
\quad \text{precondition} & : & P_S \\
\quad \text{postcondition} & : & P_G \\
\quad \text{decompose\_at} & : & (322)
\end{array}
$$

In order to obtain all optimal solutions, it suffices to solve the two subproblems optimally at the next level down and to concatenate their results. This sequence of subproblems corresponds to Wilkins's plot.

---

[1]The needle's eye (NE) is formally introduced in definition 1 of section 3.

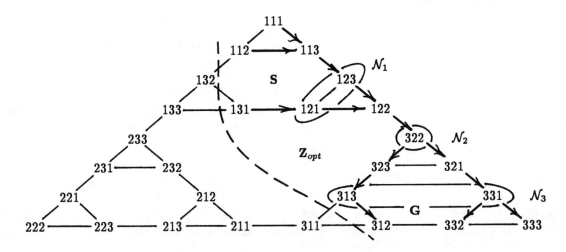

Figure 2: A Partially Ordered Section in the State Space of the *Towers of Hanoi*

Above all, we can partition ordered substructures of the state space into classes and use them for the inductive learning of such maximal problem clusters (using, for example, Quinlan's [1986] ID3 algorithm).

2.2 THE INTENSIONAL DESCRIPTION OF THE OPERATOR

Four steps are needed to generate a complete and correct abstraction:

1. For some problems of interest, NEs in the state space are acquired, either by solving problems or by expertise. We can, for instance, decompose the problem ((111),(333)) in the node (322).

2. A first induction step - in our example over the classes $S_0 := \{(111),(113),(123),(122)\}$ and $G_0 := \{(322),(321),(331),(333)\}$ - provides a most general intensional description of the operator conditions. In the example it characterizes initial states (or goal states) solely by the value $C = 1$ (or $C = 3$) of the largest disk c. This condition embraces states outside $S_0 \cup G_0$ as well, such as the initial and the goal state of problem ((112),(312)), whose optimal solution still passes through the state (322). In so far, this step provides hypotheses for further problems that may be decomposed in (322) under preservation of optimality. On the other hand, an abstract operator that is built like this will behave incorrectly if its pre- and postcondition only consider the feature c; it will decompose problems in (322) whose optimal solutions do not pass through this intermediate state, such as, for example, the problem ((133),(311)).

3. Hypothesized problems may be added to the cluster already established, if the extended set Z_{opt}

remains partially ordered (in section 3 we give a sufficient condition to this effect). In figure 2 this corresponds to the determination of the dashed line dividing Z_{opt} from the rest of the graph.

4. If the intensional description of the operator conditions generated in the second step is too general, we form classes of exceptions - here $E_S := \{(132),(133)\}$ and $E_G := \{(311)\}$ and induce again, but this time with respect to S and E_S, and G and E_G, respectively.[2]

If we insert the induced description into the predicates P_S and P_G introduced above, the operator obtains the precondition in the usual form and a postcondition comparable to the union of the STRIPS add list and the negated elements of the delete list:

decompose_at_$\mathcal{N}_2$	:	
precondition	:	$C = 1 \wedge (B \neq 3 \vee A = 1)$
postcondition	:	$C = 3 \wedge (B \neq 1 \vee A \neq 1)$
decompose_at	:	$C = 3 \wedge B = 2 \wedge A = 2$

In the last line, the intermediate goal state is given its full specification in order to require decomposition exactly in the state (322); every optimal solution to a problem $(s,g) \in S \times G$ must necessarily pass through this state (see figure 2). If a problem solving method is used that finds optimal solutions (as, for instance, "depth-first iterative-deepening"; see [Korf 1988]), the condition $C = 3 \wedge B = 2 \wedge A = 2$ over-specifies the intermediate goal, since for the problems $(s,g) \in S \times G$ an optimal forward solver cannot avoid entering the triangle $\{(3,\_,\_)\}$ via the state (322). So only those

---

[2]Note that this method does not enumerate the state space; the lower triangle on the left of figure 2 (i.e. the states with the value $C = 2$ for the largest disk c) does not occur in any of the inductions.

feature values are of interest that distinguish the intermediate state from the set S of initial states. In this example induction will, of course, find the subgoal $C = 3$ to be the suitable simplification of the over-specifying condition.[3] So the decomposition instruction in the operator above is substituted by

$$\text{achieve\_optimally}: \ C = 3$$

meaning that the stated intermediate goal is only the right one if the subproblems of the expanded operator are solved forwardly and optimally. (The intermediate goal $B = 2 \wedge A = 2$ would analogously be a suitable substitution in the case of optimal backward reasoning.)

The subproblems that arise from the expansion of the operator can be used to generate further abstract operators for the next abstraction level down, for example by means of the sets $\mathcal{N}_1$ and $\mathcal{N}_3$. Their subproblems are then solved on the base level by sequences of primitive actions.

We call this approach *structural abstraction*, since it is essentially the substructures of the state graph and purely structural properties that can be read from them (like order, optimality etc.) which are used to learn the operator conditions and its expansion. The results presented in the next section show in exemplary form that this approach is based on solid formal foundations.

3   SETS OF NEEDLE'S EYES

A necessary condition for the optimality of a plan is the optimality of all of its subplans. This discrete version of a general principle of optimality, known as Bellman's principle [Bellman 1957], has crucial consequences for the acquisition of abstract operators: in order to achieve optimality in a plan at all, the subplans obtained for the base level of an abstraction hierarchy must be optimal themselves. If abstraction results from problem decomposition in intermediate states, as in the example above, optimality can only be preserved for a narrowly defined type of intermediate goals: the concatenation of the optimal solutions to two planning problems (s, n) and (n, g) is optimal, if and only if the problem (s, g) has an optimal solution that passes through the intermediate state n. This restriction motivates the following definition of the NE [Mädler and Gust 1990].

3.1   THE NEEDLE'S EYE (NE)

By $\Pi_{opt}(s, g)$ we denote the set of all optimal solutions to the planning problem (s, g), by $Z_{opt}(s, g)$ the set of

all states passed through by these solutions. This set always shows a specific ordering: two states $x, y \in Z_{opt}(s, g)$ are partially ordered by an asymmetric and transitive relation $x \prec y$, if x precedes y in any optimal plan $p \in \Pi_{opt}(s, g)$. If $x \prec y$ holds, the two states have a well-defined, directed distance $l(x, y)$, i.e. the length of the plans in $\Pi_{opt}(x, y)$.

Definition 1: A subset $N \subset Z_{opt}(s, g)$ consisting of the states $n \in N, s \prec n \prec g$, is called a needle's eye (NE) for the problem (s, g), iff the following conditions hold

1. each plan $p \in \Pi_{opt}(s, g)$ passes through one (and only one) state $n \in N$,
2. all states $n \in N$ have the same distance $l(s, n)$ from the initial state s.

In figure 2, $N := \{(322)\}$ is a NE for each problem (s, g) with $s \prec (322) \prec g$. As a second example very problem (s, g) of the cluster $\{(s, g) | s \prec (331) \prec g\}$ has $N := \{(331)\}$ as a NE. The *Towers of Hanoi* domain has only singletons as NEs. However, the definition permits NEs to have more than one state.

The following theorem shows that for problem decomposition in NEs the converse of Bellman's principle holds: all optimal solutions can be generated by concatenating all optimal subsolutions (this, of course, is not generally true).

Theorem 1: If N is a NE for a problem (s, g), the optimal plans have a representation as a union of cartesian products

$$\Pi_{opt}(s, g) \overset{f_N}{\sim} \bigcup_{n \in N} \Pi_{opt}(s, n) \times \Pi_{opt}(n, g)$$

where $f_N((s, ..., n, ..., g)) = ((s, ..., n), (n, ..., g))$ is a bijection.

In order to describe the argument and the image of the function f_N we use the plans in their equivalent state representation.

This theorem can be generalized to multiple decomposition in the case of certain problem clusters (S, G). They are arranged in such a way that the states $Z_{opt}(S, G)$ of their solutions can be partially ordered as above. In this order we define "Needle's Eyes Sets" (NESes), which are then used to give a more general representation of the optimal plans $\Pi_{opt}(S, G)$; see theorem 2 below.

3.2   C-CLOSED PROBLEM CLUSTERS

For a single problem (s, g) the optimal plans $\Pi_{opt}(s, g)$ are closed under concatenation in the following sense (we use the state representation): if two plans $(s, z_1, z_2, .., z_j, z_{j+1}, .., z_{l-1}, g)$ and $(s', z_1', z_2', .., z_j', z_{j+1}', .., z_{l-1}', g)$ have a state $z_j = z_j'$ in common, their "crossing-over" in

---

[3]Note that this is a way for an induction tool to infer *from the structural constellation* near the node (322) that "Move the largest disk c to peg 3!" is the right subgoal at the highest abstraction level.

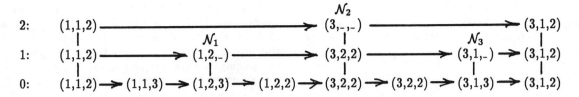

Figure 3: Hierarchical Problem Solving with Sets of Needle's Eyes

z_j also produces optimal plans from s to g, i.e. $(s, z_1, z_2, .., z_j, z'_{j+1}, .., z'_{l-1}, g) \in \Pi_{opt}(s, g)$ and $(s, z'_1, z'_2, .., z_j, z_{j+1}, .., z_{l-1}, g) \in \Pi_{opt}(s, g)$. This is sufficient for the transitivity of the order $\prec$ on $Z_{opt}(s, g)$.

Definition 2: A problem cluster (S, G) is called *closed under concatenation* (henceforth *c-closed*), iff for any two problems $(s, g), (s', g') \in (S, G)$ and any two optimal plans $(s, .., z, .., g), (s', .., z', .., g') \in \Pi_{opt}(S, G)$ having the state $z = z'$ in common the following conditions hold

1. the crossed-over problems (s, g') and (s', g) are contained in the cluster (S, G),

2. the crossed-over plans are optimal, i.e.

$$(s, .., z, .., g'), (s', .., z, .., g) \in \Pi_{opt}(S, G)$$

The problem cluster $(S, G) := S \times G$ with S and G as defined in section 2 (see figure 2) is c-closed, as is the cluster of problems having the minimal elements of $(Z_{opt}, \prec)$ as initial states and the maximal elements as goals. A somewhat more realistic example is given in the next section.

3.3 THE GENERAL CASE

For c-closed problem clusters (S, G) the relation $\prec$ is independent of the defining plan $p \in \Pi_{opt}(S, G)$ and satisfies the axioms of a partial order. Since for any problem $(s, g) \in (S, G)$ the restriction of the ordering from $Z_{opt}(S, G)$ to the subset $Z_{opt}(s, g)$ is exactly the order used in definition 1, NEs of different problems can be assembled to NESes in the common order $\prec$. For a subset $\mathcal{N}$ of the power set $\mathcal{P}(Z_{opt}(S, G))$ and for sets of states $N \in \mathcal{N}$ let the class $C_N \subset (S, G)$ consist of those planning problems (s, g) that have exactly one NE $N' \subset N$ according to definition 1. A state set $N \in \mathcal{N}$ is called a NE *for the class C_N.*

Definition 3: $\mathcal{N}$ is a *"Needle's Eyes Set"* (NES) *for the c-closed problem cluster (S, G),* iff the following conditions hold

1. the NEs $N \in \mathcal{N}$ are pairwise disjoint,

2. the classes $\{C_N | N \in \mathcal{N}\}$ are a complete and disjoint partitioning of the problem cluster, i.e.

$$(S, G) = \bigcup_{N \in \mathcal{N}} C_N \text{ and}$$

$$C_{N_1} \cap C_{N_2} = \emptyset \text{ if } N_1, N_2 \in \mathcal{N} \text{ and } N_1 \neq N_2$$

In figure 2, $\mathcal{N}_2 := \{\{(322)\}\}$ is a NES for $\{(s, g) | s \prec (322) \prec g\}$, or, in other words, for the cluster of those problems which are decomposed by the abstract operator "decompose_at_$\mathcal{N}_2$" in section 2. In order to give a second example the problem cluster $\{(s, g) | (322) \preceq s \prec (313) \prec g \text{ or } (322) \preceq s \prec (331) \prec g\}$ can be written as a disjoint union; therefore it has the NES $\mathcal{N}_3 := \{\{(313)\}, \{(331)\}\}$ with two single-element NEs. From this the following abstraction is generated:

decompose_at_$\mathcal{N}_3$:
  precondition   : $B_{Start} = 2 \wedge postcondition(\mathcal{N}_2)$
  postcondition   : $B_{Goal} \neq 2 \wedge postcondition(\mathcal{N}_2)$
  achieve_optimally : $B = B_{Goal}$

Here, the instruction for the expansion of the operator is given for optimal forward chaining. In addition to the classification into initial and goal states (using the partial order $\prec$) the complete and disjoint partitioning of the problem cluster (using the NESes) can also be used for induction. This provides the intensional description with a second "coordinate" with which the decomposing NE can be dynamically bound to the planning problem, in this operator to the position of disk b in the goal state.

The operator "decompose_at_$\mathcal{N}_3$" handles one of the subproblems arising when "decompose_at_$\mathcal{N}_2$" is expanded. Likewise, an operator "decompose_at_$\mathcal{N}_1$" can be generated from NES $\mathcal{N}_1$ to deal with the other subproblem. Then, for instance, the hierarchical optimal solution to the problem $((1, 1, 2), (3, 1, 2))$ is as shown in figure 3 above. The plans are given in their state representation. Partial states on level 2 and level 1 indicate the abstraction.

3.4 A DECOMPOSITION THEOREM

In the following decomposition theorem we restrict ourselves to the case of single-element NEs $N = \{n\}$

(a more general version is proved in [Mädler 1991b]). NESes, too, can be ordered (as, for instance, the ordered chain $\mathcal{K} := \{\mathcal{N}_1, \mathcal{N}_2, \mathcal{N}_3\}$ in figure 2). As before, but now using multi-indices $(\{n_1\}, \{n_2\}, .., \{n_m\}) \in \mathcal{N}_1 \times \mathcal{N}_2 \times ... \times \mathcal{N}_m$, we partition the cluster into classes

$$C_{n_1..n_m} := \{(s,g)|\{n_1\}, \{n_2\}, .., \{n_m\} \text{ NE for } (s,g)\}$$

The first union in the next theorem is determined by the indices $i := (\{n_1\}, \{n_2\}, .., \{n_m\})$ out of $I := \mathcal{N}_1 \times \mathcal{N}_2 \times ... \times \mathcal{N}_m$ and the second by the problems (s,g) from the classes $C_i := C_{n_1 n_2 .... n_m}$ (empty classes may occur).

Theorem 2: Let (S,G) denote a c-closed problem cluster and $\mathcal{K} := \{\mathcal{N}_1, .., \mathcal{N}_m\}$ a chain of NESes for (S,G), which have only single-element NEs. Then the optimal plans admit a representation

$$\Pi_{opt}(S,G) \overset{f_{\mathcal{K}}}{\sim} \bigcup_{i \in I} \bigcup_{(s,g) \in C_i} \Pi_{opt}(s, n_1) \times .. \times \Pi_{opt}(n_m, g)$$

under the bijection

$$f_{\mathcal{K}}((s, .., n_1, ..., n_m, .., g)) = ((s, .., n_1), ..., (n_m, .., g)).$$

A chain $\mathcal{K}$ of NESes, as given in this theorem, also represents an optimality-preserving abstract operator in its structural form. The operator conditions are hidden in the state extensions, the chain $\mathcal{K}$ represents the instructions for expansion. The "decomposition knowledge" thus acquired becomes more manageable, if we transform the structural representation of the operator into a less redundant intensional description, as we did for the operators of our example domain. Partial ordering and NESes provide us with different but supplementary classifications of state extensions that may be useful for the generation of this description via inductive learning.

4 APPLICATION

The formal version of the needle's eye principle is based upon the experiences made with its intuitive, somewhat less formal predecessor when decomposing control problems in the SOLEIL project. NEs do exist in technical processes. Rational design as well as the consideration of machinery-construction costs and, last but not least, laws of nature organize the state graph. Figure 4 (see next page) shows one of the c-closed problem clusters and its NES $\mathcal{N}$ consisting of four single-element NEs $\{39\}, \{4\}, \{27\}$ and $\{16\}$. Every number identifies a state from the part of the plasma-deposition device modelled in the SOLEIL system. The arcs are directed downwards and show the diagram of the partial order $\prec$.

Using this NES, an optimality-preserving decomposition of every planning problem (s,g), $s \prec n \prec g$, $n \in \mathcal{N}$, is accomplished. In this example the ordered set Z_{opt} splits up into four separate components which are

determined by the values of two attributes (from altogether 13 features having ranges of up to 9 values each that are modelled qualitatively). Induction with ID3 shows that the four combinations *shut/off, open/off, shut/on, open/on* of the values $\{shut, open\}$ for valve 15 and the values $\{off, on\}$ for the turbo pump completely and disjointly partition the states of figure 4 into the four columns; there is one constant combination for every column and NE. This already gives the NES-part of the intensional description. If we additionally use the partial order as a classification and take the states above $\mathcal{N}$ as start class $S = \{s \mid s \prec n, \{n\} \in \mathcal{N}\}$ and the union of the states from $\mathcal{N}$ and from below $\mathcal{N}$ as goal class $G = \{g \mid n \preceq g, \{n\} \in \mathcal{N}\}$, the following description of the abstract operator is induced:

decompose_ at_ $\mathcal{N}$:
  precondition:
    $ProcChamb = atmosphere \wedge$
    (($Valve\_15_S = shut \wedge TurbPumps_S = off$) $\vee$
      ($Valve\_15_S = open \wedge TurbPumps_S = off$) $\vee$
      ($Valve\_15_S = shut \wedge TurbPumps_S = on$) $\vee$
      ($Valve\_15_S = open \wedge TurbPumps_S = on$))
  postcondition:
    $Valve\_15_G = Valve\_15_S \wedge$
    $TurbPump_G = TurbPumps_S \wedge$
    ($ProcChamb = ar \vee ProcChamb = low$)
  achieve_ optimally:
    $ProcChamb = low$

Note that part of the postcondition is dynamically bound to the precondition, thus expressing that the initial state and the goal state of a problem have to belong to the same column and NE. The value of the variable $Valve\_15_G$ of valve 15 in the goal state, for instance, must be equal to the value of $Valve\_15_S$ in the initial state.

As for the example in section 2 the expansion instruction of this operator is stated for optimal forward chaining (see the remarks following the statement of the operator "decompose_at_$\mathcal{N}_2$" in the last part of section 2). The actions in the model of our application are context-dependent, their effects are complex and can change according to the situations in which they are performed. For instance, the opening of a valve will change the values of the process chambers it connects, if their climates are different. If in another situation the same chambers have an equal climate value, the opening of the same valve may leave them unaffected. The effects of a pump depend on the regions of the apparatus it is connected to, and these regions vary from situation to situation according to the actual values of valves and sliders. Even a running pump will have no effect on a volume as long as this volume has a connection to the atmosphere; so the closing of a valve may produce an effect of the pump or not, depending on whether there still remain other connections to the outside. More recent approaches to planning, like Pednault's [1988, 1991], that allow

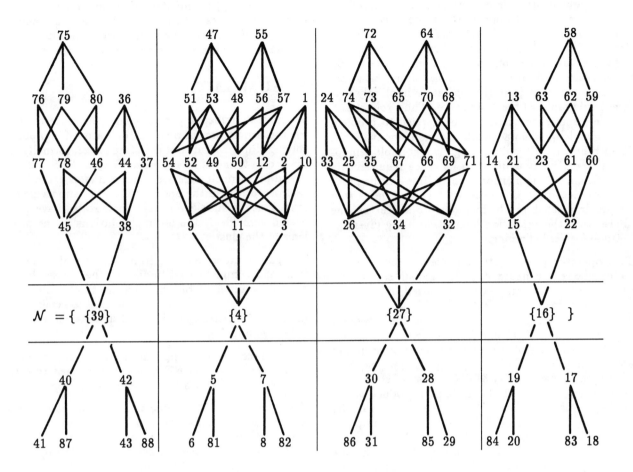

Figure 4: A Set of Needle's Eyes from the SOLEIL Prototype

decompose_ at_ $\mathcal{N}$:

precondition:

$ProcChamb = atmosphere \wedge Pipe\_2 = low \wedge$

(($Valve\_15_S = shut \wedge TurbPumps = off$) $\vee$ ($Valve\_15_S = open \wedge TurbPumps = off$) $\vee$

($Valve\_15_S = shut \wedge TurbPumps = on$) $\vee$ ($Valve\_15_S = open \wedge TurbPumps = on$)) $\wedge$

(($Pipe\_1 = low \wedge$ ($ConChamb = low \vee$ ($ConChamb = atmosphere \wedge Valve\_15_S = shut$))) $\vee$

($Pipe\_1 = atmosphere \wedge ConChamb = atmosphere \wedge Valve\_8 = shut$))

postcondition:

$Valve15_G = Valve15_S \wedge TurbPump_G = TurbPumps \wedge$

($ProcChamb = ar \wedge Pipe\_2 = low \wedge$

(($ConChamb = low \wedge Valve\_15_G = open \wedge ArValve = open \wedge TurbPump_G = on$) $\vee$

($ConChamb = ar \wedge Pipe\_1 = low \wedge ArValve = open \wedge Slider = op \wedge TurbPump_G = on$)) $\vee$

$ProcChamb = low \wedge ConChamb = low \wedge Pipe\_2 = low \wedge Pipe\_1 = air \_low \wedge TurbPump_G = on \wedge$

(($Valve\_15_G = shut \wedge Slider = op$) $\vee$

($Valve\_15_G = open \wedge$

(($Slider = op \wedge MotValve = shut$) $\vee$ $Slider = cl$))))

achieve_ optimally:

$ProcChamb = low$

Figure 5: An Induced Abstraction for the NES-Structure Shown in Figure 4

actions to be context-dependent in a fully generalized manner are rare and work is still in progress. On the other hand, however, we were able to express the actions of our application in the form of state transitions, i.e. as classes of state pairs where the action maps a partial input state into a partial output state. Sequences of these primitive operators implicitly represent subgraphs of the state space. Thus, robust and complete search methods can be applied to problem solving as long as no adequate planners are available. "Depth-first iterative-deepening" is a suitable temporary makeshift. It is linear in its space requirements and efficient - though exponential in time -, if the problems are decomposed sufficiently. This explains why we are interested in abstract operators like the one above, with the expansion instruction being given for optimal forward chaining.

This operator is complete, but correct only for the states shown in figure 4. For global correctness the intensional description is specialized in the same way as in step 4 of section 2 for the operator "decompose_ at_ $\mathcal{N}_2$". In order to build the exception classes we can restrict ourselves to *consistent* states, i.e. states that are physically meaningful according to domain knowledge. (The SOLEIL prototype, as modelled by now, has roughly 31 000 consistent states, out of some 3.3 million which the formal product of the attribute values admits.) Figure 5 shows a globally correct specialization of the operator. It is complete, i.e. it will decompose all problems intended, and globally correct in the sense that it will identify and handle only the problems it was made for: in this example 360 state pairs with more than 1100 optimal linear overall solutions.

Linear plans, however, are not the type of solutions actually wanted for our application, since they unnecessarily order the actions totally. The activities on the plasma-deposition apparatus are highly parallel. Cleaning or evacuating the chambers and other parts of the device can and should be done in parallel actions. These are time-consuming processes, and sometimes an unnecessary ordering of the operation sequences will undo desired effects that have already been established. Therefore a necessary and sufficient partial order of the actions is the right type of solution plan.

It is well-known that a partial order can be achieved by a post-processing step that removes unnecessary orderings from a totally ordered solution [Pednault 1987], [Regnier and Fade 1991], [Minton, Bresina and Drummond 1991]. Since the NEs are to be passed through by all optimal linear solutions to a problem, decomposition in NESes does not cause a loss in information needed for this post-parallelization. So nonlinear subsolutions can be derived and "concatenated", thus producing the desired type of nonlinear solutions at little expence.

Automated support for the acquisition of abstract operators via NESes (in the sense of definition 3 above) and their improved behaviour with respect to global correctness are the main aims of our current work.

5 SUMMARY

We have described a general and systematic method for the acquisition of abstract operators for problem solving. Substructures of the state space, formally expressed in terms of *sets of needle's eyes* (NESes) for c-closed problem clusters are conceived of as extensional representations of the operators. NESes subdivide the state space in such a way that their states have to be passed through by the optimal solutions to the problems of the cluster.

The partial order resulting from c-closure and the disjoint and complete partitioning of the cluster by its NESes are different but supplementary classifications of the state extentions that can be used to generate an intensional description of the abstract operators via inductive learning.

A brief account of an application was given, where an earlier version of the NE principle was used to solve control problems for a plasma-deposition apparatus.

We have called the approach *structural abstraction*, since it is essentially the substructures of the state graph and purely structural properties that can be read from them which are used to learn the operator conditions and the expansion.

Acknowledgement

I would like to thank my advisors, Helmar Gust and Claus-Rainer Rollinger, for guidance and support, and Heinz Hofmann-Illi, Günter Seidelmann and my other colleagues from the SOLEIL project for many fruitful discussions. Special thanks I owe to Alexander Horz and Josef Meyer-Fujara for their helpful comments and suggestions concerning an earlier draft of this paper.

References

[Bellman 1957]
Richard E. Bellman, *Dynamic Programming*. Princeton, New Jersey.

[Christensen 1990]
Jens Christensen, *A Hierarchical Planner that Generates its Own Hierarchies*. In: *Procceedings AAAI-90*, AAAI Press / The MIT Press, Menlo Park / Cambridge.

[Horz 1992]
Alexander Horz, *Criticalities Reconsidered*. In preparation.

[Knoblock 1990]
Craig A. Knoblock, *A Theory of Abstraction*

for Hierarchical Planning. In: D.P. Benjamin (Ed.), *Change of Representation and Inductive Bias.* Kluwer, Boston.

[Knoblock 1991]
Craig A. Knoblock, *Search Reduction in Hierarchical Problem Solving.* In: *Proceedings AAAI-91,* AAAI Press / The MIT Press, Menlo Park / Cambridge.

[Knoblock, Tennenberg and Yang 1991]
Craig A. Knoblock, Josh D. Tennenberg and Qiang Yang, *Characterizing Abstraction Hierarchies for Planning.* In: *Proceedings AAAI-91,* AAAI Press / The MIT Press, Menlo Park / Cambridge.

[Korf 1988]
Richard E. Korf, *Optimal Path Finding Algorithms.* In: Lavin Kanal and Vipin Kumar (Eds), *Search in Artificial Intelligence.* Springer.

[Mädler and Gust 1990]
Fritz Mädler and Helmar Gust, *Über ein Meta-Prinzip zur Explikation von Kontrollwissen.* In: Heinz Marburger (Ed.), *Proceedings GWAI-90,* Informatik-Fachberichte (251), Springer.

[Mädler 1991a]
Fritz Mädler, *Problemzerlegung als optimalitätserhaltende Operatorabstraktion.* In: Thomas Christaller (Ed.), *Proceedings GWAI-91,* Informatik-Fachberichte (285), Springer.

[Mädler 1991b]
Fritz Mädler, *Nadelöhrmengen, ein Konzept zur Induktion von Problemzerlegungen.* Internal working paper SOLEIL-06-PLN-02-AA, Hahn-Meitner-Institut Berlin.

[Meyer-Fujara 1992]
Josef Meyer-Fujara, *Description of Obstacles in Planning.* MOSYS-Report Nr.7, Technische Fakultät der Universität Bielefeld, Bielefeld.

[Minsky 1963]
Marvin Minsky, *Steps Toward Artificial Intelligence.* In: Edward A. Feigenbaum and Julian Feldman (Eds), *Computers and Thought.* McGraw-Hill.

[Minton, Bresina and Drummond 1991]
Steven Minton, John Bresina and Mark Drummond, *Commitment Strategies in Planning: A Comparative Analysis.* In: *Proceedings IJCAI-91, Sydney,* Morgan Kaufmann Publishers (distr.), San Mateo, California.

[Nilsson 1971]
Nils J. Nilsson, *Problem-Solving Methods in Artificial Intelligence.* McGraw-Hill.

[Pednault 1987]
Edwin P.D. Pednault, *Formulating Multiagent, Dynamic-World Problems in the Classical Planning Framework.* In: M.P. Georgeff and A.L. Lansky (Eds), *Reasoning about Actions and Plans: Proceedings of the 1986 Workshop, Los Altos, CA,* Morgan Kaufmann Publishers, San Mateo, California.

[Pednault 1988]
Edwin P.D. Pednault, *Synthesizing Plans that Contain Actions with Context-Dependent Effects.* Computational Intelligence, 4(4).

[Pednault 1991]
Edwin P.D. Pednault, *Generalizing Nonlinear Planning to Handle Complex Goals and Actions with Context-Dependent Effects.* In: *Proceedings IJCAI-91, Sydney,* Morgan Kaufmann Publishers (distr.), San Mateo, California.

[Quinlan 1986]
J.R. Quinlan, *Induction of Decision Trees.* Machine Learning 1, Kluwer, Boston.

[Regnier and Fade 1991]
Pierre Regnier and Bernard Fade, *Complete Determination of Parallel Actions and Temporal Optimization in Linear Plans of Actions.* In: Joachim Hertzberg (Ed.), *Proceedings of the European Workshop on Planning, Sankt Augustin, FRG, March 91,* Springer, Lecture Notes in AI (522).

[Sacerdoti 1974]
Earl D. Sacerdoti, *Planning in a Hierarchy of Abstraction Spaces.* Artificial Intelligence 5(2).

[Wilkins 1984]
David E. Wilkins, *Domain-Independent Planning: Representation and Plan Generation.* Artificial Intelligence 22.

[Wilkins 1988]
David E. Wilkins, *Practical Planning.* Morgan Kaufmann Publishers, San Mateo, California.

Case-based planning meets the frame problem
(case-based planning from the classical perspective)

Robert McCartney
Department of Computer Science and Engineering
University of Connecticut
Storrs, CT 06269-3155
phone: (203) 486-5232
e-mail: robert@cse1.cse.uconn.edu

Abstract

The frame problem is, arguably, the central theoretical problem in classical planning. In this paper, we present an idealized model of case-based planning that includes essential aspects shared by most case-based planning systems. Using this model, which is reasonably formal and quite simple, we show how case-based planning techniques are affected by some traditional problems facing classical planners, specifically the ramification and qualification problems. Under certain assumptions, the ramification problem is largely eliminated, while the qualification problem can take on added complexity.

1 Introduction

The frame problem is, arguably, the central theoretical problem in classical planning. In this paper, we present an idealized model of case-based planning that includes essential aspects shared by most case-based planning systems. Using this model, which is reasonably formal and quite simple, we show how case-based planning techniques are affected by some traditional problems facing classical planners, specifically the ramification and qualification problems.

In our examination, we show that the ramification problem is much reduced. The qualification problem, by contrast, is manifest in problems of *salience*, deciding which features of a situation are important, and *adaptation qualification*, the problem of determining when an adaptation is equivalence preserving.

We also examine the effects on alternative models of case-based planning corresponding to real systems: systems which "replay" plans produced by classical planners, systems which use hybrid methods of plan generation, and systems that use either parts of cases or more than one case in generating a plan. Although these models extend the idealized model, they do so

at some cost.

2 Case-based planning defined (narrowly)

In general, case-based planning is proposed as an integrated solution involving plan generation, execution, and learning. For our purposes, however, we focus on the process of *plan generation*; going from a goal to an executable plan. Moreover, we consider only the "case-based" mechanisms used in generation, and consider an ideal model of adaptation that ignores many of the efficiency considerations faced by implemented systems. The idea is to separate the mechanisms used by case-based systems from methods used elsewhere and focus attention on the characteristics of these methods, which are part of nearly all case-based planning approaches. This provides a starting point for describing systems that extend this idealization.

The representation language we use is a situation-based temporal logic that corresponds closely to the temporal representation in [Davis, 1990] (Chapter 5). Fluents, states, and event types are used to reify time-varying terms, time-varying relations, and events. The function *value-in* relates fluents to situations, the relation *true-in* relates states to situations, and the relation *occurs* relates event-types to intervals of situations.

2.1 What is a case?

The notion of *case* is central to any case-based reasoning technique. The following idealization is sufficient to illustrate the case-based technique in regards to plan generation.

A case is a propositional representation of facts and events. It includes a set of facts that hold in a distinguished initial situation, a set of facts that hold in a distinguished final situation, and a set of events and a specification of their order. The initial situation precedes all of the events; all of the events precede the final situation. A case can be represented as a tuple, $\langle \mathcal{I}, \mathcal{F}, \mathcal{P} \rangle$, where $\mathcal{I}$ and $\mathcal{F}$ are subsets of the facts in the initial and final situations, and $\mathcal{P}$ is the set of events and their ordering constraints. We will later extend this representation to include facts that occur in situations other than the initial and final ones, but that is unnecessary for the current discussion.

This model is fairly general; it allows for missing facts and events, and extra irrelevant facts and events, but does not allow incorrect information. It can associate clock times with situations by defining a "clock time" fluent and specifying its value in various situations.

2.2 Planning from cases

The basic assumption of case-based planning is that if we repeat a set of actions starting with a similar initial situation, we get a similar result. As a first cut, we consider case-based planning without adaptation under a strong similarity assumption: if a situation agrees with all of the facts in the initial situation of a case, and the events are performed in accordance with the ordering constraints, then all of the facts in the final situation of the case will hold after the execution of the events. The planning mechanism is as follows: given a goal $\mathcal{G}$ (some desired state of the world expressed as a set of facts), find a case $\langle \mathcal{I}, \mathcal{F}, \mathcal{P} \rangle$ such that

- $\mathcal{G} \subseteq \mathcal{F}$, and
- all members of $\mathcal{I}$ are true in the situation that will hold when the plan is executed.

The plan produced is the set of events and timing constraints $\mathcal{P}$: that is, a plan to replay the events of the case. Under our assumption, the goal will hold in the final situation of this execution.[1]

To make this approximation reasonable, we must restrict our cases: $\mathcal{I}$ must correspond to necessary and sufficient preconditions for the sequence of events to lead to $\mathcal{F}$, which is a subset of the set of facts that hold in *every* final situation of an execution, that is

$$\forall_{S,S_f} \text{true-in}(S, \mathcal{I}) \wedge \text{occurs}([S, S_f], \mathcal{P}) \Rightarrow \text{true-in}(S_f, \mathcal{F})$$

extending *true-in* to sets of propositions and *occurs* to sequences of events in the obvious way.

These restrictions are at odds with the definition of a case given in the previous section, but they can be reconciled as follows. We define *well-behaved* cases as those for which the strong similarity assumption holds:

$$\text{well-behaved}(\langle \mathcal{I}, \mathcal{F}, \mathcal{P} \rangle) \iff$$
$$(\forall_{S,S_f} \text{true-in}(S, \mathcal{I}) \wedge \text{occurs}([S, S_f], \mathcal{P}) \Rightarrow$$
$$\text{true-in}(S_f, \mathcal{F}))$$

Each case $\langle \mathcal{I}, \mathcal{F}, \mathcal{P} \rangle$ under our definition has associated with it a well-behaved case $\langle \mathcal{I}_w, \mathcal{F}_w, \mathcal{P}_w \rangle$. A case is a description of an actual plan execution, one whose set of events and timing constraints $(\mathcal{P}')$ is a superset of that in the case representation; the corresponding well-behaved case is the ideal description of that same execution:

$$\exists_{S,S_f} \quad \text{occurs}([S, S_f], \mathcal{P}') \wedge$$
$$\text{true-in}(S, \mathcal{I}_w) \wedge \text{true-in}(S, \mathcal{I}) \wedge$$
$$\mathcal{P} \subseteq \mathcal{P}' \wedge \mathcal{P}_w \subseteq \mathcal{P}' \wedge$$
$$\text{true-in}(S_f, \mathcal{F}_w) \wedge \text{true-in}(S_f, \mathcal{F})$$

That is, our represented cases are approximations of well-behaved cases; the facts in the initial and final situations of our cases may be missing some salient facts and include superfluous facts, and similarly may be missing salient events and/or include superfluous events (defining salient and superfluous as present in and absent from the well-behaved case).

In addition to having cases that approximate well-behaved entities, we would like to extend the replay notion to similar plans; that is, we would like to be able to *adapt* a case that does not satisfy our goals into one that does (for example, without adaptation, replay would be practically impossible for any cases with clock times). To do so, it is necessary to have a notion of "behavior preserving" transformations; transformations that can be applied to a case under certain applicability conditions. A transformation is behavior preserving if the following is true: if T is applicable to a case C, and C is well-behaved, then T(C) is well-behaved:

$$\forall_C \text{applicable}(T, C) \wedge \text{well-behaved}(C) \Rightarrow$$
$$\text{well-behaved}(T(C))$$

that is, for applicable transformations, the transform of a well-behaved case is a well-behaved case. We assume that in general, if we apply an applicable behavior preserving transformation to an approximation of a well-behaved case, the result will also approximate a well-behaved case.

Given a way of determining salience and a set of possible adaptations, planning involves finding an adaptation of a case with the goal state in the final situation and whose *salient* initial facts are true in the situation in which execution will commence. The planning algorithm becomes: Given a goal (some desired state of the world), find a case $C = \langle \mathcal{I}, \mathcal{F}, \mathcal{P} \rangle$ and a composition of applicable transformations T such that, if T(C) $= \langle \mathcal{I}_t, \mathcal{F}_t, \mathcal{P}_t \rangle$

---

[1]Actually this requirement that a goal be a subset of the final situation facts is overly restrictive; at the same complexity the goal might be allowed to include initial situation facts and events, with the subset criterion extended to $\mathcal{I}$ and $\mathcal{P}$.

- the desired state is a subset of $\mathcal{F}_t$, and

- all *salient* elements of $\mathcal{I}_t$ are true in the situation that will hold when the plan is executed.

The plan produced is the set of events and timing constraints $\mathcal{P}_t$: a "replay" of the events of the transformed case.

Summarizing the model: cases are approximations of atomic entities that work like plan operators, and those approximations are constructed from executions. Adaptations allow us to construct and use variants of cases that can be used in the same way; with adaptation, each case defines a class of plan operators. This model does not cover all case-based planning systems; it does, however, include the fundamental mechanisms used in all case-based planners.

3   Ramification and qualification

The "frame problem" as originally introduced referred to the difficulty of axiomatizing things that are not changed by actions in the situation calculus[McCarthy and Hayes, 1970], but the term has broadened to encompass a number of related problems that concern reasoning about the effects of actions. As the point of planning is to come up with action sequences that lead to particular effects, these problems are of some interest. In particular, we will examine two problems, the *ramification problem*, which deals with determining the effects of an action, and the *qualification* problem, which deals with the difficulty in enumerating all of the conditions under which an action will have a given effect. These are both practical problems faced when attempting to plan in complex domains.

3.1   The ramification (extended prediction) problem

The ramification problem deals with the practical difficulties involved in finding the logical implications of an action's effect. It is complementary to the problem of determining what does not change [Davis, 1990]; the problem is to specify how states change when others do (and use that information). An example (from [Georgeff, 1990]) involves the effects of shooting: if we have an axiom stating that breathing ceases with death it should be possible to specify death as a shooting result, but not breathing cessation, which is inferable. While this seems reasonable, it is practically very difficult in planning systems, particularly for nonlinear planners. The major problem is determining what is true (in particular, whether an action's preconditions are true) at a point in a plan before the order of the actions is fixed. In nonlinear planners, at least those with hopes of completeness (those that backtrack), this is accomplished by associating desired effects with the actions that explicitly establish them

or their negations, then reasoning about that set of actions. If effects could be inferred as well as explicitly established by an individual action, then desired preconditions could be established by combinations of actions, greatly increasing the problem's complexity. SIPE [Wilkins, 1988], unlike most classical planners, allows a restricted amount of deduction of effects; doing so while maintaining efficient performance is a real accomplishment. The *extended prediction problem* [Shoham and McDermott, 1988] is a variant on the same theme; it is "easy" to predict effects and persistences over short time intervals, but difficult over longer ones where persistences become less assured. For both of these problems, local (or immediate) prediction is reliable, but determining accumulated effects is difficult.

As defined in Section 2, the case-based planning approach handles these sorts of problems quite well based on the large grain size of cases as plan operators. A plan's ramifications ($\mathcal{F}_t$ in adapted case $\langle \mathcal{I}_t, \mathcal{F}_t, \mathcal{P}_t \rangle$) are explicit, and available for only the final situation. Deduction of results (for goals) is not used, but it would be relatively easy to include. The problematic deductions for a classical planner are those that are done at intermediate points in the plan; there are no intermediate points to reason about in a case-based planner, but only final situation results established by an arbitrarily complex group of actions. Similarly, the notion of extended prediction is less meaningful when plans are constructed from one operator: prediction takes place on the basis of a single operator (an "atomic" time unit). We cannot determine how long things persist, or when they become true, but we have a model of what is true at a particular future situation of interest.

3.2   Qualification problems

The qualification problem is this: how can we avoid enumerating all of the conditions necessary for an action to have certain effects (that is, how can we make our plan operators reasonably simple). The problem with making such simplifications in a complex domain is that sometimes exceptional situations occur (someone puts a potato in the tailpipe), and a generated plan will not be correct. This problem exists in case-based planning systems as well; it can be caused by at least three factors:

- missing important information in the initial situation of a case,

- extraneous information in the initial situation of a case—things that have no effect on results, and

- qualification problems related to the applicability conditions of adaptations.

We discuss the first two together as *salience* problems and consider adaptation problems separately.

3.2.1 Salience problems

Salience problems are due to the fact that the cases we plan from are only approximations of well-behaved cases. Given our cases, we need to ask two questions: which features of the initial situation and plan affect the results (and which of the results is actually predictable in this case), and what features *not* in the case are important in terms of prediction. These are hard problems: to determine salience exactly it would be necessary to build a causal explanation of the case; if we could do this, we could store only well-behaved cases, but then the applicability of case-based planning would be reduced to those domains where a fairly complete causal theory exists (domains within which approximate cases would be unnecessary).

Initially, salience is a case representation issue; ideally, we want all salient facts to be included [McCartney and Sanders, 1990]. This ideal is generally unachievable, and we are unable to tell which facts in a representation or a situation are salient. Instead of looking at salience directly, implemented systems use similarity as a metric; the assumption being that if one case is more similar to a situation than another, then it matches better on salient features. How similarity should be evaluated is an open research area in case-based reasoning in general [Kolodner, 1989]; among the possibilities are:

- measure similarity on the basis of agreement of "surface features", things explicitly in the representation,

- measure similarity on the basis of "deep features", things inferable from the representation and potentially relevant to the task at hand, and

- some combination of the above, perhaps with some differential weighting.

In any case, the assumption is that the more similar two cases are, the more similar their behavior. Similarity comparisons among cases in case-based systems are approximations to salience testing; they are necessitated by the qualification problems inherent in using approximate cases.

3.2.2 Adaptation problems

In our model, adaptations are general transformational plan operators with associated applicability conditions; the specification of these applicability conditions leads directly to the qualification problem in the obvious way: how to specify these conditions without getting inundated with details. The answer can be complicated by the nature (and potential generality) of these transformations as well, as the conditions that allow a transformation may be changed by a subsequent transformation. For example, consider the following example from the meal planning domain; suppose my adaptations allow the substitution of rosemary for thyme when a recipe contains chicken but not beef, and allows substitution of beef cubes for chicken whenever the chicken is hacked up; I should be able to adapt "hacked up chicken with thyme" to "hacked up chicken with rosemary", which could be adapted into "beef cubes with rosemary". Qualifying the second transformation to avoid this (allow substitution when chicken is hacked up *and* thyme has not been substituted for rosemary?) would seem to lead to excess complexity.

These problems have been ignored for the most part, and most of the attention paid to efficient implementations, like specifying substitutions in an *isa* hierarchy and using *critics* to perform the adaptation beyond substitution. These tend to be minor changes, and have general applicability, so the associated qualification problems have been minor, or fixable with simple mechanisms. As the kinds of adaptations that can be done are made more complex, however, these problems will increase.

The adaptations we consider here are termed *structural* in [Riesbeck and Schank, 1989], as opposed to *derivation-based adaptations*, which act on the derivation history of a case. We consider such methods in the next section when discussing replay; our model has insufficient information to support these.

4 Alternative CBP models

Our idealized model effectively reflects the mechanisms of non-hybrid case-based planning systems (like CHEF [Hammond, 1986] and COOKIE [McCartney, 1990]), and reflects the case-based parts of other systems, at least where they do not rely on special-purpose or domain-dependent techniques. It has a single mechanism for planning, there is a 1-1 correspondence between cases and plans, and planning is based on facts and events only. There are implemented systems that lack each of these features: systems that employ a number of planning methods, systems that use either part of a case or more than one case to develop a plan, and systems that use other information to rederive a plan. These differences affect the problems of interest.

4.1 Hybrid models

Case-based planning as idealized in this paper can be combined with other planning methods in a single system. A prime example of this approach is the JULIA system [Hinrichs, 1991] that produces plans for meals (menus and presentation); it combines a "classical" task reduction planner, a case-based reasoner, and a constraint propagation system to build its plans. Since it does task decomposition via plan operators, it is subject to the frame problem in the same way as other planners of that sort. It uses cases to point out potential problems with these plans; in a sense, this addresses the ramification problem by predicting possible undesirable effects based on the effects seen in cases. This use of cases is not goal-directed in the way we proposed in Section 2.2, but is compatible with the more general idealization in Section 5. Fairly general adaptations are supported, but without much attention to applicability conditions (a limitation noted by Hinrichs).

4.2   Replay

As mentioned earlier, it is possible to apply adaptations to the derivation structure of a plan. An example of a system using such an approach is PRIAR [Kambhampati, 1990, Hendler and Kambhampati, 1988], a domain-independent planner. The cases (which are plans produced originally by a nonlinear planner) include information on how the solution was reached. The idea is to attempt to rederive an old solution to solve a similar problem, using the same operators as in the first derivation whenever possible, and modifying the design where the old operator either does not apply (preconditions unmet) or does not produce the desired result. PRIAR uses case-based reasoning for *efficiency*: it works in conjunction with a nonlinear planner based on NONLIN[Tate, 1977]. When a plan is originally derived, certain information is stored: a hierarchical task network corresponding to the task reductions in the planning, annotations on the nodes that includes dependency and verification information for the subtasks rooted there, and states between nodes that includes the information necessary to validate the following plan steps. Simplifying somewhat, the planning mechanism is to find a plan that matches (as closely as possible) the desired situation and outcome. Then the annotations are used to determine where the plan is not applicable to the current problem, then the planner performs the local "refitting" needed to make all of the plan applicable. Since all of the useful (necessary) intermediate information is explicitly represented, this process can lead to minimum work in replanning without sacrificing any of the power of the nonlinear planner. The marked differences between this and our idealized model are largely based on the amount of internal information stored, and the reliance on other planning methods for the local adaptations. Although this work gives an example how case-based planning can lead to efficiency gains without resorting to approximations, it shares the ramification and qualification problems of NONLIN-style planners.

4.3   Using more or less than 1 case

Although certain advantages are due to plan generation from a single case, there are disadvantages as well. A case may produce more effects than desired, or only a subset of desired effects; a possible answer is to develop a mechanism whereby parts of cases are

extracted, then combined into a new plan. This capability is provided in CELIA[Redmond, 1990], which breaks cases up into subsequences of events called *snippets*. Snippets are associated with the goals that they lead to, plus the applicability conditions for their use and their effects. To use these in a plan requires

- that each snippet's applicability conditions be explicit (qualification problem), and
- that the planner be able to determine what is true at the point in the plan where the snippet is to be executed based on previous events (ramification problem).

Using a plan comprised of snippets can have advantages; the intermediate information could be very useful in monitoring the execution of a plan, for example, but it would seem that the frame problems we are considering here are as bad as in classical approaches.

5   Extending the model

With an eye toward greater functionality, we can generalize our idealized model slightly to include intermediate information and allow more general goals.

For intermediate information we add a fourth element to the case tuple, $\mathcal{M}$, which is a set of facts that are true in situations other than the initial and final situation, of the form true-in(S, P), where P is a propositional fluent and S is a situation corresponding to the beginning or end of an event. This necessitates a change in the definition of a well-behaved case to ensure that these intermediate facts are all true:

$$\text{well-behaved}(\langle\mathcal{I}, \mathcal{F}, \mathcal{P}, \mathcal{M}\rangle) \iff$$
$$(\forall_{S,S_f} \text{true-in}(S, \mathcal{I}) \wedge \text{occurs}([S, S_f], \mathcal{P}) \Rightarrow$$
$$\text{true-in}(S_f, \mathcal{F}) \wedge (\forall_\phi \phi \in \mathcal{M} \Rightarrow \phi))$$

As before, each case is related to a well-behaved case through an execution; $\mathcal{M}$ for the case is a subset of all possible facts from situations corresponding to the beginning or end of events. This extension should have no effect on the ramification or qualification problems, unless the intermediate information is used in determining the applicability of transformations; the planning process remains the same. Allowing such information broadens the range of possible goals (under the extended view of goals below), and can be used to provide guidance during execution [McCartney and Wurst, 1991].

Goals can be generalized to be a partial case specification: desired states for the initial and end situations, events, and intermediate facts (so I can specify, for example, that a particular event type occurs). With these extensions, for goal $\mathcal{G} = \langle\mathcal{I}_g, \mathcal{F}_g, \mathcal{P}_g, \mathcal{M}_g\rangle$, we find a case $\langle\mathcal{I}, \mathcal{F}, \mathcal{P}, \mathcal{M}\rangle$ and a composition of applicable transformations T such that, if T(C) = $\langle\mathcal{I}_t, \mathcal{F}_t, \mathcal{P}_t, \mathcal{M}_t\rangle$

- $\mathcal{I}_g \subseteq \mathcal{I}_t \wedge \mathcal{F}_g \subseteq \mathcal{F}_t \wedge \mathcal{P}_g \subseteq \mathcal{P}_t \wedge \mathcal{M}_g \subseteq \mathcal{M}_t$, and
- all *salient* elements of $\mathcal{I}_t$ are true in the situation that will hold when the plan is executed.

We could relax the subset requirement for goals and cases and generate plans that meet some of the goals (those present in the case).

Extending the model by generalizing the notion of goal and including intermediate information has the benefits of allowing a wider range of goals to be specified (and planned for), and leads to plans with expected intermediate conditions that can be useful in monitoring plan execution. If we try to use the increased information in adaptation, it complicates the qualification problems inherent in using transformations with applicability conditions.

5.1   Limitations in our model

This extended model has a number of representational limitations that could be addressed:

- Goals to avoid certain states are not supported, nor are desirable states (such as could be used in opportunistic planning). These should be simple to add once one determines what the semantics of such goals should be.

- The goals of a given plan are not explicit in the case. This should also be easy to add, as the goals were known when the plan (whose execution is the case) was generated. This may be useful information: being able to find a plan that *attempted* (but failed) to achieve a goal may be more useful than finding previous plan at all.

- There is no way to specify subplans, as with snippets. There is an easy representational extension (used in COOKIE), which is to define a subcase as a subset of a case, with the understanding that it approximates some well-defined case. These subcases exhibit similar qualification problems as snippets: although there are no explicit preconditions, the same salience problems exist as with the complete cases, with the added problem of determining which facts in the case are salient to the subcase. Building a plan from subplans requires that we be able to reason about the state of the world where the subplan is executed, an intermediate point in the plan, which leads to the expected ramification problems.

- There is no derivation history. Where a plan came from (what case was adapted, and what adaptations were applied) could be useful information in evaluating alternative plans as well as in analyzing reasons for success or failure.

These features could be added without great difficulty, even while paying attention to keeping clean semantics. The difficult part is determining how to use such information without losing the strengths (and simplicity) of the original case-based planning approach.

6   Conclusions

In this paper we ask whether the frame problem (specifically ramification and qualification) is manifest in case-based planning. Simple answer: ramification problem largely goes away, qualification problem shows up as problems of salience and adaptation applicability. This simple answer changes as we move away from the idealized model, as certain extensions to the basic technique share characteristics with classical planning methods.

Is the idealization presented a reasonable model of case-based planning? Yes, particularly in its extended form. In addition, it is, we hope, a starting point for the development of more formal case-based models.

Acknowledgements

This work has been supported in part by the National Science Foundation, grant IRI-9110961. Thanks to Kate Sanders for detailed discussion and criticism of these ideas, and to the reviewers for their helpful suggestions. Thanks also to the members of the COOKIE group at Connecticut: Barbara Cuthill, Madeleine Pukinskis, Dave Towers, and Karl Wurst.

References

[Davis, 1990] Ernest Davis. *Representations of Commonsense Knowledge*. Morgan-Kauffmann Publishers, Inc., San Mateo, CA, 1990.

[Georgeff, 1990] Michael P. Georgeff. Planning. In J. Allen, J. Hendler, and A. Tate, editors, *Readings in Planning*, pages 5–25, Morgan-Kauffmann Publishers, Inc., San Mateo, CA, 1990.

[Hammond, 1986] Kristian J. Hammond. *Case-based planning: an integrated theory of planning, learning, and memory*. Technical Report YALEU/CSD/RR 488, Department of Computer Science, Yale University, 1986. (PhD Thesis).

[Hendler and Kambhampati, 1988] James A. Hendler and Subbarao Kambhampati. Refitting plans for case-based reasoning. In Janet Kolodner, editor, *Proceedings of a workshop on case-based reasoning*, pages 179–181, 1988.

[Hinrichs, 1991] Thomas R. Hinrichs. *Problem solving in open worlds: a case study in design*. Technical Report GIT-CC-91/36, College of Computing, Georgia Institute of Technology, 1991. (PhD Thesis).

[Kambhampati, 1990] Subbarao Kambhampati. Mapping and retrieval during plan reuse: a validation structure based approach. In *Proceedings of the eighth national conference on artificial intelligence*, pages 170–175, Boston, MA, 1990.

[Kolodner, 1989] Janet L. Kolodner. Selecting the best case for a case-based reasoner. In *Proceedings of the 11th annual conference of the Cognitive Science Society*, pages 155–162, Ann Arbor, MI, July 1989.

[McCarthy and Hayes, 1970] John McCarthy and Patrick J. Hayes. Some philosophical problems from the standpoint of artificial intelligence. In B. Meltzer and D. Mitchie, editors, *Machine Intelligence*, pages 463–502, Edinburgh University Press, 1970.

[McCartney, 1990] Robert McCartney. Reasoning directly from cases in a case-based planner. In *Proceedings of the 12th annual conference of the Cognitive Science Society*, pages 101–108, Cambridge, MA, July 1990.

[McCartney and Sanders, 1990] Robert McCartney and Kathryn E. Sanders. The case for cases: a call for purity in case-based reasoning. In *Proceedings of the 1990 AAAI Spring Symposium on Case-based Reasoning*, pages 12–16, Palo Alto, CA, March 1990.

[McCartney and Wurst, 1991] Robert McCartney and Karl R. Wurst. Defarge: a real-time execution monitor for a case-based planner. In *Proceedings of the 1991 DARPA Case-based Reasoning Workshop*, Washington, DC, May 1991.

[McDermott, 1987] Drew McDermott. We've been framed: or, why AI is innocent of the frame problem. In Zenon W. Pylyshyn, editor, *The Robot's Dilemma: The Frame Problem in Artificial Intelligence*, pages 113–122, Ablex Publishing Corporation, Norwood, NJ, 1987.

[Redmond, 1990] Michael Redmond. Distributed cases for case-based reasoning: facilitating use of multiple cases. In *Proceedings of the eighth national conference on artificial intelligence*, pages 304–309, Boston, MA, 1990.

[Riesbeck and Schank, 1989] Christopher K. Riesbeck and Roger C. Schank. *Inside Case-based Reasoning*. Lawrence Erlbaum Associates, Hillsdale, NJ, 1989.

[Shoham and McDermott, 1988] Yoav Shoham and Drew McDermott. Problems in formal temporal reasoning. *Artificial Intelligence*, 36:49–61, 1988.

[Tate, 1977] Austin Tate. Generating project networks. In *Proceedings of the fifth international joint conference on artificial intelligence*, pages 888–893, Cambridge, MA, August 1977.

[Wilkins, 1988] David E. Wilkins. *Practical Planning*. Morgan-Kauffmann Publishers, Inc., San Mateo, CA, 1988.

Incremental Path Planning on Graphs with Cycles

Joseph C. Pemberton and Richard E. Korf
Computer Science Department
University of California
Los Angeles, CA 90024

Abstract

We present two new algorithms, LCM and IBFS, that make locally optimal incremental planning decisions for the task of finding a path to a goal state in a problem space that contains cycles. Earlier work (RTA* [Korf, 1990]) solves the incremental path planning problem when the problem space is tree structured. We precisely characterize the time and space complexity of both new algorithms, and show that they are asymptotically optimal. In addition, we present empirical evidence for a variety of maze problem spaces which shows that LCM and IBFS consistently produce shorter solutions than RTA*, and that the average computation cost of IBFS and LCM grows only slowly with the size of the problem. Finally, we show that as the lookahead depth increases, both algorithms require less computation per move decision than RTA*.

1 INTRODUCTION

Consider the following planning problem. You are in a maze, and your objective is to find your way out as efficiently as possible. Your sensory information is limited in that you can only see those locations that are adjacent to your current position. You can keep track of the portion of the maze you have seen so far, however, and recognize when you have returned to a previously visited location. The sensory limitation precludes planning an optimal sequence of moves in advance, since you can only discover the maze by moving through it. The problem is how to minimize the total distance you must travel to get out, including all exploration and backtracking.

Real-Time A* (RTA*) [Korf, 1990] solves this problem in constant time per decision when the maze is tree-structured. RTA*'s decisions are not locally optimal, however, when the problem space contains cycles.

Given this deficiency, there are three ways to proceed. The first is to apply RTA* directly to problem spaces with cycles, and accept locally suboptimal decisions. The second option is to generate an algorithm that makes locally optimal decisions on a graph, although not in constant time per decision. Two algorithms which implement this option are presented in section 3. The last option is to generate an extension of RTA* that makes locally optimal planning decisions in constant time per decision for graphs with cycles. Theoretical results presented in section 4 show that this is not possible. Empirical results in section 5 show that our new algorithms outperform RTA* when the problem space contains even relatively few cycles.

2 BACKGROUND

Traditional search algorithms, such as A*, can be used to preplan an optimal sequence of move decisions only when the entire problem space is available to the problem solver, albeit at some computational cost. This allows the problem solver to delay any action until a complete, optimal solution path is found. Although the algorithms presented here can be used instead of A* to generate globally suboptimal solution paths more efficiently than A*, their main objective is to provide incremental move decisions in situations where the sensory information is limited.

RTA* provides incremental planning decisions by storing in memory all states that have been previously visited by the problem solver, along with a heuristic estimate of each state's distance to a goal. For example, consider the graph in figure 1a. Here we assume that all edges have unit cost, that the initial static heuristic values are as shown, and that the problem solver can only "see" new nodes that are adjacent to its current state (thus the dashed edge is not initially visible). We use a lowercase h to denote initial or static heuristic values, and an uppercase H to denote stored heuristic values. For each move, RTA* generates each neighbor n' of the current state n, and computes its $f_n(n')$ value as the sum of the edge cost to the node, $k(n, n')$, plus

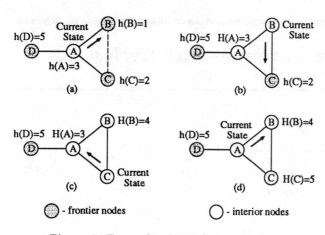

Figure 1: Example of RTA* on a Cycle.

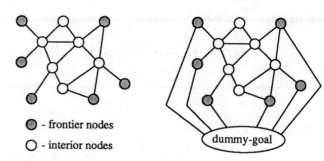

- frontier nodes

- interior nodes

Figure 2: Sample Local Graph and Corresponding Augmented Local Graph.

that node's heuristic value, $h(n')$ or $H(n')$. If the node was visited before, then it uses $H(n')$, the value that was stored with that node when it was last visited. Otherwise, its heuristic value is determined by the static evaluation function $h(n')$. Initially, A is the start node, so RTA* computes $f_A(D) = k(A, D) + h(D) = 1 + 5 = 6$, $f_A(B) = k(A, B) + h(B) = 1 + 1 = 2$, and $f_A(C) = k(A, C) + h(C) = 1 + 2 = 3$. The problem solver then moves to a neighbor n' with the lowest $f_A(n')$ value (node B), and stores the $f_A(n'')$ value of the second-best neighbor n'' (node C) as the new H-value for the previous state. Thus $H(A) = f_A(C) = 3$ is stored with node A (see figure 1b). The second-best value is stored because it represents the estimated cost of backtracking to a goal through that node. RTA* is guaranteed to eventually find a solution path in a finite graph, and makes locally optimal planning decisions when the problem space is a tree [Korf, 1990][1].

When the problem space contains cycles, however, RTA* may make locally suboptimal move decisions as can be seen by continuing the example. After moving from node A to node B (see figure 1b), RTA* will discover the edge from node B to C, compute $f_B(A) = 1 + 3 = 4$, $f_B(C) = 1 + 2 = 3$, move to node C, and store $H(B) = f_B(A) = 4$ with node B (see figure 1c). Next, it will compute $f_C(A) = 1 + 3 = 4$, $f_C(B) = 1 + 4 = 5$, move to node A, and store $H(C) = f_C(B) = 5$ with node C, resulting in the situation in figure 1d. In the next step, RTA* computes $f_A(D) = 1 + 5 = 6$, $f_A(B) = 1 + 4 = 5$, $f_A(C) = 1 + 5 = 6$, and moves to node B, storing $H(A) = f_A(C) = f_A(D) = 6$, with node A. Unfortunately, this is not a locally optimal decision, since RTA* has seen enough information at this point to realize that B and C form a dead-end loop, and that moving to node D is the correct decision. RTA* will

eventually move to node D, but by making the initial value of $h(D)$ sufficiently large, we can force RTA* to go around this loop an arbitrary number of times before it finally exits[2]. Correcting this deficiency of RTA* was the original motivation behind this work.

Before continuing, we define the following terms which are used in the remainder of the paper (see figure 2). The *local graph* is the subset of the problem space nodes and edges that the problem solver has "seen" so far. The nodes in the local graph are divided into *interior nodes*, which have been expanded by the problem solver, and *frontier nodes*, which have been generated but not yet expanded. The *augmented local graph* consists of the current local graph plus a *dummy-goal node* and one edge from each frontier node to the *dummy-goal node*, with edge costs that correspond to the static heuristic values of the frontier nodes. This augmentation is based on the face-value principle, namely that the heuristic values of frontier nodes are treated as accurate estimates of the distance to a goal node. This is a reasonable assumption when additional information about the problem space and heuristic function is not available. We define a *locally optimal* move as the first step along an optimal path, assuming the static heuristic values of the frontier nodes are exact, or in other words, a move along an optimal path towards the dummy-goal node in the augmented local graph.

3   TWO LOCALLY OPTIMAL GRAPH ALGORITHMS

In this section, we present two new algorithms that make locally optimal decisions on graphs that may contain cycles.

3.1   LOCAL CONSISTENCY MAINTENANCE

Local consistency maintenance (LCM) is based on the idea that if we maintain for each interior node a heuris-

---

[1]A similar algorithm, called Learning RTA* (LRTA*) [Korf, 1990], stores the *best* value with each visited node, but its move decisions are not guaranteed to be locally optimal, even on a tree.

[2]LRTA* performs even worse than RTA* when the problem space contains cycles.

tic value that represents the best estimate of the cost of reaching a goal from that node, then locally optimal decisions can be based on the values of the current state's neighbors. The heuristic value of a node n is *locally consistent* if and only if it is equal to the minimum $f_n(n')$ value of all its neighbors n':

$$H(n) = \min_{n'}[f_n(n') \mid f_n(n') = k(n, n') + H(n')]$$

for all adjacent nodes n', where $H(n') = h(n')$ when n' is a frontier node. A local graph is *locally consistent* if each interior node is locally consistent, in which case the heuristic value of each node represents the best estimate of the distance from that node to a goal.

The LCM algorithm operates by expanding the current state, possibly generating new frontier nodes. It then updates the stored heuristic value of the current state and recursively updates the stored heuristic values of neighbors of updated nodes as needed until all interior nodes are locally consistent. Finally, LCM moves to a neighbor with minimum f-value, where ties are broken randomly. The procedure is repeated until a goal node is visited, or all frontier nodes are expanded. For example, on the graph in figure 1, LCM initially makes the same decisions as RTA*, moving to node B and then to node C (see figure 1c). Once C is expanded, node D is the only remaining frontier node, and the updating step terminates with $H(A) = 6$, and $H(B) = H(C) = 7$. At this point, the problem solver moves to node A. Since node A was previously expanded, no updating is necessary, and the problem solver moves to node D, which is the locally optimal move.

In the worst case, where the heuristic value of every interior node must be updated, LCM reduces to calculating the shortest path from the dummy-goal node to each interior node in the augmented local graph. Our implementation maintains a queue of nodes to be updated so that it only needs to process nodes with inconsistent heuristic values, which improves the average-case running time of the algorithm. If V is the set of nodes in the local graph, then the worst-case running time is bounded by $O(|V|^2)$, which is the cost of generating the shortest-path distance to the dummy-goal node for all interior nodes.

By maintaining a locally consistent local graph, LCM can be viewed as planning a locally optimal move decision for each interior node. The end result is that each interior node is labeled with its shortest-path distance in the augmented local graph. Although this makes it possible to base move decisions only on locally stored information, it also requires the heuristic values of all inconsistent nodes to be updated after each move, whether or not they affect the current move decision, which can be inefficient.

3.2 INCREMENTAL BEST FIRST SEARCH

An alternative to LCM is Incremental Best-First Search (IBFS), which is designed to spend the least amount of effort necessary to make a single locally optimal move. The IBFS algorithm operates by performing a best-first search on the local graph starting from the current state. Interior and frontier nodes are evaluated using the A* cost function ($f = g + h$), where g is the cost of the best path from the current state and h is the static heuristic estimate of the distance to the goal. Ties between nodes with the same cost relative to the current state are broken at random, and the search process stops when a frontier node is chosen as the lowest cost node. IBFS then commits to moves along the locally optimal path toward the chosen frontier node, until the local graph is changed by the expansion of a frontier node. At this point, all intermediate results from the previous search are discarded, and the planning process is repeated until a goal state is visited (success) or until all frontier nodes have been expanded (no goal exists).

For example, on the graph in figure 1, IBFS will initially make the same decisions as RTA* and LCM, moving from node A to node B and then to node C (see figure 1c). After expanding node C, IBFS performs a best-first search on the augmented local graph by generating the neighbors of the current state (node C), marking node C as examined[3], and calculating the heuristic value of all neighbors of the current state ($f_C(A) = k(C, A) + h(A) = 1 + 3 = 4$, $f_C(B) = 1 + 1 = 2$). IBFS then continues the best-first search, examining all generated nodes in order of increasing f-value, until a frontier node is chosen for examination. Since the sensory limitation precludes generating the neighbors of a frontier node, IBFS stops searching and moves toward the chosen frontier node. In this example, node B is examined first followed by node A. Finally the frontier node D is examined, and the problem solver moves to node A which is the first step on the shortest path to D. Since node A was already expanded before, the problem solver continues moving to node D which is the next locally optimal move.

IBFS differs from A* in that it commits to partial solution paths in order to be able to further explore the problem space, whereas A* requires access to the complete problem space so it is only able to preplan the complete solution when the complete problem space is accessible. IBFS only stores the current local graph and its static heuristic values, and thus must plan the next series of moves from scratch every time a frontier node is expanded. Because it does not store any of

---

[3]We use the term "examination" when the problem solver expands a node in the local graph, and "expansion" when the problem solver moves to a frontier node and expands it, increasing the information in the local graph.

the results from previous decisions, IBFS can also be inefficient in some cases.

4   THEORETICAL PROPERTIES

For the theorems in this section, we assume that all static heuristic values are non-negative, that all edge costs are positive, and that a goal node is reachable from every node. Although many planning domains deal with the possibility of reaching a dead-end, we have assumed that this doesn't happen to simplify our analysis. Lastly, all goal nodes have heuristic values equal to zero, and they remain frontier nodes once they are generated. The first property we consider is completeness; namely, under what conditions are the move decisions by LCM and IBFS guaranteed to lead to a goal state? Proofs of the theorems have been omitted, but can be found in [Pemberton & Korf, 1992].

Theorem 1 *In a finite problem space with positive edge costs, where a goal is reachable from every state, LCM and IBFS will eventually visit a goal.*

The second theorem addresses the issue of correctness, namely that the move decisions made by LCM and IBFS are locally optimal.

Theorem 2 *Each move made by LCM and IBFS is along a path whose estimated cost of reaching a goal is minimum, based on the local graph.*

The next two properties describe the worst-case behavior of both algorithms. Since LCM and IBFS both store the local graph ($G(V, E)$) plus a constant amount of additional information per node, their space complexity is $O(|E| + |V|)$. Time complexity is addressed by the following theorem.

Theorem 3 *Given a local graph, $G(V,E)$, the worst-case time complexity of a single planning step is $O(|V|^2)$ for both IBFS and LCM .*

Next we discuss a lower bound on the complexity of making locally optimal move decisions when the problem space is a general graph with cycles. For the following theorem, we assume that the problem space can be represented as an undirected weighted graph, that the problem solver has no prior knowledge of the problem space, and that the initial heuristic information is monotone (*i.e.*, $h(n) \leq h(n') + k(n, n')$ [Pearl, 1984]).

Theorem 4 *Given a local graph, $G(V,E)$, a series of $|V|$ locally optimal move decisions requires at least $O(|V| * |E|)$ computations in the worst case.*

As a result of theorem 4, there is no general way to amortize the cost of one worst-case move decision over a series of moves, thus, in general, it is not possible to make locally optimal planning decisions in real time

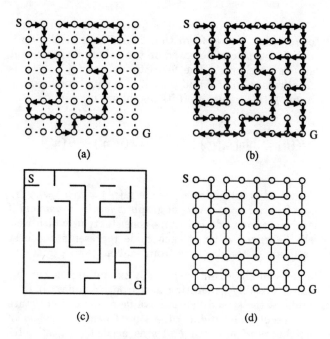

Figure 3: Sample problem space: (a) Depth-First Search on a Grid, (b) Depth-First Search Tree, (c) Maze with 20% of the Walls Removed, (d) Corresponding Graph (G is the Goal and S is the Start Node).

on a graph with cycles. This result and the fact that in the worst case $|E| = O(|V|^2)$ lead to the following corollary.

Corollary 1 *IBFS and LCM are asymptotically optimal algorithms for making a series of locally optimal move decisions.*

5   EXPERIMENTAL RESULTS

RTA*, LCM, and IBFS were tested in a number of experiments to determine how much better the locally optimal planning decisions made by LCM and IBFS are compared to RTA* when the problem space contains cycles, and the cost of this improved decision quality in terms of average computation (number of node examinations) per planning decision.

The algorithms were tested primarily on mazes created by performing a depth-first search on a graph which corresponds to a complete grid, the children are ordered randomly. As the depth-first search proceeds, graph edges are removed if they lead to a previously visited node (figure 3a shows the first edge removed). The end result is a depth-first search tree (see figure 3b) which corresponds to a maze without cycles. Cycles are then created by randomly adding edges back into the tree or similarly removing walls from the maze (see figure 3c and d). The problem spaces considered range from a tree (no walls removed) to a complete

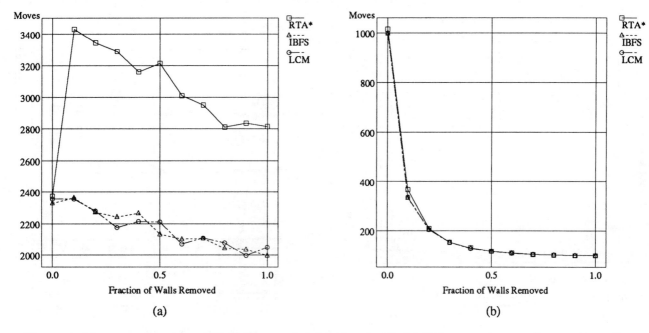

Figure 4: Moves vs. Fraction of Walls Removed, (a) $h(i) = 0$, $\forall i$; (b) $h(i) = manhattan\ distance(i, goal)$.

grid (all internal walls removed), and the start and goal states are placed at opposite corners of the problem space. Note that the fraction of walls removed is correlated with the number of cycles in the problem space.

For the following set of experiments, the problem solver was only able to "see" new nodes that are adjacent to its current location. Data was collected for two different sets of initial heuristic information: $h(i) = 0$ everywhere, corresponding to the case where the problem solver does not know the location of the exit, and $h(i) = manhattan\ distance(i, goal)$, which is the length of a shortest path if all walls were removed, corresponding to the case where the problem solver knows the relative coordinates of the exit. The mazes contain 2500 nodes (a 50 by 50 grid), and the results are averaged over 100 different random mazes with 10 trials per maze. For all three algorithms, we measured the total distance traveled to the goal and the average number of node examinations per move.

Figure 4a shows the average moves as a function of the fraction of walls removed when the initial heuristic information is zero everywhere. As expected, the number of moves required by both IBFS and LCM is fewer on the average than RTA* (e.g., one-third fewer moves for mazes with 20% of the walls removed). When the initial heuristic information is the manhattan distance (figure 4b), the number of moves required by LCM and IBFS is only slightly less than RTA* with the maximum occurring with 10% of the walls removed (roughly 8% fewer moves). This is due to the fact that, when the fraction of walls removed is greater than .30,

the manhattan distance information, plus the fact that the number of obstacles is reduced, make it possible for all three algorithms to follow a path to the goal which is nearly optimal (98 moves). When the problem space is a tree (no walls removed), all three algorithms make locally optimal decisions, and thus require roughly the same number of moves to find the goal.

Figure 5 shows the average number of node examinations per move as a function of the fraction of walls removed. In both cases, RTA* only requires one examination per move, whereas IBFS and LCM both require more. LCM requires many more examinations per move when the problem space is a tree because it often updates the stored values of each node along a branch each time the branch is extended. In general, the relative efficiency of LCM and IBFS depends on both the fraction of walls removed and the initial heuristic information. For example, when $h(i) = 0$ everywhere (figure 5a) LCM requires more examinations per move than IBFS, whereas when $h(i) = manhattan\ distance$ (figure 5b), LCM requires less examinations per move than IBFS when the fraction of walls removed is greater than 20%. This is because LCM maintains estimates of the distance to the goal for each interior node. Thus when the heuristic value is zero everywhere, some interior nodes will have to be updated after each move, whereas when the initial heuristic value is the manhattan distance, the heuristic values of the interior nodes need not to be updated as frequently.

Figure 6 shows the examinations per move versus problem space size (i.e., number of nodes). For both IBFS and LCM, when the initial heuristic information is zero

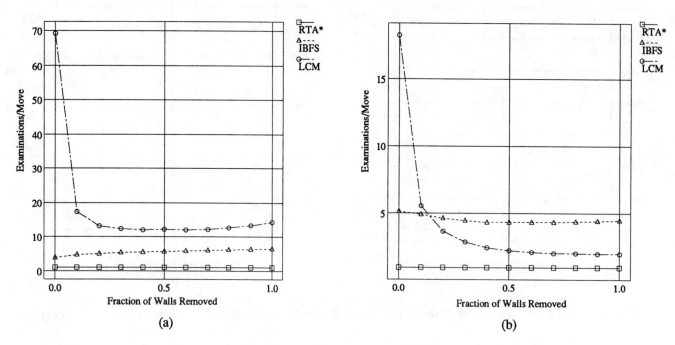

Figure 5: Average Examinations/Move vs. Fraction of Walls Removed, (a) $h(i) = 0$, $\forall i$; (b) $h(i) = manhattan\ distance(i, goal)$.

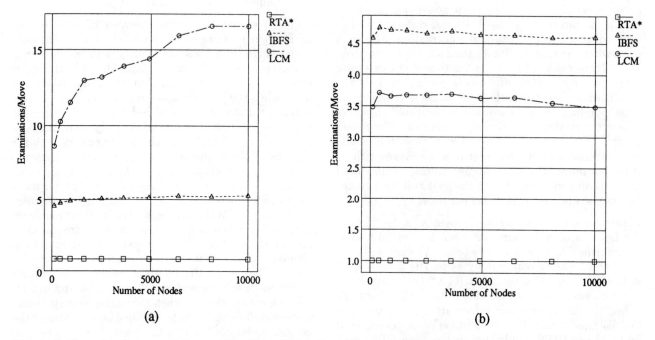

Figure 6: Examinations per Move vs. Problem Space Size (Number of Nodes) for Mazes with 20% of the Walls Removed for (a) $h(i) = 0$, $\forall i$; (b) $h(i) = manhattan\ distance(i, goal)$.

everywhere, the examinations per move grow slowly with the size of the problem space, whereas when the initial heuristic information is manhattan distance, the examination per move remain fairly constant. This behavior is typical for the problem spaces considered.

6   LOOKAHEAD SEARCH

Up to this point, we have assumed that the lookahead depth was equal to one, meaning that only the immediate neighbors of the current state are visible to the problem solver. In terms of sensory limitation, the lookahead depth can be viewed as the ratio of the range of the sensors to the distance traveled during a single move. When the lookahead depth is greater than one, RTA* examines the current state, and for each neighbor that has not been visited before, performs a depth-first search to a fixed depth, backing up the $f = g + h$ values of leaf nodes, where each node's backed-up value is the minimum value of its children (*minimin search* [Korf, 1990]). In addition, when the heuristic estimates are monotone, the best frontier node f-value can be used to prune any path whose current cost estimate equals or exceeds the current bound (*alpha pruning* [Korf, 1990]). RTA* then compares the backed-up f-values of neighbors which have not been visited before with the f-values of previously visited nodes, and moves to the neighbor with the minimum f-value.

When the problem space contains cycles, this approach has three problems. One is that a depth-first search will explore every path to a given node for which the length of the path is less than the lookahead depth. For example, if the lookahead depth is 3, then a depth-first search on the graph in figure 7(a) will examine 2^3 paths from the current state. The second problem is that a move decision can be suboptimal if the heuristic values of shallow nodes are backed up by the lookahead search. Consider the example in figure 7(b). If the current state is node A, all edges have unit cost, and the lookahead depth is 2, then *minimin* will return $h(B) = 1 + h(C) = 1 + 1 = 2$ and $h(C) = 1 + h(D) = 1 + 2 = 3$. Thus RTA* will move to node B even though node C is a better move. The third problem is that RTA* performs a full lookahead on each neighbor of the current state that was not previously visited. On a tree, this prunes a significant portion of the lookahead search space, but on a graph the amount of pruning is reduced since nodes adjacent to visited nodes can be reached through loops. For example, when the lookahead depth is 2, the filled nodes in figure 7(c) will be reexamined by the lookahead from the current state, even though they were examined to the same search depth by the lookahead from the previously visited node.

IBFS and LCM solve the first and second problems by performing the lookahead breadth first instead of

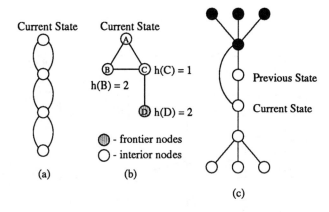

Figure 7: The Effects of Lookahead and Cycles on RTA*, (a) Depth-First Search Explores All Paths, (b) Shallow Leaf Nodes, and (c) Inefficient Pruning.

depth first. The third problem is solved by storing an additional parameter, the search depth, with each node in the local graph. The search depth is the largest depth below which a node has been previously searched. When the lookahead search encounters a node whose stored search depth is greater or equal to the current search horizon, then that node can be pruned, since a previous lookahead explored the node to an equal or greater depth.[4] By storing the search depths, IBFS and LCM are able to significantly reduce the work required by the lookahead search as the lookahead depth is increased. Since IBFS and LCM already store the local graph, the additional memory needed to store the breadth-first search graph and the search depth parameter only increase the memory required by a constant factor.

To demonstrate the effect of lookahead search, we reran some of the experiments presented earlier with different lookahead bounds. The results in figure 8 show the moves versus lookahead depth averaged over 10 trials on 100 different mazes for both initial heuristic conditions. These results show that the locally optimal decisions produced by IBFS and LCM significantly reduce the total solution length in both cases.

The effect on examinations per move is even more pronounced (see figure 9). The examinations per move grow with lookahead depth for all three algorithms, although much more quickly for RTA*, due to the lookahead inefficiencies mentioned above. It is interesting to note that with the manhattan distance heuristic, RTA* requires more examinations per move than both LCM and IBFS when the lookahead depth is greater than 7, even though it makes poorer decisions.

One additional observation is that when the lookahead depth is greater than one, IBFS generates shorter solutions on the average than LCM. This difference, which

---

[4][Russell & Wefald, 1991] made a similar observation.

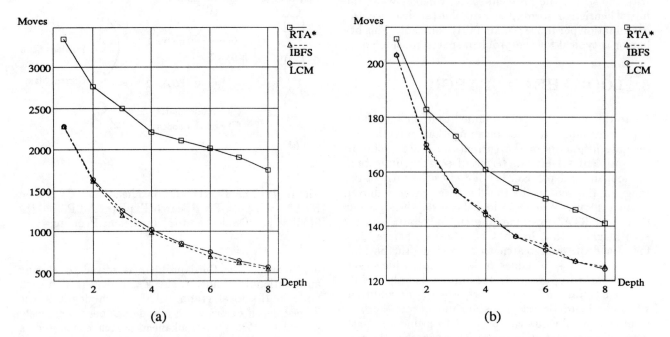

Figure 8: Moves vs. Lookahead Depth for Mazes with 20% of the Walls Removed for (a) $h(i) = 0$ everywhere, (b) $h(i) = manhattan\ distance(i, goal)$.

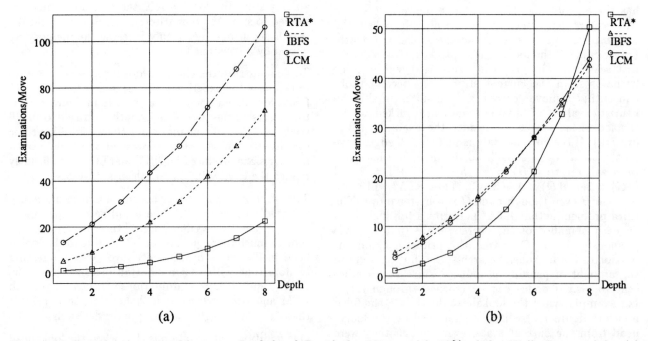

Figure 9: Examinations per Move vs. Lookahead Depth for Mazes with 20% of the Walls Removed for (a) $h(i) = 0$ everywhere, (b) $h(i) = manhattan\ distance(i, goal)$.

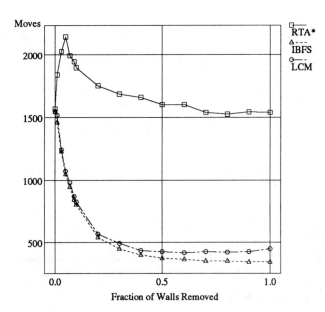

Figure 10: Moves vs. Fraction of Walls Removed (*lookahead depth* = 8, $h(i) = 0$ everywhere).

Table 1: Average moves for 1000 random 15-puzzles for RTA*, LCM and SRTA*.

Lookahead	RTA*	LCM	SRTA*
1	2715	2702	7081
2	750	692	723
3	807	654	699
4	538	475	588
5	476	351	515
6	347	291	391

can be seen in figure 8a and more noticeably in figure 10, is due to the different ways that IBFS and LCM break ties. LCM updates the interior values to be locally consistent and then chooses randomly among the minimum-value neighbors of the current state. IBFS performs a best-first search on the local graph, breaking ties when two or more nodes have the minimum heuristic value. When there are a number of frontier nodes with the same heuristic value, IBFS will choose among them randomly, even though many may share the same ancestors in the search tree. Thus if one neighbor of the current state is on one minimum cost path to the dummy-goal, and another is on many minimum cost paths, LCM will choose between them equally, whereas IBFS will weight the choice toward the neighbor that is on more minimum cost paths. This strategy results in better average decision quality. A larger lookahead depth means more frontier nodes can be expanded in a single move, further accentuating the difference between the two algorithms.

In addition to the maze problem spaces, we ran LCM and RTA* on 1000 random initial states of the 15-puzzle with different lookahead bounds. The results in Table 1 show that even for a problem space that has relatively few cycles, LCM produces solutions that require fewer moves on the average than RTA* (*e.g.* 26% fewer when the lookahead bound is 5). The SRTA* results will be discussed in the next section.

7   RELATED WORK

Sutton [Sutton, 1990, Sutton, 1991] examined a dynamic programming approach to incremental planning

which is related to our work. Although his Dyna architectures are able to eventually learn optimal plans over multiple trials, he does not address the problem of making locally optimal decisions on a single trial in order to minimize the solution length.

Others have presented work on graph algorithms that have similar properties to LCM and IBFS, although none of them address the problem of incremental path planning with limited information. For example, Mérõ's [Mérõ, 1984] B' algorithm and Bagchi and Mahanti's MarkA algorithm [Bagchi & Mahanti, 1985] both maintain consistent heuristic values for interior nodes. Another example is Chandy and Misra's [Chandy & Misra, 1982] distributed algorithm that maintains single-source shortest paths in a graph. A similar algorithm is also presented in [Ausiello *et. al.*, 1990].

Deng and Papadimitriou have considered the problem of exploring an unknown graph [Deng *et. al.*, 1990]. Although their work is related, they only consider the task of exploring edges rather than nodes, and they concentrate on directed rather than undirected graphs. In addition, their work is only concerned with finding all edges in a graph, rather than finding a goal state.

Russell and Wefald [Russell & Wefald, 1991] have presented an extension of RTA*, called Simplified RTA* (SRTA*), that stores the best f-value +10% (*i.e.*, $1.1 * f(best\ neighbor)$) rather than the second-best f-value. We have performed experiments which show that the solution lengths using SRTA*'s stored heuristic values are consistently worse than RTA* on maze problem spaces. In addition, SRTA* requires more moves than LCM to solve random instances of the 15-puzzle (see Table 1). Note that the decisions made by SRTA* are not locally optimal even on tree-structured problem spaces.

8   CONCLUSIONS AND DISCUSSION

The main contributions of this paper are the two incremental planning algorithms for making locally optimal move decisions on graphs when information is limited, and the theoretical results on the inherent complexity of this problem. While the decisions produced by RTA* are locally optimal when the problem space is a tree, both LCM and IBFS extend this result to graphs with cycles, at the expense of additional space and time complexity. The complexity of making a series of $|V|$ locally optimal decisions is at least $O(|V| * |E|)$ in the worst case, where $G(V, E)$ is the local graph. As a result, LCM and IBFS make locally optimal decisions with a worst-case complexity that is asymptotically optimal.

In our experiments, the average length of the paths produced by both LCM and IBFS was significantly shorter than the paths produced by RTA*. The amount of improvement depends on the problem space and the quality of the heuristic information. The costs of this improvement are a constant-factor increase in memory, and a greater number of examinations per move decision. Although in the worst case the number of examinations per move for LCM and IBFS grow linearly with the problem size, our empirical results show that the average examinations per move grow much slower for the problem spaces we considered.

Our later experiments with lookahead search showed that IBFS and LCM can make better use of the additional information provided by lookahead than RTA*. In addition, due to the nature of the algorithms, LCM and IBFS are able to use the additional information more efficiently than RTA*. Finally, the results showed that the method of tie-breaking used by IBFS results in consistently shorter solutions than LCM for the problems we examined when the lookahead depth is greater than one.

Acknowledgements

We would like thank Rob Collins, Tanya Pemberton, and Weixiong Zhang for many helpful discussions, the referees for their comments, and David Harrison for *xgraph* and William Cheng for *tgif*. This research was supported by an NSF Presidential Young Investigator Award and a grant from Rockwell International.

References

Ausiello, G., Italiano, G. F., Spaccamela, A. M., and U. Nanni, Incremental Algorithms for Minimal Length Paths, in: Proceedings of the First ACM-SIAM Symposium on Discrete Algorithms, San Francisco, California (1990) 12-21.

Bagchi, A. and A. Mahanti, Three Approaches to Heuristic Search in Networks, JACM 32 (1) (1985) 1-27.

Boddy, M., Problem Solving Using Dynamic Programming, in: Proceedings AAAI-91, Anaheim (1991) 738-743.

Chandy, K. M. and J. Misra, Distributed Computation on Graphs: Shortest Path Algorithms, Communications of the ACM, 25 (11) (1982) 833-837.

Dean, T. and M. Boddy, An Analysis of Time-Dependent Planning, in: Proceedings AAAI-88, St. Paul, Minnesota (1988), 49-54.

Deng, X. and C. H. Papadimitriou, Exploring an Unknown Graph, in: Proceedings of the Thirty-First Annual Symposium on Foundations of Computer Science (FOCS-90), St. Louis, (1990) 355-361.

Dijkstra, E. W., A note on two problems in connexion with graphs, Numerische Mathematik, 1 (1959) 269-271.

Hart, P.E., N.J. Nilsson, and B. Raphael, A formal basis for the heuristic determination of minimum cost paths, IEEE Transactions on Systems Science and Cybernetics, 4 (2) (1968) 100-107.

Korf, R.E., Real-time heuristic search, Artificial Intelligence, 42 (2-3) (1990) 197-221.

Martelli, A., On the Complexity of Admissible Search Algorithms, Artificial Intelligence, 8 (1977) 1-13.

McDermott, D., Robot Planning, in: Proceedings AAAI-91, Anaheim (1991) 930-931.

Mérõ, L., A Heuristic Search Algorithm with Modifiable Estimate, Artificial Intelligence, 23 (1) (1984) 13-27.

Pearl, J., Heuristics (Addison-Wesley, Reading, Massachusetts, 1984).

Pemberton, J. C. and R. E. Korf, Making Locally Optimal Decisions on Graphs with Cycles, UCLA Computer Science Technical Report Number 920004.

Russell, S., and E. Wefald, Do the Right Thing; Studies in Limited Rationality, (M.I.T. Press, Cambridge, Massachusetts, 1991).

Spira, P. M. and A. Pan, On Finding and Updating Spanning Trees and Shortest Paths, SIAM J. Comput. 4 (1975) 375-380.

Sutton, Richard S., Integrated Architectures for Learning, Planning, and Reacting Based on Approximating Dynamic Programming, in: Proceedings of the Seventh International Conference on Machine Learning (1990) 216-224.

Sutton, Richard S., Planning by Incremental Dynamic Programming, in: Proceedings of the Eighth International Conference on Machine Learning (1991) 353-357.

Tarjan, R. E., Data Structures and Network Algorithms, CBMS-NSF Regional Conference Series in Applied Mathematics, SIAM (1983).

Conditional Nonlinear Planning

Mark A. Peot
Stanford University
Department of Engineering-Economic Systems
Stanford, CA 94305
peot@rpal.rockwell.com
(415) 325-7143

David E. Smith
Rockwell International
444 High St.
Palo Alto, CA 94301
de2smith@rpal.rockwell.com
(415) 325-7162

Abstract

Work-in-progress on the design of a conditional nonlinear planner is described. CNLP is a nonlinear planner that develops plans that account for foreseen uncertainties. CNLP represents an extension of the conditional planning technique of Warren [75] to the domain of nonlinear planning.

1 Problem

Most classical AI planners develop unconditional sequences of actions. Observations of the environment during plan execution have no effect on the sequence of actions executed during the course of that plan. In many planning domains, it is desirable to develop a plan that takes advantage of observations made during plan execution to select the actions that are executed. This is a conditional plan. The actions in the plan are conditioned on observations made prior to their execution.

A conditional plan is necessary when uncertainties in the environment or in the results of actions preclude the selection of a single course of action to accomplish a goal. A conditional plan tests the environment to determine whether a planned sequence of actions is appropriate or not. Rather than replanning at runtime, the conditional planner develops a set of plans for every projected contingency. Note that this is not quite the same as reactive planning. A conditional planner develops plans that are reactive only to a few predicted sources of uncertainty. Reactive planners improvise solutions at run time as uncertainties, predicted or unpredicted, arise. A conditional plan does not exhibit the 'persistent goal-seeking behavior' of a reactive plan [Schoppers 89]. Still, a conditional planner may develop good plans for those predicted sources of uncertainty because it considers the effects of actions on several possible futures simultaneously. For example:

–A conditional planner can prepare for contingencies by ensuring that items needed for the execution of more than one possible plan branch are collected when it is convenient to do so. (Example: "I better take something to do in case the coffee house is closed.")

–A conditional planner can avoid "painting itself into a corner" by considering the impact of actions on the feasibility of contingency plans. (Example: "I'm glad that I remembered to bring an extra key!")

–A contingent planner can consider explicitly the benefit of seeking out and observing information. In conjunction with a decision-theoretic plan evaluator, it can identify the optimal information collection policy by implicitly calculating the value of information [Howard 66].

2 WARPLAN-C

Warplan-C [Warren 76] uses a simple approach for developing conditional *linear* plans. Certain of the actions that comprise a plan are tagged as conditional. Conditional actions have two possible outcomes P or $\neg$ P. During the first planning pass, the planner assumes that all of the conditional actions are unconditional with a single outcome P. Warplan-C attempts to develop a plan using one branch of each conditional and then reinvokes the planner to plan for each dangling 'else' branch. This is illustrated below.

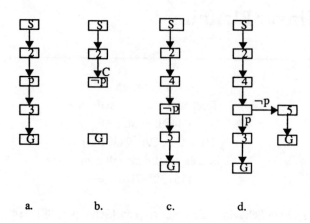

Figure 1: Operation of Warplan-C

The planner develops an unconditional plan assuming that the conditional action has outcome P (Fig 1.a.). After such a plan is found, the planner is reinvoked to plan for the other branch of the conditional. The initial segment used for this plan is the initial segment of the previous plan except that the conditional action is replaced by an action whose preconditions are the protected conditions of the initial segment that were used by action 3 or the goal. The outcome of this new action is ¬P (shown in Fig 1.b). A new plan is found for this branch of the conditional (Fig 1.c) and the result is combined with the original plan to form the final conditional plan (Fig 1.d). Note that actions can be added before the conditional action in order to satisfy the 'else' part of the conditional (for example, step 4 in Fig 1.c, 1.d). Also note that Warplan-C makes no attempt to fuse the branches of the conditional plan.

3 Conditional Nonlinear Plans

The planner that we are developing is a conditional version of the Systematic Nonlinear Planner (SNLP) [McAllester and Rosenblitt, 91; Soderland and Weld, 91]. In the following discussion, we will describe enough of the terminology to understand an extended example. The complete description of the planner follows the example.

An *operator* is a STRIPS operator [Fikes+Nilsson, 71]. Operators are used to describe actions. An operator consists of a set of preconditions and a set of postconditions. We do not use an add and a delete list.

Instead we use three truth values for P. P may be true, false or unknown denoted by P, ¬ P, and Unk(P) respectively.

Actions may have several different, mutually exclusive sets of outcomes for postconditions. The operator Observe (described below) has two possible outcomes: either the road from x to y is clear or it isn't. The postconditions associated with a single greek letter are mutually exclusive and are collectively exhaustive. Exactly one of the sets of postconditions denoted by $\alpha_1...\alpha_n$ are observed. We will call this type of action a *conditional action*.

```
(Observe (Road ?x ?y))

    Pre:      Unk(Clear ?x ?y)

              (at ?x)

 +α₁:      (Clear ?x ?y)

 +α₂:      ¬(Clear ?x ?y)
```

A plan *step* is what we call an operator when it appears in a plan. A step is identical to an operator except that it is tagged with labels representing the action's *reason* and the *context*. Reason contains the list of goals that the plan step contributes to. Context captures the set of events in the environment that the action is conditioned on. An action may be executed in a plan if the observations made during execution thus far are consistent with the context of that action. Reason and context will be described more fully later in the paper.

A *causal link* is a triple <E, P, C> where P is a proposition, E is a step that has P in its postcondition, and C is a step that has P as a precondition.   We will refer to E as the *establisher* of the condition P and refer to C as the *consumer* of that condition. A causal link represents a commitment that the P precondition of step C will be satisfied by a postcondition of step E and that no other action should interfere in the time between the execution of C and E. Causal links are sometimes referred to as *protection intervals*.

A *conditioning link* is a triple {A, α, B} where A and B are actions and α is a condition. Action B may not be executed unless the outcome of action A is α.

An *ordering constraint* is a constraint on the order of two steps in a plan. (McAllester calls this a *safety condition*.) A > B means that A must be executed at some point after B is executed. There are ordering constraints implicit in causal links and conditioning links. C > E in the causal link <E, P, C> or the conditioning link {E, α, C}.

A *conditional plan* consists of a set of steps, reason and context labels for those steps, a set of ordering constraints, a set of bindings for variables in the plan, a set of causal links and a set of conditioning links.

4 Overview of CNLP

The following simple example demonstrates the operation of our nonlinear planner, CNLP.

Let's say that our objective is to ski. In order to ski, we need to get our skis and drive to a place that has a ski resort. In the simple example diagrammed below, there are only two ski resorts, Snowbird and Park City (abbreviated S and P). It is possible that the road from B to S or the road from C to P will be covered with snow. All of the other roads are clear. If the road is snow covered then it is impassable. If the road from B to S or the road from C to P is snowed in, then we can observe this fact from B or C respectively. There are three operators in this domain: the Observe operator described above, (Drive ?x ?y) and (Get Skis). In order to drive from x to y, we must be at x when the action is executed and the road from x to y must be clear. In order to get our skis, we must be at home. Our goal is to be at a resort with our skis: (At ?x) and (Resort ?x) and (Have Skis). Note that it may not always be possible to achieve the goal.

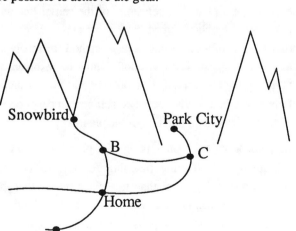

The planner starts with two dummy operators. The first operator, **IC**, has the initial conditions as its postconditions. The second operator has preconditions corresponding to the conjunctive clauses of the goal. We call our first attempt to instantiate the goal G_1. Initially, the context for G_1 is true. This means that we expect to derive a plan that results in the goal being satisfied in every context. The planner works by adding causal links from actions to *open conditions*, resolving conflicts whenever they arise. An open condition is a precondition that has not been established through a causal link. There are two ways of adding a causal link to a plan. The first, **add-link**[1], adds a causal link between an existing action and an open precondition. **Add-step** adds a new action to a plan. The other planning operators resolve conflicts between pieces of the plan.

The figure on the next page illustrates a conditional nonlinear plan that solves the example problem. IC and the links from IC to other nodes have been omitted for clarity. Solid lines, dashed lines and thick lines represent causal links, ordering constraints and conditioning links, respectively.

CNLP is a nondeterministic planner much like SNLP [McAllester+Rosenblitt 91] or TWEAK [Chapman 87]. This type of planner nondeterministically selects a completions for incomplete plans. We will not attempt to describe how a nondeterministic planning algorithm works and assume that the reader is familiar with [McAllester+Rosenblitt 91, or Soderland+Weld 91].

The plan consists of three different conditional branches corresponding to the case when the road from **b** to **s** is clear, the case when **b** to **s** is not clear and the road from **c** to **p** is clear and the case when neither road is clear. These branches are labelled with the contexts α_1, $\alpha_2\beta_1$, and $\alpha_2\beta_2$ respectively.   The actions that comprise a given conditional branch are labelled with the context of that conditional branch. There is a separate goal attempt for every conditional branch. No attempt is made to merge branches after they split.

---

[1] We have borrowed the names for most of our planning operations from [Soderland+Weld, 91].

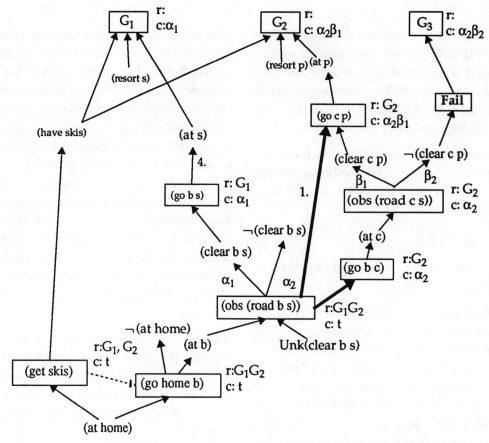

Figure 2 -- A conditional nonlinear plan for skiing.

Before discussing the planner itself, we'll discuss some of the unique features of a conditional nonlinear plan. The first is that actions are tagged with reason and context labels. Consider the action **(get skis)**. This action has a context of 'true' and a reason G_1G_2. A context of 'true' in this situation means that the action can be executed regardless of the result of any observations made during plan execution. Reason G_1G_2 means that the action is used in the first and second attempts to achieve the goal. There is no need to execute an action if the goal actions in its reason become impossible to achieve. When this happens, the action is no longer necessary for any of the goal attempts that are still feasible.

An action like **(Observe (road b s))** has multiple possible outcomes. The outcomes are each labelled with a unique identifier called an *observation label*. Subsequent actions that depend on this observation are tagged with a context that contains an observation label from this action. For example, **(go b s)** has a

context containing α_1. This means that **(go b s)** should only be executed when the observation denoted by α_1, **(clear b s)**, has been observed.

The contexts are also used in determining whether a postcondition of an action can clobber a causal link. There is no need to resolve a clobberer if the clobberer and the causal link that it clobbers never occur together in the execution of a plan. The consumer of the causal link and the potential clobberer must have *compatible* contexts in order for a conflict to occur. A new method for resolving clobberers suggests itself. A conflict may be resolved by restricting the contexts of the clobberer and the consumer of the causal link so that these two actions can never occur together in a valid completion of the plan.

The planner starts by attempting to a plan for the initial goal attempt G_1. During planning for G_1, its context becomes something other than true. This means that the goal attempt G_1 cannot be achieved in every completion of the plan. When this happens the planner attempts to achieve the goal in another way. It adds another dummy goal operator, G_2, and attempts to achieve G_2 using only new actions and actions that are consistent with some unexplored context in the plan. This context becomes the *global context* for the planning process. Adding new goal operators rather than fusing all of the branches into the same goal node simplifies the planner, particularly when the planner uses variables. In the skiing example, the actual variable bindings are different in G_1 and G_2. G_1 is the goal for skiing at Snowbird and G_2 represents the goal for skiing at Park City. The global context is used to control the process of adding links to previously planned steps in the plan. A link may only be made to a plan step that has a context that is compatible with the global context. For example, if we are planning for the case where α_2 is true, then we should not be able to link to a plan step that is conditional on α_1 being true since α_1 and α_2 can never become true at the same time.

Finally, there is no possible plan that accomplishes the goal when both roads are blocked. We cannot count on the planner terminating in this situation since planning is undecidable [Chapman, 87]. We suggest that some upper bound be placed on the cost of the steps that can be added to a plan in order to accomplish a particular goal. When this bound is exceeded, the plan branch is considered impossible to achieve. We annotate the plan with a *Fail* operator that has as its precondition the observation(s) that could not be tied into a plan that accomplishes the goal. *Fail* satisfies all of the preconditions of the goal that it corresponds to. In this case, *Fail* is linked to all of the preconditions of G_3, the goal that is impossible to achieve. The context for the Fail operator is set to the current global context. When the plan is executed, the Fail operator signals that it is no longer possible to pursue the goal.

5 CNLP

In this section, we make the definitions suggested in the example more formal and define the planner. For simplicity, we will ignore variable bindings. The planner may be easily extended to include variables using the technique outlined in [McAllester+Rosenblitt 91].

Definition 1: An *observation label* is a unique identifier associated with one of the outcomes of a plan step that has multiple mutually-exclusive outcomes. An observation label is *compatible* with another observation label when the two labels are identical or when they come from different sets of outcomes. We have been denoting observation labels with small, subscripted greek letters (α_3, β_2, γ_1, etc.). For example, if the greek letter denotes an observation, then the subscript would denote the specific result of that observation. α_x refers to the situation where x is the specific outcome of the outcome set denoted by α. Note that α_x is compatible with α_y only when x = y. α_x is always compatible with β_y when $\alpha \neq \beta$ since these labels refer to different observations.

Definition 2: A *context* is a set of observation labels.

A context summarizes a set of observations. When the observations that have been made thus far match the observations denoted by the context of a plan step then that plan step may be executed. For example, if a plan step contains a context $\alpha_2\beta_1$ then that plan step should only be executed if observation event α was observed to have outcome 2 and observation event β was observed to have outcome 1. In our example, the operator (go c p) is contingent on observing $\neg$ (clear b s) and (clear c p), denoted by α_2 and β_1 respectively. The idea of a context seems similar in spirit to the idea of a *chronoset* [McDermott 82]. It is used to identify the possible future that the plan step is a part of.

Observation labels are propagated from the contexts of a plan step to the contexts of following plan steps using the following rules. The context of a plan step, A, includes the observation labels of a plan step, B, whenever there exists a causal link of the form <B, X, A> or a conditioning link of the form {B, α, A}. If B is a conditional plan step, then A also includes the observation label corresponding to the post condition X of step B. Additional observation labels may be added to a context as long as they are compatible with the labels already in the context. The *context of a condition* is the context derived by merging the context of the plan step that establishes the condition with the observation label (if any) associated with the condition itself. This is simpler than it sounds. We are concerned with labelling future branches of a 'chronicle tree'-like structure with events that occurred in the past [McDermott 82]. See Figure 3.

Past   Future

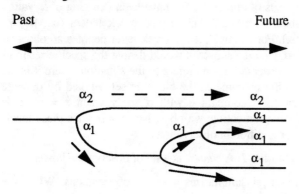

Figure 3: Label propagation in the plan network.

Definition 3: A *descendent* of a step is a plan step that can be reached by following causal links or conditioning links forward in time. An *ancestor* of a step is a plan step that can be reached by following causal links or conditioning links backwards in time.

Definition 4: A *topological sort* of a plan graph is a linear ordering of the steps in the graph that respects the temporal constraints denoted by the graph's causal links, conditioning links, and the ordering constraints.

Definition 5: Plan step A is *possibly after* a plan step B when A is after B in at least one topological sort of the plan graph. A is *possibly before* B when A is before B in at least one topological sort of the plan graph. A is *possibly between* plan steps B and C, if A is possibly after B and A is possibly before C.

Definition 6: The *kernel* of a proposition is the proposition left over after all of the 'negation' and 'unknown' symbols are stripped from it. |p| denotes the kernel of p. For any p, | ¬p| = |Unk(p)| = |p|.

Definition 7: A plan step C *clobbers* a causal link <A, p, B> if

1. C is possibly between A and B.
2. The kernel of a postcondition of C, |q|, equals |p| and p ≠ q.
3. The context of C and B are compatible.

The three parts of this definition are worth some discussion. A clobberer indicates that there is a condition that possibly conflicts with a condition needed for the execution of an action. In order to clobber a causal link, the clobbering action must be able to occur between the

time that the establishing action of a causal link occurs and the time that the consuming action occurs. Two conditions are in conflict only when their kernels unify but their truth values differ. SNLP [McAllester+Rosenblitt, 91] declares that two conditions are in conflict whenever the kernels unify even if the clobber condition is identical to the condition that it clobbers. This is done in order to guarantee systematic generation of partial plans. When we tested our version of SNLP we discovered that the time spent in planning dropped dramatically when we modified the planner so that two conditions with identical kernels and truth values are never in conflict. The overhead spent exploring duplicate plans seems much smaller than the overhead spent in declobbering 'nonconflicting' conditions.

Definition 8: An *open condition* is a pair <P, X> where P is a precondition of a plan step X that is not established by a causal link. That is, there is no causal link of the form <A, R, X> where R unifies with P under the bindings of the plan.

The planner works by eliminating conflicts in the plan (eliminating clobberers) and by proving that the preconditions of each plan step are true when that plan step is executed (attaching causal links to open conditions).

Definition 9: A conditional nonlinear plan is called *complete* if the following conditions hold:

1) There are no clobberers, that is, no action clobbers a causal link.

2) There are no open conditions. Every precondition of every step in the plan is linked to an action that establishes it.

3) There exists a topological sort of the plan graph.

4) The contexts for the goals in the plan form a tautology. The context of every postcondition in the plan must be compatible with at least one of the goal operators.

6 Plan Construction Operations

The planning algorithm defined below attempts to make a plan complete by incrementally and nondeterministically repairing all of the sources of incompleteness. A plan can be incomplete whenever it possesses a clobberer, an open condition or there is an observation context that is not compatible with the context of any of the goal operators.

6.1 Resolving Open Conditions.

In order to resolve an open condition, a causal link must be established from a new plan step to the open condition or from an existing plan step. The planner operations that do this are called **add-step** and **add-link**. Both of these operators take an open condition <P, S>, a partial plan, and a cost bound as arguments. Add-link requires the global context, g-context, as an argument so that it may decide which operators may be used to satisfy a subgoal of the current goal. The global context prevents the planner from linking the goal to conditional plan branches that have already been expanded.

Add-Step(<P, S>, plan)

    1) Nondeterministically select an operator, O, that possesses a postcondition that matches the unsatisfied precondition, P. This is the new plan step, N.

    2) Let new-plan be plan + N + <N, P, S> . That is, bind new-plan to the partial plan constructed by adding step N, and causal link <N, P, S> to the old plan. Update the context of each of the descendents of N to include the context of the condition P. If the new causal link touches a goal node, add the goal node to the reason of N. Return new-plan.

Add-Link(<P, S>, plan, g-context)

    1) Nondeterminstically select a step O from plan that is possibly before S, has a context that is compatible with g-context and possesses a postcondition that unifies the precondition P.

    2) Let new-plan be plan + <O, P, S> . Update the context of each of the descendents of S as in **Add-Step**. Update the reasons of O and each of the ancestors of O so that they include the reasons of S. Return new-plan.

6.2 Resolving Clobberers

A clobberer can be resolved by attacking any one of the necessary conditions for the clobberer to exist. These are: restricting the clobberer to occur before or after the causal link it clobberers, or restricting the contexts of the clobberer and the link consumer so that they are incompatible. In the following routines, X is the clobbering action, <E, P, C> is the causal link that is clobbered, and Q is the postcondition of X that is doing the clobbering.

Promote(X, <E, P, C>, plan)

    1) If C is not a goal and X is possibly after C, let new-plan be plan + (X > C). Return new-plan.

Demote(X, <E, P, C>, plan)

    1) If E is not IC, the plan step that contains the initial conditions, and X is possibly before E, let new-plan be plan + (X < E). Return new-plan.

Condition(X, <E, P, C>, plan)

    1) Nondeterministically select a conditional plan step A such that A is possibly before both X and C.

    2) Nondeterministically select two of the observation labels, α_i and α_j of A such that $i \neq j$.

    3) Let the context of A be C_A. If $C_A \cup \alpha_i$ is compatible with the context of X and $C_A \cup \alpha_j$ is compatible with the context of C, then bind new-plan to plan + {A, α_i, X} + {A, α_j, C}. Update the context of X and the contexts of the descendents of X to include $C_A \cup \alpha_i$ and update the context of Y and the contexts of the descendents of Y to include $C_A \cup \alpha_j$. Return new-plan.

6.3 The Top Level.

This is an auxiliary function to edit the plan when a goal cannot be established with a plan that satisfies the current cost bound.

Fail(Plan, Global-Context, Current-Goal)

Fail conditions a *Fail* action on the global-context and links the *Fail* to the current goal. All actions that have Current-Goal as their only reason are pruned from the plan. The current-goal's context is set to the global-context and the resulting plan is returned.

The procedure Find-Conditional-Completion (F-C-C) attempts to complete the plan by fixing flaws in it nondeterministically. G-C is the global context. Goal is the current goal attempt, and Bound is the cost bound. Note that an attempt to plan for a goal is failed if the actions required to accomplish that goal exceed the cost bound.

F-C-C(Plan, G-C, Goal, Bound)

    1. If the cost of the portions of Plan that are consistent with the global context exceeds the current cost bound, then return

        F-C-C(Fail(Plan, G-C, Goal), G-C, Goal, Bound).

    2. If the plan is complete then exit returning the plan.

3. If the postcondition Q of plan-step X in Plan clobbers a causal link <E, P, C> then bind new-plan nondeterministically to one of the following:

    a. Promote(X, <E, P, C>, Plan)

    b. Demote(X, <E, P, C>, Plan)

    c. Condition(X, <E, P, C>, Plan)

Return F-C-C(new-plan, G-C, Goal, Bound).

4. If there is an open condition <P, S> in the plan then bind new-plan nondeterministically to one of the following:

    a. Add-Step(<P, S>, Plan)

    b. Add-Link(<P, S>, G-C, Plan)

Return F-C-C(new-plan, G-C, Goal, Bound).

5. Else, there is a post condition with a context, C_{new}, that is not compatible with the context of any goal. Add a new goal step, G_{new}, to the plan and

return F-C-C(Plan, C_{new}, G_{new}, Bound).

7 Discussion

We have described an algorithm to develop conditional nonlinear plans. We are currently implementing the algorithm to confirm that it does in fact work. We also still need to assemble the proofs that show that the algorithm is correct and complete.

There are several novel features of the planning approach proposed. The approach proposed uses a labelling technique similar to that used by an ATMS [DeKleer, 86] in order to keep track of when actions are visible to other actions. We have developed a notion of completeness for conditional planning that does not require that the planner be able to accomplish a goal in all possible circumstances. Finally, we have introduced a new declobbering method that is unique to conditional planning, the **condition** operator.

We believe that the CNLP algorithm will rarely be useful on its own. The size and complexity of the plans generated by CNLP increase exponentially with the number of observation actions in the plan. The amount of computation may be reduced by attaching a relative likelihood measure to the various contexts in the plan. The planner may elect to skip contexts that are sufficiently unlikely, reducing the number of extensions that must be explored by a significant amount. There are other strategies that may be applicable for reducing the time spent in planning such as the use of abstraction or dynamic programming [Einav 91]. We view the development of CNLP as the first step in the development of a decision-theoretic nonlinear planner.

Acknowledgments

The authors would like to thank Jack Breese and Ross Shachter for their contributions to our work. We also thank the anonymous reviewers for their comments and criticism. This work is partially funded by DARPA contract F30602-91-C-0031 and by the National Science Foundation through a Graduate Fellowship.

References

[Chapman, 87] Chapman, D. Planning for Conjunctive Goals, *Artificial Intelligence* **32**, pp 333-377.

[de Kleer, 86] de Kleer, J. An Assumption-based TMS, *Artificial Intelligence* **28**, pp 127-162.

[Einav, 91] Einav, D., Reasoning with Uncertainty and Resource Constraints, PhD Dissertation, Department of Engineering-Economic Systems, Stanford University, 1991.

[Fikes+Nilsson, 71] Fikes, R. E. and Nilsson, N. J. STRIPS: A New Approach to the Application of Theorem Proving to Problem Solving, *Artificial Intelligence* **2**(3/4), pp 189-208.

[Howard, 66] Howard, R. E., Information value theory, *IEEE Transactions on Systems Science and Cybernetics*, vol. SSC-2, pp. 22-26, 1966.

[McAllester+Rosenblitt, 91] McAllister, D. and Rosenblitt, D. Systematic Nonlinear Planning, *Proceedings of AAAI-91*, Anaheim.

[Schoppers, 89] Schoppers, M. E., *Representation and Automatic Synthesis of Reaction Plans*, Report No.89-1546, Department of Computer Science, University of Illinois at Urbana-Campaign, 1989.

[Soderland+Weld, 91] Soderland, S. and Weld, D. S., Evaluating Nonlinear Planning, Technical Report 91-02-03, Department of Computer Science and Engineering, University of Washington.

[Waldinger, 77] Waldinger, R. J., Achieving Several Goals Simultaneously, *Machine Intelligence 8*, Chichester: Ellis Norwood Limited.

[Warren, 76] Warren, D. H. D., Generating Conditional Plans and Programs, in *Proceedings of the Summer Conference on AI and Simulation of Behavior*, Edinburgh, 1976.

[Warren, 74] Warren, D. H. D., Warplan: A System for Generating Plans, in Allen, J., Hendler, J, and Tate, A. eds, *Readings in Planning*, San Mateo, California: Morgan Kaufmann, 1990.

The Projection Problem in the Situation Calculus: A Soundness and Completeness Result, with an Application to Database Updates

Raymond Reiter
Department of Computer Science
University of Toronto
Toronto, Canada M5S 1A4
and
The Canadian Institute for Advanced Research
email: reiter@ai.toronto.edu

Abstract

We describe a novel application of planning in the situation calculus to formalize the evolution of a database under update transactions. In the resulting theory, query evaluation becomes identical to the temporal projection problem. We next define a class of axioms for which the classical AI planning technique of goal regression provides a sound and complete method for solving the projection problem, hence for querying evolving databases. Finally, we briefly discuss several issues which naturally arise in the settings of databases and planning, namely, proofs by mathematical induction of properties of world states, logic programming implementations of the projection problem, and historical queries.

1 Introduction

The situation calculus (McCarthy [7]) is enjoying new popularity these days. One reason is that its expressiveness is considerably richer than has been commonly believed (Gelfond, Lifschitz, Rabinov [2]). Another is the possibility of precisely characterizing the strengths and limitations of various general theories of actions expressed within its formalism (see [6, 5, 13] for examples). In this paper we propose yet another reason for not giving up too hastily on the situation calculus. Specifically, we propose a novel application of it to the problem of specifying the evolution of a database under update transactions. Our proposal is to represent a database in the situation calculus. Updatable database relations will be fluents; transactions will be functions, and will be treated exactly as are actions in the usual situation calculus formalizations of dynamic worlds. As we shall see, querying an evolving database is precisely the *temporal projection problem* in AI planning. This motivates the theoretical focus of this paper, which presents a sound and complete regression-style procedure for solving the projection problem in the case of a limited, but sizable class of background axiomatizations.

The theoretical results of this paper complement those of (Reiter [10]), where a sound and complete plan synthesis procedure is described, based on goal regression. Proofs of our results, and further discussion, may be found in (Reiter [13]).

2 Formalizing Database Evolution in the Situation Calculus: An Example

In this section we describe a novel application of the situation calculus and its relationship to the temporal projection problem in planning. In the theory of databases, the evolution of a database is determined by *transactions*, whose purpose is to update the database with new information. For example, in an educational database, there might be a transaction specifically designed to change a student's grade. This would normally be a procedure which, when invoked on a specific student and grade, first checks that the database satisfies the transaction's preconditions (e.g., that there is a record for the student, and that the new grade differs from the old), and if so, records the new grade. In current database practice, transactions are procedures which physically modify data structures representing the current database state, much like STRIPS operators. Our objective in this section is to provide a *specification* of the effects of transactions on database states. Our proposal is to represent a database in the situation calculus. Updatable database relations will be fluents; transactions will be functions, and will be treated exactly as are actions in the usual situation calculus formalizations of dynamic worlds.

To illustrate our approach to specifying database transactions, we consider the following toy education database.

Relations The database involves the following three relations:

1. *enrolled*(*st, course, s*): Student *st* is enrolled in course *course* when the database is in state *s*.

2. *grade*(*st, course, grade, s*): The grade of student *st* in course *course* is *grade* when the database is in state *s*.

3. *prerequ*(*pre, course*): *pre* is a prerequisite course for course *course*. Notice that this relation is state independent, so is not expected to change during the evolution of the database.

Initial Database State We assume given some first order specification of what is true of the initial state S_0 of the database. These will be arbitrary first order sentences, the only restriction being that those predicates which mention a state, mention only the initial state S_0. Examples of information which might be true in the initial state are:

$$enrolled(Sue, C100, S_0) \vee enrolled(Sue, C200, S_0),$$

$$(\exists c)enrolled(Bill, c, S_0),$$

$$(\forall p).prerequ(p, P300) \equiv p = P100 \vee p = M100,$$

$$(\forall p)\neg prerequ(p, C100),$$

$$(\forall c).enrolled(Bill, c, S_0) \equiv$$
$$c = M100 \vee c = C100 \vee c = P200,$$

$$enrolled(Mary, C100, S_0),$$

$$\neg enrolled(John, M200, S_0), \ldots$$

$$grade(Sue, P300, 75, S_0),$$

$$grade(Bill, M200, 70, S_0), \ldots$$

$$prerequ(M200, M100), \quad \neg prerequ(M100, C100), \ldots$$

Database Transactions Update transactions will be denoted by function symbols, and will be treated in exactly the same way as actions are in the situation calculus. For our example, there will be three transactions:

1. *register*(*st, course*): Register student *st* in course *course*.

2. *change*(*st, course, grade*): Change the current grade of student *st* in course *course* to *grade*.

3. *drop*(*st, course*): Student *st* drops course *course*.

Transaction Preconditions Normally, transactions have preconditions which must be satisfied by the current database state before the transaction can be "executed". In our example, we shall require that a student

can register in a course iff she has obtained a grade of at least 50 in all prerequisites for the course:[1]

$$Poss(register(st, c), s) \equiv \{(\forall p).prerequ(p, c) \supset$$
$$(\exists g).grade(st, p, g, s) \wedge g \geq 50\}.$$

It is possible to change a student's grade iff he has a grade which is different than the new grade:

$$Poss(change(st, c, g), s) \equiv$$
$$(\exists g').grade(st, c, g', s) \wedge g' \neq g.$$

A student may drop a course iff the student is currently enrolled in that course:

$$Poss(drop(st, c), s) \equiv enrolled(st, c, s).$$

Transaction Specifications These are the central axioms in our formalization of update transactions. They specify the effects of all transactions on all updatable database relations. As usual, all lower case roman letters are variables which are implicitly universally quantified. In particular, notice that these axioms quantify over transactions.

$$Poss(a, s) \supset [enrolled(st, c, do(a, s)) \equiv$$
$$a = register(st, c) \vee \qquad (1)$$
$$enrolled(st, c, s) \wedge a \neq drop(st, c)],$$

$$Poss(a, s) \supset [grade(st, c, g, do(a, s)) \equiv$$
$$a = change(st, c, g) \vee$$
$$grade(st, c, g, s) \wedge (\forall g')a \neq change(st, c, g')].$$

Although incidental to the main thrust of this paper, notice that it is these transaction specification axioms which "solve" the frame problem in the database setting. The equivalences in these axioms were motivated by Pednault's approach to the frame problem [9], and the appeal to quantification over transactions stems from the *explanation closure axioms* of Haas [3] and Schubert [15]. See (Reiter [10, 13]) for further discussion.

Querying a Database Notice that in the above account of database evolution, all updates are *virtual*; the database is never physically changed. To query the database resulting from some sequence of transactions, it is necessary to refer to this sequence in the query. For example, to determine if John is enrolled in any courses after the transaction sequence

$$drop(John, C100), register(Mary, C100)$$

has been 'executed', we must determine whether

$$Database \models (\exists c).enrolled(John, c,$$
$$do(register(Mary, C100),$$
$$do(drop(John, C100), S_0))).$$

Thus, querying an evolving database is precisely the *temporal projection problem* in AI planning [4]; this motivates the theoretical focus of this paper.

---

[1]In the sequel, lower case roman letters will denote variables. All formulas are understood to be implicitly universally quantified with respect to their free variables whenever explicit quantifiers are not indicated.

3   An Axiomatization

In this section we precisely characterize the class of axioms which the theory of this paper addresses. The axioms of Section 2 all fit these patterns. Throughout, we assume a sorted second order language $\mathcal{L}$, with sorts for states and for actions.[2] We omit the details of this language, which are described in (Reiter [13]).

Unique Names Axioms for Actions For distinct action names T and T',

$$T(\vec{x}) \neq T'(\vec{y})$$

Identical actions have identical arguments:

$$T(x_1, ..., x_n) = T(y_1, ..., y_n) \supset x_1 = y_1 \wedge ... \wedge x_n = y_n$$

for each function symbol T of $\mathcal{L}$ of sort *action*.

Unique Names Axioms for States

$$(\forall a, s) S_0 \neq do(a, s),$$

$$(\forall a, s, a', s').do(a, s) = do(a', s') \supset a = a' \wedge s = s'.$$

Definition: The Simple Formulas The *simple* formulas of $\mathcal{L}$ are those first order formulas which do not mention the predicate symbols *Poss*, $<$ or $\leq$, whose fluents do not mention the function symbol *do*, and which do not quantify over variables of sort *state*.

Definition: Action Precondition Axiom An action precondition axiom is a sentence of the form

$$(\forall \vec{x}, s).Poss(T(x_1, \cdots, x_n), s) \equiv \Pi_T,$$

where T is an n-ary function of sort *action* of $\mathcal{L}$, and Π_T is a simple formula of $\mathcal{L}$ whose free variables are among $x_1, \cdots, x_n, s$.

Definition: Successor State Axiom A successor state axiom for an $(n+1)$-ary fluent F of $\mathcal{L}$ is a sentence of $\mathcal{L}$ of the form

$$(\forall a, s).Poss(a, s) \supset$$
$$(\forall x_1, \ldots, x_n).F(x_1, \ldots, x_n, do(a, s)) \equiv \Phi_F$$

where, for notational convenience, we assume that F's last argument is of sort *state*, and where Φ_F is a simple formula, all of whose free variables are among $a, s, x_1, \ldots, x_n$.

Notice that these successor state axioms are suitable only for formalizing *determinate* actions, i.e. actions whose effects on all fluents are completely known. We could not appeal to axioms of this form for characterizing the action of putting down an object, when the

resulting precise location of the object is unknown.[3] While this is a severe restriction in practice, database applications normally appeal to determinate transactions, in which case these successor state axioms are precisely what we want.

Notice also, as remarked in Section 2, these axioms deal with the frame problem. They do not, alas, address the *ramification problem* (Finger [1]), which is to say that the ramifications of any action must be explicitly represented in the successor state axioms. Recent results by Lin and Shoham [6] appear to address this problem in our setting.

4   Regression and the Projection Problem

> "In solving a problem of this sort, the grand thing is to be able to reason backward."
>
> Sherlock Holmes, *A Study in Scarlet*

This section describes our formal results for the temporal projection problem in the situation calculus. It defines a regression operator, and uses it to characterize legal plans, as well as a systematic procedure for solving the projection problem.

4.1   Legal Plans

Not all plans need be legal. Intuitively, an action sequence is legal iff, beginning in state S_0, the preconditions of each action in the sequence are true in that state resulting from performing all the actions preceeding it in the sequence. To formalize this notion of a legal plan, we first define an ordering relation $<$ on states . The intended interpretation of $s < s'$ is that state s' is reachable from state s by some sequence of actions, each action of which is possible in that state resulting from executing the actions preceeding it in the sequence. Hence, we want $<$ to be the smallest binary relation on states such that:

1. $\sigma < do(a, \sigma)$ whenever action a is possible in state σ, and

2. $\sigma < do(a, \sigma')$ whenever action a is possible in state σ' and $\sigma < \sigma'$.

This we can achieve with a second order sentence, as follows:[4]

---

[2]We require a second order language in order to define the concept of a legal action sequence. See Section 4.1 below.

[3]At least, we could not do so whenever a fluent $location(x, l, s)$ is part of the theory.

[4]This cannot be done with a first order sentence since it requires transitive closure, which is well known not to be first order definable.

Definitions: $s < s'$, $s \leq s'$

$$(\forall s, s').s < s' \equiv$$
$$(\forall P).\{[(\forall a, s_1).Poss(a, s_1) \supset P(s_1, do(a, s_1))] \wedge$$
$$[(\forall a, s_1, s_2).Poss(a, s_2) \wedge P(s_1, s_2) \supset$$
$$P(s_1, do(a, s_2))]\}$$
$$\supset P(s, s').$$
$$(2)$$

$$(\forall s, s').s \leq s' \equiv s < s' \vee s = s'. \qquad (3)$$

Intuitively, $S_0 \leq s$ states that s is an executable plan, i.e., it is a sequence of plan steps, each of whose action preconditions is true in the previous state.

Notation: Let $a_1, \ldots, a_n$ be terms of sort *action*. Define

$$do([\,], s) = s,$$

and for $n = 1, 2, \ldots$

$$do([a_1, \ldots, a_n], s) = do(a_n, do([a_1, \ldots, a_{n-1}], s)).$$

$do([a_1, \ldots, a_n], s)$ is a compact notation for the state term

$$do(a_n, do(a_{n-1}, \ldots do(a_1, s) \ldots))$$

which denotes that state resulting from performing the action a_1, followed by $a_2, \ldots$, followed by a_n, beginning in state s.

Definition: The Legal Action Sequences Suppose $\tau_1, \ldots, \tau_n$ is a sequence of ground terms (i.e. terms not mentioning any variables) of $\mathcal{L}$, where each τ_i is of sort *action*. Then this sequence is *legal (with respect to some background axiomatization $\mathcal{D}$)* iff

$$\mathcal{D} \models S_0 \leq do([\tau_1, \ldots, \tau_n], S_0).$$

Definition: In the sequel, we shall only consider background axiomatizations $\mathcal{D}$ of the form:

$$\mathcal{D} = less\text{-}axioms \cup \mathcal{D}_{ss} \cup \mathcal{D}_{ap} \cup \mathcal{D}_{uns} \cup \mathcal{D}_{una} \cup \mathcal{D}_{S_0} \quad (4)$$

where

- *less-axioms* are the axioms (2), (3) for $<$ and $\leq$.
- $\mathcal{D}_{ss}$ is a set of successor state axioms.
- $\mathcal{D}_{ap}$ is a set of action precondition axioms.
- $\mathcal{D}_{uns}$ is the set of unique names axioms for states.
- $\mathcal{D}_{una}$ is the set of unique names axioms for actions.
- $\mathcal{D}_{S_0}$ is a set of first order sentences with the property that S_0 is the only term of sort *state* mentioned by the fluents of a sentence of $\mathcal{D}_{S_0}$. See Section 2 for an example $\mathcal{D}_{S_0}$. Thus, no fluent of a formula of $\mathcal{D}_{S_0}$ mentions a variable of sort *state* or the function symbol do. $\mathcal{D}_{S_0}$ will play the role of the initial database (i.e. the one we start off with, before any actions have been "executed").

Definition: A Regression Operator Let W be first order formula. Then $\mathcal{R}[W]$ is that formula obtained from W by replacing each fluent atom $F(\vec{t}, do(\alpha, \sigma))$ mentioned by W by $\Phi_F(\vec{t}, \alpha, \sigma)$ where F's successor state axiom is

$$(\forall a, s).Poss(a, s) \supset (\forall \vec{x}).F(\vec{x}, do(a, s)) \equiv \Phi_F(\vec{x}, a, s).$$

All other atoms of W not of this form remain the same.

The use of the regression operator $\mathcal{R}$ is a classical plan synthesis technique (Waldinger [16]). Regression also corresponds to the operation of *unfolding* in logic programming.

Notation: When G is a formula of $\mathcal{L}$,

$$\mathcal{R}^0[G] = G,$$

$$\mathcal{R}^n[G] = \mathcal{R}[\mathcal{R}^{n-1}[G]] \quad n = 1, 2, \ldots$$

Recall that for each function T of sort *action*, $\mathcal{D}_{ap}$ will contain an axiom of the form

$$(\forall \vec{x}, s).Poss(T(\vec{x}), s) \equiv \Pi_T(\vec{x}, s),$$

Theorem 1 (Reiter [13]) *Let $T_1, \ldots, T_m$ be function symbols of sort action. Then the sequence $T_1(\vec{g}_1), \ldots, T_m(\vec{g}_m)$ of ground terms is legal wrt $\mathcal{D}$ iff*

$$\mathcal{D}_{uns} \cup \mathcal{D}_{una} \cup \mathcal{D}_{S_0} \models$$
$$\bigwedge_{i=1}^{m} \mathcal{R}^{i-1}[\Pi_{T_i}(\vec{g}_i, do([T_1(\vec{g}_1), \ldots, T_{i-1}(\vec{g}_{i-1})], S_0))].$$

Theorem 1 reduces the test for the legality of an action sequence to a first order theorem proving task *in the initial database $\mathcal{D}_{S_0}$*, together with suitable unique names axioms.

Example: Legality Testing
In connection with the example database of Section 2, we determine the legality of the transaction sequence

$$change(Bill, C100, 60), register(Sue, C200),$$
$$drop(Bill, C100).$$

We first compute

$$\mathcal{R}^0[(\exists g')grade(Bill, C100, g', S_0) \wedge g' \neq 60] \wedge$$
$$\mathcal{R}[(\forall p)prerequ(p, C200) \supset$$
$$(\exists g).grade(Sue, p, g, do(change(Bill, C100, 60), S_0))$$
$$\wedge g \geq 50] \wedge$$
$$\mathcal{R}^2[enrolled(Bill, C100, do(register(Sue, C200),$$
$$do(change(Bill, C100, 60), S_0)))].$$

This simplifies to

$$\{(\exists g').grade(Bill, C100, g', S_0) \wedge g' \neq 60\} \wedge$$
$$\{(\forall p).prerequ(p, C200) \supset Bill = Sue \wedge p = C100 \vee$$
$$(\exists g).grade(Sue, p, g, S_0) \wedge g \geq 50\} \wedge$$
$$\{Sue = Bill \wedge C200 = C100 \vee$$
$$enrolled(Bill, C100, S_0)\}.$$

So the transaction sequence is legal iff this formula is entailed by the initial database, together with unique names axioms for states and actions.

4.2   A Solution to the Projection Problem

The following provides a systematic regression-based procedure for solving the projection problem for the class of axioms (4) defined above.

Theorem 2 (Soundness and Completeness (Reiter [13])) *Suppose $Q(s) \in \mathcal{L}$ is simple, and that the state variable s is the only free variable of $Q(s)$. Suppose $\tau_1, \ldots, \tau_n$ is a sequence of ground terms of $\mathcal{L}$ of sort action. Then if $\tau_1, \ldots, \tau_n$ is a legal action sequence,*

$$\mathcal{D} \models Q(do([\tau_1, \ldots, \tau_n], S_0))$$

iff

$$\mathcal{D}_{uns} \cup \mathcal{D}_{una} \cup \mathcal{D}_{S_0} \models \mathcal{R}^n[Q(do([\tau_1, \ldots, \tau_n], S_0))].$$

As in the case of verifying legality, the projection problem reduces to first order theorem proving *in the initial database* $\mathcal{D}_{S_0}$, together with unique names axioms.

Corollary 1 (Relative Consistency) $\mathcal{D}$ *is satisfiable iff* $\mathcal{D}_{uns} \cup \mathcal{D}_{una} \cup \mathcal{D}_{S_0}$ *is.*

Corollary 1 provides an important relative consistency result. It guarantees that we cannot introduce an inconsistency to a "base" theory $\mathcal{D}_{uns} \cup \mathcal{D}_{una} \cup \mathcal{D}_{S_0}$ by augmenting it with the axioms for $<$ and $\leq$, together with successor state and action precondition axioms.

Example: Query Evaluation

Continuing with the example education database, consider again the transaction sequence

$$\mathbf{T} = change(Bill, C100, 60), register(Sue, C200),$$
$$drop(Bill, C100).$$

Suppose the query is

$$(\exists st).enrolled(st, C200, do(\mathbf{T}, S_0)) \wedge$$
$$\neg enrolled(st, C100, do(\mathbf{T}, S_0)) \wedge$$
$$(\exists g).grade(st, C200, g, do(\mathbf{T}, S_0)) \wedge g \geq 50.$$

We must compute $\mathcal{R}^3$ of this query. After some simplification, assuming that $\mathcal{D}_{S_0} \models C100 \neq C200$, we obtain

$$(\exists st).[st = Sue \vee enrolled(st, C200, S_0)] \wedge$$
$$[st = Bill \vee \neg enrolled(st, C100, S_0)] \wedge$$
$$[(\exists g).grade(st, C200, g, S_0) \wedge g \geq 50].$$

Therefore, assuming that the transaction sequence $\mathbf{T}$ is legal, the answer to the query is obtained by evaluating this last formula in $\mathcal{D}_{S_0}$.

5   Discussion

The striking similarities between databases evolving under update transactions and dynamically changing worlds in the situation calculus raises a number of additional issues of common interest to the database and planning communities:

- **Proving properties of world states:** In commonsense reasoning about the physical world, we often want to establish properties which will be true no matter what the state of the world is, for example, that if an object is broken and it never gets repaired, then it will always be broken:

$$(\forall x).broken(x, S_0) \wedge$$
$$[(\forall s).S_0 \leq s \supset \neg occurs(repair(x), s)] \supset$$
$$(\forall s').S_0 \leq s' \supset broken(x, s').$$

Here, $occurs(a, s)$ means that action a occurs in the sequence of actions leading from S_0 to s. An analogous problem arises in connection with *integrity constraints* in database theory. Informally, an integrity constraint specifies what counts as a legal database state; it is a property that every database state must satisfy. One of the classic examples of such a constraint is that no one's salary may decrease during the evolution of the database:

$$(\forall s, s')(\forall p, \$, \$').S_0 \leq s \wedge s \leq s' \supset$$
$$sal(p, \$, s) \wedge sal(p, \$', s') \supset \$ \leq \$'.$$

As might be expected, proving such properties of states in the situation calculus requires mathematical induction. Using the axioms (2) and (3) for $<$ and $\leq$, Reiter [12, 11] derives suitable induction axioms for this task, and gives various examples of integrity constraints and their proofs.

- **Logic programming implementation:** As it happens, there is a natural translation of the axioms of Section 3 into Prolog clauses, thereby directly complementing the logic programming perspective on databases (Minker [8]). For example, the successor state axiom (1) of Section 2 is represented by two Prolog clauses:

$$enrolled(st, c, do(a, s)) \leftarrow$$
$$a = register(st, c), Poss(a, s).$$

$$enrolled(st, c, do(a, s)) \leftarrow$$
$$a \neq drop(st, c), enrolled(st, c, s), Poss(a, s).$$

Similar clauses may be proposed for the other axioms of Section 2 (see Reiter [12, 14]). With a suitable clausal form for $\mathcal{D}_{S_0}$, it would then be possible to evaluate queries against updated databases, for example

$$\leftarrow enrolled(John, C200,$$
$$do(register(Mary, C100),$$
$$do(drop(John, C100), S_0))).$$

In other words, there appears to be a natural logic programming implementation of the temporal projection problem. Presumably, all of this can be made to work under suitable conditions. The remaining problem is to characterize what these conditions are, and to prove correctness of such an implementation with respect to the logical specification of this paper.

- **Historical queries:** Using the relations $<$ and $\leq$ on states, it is possible to pose *historical* queries to a database. For example, if $\mathbf{T}$ is the transaction sequence leading to the current database state (i.e., the current database state is $do(\mathbf{T}, S_0)$), the following asks whether Mary's salary was ever less than it is now:

$$(\exists s, \$, \$').S_0 \leq s \wedge s < do(\mathbf{T}, S_0) \wedge$$
$$sal(Mary, \$, s) \wedge sal(Mary, \$', do(\mathbf{T}, S_0)) \wedge$$
$$\$ < \$'.$$

Such queries are of some interest for databases. The analogous questions for planning would be something like: If this plan is executed, would such and such ever be true during the plan execution? (Will block A ever be on block B during the execution of this plan?) Within the framework of this paper, it is possible to develop a theory of such queries (Reiter [14]).

Acknowledgements

Many of my colleagues provided important conceptual and technical advice. My thanks to Leo Bertossi, Alex Borgida, Craig Boutilier, Charles Elkan, Michael Gelfond, Gösta Grahne, Russ Greiner, Joe Halpern, Hector Levesque, Vladimir Lifschitz, Fangzhen Lin, Wiktor Marek, John McCarthy, Alberto Mendelzon, John Mylopoulos, Javier Pinto, Len Schubert, Yoav Shoham and Marianne Winslett. Funding for this work was provided by the National Science and Engineering Research Council of Canada, and by the Institute for Robotics and Intelligent Systems.

References

[1] J. Finger. *Exploiting Constraints in Design Synthesis*. PhD thesis, Stanford University, Stanford, CA, 1986.

[2] M. Gelfond, V. Lifschitz, and A. Rabinov. What are the limitations of the situation calculus? In *Working Notes, AAAI Spring Symposium Series on the Logical Formalization of Commonsense Reasoning*, pages 59–69, 1991.

[3] A. R. Haas. The case for domain-specific frame axioms. In F. M. Brown, editor, *The frame problem in artificial intelligence. Proceedings of the 1987 workshop*, pages 343–348, Los Altos, California, 1987. Morgan Kaufmann Publishers, Inc.

[4] S. Hanks and D. McDermott. Default reasoning, nonmonotonic logics, and the frame problem. In *Proceedings of the National Conference on Artificial Intelligence*, pages 328–333, 1986.

[5] V. Lifschitz. Toward a metatheory of action. In J. Allen, R. Fikes, and E. Sandewall, editors, *Proceedings of the Second International Conference on Principles of Knowledge Representation and Reasoning (KR'91)*, pages 376–386, Los Altos, CA, 1991. Morgan Kaufmann Publishers, Inc.

[6] F. Lin and Y. Shoham. Provably correct theories of action. In *Proceedings of the National Conference on Artificial Intelligence*, 1991.

[7] J. McCarthy. Programs with common sense. In M. Minsky, editor, *Semantic Information Processing*, pages 403–418. The MIT Press, Cambridge, MA, 1968.

[8] J. Minker, editor. *Foundations of Deductive Databases and Logic Programming*. Morgan Kaufmann Publishers, Inc., Los Altos, CA, 1988.

[9] E.P.D. Pednault. ADL: Exploring the middle ground between STRIPS and the situation calculus. In R.J. Brachman, H. Levesque, and R. Reiter, editors, *Proceedings of the First International Conference on Principles of Knowledge Representation and Reasoning (KR'89)*, pages 324–332. Morgan Kaufmann Publishers, Inc., 1989.

[10] R. Reiter. The frame problem in the situation calculus: a simple solution (sometimes) and a completeness result for goal regression. In Vladimir Lifschitz, editor, *Artificial Intelligence and Mathematical Theory of Computation: Papers in Honor of John McCarthy*, pages 359–380. Academic Press, San Diego, CA, 1991.

[11] R. Reiter. Proving properties of states in the situation calculus. 1992. submitted for publication.

[12] R. Reiter. On specifying database updates. Technical report, Department of Computer Science, University of Toronto, in preparation.

[13] R. Reiter. A simple solution to the frame problem (sometimes). Technical report, Department of Computer Science, University of Toronto, in preparation.

[14] R. Reiter. Formalizing database evolution in the situation calculus. In *Proc. Fifth Generation Computer Systems*, Tokyo, June 1 - 5, 1992.

[15] L.K. Schubert. Monotonic solution of the frame problem in the situation calculus: an efficient method for worlds with fully specified actions. In H.E. Kyberg, R.P. Loui, and G.N. Carlson, editors, *Knowledge Representation and Defeasible Reasoning*, pages 23–67. Kluwer Academic Press, 1990.

[16] R. Waldinger. Achieving several goals simultaneously. In E. Elcock and D. Michie, editors, *Machine Intelligence 8*, pages 94–136. Ellis Horwood, Edinburgh, Scotland, 1977.

Building Plans to Monitor and Exploit Open-Loop and Closed-Loop Dynamics

Marcel Schoppers
Advanced Decision Systems
1500 Plymouth Street
Mountain View, CA 94043

Abstract

This paper presents a simple but effective approach to automatically producing highly concurrent and potentially intricate embedded behavior. First, the first-order terms generally used to encode domain models for planners are infiltrated with several modal operators, thus greatly extending the expressiveness of declarative domain models, while preserving the value of logical deduction for plan synthesis purposes. Then, the Universal Plans interpreter is modified to operationalize the achievement of various modal terms. I show how a modal logic of knowledge can provide for plans containing sensing actions, to monitor the changing state of the environment; how a modal logic of belief can provide for activity based on state estimates derived from previous sense data and/or action attempts; and how a fragment of a modal logic of branching time can allow a plan to anticipate the environment's expected future behavior. The result is a formalism that supports the compact specification and implementation of embedded agents that can, efficiently and concurrently, monitor and react to, the progress and eventual outcomes of, environmental processes and the agent's own actions (including sensing actions). When employed in Universal Plans, the formalism supports the exploitation of known dynamics without impairing recovery after unknown dynamics. Architectural consequences are also discussed. The approach has been used to synthesize a control and coordination plan for the distributed sensor and effector subsystems of the space-faring NASA EVA Retriever robot.

1 INTRODUCTION

1.1 FORMALIZING PLAN MONITORING

When a plan or procedure is being carried out by a system embedded in the real world (e.g. a robot), there must be some way to determine whether the plan is working. Given that sensing is necessary and that the *flexible* use of a sensor will require effector activity (such as moving the sensor platform relative to the robot body, or moving the whole robot body), the sensory activities and their supporting effector activities had better become part of the plan, and both had better be represented in such a way that their effects and interactions can be reasoned about during plan construction.

My formalization of sensing actions lies in a gap between two non-overlapping bodies of planning work. On the side of formalisms for reasoning about knowledge and action, none had planned the execution of knowledge-generating actions to check whether other planned and executed actions had worked as desired. For example, when [Moore, 1980, pp.121f] had a safe-opening action produce the knowledge that the safe was open, he did it not by performing a sensing action to find out at execution time whether the safe was open or closed, but by showing that if the safe were *assumed* open (or closed) then, after simulating the safe-opening action, *the planner* would "know" that the safe was open (or closed). Of course, the planner could equally well assume that the safe was still closed, and actually had no reason to make either assumption. Similarly, none of the formalisms of [Konolige, 1980], [Drummond, 1986, sec 5.12], [Haas, 1986] or [Morgenstern, 1987] were used to represent actions whose execution would check the outcomes of other planned actions.

On the other side of the gap there was a body of work on situated agency and plan monitoring in which execution-time sensing was common-place. However, most of the people engaged in building situated agents have done so by hand, e.g. [Agre and Chapman,

1987] [Brooks, 1986] [Firby, 1987] [Georgeff et al, 1985] [Hendler and Sanborn, 1987] [Kaelbling, 1988] [Nilsson, 1988]. Their "representations" are actually programming languages, possibly with special compilers; there is no planner that manipulates the programming language. A similar comment applies to decision-theoretic work on what to sense and how often: currently, in this approach, the decision model for plan execution must be built by hand, e.g. [Dean et al, 1990].[1] Finally, among the approaches that do represent sensing actions for use by automatic planners, none have supported logical deduction, e.g. [Brooks, 1982] [Doyle et al, 1986] [Gervasio, 1990].

In a previous paper [Schoppers, 1992] this gap was closed by infiltrating the first-order terms of an otherwise ordinary planning representation with modal operators for knowledge and belief. Consequently, the pre- and post-conditions of actions, and the declarative domain constraints, could all make use of modal terms. This preserved the value of logical deduction for plan synthesis purposes. Then, "knowledge" was interpreted as "perceptually verified information", and the achievement of knowledge goals was operationalized in such a way that the planner had to build sensing actions into the plan. Nevertheless, the promised knowledge could only be obtained by actually performing the sensing actions during plan execution. In this way I avoided the tar-pit of previous knowledge-and-action formalisms. Details of my approach will be given later.

1.2 TEMPORAL ISSUES

At the end of [Schoppers, 1992] I noted that my formalization of plan monitoring did not overcome a number of difficulties that would seriously impair the competence of embedded agents. In particular,

1. The approach did not say how often a particular goal should be sensed.

2. The approach monitored the outcomes of actions, but did not monitor their progress: if no progress was being made, the plan would wait forever.

3. The approach did not permit a condition to be monitored in parallel with the performance of the action chosen to achieve that condition.

4. The approach did not permit a condition to be monitored in parallel with the performance of an action needing that condition as a precondition.

5. The approach did not allow for the environment being so cooperative that a goal could be achieved by simply waiting.

6. The approach did not allow that an already true condition might require sustained effort to keep it true.

---

[1][Hansson et al, 1990] use a decision model for plan synthesis to automatically build a plan, but do not discuss plan execution.

This list of difficulties is an elaboration of my previous list. Here, this list serves to state the problems that the present paper will solve.

Of these problems, numbers #3 through #6 might be regarded as having been rendered solvable by various approaches to modelling processes and concurrency, e.g. [McDermott, 1982] [Georgeff, 1986] [Sandewall and Ronnquist, 1986] [Pelavin, 1991]. However, none of the relevant works include sensing actions in their formalisms, and there is reason to believe that it will be a major undertaking to augment their formalisms with sensing actions. The argument is as follows.

The outcome of any sensing action worth having is unpredictable: maybe the car will start, maybe it won't. If one takes seriously the idea that a plan executor must sense the truth of at least *some* conditions needed by the plan, and if each sensory test can come out in two or more ways, then there is an obvious implication that plans must cope with exponentially large numbers of possible futures. If, further, one believes that the temporal order of planned events must be explicitly represented in plans, then there is no escape from plans containing large numbers of conditional branches and loops. Unfortunately, all of the existing approaches to planning with processes and concurrency have accepted the notion that the temporal order of planned events must be explicitly represented. Consequently, those approaches cannot represent the heavy use of sensing actions required by embedded applications.

The explosive branching issue disappears completely in the context of the classification-based "reaction plans" now controlling some situated agents, because such plan structures are inherently highly conditional and iterative (like production systems) without actually containing any explicit conditionals or loops. That such highly conditional plans may be built automatically has been shown by the author's Ph.D. thesis [Schoppers, 1989]. Therefore, the time is right to formalize and integrate continuous processes, concurrency, and bona fide sensing actions (or other actions having nondeterministic outcomes), for presentation to an automatic planner, and for inclusion into automatically constructed reaction plans. This paper is the first to report such an integration. Furthermore, the approach taken herein has already been successfully exercised in a practical robotic application.

1.3 OVERVIEW

The uniqueness of my approach is most easily visible in the intuitive meaning assigned to the modal operators of knowledge, belief, and time:

- *Beliefs* about the current state of the world arise solely as model-based projections of earlier beliefs (or knowledge) forward through time.

- After initiating an action, the execution monitor may believe the *eventual* attainment of desired effects, but may specifically *not* believe that the desired effects have been obtained, unless the action is described as being instantaneous.
- *Knowledge* of the state of the world is obtainable only by performing sensing actions at plan execution time.
- Sensing actions are usually described as enabling the belief that it will eventually be the case that P is known to be true *or* P is known to be false, so that the planner cannot tell whether the knowledge will be of P or of ¬P, since that will be decided at plan execution time.
- All actions (including sensing actions) are monitored not only for their success but also for their progress, and are controlled and timed by means of beliefs about anticipated open- and closed-loop dynamics.

The next Section describes the modal logic of knowing-whether, relates it to a logic of belief, and then adds the modal logic of branching time that is used to monitor and control the timing of all actions. The remainder of the paper then applies those logics to representing the actions and domain constraints needed for part of the control plan of a space-faring retriever robot.

2   THE MODAL LOGICS

I have chosen the modal system S5 for the knowledge modality, and weak S5 for the belief modality. This choice rests in part upon the derivation given in [Rosenschein, 1985], and in part on the fact that S5 is the simplest logic having the desired expressiveness (see [Halpern and Moses, 1985] for an introduction to modal logics).

2.1   KNOWING-WHETHER

It is shown in [Montgomery and Routley, 1966] that a modal operator for "knowing-whether", there called the "non-contingency" operator, can be used to produce modal logics deductively equivalent to T, S4 and S5. Here it is sufficient to define the "logic of knowing-whether" as a simple extension of a logic of knowledge.

Let "it is known that P" be expressed as usual by the formula "k P". Then "it is known whether (or not) P" is definable in the obvious way:

$$\mathbf{kw}\ P \equiv \mathbf{k}\ P \vee \mathbf{k}\neg P\ .$$

The formula "kw P" may also be read as "the truth value of P is known" (i.e. for my purposes, is perceptually obtained).

Now, to know whether a certain condition P is true at plan execution time, the plan executor may perform an action that is described as achieving **kw** P. Actions described as achieving P are no use when the goal is **kw** P, because the achievement of P is not an achievement of knowledge of P. Conversely, actions described as achieving **kw** P are no use when the goal is to achieve P itself, for the achievement of **kw** P might yield either **k** P or **k**¬P. Consequently it is easy for planners and plan executors to tell whether an achievement of P is a verified reality (when P ∧ **kw** P) or merely an expectation (when P ∧ ¬**kw** P).

For some axioms and theorems pertaining to **kw**, see [Schoppers, 1992].

2.2   ALLOWING FOR BELIEFS

Usually, a system will maintain some estimates or beliefs about things that aren't being sensed at that precise moment, e.g. by projecting an object's known motion forward through time while the object is not actually being tracked. Here a modal belief operator is used to allow the representation of such unverified projections.

The belief operators are **b** and **bw** (read as "believed whether"). For the relevant axioms and theorems see [Schoppers, 1992].

2.3   OPEN- AND CLOSED-LOOP DYNAMICS

Conditions that are currently true may or may not stay that way without appropriate continued action. A door may or may not stay open by itself, depending on the presence of a spring or door-stop. The idea of a dynamic — a rule about change over time — is at the heart of this issue, and control theorists have further distinguished between open-loop and closed-loop dynamics. Open-loop dynamics are rules for a system's behavior when it is not subject to ongoing direct influence from our plan executor or controller. A spring-loaded door's open-loop dynamics cause the door to close. A system's closed-loop dynamics are the rules that govern the system's behavior when it *is* subject to ongoing direct influence from our plan or control law. When our robot continuously holds the door open, the door's response to the ongoing action of our robotic agent is a closed-loop dynamic.

Reaction plans must be able to exploit both open- and closed-loop dynamics for several reasons, but the reasons most salient to this paper are the following three:

1. If a system's open-loop dynamics are such that the system will evolve toward certain desired conditions of its own accord, then a robotic agent may not need to act on the system at all to achieve the desired ends.

2. If a system's open-loop dynamics are such that the system will evolve away from certain desired con-

ditions of its own accord, then a robotic agent may have to keep acting on the system even though the desired conditions are already true. That is, the plan must be able to react to the unwanted open-loop dynamic by replacing it with a suitable closed-loop dynamic.

3. The distinction between open-loop and closed-loop dynamics bears directly on the issue of how often to sense something. This bearing is explained immediately below.

An agent's beliefs about current environmental state can be viewed as a dynamical system whose open-loop dynamics have to do with a decay of accuracy and/or certainty over time. If an agent's beliefs about environmental state are subject to decay, and if those same beliefs must be maintained for plan execution purposes, then the plan is faced with a situation that is exactly analogous to a closing door that should be kept open. Then, one appropriate response is to resort to a closed-loop dynamic, e.g. by occasionally updating the decaying information. The distinction between open-loop and closed-loop dynamics, and the ability to occasionally update decaying information through sensing, can both be built into reaction plans by means of a modal logic of branching time, as follows.

We need a standard model of branching time, and define three modal operators. **soon** P is a modification of the standard operator $\forall \Diamond$ P, and is true at a world if, in all possible *open-loop* futures that do *not* include the present world, P is true eventually. **sust** P (for "sustainable") is just the standard operator $\exists \Box$ P, and is true at a world if, in some possible future including the present world, P is true forever. Since **sust** is not restricted to open-loop futures, it permits closed-loop futures. When these two operators are composed we find that **soon sust** P is true at a world if, without the plan's having to bring it about, it will eventually be the case that P is true and can be kept that way. More importantly, **soon sust** P is false at a world when

1. the plan must perform some action to make P true in a sustainable way, or

2. P is already true and sustainable but will become false or unsustainable unless the plan does something immediately.

Thus, the falsity of **soon sust** P is a signal that action is required.

As a special case, the falsity of **soon sust kw** Q leads to a sensing action. Moreover, the update frequency of each piece of sensed information can be determined by that information's decay rate. If a condition Q is known to be true and is not subject to decay, **soon sust kw** Q can stay true forever and Q need never be sensed again.

The third temporal operator is **cont** P, which is a mod-

ification of the standard operator $\forall \Box$ P, and is true at a world if, in all possible *open-loop* futures including the present world, P is true forever. This operator is used to describe conditions that will remain stable unless forced to change.

2.4   HOW THE LOGICS ARE USED

To understand the plan fragment discussed in the next Section, the reader should first know how the logics of this Section cooperate. Conceptually, we can begin with a plan that contains none of the above logics; it simply states what should be done in various circumstances, much like a production system. But because we wish to build embedded systems, we are immediately forced to diverge from production systems by including some way to describe actions that bring information from the outside world into the executing plan. The modal logic of knowledge plays that role. However, some actions are valuable even if some of their preconditions have not been recently sensed, so we need a way to represent information that has been derived from earlier knowledge using a dynamics model. The modal logic of belief fills that gap. Finally, it is necessary to represent some of the dynamics of the application domain, so that approaching events can be anticipated and appropriate measures taken, whether those measures consist of doing nothing, of initiating corrective action, or of continuing existing activities. This last role is played by the modal logic of branching time, adapted to model both open- and closed-loop dynamics.

The reader will also find it useful to know certain cliches that arise frequently in Universal Plans. The cliches used in the next Section are the following:

- Instead of achieving **k** P directly, the plan achieves the conjunction (P and **kw** P), which is logically equivalent but makes very clear that achievement of knowledge of P may require several interdependent actions, namely
  - perceiving whether P is perhaps already true before anything has been done,
  - acting to make P true, and
  - perceiving whether P has successfully been made true.

  Consequently, the plan contains many instances of the following fragment (here shown without temporal modifications):

  ```
  kw P ?
  T: P ?
      T: RUN A
      F: ACT TO ACHIEVE P
  F: ACT TO ACHIEVE kw P
  ```

- Instead of directly achieving a *momentary* precondition P of action A (whether that precondition is a knowledge condition, belief condition, or nonmodal) the plan actually achieves **b soon** P, thus inherently exploiting any relevant open-loop dynamics. Nevertheless, the action A of which P is a precondition can only be performed when P is in fact true-at-the-time. Consequently, the plan contains many instances of the following decision fragment:

```
P ?
T: RUN A
F: b soon P ?
    T: NO-OP     % wait for P
    F: ACT TO ACHIEVE P
```

- Instead of directly achieving a *sustained* precondition P of action A (whether that precondition is a knowledge condition, belief condition, or non-modal) the plan actually achieves **b soon sust** P, thus inherently exploiting any relevant open-loop dynamics. Nevertheless, the action A of which P is a precondition can only be performed when both of the following hold:
  - P is true-at-the-time, and
  - circumstances are such that P can be kept true indefinitely (barring disturbances).

Furthermore, in order to run the action A that requires the truth of P, and simultaneously act to sustain the truth of P, the plan may have to do several things in parallel. Consequently, the plan contains many instances of the following decision fragment:

```
{ b sust P ?
  T: RUN A
  F: NO-OP      % wait for sust P
||
  b soon sust P ?
  T: NO-OP      % wait for sust P
  F: ACT TO ACHIEVE sust P
}
```

More complex plan fragments occur when an action requires the achievement of a knowledge condition, i.e. **k** P for some P. Goals of this form can be factored into four subgoals: **b soon kw** P, **b soon** P, **b kw** P, and **b** P. The plan then tests all four of these conditions, and their significance can be perplexing — and the plan unreadable! — unless their relationship to the original goal is recalled.

Similarly complex plan fragments arise in the achievement of sustained knowledge conditions.

The most complex fragments plan fragments occur when an action requires achievement of a belief condition, **b** P. Under the above rules this goal expands into the two goals **b** P and **b soon b** P. If the latter is false, the plan can make it true only by achieving **k** P, which then expands into three of the four subgoals just mentioned — the fourth, **b soon b** P, can be omitted because it is already known to be false.

The degree of parallelism that emerges from the composition of these plan fragments can be surprising. For

example, consider an action A that is being performed to achieve a goal G, and that has a precondition **b sust k** P. All of the following activities may be occurring in parallel:

- checking beliefs about the current truth of P,
- checking beliefs about the expected continued truth of P,
- sensing the current truth value of P,
- checking beliefs about expected continued availability of sensory information about the truth of P,
- acting to sustain the truth of P,
- performing A to achieve the truth of G,
- checking beliefs about the current falsehood of G,
- checking beliefs about the expected continued falsehood of G (or, monitoring the progress of A toward achieving G),
- sensing the current truth value of G.

3   APPLICATION TO AN EVA RETRIEVER ROBOT

This Section shows how the logics described above allow the synthesis of Universal Plans intermixing sensing and effecting. The planning machinery itself will not be described here; for that, see [Schoppers, 1989].

The NASA Extra Vehicular Activity (EVA) Retriever robot (known as "EVAR") will be housed on a Shuttle or the Space Station, and will retrieve tools and astronauts that become untethered during EVA. Each retrieval mission will involve sensor acquisition of the target object, rendezvous with the object, grappling, return home with the object, and delivery.

To understand the domain description given below it is necessary to know something of EVAR's capabilities and construction. EVAR is a free-flying robot. It can accelerate in any direction at any time, and can rotate about all three of its body axes at the same time, if required. It has two arms, one of which is equipped with a clamp. The clamp is instrumented with a sensor to indicate whether the clamp is open; at present there is no contact or proximity sensor. EVAR has three chest cameras mounted side by side so that their fields of view overlap slightly, and so that their combined fields of view span 180 degrees horizontally. (This arrangement allows EVAR to perform a visual scan in all directions by doing a backwards somersault.) A directable scanning laser range finder is mounted on top of EVAR's "shoulders", and has a rectangular field of view 60 degrees wide and high. The laser can be pointed at anything above the plane of EVAR's shoulders, hence cannot look at anything that is more than 30 degrees below that plane.

The rules required to specify the acquisition, rendezvous, and grappling phases of an EVAR mission are shown in Figure 1. The meaning of most predicates should be obvious from their names. Some predicates needing explanation are:

- located(X) is true if the object's azimuth and elevation are more or less precisely known.
- laserable(X) is true iff the object has an elevation of $>= -30$ degrees in EVAR's body-centered coordinate system, i.e. iff the object's location is accessible to the laser range finder without rotating the whole robot.
- facing(X) is a low-pass filter on the object's azimuth and elevation in EVAR body coordinates.
- standing-off(X) is a low-pass filter on the object's distance and speed relative to EVAR.
- "fov" is an abbreviation for "field of view".

```
% rules constraining both knowledge & belief

k( clamp-open <-> ~ clamp-closed ) ).

k( facing(X) -> in-camera-fov(X) ).
k( in-fov(X) <->
      in-camera-fov(X) | in-laser-fov(X) ).
k( in-fov(X) -> laserable(X) ).
k( laserable(X) -> located(X) ).


% rules constraining knowledge only

k located(X) -> k in-fov(X).
k located(X) -> kw in-laser-fov(X).
k located(X) -> kw in-camera-fov(X).
k in-fov(X) <-> kw facing(X).

k in-laser-fov(X) <-> kw clamp-near(X).
k in-laser-fov(X) <-> kw standing-off(X).
k in-camera-fov(X) <-> kw low-spin(X).


% some of the above rules hold for belief too

b located(X) -> bw in-laser-fov(X).
b located(X) -> bw in-camera-fov(X).
% hence b located(X) -> bw in-fov(X).
b in-fov(X) <-> bw facing(X).


% rules about persistence

% the clamp never moves by itself
clamp-open -> cont clamp-open.
clamp-closed -> cont clamp-closed.
% an inert object can't accelerate
low-spin(X) -> cont low-spin(X).
~ low-spin(X) -> cont ~ low-spin(X).
```

Figure 1: Grappling Rules for the EVA Retriever.

The rest of this Section examines Figures 1 from a

knowledge representation viewpoint.

By virtue of the axiom ($\mathbf{k}$ P $\supset$ $\mathbf{b}$ P), the first set of rules in Figure 1a can be used to derive either knowledge or belief.

```
% action descriptions

opening --              % open the clamp
   clamp-open <+ true.

closing --              % close the clamp
   clamp-closed <+ true
&& captured(X) <+ b clamp-open, b clamp-near(X).

extending --           % extend arm with clamp
   b soon sust arm-out <+ true.

translating1(X) --     % move to standoff
   b soon sust standing-off(X)
              <+ b sust k located(X).

translating2(X) --     % move to contact
   b soon sust clamp-near(X)
              <+ b sust k low-spin(X),
                 b sust k facing(X),
                 b sust k standing-off(X),
                 b sust b arm-out.

rotating1(X) --        % turn to look at X
   b soon sust laserable(X) <+ b located(X).

rotating2(X) --        % turn to face X
   b soon sust facing(X) <+ b located(X).

rotating3(X) --        % somersault
   b soon sust in-camera-fov(X) <+ true.

tracking(X) --         % track with range finder
   b soon sust in-laser-fov(X)
              <+ b sust b laserable(X).

get-status --          % read internal sensors
   b soon sust kw clamp-open,
   b soon sust kw arm-out <+ true.

get-info(X) --         % get data from sensors
   b soon sust kw located(X) <+ true.
```

Figure 1b: Grappling Rules for the EVA Retriever.

An example of a (domain constraint) rule that holds for knowledge only is

$$\mathbf{k} \text{ located}(X) \to \mathbf{k} \text{ in-fov}(X).$$

This rule holds for knowledge because an object can only be *known* to be located, at a given time, if it is being perceived at that time, and it can only be perceived if it is in some sensor's field of view. The corresponding rule for belief does not hold because EVAR is entitled to have beliefs about an object's location without that object being visible at the time.

The action descriptions are written action-name first, followed by goal-reduction rules in Prolog style, with postconditions on the left, a state transition arrow "<+" in the middle, and preconditions on the right. For all actions but the last two, the postconditions are free of knowledge modalities; the last two actions are knowledge-generating. On the other hand, the (non-trivial) preconditions of actions are all qualified by a belief (or knowledge) modality, subject to the domain engineer's view that each action may (or may not) be performed on the strength of unverified projections derived from earlier states.

The temporal modalities on action postconditions indicate the expected duration of actions. Only the actions of opening and closing the clamp are instantaneous, all the rest take some time. The temporal modalities on action preconditions indicate whether the preconditions must be true only initially or throughout the action. In the case of translation and tracking, the preconditions must not only be true, they must be (believed to be) sustainably true. For all the other actions it is sufficient if their preconditions are only momentarily true.

In this application, due to project constraints, there are only two actions that deliver knowledge. The camera and laser image interpretations are developed by software provided by NASA. Those interpretations are exhaustive, i.e. the software extracts as much information as possible about each object, packages the information for each object into a record format, and then sends (on request) the whole record to my control plan. As a result, my control plan needs to perform only one action, GET-INFO(X), to find out everything currently known about the object designated by X.

Notice that despite the deluge of information it produces, GET-INFO(X) is described as achieving only **kw** located(X). It is easy to show, using the deductive rules provided, that when **kw** located(X), all of the following must also hold: **kw** in-camera-fov(X), **kw** in-laser-fov(X), **kw** in-fov(X), **kw** laserable(X), and **kw** facing(X). These are unconditional side effects of GET-INFO(X), and will be recognized as such whenever they are needed by the Universal Plans synthesis machinery. This deduction ability was one of the main motivations for the modal formalization.

4   THE RESULTING BEHAVIOR

The rules of Figures 1 give rise to a sizeable Universal Plan. Here I present only a small piece of that plan, further simplified for readability.

Figure 2 shows the sequence of decisions made by the

Universal Plans interpreter as it backchains from the goal **kw** clamp-near(X), which arises as a subgoal in the task of capturing the object referred to by X. clamp-near(X) is a threshold on the distance between EVAR's clamp and the object X. A goal to know the truth *or* falsity of clamp-near(X) thus amounts to a goal to know the range to X. Ranges can only be known by using the directable laser.

```
1   k-in-laser-fov-TREE(X) =
2     kw in-laser-fov(X) ?
3     T: in-laser-fov(X) ?
4       T: NO-OP                        % finished
5       F: b soon in-laser-fov(X) ?
6         T: NO-OP                      % waiting
7         F: CALL b-sust-b-laserable-TREE(X)
8     F: b soon kw in-laser-fov(X) ?
9       T: NO-OP                        % waiting
10      F: GET-INFO(X)

11  b-sust-b-laserable-TREE(X) =
12    { b sust b laserable(X) ?
13      T: TRACKING(X)
14      F: NO-OP                        % waiting
15    ||
16      b soon sust b laserable(X) ?
17      T: NO-OP                        % waiting
18      F: % achieve sust-k-laserable(X)
19        { b sust kw laserable(X) ?
20          T: b sust b laserable(X) ?
21            T: CALL b-located-TREE(X)
22            F: NO-OP
23          F: NO-OP                    % waiting
24        ||
25          b soon sust kw laserable(X) ?
26          T: NO-OP                    % waiting
27          F: GET-INFO(X)
28        }
29    }

30  b-located-TREE(X) =
31    b located(X) ?
32    T: ROTATING1(X)
33    F: b soon b located(X) ?
34      T: NO-OP                        % waiting
35      F: % achieve k located(X)
36        kw located(X) ?
37        T: ROTATING3
38        F: b soon kw located(X) ?
39          T: NO-OP                    % waiting
40          F: GET-INFO(X)
```

Figure 2: Decision Tree Form of Range Finding Plan.

In the decision tree, predicates are typed in small letters and are followed by a question mark; actions are typed in capitals. Every condition either must be deducible using the domain constraints, or must be implemented as a piece of code (e.g. a C function) that evaluates the named condition and returns either True or False.[2] Similarly, every action must be implemented as a piece of code that sends commands to the relevant sensors or effectors. The parameter X is bound, at execution time, to a data structure that is accessible to the code implementing the predicates and actions. That data structure contains the known or expected position (if any) of the object that EVAR is pursuing, and supports indexical-functional reference [Schoppers and Shu, 1990].

The line numbers beside the decision tree exist to facilitate the following comments. The most salient points of the plan are that it can:

1. apply actions for their implicit, deductively derived, effects, including the deduction of knowledge conditions (the GET-INFO(X) on line 10 was selected to achieve the **b soon kw** in-laser-fov(X) condition on line 8, and the GET-INFO(X) on line 27 was selected to achieve the **b soon sust kw** laserable(X) condition on line 25),

2. cause a somersaulting behavior, in the absence of any beliefs about the target's location, to (re)acquire the target (the ROTATING3 on line 37 was selected to achieve the **b soon b** located(X) condition on line 33),

3. rotate EVAR's whole body, given a belief about the target's location, so as to bring the target into a position where the laser can scan it (the ROTATING1(X) on line 32 was selected to achieve the **b soon sust b** laserable(X) condition on line 16),

4. point the laser at the target, given a belief that the target is in a laserable region of space, to determine whether or not the target is really there (the TRACKING(X) on line 13 was selected to achieve the **b soon** in-laser-fov(X) condition on line 5),

5. make use of plant dynamics to determine whether effector actions are proceeding as expected (the NO-OPs on lines 14 and 17 do nothing when it is believed that the object X is not yet laserable but will soon be so, e.g. after performing the ROTATING1(X) action on line 32, and provided that EVAR is actually rotating as desired),

6. make use of sensor dynamics (including timeouts) to determine whether sensing actions are proceeding as expected (the NO-OPs on lines 23 and 26 do nothing when it is believed that the plan executor does not yet know-whether laserable(X) but will soon know it, e.g. after performing the GET-INFO(X) on line 27),

7. make use of "belief decay dynamics" to determine whether updates and sensing actions are necessary (the GET-INFO(X) on line 10 is performed only

when it is *not* believed that **kw** in-laser-fov(X) will stay true for a while by itself, and similarly, the GET-INFO(X) on line 27 is performed only when it is *not* believed that **sust kw** laserable(X) will stay true for a while by itself).

Points 2 – 4 are examples of acting to enable sensing. The purpose of the whole plan is to determine whether some target object is currently graspable, i.e. the plan is an example of sensing in support of action. Indeed, arbitrary recursion of sensing and acting is possible.

The ability to direct the laser range finder on the strength of a belief about the target's location (point 4) is an example of performing an experiment to test the veracity of some beliefs. If the beliefs about the target's location turn out to be correct and the target is seen, the somersault can be skipped and more efficient behavior results; if the target is not seen where it was expected, the actual consequence of the TRACKING attempt will be **k¬**located(X) and EVAR will then resort to somersaulting to find the target.

Points 5 – 7 are about the interaction of dynamics with both effector and sensor actions. This interaction is useful in distinguishing progress monitoring from results perception, and in filtering out redundant action attempts. The sensor load is kept in check through the filtering out of redundant sensing actions.

5 SUMMARY AND LOOSE ENDS

In a previous paper [Schoppers, 1992] I argued that the planner's projections and the real world must be kept clearly separate, even to the extent of saying that action descriptions carry no more promisory force than heuristics. That paper's distinctions between estimated/believed and perceived/known information, together with the present paper's beliefs about expected behavior under open- and closed-loop dynamics, allow the representation and construction of plans in which projecting, sensing, acting and timing can support each other in new and relatively sophisticated ways. Furthermore, a complex and highly parallel Universal Plan, built using the formalisms described herein, has been demonstrated. It exploits known helpful dynamics for economy of effort; neutralizes known counterproductive dynamics; recovers robustly from unmodelled dynamics[3]; also recovers robustly from mistaken perceptions[4]; and runs very efficiently.

That said, the formalism also has obvious limitations in that it does not support the explicit representation

---

[2]For example, the condition **b sust kw** laserable(X) maps into a call to the C function b_s_kw_laserable(X).

[3]Unmodelled helpful dynamics are never a problem. Unmodelled counter-productive dynamics can be a problem if they are persistent (i.e. if they should have been modelled).

[4]From the plan's point of view, mistaken perceptions are indistinguishable from unmodelled dynamics.

of metric information about either certainty or time. Thus it is not possible to automatically make use of two sensors simultaneously when that would deliver higher certainty than either sensor used alone. Similarly, there is a built-in assumption that perceived information is always more reliable than information obtained by model-based estimation. On the topic of metric time, it is not possible to symbolically represent the amount of time it usually takes to complete an action. Fortunately, these limitations turned out to be nearly irrelevant to the EVA Retriever domain. The inability to use two sensors never became an issue because no two sensors delivered readings of the same quantity; the assumption that perceived information is more reliable than projected information turned out to be true because projections were based on earlier readings whose certainty was no higher than that of new readings; and a lot of metric temporal information could be built into the C code that evaluated the plan's conditions. An example of the latter is that it was possible to evaluate the condition **b soon** P as true for 1 second after attempting to achieve P, and thereafter to evaluate it as true if observed movements were appropriate.

Indeed, the formalism exhibited only one serious problem deriving from the lack of metric information. The plan sometimes wanted to carefully measure distance to the Space Station (to avoid a collision) while also watching the retrieved astronaut (to make sure we still had him), but could not watch them both at once. The resulting behavior was that the robot looked at the Space Station, got the knowledge it wanted, believed that knowledge to be good for some time and so turned to look at the astronaut, then lost confidence in the Space Station's position before the astronaut had actually been seen, and so looked back at the Space Station, losing track of the astronaut entirely. This problem was solved with a hand-coded hack because the formalism did not represent enough information to support automated detection of the problem. On the other hand it is also not clear that a more explicit formalism is the only answer: a dynamic resource scheduler/arbitrator such as that of [Bestavros et al, 1990] might do as well.

The above discussion brings us to the issue of optimal behavior and the utility of actions. Why not regard information as a valuable commodity, and utilize Decision Theory to decide which sensors to use when, e.g. [Dean et al, 1990]? Because the use of Decision Theory for plan execution faces two practical hurdles: **1.** how to *automatically* synthesize the necessary decision models, and **2.** how to compute action decisions *efficiently* without resorting to poor decision models.

I now turn to architectural issues. There is in the literature a distinction between situated agents that have sense/plan/act cycles and those in which monitoring is an ongoing asynchronous activity. The newly elaborated Universal Plans cut across this issue in an interesting way. Under Universal Plans, an initiated action is presumed to be carried out by distributed controllers, and is usually ongoing. Furthermore, Universal Plans support the concurrent initiation and monitoring of any number of actions, all of which can be ongoing simultaneously. When some of those actions are sensing actions, their results are dumped into the plan executor's knowledge base between plan execution cycles — that part of the machinery is synchronous. However, because of its exploitation of dynamics information to filter out superfluous action requests, the plan executor actually spends most of its time performing NO-OP actions (while the existing beliefs are considered still valid), and the plan executor is fast enough so that there is seldom any new perceptual information between plan execution cycles. Indeed, since sensing is a requestable action, the plan executor's *only* reason for running is to use the realtime clock to monitor the "decay dynamics" of whatever beliefs are currently relevant. Meanwhile, the controllers that carry out the previously initiated sensing actions proceed asynchronously. To summarize: sensing and acting are concurrent and asynchronous with respect to each other, but the information produced by sensing is made available to the plan executor on a synchronous basis. The result is not a sense/plan/act cycle, nor is monitoring asynchronous with respect to plan execution.

Another way of describing the current approach is to say that plan execution and action performance proceed asynchronously — a rather odd circumstance, until it is realized that "plan execution" now consists mostly of monitoring belief decay dynamics, and only occasionally *initiating* actions.

The main reason for this division of labor is that the time constraints on action performance are much more severe than those on action initiation, often demanding the use of dedicated controllers. Since the EVA Retriever has a multiplicity of such high-speed controllers, the role of the plan was primarily to coordinate their activities by managing their modes and setpoints. Universal Plan execution is currently only "coincidentally real-time", however: it is empirically an order of magnitude faster than the dynamics of the EVA Retriever domain, but there are no performance guarantees.

Acknowledgements

The work reported herein was funded by NASA under contract NAS9-18162. Dan Shapiro and Dave Gaw contributed helpful discussions. The reviewers' comments were also appreciated.

References

[Agre and Chapman, 1987] P. Agre and D. Chapman. Pengi: an implementation of a theory of activity.

Proc AAAI National Conf, pages 268–272, 1987.

[Bestavros et al, 1990] A. Bestavros, J. Clark and N. Ferrier. Management of sensori-motor activity in mobile robots. *Proc IEEE Internat'l Conf on Robotics and Automation*, pages 592–597, 1990.

[Brooks, 1982] R. Brooks. Symbolic error analysis and robot planning. AI Memo 685, MIT, 1982.

[Brooks, 1986] R. Brooks. A layered control system for a mobile robot. *IEEE Journal of Robotics and Automation* 2:1, pages 14–23, 1986.

[Davis, 1988] E. Davis. Inferring ignorance from the locality of visual perception. *Proc AAAI National Conf*, pages 786–791, 1988.

[Dean et al, 1990] T. Dean, K. Basye and M. Lejter, Planning and active perception. *Proc DARPA Workshop on Innovative Approaches to Planning, Scheduling and Control*, pages 271–276, 1990.

[Doyle et al, 1986] R. Doyle, D. Atkinson and R. Doshi. Generating perception requests and expectations to verify the execution of plans. *Proc AAAI National Conf*, pages 81–87, 1986.

[Drummond, 1986] M. Drummond. *Plan Nets: a Formal Representation of Action and Belief for Automatic Planning Systems*. PhD thesis, Dept of AI, University of Edinburgh, UK, 1986.

[Firby, 1987] R.J. Firby. An investigation into reactive planning in complex domains. *Proc AAAI National Conf*, pages 202ff, 1987.

[Georgeff et al, 1985] M. Georgeff, A. Lansky and P. Bessiere. A procedural logic. *Proc 9th IJCAI*, pages 516ff, 1985.

[Georgeff, 1986] M. Georgeff. The representation of events in multiagent domains. *Proc AAAI National Conf*, pages 70ff, 1986.

[Gervasio, 1990] M. Gervasio. Learning general completable reactive plans. *Proc AAAI National Conf*, pages 1016–1021, 1990.

[Gettier, 1963] E. Gettier. Is justified true belief knowledge? *Analysis* 23:6, pages 121–123, 1963.

[Haas, 1986] A. Haas. A syntactic theory of belief and action. *AI Journal* 28, pages 245–292, 1986.

[Halpern and Moses, 1985] J. Halpern and Y. Moses. A guide to the modal logics of knowledge and belief. *Proc 9th IJCAI*, pages 480ff, 1985.

[Hansson et al, 1990] O. Hansson, A. Mayer and S. Russell. Decision-theoretic planning in BPS. In J. Hendler (ed) *Planning in Uncertain, Unpredictable or Changing Environments*. Tech Report 90-45, Systems Research Center, U of Maryland, 1990.

[Hendler and Sanborn, 1987] J. Hendler and J. Sanborn. A model of reaction for planning in dynamic environments. *Proc DARPA Knowledge-Based Planning Workshop, Austin, TX*, pages 24.1–24.10, 1987.

[Kaelbling, 1988] L. Kaelbling. Goals as parallel program specifications. *Proc AAAI National Conf*, pages 60–65, 1988.

[Konolige, 1980] K. Konolige. A first-order formalization of knowledge and action for a multi-agent planning system. Tech Note 232, AI Center, SRI International, 1980.

[McDermott, 1982] D. McDermott. A temporal logic for reasoning about processes and plans. *Cognitive Science* 6, pages 101ff, 1982.

[Montgomery and Routley, 1966] H. Montgomery and R. Routley. Contingency and non-contingency bases for normal modal logics. *Logique et Analyse* 9:35, pages 318ff, 1966.

[Moore, 1980] R. Moore. Reasoning about knowledge and action. Tech Note 191, AI Center, SRI International, 1980.

[Morgenstern, 1987] L. Morgenstern. *Foundations of a Logic of Knowledge, Action and Communication*. PhD thesis, Dept of Computer Science, New York University, 1987.

[Nilsson, 1988] N. Nilsson. Action networks. *Proc Rochester Planning Workshop, U of Rochester, NY*, pages 21ff, 1988.

[Pelavin, 1991] R. Pelavin. Planning with concurrent actions and external events. In J. ALLEN et al, *Reasoning About Plans*, Morgan Kaufmann, 1991.

[Rosenschein, 1985] S. Rosenschein. Formal theories of knowledge in AI and robotics. *New Generation Computing* 3:4, pages 345–357, 1985.

[Sandewall and Ronnquist, 1986] E. Sandewall and R. Ronnquist. A representation of action structures. *Proc AAAI National Conf*, pages 89ff, 1986.

[Schoppers, 1989] M. Schoppers. *Representation and Automatic Synthesis of Reaction Plans*. Report, Dept of Computer Science, University of Illinois at Urbana-Champaign, 1989.

[Schoppers and Shu, 1990] M. Schoppers and R. Shu. An implementation of indexical-functional reference for the embedded execution of symbolic plans. *Proc DARPA Workshop on Innovative Approaches to Planning, Scheduling and Control*, pages 490–496, 1990.

[Schoppers, 1992] M. Schoppers. Representing the plan monitoring needs and resources of robotic systems. *Proc 3rd IEEE Conf on AI, Planning and Simulation in High Autonomy Systems*, 1992.

Vague Data Management in Production Process Scheduling applied to High-Grade Steelmaking

Wolfgang Slany   **Christian Stary**   **Jürgen Dorn**

Christian Doppler Laboratory for Expert Systems
E184/2, TU Wien, A-1040 Vienna, Austria, Europe
Phone: +43-1-58801/{6123|6124|6127}   Fax: +43-1-5055304
E-Mail: {wsi|stary|dorn}@vexpert.dbai.tuwien.ac.at

Abstract

Mathematical-analytical methods as used in Operations Research approaches are often insufficient for planning problems. This is due to three reasons: The imprecise informations in the production process, combinatorial complexity of the search space, and conflicting objectives for production optimizing. The combination of several knowledge-based techniques, especially approximate reasoning and constraint relaxation, is a promising way to handle these problems.

We use a case study to demonstrate how knowledge-based scheduling works with the desired capabilities. The applied knowledge representation technique covers the vagueness inherent in the problem domain by using fuzzy set theory. Based on this knowledge representation, the importance of jobs is defined. This classification of jobs is used for the straightforward generation of a schedule.

We introduce a control strategy which comprises several types of constraints, namely organizational, spatial, and chemical ones. This strategy supports the dynamic relaxation of conflicting constraints in order to improve the schedule. To show the benefits of this strategy, the generation of a schedule for one day is explained in detail.

1   INTRODUCTION

Planning, and thus scheduling of factory processes involves the simultaneous consideration of jobs to be performed and resources which those jobs require. Usually, a job is identified with a deliverable product which has to meet a certain quality. Hence, each job is correlated to some formal specification of the intended product.

Resources are typically those materials, tools, units, and individuals, which are in the factory to be consumed, to be used, or to work for the production process. Each resource is associated with some formal specification of its characteristics and capabilities.

The planner's task is to correlate these specifications, and to generate a set of operations called a process plan which leads to the production of the desired product. Additionally, it leads to a set of explicit constraints concerning the sequence of operations, and a set of resource requirements for the operations.

When a number of jobs has to be executed together, the composition of their resource requirements imposes additional constraints on the sequence of operations. These constraints prohibit simultaneous use of non-sharable resources. A planner (scheduler) has to consider both the explicit constraints concerning the sequence of operations imposed by the plans, and the implicit constraints concerning the sequence of operations, which are determined by the availability of the resources. The scheduler must also take into account expected delivery and maintenance dates, as well as human factors.

The task of scheduling jobs and resources in a factory is difficult for at least three reasons. First, we have to deal with the combinatorial complexity due to multiple ways of job accomplishment [Fox 1990, Garey 1979]. Second, conflicting objectives may hinder the definition of an undisputed optimality measure [Smith 1986]. Finally, there is uncertainty in the execution of jobs due to the lack of an accurate causal model of the production process. Often, reactive scheduling is proposed as a solution to this problem [Prosser 1989]. Thus, it becomes senseless to compute exact scheduling solutions. To illustrate these problems, we describe an existing scheduling task.

In a joint project between the Alcatel-Elin Research Center Vienna and the CD-Laboratory for Expert Systems, an expert system has been developed. It supports the technical staff of the steelmaking plant of Böhler Company in Styria (Austria) in generating schedules for steel heats for a period of one week [Dorn 1991].

Böhler is one of the most important European producers of high-grade steel. The plant produces tool steel, high-speed steel, and stainless steel. There are hundreds of different kinds of steel, with 42 chemical elements varying in their specification. The requirements concerning their quality are very strong.

In the course of a schedule construction several constraints have to be taken into account. These constraints are often vague and moreover, they conflict with each other. Human experts have no pretension to generate an optimal schedule, because they know that the uncertainty in the execution of the schedule would break this optimality anyway. Human experts can decide that some schedules are better than others, but they can not give straightforward algorithms to construct the optimal schedule.

One problem in scheduling is that residuals of one heat in the electric arc furnace may pollute the next heat. As a general rule of thumb, it can be said that 3% of a chemical element in a heat remain on the electric arc furnace's wall, and 3% of the difference of this element in the first heat and the second heat will be assimilated by the second heat. Two heats that have similar shares of the element in question pose no problem. However, if the second heat has a much smaller percentage than the preceding one, the pollution by the residual from the first becomes too large to be compensated by decreasing the amount added to the second heat. This either means that the quality of the second heat will be badly influenced, or if the polluting element is expensive, that it will be wasted, and money is lost. In the following these two constraints are called compatibility rule. The compatibility rule is effective for all 42 chemical elements, but usually only 8 main elements are considered, since the others generally are not expensive, do not vary significantly, or have no great impact on the steel quality. This general rule nevertheless has some exceptions that have to be handled separately.

For some steel qualities, it is necessary that the steel is still hot after casting for subsequent treatments like forging. In this case, there will be an appointment between the steelmaking plant and the subsequent plant. This appointment has to be kept within a variation of ± 2 hours. The average number of jobs with appointments is about 10%. For some jobs no appointments are made, although their subsequent treatment should be done immediately after casting. These jobs should not be scheduled at the end of the week, because the subsequent plants are not working throughout weekends. Some jobs with difficult treatments should be performed during day shifts, because an engineer should supervise these jobs.

If a heat should be cast in many small ingots, the burden for the workers that set up und strip off the moulds is larger than for a few large ingots, because the handling of every mould takes approximately the same time. One objective of the expert system is to achieve a uniform distribution of the burden over the planning horizon.

Further constraints for the scheduling process are spatial and resource restrictions on and among the aggregates.

One important aspect and problem we have mentioned is the vagueness in the production process itself. Often, a certain amount of scrap iron is used for economical reasons for some heats. Scrap iron is classified regarding its presumed ingredients. For a given job, scrap iron that contains already some desired elements is chosen. Unfortunately, these ingredients can only be identified approximately. If a specification for a heat exists, it is not certain whether the actual heat fulfils these requirements. Sometimes additional treatments have to be performed after the scrap is melted in the furnace. Hence, the overall duration of a job as well as the actual steel quality are uncertain.

The second problem we want to cope with is the complexity of the scheduling process. There are about 45 jobs with different steel quality requirements for every furnace for one week. There are 45! or about 1.2×10^{56} permutations how the jobs could be scheduled without observing the constraints. Clearly too many to try to evaluate and compare them all. Unfortunately, constraints mainly reduce pairs of possible subsequent jobs and can only be applied if some jobs have already been scheduled. In many cases, the first jobs scheduled will not necessarily ideally fit in the preliminary schedule, and therefore they are likely to become candidates for backtracking. Applying chronological backtracking would result in an exponential problem that could not be solved in reasonable time. Further complexity arises from interactions between the four furnaces which cannot be discussed in this paper.

2 VAGUE DATA MANAGEMENT

Our approach to solve the problems mentioned in the introduction is as follows: A first schedule is generated straightforward by considering most important jobs first. In order to cope with the given complexity, the schedule is constructed without chronological backtracking. The importance of jobs is fuzzy and dynamic, which means that the importance of one job may grow over time. The preliminary schedule may not contain all jobs and still violate some constraints. In such a case, jobs in the schedule will be exchanged to find a proper schedule. A hill climbing search method is used to control this exchange. To compare solutions, we need an evaluation function that is based on the given constraints. We use fuzzy logic for modeling this evaluation. Since we cannot discuss pros and cons of fuzzy logic in this paper, we

Table 1: Characteristics Of Given Heats In The Example

No.	Name	Time	Type	Ni	Cr	Co	Mn	Fe	V	W	Mo
h_0	M100	5am		.1	1.2	.005	1.3	95	.1	.005	.005
h_1	A101			12.0	17.8	.25	1.8	69	.005	.005	2.8
h_2	S600			.2	4.3	.0005	.35	78	1.9	6.7	5.2
h_3	K460	11am	CC	.1	.6	.0005	1.15	94	.1	.15	.005
h_4	A506			8.0	17.5	.005	2.0	69	.005	.005	0.05
h_5	M238		BEST	1.2	2.1	.005	1.6	90	.005	.005	.25
h_6	M238		BEST	1.2	2.1	.005	1.6	90	.005	.005	.25
h_7	K116			.1	12	.0005	.4	83	.005	.005	.005

refer to [Negoita 1985, Zadeh 1989].

In section 2.1, we propose a method how the given constraints may be represented by fuzzy sets and how an evaluation for a complete schedule is computed. Section 2.2 explains the generation of a preliminary schedule and the search for a better schedule. Such a schedule can only be found if constraints are relaxed, because many constraints are antagonistic. This relaxation will again be based on fuzzy sets.

We describe a small example of our application to illustrate the used techniques. We restrict the example to one furnace and the planning horizon to one day. Additionally, we consider only a subset of the given constraints in order to reduce the complexity of the example. We assume that there exists already a schedule until 5am. Our input is a list of jobs that should be scheduled. The first heat h_0 in the list is the latest job scheduled from the last scheduling process. The main ingredients of each order are given in table 1.

Three heats of table 1 have special characteristics that imply their classification as very important jobs. Heat h_3 is processed on the continuous caster (CC) and has a delivery date. The delivery date is 4pm, the overall treatment takes about five hours, and therefore the processing should start at 11am. Heats h_5 and h_6 shall be cast into big ingots with a special BEST[1]-treatment. This implies that they cannot be produced immediately one after the other. Instead, there should be a time interval of at least ten hours between them.

2.1 QUALITATIVE REPRESENTATION AND EVALUATION OF CONSTRAINTS WITH FUZZY LOGIC

The constraints of the given application can be put into three main groups: Constraints on a particular job, temporal constraints, and constraints on the compatibility of jobs.

Constraints on a particular job are constraints based on required resources or aggregates. They are used to describe the importance of jobs. This importance of jobs is used later to control the generation of a prelim-

---

[1]BEST stands for Böhler Electro Slag Topping.

inary schedule by scheduling the most important job first. In our sense, the importance is a combination of the difficulty to schedule a job in general and the importance to schedule it for the actual planning horizon. A job that requires a bottle-neck resource like the continuous caster is usually difficult to schedule. A job with a certain delivery date is important, because it has to be scheduled in the planning horizon in which the delivery date falls. As a matter of fact, jobs that are not that important may be shifted to the next planning horizon. To get such a shifted job ever scheduled, it is necessary that the importance of the job increase over time. The range of fuzzy values to represent this importance is: *urgent*, *very important*, *important*, *medium*, and *not important*.

The classification of jobs in the list is dependent on the situation in the actual planning horizon. For instance, if for the actual planning horizon many jobs with a high chromium-nickel-alloy exist, then a high percentage of nickel (Ni) is no problem. On the other hand, when there are only few jobs with high nickel percentages, these jobs can be difficult to schedule.

One objective of our strategy is to schedule as many jobs as possible. In order to get the most important jobs scheduled, the evaluation function for an entire schedule has to contain a factor representing the importance of jobs. Hence, an evaluation function is defined to assign an importance value to a schedule, with N the number of jobs:

$$importance(S) = \bigcap_{i=1}^{N} importance(H_i)$$

The fuzzy-operator *bigcap* is used here in the usual fuzzy set theoretic meaning. For actual computations, an infinite number of appropriate T-norm operators for this purpose has been extensively described in the literature, see for example[Negoita 1985, Zadeh 1989]. We settled for the minimum-operator, which is the most commonly used in actual applications.

Temporal fuzzy values can be used to describe that jobs are too early or too late. The fuzzy value describes a degree of uncertainty in both direction. We can identify the following values: *very early*, *early*, *in time, late, very late.* For the evaluation of a schedule it makes no difference whether jobs are too early or too late. Therefore, the five values are mapped onto three values: *in time, nearly in time,* and *not in time.* From these values a schedule can be evaluated with respect to its temporal constraints:

$$timeliness(S) = \bigcap_{i=1}^{N} timeliness(H_i)$$

Representation of temporal constraints with fuzzy sets is discussed in detail in [Bel 1989, Dubois 1989a, Dubois 1989b, Prade 1979]. We therefore do not further investigate this aspect.

The compatibility of two jobs integrates several factors: Different chemical elements, and the work load of workers. The compatibility between two jobs is calculated by first evaluating the compatibility for each factor separately, in order to get restricted compatibility measures. Accordingly, we define six fuzzy sets for the global as well as for each restricted compatibility: *very high, high, medium, low, very low,* and *no* compatibility. The latter is a special case, since a sequence being classified incompatible can never be scheduled in this order because of hard chemical constraints to be observed.

In the lower part of table 2, several rules defining this compatibility measure have been listed. These rules can be interpreted directly as fuzzy inference rules. The compatibility calculation for nickel is shown in the upper part of table 2. The condition parts of the rules contain statements about the percentage of some chemical element in the first heat compared to the following heat. With the example taken from table 1, the heat h_5 has to contain $h_5[Ni] = 1.2\%$ of the chemical element nickel, whereas heat h_7 should contain only $h_7[Ni] = 0.1\%$. The relative percentage of $h_5[Ni]$ is therefore 1200% of $h_7[Ni]$. The question is now, considering only nickel, whether the sequence h_5 preceding h_7 is allowed or not, and if yes, how good this sequence is compared to other sequences. To decide this with the given fuzzy inference rules, somehow the linguistic variables and numeric values have to be matched. This is achieved by applying a fuzzy membership function as defined in table 2, both for the condition and for the conclusion part. In our example, the numeric input of 1200% relates more or less with the linguistic variables *more* and *much more*. Following the dotted lines to the conclusion membership functions for rules 5 and 6, two membership functions $low_{[Ni]}(h_5, h_7)$ and $medium_{[Ni]}(h_5, h_7)$ appear as a result of the calculation. Their combination

$$comp_{[Ni]}(h_5, h_7) = \max(low_{[Ni]}(h_5, h_7),$$
$$medium_{[Ni]}(h_5, h_7))$$

is a new membership function defining the nickel-compatibility of h_5 preceding h_7, which is generally spoken more low than medium. In order to compare the result with other compatibilities, it has to be defuzzified. This step can be achieved by calculating the center of gravity of the surface and then taking the value of its x-coordinate as the result.

As one observes, the conditions of the fuzzy inference rules consider only relative values for the percentage of elements like nickel in the two compared heats. Absolute values are for the compatibility problem of minor interest, but could easily be modeled by introducing more complex three dimensional membership functions. We chose a half-logarithmic graduation to be able to handle those relative values. Since the compatibility rule is asymmetric and only restricts the second heat to a minimal value for a certain chemical element, which have to at least be present in this heat, the graduation is asymmetric, too, and only logarithmic on the right half. Beside simplifying the visualization, this logarithmic scale has an additional positive effect, since positions on the right side of the 100% mark that are still near the center, are preferred and get more attention per unit than positions more close to the physical limit on the far right. This reenforces the natural meaning of the fuzzy linguistic variables positively.

The fuzzy inference rules like those in table 2 give several fuzzy judgements how compatible the heats are. These judgements in form of membership functions can be simplified to the linguistic variable to which the judgement mainly pertains. The resulting fuzzy-values can all be combined by computing a weighted mean of the defuzzified values to get one overall value for the two heats:

$$comp(H_i, H_j) = \sum_{E \in \{Wl, Ni, Cr, \ldots\}} g(E)comp_{[E]}(H_i, H_j)$$

In this formula, $g(E)$ is the normalized weight of a rule and E is a member of the set of all factors influencing the compatibility, namely work load (Wl) and the 42 chemical elements like nickel or chromium.

This computation is performed for each pair of jobs that may be scheduled. The result is a matrix of fuzzy values where the fuzzy values describe how compatible the sequence of the job of a column after the job in a row is according to all rules.

Table 3 shows this matrix for our example. It will be used for the construction of the preliminary schedule and during the improvement process. To evaluate schedules during improvement steps, it is necessary to compute an evaluation function for the compatibility of the entire schedule. This can be achieved with a fuzzy and-operator.

Table 2: Fuzzy Inference To Compute Chemical Compatibility Between Two Heats

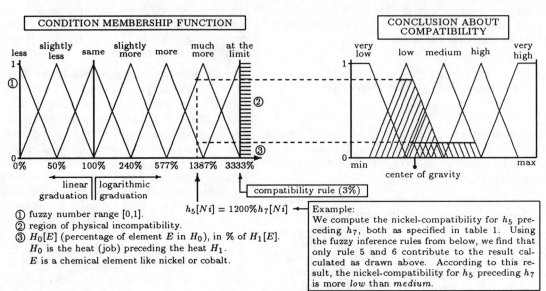

① fuzzy number range [0,1].
② region of physical incompatibility.
③ $H_0[E]$ (percentage of element E in H_0), in % of $H_1[E]$.
H_0 is the heat (job) preceding the heat H_1.
E is a chemical element like nickel or cobalt.

$h_5[Ni] = 1200\% h_7[Ni]$

Example:
We compute the nickel-compatibility for h_5 preceding h_7, both as specified in table 1. Using the fuzzy inference rules from below, we find that only rule 5 and 6 contribute to the result calculated as drawn above. According to this result, the nickel-compatibility for h_5 preceding h_7 is more *low* than *medium*.

The fuzzy inference rules with fuzzy linguistic variables:

1. IF the percentage of chemical element E in heat H_0 is *less* than in heat H_1,
   THEN the E-compatibility of H_0 preceding H_1 is *medium*.
2. IF the percentage of chemical element E in heat H_0 is *slightly less* than in heat H_1,
   THEN the E-compatibility of H_0 preceding H_1 is *high*.
3. IF the percentage of chemical element E in heat H_0 is the *same* as in heat H_1,
   THEN the E-compatibility of H_0 preceding H_1 is *very high*.
4. IF the percentage of chemical element E in heat H_0 is *slightly more* than in heat H_1,
   THEN the E-compatibility of H_0 preceding H_1 is *high*.
5. IF the percentage of chemical element E in heat H_0 is *more* than in heat H_1,
   THEN the E-compatibility of H_0 preceding H_1 is *medium*.
6. IF the percentage of chemical element E in heat H_0 is *much more* than in heat H_1,
   THEN the E-compatibility of H_0 preceding H_1 is *low*.
7. IF the percentage of chemical element E in heat H_0 is *just below*
   the physical limit imposed by the element's presence in H_1,
   THEN the E-compatibility of H_0 preceding H_1 is *very low*.
8. IF the percentage of chemical element E in heat H_0 is *over*
   the physical limit imposed by the element's presence in H_1,
   THEN there is *no compatibility* for H_0 preceding H_1.

Table 3: Compatibility Matrix For Heat Sequences

$H_0 \backslash H_1$	h_1	h_2	h_3	h_4	h_5	h_6	h_7
h_0	low	medium	high	low	high	high	medium
h_1	–	very low	very low	very high	low	low	very low
h_2	very low	–	very low	low	very low	very low	very low
h_3	medium	high	–	medium	high	high	high
h_4	high	very low	very low	–	medium	medium	medium
h_5	medium	high	high	medium	–	very high	medium
h_6	medium	high	high	medium	very high	–	medium
h_7	medium	medium	low	medium	medium	medium	–

Note: H_0 precedes H_1, e.g., the compatibility of heat h_3 preceding h_2 is *high*, whereas h_2 preceding h_3 is *very low*.

Table 4: Preliminary Schedule For Example Heats

compatibility:	high	medium	low	high	very low	low	
	h_0	h_5	h_7	h_3	h_2	h_1	h_6
time:	5am	7am	9am	11am	1pm	3pm	5pm

2.2 GENERATING A SCHEDULE

To generate a preliminary schedule, the jobs are classified regarding their importance. Then they are scheduled in the sequence of their importances. The *urgent* and *very important* jobs are scheduled first. To be scheduled means that a temporal interval is assigned to them. These intervals are spread over the entire planning horizon because of temporal and resource constraints. During this scheduling process, empty intervals are created between scheduled jobs. The compatibilities with the jobs before and behind this empty interval are not considered. If empty intervals with a duration of approximately one job are created, they are filled with compatible jobs as soon as possible. During this scheduling process, the compatibility matrix as shown in table 3 is used.

Usually, some jobs can not be scheduled, because no interval exists where they would not violate some compatibility constraints. In addition, some empty intervals remain in the schedule, and the compatibility between the jobs adjacent to this interval is usually bad. Instead of backtracking the last scheduling decisions, we try to repair or improve such a preliminary schedule.

In the list of jobs given in table 1, job h_3 has a delivery date. It will be scheduled first. Thereafter, jobs h_5 and h_6 will be scheduled, because they are very difficult jobs. They include a special treatment and therefore need a long time span between each other. Fortunately, one of them fits well after h_0. We choose h_5 to be the successor of h_0. The other is scheduled at the end of the planning horizon. The job h_7 is scheduled between h_5 and h_3 to close the empty interval between them. Heat h_2 is another difficult job for the actual week, because most heats have high percentages of nickel (Ni) and chromium (Cr), and h_2 has only small amounts of both. Moreover, h_2 has large amounts of vanadium (V) and tungsten (W). The best place for h_2 is behind heat h_3. An empty interval remains between h_2 and h_6. There exists no heat in the given list that fits between h_2 and h_6. To fill the interval, we schedule h_1 between h_2 and h_6. Heat h_4 remains for the next planning horizon. This preliminary schedule is illustrated in table 4.

To improve a schedule, we need a measure that evaluates two schedules against each other. Unfortunately, the violation of constraints has far-reaching consequences. The violation of a temporal constraint can cause the need for more resources such as additional energy, or rescheduling in subsequent plants. The violation of chemical compatibility can result in the loss of a heat which would be a great financial damage. On one hand, we have to consider hard constraints that may not be relaxed, and on the other hand constraints may be relaxed to a certain degree in order to get a feasible schedule with as many jobs as possible. In order to evaluate all these antagonistic constraints, we need an evaluation function based on the introduced fuzzy values.

We call the actual schedule the "currently best schedule". This "currently best schedule" is usually not that good. To improve a given schedule, we look for a potential constraint violation that could be improved. In the example, such a violation is found between heat h_2 and h_1. We will therefore take one of them out of the schedule. If we take h_1, no other heat is found in the whole list that would fit better. Therefore we take h_2 out of the schedule and look for another heat that fits better here. We can replace h_2 by h_4 and get as a result the schedule shown in table 5 which is the "current best schedule", because our evaluation function based on fuzzy sets assigns a better value to this schedule than to the old one.

In the next step, we find that the compatibility of h_7 preceding h_3 is low. Therefore we look for a job that would be a better predecessor of h_3. Heat h_5 is the best choice. We thus have two possibilities: We can look for a heat that can be processed between h_0 and h_5, or we simply shift h_3 in time. Regarding only the compatibility constraints, the best solution would be to exchange h_5 and h_7. Unfortunately, another constraint is violated in this case: The interval between the heats h_5 and h_6 should be at least 10 hours. Therefore we try to shift heat h_3. Since delivery dates may be shifted up to two hours, we can start with heat h_3 at 9am and start heat h_7 after h_3. The result is the schedule shown in table 6.

Every exchange of jobs in the schedule can be interpreted as one operator in a search process. The search for better schedules can be guided by heuristics based on our evaluation function. This heuristic search is a kind of hill climbing method. Unfortunately, the disadvantage of a hill climbing method is that it can be caught in local maxima. In [Glover 1989a, Glover 1989b] a technique called TABU search is described that can be used to overcome this problem.

The search will end if no further constraint violations can be detected any more, or no further improvement

Table 5: Intermediate Schedule For Example Heats

compatibility:	high	medium	low	medium	high	low
	h_0	h_5	h_7	h_3	h_4	h_1	h_6
time:	5am	7am	9am	11am	1pm	3pm	5pm

Table 6: Final Schedule For Example Heats

compatibility:	high	high	high	medium	high	low
	h_0	h_5	h_3	h_7	h_4	h_1	h_6
time:	5am	7am	9am	11am	1pm	3pm	5pm

can be achieved. It is not that easy to predict that no further improvement can be achieved. In this case it makes sense to define a distance function between an optimal schedule where all compatibilities would be very high, and all the other constraints would be observed too. If we have such a distance function, we can restrict the search effort by a ratio between distance and search effort. It would be fruitless to invest much more search effort if only a small distance exists. On the other hand, if the distance is large, one should search longer for a better schedule.

3   CONCLUSION

Due to the highly unreliable knowledge and conflicting objectives in scheduling applications, mathematical-analytical methods as used in Operation Research approaches are insufficient in many cases. We have illustrated this very problem for a steelmaking plant. In order to overcome this deficiency we have developed a solution which combines two practical AI-techniques for problem solving: Approximate reasoning and constraint relaxation.

Our applied knowledge representation technique, namely fuzzy sets, covers the vagueness of domain knowledge and supports the straightforward generation of a schedule based on the importance of the jobs considered. However, due to this ad hoc generation of schedules, some jobs usually remain unscheduled. In order to utilize the compatibility of jobs, we have also proposed a control strategy, which comprises several types of constraints (organizational, spatial, chemical), and supports the dynamic relaxation of conflicting constraints.

This control strategy can be used to handle emergency cases, too. Hence, it becomes possible to react to events in the course of job execution. In particular, improper conditions for subsequent jobs, require immediate and dynamic adaptation, i.e. reactivity in scheduling. We have achieved this adaptation by supporting the human expert in relaxing those conditions which may solve the case at hand. Using this approach, it becomes possible to evaluate possible scenarios before

actual activities are performed. We call this kind of problem solving 'what-if' games. Such a simulation prevents the human expert from causing more troubles by an improper decision. Finally, the decision process is more transparent.

However, in order to support the evaluation and experiments with different constellations of chemical elements as well as constraints concerning the production, we have to develop a sophisticated interaction concept. In particular, the condition membership function for inference rules as shown in table 2 should remain under complete control of the human expert. The compatibility rule, the element constellation, the shape of the membership functions, and the weights of the fuzzy inference rules should be considered in the course of what-if games with the schedule to support estimates of schedule modifications. The condition membership functions in table 2 for example are to be adapted for each element in two ways. First, their general shape can be altered in order to get sharper or softer transitions from one linguistic variable to the next. Second, the compatibility rule can be changed for one element from 3% to 2.5%, which would mean that this latter element does not remain in the furnace as a residual to the same extent as the other. Additionally, the relative weights of the fuzzy inference rules can be changed to better represent the relative importance of the playing factors, e.g., the work load constraint could be classified more important and thus receive higher weights than chemical constraints. All these adaptations need a lot of tuning, therefore the engineers should have the opportunity to experiment with the system in order to be able to match their own way of decision making more accurately. An enriched, spreadsheet-like environment seems to be the proper interaction technique for this type of correlated information. In such an environment, the change of one dimension can be traced simultaneously with the remaining dimensions. This immediate feedback enhances considerably the way the engineers can experiment with their assumptions in order to find better values for the system's parameters.

Our team currently is composed of ten members working on the realization of a similar scheduling environment in a steel plant of the Austrian Industries holding. Based on an existing scheduling expert system developed by their industrial construction department that was eventually not adopted by the steelmaking plant because of problems with vague data handling and an inappropriate user interface, we now intend to build a general fuzzy-scheduling environment to support the development of other expert systems in the domain of industrial production scheduling. We believe that, using the described techniques, the development cycle for scheduling expert system becomes shorter, and the knowledge representation is facilitated. Moreover, we assume that with the given techniques, better schedules can be generated.

References

[Bel 1989] G. Bel, E. Bensana, D. Dubois, J. Erschler and P. Esquirol: "A Knowledge-Based Approach to Industrial Job-Shop Scheduling" In: *Knowledge-Based Systems in Manufacturing, Andrew Kusiak (ed.)*, Taylor & Francis, pp 207–246, 1989.

[Chen 1987] Dahai Chen, Yuhuan Pan and Jinsong Xue: "A Fuzzy Production System with Backtracking Control Strategy for Multiobjective Scheduling to a One-Machine-N-Parts Problem" In: *Modern Production Management Systems, Andrew Kusiak (ed.)*, Elsevier, pp 135–145, 1987.

[Dorn 1991] Jürgen Dorn and Reza Shams: "An Expert System for Scheduling in a Steelmaking Plant" In: *Proceedings of the World Congress on Expert Systems, Orlando Fla.*, Pergamon Press, 1991.

[Dubois 1989a] Didier Dubois: "Fuzzy Knowledge in an Artificial Intelligence System for Job-Shop Scheduling" In: *Applications of Fuzzy Set Methodologies in Industrial Engineering, Gerald W. Evans et al. (eds.)*, Elsevier, pp 73–89, 1989.

[Dubois 1989b] Didier Dubois and Henri Prade: "Processing Fuzzy Temporal Knowledge" In: *IEEE Transactions on Systems, Man, and Cybernetics, Vol. 19, No. 4*, pp 729–744, July/August 1989.

[Fox 1987] Mark S. Fox: *Constraint-Directed Search: A Case Study of Job-Shop Scheduling.* Pitman, London, 1987.

[Fox 1990] Mark S. Fox and Norman Sadeh: "Why Is Scheduling Difficult? A CSP Perspective" In: *Proceedings of the European Conference on Artificial Intelligence*, pp 754–767, 1990.

[Garey 1979] Michael R. Garey and David S. Johnson: *Computers And Intractability: A Guide to the Theory of NP-Completeness.* Freeman and Co., 1979.

[Glover 1989a] Fred Glover: "Tabu Search–Part I" In: *ORSA Journal on Computing, Vol. 1, No. 3*, pp 190–206, 1989.

[Glover 1989b] Fred Glover: "Tabu Search–Part II" In: *ORSA Journal on Computing, Vol. 2, No. 1*, pp 4–32, 1989.

[Kanemoto 1990] Michitaka Kanemoto, Hiroshi Yamane, Tooru Yoshida and Hideo Tottori: "An Application of Expert System to LD Converter Processes" In: *Journal of the Iron and Steel Institute of Japan, ISIJ International, Vol. 30, No. 2*, pp 128–135, 1990.

[Kerr 1989] R. M. Kerr and R. N. Walker: "A Job Shop Scheduling System Based on Fuzzy Arithmetic" In: *Proceedings of the 2nd International Conference on Expert Systems and Leading Edge in Production and Operations Management, Hilton Head Island, S.C.*, pp 433–450, May 1989.

[Maki 1989] Yunosuke Maki, Yasuo Masuda, T. Sawada, T. Matsumoto, Hiroshi Obata and N. Takashima: "Application of Fuzzy Theory for Automatic Control of Hot Stove Combustion Gas Flow" In: *Proceedings of the 6th IFAC Symposium on Automation in Mining, Mineral and Metal Processing (IFAC MMM 1989), 4–8 September 1989, Buenos Aires, Argentina*, pp 278–284, 1989.

[Negoita 1985] Constantin V. Negoiţă: *Expert Sytems and Fuzzy Systems.* Benjamin/Cummings 1985.

[Prade 1979] Henri Prade: "Using Fuzzy Set Theory in a Scheduling Problem: A Case Study" In: *Fuzzy Sets and Systems, Vol. 2, No. 2*, pp 153–165, April 1979.

[Prosser 1989] Patrick Prosser: "A Reactive Scheduling Agent" In: *Proceedings of the Eleventh International Joint Conference on Artificial Intelligence*, pp 1004–1009, 1989.

[Smith 1986] Stephen F. Smith, Mark S. Fox and Peng Si Ow: "Constructing and Maintaining Detailed Construction Plans: Investigations into the Development of Knowledge-Based Factory Scheduling Systems" In: *AI Magazine 7(4) Fall*, pp 45–61, 1986.

[Zadeh 1989] Lotfi A. Zadeh: "Knowledge Representation in Fuzzy Logic" In: *IEEE Transactions on Knowledge and Data Engineering, Vol. 1, No. 1*, pp 89–100, March 1989.

When is Planning Decidable?*

Kutluhan Erol
kutluhan@cs.umd.edu

Dana S. Nau†
nau@cs.umd.edu

V. S. Subrahmanian‡
vs@cs.umd.edu

Computer Science Department
University of Maryland
College Park, MD 20742

Abstract

In this paper, we show conditions under which planning is decidable and undecidable. Our results on this topic solve an open problem posed in (Chapman 1987), and clear up some difficulties with his undecidability theorems.

1 Introduction

Much planning research has been motivated, in one way or another, by the difficulty of producing complete and correct plans. For example, abstraction (Sacerdoti 1974, Charniak & McDermott 1985, Nilsson 1980, Tate *et al.* 1990) and task reduction (Sacerdoti 1975, Charniak & McDermott 1985, Tate *et al.* 1990) were developed in an effort to make planning more efficient, and concepts such as deleted-condition interactions were developed to describe situations which make planning difficult.

Here we examine how the decidability of domain-independent planning depends on the nature of the planning operators. We consider planning problems in which the current state is a set of ground atoms, and each planning operator is a STRIPS-style operator consisting of three lists of atoms: a precondition list, an add list, and a delete list. Our results can be summarized as follows:

1. If function symbols are allowed or if the language contains infinitely many constant symbols, then determining, in general, whether a plan exists is *undecidable* (more specifically, semidecidable)[1]. This is true even if we have no delete lists and the precondition list of each operator contains at most one (non-negated) atom. If no function symbols are allowed and only finitely many constant symbols are allowed, then plan existence is *decidable*, regardless of the presence or absence of delete lists.

2. The above results resolve an open problem stated by Chapman in (Chapman 1987): whether or not planning is undecidable if the initial state is finite. If the initial state is finite and the language has finitely many ground terms, then the general planning problem is decidable, but if the initial state is finite and the language has infinitely many ground terms, then planning is undecidable in general.

3. Chapman's Second Undecidability Theorem states that "planning is undecidable even with a finite initial situation if the action representation is extended to represent actions whose effects are a function of their situation" (Chapman 1987). This theorem, as stated, is misleading. Whether or not planning is undecidable has nothing to do with whether or not the operators have conditional effects—instead, planning is decidable if and only if the language contains finitely many ground terms.

Section 2 contains the basic definitions. Section 3 contains the decidability and undecidability results, and Section 4 compares and contrasts them with Chapman's results. Section 5 contains concluding remarks. For proofs of the theorems, the reader is referred to (Erol *et al.* 1991).

2 Preliminaries

Throughout this section, we let $\mathcal{L}$ be an ordinary first-order language generated by finitely many constant,

---

*This work was supported in part by NSF Grant NSFD CDR-88003012 to the University of Maryland Systems Research Center, as well as NSF grants IRI-8907890 and IRI-9109755.

†Also in the Systems Research Center and the Institute for Advanced Computer Studies.

‡Also in the Institute for Advanced Computer Studies

[1]The formal definition of the plan existence problem is given at the end of the section entitled "Preliminaries."

Fig. 1: Initial   Fig. 2: Goal
configuration   configuration

function and predicate symbols. $\mathcal{L}$ has an infinite number of variable symbols together with the usual logical symbols.

A *state* is a set of ground atoms. Intuitively, a state tells us which ground atoms are currently true. Thus, if a ground atom A is in state S, then A is true in state S; if $B \notin S$, then B is false in state S. Thus, a state is simply an Herbrand interpretation for the language $\mathcal{L}$, and hence each formula of first-order logic is either satisfied or not satisfied in S according to the usual first-order logic definition of satisfaction.

We consider a STRIPS-style *planning operator* α to be a 4-tuple $(\mathrm{Name}(\alpha), \mathrm{Pre}(\alpha), \mathrm{Add}(\alpha), \mathrm{Del}(\alpha))$, where

1. $\mathrm{Name}(\alpha)$ is a syntactic expression of the form $\alpha(X_1, \ldots, X_n)$ where each X_i is a variable symbol of $\mathcal{L}$;

2. $\mathrm{Pre}(\alpha)$ is a finite set of literals, called the *precondition list* of α, whose variables are all from the set $\{X_1, \ldots, X_n\}$;

3. $\mathrm{Add}(\alpha)$ and $\mathrm{Del}(\alpha)$ are both finite sets of atoms (possibly non-ground) whose variables are taken from the set $\{X_1, \ldots, X_n\}$. $\mathrm{Add}(\alpha)$ is called the *add list* of α, and $\mathrm{Del}(\alpha)$ is called the *delete list* of α.

Observe that atoms and negated atoms may occur in the precondition list, but negated atoms may not occur in either the add list or the delete list.

A *planning domain* is a pair $\mathbf{P} = (S_0, \mathcal{O})$, where S_0 is the *initial state* and $\mathcal{O}$ is a finite set of operators. A *goal* is an existentially closed conjunction of atoms. A *planning problem* is a triple $\mathbf{P} = (S_0, \mathcal{O}, G)$, where $(S_0, \mathcal{O})$ is a planning domain and G is a goal.

Example 1 (Blocks World) Consider a blocks-world domain containing three blocks a, b, c, along with Nilsson's "stack", "unstack", "pickup", and "putdown" operators (Nilsson 1980). Suppose the initial and goal configurations are as shown in Figs. 1 and 2. This domain can be represented as follows:

- *Language.* The language $\mathcal{L}$ contains a supply of variable symbols $X_1, X_2, \ldots$, and three constant symbols a, b, c to represent the three blocks. $\mathcal{L}$ contains a binary predicate symbol "on", unary predicate symbols "ontable", "clear", and "holding", and a 0-ary predicate symbol "handempty". Operator names, such as "stack", "unstack", etc., are not part of $\mathcal{L}$.

- *Operators.* The "unstack" operator is the following 4-tuple (the "stack", "pickup", and "putdown" operators are defined analogously):

  Name : $\mathrm{unstack}(X_1, X_2)$
  Pre $\{\mathrm{on}(X_1, X_2), \mathrm{clear}(X_1), \mathrm{handempty}()\}$
  Del : $\{\mathrm{on}(X_1, X_2), \mathrm{clear}(X_1), \mathrm{handempty}()\}$
  Add : $\{\mathrm{clear}(X_2), \mathrm{holding}(X_1)\}$

- *Planning Domain.* The planning domain is $(S_0, \mathcal{O})$, where S_0 and $\mathcal{O}$ are as follows:

$$S_0 = \{\mathrm{clear}(a), \mathrm{on}(a,b), \mathrm{ontable}(b),$$
$$\mathrm{clear}(c), \mathrm{ontable}(c), \mathrm{handempty}()\};$$
$$\mathcal{O} = \{\mathrm{stack}, \mathrm{unstack}, \mathrm{pickup}, \mathrm{putdown}\}.$$

- *Planning Problem.* The planning problem is $(S_0, \mathcal{O}, G)$, where $G = \{\mathrm{on}(b, c)\}$.

Let $\mathbf{P} = (S_0, \mathcal{O})$ be a planning domain, α be an operator in $\mathcal{O}$ whose name is $\alpha(X_1, \ldots, X_n)$, and θ be a substitution that assigns ground terms to each $X_i, 1 \leq i \leq n$. Suppose that the following conditions hold:

$$\{A\theta \mid A \text{ is an atom in } \mathrm{Pre}(\alpha)\} \subseteq S;$$
$$\{B\theta \mid \neg B \text{ is a negated literal in } \mathrm{Pre}(\alpha)\} \cap S = \emptyset;$$
$$S' = (S - (\mathrm{Del}(\alpha)\theta)) \cup (\mathrm{Add}(\alpha))\theta.$$

Then we say that α is *θ-executable* in state S, *resulting in state S'*. This is denoted symbolically as $S \stackrel{\alpha, \theta}{\Longrightarrow} S'$.

Suppose $\mathbf{P} = (S_0, \mathcal{O})$ is a planning domain and G is a goal. A *plan that achieves* G is a sequence $S_0, \ldots, S_n, S_{n+1}$ of states, a sequence $\alpha_0, \ldots, \alpha_n$ of planning operators, and a sequence $\theta_0, \ldots, \theta_n$ of substitutions such that

$$S_0 \stackrel{\alpha_0, \theta_0}{\Longrightarrow} S_1 \stackrel{\alpha_1, \theta_1}{\Longrightarrow} S_2 \cdots \stackrel{\alpha_n, \theta_n}{\Longrightarrow} S_{n+1} \qquad (1)$$

and G is satisfied by S_n, i.e. there exists a ground instance of G that is true in S_n. The *length* of the above plan is n.

We will often say that (1) above is a plan that achieves G.

Let $\mathbf{P} = (S_0, \mathcal{O})$ be a planning domain or $\mathbf{P} = (S_0, \mathcal{O}, G)$ be a planning problem; and let $\mathcal{L}$ be the language of $\mathbf{P}$. Then:

1. $\mathcal{O}$ (and thus $\mathbf{P}$) is *positive* if for all $\alpha \in \mathcal{O}$, $\mathrm{Pre}(\alpha)$ is a finite set of *atoms* (i.e. negations are not present in $\mathrm{Pre}(\alpha)$).

2. $\mathcal{O}$ (and thus $\mathbf{P}$) is *deletion-free* if for all $\alpha \in \mathcal{O}$, $\mathrm{Del}(\alpha) = \emptyset$.

3. $\mathcal{O}$ (and thus $\mathbf{P}$) is *context-free* if for all $\alpha \in \mathcal{O}$, $|\mathrm{Pre}(\alpha)| \leq 1$, i.e., $\mathrm{Pre}(\alpha)$ contains at most one atom.

4. $\mathcal{O}$ (and thus $\mathbf{P}$) is *side-effect-free* if for all $\alpha \in \mathcal{O}$, $|\text{Add}(\alpha) \cup \text{Del}(\alpha)| \leq 1$, i.e., α has at most one postcondition.

5. $\mathcal{L}$ (and thus $\mathbf{P}$) is *function-free* if $\mathcal{L}$ contains no function symbols.

PLAN EXISTENCE is the following problem: "given as input, a planning problem $\mathbf{P} = (S_0, \mathcal{O}, G)$, is there a plan in $\mathbf{P}$ that achieves G?" It is important to note that in this formulation, planning is undecidable if there is no algorithm that halts on *all* possible input values of S_0, $\mathcal{O}$ and G. The fact that certain specific planning *domains* are decidable does not mean that the general planning problem, where arbitrary planning domains may occur in the input, is decidable.

3 Decidability and Undecidability Results

In this section, we show that logic programming is essentially the same as planning without delete lists. This is established by showing how to transform a deletion-free planning domain into a logic program such that for all goals G, the goal G is achievable from the planning domain iff the logical query that G represents is provable from the corresponding logic program.[2] As a consequence of this equivalence, we can use results on the complexity of logic programs and deductive databases to demonstrate the following results:

- PLAN EXISTENCE is *undecidable*, even if all operators have at most one precondition, and regardless of whether the operators have delete lists and/or negative preconditions.

- PLAN EXISTENCE is *decidable* if our first-order language contains no function symbols and is finitely generated (in particular, this means that only finitely many constants are present in the language). The presence or absence of delete lists does not affect the decidability result.

---

[2]This should be intuitively true, anyway, but the formal establishment of this equivalence is necessary before attempting to apply results from logic programming and deductive databases to planning problems. An important point to note is that we will only be considering truth in *Herbrand* models (cf. Shoenfield 1967) in this paper. It doesn't make much sense to consider non-Herbrand models for planning problems because the domains of such models often contain objects that do not occur in the language. In the case of blocks world, for instance, this corresponds to assuming (inside the model) that there are blocks on the table that cannot be referred to in the language. Obviously, this is not relevant to planning. Thus, when we talk of logical consequences of programs, we will be referring to those sentences that are true in all Herbrand models of the program. For function-free languages, this condition is well known to yield decidability of logical consequence (Plaisted 1984, Vardi 1982).

- When our planning domain $\mathbf{P} = (S_0, \mathcal{O})$ is fixed in advance, then the problem "given goal G, does there exist a plan that achieves G?" may still be undecidable depending on $\mathbf{P}$. The presence or absence of delete lists does not affect this result.

We now proceed to establish the equivalence between logic programming and planning without delete lists. Subsequently, we show how to do away with delete lists when function symbols are absent.

If $\mathbf{P}$ is deletion-free, then the *logic program translation* of an operator $\alpha \in \mathcal{O}$, denoted by $\text{LP}(\alpha)$, is the set of clauses

$$\text{LP}(\alpha) = \{(\forall)(A \leftarrow B_1 \,\&\, \ldots \,\&\, B_n) \mid A \in \text{Add}(\alpha)\},$$

where $\text{Pre}(\alpha) = \{B_1, \ldots, B_n\}$. The *logic program translation* of $\mathbf{P} = (S_0, \mathcal{O})$, denoted $\text{LP}(\mathbf{P})$, is the set of clauses

$$\text{LP}(\mathbf{P}) = S_0 \cup \bigcup_{\alpha \in \mathcal{O}} \text{LP}(\alpha).$$

Remark 1 Note that if we consider planning domains $\mathbf{P} = (S_0, \mathcal{O})$ where S_0 is infinite, then $\text{LP}(\mathbf{P})$ would contain infinitely many unit clauses. The infinite nature of $\text{LP}(\mathbf{P})$ will turn out to be irrelevant when $\mathbf{P} = (S_0, \mathcal{O})$ contains no operators that have negations in their preconditions. This irrelevance is due to the compactness theorem for first-order logic.

Lemma 1 Suppose that $\mathbf{P} = (S_0, \mathcal{O})$ is any *positive, deletion-free* planning domain, and

$$S_0 \overset{\alpha_0, \theta_0}{\Longrightarrow} S_1 \overset{\alpha_1, \theta_1}{\Longrightarrow} S_2 \cdots \overset{\alpha_n, \theta_n}{\Longrightarrow} S_{n+1}$$

is a plan that achieves some goal G (we really don't care what G is as far as this lemma is concerned). Then:

1. $S_0 \subseteq S_1 \subseteq S_2 \cdots \subseteq S_{n+1}$.

2. If operator α is θ-executable in state S_j, then α is θ-executable in state S_k for all $k \geq j$.

If $\mathbf{P} = (S_0, \mathcal{O})$ is a positive deletion-free planning domain, then $\text{LP}(\mathbf{P})$ is a *pure* (i.e., negation-free) logic program. The following theorem shows that achievability of a goal G in $\mathbf{P}$ is identical to provability of G from $\text{LP}(\mathbf{P})$.

Theorem 1 (Equivalence Theorem) Suppose $\mathbf{P} = (S_0, \mathcal{O})$ is a positive, deletion-free planning domain and G is a goal. Then there is a plan to achieve G from $\mathbf{P}$ iff $\text{LP}(\mathbf{P}) \models G$.

Corollary 1 (Semi-Decidability Results)

1. $\{G \mid G$ is an existential goal such that there is a plan to achieve G from $\mathbf{P} = (S_0, \mathcal{O})\}$ is a recursively enumerable subset of the set of all goals.

2. Given any recursively enumerable collection X of ground atoms (which, of course, are goals), there is a positive deletion-free planning domain $\mathbf{P} = (S_0, \mathcal{O})$ such that $\{A \mid A$ is a ground atom such that there is a plan to achieve A from $\mathbf{P}\} = X$

3. If we restrict $\mathbf{P}$ to be positive and deletion-free, then PLAN EXISTENCE is strictly semi-decidable.

Corollary 2 The problem "given a positive deletion-free planning domain $\mathbf{P} = (S_0, \mathcal{O})$, is the set of goals achievable from $\mathbf{P}$ decidable?" is Π_2^0-complete.

Corollary 3 If we restrict $\mathbf{P}$ to be positive, deletion-free, and context-free, then PLAN EXISTENCE is still strictly semi-decidable.

Corollary 4 Suppose $\mathbf{P} = (S_0, \mathcal{O})$ is a fixed positive, deletion-free planning domain. Then the problem: "given a goal G, does there exist a plan to achieve G?" is decidable iff the set of goals provable from $LP(\mathbf{P})$ is decidable.

Theorem 1 holds only when $\mathbf{P}$ is positive. The reason for this is that if $\mathbf{P}$ is not positive, then $LP(\mathbf{P})$ is a logic program that may contain negation in its body. Logic programming interprets negation in $LP(\mathbf{P})$ as "failure to prove", which is different than the interpretation of negation in the planning domain $\mathbf{P}$. Intuitively, negation in logic programming says "conclude $\neg p$ if it is impossible to prove p". The corresponding notion of negation in planning would be "conclude $\neg p$ if there is no plan to achieve p" which is much stronger than saying "p is false in the current state." Thus, if $\mathbf{P}$ is not positive, then in some cases G will be achievable in $\mathbf{P}$ but $LP(\mathbf{P}) \models G$ will be false. To see this, consider the following example:

Example 2 Consider the planning domain $\mathbf{P} = (S_0, \mathcal{O})$ that contains the two operators α_1, α_2 described below:

$$\text{Pre}(\alpha_1) = \{\neg b\}, \qquad \text{Add}(\alpha_1) = \{a\}$$
$$\text{Pre}(\alpha_2) = \{c\}, \qquad \text{Add}(\alpha_2) = \{b\}$$

Suppose our initial state is the state $\{c\}$. Clearly, there is a plan to achieve a by simply executing operation α_1 in the initial state.

Now consider $LP(\mathbf{P})$, which is the logic program:

$$a \leftarrow \neg b$$
$$b \leftarrow c$$
$$c \leftarrow$$

The set of atoms provable from this program according to logic programming (all major semantics for logic programs agree on this) is $\{b, c\}$, i.e. a cannot be obtained even though our planning domain admits a plan that achieves a.

Lemma 2 Suppose I is a decidable Herbrand interpretation, i.e. I is a decidable set of ground atoms, and G is a goal. Then

1. The problem "is goal G true in interpretation I?" is semi-decidable.

2. If the language $\mathcal{L}$ is known to be function free, then the above problem is decidable.

Theorem 2 (Decidability of Deletion-Free, Function-Free Planning) If we restrict $\mathbf{P}$ to be deletion-free and function-free, then PLAN EXISTENCE is decidable.

Theorem 3 (Theorem on Infinite Initial States) PLAN EXISTENCE is semi-decidable if we restrict $\mathbf{P} = (S_0, \mathcal{O})$ to be positive and deletion-free, and S_0 to be a *decidable* set of ground atoms of language $\mathcal{L}$ (even though S_0 may be infinite).

We now show that when $\mathcal{L}$ contains no function symbols, we can do away with delete lists. The idea is intuitively the same as that of Green (Green 1969, Nilsson 1980) (vis-a-vis the famous "Green's formulation of planning"), with one difference: Green introduces function symbols even if the original language contained none: we introduce new constants. When the language is function-free, only finitely many new constants are included.

Theorem 4 (Eliminating Delete Lists) Suppose $\mathbf{P}$ is a function-free planning domain. Then there is a positive deletion-free planning domain $\mathbf{P}' = (S_0', \mathcal{O}')$ such that for each goal $G \equiv (\exists)(A_1 \& \ldots \& A_n)$, there is a goal $G' \equiv (\exists)(A_1' \& \ldots \& A_n' \& \text{poss}(S))$, where "poss" is a new unary predicate symbol and for all $1 \le i \le n$, if $A_i \equiv p(t_1, \ldots, t_n)$, then $A_i' \equiv p(t_1, \ldots, t_n, S)$ where S is a variable symbol. Furthermore, G is achievable from $\mathbf{P}$ iff G' is achievable from $\mathbf{P}'$.

An important point to note is that even though delete lists may be removed, the size of $\mathbf{P}'$ is much larger than $\mathbf{P}$.

Theorem 5 (Decidability of Function-Free Planning) If we restrict $\mathbf{P}$ to be function-free, then PLAN EXISTENCE is decidable.

4   Chapman's Undecidability Results

To date, the best-known results on decidability and undecidability in planning systems are those of (Chapman 1987). However, there is a certain amount of confusion about what Chapman's undecidability results actually say, because some of his assumptions become clear only after a careful reading of the paper. To clarify the meaning of Chapman's undecidability results, we now compare and contrast his results with ours.

First Undecidability Theorem. Chapman's first undecidability theorem (Chapman 1987, pp. 370–371) says that all Turing machines with their inputs may be encoded as planning problems in the TWEAK representation, and hence planning is undecidable. Our results compare and contrast with this result in the following respects:

1. Chapman assumes that "an infinite set of constants t_i are used to represent the tape squares" (Chapman 1987, p. 371), but in his discussion of the result, he points out that this set of constants is recursive.

   Our language $\mathcal{L}$ contains only finitely many constants, but it may contain function symbols. This is essentially the same as having a recursive set of constants, because the function symbols can be used to generate countably many ground terms. Thus in this respect, our result doesn't differ from Chapman's first undecidability theorem.

2. Chapman uses an infinite initial state to prove his result. In particular, "there must be countably many successor propositions to encode the topology of the tape (and also countably many contents propositions to make all but finitely many squares blank)" (Chapman 1987, p. 371). He also says (Chapman 1987, p.344):

   > This result is weaker than it may appear ... the proof uses an infinite (though recursive) initial state to model the connectivity of the tape. It may be that if problems are restricted to have finite initial states, planning is decidable. (This is not obviously true though. There are infinitely many constants, and an action can in effect "gensym" one by referring to a variable in its post-conditions that is not mentioned in its preconditions.)

We now describe how our results solve the open problem posed in the above quote.

First, our Corollary 1 shows that if the language contains infinitely many ground terms, then planning is undecidable even if initial states are finite. This is true regardless of whether the infinite number of ground terms occurs because infinitely many constants are present in the language as is the case with (Chapman 1987), or because there are finitely many constants together with finitely many function symbols, as is true in our case.

Second, our result Theorem 5 shows that if the language contains only finitely many ground terms, then planning is decidable. Planning with only finitely many ground terms in the language makes a lot of sense, because it applies to all domains where a finitely bounded number of "entities" are being manipulated (the usual formulation of the blocks world is one such example). We

can make the number of these entities large, but as long as we keep it finite, these results apply.

3. Our Corollaries 1 and 3 demonstrate that planning with infinitely many terms is undecidable in general even if every planning operator contains no delete lists, at most one positive precondition, and no negative preconditions. Chapman's result (Chapman 1987, p. 371) is more restrictive: he needs four preconditions, and he explicitly uses negative post-conditions, which is equivalent to having delete lists.

Second Undecidability Theorem. The statement of Chapman's second undecidability theorem is that "planning is undecidable even with a finite initial state if the action representation is extended to represent actions whose effects are a function of their input situation" (Chapman 1987, p. 373). From his discussion on p. 371, it appears that Chapman is referring to the following kind of conditional operator:

> Name: $\alpha(...)$
> **if** P_α **then** add A_α and delete D_α
>   **else** add A'_α and delete D'_α

where P is a set of literals, and A_α, D_α, A'_α, and D'_α are sets of atoms.

A careful reading of Chapman's proof makes it clear that there is an additional assumption. In his proof, he makes use of operators that increment and decrement two counters, but there is no upper bound on the value of those counters—and thus it is necessary that the language contain infinitely many terms. But if there are infinitely many terms, then our Corollary 1 shows that planning is undecidable even with ordinary STRIPS-style planning operators.

On the other hand, suppose that the language contains only finitely many terms, but that there are conditional operators of the kind described above. Let α be any one of these conditional operators, and suppose that $P_\alpha = \{p_1, p_2, \ldots, p_n\}$. We now define an equivalent set of STRIPS-style operators $\{\alpha_N | N \subseteq P_\alpha\}$, none of which has conditional effects.

$\alpha_\emptyset$ is the following operator:

$$
\begin{array}{rl}
\text{Name}: & \alpha_0(\ldots) \\
\text{Pre}: & P_\alpha \\
\text{Add}: & A_\alpha \\
\text{Del}: & D_\alpha
\end{array}
$$

For every nonempty set $N \subseteq P$, α_N is the following operator:

$$
\begin{array}{rl}
\text{Name}: & \alpha_i(\ldots) \\
\text{Pre}: & \{\neg p_i | p_i \in N\} \cup (P - N) \\
\text{Add}: & A'_\alpha \\
\text{Del}: & D'_\alpha
\end{array}
$$

The set of "unconditional" operators $\{\alpha_N | N \subseteq P\}$ is equivalent to α, in the sense that $S \overset{\alpha,\theta}{\Longrightarrow} S'$ if and only if there is exactly one α_i that is θ-executable in S, and $S \overset{\alpha_i,\theta}{\Longrightarrow} S'$.

Replacing each conditional operator by the equivalent set of unconditional operators produces a planning domain whose language has finitely many ground terms—and according to Theorem 5, planning is decidable for such domains.

From the above, it follows that the statement of Chapman's Second Undecidability Theorem is misleading. His proof of undecidability has nothing to do with whether the operators are conditional—it instead depends on the fact that his planning domain requires an infinite number of terms.

5 Conclusion

The primary aim of this paper has been to examine the decidability of planning with STRIPS-style planning operators (i.e., operators comprised of preconditions, add lists, and delete lists).

Our primary result is that planning is decidable if and only if the language has finitely many ground terms. This relates in several ways to Chapman's work (Chapman 1987):

1. It solves an open problem posed in (Chapman 1987), regarding the decidability of planning with a finite initial state. The answer depends on whether the language has finitely many ground terms.

2. It shows that one of the results in (Chapman 1987) is misleading. The undecidability of planning with STRIPS-style operators has nothing to do with the presence or absence of conditional effects. If the language has finitely many ground terms, then planning is decidable even if the operators have conditional effects. If the language has infinitely many ground terms, then planning is undecidable even if no operators have no conditional effects, no delete lists, and no negative preconditions.

References

H.A. Blair. "Canonical Conservative Extensions of Logic Program Completions," *Proc. 4th IEEE Symposium on Logic Programming*, 1989, pp. 154–161.

Eugene Charniak and Drew McDermott. *Introduction to Artificial Intelligence*. Addison-Wesley, Reading, MA, 1985.

D. Chapman. "Planning for Conjunctive Goals," *Artificial Intelligence* **32**, 1987, pp. 333-377.

K. Erol, D. S. Nau, and V. S. Subrahmanian. "Complexity, Decidability and Undecidability Results for First-Order Planning," submitted for journal publication, 1991.

C. Green. "Application of Theorem-Proving to Problem Solving," *Proc. IJCAI-69*, 1969.

Naresh Gupta and Dana S. Nau. "Complexity results for blocks-world planning," *Proc. AAAI-91*, 1991. Honorable mention for the best paper award.

Naresh Gupta and Dana S. Nau, *Artificial Intelligence*, accepted for publication, 1992.

N. J. Nilsson 1980. *Principles of Artificial Intelligence*. Tioga, Palo Alto, 1980.

Earl D. Sacerdoti. "Planning in a hierarcy of abstraction spaces." In James Allen, James Hendler, and Austin Tate, editors, *Readings in Planning*, pages 98–108. Morgan Kaufman, 1990. Originally appeared in *Artificial Intelligence* **5** (1974), 115–135.

D.A. Plaisted. "Complete Problems in the First-Order Predicate Calculus," *Jour. Computer and Systems Sciences* **29** (1984), pp. 8–35.

Earl D. Sacerdoti. "The nonlinear nature of plans." In James Allen, James Hendler, and Austin Tate, editors, *Readings in Planning*, pages 206–214. Morgan Kaufman, 1990. Originally appeared in *Proc. IJCAI-75*.

J. Sebelik and P. Stepanek. "Horn Clause Programs for Recursive Functions." In K. Clark and S.-A. Tarnlund, editors, *Logic Programming*, pp. 325–340, Academic Press, 1980.

J. Shoenfield. *Mathematical Logic*, Academic Press, 1967.

A. Tate, J. Hendler, and M. Drummond. "A review of AI planning techniques." In James Allen, James Hendler, and Austin Tate, editors, *Readings in Planning*, pages 26–49. Morgan Kaufman, 1990.

M. Vardi. "The Complexity of Relational Query Languages," *Proc. 14th ACM Symp. on Theory of Computing*, San Francisco, 1982, pp. 137–146.

A Semi-Reactive Planner
Based on a Possible Models Action Formalization

Sylvie Thiébaux*
Computer Science Department
FIT
Melbourne, FL 32901-6988, U.S.A.
e-mail: sylvie@cs.fit.edu

Joachim Hertzberg
AI Research Division
GMD
5205 Sankt Augustin 1, F.R.G.
e-mail: hertz@gmdzi.gmd.de

Abstract

We describe the basics of a semi-reactive planner that is based on a possible models action formalization. By semi-reactive planner, we mean a planning system that is able to incrementally generate plans in a classical way, thereby extending, when necessary, the compiled knowledge available for reactive execution. The action formalization, which is a correction of the possible worlds approach by Ginsberg and Smith, allows one to cope with lacking information, ambiguity and context dependency in the planning domain by considering different courses of action. This enables the planner to handle certain forms of uncertainty at planning time. Plans developed under this model are compiled into finite state automata for execution, as a basis for reacting to less expected effects at execution time. Moreover, we explain how replanning fits into the framework, thereby opening it towards handling unexpected effects which occur during plan execution, and for which no reaction plan is available.

1 MOTIVATION

Much of the more recent work in AI planning can be subsumed under the following two topics, both of which are in fact old, dating back to research on STRIPS [Fikes and Nilsson, 1971; Fikes *et al.*, 1972] and before.

Formalization, i.e., formal calculi for planning, for describing planning systems, or planning using formal calculi for more or less complete parts of a planner. (See [Bibel, 1986], [Lifschitz, 1987], [Reichgelt and Shadbolt, 1990; Chapman, 1987] for examples of the respective directions.) The idea is that formalization helps to understand or to communicate one's

understanding of planning in detail; more practically, descriptions of some degree of formality might be a basis for sound software engineering. Moreover, there is the related work on formalizing action and change, which, however, is not always put into relation to planning as closely as possible. (An example for such work is [Ginsberg and Smith, 1988], which will be talked of later; see [Sandewall, 1991] for further references.)

Reactivity, i.e., reactive planning and reaction planning. ([Schoppers, 1989a], from which we borrow the terminology, contains further references.) The idea is the following. In general, it is wrong to assume that every conceivable course of things can be properly kept track of at planning time and that all and only the events considered at planning time will happen at plan execution time. Reaction planning tackles the problem by (sometimes automatically) encoding goal directed behavior not only for a single planning problem but for whole parts of the problem domain (e.g., [Georgeff and Lansky, 1987; Agre, 1988; Schoppers, 1989b]). Reactive planning follows the idea of providing rough plans that are used, reacting to unforeseen or unforeseeable events in the world at execution time (e.g., [Dean and Boddy, 1988]).

If you agree with the reasons for working on the individual topics, then it seems obvious that their combination is worth being examined; work in this direction is, e.g., [Downs and Reichgelt, 1991]. The objective of the work reported in our paper is to develop a planner exhibiting some degree of reactivity, and having a well defined semantics, not by an *ex post* formalization, but by virtue of being based on a well understood action calculus. You will even notice that our formalization resembles Winslett's [1988] and that the basics of our semi-reactive system is similar to, e.g., Drummond and Bresina's [1990] projection graphs and Kabanza's [1990] world automata. (The differences are sketched in the sections 2 and 3, respectively). However, the point here is not to develop yet another variant of well-known action formalizations or reactive systems, thereby pushing forward reaction planning or planner formalization individually, but to attempt exploring

---

*Work done while the author was at GMD

what Drummond and Bresina [1990] call the

> continuum of plan-guided systems from those ..., where complete plans are produced in advance and later used by independently competent execution systems, to those systems that are embedded in the situations for which their plans are generated.

In particular, we propose to build a semi-reactive planning system, i.e., a system that is able to generate reaction plans to extend its "compiled" knowledge, when no reaction plan is available. Our planner is based on a particular formalization of actions [Brewka and Hertzberg, 1991] that allows taking several forms of uncertainty into account at planning time. In accordance with a theory about the world stating some of the most frequent unwanted effects occuring when applying an action, it develops plans that include alternative actions. As it is unthinkable to envisage *all* possible cases in advance, the remaining part of uncertainty will be handled at execution time, by using the reaction plans available, or by generating new ones incrementally. The reaction plans are represented as classical finite automata.

The computer program PASCALE illustrates and implements the ideas presented here; [Thiébaux, 1991] describes it and elaborates on these ideas.

The paper is organized as follows. In section 2, we present the possible models formalization as the formal background for our approach. Section 3 describes the plan representation we use. In section 4, we describe the concept of a semi-reactive system built within the framework. Section 5 concludes with some notes about related work.

2   A POSSIBLE MODELS FORMALIZATION OF ACTION

To start with, we briefly present the key concepts of the formalization of actions our work is based on. The formalization is described in [Brewka and Hertzberg, 1991] to which we refer for details, a discussion of its strenghts and weaknesses, and a comparison to related work.[1] We first give the intuition of the approach informally, turning to formal definitions afterwards.

---

[1]In [Brewka and Hertzberg, 1991], what we call possible *model* here is called possible *world,* following the terminology of Ginsberg and Smith. To stress the difference to Ginsberg and Smith's approach and the similarity with Winslett's, we change the terminology. Moreover, in view of implementation, we make a few very slight modifications in the formalism described by Brewka and Hertzberg.

2.1   INTUITION

Starting point for our action model is the state based approach of Ginsberg and Smith [1988]. Their idea is to use standard first order logic to model action effects, where the frame problem is solved by making the STRIPS assumption explicit: Given a state, which is described by a set S of formulae (denoting their conjunction), and an action whose postconditions P are also given as a set of formulae, a possible world T for P in S is a maximal consistent subset of $S \cup P$ containing all the formulae in P. That means: Compute $S \cup P$, and then delete non-elements of P from the whole set until the rest is consistent. As there may be different ways to make $S \cup P$ consistent, T is not unique.

The appeal of this formalization is that it looks close to what may be used in a planner implementation. However, it may yield highly unintuitive results, as was first noticed by Winslett [1988] and described in more detail in [Brewka and Hertzberg, 1991]. Ginsberg and Smith's approach tends to have problems with obtaining the intended results of actions in the presence of lacking or ambiguous information about the situation or about action postconditions.

Consider an example. In a room, there are a door and a window, at least one of which is currently open, i.e., $open(d) \vee open(w)$. You are now told that someone has—by an action that may or may not have changed something—cared for the door being closed. Intuitively, only $\neg open(d)$ should be concluded now, as nothing is known about the window. According to Ginsberg and Smith's approach, however, closing the door would magically open the window: as $open(d) \vee open(w)$ and $\neg open(d)$ are consistent, the new information would just be added to the situation description, and $open(w)$ becomes derivable.

As argued in [Winslett, 1988], the remedy for this problem is to calculate successor state descriptions not in terms of sets of arbitrary formulae but in terms of ground instances of literals occurring in the theory. (These can be understood as partial Herbrand models of the theory, hence the term possible *models.*) The idea is that instead of the description S of the recent world state you take the set of possible models of S, which may be unary or not, and apply the action in each of these possible models. Moreover, action effects must be represented as subsets of possible models (partial possible models, for short), not as arbitrary formulae. This is a difference to Winslett's approach, which is necessary to handle alternative action effects properly. Again, see [Brewka and Hertzberg, 1991] for examples and a discussion of this point.

An ambiguous outcome of an action is captured as a set of alternative outcomes, formulated as different partial possible models. The idea of calculating successor states by considering maximally consistent sets of formulae containing the just obtained action effects is imported from Ginsberg and Smith, but is applied only to possible models, not to arbitrary formulae.

In the example of closing the door, the description of the initial situation yields three possible models, involving essentially: either the door is open, or the window is open, or both of them are open. After closing the door, we have two possible worlds, involving essentially: either the door is closed and the window is open, or the door is closed and the window is closed.

We will now describe the basics of the approach formally.

2.2   FORMAL DEFINITION

We assume a first order logical language $\mathcal{L}$ of closed formulae. A subset of $\mathcal{L}$ is the finite set $L = \{s_1, \ldots, s_n\}$ of ground atomic sentences. L must be sufficient to describe all relevant aspects of different states of the world as a conjunction of ground literals l_i built from these atomic sentences, i.e., $l_i = s_i$ or $l_i = \neg s_i$. Each n-elementary conjunction $l_1 \wedge \cdots \wedge l_n$ of literals from all elements of L is called an L-model.[2] If this causes no confusion, we will switch between the conjunctive notation for L-models or partial L-models as defined and set notation, e.g., $\{l_1, \ldots, l_n\}$, which is to be interpreted as the conjunction of its elements.

We assume a set $K \subseteq \mathcal{L}$ representing the domain *background knowledge*, i.e., knowledge about what is true in all situations. Assuming furthermore that a situation is described as a formula of $\mathcal{L}$, we now define

Def. 2.1 (Possible model) *Let $S \in \mathcal{L}$ be a formula and K the background knowledge. The possible models in S with respect to K are*
$Poss_K(S) = \{pm | pm$ *is an L-model and $K \cup \{S\} \cup pm$ is satisfiable.*$\}$

We use $Poss(K)$ as a shorthand for the possible models of the conjuction of formulae in K.

Consider again the door and window world. Let $L_0 = \{open(d), open(w)\}$; the background knowledge $K_0 = \{open(d) \oplus closed(d), open(w) \oplus closed(w)\}$;[3] $\mathcal{L}_0$ is defined appropriately. Let now $S_0 = open(d)$, i.e., all you know is that the door is open. Then
$$Poss_{K_0}(S_0) = \{ \{open(d), open(w)\}, \\ \{open(d), \neg open(w)\} \}$$
The respective complete situation descriptions are obtained using K_0, enforcing, e.g., the conclusion $\neg closed(d)$ in both possible models.

---

[2]This definition clearly overloads the term model which keeps its usual logical definition. The excuse for this overloading is that the concept is very close to the usual notion of Herbrand model and that [Winslett, 1988] does the same. Moreover, there will be no confusion of our models with the usual notion of model as we will primarily use *possible* models, which will be defined next.

[3]⊕ is the exclusive disjunction.

Our actions are generalized variants of STRIPS operators with pre and postconditions, without distinguishing between added and deleted postconditions. We allow for alternative outcomes of actions applied in the same situation; an example is the action of tossing a coin. Independently from that, an action may produce different effects when applied in different situations; consider as an example the action of toggling a lightswitch: the light is on if it was off before, and vice versa. The general format of actions, then, is:

$$[\quad Pre_1 \quad | \quad Post_{1,1}, \ldots, Post_{1,l(1)};$$
$$\vdots$$
$$Pre_m \quad | \quad Post_{m,1}, \ldots, Post_{m,l(m)};$$
$$true \quad | \quad Post_{true} \qquad\qquad]$$

The preconditions Pre_i are arbitrary formulae from $\mathcal{L}$; each postcondition element $Post_{i,j}$ is a set (conjunction) of literals of ground atoms from L. The preconditions are tested in the order they appear. The first precondition that holds determines the possible effects of the action. By default, $Post_{true}$ is the empty set. This captures one of the potential intuitions about what may result from—well—applying an action in a situation where it is not applicable: The action changes nothing. Different intuitions are possible, but this is not an issue here. As a shorthand, the *true* case is skipped, i.e., $[Pre|Post]$ stands for $[Pre|Post; true|\{\}]$. In this action format, nothing is said about the relative probabilities with which the different postconditions in one branch will occur. This might be done along the lines of [Hanks, 1990], but we will not do so here.

As an example, consider the action *nocirculation* of preventing circulation in the door and window world: If the door and window are both open, one of them will be arbitrarily shut, otherwise nothing is done.

$$nocirculation =$$
$$[\; open(d) \wedge open(w) \; | \; \{\neg open(d)\}, \{\neg open(w)\} \;]$$

Note that there is no need to specify that something is closed when it is not open any more: this will follow from the background knowledge. Thus, we provide a solution to both frame and ramification problems. See [Brewka and Hertzberg, 1991] for details about when this solution is sound.

We will now define the result of an action; before doing so, however, we need the intermediate concept of p-conformity for a set of literals p made from L. This is needed to capture the intuition that a possible model, that results from applying an action making p true, contains p but differs as little as possible from the possible model representing the original situation.

Def. 2.2 (Maximal p-conformity)
Let pm and pm' be elements of $Poss(K)$, and p a partial model. pm' is maximally p-conform with pm iff $pm \cap pm'$ is (set inclusion) maximal, subject to the condition that $p \subseteq pm'$.

For example, the possible model $\{open(d), \neg open(w)\}$ is maximally $\{\neg open(w)\}$-conform with the possible model $\{open(d), open(w)\}$, whereas, though being an element of $Poss(K)$, $\{\neg open(d), \neg open(w)\}$ is not.

Def. 2.3 (Result of an action)

Let S be a formula, and let a be an action such that

$$a = \begin{bmatrix} Pre_1 & | & Post_{1,1}, \ldots, Post_{1,l(1)}; \\ & \vdots & \\ Pre_m & | & Post_{m,1}, \ldots, Post_{m,l(m)} \end{bmatrix}$$

The result of applying a in S given K, denoted $r_K(a, S)$, is the set:
$\{pm' \in Poss(K) | \exists pm \in Poss_K(S) \text{ such that } pm' \text{ is maximally } Post_{i,j}\text{-conform with } pm, \text{ where } i \text{ is the smallest integer such that } K \cup pm \models Pre_i \text{ and } j \in \{1, \ldots, l(i)\}\}.$

As an example, let us apply the action *nocirculation* to the incomplete situation S_0 and the K_0 given previously. We have:

$$r_{K_0}(nocirculation, S_0) = \{ \{open(d), \neg open(w)\}, \\ \{\neg open(d), open(w)\} \}$$

In the first possible model of $Poss_{K_0}(S_0)$, the door and window are both open. Thus, the action can produce one of the two possible models, depending on whether the door or else the window is closed. For the second possible model of $Poss_{K_0}(S_0)$, there is already no circulation. Here, the action changes nothing, and the model equals the one resulting from closing the window.

Naturally enough, the result of a linear plan, i.e., a total ordering of actions, is the set of possible models resulting from the successive application of the actions in the plan. The result of a nonlinear plan, i.e., a partial ordering of actions, then, is the union of possible worlds resulting from all linearizations.

This suffices as a description of the possible models action formalization; consult [Brewka and Hertzberg, 1991] for further information. We showed that this formalization copes with certain forms of uncertainty at planning time: lacking information (disjunctions in or incomplete specification of the start situation), ambiguity (alternative operator effects), and context dependency of operator effects. That is quite powerful; but it is not enough. The possible models give no help for dealing with uncertainty at execution time that would require to react flexibly to failure, sabotage, or serendipity which are impossible to think of at planning time by definition. Developing a framework additionally facilitating this is what we will do now.

3   REPRESENTING ALTERNATIVE PLANS AS FINITE AUTOMATA

We start with the question how to *represent* plans, which are in accordance with the possible models formalization, such that they can be reused flexibly and guide their execution monitoring. We will then briefly describe how to *generate* these plans.

As for plan representation, the idea is to define an analogue to STRIPS triangle tables [Fikes *et al.*, 1972] that supports handling alternative action effects as defined in the possible models framework. The key observation concerning the representation is that possible models are finite by definition. So the task is to represent a structure of finitely many actions, applicable in a subset of finitely many possible models, where each action application produces another subset of the possible models; there is a set of start and a set of finish models.

It is easy to see that such a structure can be understood as a finite automaton (FA): actions correspond to states of the automaton, the possible worlds to the finite alphabet, a dummy start action resulting in the initial possible models corresponds to the initial state, another dummy action with the goal description as precondition to the final state of the automaton, and the results of the actions define the transition function. The resulting FA is even deterministic.

The plan representation we actually use is a variant of a FA, where it is mostly technical to show the correspondence, see [Thiébaux, 1991]. The idea is first to define a graph type, called *T-M* graph, mirroring the interplay between tasks, i.e., occurrences of actions in a plan, and possible models; and then to represent individual planning problems given by a formula S defining the start situation, the background knowledge K and a set of actions A, as a special *T-M* graph.

Def. 3.1 (*T-M* Graph)

A T-M graph is a bipartite directed graph consisting of T- and M-nodes with a unique root, where:

- *The root is a T-node; all leaves are M-nodes.*

- *T-nodes have only M-nodes as successors.*

- *Non-leaf M-nodes have exactly one T-node as successor; all non-root T-nodes have exactly one predescessor.*

Def. 3.2 ((S, K, A) Graph)

Given two formulae S and K, a set of actions A, and Start, a task built from the action that is defined by:

$$start = \begin{bmatrix} true & | & pm_1, \ldots, pm_n \text{ such that} \\ & & \{pm_1, \ldots, pm_n\} = Poss_K(S) \end{bmatrix}$$

An (S, K, A) graph is a T-M graph consisting of exactly the following nodes:

- *M-nodes are possible models from Poss(K).*

- *T-nodes are Start and·tasks built from actions in A. Start occurs exactly once in the graph.*

- *Start is the root; all $Poss_K(S)$ elements are its sucessors, and only these.*

- *Let m be a non-leaf M-node and t its successor T-node. The successors of t are the M-nodes corresponding to all the elements of $r_K(t, m)$ (extending the r_K function to T- and M-nodes in the obvious way).*

The last item is the really interesting one, guaranteeing that all and only the results of tasks are included in the graph. To use an (S, K, A) graph as a plan, you must make sure that its leaves correspond to goal states and that there is at least one path to a leaf from each of its nodes. More formally:

Def. 3.3 (g-Achievingness, Validity, Plan)
Given a formula g, an (S, K, A) graph achieves g if and only if for all of its leaves m: K together with the possible model corresponding to m entail g.
An (S, K, A) graph is valid if and only if from each of its nodes there is at least one path to a leaf.
Given a planning problem specified by a formula S representing the initial state, a background knowledge K, a set of actions A, and a formula g representing the goal, a plan solving this problem is a valid g-achieving (S, K, A) graph.

As an informal lemma, note that a valid graph cannot include a T-node corresponding to a task that is not applicable under the possible model corresponding to its predecessor M-node, i.e., it changes nothing. The reason is that the loop formed by these two T and M-nodes would be a blind alley in the graph.

Consider the following example. Starting a lecture in a room in a building on a noisy street requires that the window be closed. Sometimes, a janitor would open it between lectures, but not always, so nothing is known initially about the window being open or closed. Moreover, you must turn on the light, which the janitor would switch off between lectures; the light is operated by two toggle switches *sw1* and *sw2* both of which can be in positions *swi, ¬swi*. The light is *on* if and only if *sw1* and *sw2* are in equal positions. Both switches are old and unreliable: immediately after flipping them, they may flip back into their former position, i.e., toggling a switch may or may not have an effect.

The language L_1 for describing possible models consists of *open*, *sw1*, and *sw2*; ¬*open* is, outside of possible models, called *closed*, and ¬*on* is called *off*. The available action set A_1 consists of *toggle1* for toggling *sw1* and *close-window* for closing the window if open.

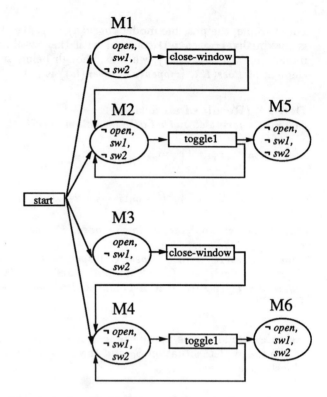

Figure 1: An (S, K, A) graph representing an alternative plan for the lecture example.

In summary, we have

$$close\text{-}window = [\quad open \quad | \quad \{\neg open\} \quad]$$
$$toggle1 = [\quad sw1 \quad | \quad \{\neg sw1\}, \{\}; $$
$$\neg sw1 \quad | \quad \{sw1\}, \{\} \quad]$$

$K_1 = \{open \oplus closed, on \leftrightarrow (sw1 \leftrightarrow sw2), on \oplus off\}$,
$S_1 = \{off\}$,
$g_1 = closed \wedge on$

A plan for solving the problem is shown in figure 1. This plan is to be interpreted as follows: Finding yourself in one of the possible start situations where the window is closed, toggle *sw1* until it works; else close the window first and continue as before. So, this plan, as one would intuitively expect from something *planned*, does *not* describe all possible courses of action but follows a rationale: close the window first and switch on the light then. Of course, it would have been possible to find other plans.

Note that *M* nodes occur only once in the graph, even if generated by different *T* nodes. This keeps the graph finite, because there are only finitely many possible models. Note further that the graph looks a bit like the representation of a part of the state space, where not all applicable tasks are included. However, it is different from a state space representation in that the representation of a state is restricted to the vocabulary *L* for describing the possible models. In fact, the graph is a finite part of the state space where states are restricted to *essential* [Lifschitz, 1987] ground atoms or to *frame fluents* [Lifschitz, 1990].

Our (S, K, A) graphs are comparable to Kabanza's [1990] branching time temporal logics based *world automata* in that we use actions (events) with alternative effects. (S, K, A) graphs are different in that they have a bipartite node set. The reason behind this difference is a difference in ontology: what we would view as alternative outcomes of an action applied in a situation, would be viewed as a single action (event) followed by different external events by Kabanza. An advantage of his approach is that world automata describing "purely external" courses of events and world automata involving agent induced events, i.e., plans, have an identical structure and can thus be handled identically. The advantages of our graphs will become apparent when we talk in section 4 about replanning and plan reuse, which seem to be a little cumbersome in Kabanza's approach.

The requirement that non-leaf M-nodes have exactly one successor T-node in T-M graphs makes the execution of a plan deterministic. That has its advantages. On the other hand, it enforces that only the analogs of linear plans can be represented here; e.g., if either of the two execution sequences of two commutatively executable actions would lead to the goal, then the very format of our plans forces the planner to commit itself to one of these sequences. Experimenting with ways to introduce non-linearity into the plans and investigating the implications is part of our future research.

How can these plans be generated? As we have not yet defined an appropriate version of regression [Waldinger, 1977] for our action format, we presently generate the plans in forward fashion in PASCALE. Moreover, we haven't worried about clever control heuristics, so one should not have high expectations about PASCALE's performance. In fact, PASCALE performs A^* search through the space of partial valid (S, K, A) graphs. Such a search always terminates as the search space is finite, which is inherited from the finiteness of the state space. Moreover, restricting the search to *valid* graphs reduces the search space considerably.

The approach allows for an *anytime* planning behavior [Dean and Boddy, 1988], if you introduce a possibility ordering of action postconditions, and plan for the most probable outcomes first. This is in fact done in [Drummond and Bresina, 1990]. Introducing probability into (S, K, A) graphs is part of our future research.

Finally, it is unnecessary to work on the whole space of possible models at once. An agreeable feature of g-achieving (S, K, A) graphs is that they can be generated incrementally and reused later, which is a topic for the next section.

4 BUILDING A SEMI-REACTIVE SYSTEM

It is commonplace that not all possible events can be accounted for at planning time. This remains true when using (S, K, A) graphs: you can plan for anticipated execution failures such as sticking toggles, or for lacking information such as the light's initial state. But the plans don't deal with every conceivable course of events. This is no bug, but a matter of efficiency.

Hence, the point here is *not* that executing (S, K, A) graphs doesn't require the ability to recover from execution failures and to replan. The point *is* that these plans are already close to what is needed for execution monitoring and are a good basis both for monitoring and for replanning in the case of execution failures. Thus, facilitated by the possible models approach, planning, execution, and plan reuse are intimately intertwined, motivating the term of *semi-reactive* planning. All this shall be made plausible now, starting with execution monitoring and turning to replanning and plan reuse afterwards. All this will be described informally; consult [Thiébaux, 1991] for a more formal treatment.

4.1 EXECUTION MONITORING

To see what the problems are, let us modify our lecture preliminaries example. Consider that while fumbling with *sw1*, the window gets reopened (by some obstructive student). Let us first assume that *sw1* is in its original position and that the light is still off. Hence, we find ourselves in another state which may or may not (depending on whether the window was initially open or not) equal the one which executing the plan started at.

Obviously, an execution monitoring component should resume the plan execution from the M-node corresponding to the most recent world state, i.e., execute (or reexecute) the action *close-window*. In this respect, the functionality of our system is as powerful as STRIPS's [Fikes *et al.*, 1972] facilities based on triangle tables.

Thus, monitoring the plan execution is focused on monitoring possible models. Note that this feature of our approach also constrains the choice of L: Basing a planner plus execution monitor on the possible models framework will work only if the atomic sentences set L consists of all relevant observables, where relevant means that these observables allow to conclude that the plan execution is still on the right track if they have the expected truth values.

Another form of focusing concerns the part of the (S, K, A) graph, that can be kept in the focus of the execution monitor. At planning time, many features of the actual start situation for plan execution may be unknown, resulting in alternative paths through the graph. At the start of the execution, many of these unknown features may become known; in our example, the values of *open*, *sw1*, and *sw2* (and other derived features) can be observed, resulting in a unique possible start model. If the plan execution can be assumed to be sufficiently reliable, then the plan executor can strip off everything from the plan which is not on the possible paths from the current M-node to goal M-nodes. If, e.g., the start situation in the lecture scenario corresponds to the M-node M2 in figure 1, all non-successors of this node can be stripped off.

The straightforward algorithm for extracting the relevant part of a graph for a particular situation is given in [Thiébaux, 1991]. Note that extraction can proceed as execution proceeds and more and more information becomes available, narrowing down the plan and describing the expected course of things less and less ambiguously. Should, as by obstructive students, a world state occur that does not correspond to an M-node in the current focus, then you have to download the original plan and try to locate the now current M-node.

4.2   REPLANNING

However, you may fail to locate such node in the original plan, which leads to replanning. In our lecture example consider the case of the aforementioned obstructive student opening the window right after you managed to turn on the light. The resulting world state includes both *on* and *open*, and there is no corresponding M-node in the complete plan. To get out of this situation, you have to replan.

As usual, replanning is similar to planning, and the only interesting question is to what extent you can inherit effort from the previous planning. Concerning this, note that an (S, K, A) graph can be extended incrementally to include more M-nodes; in order to ascertain g-achievingness of the new graph, you only must make sure that there is a path from every new M-node to an old M-node or to a newly introduced goal node. Again, the finiteness of the set of M-nodes provides this process with an upper limit. In PASCALE, we use the strategy to stop replanning as soon as the resulting graph is g-achieving. This may be achieved by inserting new M-nodes corresponding to unexpected world states as successors of the *Start* task and connecting these new M-nodes to old ones. As there might have been a shorter path from the new M-node to a *new* goal M-node, the new plan may be suboptimal. This strategy for reusing the old plan is convenient, but it is not enforced by the use of possible models, and other strategies are conceivable.

In our example, assuming that the initial state of the world corresponded to node M2 in figure 1, the unexpected situation with the light on and the window open would lead to introducing another M-node $\{open, \neg sw1, \neg sw2\}$, which would be connected via a new *close-window* T-node to the old goal node M5.

4.3   REUSING OLD PLANS

In fact, replanning as described here is just a special case of the more general technique of reusing a plan from an existing library of plans. Let us start with describing a simple case of plan reuse.

Given two goals g and h, if $g \vdash h$, then every g-achieving graph is also h-achieving, i.e., you can reuse a plan achieving g for obtaining h. To make a silly lecture scenario example, you can reuse the graph in figure 1 to achieve $sw1 \leftrightarrow sw2$. But note two things: First, the resulting plan need not be optimal (there may be simpler ways to generate h); and second, reusing here doesn't mean that the plan is really finished (there may be possible initial worlds not contained in the old M-nodes, for which you must replan to achieve h).

In general, you will not simply find solutions to instances of your current problem in your plan library. In this case, it is still possible to find "useful" parts of old plans, extract them using the extraction mechanism sketched above, and extend the resulting plan embryos to become valid h-achieving. The crucial question is the definition of usefulness; in [Thiébaux, 1991], a numerical measure is used to state to what extent leaves of old plans and possible models for the recent goal overlap. A detailed discussion, however, lies out of scope here.

5   FURTHER RELATED WORK

Let us conclude with some further remarks comparing our concepts with related ones. For a summary, please reread the abstract.

Situation-action rules. Another approach to encoding reactivity are situation-action rules, e.g., [Drummond, 1989; Drummond and Bresina, 1990; Downs and Reichgelt, 1991]. An (S, K, A) graph can obviously be translated into a set of situation-action rules (both for achieving the same goal) by interpreting the possible models corresponding to the M-nodes as IF parts of a rule, and the T-node task as the THEN part. A graph has just more structure than a set of rules—no more and no less. The particular struture of T-M graphs prevents what would be conflicts between two applicable rules. Thus, the graph focuses the execution monitor, allowing to choose the next execution step deterministically. Moreover, the technique of extraction is obvious in the graphs, but far less obvious in rule sets. Finally, the (S, K, A) graphs are conceptually closer to classical plans than are rule sets, allowing direct replanning.

Universal Plans. To provide the extreme case of plan reuse for a goal g, you can generate (S, K, A) graphs containing M-nodes corresponding to the whole of $Poss(K)$ in advance. This could be done by giving no information about the start situation, i.e., the *Start* node of the (S, K, A) graph to be generated has successor M nodes corresponding to all $Poss(K)$ elements. Thus, you generate a kind of universal plan [Schoppers, 1989b] for the domain for achieving g. However, this remark is not intended to actually recommend generating these universal plans, but just to state that our theory contains this as an extreme case.

Acknowledgements

This work is partially funded by the German Federal Ministry for Research and Technology (BMFT) in the joint project TASSO under grant ITW8900A7. TASSO is also part of the GMD Assisting Computer (AC) *Leitvorhaben.*

Thanks to the following persons for commenting on drafts: Marie-Odile Cordier, Tom Gordon, Hans Werner Güsgen, Robert Morris, Eric Rutten, Josef Schneeberger.

References

[Agre, 1988] P.E. Agre. *The Dynamic Structure of Everyday Life.* PhD thesis, MIT Artificial Intelligence Laboratory, 1988.

[Bibel, 1986] W. Bibel. A deductive solution for plan generation. *New Generation Computing*, 4:115–132, 1986.

[Brewka and Hertzberg, 1991] G. Brewka and J. Hertzberg. How to do things with worlds: On formalizing actions and plans. Submitted for publication, 1991.

[Chapman, 1987] D. Chapman. Planning for conjunctive goals. *J. Artificial Intelligence*, 32:333–377, 1987.

[Dean and Boddy, 1988] T.L. Dean and M. Boddy. An analysis of time-dependent planning. In *Proc. AAAI-88*, pages 49–54, 1988.

[Downs and Reichgelt, 1991] J. Downs and H. Reichgelt. Integrating classical and reactive planning within an architecture for autonomous agents. In J. Hertzberg, editor, *European Workshop on Planning. EWSP '91, Sankt Augustin, FRG, March 1991, Proceedings*, pages 13–26. Springer Verlag (Lecture Notes in AI vol. 522), 1991.

[Drummond and Bresina, 1990] M. Drummond and J. Bresina. Anytime synthetic projection: Maximizing the probability of goal satisfaction. In *Proc. AAAI-90*, pages 138–144, 1990.

[Drummond, 1989] M. Drummond. Situated control rules. In *Proc. 1st Intl. Conference on Principles of Knowledge Representation and Reasoning (KR-89)*, pages 103–113, 1989.

[Fikes and Nilsson, 1971] R.E. Fikes and N.J. Nilsson. STRIPS: A new approach to theorem proving in problem solving. *J. Artificial Intelligence*, 2:189–208, 1971.

[Fikes et al., 1972] R.E. Fikes, P.E. Hart, and N.J. Nilsson. Learning and executing generalized robot plans. *J. Artificial Intelligence*, 3:251–288, 1972.

[Georgeff and Lansky, 1987] M.P. Georgeff and A.L. Lansky. Reactive reasoning and planning. In *Proc. AAAI-87*, pages 677–682, 1987.

[Ginsberg and Smith, 1988] M.L. Ginsberg and D.E. Smith. Reasoning about action I: A possible worlds approach. *J. Artificial Intelligence*, 35:165–195, 1988.

[Hanks, 1990] S. Hanks. Practical temporal projection. In *Proc. AAAI-90*, pages 158–163, 1990.

[Kabanza, 1990] F. Kabanza. Synthesis of reactive plans for multi-path environments. In *Proc. AAAI-90*, pages 164–169, 1990.

[Lifschitz, 1987] V. Lifschitz. On the semantics of STRIPS. In M.P. Georgeff and A.L. Lansky, editors, *Proc. 1986 Workshop Reasoning about Actions and Plans, Timberline, OR*, pages 1–9, Los Altos, 1987. Morgan Kaufmann.

[Lifschitz, 1990] V. Lifschitz. Frames in the space of situations. *J. Artificial Intelligence*, 46:365–376, 1990.

[Reichgelt and Shadbolt, 1990] H. Reichgelt and N. Shadbolt. A specification tool for planning systems. In *Proc. ECAI-90*, pages 541–546, 1990.

[Sandewall, 1991] E. Sandewall. Features and fluents. Technical Report LiTH-IDA-R-91-29, Dept. of Computer and Information Sciences, Linköping University, 1991.

[Schoppers, 1989a] M.J. Schoppers. In defense of reaction plans as caches. *AI Magazine*, 10(4):51–60, 1989.

[Schoppers, 1989b] M.J. Schoppers. *Representation and Automatic Synthesis of Reaction Plans.* PhD thesis, Dept. of Computer Science, Univ. of Illinois at Urbana-Champaign, 1989. also as Tech. Rep. UIUCDCS-R-89-1546.

[Thiébaux, 1991] S. Thiébaux. PASCALE: A system for planning under uncertainty. TASSO-Report 28, GMD, 1991.

[Waldinger, 1977] R. Waldinger. Achieving several goals simultaneously. *Machine Intelligence*, 8:94–136, 1977.

[Winslett, 1988] M. Winslett. Reasoning about action using a possible models approach. In *Proc. AAAI-88*, pages 89–93, 1988.

Modular Utility Representation for Decision-Theoretic Planning

Michael P. Wellman
USAF Wright Laboratory
WL/AAA-1
Wright-Patterson AFB, OH 45433
(513) 255-5800
wellman@wl.wpafb.af.mil

Jon Doyle
MIT Laboratory for Computer Science
545 Technology Square
Cambridge, MA 02139
(617) 253-3512
doyle@zermatt.lcs.mit.edu

Abstract

Specification of objectives constitutes a central issue in knowledge representation for planning. Decision-theoretic approaches require that representations of objectives possess a firm semantics in terms of utility functions, yet provide the flexible compositionality needed for practical preference modeling for planning systems. Modularity, or separability in specification, is the key representational feature enabling this flexibility. In the context of utility specification, modularity corresponds exactly to well-known independence concepts from multiattribute utility theory, and leads directly to approaches for composing separate preference specifications. Ultimately, we seek to use this utility-theoretic account to justify and improve existing mechanisms for specification of preference information, and to develop new representations exhibiting tractable specification and flexible composition of preference criteria.

1 REPRESENTING UTILITY FOR PLANNING

As generally conceived, the AI planning task aims to use beliefs about the world and predicted effects of available actions to synthesize a course of action furthering some objectives. *Decision-theoretic* planning, which measures beliefs in terms of Bayesian probability and objectives in terms of expected utility, challenges the architect of planning systems to design representation constructs that can be interpreted faithfully in terms of probabilities and utilities, that can be scaled to facilitate expression of general knowledge about broad domains, and that support computationally tractable inference about plans and partial plans.

Multiple objectives, partially achievable objectives, and uncertainty about the effects of actions all pose difficult problems for traditional goal-based planning systems. In themselves, goal conditions provide no means for resolving tradeoffs among competing objectives or for expressing varying degrees of partial satisfaction. Since these difficulties arise in most (if not all) realistic planning problems, builders of practical planning systems commonly augment goal-based representations with heuristic measures of goal importance, partial goal achievement, or other priority relationships. These augmentations might assign, for example, numeric achievement values to individual goals, costs to individual actions, and penalties proportional to the measured distance from a goal. The planner then combines them in some straightforward way (e.g., achievement values minus costs minus penalties) to evaluate an overall plan. Although such *ad hoc* mechanisms might provide reasonable performance in particular planning systems, they typically lack any precise meaning, and so provide neither a basis for evaluating their coherence and appropriateness for other problem domains, nor a justification for the inference operations and choices executed by the underlying planning architecture.

In contrast, interpreting specifications of objectives in terms of decision-theoretic preferences permits the designers of planning systems to judge both the coherence of the objectives and the effectiveness of the planning system in furthering these objectives. But decision theory per se does not address the problem of designing convenient representations for preference, or its corresponding measure, utility. Applying the concepts of decision theory directly (as in *decision analysis*) requires specifying a utility function over the entire domain, ranking plan results by their desirability in any conceivable planning situation. This places unwarranted burdens on the modeler, since different features of the situation are relevant with respect to decisions made at different levels of abstraction or at intermediate stages of plan synthesis. To make utility specifications more convenient, we seek *modular* representations that separately specify preference information concerning particular factors, so that we can dynamically combine those factors deemed relevant to a particular problem and level of abstraction.

The following builds a framework for modular specification of utilities on firm decision-theoretic foundations. We begin by presenting our view of modularity in knowledge representation as specification of flexibly composable model elements. Next, we present some background material on multiattribute utility theory prerequisite to our account of modular utility specification. We then demonstrate the correspondence between separability in specification and well-established independence concepts from utility theory, and exhibit the consequences of the theory for composition operations on utility representations. We conclude with a summary discussion of related issues and work.

2 MODULARITY AND MODEL COMPOSITION

AI planning distinguishes itself from other approaches to automated decision making by emphasizing compositional synthesis of a course of action from primitive action elements (i.e., operators) together with specifications of the effects of each of these primitive elements in isolation. To synthesize a composite plan, a planner must determine the overall effects of the composite plan as a modular combination of the effects of its constituent actions. Modular specification of effects is essential to giving planners the freedom to compose primitives as necessary. But modular specification of planning *objectives* is equally important. Access to preferences regarding specific outcome features (without specifying them over complete outcomes) is essential when it is impossible or infeasible to characterize the entire outcome space in advance, when different features are relevant for different decision problems, and when preferences for particular aspects of the outcome depend on background context.

For example, consider the problem of planning large-scale military transportation operations. At a high level, we might consider monetary costs and whether the specified movement requirements are met, whereas a more detailed analysis would consider the timeliness of cargo movements, the amount and type of cargo moved, stress on transportation resources, and safety. When making isolated decisions about parts of the operation (the usual case), it often proves advantageous to treat resource reservations that impact the rest of the plan as part of the outcome, and to summarize the value of those resources as opportunity costs.

Assessing a global utility function covering all of these outcome features and their subconcepts seems impractical. We believe it more reasonable to specify utility functions over individual features or small groups of features, combining these as needed for making tradeoffs in decision problems involving sets of features. For example, we might have a measure of the value

of moving various types of cargo and a relation describing the tradeoff between monetary cost and tardiness for particular movement classes. When faced with a particular decision problem, the planner assembles the relevant outcome features and corresponding utility specifications, then constructs a comprehensive utility model by composing the individual utilities.[1]

To realize this approach, we must develop interpretations for isolated preference specifications, and methods for defining composition operators and composing selected partial specifications. Fortunately, utility theorists have developed a rich framework for analyzing the composition of utility functions over multiple attributes, motivated by the need to simplify assessment even when attributes are fixed in advance.[2] We can exploit this theory for more flexible utility representation as well, both to make sense of modular specifications and to determine the appropriate form of composition operators. In the remainder of this paper, we present the relevant utility theory, and demonstrate its application to the problem of flexible composition of modular utility specifications.

3 PREFERENCES AND UTILITY FUNCTIONS

Utility theory starts with the notion of *preferences* over *outcomes* (Keeney and Raiffa, 1976). Outcomes represent the possible consequences of the agent's decisions. In the planning context, an outcome might be taken to be the state resulting from execution of a plan, or perhaps an entire history of instantaneous states over the lifetime of the agent. To provide an adequate basis for decision, the set Ω of (mutually incompatible) possible outcomes must distinguish all consequences that the agent cares about and are possibly affected by its actions. We define the agent's preferences by a total preorder (a complete, reflexive, and transitive relation), $\succsim$, over possible outcomes, called the *preference order*.

Given a few topological restrictions on $\succsim$, the preference order can be captured by an order-preserving, real-valued *utility function*, u. The function u *represents* $\succsim$ in the sense that outcomes can be ranked by comparing the numeric values of the utility function

---

[1]The task of dynamically constructing decision models for particular problem instances from general domain knowledge is gaining increasing attention from researchers (Wellman *et al.*, 1992). Most of the work to date concerns probabilistic modeling, but some addresses the equally important problem of generating utility models (Haddawy and Hanks, 1990; Loui, 1990).

[2]Researchers in multiattribute utility theory tend to refer to *de*composition rather than composition because they look to assess a fixed outcome space in a top-down manner, rather than the bottom-up assembly of primitive utility specifications.

applied to those outcomes, with $\omega \succsim \omega'$ iff $u(\omega) \geq u(\omega')$ for $\omega, \omega' \in \Omega$. However, the utility-function representation is not unique. If $u(\omega) \geq u(\omega')$, then it must also be the case that $\varphi(u(\omega)) \geq \varphi(u(\omega'))$, for any monotonically increasing function φ. Since they represent the same preference order—and thus would sanction identical decisions (under certainty)—we say that u and $\varphi \circ u$ are *strategically equivalent*.

When there is *uncertainty*, plans influence outcomes only probabilistically, and we must represent the anticipated result of a plan by a probability distribution over Ω, or *prospect*, and extend $\succsim$ to order prospects. The central result of utility theory is a representation theorem that establishes (given some restrictions on $\succsim$) the existence of a utility function $u : \Omega \to \mathbf{R}$ such that preference over prospects is represented by the *expectation* of u over those prospects. The key point here is that u is defined over outcomes alone; the extension to prospects via expectation is a consequence of the axioms of probability and utility (Savage, 1972).

As in the deterministic case, the utility-function representation for a preference order over uncertain prospects is not unique. However, monotone transformations do not generally preserve expectation orderings, and hence the class of strategically equivalent functions is more limited in the uncertain case. Specifically, expected utility functions[3] are unique up to a positive linear transformation. That is, for positive linear function ψ (i.e., $\psi(x) = ax + b$, $a > 0$), the utility functions u and $\psi \circ u$ are strategically equivalent.

In principle, we could avoid utility functions altogether and perform decision-theoretic reasoning directly in terms of preference orders, but numeric representations offer distinct advantages in compactness and analytic manipulability. Multiattribute utility theory exploits these advantages as far as possible, by decomposing complex outcome spaces into modular structures and specifying complex utility functions in terms of combinations of lower-dimension functions.

4   MULTIATTRIBUTE OUTCOMES

In realistic decision situations, there are commonly many objectives, and hence an outcome would represent a highly complex set of features describing the plan's result. In utility theory, preference-relevant features of an outcome are called *attributes*, and a substantial body of work has been devoted to relating preference on individual attributes to preference for complex outcomes. The first requirement for separating overall preference into that for individual attributes is some structure on the outcome space. This structure is provided by a *framing*, which defines a

multiattribute representation of the given outcome space (Wellman and Doyle, 1991). A framing represents each outcome ω as a vector $\langle \omega_1, \ldots, \omega_n \rangle$ of attributes, where each outcome attribute ω_i is drawn from an *attribute space* A_i. The framing thus views the set of outcomes Ω as a subset of the multiattribute space $A = \prod_{i=1}^{n} A_i$. In the following, we assume that every attribute vector corresponds to some outcome, that is, that the attributes characterize the outcomes exactly.[4]

Given a particular framing, the utility function over Ω can be expressed as a multi-dimensional function over A. The modularity advantages of the multiattribute representation accrue if this multi-dimensional function can in turn be decomposed into some regular combination of lower dimension *subutility* functions, each representing preferences over one or more attributes.

5   SEPARABILITY AND UTILITY INDEPENDENCE

Indirect specification of a multi-dimensional function as a combination of functions of lower dimension depends on separability of the various dimensions. In the context of utility theory, we are further concerned that the lower-dimension functions themselves have some meaningful interpretation in terms of preferences, ideally that they be considered subutility functions in some sense. What, then, does it mean to say that u_i is a subutility function for attribute i? We can answer this question in terms of invariance of decisions, or strategic equivalence.

If we wish to interpret $u_i : A_i \to \mathbf{R}$ as a utility function, then it must correspond to some preference order, $\succsim_i$, over prospects involving A_i. To talk sensibly about preferences over A_i without referring to the remainder of the outcome vector, preferences for attribute i must be invariant in some sense with respect to the other attributes. If we indeed specify an entire utility function for that attribute, we are uniquely determining $\succsim_i$, and in effect determining all decisions involving that attribute, assuming that all others are fixed. In other words, u_i determines the optimal decision (or decisions, in case of ties) for all choices involving prospects where outcomes differ only in attribute i. Moreover, this decision does not depend on what fixed values the other attributes take.

This invariance property is a fundamental concept in multiattribute utility theory, called *utility independence* (UI) (Keeney and Raiffa, 1976).

---

[3]Henceforth, we assume the more general, uncertain, case, and refer exclusively to utility functions that exhibit the expectation property.

[4]For our purposes here (although not for other purposes (Wellman and Doyle, 1991)), we can safely satisfy this assumption by padding the outcome space and extending the preference order in a manner consistent with other given constraints.

Definition 1 (UI) *One attribute is utility independent (UI)[5] of the remaining attributes if preferences for prospects over this attribute, holding other attribute values fixed, do not depend on the fixed values of those attributes.*

We can generalize this to UI between two sets of attributes by considering prospects where attributes in the first set vary and those in the second set are fixed. Note that UI is not symmetric—for instance, when $n = 3$, it is quite possible that $\{A_1\}$ be UI of $\{A_2, A_3\}$, but $\{A_2, A_3\}$ not be UI of $\{A_1\}$.

Utility independence appears to be a minimal requirement for modular specification of preferences. The reason is that without implicitly invoking UI relationships, it is generally not coherent to refer to preferences on individual outcome features via subutility functions. If we accept the view that specifying properties of subutility functions on individual features or small groups of features is the essence of modularity, we find that extensive application of utility independence is pragmatically unavoidable.

Fortunately, the UI condition justifies some strong separability results, leading to well-structured utility representations. The separable form of a utility function over UI attributes follows directly from the invariance condition. Suppose $n = 2$, and A_1 is UI of A_2. The overall utility is a function of both attributes, $u : A_1 \times A_2 \to \mathbf{R}$. We know from the UI condition that the conditional utility function $u(\cdot, \omega_2')$ where the second attribute is fixed at the constant value ω_2' must be strategically equivalent (with respect to the first attribute) to the conditional utility function corresponding to any other value. Because utility is unique up to a positive linear transformation, this implies, for utility conditioned on ω_2'', that

$$u(\omega_1, \omega_2'') = a u(\omega_1, \omega_2') + b$$

for some constants $a > 0$ and b. Indeed, such a relationship must hold for any value $\omega_2 \in A_2$, although the a and b parameters may depend on ω_2. This observation yields a general form for the overall utility function,

$$u(\omega_1, \omega_2) = g(\omega_2) u(\omega_1, \omega_2') + h(\omega_2).$$

Defining the subutility function $u_1(\omega_1)$ as $u(\omega_1, \omega_2')$, for the particular constant ω_2', we have

$$u(\omega_1, \omega_2) = g(\omega_2) u_1(\omega_1) + h(\omega_2). \tag{1}$$

In fact, the functions g and h can also be expressed in terms of conditional utility functions for attribute 2, with the first attribute fixed at particular values. (See Keeney and Raiffa (1976, Chapter 5) for the details of this decomposition.)

---

[5]We use the same abbreviation for both noun and adjective forms of the concept.

6 MULTIATTRIBUTE UTILITY FORMS

The development above establishes the separability of an attribute subset from its complement in the framing, when UI holds. In framings with many attributes, we would expect to have partial preference information in the form of subutility functions (hence implicit UI conditions) corresponding to a variety of attribute subsets and individual attributes. When certain patterns of UI hold over the entire multiattribute space, general forms for the overall utility function follow. There are two elementary forms of multiattribute decomposition, in both of which the overall utility function can be expressed as a modular combination of single-attribute subutility functions.[6]

In the *multilinear* decomposition, the n-dimensional utility function is separable into $n - 1$ subutility functions for individual attributes, with perhaps one other (which we take to be the first, without loss of generality) not expressible as a subutility,

$$u(\omega_1, \ldots, \omega_n) = f(\omega_1, u_2(\omega_2), \ldots, u_n(\omega_n)).$$

The form is called multilinear because the function f is linear in each argument save the first, holding the remaining arguments fixed. It is a valid decomposition as long as each attribute (except possibly the first) is UI of the rest, that is, has preferences validly expressed as a subutility function. The disadvantage of the multilinear form is that it requires that we specify $O(2^n)$ parameters (called *scaling constants*) in addition to the single-attribute functions.

The *multiplicative* form corresponds to the sum or product of the subutility functions, each weighted by a scaling constant. Since this form requires only $O(n)$ parameters, it is far easier to specify (i.e., more modular) than the multilinear form. The price paid for this simplicity is that each subset of the attributes must be UI of its complement. Of course, we could not expect to have explicit UI assertions or subutilities corresponding to all subsets; specifying these would defeat the purpose of modularity anyway. Fortunately, the utility independence of some sets of attributes often entails the UI of related sets. The theory of UI relations provides a basis for deriving the most modular form corresponding to a given set of fundamental independence relations.

The basic mechanism for deriving new separability conditions from a set of UI relations is based on a result originally due to Gorman (1968). Suppose we have two attribute sets, each UI of its complement,

---

[6]The decompositions actually require a slightly weaker condition than UI, called *generalized utility independence* (GUI) (Keeney and Raiffa, 1976) or *autonomy* (von Stengel, 1988). In the following discussion, we continue to appeal to UI, since the preferential interpretation of subutility functions implicitly invokes the stronger concept.

with a nonempty intersection, Y. We can write the first set as $X \cup Y$ and the second as $Y \cup Z$, with X, Y, and Z disjoint attribute sets. Then it follows that all combinations of these sets—X, Y, Z, $X \cup Z$, and $X \cup Y \cup Z$—are also UI[7] of their respective complements. From this fact, we see that a small number of UI conditions for overlapping attribute sets can implicitly entail a large number of independence relations.

7   MODULAR COMPOSITION OF UTILITY FUNCTIONS

The general utility-model composition problem is as follows. Suppose we are given a collection of subutility functions and other preference information involving attributes from a given framing.[8] Taking the existence of subutility functions to implicitly assert a corresponding UI condition, our task is to find a modular composition of these subutilities into an overall utility function. In doing so, we exploit the UI conditions entailed by those implicit in the given subutility functions according to the rule described above.

First, note that determining the form of the overall utility function is not simply a matter of verifying whether the given UI conditions collectively justify an n-attribute multiplicative or multilinear decomposition. There is actually a structural continuum between these forms, defined by the space of hierarchical decompositions in which each node is a multiplicative or multilinear function of some partition of the attribute set. For example, with $n = 5$, the top-level decomposition might be a multilinear combination of the form

$$u(\omega_1, \ldots, \omega_5) = f(\omega_1, u_2(\omega_2), u_{3,4,5}(\omega_3, \omega_4, \omega_5)),$$

and $u_{3,4,5}$ might be recursively decomposable as a multiplicative combination of its three attributes.

In fact, there exists a unique decomposition hierarchy, or *utility tree*, corresponding to any set of UI conditions (Gorman, 1968; von Stengel, 1988). Moreover, we can derive this tree from a given set of UI premises without enumerating all of the UI relationships that follow from these premises. We have developed an algorithm (to be reported in detail elsewhere) that computes the decomposition hierarchy corresponding to an arbitrary collection of UI assertions in an incremental manner, permitting a "structural sensitivity analysis" of the implications of additional UI axioms or subutility functions. The basic ideas in the algorithm follow from the constructive demonstration of the de-

composition theorems by Gorman (1968), Keeney and Raiffa (1976), and von Stengel (1988).

8   AN EXAMPLE

To illustrate the hierarchical structure of a multiattribute utility function, we adduce an example from the transportation domain. The attributes and independence relations we employ are selected purely for expository purposes and are not intended to represent real salience or independence in this domain.

Suppose we are considering alternate modes of transportation for a particular cargo movement, say M. To evaluate the results of this movement, we might consider the following outcome attributes: (1) amount of bulk cargo transported in M, (2) monetary expenses associated with M, (3) tardiness of M with respect to some target arrival time, (4) opportunity costs associated with vehicles employed in M, (5) opportunity costs of facilities (e.g., warehouses, loading equipment) employed in M, (6) human resources (e.g., vehicle crews) used in M, and (7) safety. In a more concrete instance, these attributes would be directly associated with particular resource and cargo types.

Suppose further that we have preference information about these attributes in the form of subutility functions. Let $u_{i,j,\ldots}$ denote the subutility function corresponding to attributes $i, j, \ldots$ in the numbering above. In our example, suppose that we have (given or perhaps derived from some more fundamental information) the subutility functions:

$$u_1, \quad u_{2,3}, \quad u_{2,4,5,6}, \quad u_{4,5}, \quad \text{and } u_7.$$

That is, we have subutility functions for the individual attributes bulk cargo movement and safety, and joint subutility functions describing the tradeoff between monetary expenses and tardiness, as well as among monetary expenses and the various resource costs. We also have a specification of the particular tradeoff between vehicle and facility resource usage.

We interpret the existence of these subutility functions as implicitly asserting UI between the domain of each function and the rest of the attributes. These UI conditions, in turn, lead to a unique utility tree describing the modular composition of these subutilities into an overall utility function. Figure 1 depicts the tree corresponding to the subutility functions listed above.

At the top level, the utility function is a multilinear combination of the given subutilities u_1 and u_7, along with a joint subutility function for the remaining attributes. This in turn is composed of subutilities u_2, u_3, and $u_{4,5,6}$, none of which are among those originally specified. However, all of the leaf subutilities are derivable from the originals given the implied UI conditions.[9] For example, u_2 and u_3 are condi-

---

[7]Technically, only in the generalized sense noted above.

[8]A more flexible approach would be to construct the framing dynamically based on attributes for which we have preferential information. In this discussion, we abstract from the problem of defining the framing, as well as that of obtaining the subutility functions, although both are critical steps in utility model composition.

[9]As are many of the necessary scaling constants.

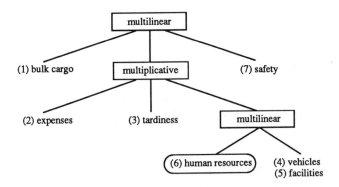

Figure 1: The utility tree for the transportation example. Except for *human resources*, each of the leaves corresponds to a separable subutility function.

tioned versions of $u_{2,3}$, obtained by fixing attributes 3 and 2, respectively, at arbitrary levels. These are indeed subutilities—hence the freedom in choosing conditioning values—by virtue of the UI relations implicit in the overlapping UI index sets $\{2,3\}$ and $\{2,4,5,6\}$. If in fact $u_{2,3}$ is not separable, then this subutility function is incompatible with the existence of subutility $u_{2,4,5,6}$.[10] Finally, the subutility $u_{4,5,6}$ is separable via a two-attribute multilinear form. This composition corresponds to the UI form (Equation (1)) separating $\{4,5\}$ from $\{6\}$. Note that $\{6\}$ is not UI of $\{4,5\}$, and therefore preference for attribute 6 is not expressible as a subutility. And note also that attributes 4 and 5 are not separable; the utility tree employs the joint subutility $u_{4,5}$.

9   CONCLUSIONS

In summary, we have argued that modularity is an essential feature of utility representation for decision-theoretic planning, and that separate specification of utility for isolated outcome features is tantamount to an assertion of utility independence. The independence relations implicit in a collection of modular utility components dictate the form in which they should be composed to define an overall utility function. Customized utility models can be constructed dynamically to reflect the relevant factors in a particular decision situation via bottom-up composition according to rules of multiattribute utility theory.

When the modular preference specifications are partial (i.e., not complete subutility functions), the corresponding invariance property implicit in the separation is generally weaker than utility independence. For example, specifying only ordinal subutilities (e.g., monotonicity conditions) is tantamount to *preferential independence*, another well-known concept of utility

---

[10]The problem of dealing with overconstrained or otherwise inconsistent utility specifications is an important issue in utility composition but beyond the scope of this paper.

theory. In principle, we could extend this analysis to cover a broad spectrum of independence concepts with a variety of implications for utility composition.

Our investigation is in the spirit of analogous analyses relating modularity and probabilistic independence (Heckerman, 1990; Heckerman and Horvitz, 1988; Wellman, 1990). In both cases, we must invoke independence to justify scalable representation schemes, and we may exploit the independence relations to define valid composition rules. Utility trees can be viewed as an analog of probabilistic dependence graphs, the underlying basis for the most prevalent modeling scheme for probabilistic reasoning (Charniak, 1991; Pearl, 1988).

The notion of incremental utility specification and combination has also been advocated by Loui (1989; 1990). Our analysis serves to determine when such combination is sanctioned by utility theory, and to constrain the form that it might take. It may also be reasonable to heuristically apply modular combination rules when they are not theoretically justified, as the computational benefits may outweigh the cost of potential errors.

We are currently attempting to incorporate these ideas in the design of a scheme for utility representation to be used as part of common Knowledge Representation Specification Language for the DARPA/Rome Laboratory initiative on Transportation Planning. The experience gained in using these techniques to build a substantial KB for use by several research groups will be invaluable in developing more refined representations for decision-theoretic planning.

Acknowledgments

Our investigation of this topic arose from an effort to design a general utility representation for transportation planning. We have benefited from collaborations with the other members of this project: Jack Breese, Tom Dean, and Max Henrion. We are also grateful to Ron Loui and Bernhard von Stengel for past discussions about central aspects of this work. Jon Doyle is supported by the USAF Rome Laboratory and DARPA under contract F30602-91-C-0018, and by National Institutes of Health Grant No. R01 LM04493 from the National Library of Medicine.

References

[1] Eugene Charniak. Bayesian networks without tears. *AI Magazine*, 12(4):50–63, 1991.

[2] W. M. Gorman. The structure of utility functions. *Review of Economic Studies*, 35:367–390, 1968.

[3] Peter Haddawy and Steve Hanks. Issues in decision-theoretic planning: Symbolic goals and numeric utilities. In *Proceedings of the DARPA*

Workshop on Innovative Approaches to Planning, Scheduling, and Control, pages 48–58, 1990.

[4] David E. Heckerman. Probabilistic similarity networks. *Networks*, 20:607–636, 1990.

[5] David E. Heckerman and Eric J. Horvitz. The myth of modularity in rule-based systems for reasoning with uncertainty. In John F. Lemmer and Laveen N. Kanal, editors, *Uncertainty in Artificial Intelligence 2*, pages 23–34. North-Holland, 1988.

[6] Ralph L. Keeney and Howard Raiffa. *Decisions with Multiple Objectives: Preferences and Value Tradeoffs*. John Wiley and Sons, New York, 1976.

[7] R. P. Loui. Defeasible decisions: What the proposal is and isn't. In *Proceedings of the Workshop on Uncertainty in Artificial Intelligence*, pages 245–252, Windsor, ON, 1989.

[8] Ronald Loui. Defeasible specification of utilities. In Henry E. Kyburg, Jr., Ronald P. Loui, and Greg N. Carlson, editors, *Knowledge Representation and Defeasible Reasoning*, pages 345–359. Kluwer Academic Publishers, 1990.

[9] Judea Pearl. *Probabilistic Reasoning in Intelligent Systems: Networks of Plausible Inference*. Morgan Kaufmann, San Mateo, CA, 1988.

[10] Leonard J. Savage. *The Foundations of Statistics*. Dover Publications, New York, second edition, 1972.

[11] Bernhard von Stengel. Decomposition of multiattribute expected-utility functions. *Annals of Operations Research*, 16(4):161–184, 1988.

[12] Michael P. Wellman. The STRIPS assumption for planning under uncertainty. In *Proceedings of the National Conference on Artificial Intelligence*, pages 198–203, Boston, MA, 1990. AAAI.

[13] Michael P. Wellman, John S. Breese, and Robert P. Goldman. From knowledge bases to decision models. *Knowledge Engineering Review*, 7(1), 1992.

[14] Michael P. Wellman and Jon Doyle. Preferential semantics for goals. In *Proceedings of the National Conference on Artificial Intelligence*, pages 698–703, Anaheim, CA, 1991. AAAI.

Automatically Abstracting the Effects of Operators

Eugene Fink
Department of Computer Science
University of Waterloo
Waterloo, Ontario, Canada N2L3G1
efink@violet.waterloo.edu

Qiang Yang
Department of Computer Science
University of Waterloo
Waterloo, Ontario, Canada N2L3G1
qyang@logos.waterloo.edu

Abstract

The use of abstraction in problem solving is an effective approach to reducing search, but finding good abstractions is a difficult problem. The first algorithm that completely automates the generation of abstraction hierarchies is Knoblock's ALPINE, but this algorithm is only able to automatically abstract the *preconditions* of operators. In this paper we present an algorithm that automatically abstracts not only the preconditions but also the *effects* of operators, and produces finer-grained abstraction hierarchies than ALPINE. The same algorithm also formalizes and selects the *primary effects* of operators, which is thus useful even for planning without abstraction. We present a theorem that describes the necessary and sufficient conditions for a planner to be complete, when guided by primary effects.

1 INTRODUCTION

Recently, there has been an increasing amount of interest in formalizing abstraction and abstract problem-solving. Much work has stemmed from Sacerdoti's ABSTRIPS system [Sacerdoti, 1974], which builds an abstraction hierarchy by systematically eliminating preconditions of operators. Given a problem space and a hierarchy of abstractions, a hierarchical problem-solver first solves a problem in an abstract space, and then refines it in successively more detailed spaces. Abstraction often reduces the complexity of search by dividing up a problem into smaller subproblems.

A notable achievement in recent research is Knoblock's ALPINE system [Knoblock, 1991], which completely automates the formation of abstraction hierarchies. The hierarchies that ALPINE constructs satisfy the *ordered property* [Knoblock et al., 1991], which states that while refining an abstract plan on a concrete level, no abstract-level predicate will be changed.

To a large extent, the property is successful in formalizing an important intuition behind the use of abstraction: one wants to preserve the abstract-plan structure while adding concrete-level operators. Experiments [Knoblock, 1991] have demonstrated that in many problem domains, ALPINE gains an exponential amount of savings in planning time.

The ability for a problem-solver to reduce search relies heavily on the quality of an abstraction hierarchy it generates. A problem with ALPINE is that it often generates a hierarchy with too few levels. In some cases, the entire hierarchy collapses into a single level. The "collapsing-problem" of ALPINE makes it incapable of handling many real-life domains.

In this paper, we present a new algorithm for generating abstraction hierarchies that satisfy the ordered property. The new algorithm addresses the collapsing problem of ALPINE by providing more levels of hierarchies than ALPINE does. It often succeeds in cases where ALPINE fails to create a multi-level hierarchy. The intuition behind our success is due to the fact that our algorithm automatically abstracts not only preconditions but also the *effects* of operators. On the other hand, ALPINE only abstracts the *preconditions* of operators automatically, while its abstraction of effects depends critically on a set of user-provided primary-effects.

The paper starts by reviewing the terminology used in the planning literature and a brief discussion of the ALPINE system. Then we provide a theory for constructing abstraction hierarchies, and demonstrate the application of the described method via theorems and examples. Finally, we will discuss the advantages and possible shortcomings of our approach, and methods for fixing the shortcomings.

2 ABSTRACTION IN PLANNING: A REVIEW

We follow the terminology used in [Knoblock et al., 1991]. A *planning domain* consists of a set of literals and a set of operators. Each *operator* α is defined by a set of *precondition literals* $Pre(\alpha)$ and *effect literals* $Eff(\alpha)$.

A *state* of the world is a set of literals. Applying an operator α produces a new state, where all literals from $Eff(\alpha)$ hold, and all literals that do not conflict with $Eff(\alpha)$ are left unchanged. For example, suppose p_1 and p_2 are some atomic statements in a problem domain. The corresponding literals are p_1, p_2, $\neg p_1$, and $\neg p_2$. Let $Eff(\alpha) = \{\neg p_1\}$. Then applying α to a state $S = \{p_1, p_2\}$ produces a new state $S = \{\neg p_1, p_2\}$.

A *plan* $\Pi = (\alpha_1, \ldots, \alpha_n)$ is a sequence of operators, which can be applied to a state by executing each operator in order. An *initial state* S_0 is a state of the world before executing plan, and S_i is the state achieved by executing first i operators of Π. A plan $\Pi = (\alpha_1, \ldots, \alpha_n)$ is *legal* relative to an initial state if the preconditions of each operator are satisfied in the state in which the operator is applied, i.e. $(\forall i \in [1 \ldots n])$ $Pre(\alpha_i) \subseteq S_{i-1}$.

A *planning problem* is a pair (S_0, S_g), where S_0 is an initial state, and S_g is a *goal state*. A plan Π is *correct* relative to the planning problem (S_0, S_g) if Π is legal relative to S_0 and the goal is satisfied in the final state: $S_g \subseteq S_n$.

To build an abstraction hierarchy, one can associate some natural number, called *criticality*, with every literal in the problem domain. While solving problem at *the i-th level of abstraction*, we ignore all literals with criticality less than i. Abstract planning is usually done in a top-down manner: first we find an abstract solution at the highest level of abstraction. Then we refine it to account for successive levels of details. The process of transforming a correct plan Π from level i to a correct plan at a lower level is called *refinement*. Given a correct plan Π at level i of abstraction, the refinement process can be briefly described as follows:

1. Add the level $i-1$ literals into both the preconditions and effects of operators, and initial and goal states in Π

2. Add operators that achieve these new literals.

This concept of refinement captures the intuition behind plan refinements not only in ABSTRIPS, but also in the task-network based planning systems, such as SIPE [Wilkins, 1984] and NONLIN [Tate, 1977].

For a given set of operators, different criticality assignments may result in different behavior in problem solving. We would like an abstraction hierarchy to help reduce the complexity of planning. *Ordered hierarchies*, introduced in [Knoblock *et al.*, 1991], are aimed at achieving this goal. Informally, an abstraction hierarchy is an ordered hierarchy if every refinement of an abstract plan leaves the abstract plan structurally unchanged. Experiments have shown that the ordered

hierarchies often increase the efficiency of planning algorithms exponentially [Knoblock, 1991]. ALPINE has been implemented by Knoblock to automatically generate ordered hierarchies that conform with human intuition behind "good" hierarchies. Hierarchies generated by ALPINE are based on the following syntactic restriction:

Restriction 1 (Ordered restriction)
Let O be the set of operators in a domain. $\forall \alpha \in O$, $\forall e_1, e_2 \in Eff(\alpha)$, and $\forall p \in Pre(\alpha)$ such that p is achieved by some operator,
(1) $\mathrm{crit}(e_1) = \mathrm{crit}(e_2)$, and
(2) $\mathrm{crit}(e_1) \geq \mathrm{crit}(p)$.

Intuitively, all effects of an operator have the same criticality, and their criticality is at least as great as the criticalities of operator's preconditions (except the preconditions that cannot be achieved by any operator).

Consider the Tower of Hanoi domain with 3 pegs and 3 disks. Let the three pegs be P_1, P_2, and P_3, and let the disks be *Large*, *Medium* and *Small*. We can represent the locations of the disks using literals of the form $OnLarge(x)$, $OnMedium(x)$, and $OnSmall(x)$. The operators for moving disks can be represented as shown in Table 1. Observe that the literals of the form $IsPeg(x)$ cannot be achieved by any operator, while all other literals may be achieved by some operator.

We may assign criticality 3 to each $IsPeg$ literal, criticality 2 to each $OnLarge$ literal, criticality 1 to each $OnMedium$ literal, and criticality 0 to each $OnSmall$ literal. It is not hard to verify that this assignment satisfies the Ordered Restriction.

3   A MOTIVATING EXAMPLE

Suppose that in the Tower of Hanoi example, we add the operators that can move *two disks* at a time, as long as both disks are on the same peg, and there are no disks between them. The extra operators are listed in Table 2.

ALPINE fails to generate a hierarchy for this new domain: all literals collapse into a single level of abstraction. To see this, observe that according to Statement 1 of the Ordered Restriction, all effects of operators must have the same criticality. The operator *MoveLM* has effects *OnLarge* and *OnMedium*, and therefore $crit(OnLarge) = crit(OnMedium)$. Similarly, for effects of the operator *MoveMS* we have $crit(OnMedium) = crit(OnSmall)$.

So the only criticality assignment satisfying the Ordered Restriction is

$$crit(OnLarge) = crit(OnMedium) = crit(OnSmall).[1]$$

---

[1] One may easily verify that a hierarchy collapses into a

Table 1: Operators For the Tower Of Hanoi

Preconditions		Effects
MoveL(x,y)		
IsPeg(x), IsPeg(y), ¬OnSmall(x), ¬OnSmall(y), ¬OnMedium(x), ¬OnMedium(y), OnLarge(x)		¬OnLarge(x), OnLarge(y)
MoveM(x,y)		
IsPeg(x), IsPeg(y), ¬OnSmall(x), ¬OnSmall(y), OnMedium(x)		¬OnMedium(x), OnMedium(y)
MoveS(x,y)		
IsPeg(x), IsPeg(y), OnSmall(x)		¬OnSmall(x), OnSmall(y)

Table 2: New Operators For the Tower Of Hanoi

Preconditions		Effects
MoveLM(x,y)		
IsPeg(x), IsPeg(y), ¬OnSmall(x), ¬OnSmall(y), *OnLarge(x)*, *OnMedium(x)*		¬OnLarge(x), OnLarge(y), ¬OnMedium(x), OnMedium(y)
MoveMS(x,y)		
IsPeg(x), IsPeg(y), OnSmall(x), OnMedium(x)		¬OnMedium(x), OnMedium(y), ¬OnSmall(x), OnSmall(y)
MoveLS(x,y)		
IsPeg(x), IsPeg(y), OnLarge(x), OnSmall(x), ¬OnMedium(x)		¬OnSmall(x), OnSmall(y), ¬OnLarge(x), OnLarge(y)

Notice that even with the operators for moving two disks, intuitively it is still true that moving the large disk is more difficult than moving the small one. Thus, intuitively one should still consider the movement of a large disk at an abstract level. This example shows a shortcoming of ALPINE: the addition of a few new operators may collapse an abstraction hierarchy into a single level, even though intuition tells us that the abstraction hierarchy should stay intact.

The purpose of this paper is to remove this deficiency of ALPINE. In the sections below, we achieve this by presenting a new algorithm that constructs abstraction hierarchies and still preserves the ordered monotonicity property.

4 ORDERED HIERARCHIES WITH PRIMARY EFFECTS

A key point to observe in the above example is that, if we want to move the small disk alone, we do not use the operator MoveLS or MoveMS. It is more natural to move the small disk with the operator MoveS. Similarly, we use the MoveLM operator if we want to

move either the large disk[2], or the large and medium disks together. But we do not use MoveLM to move the medium disk alone. In other words, an operator is used for the sake of its *primary effects*. In the Tower of Hanoi example, we can envision $OnLarge(y)$ as the primary effect of the operator $MoveLS(x, y)$, and $OnSmall(y)$ as its *side effect*. The set of primary effects of the Tower of Hanoi operators are listed in Table 3.

As another example, suppose you are going to a computer shop to buy diskettes. The primary effect of this action is obtaining diskettes — this is your main goal. Side effects are spending $20, having a pleasant walk on a sunny day, wearing your shoes, and so on.

The purpose of recognizing primary effects is to reduce the complexity of a problem-solving process by reducing the branching factor of search space. When achieving some literal, a problem-solver needs to consider only operators whose primary effects contain this literal. If a problem-solver uses operators only for the sake of their primary effects, it is said to be *primary-effect restricted*. ALPINE is primary-effect restricted,

---

single level even if we use *problem-specific* ordered restrictions [Knoblock, 1991].

---

[2]The reason to use MoveLM when we need to move only the large disk is that the medium disk may be above the large one, in which case we cannot use MoveL without removing the medium disk first.

Table 3: Primary Effects Of Operators In the Extended Tower Of Hanoi.

Operators	Primary Effects	Operators	Primary Effects
$MoveL$(x,y)	OnLarge(y)	$MoveLM$(x,y)	OnLarge(y)
$MoveM$(x,y)	OnMedium(y)	$MoveMS$(x,y)	OnMedium(y)
$MoveS$(x,y)	OnSmall(y)	$MoveLS$(x,y)	OnLarge(y)

but the primary effects of operators have to be provided by the user. Therefore, an extension of ALPINE would be to consider methods for automatically finding the primary effects that facilitate abstraction.

In the next section we present an algorithm for *automatically* finding the primary effects of operators. But for now, we assume that the primary effects of the operators in a domain have been found. The set of primary effects of an operator α is denoted by *Prim-Eff*(α). We now consider how to construct a finer-grained ordered abstraction hierarchy based on the primary effects. Consider the following modified ordered restriction:

Restriction 2 *Let O be the set of operators in a domain. $\forall \alpha \in O$, $\forall e \in$ Eff(α), $\forall e_1, e_2 \in$ Prim-Eff(α), and $\forall p \in$ Pre(α) such that p is achieved by some operator,*
  (1) crit(e_1) = crit(e_2),
  (2) crit$(e_1) \geq$ crit(e), *and*
  (3) crit$(e_1) \geq$ crit(p).

This restriction formalizes the syntactic conditions behind the algorithm used by ALPINE ([Knoblock, 1991], page 83). For a primary-effect restricted problem-solver, Restriction 2 provides a sufficient condition to guarantee a hierarchy to be ordered:

Theorem 1 *If a planner is primary-effect restricted, then every abstraction hierarchy satisfying Restriction 2 is ordered.*

That is, if an abstraction hierarchy satisfies Restriction 2, then no new operators in the refinement of an abstract plan achieves an abstract literal, as long as the problem-solver is primary-effect restricted. To see that the theorem holds, consider the achievement of a precondition literal l at level $(i-1)$ during the refinement of an abstract plan. Suppose an operator α is selected for achieving l. Since our problem-solver is primary-effect restricted, l is a primary effect of α. The criticalities of all other effects of α are not greater than $(i-1)$, and therefore no higher-level literals are achieved by α. For a more formal proof, see [Fink, 1992]. It is easy to create an algorithm that automatically generates an abstraction hierarchy based on Restriction 2.

5 AUTOMATICALLY SELECTING PRIMARY EFFECTS

The construction of an ordered abstraction hierarchy for a primary-effect restricted problem-solver is based on a definition of primary effects for the set of operators in a domain. For each planning domain, there are different ways to define primary effects, which can be grouped into the following three categories:

1. **All Effects Are Primary Effects.** This option is implicitly used in the syntactic restriction given in [Knoblock *et al.*, 1991], and used as default by ALPINE if no primary effects are provided by the user. As we have demonstrated, it often creates too few number of abstraction levels.

2. **User-Defined Primary Effects.** This is the approach taken by ALPINE, and many other systems. For example, the ABTWEAK system [Yang *et al.*, 1991] depends on the user to define the set of primary effects of operators.

3. **Automatically Selecting Primary Effects.** This is the approach we are taking. We now give a more detailed description of the algorithm.

For each operator, a definition of primary effects should make a clear distinction between those effects that are important, and those that are not. A good distinction thus relies on a formalization of what is important. The notion of importance that we follow is based on the intuition of ordered hierarchies:

> Given two effects e_{pri} and e_{sec} of an operator α, e_{pri} is more important (i.e., primary) than e_{sec} if it is possible to achieve e_{sec} without violating e_{pri}, while to achieve e_{pri} one has to violate e_{sec}.

In other words, e_{sec} is easier to achieve compared to e_{pri}, because it is possible to achieve it without violating e_{pri}. As an example, one can have a pleasant walk without going to a computer shop, but to buy diskettes, one has to go to a computer shop. Thus, taking a walk is a secondary effect of going to a computer shop as compared with buying diskettes.

From Theorem 1, every choice of primary effects that satisfies Restriction 2 results in an ordered hierarchy. But different choices of primary effects give rise to different hierarchies. The finest distinction between primary and secondary effects also corresponds to an ordered hierarchy with the greatest number of abstraction levels. Therefore, when finding the primary effects of operators, we strive to maximize the total number of abstraction levels for an ordered hierarchy.

Our strategy is to augment the ALPINE algorithm by providing it with a facility of choosing primary effects. ALPINE constructs an abstraction hierarchy by building a constraint graph of literals. The literals in a problem domain are represented as nodes of a directed graph. Constraints are represented as directed edges. An edge from l_1 to l_2 indicates that $crit(l_1) \geq crit(l_2)$. Initially, the graph is a set of literals without any constraints. When the algorithm terminates, the strongly connected components of the graph correspond to abstraction levels. The abstraction levels also relate closely to the primary effects for each operator: an effect e_1 is primary if it has a criticality value no less than the other effects of the same operator. Our algorithm will thus try to leave as many strongly connected components as possible.

To avoid an exhaustive search, we use a greedy algorithm. The algorithm uses a heuristic for incrementally adding edges to the graph, attempting to impose as few constraints as possible. To do this, the algorithm processes operators which impose the fewest number of constraints first, and consider the operators which have the potential to impose a large number of constraints later. A heuristic function for determining the amount of constraints equals the total number of effects of an operator. At the same time, we also try to guarantee planning completeness, by making sure that every operator has a primary effect, and every literal is the primary effect of at least one operator.

To sum up, our algorithm first sorts the operators in ascending order of the number of their effects. While building the constraint graph and choosing primary effects, the algorithm starts by considering operators each of which achieves exactly one literal. Thus, for each operator α that has a unique effect e, we make e the primary effect of α, and add directed edges from e to all preconditions of α. Then we consider each literal achieved by a unique operator. Since each achievable literal must be a primary effect of some operator, we make every literal achieved by a unique operator a primary effect of the corresponding operator. In the next iteration, we consider the set of operators that establishes two distinct literals, and the literals that are achieved by two different operators. At the i-th step, the algorithm performs the following two operations:

- choose primary effects of each operator that establishes i different literals, and

- for every literal l that is achieved by i different operators, make l a primary effect of one of the corresponding operators.

Each choice of a primary effect will add edges to the constraint graph. Given an operator with m effects, there are m possible choices. The best choice is dictated by maximizing the total number of strongly connected components in the constraint graph. In other words, the algorithm uses a greedy strategy by making locally optimal choice at each step.

Our algorithm, *Choose_Primary_Effects*, is shown in Table 4. Its input is a set of operators in a domain, and it outputs a selection of primary effects for each operator. It gives the user the option to define primary effects of some (not necessarily all) operators, and then chooses primary effects of the remaining operators. The notation $\|Graph\|$ refers to the total number of strongly connected components in the graph.

We now give a more detailed description of the algorithm. Line 2 of the main algorithm adds edges defined by Restriction 2 for the user-defined primary effects. Then the algorithm chooses primary effects of the remaining operators. At the i-th step, we choose primary effects of operators that achieve i literals. This is performed by the algorithm *Choose_Prim_Effects_Of_Operator*. Let α be an operator, $e_1, e_2, \ldots, e_i$ be effects of α, and *Graph* be the constraint graph before a primary effect of α is chosen. First the algorithm tries to make e_1 a primary effect of an operator, by adding directed edges from e_1 to all other effects of α and to all preconditions of α, thus creating a new graph $Graph_1$. Then the algorithm tries to make e_2 a primary effect of α and creates the corresponding graph $Graph_2$. Similarly, it generates $Graph_3, \ldots, Graph_i$. After all graphs are generated, the algorithm counts the number of strongly connected components in each of the graphs, and chooses the graph $Graph_j$ with the largest number of components. e_j is then chosen as a primary effect of α. This operation is performed for all operators that achieve i distinct literals.

The algorithm next considers all literals achieved by i different operators, and make each literal a primary effect of one of the corresponding operators. This is performed by the procedure *Make_Literal_Be_Prim_Effect*, which is similar to *Choose_Prim_Effect_Of_Operator*. For the lack of space, we do not present it here. Interested readers can refer to [Fink, 1992].

After the *Graph* is completely built, line 10 of the main algorithm chooses the remaining primary effects of operators according to the imposed constraints: for each operator α, the criticality of every effect of α is compared with the criticality of the primary effect found by the procedure *Choose_Prim_Effect_Of_Operator*. All effects of α whose criticalities are equal to the criticality value of the primary effect, are added to the set of primary effects of α.

It can be shown that the running time of the algorithm is $O(|\mathcal{L}|^2 \cdot \sum_{\alpha \in O} |Eff(\alpha)|)$, where $\mathcal{L}$ is the set of all literals in the problem domain, and O is the set of all operators in the problem domain.

As an example, we consider the Extended Tower of Hanoi domain. Each of the operators *MoveL*, *MoveM*, and *MoveS* achieves one literal, and at the first step the algorithm makes this literal a primary effect. After performing this step the graph G is as shown on Figure 1a. Then the algorithm considers operators that achieve two distinct literals. These operators are *MoveLM*, *MoveMS*, and *MoveLS*. The effects of *MoveLM* are *OnLarge* and *OnMedium*. One of them must be chosen as a primary effect. If *OnLarge* is a primary effect, its criticality must be at least as great as the criticality of *OnMedium* and the criticalities of all preconditions of *MoveLM*. These restrictions already hold in G, so it is not necessary to add new constraints. If *OnMedium* is chosen as a primary effect of *MoveLM*, we must have $crit(OnMedium) \geq crit(OnLarge)$. After the constraint defined by this inequality is added to G, we receive a new graph G' shown in Figure 1b. G' contains fewer strongly connected components than G. Since the purpose is to maximize the number of strongly connected components, the algorithm finally chooses *OnLarge* to be a primary effect of *MoveLM*. Then the algorithm uses the same method to choose primary effects of *MoveMS* and *MoveLS*. One may check that the algorithm chooses *OnMedium* to be a primary effect of *MoveMS*, and *OnLarge* to be a primary effect of *MoveLS*. According to Restriction 2, the predicates *OnLarge*, *OnMedium* and *OnSmall* have criticality values 2, 1, and 0, respectively.

6   ADVANTAGES AND LIMITATIONS OF USING PRIMARY EFFECTS

In this section, we discuss the advantages and limitations of an abstraction hierarchy based on Restriction 2, as compared to a hierarchy built by ALPINE. We compare two types of abstraction levels in terms of the number of hierarchies generated by each algorithm, and discuss the completeness of the resulting planning system.

First observe that the number of abstract levels generated by our algorithm is always no less than that generated by ALPINE. This is because our algorithm imposes criticality constraints only for *primary effects*, while ALPINE imposes constraints for *all* effects of an operator, unless the primary effects are provided by the user.

Second, if we need to establish some literal l, we may use only operators with a *primary* effect l, not all the operators that achieve l. This reduces the branching factor of search.

Table 4: Creating an Ordered Hierarchy

Choose_Primary_Effects
1. $Graph$:= create a directed graph where
    (a)   every literal in the problem domain
              is represented as a node, and
    (b)   there are no edges between the nodes
2. Add_Constraints_For_User-Defined_Prim_Effects;
3. for $i := 1$ to n do
    begin
4.   for each α that achieves i distinct literals do
5.   if the user have not defined prim. effects of α
6.   then Choose_Prim_Effect_Of_Operator(α);
7.   for each l achieved by i distinct operators do
8.   if l is not yet a prim. effect of some operator
9.   then Make_Literal_Be_Prim_Effect(l);
    end;
10. Choose_Prim_Effects_According_To_Graph
11. Topological_Sort

Choose_Prim_Effect_Of_Operator(α)
1. $Max\_Number\_Of\_Comps := 0$;
2. for each $e_1 \in Eff(\alpha)$ do
    begin
3. $Graph1 := Graph$;
4.   for each $e_2 \in Eff(\alpha)$ do
5.   add an edge in $Graph1$ from e_1 to e_2;
6.   for each $p \in Pre(\alpha)$ do
7.   if p can be achieved by some operator
8.   then add an edge in $Graph1$ from e_1 to p;
9.   Combine_Strongly_Connected_Comps($Graph1$);
10.   if $||Gr1|| > Max\_Number\_Of\_Comps$
            then
                begin
11. $Graph2 := Graph1$;
12. $primary := e_1$;
13. $Max\_Number\_Of\_Comps := ||Graph1||$
                end
    end;
14. $Graph := Graph2$;
15. $Prim\text{-}Eff(\alpha) := \{primary\}$

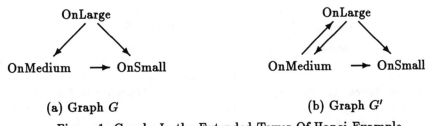

(a) Graph G (b) Graph G'

Figure 1: Graphs In the Extended Tower Of Hanoi Example

Now we discuss the *completeness* of a system based on the abstraction hierarchy produced by our algorithm. Ideally, we would like an abstraction hierarchy to have the *monotonic property*. The monotonic property holds if for every solvable problem there exists a *justified* [3] abstract-level plan that can be refined to a concrete-level plan that solves the problem. Yang and Tenenberg have shown that every abstraction hierarchy satisfy this property [Yang et al., 1991]. However, this claim holds only for problem-solvers that do not use primary effects. A primary-effect restricted planner applied to an abstraction hierarchy may not satisfy the monotonic property.

To solve the completeness problem, we present a theorem that allows us to test whether given hierarchy (built with primary effects) has the monotonic property. Let S be a state, and α be an operator whose preconditions are satisfied in S. Let $l_1, \ldots, l_k$ be primary effects of α, and $l_{k+1}, \ldots, l_n$ be its side effects. We say that α is *replaceable on a lower level* for an initial state S if there exists some plan Π with an initial state S such that Π achieves all *side* effects of α and leaves all other predicates unchanged. In other words, all side effects of α may be achieved on some lower level of abstraction without violating any higher-level literals and any other low level literals. In our example with the computer shop, this means that you can spend $20 and have a walk *without* bying diskettes.

Theorem 2 *A hierarchy has the monotonic property if and only if for every state S and for every operator α whose preconditions are satisfied in S, α is replaceable on a lower level for the initial state S.*

The reason why this theorem holds may be explained informally as follows. Suppose we have some planning problem and a concrete-level plan Π that solves this problem. Let Π' be a justified version of Π on the abstract level. Such a version always exists by the Upward Solution Property [Tenenberg, 1988]. We wish to show that Π' may be refined on the concrete level. Π may not be a concrete-level refinement of Π', since it may contain additional operators that achieve abstract-level literals. But all operators inserted into Π' are used to achieve concrete-level literals. So if some

inserted operator has primary effects on the abstract level, it is inserted only for the sake of its side effects. The operator is replaceable, so we may replace it with a sequence of operators that achieve only its side effects, and leave all abstract-level literals intact. Let us replace all the newly inserted operators that have abstract-level effects with sequences of operators that achieve only their side effects. Our plan is still correct, and all operators inserted into Π' now have only concrete-level effects. So, this new plan is a concrete level refinement of Π'.

Based on this theorem, we can build an algorithm to test whether a particular selection of primary effects yield a monotonic hierarchy. It can be verified that the Tower of Hanoi domain, with the extended operators and the chosen primary effects satisfies the conditions of the theorem.

7   A ROBOT-DOMAIN EXAMPLE

In this section we demonstrate the result of applying our algorithm to a simple robot domain taken from [Yang et al., 1991], which is a simplification of the domain from [Sacerdoti, 1974]. In this domain there is a robot that can walk within several rooms. Some rooms are connected by doors, which may be open or closed. In addition, there are a number of boxes, which the robot can push either within a room or from one room to another. Figure 2 shows an example of a robot domain. The domain may be described by the following predicates:

$open(d)$	door d is open
$box\text{-}inroom(b, r)$	box b is in room r
$box\text{-}at(b, loc)$	box b is at location loc
$robot\text{-}inroom(r)$	the robot is in room r
$robot\text{-}at(loc)$	the robot is at location loc
$location\text{-}inroom(loc, r)$	location loc is in room r
$is\text{-}door(d)$	d is a door
$is\text{-}box(b)$	b is a box

(Observe that the last three predicates are not achievable.) The list of operators in this domain, described on LISP, is given in Table 5.

A straightforward application of Restriction 1 to this domain fails to produce a multilevel hierarchy,

---
[3] A plan is justified if every operator either directly or indirectly contributes to achievement of a goal. In other words, a justified plan does not contain "useless" operators.

Table 5: The Operators Of the Robot World

---- Operators For Moving Within a Room ----

```
; Go to Location within room                 ||  ; Push box between locations within a room
(setq o1 (make-operator                      ||  (setq o2 (make-operator
  :name '(goto-room-loc $from $to $room)      ||    :name '(push-box $box $room $box-from-loc
  :preconditions '(                           ||                   $box-to-loc robot)
    (location-inroom $to $room)               ||    :preconditions '(
    (location-inroom $from $room)             ||      (is-box $box)
    (robot-inroom $room)                      ||      (location-inroom $box-to-loc $room)
    (robot-at $from))                         ||      (location-inroom $box-from-loc $room)
  :effects '(                                 ||      (box-inroom $box $room)
    (not robot-at $from)   ;**                 ||      (robot-inroom $room)
    (robot-at $to))))      ;**                 ||      (robot-at $box $box-from-loc))
                                              ||    :effects '(
                                              ||      (not robot-at $box-from-loc)
                                              ||      (not box-at $box $box-from-loc)  ;**
                                              ||      (robot-at $box-to-loc)
                                              ||      (box-at $box $box-to-loc))))     ;**
```

---- Operators For Moving Between Rooms ----

```
; Push box through door between two rooms     ||  ; Go through door between two rooms
(setq o3 (make-operator                      ||  (setq o4 (make-operator
  :name '(push-thru-dr $box $door-nm          ||    :name '(go-thru-dr $door-nm $from-room
                $from-room $to-room            ||                   $to-room $door-loc-from
                $door-loc-from                 ||                   $door-loc-to)
                $door-loc-to robot)            ||    :preconditions '(
  :preconditions '(                           ||      (is-door  $door-nm $from-room $to-room
    (is-door  $door-nm $from-room $to-room     ||              $door-loc-from $door-loc-to)
            $door-loc-from $door-loc-to)       ||      (robot-inroom $from-room)
    (is-box $box)                             ||      (robot-at $door-loc-from)
    (box-inroom $box $from-room)               ||      (open $door-nm))
    (robot-inroom $from-room)                  ||    :effects '(
    (box-at $box $door-loc-from)               ||      (robot-at $door-loc-to)          ;**
    (robot-at $door-loc-from)                  ||      (not robot-at $door-loc-from)    ;**
    (open $door-nm))                           ||      (not robot-inroom $from-room)    ;**
  :effects '(                                 ||      (robot-inroom $to-room))))       ;**
    (not robot-inroom $from-room)              ||
    (robot-inroom $to-room)                    ||
    (not box-inroom $box $from-room)   ;**     ||
    (box-inroom $box $to-room)         ;**     ||
    (robot-at $door-loc-to)                    ||
    (box-at $box $door-loc-to)         ;**     ||
    (not robot-at $door-loc-from)              ||
    (not box-at $box $door-loc-from))))  ;**   ||
```

---- Operators For Opening and Closing Doors ----

```
; Open door                                   ||  ; Close door
(setq o5 (make-operator                      ||  (setq o6 (make-operator
  :name '(open $door-nm $from-room $to-room    ||    :name '(close $door-nm $from-room $to-room
            $door-loc-from $door-loc-to)       ||                $door-loc-from $door-loc-to)
  :preconditions '(                           ||    :preconditions '(
    (is-door $door-nm $from-room $to-room      ||      (is-door $door-nm $from-room $to-room
            $door-loc-from $door-loc-to)       ||              $door-loc-from $door-loc-to)
    (not open $door-nm)                        ||      (open $door-nm)
    (robot-at $door-loc-from))                 ||      (robot-at $door-loc-from))
  :effects '(                                 ||    :effects '(
    (open $door-nm))))   ;**                   ||      (not open $door-nm))))   ;**
```

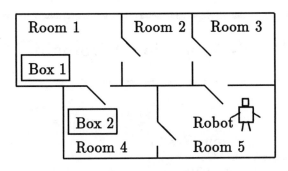

Figure 2: Example of a Robot Domain

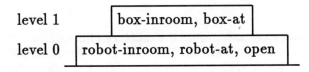

Figure 3: Abstraction Hierarchy In the Robot Domain

while the algorithm *Choose_Primary_Effects* divides the achievable predicates of the robot domain into two abstraction levels shown in Figure 3. The primary effects of operators chosen by the algorithm are marked by ";**" in Table 5.

8   CONCLUSION

This paper presents an extension of Knoblock's ALPINE algorithm for automatically generating abstraction hierarchies. Using the notion of primary effects and primary-effect restricted problem-solvers, we are able to generate ordered hierarchies where ALPINE fails. The algorithm for finding primary effects is also novel in *automatically* selecting primary effects in a given domain. We also discussed possible shortcomings and advantages of our system as compared to ALPINE.

An important extension of the described method is the algorithm that generates *problem-specific* ordered hierarchies based on primary effects. Such hierarchies are built based on individual problem instances. We have found such an algorithm, a description of which is presented in [Fink, 1992]. It allows one to generate an ordered hierarchy for a specific goal, while permitting the resulting hierarchy to be finer-grained than a problem-independent hierarchy.

The method for finding primary effects presented in the paper is purely syntactic. A possible direction of future work is to address the semantic meaning of primary effects. Another open problem is to find an algorithm that generates a hierarchy with the *maximal* possible number of levels, using the A* algorithm. Such a hierarchy will be particularly useful in a domain

where the same hierarchy will be used many times.

Acknowledgements

The authors are supported in part by a scholarship and grants from the Natural Sciences and Engineering Research Council of Canada and ITRC.

References

[Fink, 1992] Eugene Fink. Justified plans and ordered hierarchies. Master's thesis, University of Waterloo, Department of Computer Science, Waterloo, Ont. Canada, Forthcoming 1992.

[Knoblock *et al.*, 1991] Craig Knoblock, Josh Tenenberg, and Qiang Yang. Characterizing abstraction hierarchies for planning. In *Proceedings of the 9th AAAI*, Anaheim, CA, 1991.

[Knoblock, 1991] Craig A. Knoblock. *Automatically Generating Abstractions for Problem Solving*. PhD thesis, School of Computer Science, Carnegie Mellon University, May 1991. Tech. Report CMU-CS-91-120.

[Sacerdoti, 1974] Earl Sacerdoti. Planning in a hierarchy of abstraction spaces. *Artificial Intelligence*, 5:115–135, 1974.

[Tate, 1977] Austin Tate. Generating project networks. In *Proceedings of the 5th IJCAI*, pages 888–893, 1977.

[Tenenberg, 1988] Josh Tenenberg. *Abstraction in Planning*. PhD thesis, University of Rochester, Dept. of Computer Science, May 1988.

[Wilkins, 1984] David Wilkins. Domain-independent planning: Representation and plan generation. *Artificial Intelligence*, 22, 1984.

[Yang *et al.*, 1991] Qiang Yang, Josh Tenenberg, and Steve Woods. *Abtweak: Abstracting a nonlinear, least commitment planner*. Dept. of Computer Science, University of Waterloo, Dec. 1991. Research Report CS-91-65.

Constraint Satisfaction with a Multi-Dimensional Domain

Masazumi Yoshikawa   Shin-ichi Wada
C&C Systems Research Laboratories, NEC Corporation
4-1-1 Miyazaki, Miyamae-ku, Kawasaki 216
JAPAN

Abstract

This paper presents a novel approach to a class of *constraint satisfaction problems (CSPs)*. First, it defines *Multi-Dimensional Constraint Satisfaction Problem (MCSP)*, which is a useful model applicable to many scheduling problems. Second, it proposes an approach for MCSPs. The approach employs both a general problem-solving method and an automatic generation method for problem-solving programs. The problem-solving method is a combined method with backtracking and constraint propagation, based on the features of MCSPs. The automatic generation method analyzes the meaning of constraints and generates a problem-solving program, which is especially efficient for the given problem. Finally, the proposed approach is evaluated by several experiments including scheduling applications and well-known toy problems. Employing both the two methods enables solving a hard MCSP in a reasonable time, merely by describing it in a declarative form.

1 INTRODUCTION

In recent years, a scheduling problem is increasingly being viewed as a *constraint satisfaction problem (CSP)* [Fox 1989]. The CSP has a simple well-defined model and general problem-solving algorithms. Since many scheduling problems can be formulated as CSPs, they can be solved by these algorithms, in a general way.

In order to solve a CSP, two classes of algorithms have been developed. The first group involves *backtracking* algorithms and the second group involves *constraint propagation* algorithms. Backtracking algorithms are guaranteed to solve any CSP, but they suffer from thrashing [Nudel 1983]. On the other hand, several *network-based* constraint propagation algorithms have been developed, using the topology of *constraint networks* [Mackworth 1977, Freuder 1982, Freuder 1990]. They are guaranteed to solve a class of CSPs with a *tree-like* constraint network in polynomial time [Mackworth 1985].

Recently, combined algorithms with backtracking and constraint propagation have been developed [Dechter 1988, Dechter 1990]. They use constraint propagation on tree-like subgraphs of a constraint network in order to reduce the search space for backtracking. They can solve any CSP and are efficient for tree-like constraint networks. They have been the most powerful algorithms to solve CSPs in a general way.

However, even with these algorithms, most scheduling problems are hard problems. This is because, they have a *disjointness* constraint, that prohibits assigning a same *value* (resource) to more than one *variable* (task). Since this constraint is concerned with every combination of two variables, their constraint networks become a *complete graph*, which is the most complex one. In general, a CSP is the more difficult, if the constraint network is the more complex [Zabih 1990]. This is the most critical difficulty for solving scheduling problems in a general way.

In order to overcome this difficulty, the authors took an approach from two points of view:

1. Since there is no algorithm which solves any CSPs efficiently, a problem-solving method, based on the features of the application problems, is required.

2. The network-based algorithms use only the topological features of the constraints. However, focusing on the meaning of constraints, there may be more efficient ways to process them.

This paper presents a novel approach to a class of CSPs. First, it defines *Multi-Dimensional Constraint Satisfaction Problem (MCSP)*, which is a useful model applicable to many scheduling problems. A declarative framework to describe MCSPs is also presented. Second, it proposes an approach for MCSPs. The

Variables: $\rightarrow n$

variable 1	variable 2	...	variable N

Domain: $\rightarrow j$

	value $(1,1)$	value $(1,2)$	...	value $(1,J)$
	value $(2,1)$	value $(2,2)$	...	value $(2,J)$
$\downarrow$	...	...	...	...
i	value $(I,1)$	value $(I,2)$	...	value (I,J)

Figure 1: Multi-Dimensional Constraint Satisfaction Problem

approach employs a general problem-solving method for MCSPs and an automatic generation method for problem-solving programs.

The problem-solving method is a combined method with backtracking and constraint propagation. It is an efficient method, based on the features of MC-SPs. The automatic generation method generates a problem-solving program, which is especially efficient for the given problem. It analyzes constraints in a logical form and selects efficient procedures, according to the meaning of constraints.

Finally, the proposed approach is evaluated by experiments including school curriculum scheduling, production scheduling, work assignment problems, and several well-known MCSP problems.

Employing the two methods enables solving a hard MCSP in a reasonable time, merely by describing it in a declarative form.

The following section defines the MCSP and presents the declarative framework to describe MCSPs. In Section 3, the problem-solving method for MCSPs is proposed. The automatic program generation method is described in Section 4. Section 5 shows and discusses the experimental results. A summary and conclusion are given in Section 6.

2 PROBLEMS

As described in the previous section, most scheduling problems belong to the most difficult class of CSPs. Therefore, the authors focused their attention on a class of CSPs, that is applicable to many scheduling problems. This section defines *Multi-Dimensional Constraint Satisfaction Problem (MCSP)* and presents a declarative framework to describe MCSPs.

2.1 Multi-Dimensional Constraint Satisfaction Problem

A CSP involves a set of N *variables* $v_1, ..., v_N$ having *domains* $D_1, ..., D_N$, where each D_n defines the set of

```
1  (define-set area     area1 area2 area3 area4...)
2  (define-set color    red blue green yellow)
3  (define-set-of-sets neighbors
4     (area1 area2) (area1 area3) (area2 area4)...)
5  (define-constraint exclusive-color
6     ((area color) (area1 color1) (area2 color2))
7     (if (in-same-set-of neighbors area1 area2)
8        (not (= color1 color2))
9        true))
10 (define-problem four-color-problem
11      (:variables area)
12      (:domain (color))
13      (:constraints exclusive-color))
```

Figure 2: Declarative Description of a Four Color Problem

available values for the variable v_n. An MCSP is a CSP, in which the all domains are same. Namely, $D_1 = D_2 = ... = D_N$.

For example, a *Four Color Problem* is an MCSP. It is a problem to assign four colors on every bounded area on a plane, satisfying the constraint that no area has the same color as it's neighboring area. This problem has variables for every area, and a shared domain that is the set of four colors.

Moreover, the domain may be represented by an $I \times J$ array with two (or more) dimensions. Figure 1 illustrates the MCSP variables and domain.

For example, a school curriculum scheduling problem, by which to assign a teacher and a time for every classroom, is a two-dimensional MCSP. In this case, variables are given classrooms. The domain is represented by an array with two dimensions corresponding to teachers and times. Another example is a production scheduling problem, that consists of N tasks, I production machines, and J time-intervals in a scheduling period.

Many other scheduling problems, such as work assignment problems, can be formulated as MCSPs. Consequently, MCSP is an important subclass of CSPs for scheduling applications.

2.2 DECLARATIVE DESCRIPTION OF MCSPS

This section presents a declarative framework to describe MCSPs. An MCSP consists of a set of variables, a multi-dimensional domain, and a set of constraints.

For example, the declarative description of a Four Color Problem is presented in Fig. 2. Lines 1-2 define the sets of variables and a domain. Lines 3-4 define a class used in the constraint definition in lines 5-9. The problem is defined in lines 10-13. The body (lines 7-9) of the constraint definition is a logical form. The meaning of the constraint definition is that:

For every pair of two different assignments (area color)s, let the assignments be (area1 color1) and (area2 color2),
if area1 and area2 form a pair of neighbors,
    color1 and color2 must be different,
otherwise OK.

Line 12 defines the shared domain for this MCSP. A Four Color Problem has a one-dimensional domain (a set color).

In case of school curriculum scheduling, the domain may have two-dimensions (teachers and time involved). The problem definition may be as follows:

```
(define-problem school-scheduling
    (:variables classroom)
    (:domain (teacher time)) ;; 2-dimension
    (:constraints ...))
```

The problem is to assign a value, in the two-dimensional domain made up with the sets teacher and time, to each variable in the set classroom, satisfying the all constraints specified in the :constraints option.

3   A METHOD TO SOLVE MCSPS

As described in Section 1, most scheduling problems belong to the most difficult class of CSPs. Therefore, the authors developed an efficient method for MCSPs, based on the MCSP features. This section describes two MCSP features and proposes a problem-solving method, based on the features.

3.1   FEATURES OF MCSPS

As mentioned in the preceding section, an MCSP has a multi-dimensional (or single-dimensional) domain that consists of a set of dimensions. In the case of a multi-dimensional domain, the dimensions have independent meanings in the application problem, e.g., teachers and times. Therefore, many constraints refer to only one dimension of the domain.

For example, a school curriculum scheduling problem has the following constraints:

science-classroom-science-teacher
    A science teacher must be assigned to a science classroom.

same-class-different-time
    Different times must be assigned to two classrooms of the same class.

Constraint science-classroom-science-teacher does not refer to the domain dimension time, but to the other dimension teacher. On the other hand, same-class-different-time refers to only time.

The constraints, which refer to only one domain dimension, are called *one-dimensional constraints*, while other constraints are called *multi-dimensional constraints*.

Since domain dimensions have independent meanings, most constraints are one-dimensional. This is an important feature of MCSPs. The proposed method is based on this *dimension independence* of MCSPs.

Another MCSP feature is *problem duality*. Since an MCSP has a two (or more) dimensional domain, the problem is assigning a two-dimensional value (i, j) to each variable v_n. Therefore, it can be reformulated into another CSP, in which a (one-dimensional) value i is assigned to a variable vi_n and j is assigned to vj_n. For example, since the school curriculum scheduling problem is assigning a value (teacher, time) to each classroom, it can be reformulated into another CSP with $2N$ variables, N variables vi_n (classrooms) for I values (teachers) and N variables vj_n (classrooms) for J values (times). This problem duality is also used in the problem-solving method for MCSPs.

3.2   A PROBLEM-SOLVING METHOD BASED ON MCSP FEATURES

The problem-solving method is based on the MCSP features, dimension independence and problem duality.

The method decomposes an MCSP into three (or more) subproblems, using *problem duality*. The subproblems are:

SP-M A subproblem, which is same as the original MCSP, except that it has only multi-dimensional constraints.

SP-I A subproblem, which corresponds to the dimension i, with N variables vi_n, a domain with size I, and one-dimensional constraints that refer to i.

    In the school curriculum scheduling problem, it has N classrooms as variables, I teachers as values, and one-dimensional constraints that refer to only teachers, e.g., science-classroom-science-teacher.

SP-J A subproblem, which corresponds to the dimension j, with N variables vj_n, a domain with size J, and one-dimensional constraints that refer to j.

    In the example, it has N classrooms as variables, J times as values, and one-dimensional constraints that refer to only times, e.g., same-class-different-time.

Then, the method assigns values to variables using a backtracking algorithm and a constraint propagation algorithm, as follows:

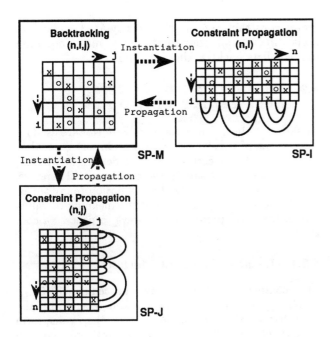

Figure 3: A Problem-Solving Method for MCSPs

1. A backtracking algorithm creates assignment on subproblem SP-M, checking multi-dimensional constraints.

2. A constraint propagation algorithm processes one-dimensional constraints on subproblems SP-I and SP-J.

   In the example, one-dimensional constraints about `times` are propagated in SP-J.

The constraint propagation is triggered when the backtracking assigns a value to a variable. The backtracking selects the candidate values for a variable according to the constraint propagation results. Figure 3 illustrates the problem-solving method.

Here, it should be noticed that the problem-solving method does not specify a certain backtracking algorithm or a constraint propagation algorithm. Existing backtracking algorithms can be joined into this method with small modification. Also, several constraint propagation algorithms can be combined in the problem-solving method. Current experimentation uses a *most-constraint min-conflicts* backtracking algorithm, as described in [Keng 1989], and a naive constraint propagation algorithm AC-3 in [Mackworth 1977].

3.3   DISCUSSION

In order to evaluate the problem-solving method, how existing CSP algorithms work on an MCSP must be considered. Several efficient algorithms have been developed using the topology of *constraint networks*, e.g., [Freuder 1982], [Mackworth 1985], [Dechter 1988], and

[Dechter 1990]. They are applicable or efficient with *tree-like* constraint networks. However, most scheduling problems have a disjointness constraint that makes a constraint network form a *complete graph*. Since they belong to the most difficult class of CSPs [Zabih 1990], these algorithms have few merits.

On the other hand, SP-I and SP-J in the proposed problem-solving method have small domain sizes I and J, while the domain size for the original MCSP is $I \times J$. If we propagate e one-dimensional constraint edges on an MCSP, using AC-3, then the complexity is $O(eI^3J^3)$ (See [Dechter 1988]). On the other hand, the complexity on SP-I and SP-J is $O(e_iI^3 + e_jJ^3)$, where e_i and e_j are number of edges on SP-I and SP-J, namely $e = e_i + e_j$. Consequently, the proposed method dramatically decreases the computational time.

Here, it must be considered carefully that SP-I and SP-J have only one-dimensional constraints. Since MCSPs have dimension independence, most constraints are one-dimensional. However, if there are heavy multi-dimensional constraints in an MCSP, the proposed method has few merits. This is the limitation of this method. An example of heavy multi-dimensional constraints is the disjointness constraint, which can be checked in a cheaper manner, using an $I \times J$ array, as described in the next section.

In addition, *the combination of local propagation and backtracking (LPB)* in [Guesgen 1989] is similar to the proposed method, except that it does not use domain dimensions.

4   AN AUTOMATIC PROGRAM GENERATION METHOD

This section describes an automatic program generation method. The method analyzes the meaning of given constraints and generates appropriate procedures to process them. Then, it integrates them into a program to solve the problem. First, a naive program generation method is described. Then, a method to refine a constraint process is proposed.

4.1   A NAIVE PROGRAM GENERATION METHOD

The naive program generation method analyzes a given constraint and generates a constraint process procedure, as follows.

Step 1: A constraint is defined with a logical form. For example, the `exclusive-color` constraint for a Four Color Problem has the following form:

```
(if (in-same-set-of neighbors area1 area2)
    ;; if area1 and area2 is a neighbors pair.
    (not (= color1 color2))
    true)
```

Step 2: What is prohibited by the constraint can be represented by the negation of the logical form. The logical form is negated and normalized into a *conjunctive normal form*:

```
(and (in-same-set-of neighbors area1 area2)
     (= color1 color2))
```

Step 3: The subforms for the conjunctive form (the **and** form) are divided into two sets, *variable-forms* and *value-forms*.

Variable-forms: Subforms, which refer to no domain values (**colors**), but variables (**areas**).
```
(in-same-set-of neighbors area1 area2)
```
Value-forms: Subforms, which refer to domain values (**colors**), may also refer to variables (**areas**).
```
(= color1 color2)
```

Step 4: Variable-forms restrict related (combinations of) variables to those which satisfy them. The method generates a procedure which associates the constraint to the related variables, using the variable-forms. In this example, the generated procedure creates constraint edges between all pairs of **neighbors**.

Step 5: Value-forms specify what (combinations of) values are prohibited by the constraint. The method generates a procedure which processes the constraint, using the value-forms. There are three kinds of constraint processes and the category is determined by the problem-solving method, described in Section 3.

The three kinds of constraint processes are, domain-value removal for unary constraints, constraint propagation for one-dimensional binary constraints, and constraint checking for multi-dimensional constraints.

In the case of one-dimensional binary constraints, the value-forms are processed by constraint propagation. The method generates the following propagation procedure:

> **PROC-N:** For each available *value2* (**color2**) value, if there is no available value *value1* (**color1**) such that the *value-form* (= color1 color2) is evaluated to be false, remove *value2* (**color2**) value from the domain, otherwise do nothing.

Note that this is the same as the procedure REVISE of AC-3. If an implementation uses another constraint propagation algorithm, this procedure may be modified, according to the algorithm in use.

The constraint procedures, generated by the generation method, are integrated into a problem-solving program, that uses the problem-solving method, described in Section 3. Current experimentation generates a program which preprocesses unary constraints by domain-value removal, propagates one-dimensional

binary constraints on subproblems by AC-3, and checks multi-dimensional constraints in a most-constraint min-conflicts backtracking algorithm.

4.2   A CONSTRAINT PROCESS REFINEMENT METHOD

As shown in the naive method, *value-forms* are used for three kinds of constraint processes. In any case, they are evaluated with certain values to determine whether or not these values satisfy the constraint. Therefore, the naive method repeats the evaluation many times. On the other hand, considering the meaning of value-forms, there are more efficient ways to process a constraint.

4.2.1   Local Refinement Method

The complexity of the naive procedure PROC-N is $O(I^2)$, where I is the domain size. In the **exclusive-color** example, since the value-form (= color1 color2) prohibits **color1** and **color2** from taking the same value, it can be propagated as follows:

> **PROC-1:** Check whether the available value for *value1* (**color1**) is unique or not. If unique, remove the unique value from the domain of *value2* (**color2**), otherwise do nothing.

Using this procedure, the constraint can be propagated in constant time when an implementation provides a domain size counter for every variable.

For another example, a job-shop production scheduling problem has a constraint that specifies the ordering among two tasks. The value-form of this constraint may be (not (< time1 time2)). An $O(I)$ procedure, to propagate the constraint, is:

> **PROC-2:** Find the minimum available value of *value1* (**time1**), remove the values less-than-or-equal-to the minimum value from the domain of *value2* (**time2**).

As shown in the examples, several common value-forms have an efficient procedure to process them. The refinement method provides such efficient procedures associated with a pattern for a value-form, such as (= *value1 value2*). The refinement method takes matching between a given value-form and provided patterns. If a matching pattern is found, then the associated procedure is used in place of the naive procedure. They are provided separately, according to the three kinds of constraint processing.

Here, it should be noticed that procedures PROC-1 and PROC-2 depend on propagation algorithm AC-3. These procedure must be modified, corresponding to the propagation algorithm in use.

4.2.2 Global Refinement Method

The method described above refines a propagation process for one constraint edge. On the other hand, it is possible to refine the propagation process for a set of constraint edges into an efficient procedure. This refinement is accomplished in almost the same manner, but it uses variable-forms, as well as value-forms.

Consider the `same-class-different-time` constraint for the school curriculum scheduling in Section 3. It has a value-form and a variable- form as follows:

Variable-form:
    (in-same-set-of classrooms-for-the-same-class
                    classroom1 classroom2)
Value-form:
    (= time1 time2)

The constraint propagation from one variable to all the other variables in a `classrooms-for-the-same-class` set is refined into a procedure:

> **PROC-3**: Check whether or not the available *value1* (`time1`) value is unique. If unique, remove the unique value from the domains for all the other variables in a *set* (`classrooms-for-the-same-class`), otherwise do nothing.

This refinement reduces the complexity from $O(mI^2)$ into $O(m)$, where m is the size of a *set*.

As described in Section 3, thorough checking of a disjointness constraint has large costs in the problem-solving method. The constraint checking can be replaced by the following procedure.

> **PROC-4**: Provide an $I \times J$ Boolean array that expresses the domain. Look up an array entry in order to check the disjointness constraint. When backtracking assigns a value, mark a corresponding array entry in order to specify that the value is unavailable.

If there were no backtrack to assign values to all variables, PROC-4 reduces the total checking cost from $O(N^3)$ into $O(N^2)$. This refinement is more effective in general cases.

4.3 DISCUSSION

The effectiveness of the refinement method has already been shown. Here, the novelty and limitation for this method are discussed.

Guesgen's CONSAT also provides a constraint description language and a constraint compiler, which improves constraint propagation processes [Guesgen 1989]. The compiler eliminates checking variables, which has no relation to a given constraint. However, it does not refine the propagation process with the related variables. The improvement of CONSAT compiler is similar to Step 4 of the naive program generation method in Section 4.1.

The most close research to the refinement method is an arc consistency algorithm AC-5 in [Deville 1991]. AC-5 uses the feature of *functional* and *monotonic* constraints in order to reduce the complexity. It is based on almost the same idea as the *local* refinement method for constraint propagation, except that it does not handle *disequation* constraints, such as disjointness. Moreover, AC-5 does not include the *global* refinement method or refinements for domain-value removal and constraint checking.

It is trivial that this refinement method is effective only when a value-form matches a provided pattern. This is the limitations of the method.

5 EXPERIMENTAL RESULTS

This section evaluates the proposed approach with several experiments including school curriculum scheduling, production scheduling, work assignment, and several well-known CSP problems (See Appendix).

The computational times used for a school curriculum scheduling and a production scheduling problem are shown in Table 1. For each problem, both a two-dimensional and a one-dimensional formalization are examined. A one-dimensional formalization represents the same problem as a two-dimensional one, except that the two-dimensional domain is elongated into a one-dimensional domain. This elongation causes that the proposed problem-solving method works in the same way as LPB in [Guesgen 1989] works (See Section 3.3). Therefore, a comparison between one-dimensional and two-dimensional formalization shows the improvement by using domain dimensions. Here, the constraint process refinement method, proposed in Section 4, is not used, except PROC-4 for the disjointness constraint. [1]

In the case of Problem A, using a multi-dimensional domain causes almost 80 times the previous efficiency. This marked result indicates the great effect of the proposed problem-solving method. On the other hand, the ratio is 1.78 for Problem B. This is because that Problem B is smaller than Problem A. As discussed in Section 3, the complexity of propagating one-dimensional constraints is $O(eI^3J^3)$ vs. $O(e_iI^3 + e_jJ^3)$. Therefore, the method is more effective for a larger problem, namely larger values e, I, and J. Consequently, the problem-solving method is more effective for a larger and more tightly constrained problem.

---

[1]This is because the one-dimensional curriculum scheduling problem (Problem A') can not be solved in four days, without PROC-4.

Table 1: Experimental Results of the Problem-Solving Method

Problem		a. Two-dims. (seconds)	b. One-dim. (seconds)	Ratio (b/a)
A,A'	Curriculum Scheduling	1,921	151,900	79.04
B,B'	Production Scheduling	3.94	7.01	1.78

Table 2: Experimental Results of the Constraint Process Refinement Method

Problem		a. Refined (seconds)	b. Naive (seconds)	Ratio (b/a)	Procedures
A	Curriculum Scheduling	866.60	30400	35.07	PROC-2, 3, 4, etc.
B	Production Scheduling	3.73	47.71	12.79	PROC-2, 4, etc.
C	Work Assignment	82.48	87.62	1.06	PROC-1, 3, etc.
D	Work-Pattern Assignment	1.96	2.38	1.22	PROC-1, etc.
E	50-Queen	148.20	1110	7.49	PROC-4, special proc.
F	Four Color Problem	217.60	598.60	2.80	PROC-1.
G	Four Color Problem (no solution)	0.42	10.34	24.60	PROC-1.
H	Zebra Problem	0.41	0.60	1.44	PROC-3, etc.

Table 2 compares the computational times for the same problem in two cases: one is when the constraint process refinement method is applied, and only the naive program generation method is used in the other case. [2] These results for each problem are taken from exactly the same problem definition. The procedures used in the refinement method are also listed in the table.

One of the most remarkable results is that the PROC-4, which refines checking the disjointness constraint, has a great advantage (in Problem A, B, and E). Comparing the results of D and H, since PROC-3 (in Problem H) is a global refinement procedure, the gains are larger than a local refinement procedure PROC-1 in Problem D. As discussed in Section 4.3, AC-5 does not include the refinement of constraint checking and global refinement method. Consequently, the proposed refinement method is more effective than merely employing AC-5.

Consider the Four Color Problems (F and G). Since the unique constraint is refined by PROC-1, the gains for the refinement method are comparatively large. In the case of Problem G, an arc consistency algorithm as AC-3 proves that it has no solution without any backtracking. Namely, almost all the time is spent in constraint propagation. Therefore, the refinement method causes a high efficiency.

In addition, it should be mentioned that the same procedures are used in several problems involving different application fields. This means that the constraint

process refinement method is applicable for many applications.

Although the constraint process refinement method refines only a part of constraint processes, it has considerable merits for many application problems. Moreover, it is very effective especially for hardly constrained problems. Consequently, two proposed methods enable solving a hard problem in a dramatically efficient way.

6   CONCLUSION

In this paper, a novel approach to a class of CSPs is presented. First, it defines *Multi-Dimensional Constraint Satisfaction Problem (MCSP)*, which is a useful model applicable to many scheduling problems. Second, it proposes an approach for MCSPs, focusing on the features of MCSPs and the meaning of constraints. The approach employs a general problem-solving method for MCSPs and an automatic generation method of problem-solving programs. Finally, the proposed approach is evaluated by several experiments including scheduling applications and well-known toy problems. Employing these methods enables solving a hard MCSP in a reasonable time, merely by describing it in a declarative form.

Appendix: Test Problems

A *A school curriculum scheduling problem* is presented as an example. It has 160 variables (32 classrooms for every 5 classes) and 352 values (11 teachers × 32 times). The constraints are, `science-classroom-science-teacher`,

---

[2] Current experimentation uses a most-constraint min-conflicts backtracking algorithm and a naive constraint propagation algorithm AC-3.

`same-class-different-time`, `disjointness`, a constraint specifying continuous classrooms, a constraint specifies that classrooms in the same class and the same subjects must not be assigned in the same day, etc.

A' The same problem as **A**, except that the two-dimensional domain (11 × 32) is elongated into a one-dimensional domain (352).

B *A job-shop production scheduling problem* with 44 variables (tasks), 6 production machines × 10 time-intervals. It is a very simple test problem developed for experimental purpose. It includes, specification regarding off-days and scheduled machine maintenance, relation among a task and a machine, due dates, task orderings, and a few constraints.

B' The same problem as **B**, except that the two-dimensional domain (6 × 10) is elongated into a one-dimensional domain (60).

C *A work assignment problem* with 114 variables (works) and one-dimensional domain (21 workers). Since the time of a work is given, there are no time dimension for the domain. Constraints are, exclusive assignments for the same work time, specification of workers' available times, license for workers, standard working time length, etc.

D The same problem as **C**, except that the 114 works are preprocessed and combined into 22 work-patterns.

E *N-Queen problems*. They have *N* variables (rows) and a one-dimensional domain with *N* values (columns).

F *A Four Color Problem* with 560 variables (areas), 4 values (colors), and 1583 pairs of neighboring areas. It is a one-dimensional problem.

G *A Four Color Problem*. It has 152 variables (areas) and 413 neighborings. Since the available set of colors for each area is restricted, it has no solution.

H *Zebra Problem* in [Dechter 1990]. It is a one-dimensional problem with 25 variables (5 cigarettes, 5 pets, 5 persons, 5 houses, and 5 drinks) and 5 values (positions). It has only one solution.

Acknowledgments

The authors would like to express their thanks to Tatsuo Ishiguro, Masahiro Yamamoto, Takeshi Yoshimura, Masanobu Watanabe and Tomoyuki Fujita for their encouragement in this work. Further, they also thank Yoshiyuki Koseki for his valuable advice.

References

[Dechter 1988] R. Dechter and J. Pearl, "Network-Based Heuristics for Constraint-Satisfaction Problems", *Artificial Intelligence*, Vol. 34, 1988, pp. 1-38.

[Dechter 1990] R. Dechter, "Enhancement Schemes for Constraint Processing: Backjumping, Learning, and Cutset Decomposition", *Artificial Intelligence*, Vol. 41, 1990, pp. 273-312.

[Deville 1991] Y. Deville and P.V. Hentenryck, "An Efficient Arc Consistency Algorithm for a Class of CSP Problems", *Proceedings of the Twelfth International Joint Conference on Artificial Intelligence*, 1991, pp. 325-330.

[Fox 1989] M.S. Fox, N. Sadeh, and C. Baykan, "Constrained Heuristic Search", *Proceedings of the Eleventh International Joint Conference on Artificial Intelligence*, 1989, pp. 309-315.

[Freuder 1982] E.C. Freuder, "A Sufficient Condition for Backtrack-Free Search", *Journal of the Association for Computing Machinery*, Vol. 29, No. 1, January 1982, pp.24-32.

[Freuder 1990] E.C. Freuder, "Complexity of K-Tree Structured Constraint Satisfaction Problems", In *Proceedings of the Eighth National Conference on Artificial Intelligence*, 1990, pp.4-9.

[Guesgen 1989] H.W. Guesgen, "A Universal Constraint Programming Language", In *Proceedings of the Eleventh International Joint Conference on Artificial Intelligence*, 1989, pp. 60-65.

[Keng 1989] N. Keng and D.Y.Y. Yun, "A Planning/Scheduling Methodology for the Constrained Resource Problem", In *Proceedings of the Eleventh International Joint Conference on Artificial Intelligence*, 1989, pp. 998-1003.

[Mackworth 1977] A.K. Mackworth, "Consistency in networks of relations", *Artificial Intelligence*, Vol. 8, 1977, pp. 99-118.

[Mackworth 1985] A.K. Mackworth and E.C. Freuder, "The Complexity of Some Polynomial Network Consistency Algorithms for Constraint Satisfaction Problems", *Artificial Intelligence*, Vol. 25, 1985, pp. 65-74.

[Nudel 1983] B. Nudel, "Consistent-Labeling Problems and their Algorithms: Expected-Complexities and Theory-Based Heuristics", *Artificial Intelligence*, Vol. 21, 1983, pp. 135-178.

[Zabih 1990] R. Zabih, "Some Applications of Graph Bandwidth to Constraint Satisfaction Problems", In *Proceedings of the Eighth National Conference on Artificial Intelligence*, 1990, pp.46-51.

Efficient Resource-Bounded Reasoning in AT-RALPH

Shlomo Zilberstein and Stuart J. Russell
Computer Science Division
University of California
Berkeley, CA 94720

Abstract

Anytime algorithms have attracted growing attention in recent years as a key mechanism for implementing models of bounded rationality. The main problem, however, as with planning systems in general, is the integration of the modules and their interface with the other components of the system. We have implemented a prototype of AT-RALPH (Anytime Rational Agent with Limited Performance Hardware) in which an off-line compilation process together with a run-time monitoring component guarantee the optimal allocation of time to the anytime algorithms. The crucial meta-level knowledge is kept in the *anytime library* in the form of *conditional performance profiles*. These are extensions of an earlier notion of performance description – they characterize the performance of each elementary anytime algorithm as a function of run-time and input quality. This information, used by the compiler to produce the performance profile of the complete system, is also used by the run-time system to measure the *value of computation* and monitor the execution of the top-level procedure in the context of a particular domain. The result is an efficient and cheap meta-level control for real-time decision making that separates the performance components from the schedule optimization mechanism and automates the second task.

1 Introduction

Our objective has been to develop an efficient meta-level control for utility-driven, real-time agents. These agents are designed to operate in complex domains where future states and utility change over time are unpredictable. The complexity of these domains on the one hand and the limited computational resources available to the agents on the other hand have led us to a solution based on bounded rationality and anytime computation. Anytime algorithms[1] have attracted growing attention in recent years as a key mechanism for implementing models of bounded rationality. The main problem, however, as with planning systems in general, is the integration of the anytime components into a single, efficient, decision making procedure and interfacing this procedure with the other components of the agent – perception and action. In AT-RALPH, this problem is solved through an off-line compilation process together with a run-time monitoring component that guarantee the optimal allocation of time to the elementary anytime algorithms.

Anytime computation introduces a tradeoff between run-time and quality of results. In order to optimally control this new degree of freedom we introduce *conditional performance profiles* that give a probabilistic description of the quality of the results of an algorithm as a function of run-time and input quality (or a set of properties of the input). This is an extension of an earlier notion of performance profile that depends on run-time only.

Consider for example an anytime hierarchical planner whose quality of results is measured by the level of specificity of the plan. Obviously, the specificity of a plan affects its execution time and hence has influence on the efficiency of the agent. We have recently implemented such an algorithm for hierarchical path planning. Its conditional performance profile describes how the quality of the plan depends on run-time as well as on input quality, that is, the precision of the domain description.

Basic applications of anytime algorithms have been introduced by Boddy and Dean [1989] for solving a path planning problem and by Horvitz [1987] for real-time decision making in the health care domain. In this work we extend the use of anytime algorithms to the construction of complex planning systems. It is un-

---

[1]Anytime algorithms are algorithms whose quality of results improves gradually as computation time increases.

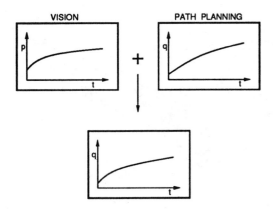

Figure 1: Path planning example

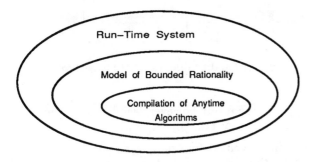

Figure 2: The three conceptual layers of AT-RALPH

likely that a complex system would be developed by implementing one large anytime algorithm. Systems are normally built from components that are developed and tested separately. In standard algorithms, the expected quality of the output is fixed, so composition can be implemented by a simple call-return mechanism. However, when algorithms have resource allocation as a degree of freedom, incremental scheduling and constant monitoring are required to guarantee optimal utilization of resources.

Figure 1 illustrates our approach. It shows an anytime path planning algorithm that receives its input from an anytime vision module. The quality of vision is measured in terms of precision of the domain description. The quality of path planning is measured in terms of specificity of the suggested plan. Our compilation scheme combines these two modules into one anytime path planning algorithm that can automatically distribute any given amount of time between the two components so as to maximize the overall quality of results. The rest of this paper describes in detail our solution to the problem of integrating and controlling anytime algorithms. The result is an efficient and cheap meta-level control for real-time decision making that separates the performance components from the schedule optimization mechanism and automates the second task.

The next three sections of the paper correspond to the three conceptual layers of AT-RALPH as illustrated in Figure 2. In Section 2, we describe the compilation of anytime algorithms – a process that creates an optimal anytime algorithm from a program composed of anytime components. Section 3 describes the theoretical framework used to determine the value of computation and the meta-level control of AT-RALPH. In Section 4, we describe the programming environment and run-time system. Finally, we summarize the benefits of our approach and discuss further work.

2 Compilation of anytime algorithms

The compilation of anytime algorithms, a central concept in our system, is an automated process that extends the idea of functional composition to anytime computation. Before explaining it in detail, we must make a distinction between *interruptible* algorithms and *contract* algorithms. Interruptible algorithms produce results of the quality "advertised" by their performance profiles even when interrupted unexpectedly; whereas contract algorithms, although capable of producing results whose quality varies with time allocation, must be given a particular time allocation in advance. The greater freedom of design makes it easier to construct contract algorithms than interruptible ones. In fact the compilation process described below produces a contract algorithm. To make this algorithm interruptible we use the result from [Russell and Zilberstein, 1991]:

Theorem 1 *For any contract algorithm $\mathcal{A}$, an interruptible algorithm $\mathcal{B}$ can be constructed such that for any particular input $Q_{\mathcal{B}}(4t) \geq Q_{\mathcal{A}}(t)$.*

Note that $Q_{\mathcal{A}}(t)$ represents the actual quality of the results of $\mathcal{A}$ with time allocation t. The construction of the interruptible algorithm is based on repeatedly restarting the contract algorithm with exponentially increasing allocation of time. Some readers may wonder whether the constant, 4, could result in a significant degradation of performance. Our experience, however, shows that in dynamic situations the flexibility of using an anytime interruptible algorithm can offset the slowdown caused by its construction. In addition, this constant can be reduced by scheduling the contract algorithm on a parallel machine. We have derived, for example, an optimal schedule that reduces the constant to 3 with 2 processors. The parallel scheduling options are, however, not trivial. We now turn to a detailed look at the compilation process.

Definition 1 Compilation of anytime algorithms *is the process of deriving a contract algorithm with an optimal performance profile from a program composed of several anytime algorithms whose performance profiles are given.*

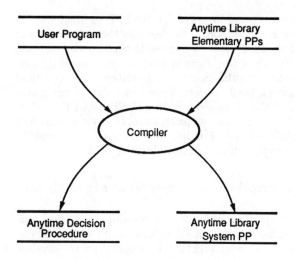

Figure 3: Compilation of decision procedures

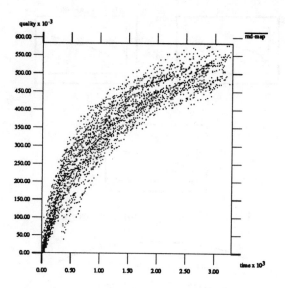

Figure 4: Quality map of TSP algorithm

Figure 3 shows the input and output of the compiler. Its input includes a user defined Lisp program composed of anytime components and a set of *conditional performance profiles* stored in a library. The task of the compiler is to produce a new version of the program that includes code to control the distribution of time between the components so as to maximize the overall performance for any given time allocation. It also creates a performance profile for the complete program based on optimal time allocation. The rest of this section describes the compilation process in detail.

2.1   Library of performance profiles

Once an elementary anytime algorithm is completed, its performance profile has to be computed and entered into the *anytime library*. The task of finding the performance profile of an algorithm can be quite complicated. In some cases, performance profiles can be constructed by a mathematical analysis of the anytime algorithm. For example in many iterative algorithms, such as Newton's method, the error in the result is (bounded by) a function of the number of iterations hence the performance profile can be constructed once the run-time of a single iteration is determined. In general, however, a mathematical analysis of the code is impossible. A general and practical approach is to compute the performance profile by gathering statistics on the performance of the algorithm in representative cases[2] (or learning it while the agent acts in the world). The performance profiles stored in the library can also be approximations to be refined within the context of a particular domain of application. At present we compute conditional performance profiles of the elementary anytime components by running a user-defined special program to gather the necessary

statistics. In the future however, we plan to automate this task within our system.

We have implemented, for example, a randomized anytime algorithm for the Traveling Salesman Problem (TSP) that is based on tour improvement[3]. Quality in this case was measured by the percentage of tour length reduction (with respect to the original random tour). Figure 4 shows the quality map that we generated by running the algorithm with randomly generated input instances. Each point (t, q) represents an instance for which quality q was achieved with runtime t. These statistics form the basis for the construction of the performance profile of the algorithm.

Quality measures

Russell and Zilberstein [1991] present three types of performance profiles and argue that the *performance interval profile* is the most appropriate for integrating anytime algorithms. However, for the purpose of this paper it will be easier for the reader to think about a performance profile as a mapping from computation time to the *expected* quality of results. This quality can be measured in three different ways: *Certainty* – where probability of correctness determines quality; *Accuracy* – where error bound determines quality; or *Specificity* – where the amount of detail determines quality. In principle, performance profiles can also be multidimensional, expressing, for example, both the certainty and accuracy of the results. However, we do not support multidimensional performance profiles in

---

[2]Representative problem instances are randomly generated based on prior knowledge of the problem domain.

[3]In the general case of tour improvement procedures, r edges in a feasible tour are exchanged for r edges not in that solution as long as the result remains a tour and the length of that tour is less than the length of the previous tour. See also [Lawler *et al.*, 1987].

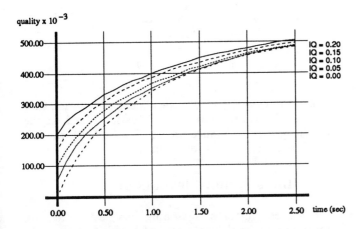

Figure 5: Conditional performance profile of TSP

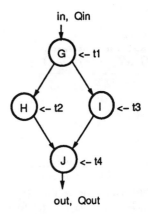

```
(defun F (u &aux x y z)
   (setf x (G u))
   (setf y (H x))
   (setf z (I x))
   (J y z))
```

```
(defun F (u)
   (J (H (G u)) (I (G u))))
```

6(a) Lisp definition of F

6(b) DAG representation of F

Figure 6: Compiling a straight line program

the current version of AT-RALPH.

Conditional performance profiles

To be able to properly combine anytime algorithms one has to take into account the fact that the quality of the results depends not only on time allocation but also on properties of the input, most notably its quality. Performance profiles in our system are therefore conditional. They consist of mappings from input quality and run-time to probability distribution of output quality:

$$\mathcal{CPP} \; : \; Q_{in} \times T \rightarrow Pr(Q_{out})$$

Figure 5 shows the conditional performance profile that we got for the TSP algorithm with several different initial input qualities[4].

2.2   Compilation

In the current prototype of AT-RALPH we solved the compilation problem for the case where compound (non-elementary) anytime algorithms are restricted to composition of other anytime algorithms. An equivalent assumption is that the code of a compound algorithm can be written as a *straight line program*[5] with anytime algorithms as basic operations. For example, Figure 6(a) shows a definition of a compound anytime function **F** both as a straight line program (top version) and as a composition of anytime functions. Every straight line program has a corresponding DAG (Directed Acyclic Graph) representation where each

node corresponds to one variable evaluation with a directed arc going to each function using that value. Figure 6(b) shows the DAG representing of **F**. The task of the compiler in this case is to find for each total allocation of time t, and input quality Q_{in}, the run-times t_1, t_2, t_3, t_4 ($t_1 + t_2 + t_3 + t_4 = t$) for the modules **G**, **H**, **I**, and **J** that maximize the expected quality of results Q_{out}. For each given allocation of time it is simple to find the expected quality of results based on the DAG representation and the performance profiles of the elementary anytime functions. In order to find the optimal allocation we have implemented an efficient search algorithm described below.

The time allocation algorithm is based on hill-climbing search. It starts with an equal amount of time allocated to each anytime component. Then it considers trading s time units between two modules so as to increase the expected quality of the results. As long as it can improve the expected quality, it trades s time units between the two modules that have maximal effect on output quality. When no such improvement is possible with the current value of s, it divides s by 2 until s reaches a certain minimal value. At that point, it reaches a local maxima and returns the best time allocation it found. As with any hill-climbing algorithm, it suffers from the problem of converging on a local maxima.

---

[4]Problems with a particular desired initial quality were generated using a different TSP algorithm.

[5]A straight line program is a sequence of expressions of the form *(setf u (f $v_1...v_n$))* where *u* is a new variable and $v_1...v_n$ are program arguments or existing variables. There is a trivial one-to-one mapping between functional composition and straight line code.

Time Allocation Algorithm

```
for each Q_in ∈ QUALS-TABLE
    for each T ∈ TIME-TABLE
        s ← initial-resolution(T)
        t_i ← T/n   ∀i : 1 ≤ i ≤ n
        repeat
            while ∃i, j such that
                E(Q_out(Q_in, t_1, ..., t_i − s, ..., t_j + s, ..., t_n))
                    > E(Q_out(Q_in, t_1, ..., t_n))
                let i, j be the ones that maximize E(Q_out)
                t_i ← t_i − s
                t_j ← t_j + s
            end
            s ← s/2
        until s < min-time-resolution
        CPP[Q_in, T] ← [Pr(Q_out), t_1, ..., t_n]
    end
end
```

Complexity

The current version of the system uses discrete performance profiles stored in a two dimensional table (with input quality and run-time as indices). Linear approximation is used to compute the performance distribution for points that do not match exactly one of the table entries. The allocation algorithm therefore has to fill-in this two dimensional table. For each entry in the table, the complexity of the algorithm is $O(Kn^2 logT)$, where K is a small constant representing the number of times s units of time are traded before s is divided by 2, n is the number of modules and T is the total run-time. Since the number of modules used to define a new function is normally small the overall complexity of the algorithm is dominated by the accuracy of the compiled performance profile (a system parameter) and is independent of the program itself.

Finally, the compiler inserts in the original function the necessary code to control internal time allocation. For this purpose, the compiler replaces each call to an anytime algorithm by an activation of the following form:

```
(at '<anytime-function> :time <run-time>)
```

It activates the algorithm <anytime-function> as a contract algorithm with time allocation <run-time>. The amount of time allocated to each module is determined at run time by the total allocation and a simple lookup in the compiled performance profile. For example, the function defined in Figure 6 would be redefined as:

```
(defun F (u &key iq time &aux x y z)
  (setf x (at '(G u) :time
    (TA CPP-F iq time 1)))
  (setf y (at '(H x) :time
```

```
    (TA CPP-F iq time 2)))
  (setf z (at '(I x) :time
    (TA CPP-F iq time 3)))
  (at '(J y z) :time
    (TA CPP-F iq time 4)))
```

Note that TA is a general time allocation function that returns the appropriate time allocation based on the conditional performance profile of F (CPP-F), the initial input quality and total run-time.

3   Efficient meta-level control

Meta-level control of reasoning has been a leading technique in implementations of bounded rationality [Dean and Boddy, 1988; Doyle, 1990; Horvitz, 1987; Russell and Wefald, 1991]. In an early stage of these implementations it became apparent that gathering the necessary meta-level knowledge is a complicated task that can dominate the base-level problem itself. It was necessary therefore to develop a system in which the meta-level knowledge could be gathered automatically. Another goal was to be able to solve the meta-level decision problem quickly. This is exactly what we achieve by using conditional performance profiles. The compiler can automatically use them to generate the performance profile of the complete system and the monitor can use them for a quick evaluation of the utility of continued computation. This utility, also defined as the *value of computation*, is determined in the following way:

Given an algorithm $\mathcal{A}$, let S_{t_i} represent the state of the domain at time t_i, let q_{t_i} represent the quality of the results of the top-level interruptible anytime algorithm at time t_i. $U_{\mathcal{A}}(S, q)$ represents the utility of results of quality q in state S. The purpose of the meta-level control is to maximize $U_{\mathcal{A}}(S_{t_i}, q_{t_i})$. Due to uncertainty concerning the quality of the results of the algorithm, the expected utility of the results in a given state S at some future time t_i is computed by:

$$U'_{\mathcal{A}}(S, t_i) = \sum_q p(q_{t_i} = q) U_{\mathcal{A}}(S, q)$$

The probability $p(q_{t_i} = q)$ is provided by the performance profile of the algorithm. Due to uncertainty concerning the future state of the domain, the expected utility of the results at some future time t_i is computed by:

$$U''_{\mathcal{A}}(t_i) = \sum_S p(S_{t_i} = S) U'_{\mathcal{A}}(S, t_i)$$

The condition for continuing the computation at time t for an additional Δt time units is therefore $VOC > 0$ where:

$$VOC = U''_{\mathcal{A}}(t + \Delta t) - U''_{\mathcal{A}}(t)$$

In some cases it is possible to separate the utility of the results from the time used to generate them. In

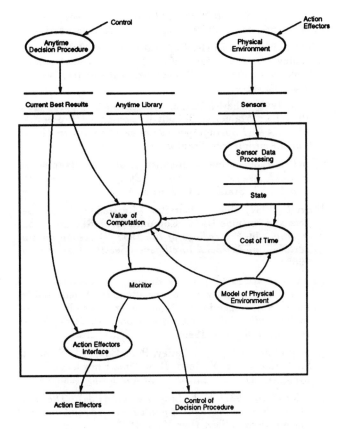

Figure 7: Data flow diagram of the run-time system

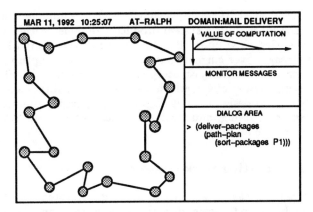

Figure 8: The user interface

such cases the value of computation can be expressed simply by:

$$VOC = U_{\mathcal{A}}'''(q_{t+\Delta t}) - U_{\mathcal{A}}'''(q_t) - TC(t, \Delta t)$$

where $U_{\mathcal{A}}'''(q)$ is the utility of results of quality q, and $TC(t, \Delta t)$ is the time cost of Δt time units at time t. This assumption, when valid, simplifies the calculation of the value of computation.

4   The run-time system

The purpose of the run-time system is primarily to monitor the execution of the compiled anytime algorithm. It also provides a standard interface between the implemented agent, the physical environment, and the user interface. Figure 7 shows the data flow between the main components of the run-time system. Sensory input is used to update the state of the environment as perceived by the agent. The state is then used in order to compute the cost of time that, together with the current best results and the performance profile of the main decision procedure, is used to determine the value of computation. The monitor decides, based on the value of computation, whether to interrupt the decision procedure and apply the current best results. The system has two different modes: (1) Single decision mode; and (2) Continuous decision

mode. In the first case the anytime algorithm is provided with a single set of inputs. It computes the results and may be interrupted by the monitor when the value of computation becomes negative. In the second case the algorithm is provided with an *input generator* that generates many instances of a problem. The run-time system restarts the algorithm with a new instance of the problem after each interruption/termination. This case models the behavior of an autonomous robot optimizing performance over a "history".

Another component of the run-time system, to be added in the future, is a debugging tool to allow the programmer to perform special operations that are unique to anytime computation such as: interrupting an algorithm and forcing its termination, examining the best result so far while the algorithm is running, or initiating events that change the cost of time to see how they affect the behavior of the monitor and the agent.

Figure 8 shows how the user interface of AT-RALPH will look in its complete implementation. The user will be able to load a particular domain definition and then run the system by specifying a particular problem using the dialog area. The system will then simulate the physical domain and the agent's behavior. The value of computation and a visual representation of the physical domain will be displayed during the simulation.

5   Conclusion

We have presented the three layers of AT-RALPH that together offer an integrated programming environment for constructing utility-driven, real-time agents. The central reasoning component of AT-RALPH is composed of elementary anytime algorithms that are combined together by the compiler into one anytime decision procedure. Our efficient meta-level control solves the problem of scheduling the elementary anytime components so as to maximize the overall performance.

Laffey *et al* [1988] claim that "ad hoc techniques are used for making a system produce a response within a specified time interval". Our approach has many advantages over current techniques: it achieves optimal performance not just acceptable performance; it can handle situations in which resource availability is unknown at design time; it effectively integrates planning and scheduling; and it provides machine independent real-time modules.

5.1 Further work

There is still a significant amount of system work to be done to generalize the various components of AT-RALPH. Another important task is to expand the "anytime" concept to include sensing and action. Moving toward a target in order to get a better view and aiming a gun at a target are examples of interruptible anytime actions. Similarly an anytime sensing procedure to estimate the size and location of an object can be developed by varying the number of samples and their resolution.

There is however an important distinction between sensing and action. Sensing may be assumed to have no relevant effect on the state of the domain while actions are intended to transform the state of the domain. As a result, it is possible to treat an anytime sensing component just as anytime computation and to apply to it the same compilation method. The contract-to-interruptible conversion cannot apply to actions, however, because re-initiating the action may result in different effects because of the changed initial state (consider, for example, gem polishing with increasingly fine abrasives). Further work is needed in order to integrate sensing and action into the framework. Our ultimate goal in this project is to construct an integrated programming environment for developing real-time agents that act by performing anytime actions and make decisions using anytime computation.

Acknowledgements

Support for this work was provided in part by the National Science Foundation under grants IRI-8903146 and IRI-9058427 (Presidential Young Investigator Award). The first author was also supported by the Malcolm R. Stacey Scholarship.

References

[Boddy and Dean, 1989] M. Boddy and T. Dean. Solving time-dependent planning problems. Technical Report CS-89-03, Department of Computer Science, Brown University, Providence, 1989.

[Dean and Boddy, 1988] Thomas Dean and Mark Boddy. An Analysis of Time-Dependent Planning. In *Proceed-ings of the Seventh National Conference on Artificial Intelligence*, pages 49–54, Minneapolis, Minnesota, 1988.

[Doyle, 1990] Jon Doyle. Rationality and its Roles in Reasoning. In *Proceedings of the Eighth National Conference on Artificial Intelligence*, pages 1093–1100, Boston, Massachusetts, 1990.

[Elkan, 1990] Charles Elkan. Incremental, Approximate Planning: Abductive Default Reasoning. In *Proceedings of the AAAI Spring Symposium on Planning in Uncertain Environments*, Stanford, California, 1990.

[Hendler, 1989] James A. Hendler. Real Time Planning. In *Proceedings of the AAAI Spring Symposium on Planning and Search*, Stanford, California, 1989.

[Horvitz, 1987] Eric J. Horvitz. Reasoning About Beliefs and Actions Under Computational Resource Constraints. In *Proceedings of the 1987 Workshop on Uncertainty in Artificial Intelligence*, Seattle, Washington, 1987.

[Horvitz et al., 1989] Eric J. Horvitz, H. Jacques Suermondt and Gregory F. Cooper. Bounded Conditioning: Flexible Inference for Decision Under Scarce Resources. In *Proceedings of 1989 Workshop on Uncertainty in Artificial Intelligence*, 1989.

[Laffey et al., 1988] T. J. Laffey, P. A. Cox, J. L. Schmidt, S. M. Kao and J. Y. Read. Real-Time Knowledge Based Systems. *AI Magazine*, 9(1), 27-45, Spring 1988.

[Lawler et al., 1987] E. L. Lawler et al., (Eds). *The traveling salesman problem: a guided tour of combinatorial optimization*. Wiley, New York, 1987.

[Russell and Wefald, 1991] Stuart J. Russell and Eric H. Wefald. *Do the Right Thing: Studies in limited rationality*. MIT Press, Cambridge, Massachusetts, 1991.

[Russell, 1991] Stuart J. Russell. An architecture for bounded rationality. In *Proceedings of the AAAI Spring Symposium on Integrated Architectures for Intelligent Agents*, Stanford, California, 1991.

[Russell and Zilberstein, 1991] Stuart J. Russell and Shlomo Zilberstein. Composing Real-Time Systems. In *Proceedings of the 12th International Joint Conference on Artificial Intelligence*, Sydney, Australia, 1991.

[Zilberstein, 1991] Shlomo Zilberstein. Integrating Hybrid Reasoners through Compilation of Anytime Algorithms. In *Proceedings of the AAAI Fall Symposium on Principles of Hybrid Reasoning*, pages 143-147, Pacific Grove, California, November 1991.

Posters

Using Abstraction-Based Similarity to Retrieve Reuse Candidates

Amedeo Cesta[1]
IP-CNR, National Research Council
Viale Marx 15, I-00137 Rome (Italy)
amedeo@irmkant.bitnet

Giovanni Romano
Fondazione Ugo Bordoni
Via B. Castiglione 59, I-00142 Rome (Italy)
fubdpt5@itcaspur.bitnet

Abstract

A case study from an application in man-machine interfaces is presented in which a previous reusing algorithm (Kambampathi 1989) turns out to be insufficient. An extension to that algorithm is provided which solves the problem. The extension is grounded on the use of domain knowledge to define "similar" plans. This similarity criterion is based on an abstraction hierarchy that represents the domain knowledge and is applied to retrieve suitable reuse candidates.

1 INTRODUCTION

We are currently investigating the possibility of applying planning techniques to an intelligent help system for Macintosh computer applications (Cesta and Romano 1989). In such a system, planning is called into play when the sequence of commands that achieves the user's goal is to be constructed. The problem we face with is that of planning in real-time. In order to overcome this computational complexity, we decided to exploit the regular structure of the domain in order to reuse past planning experience.

The initial object of our studies has been the PRIAR system (Kambampathi 1989), because of its extreme analytical capability, which is strictly linked to previous works on planning. In PRIAR, plans generated by a NONLIN-like planner are stored with all their annotations, i.e. their "range" links (Tate's terminology (Tate 1977)) between the producers and consumers of the various predicates. Given a new problem, PRIAR performs a sort of dependency-directed backtracking of an old plan in order to find a better partial plan as a starting point for the search process.

The difficulties we have met in applying PRIAR's algorithm are exemplified by the following problem: the system is asked to build a plan to copy a graphic element within the Claris MacDraw application. The goal will be represented as follows:

$$(Graphic\text{-}Element\text{-}Copied\ X\ Y)$$

where X represents the graphic element to be copied and Y is the position it will be copied to (*D-Position* in our terminology). People who usually work with Macintosh are likely to catch the analogy with respect to the problem of text copying in a wordprocessor (MS Word for example) when they recognize the similarity between lines of text in Word and graphic elements in MacDraw.

The PRIAR's retrieving algorithm ((Kambampathi 1989) Chapter 6), is based on a syntactic match between goals. Reuse candidates are evaluated by constructing three validations classes with respect to the new problem: goal validations (*g-features*), filter condition validations (*f-features*), and precondition validations (*pc-features*). The system searches for the plan which achieves the highest number of goals, and presents the lowest number of initial conditions to be met, so as to minimize the process of adaptation. The matching function recognizes equality but not similarity between predicates. That algorithm, when applied to our example, does not retrieve the plan for text copying, because the respective goals are represented by using two distinct predicates: *Text-Copied* and *Graphic-Element-Copied*.

Our attention has been focused on modifying the retrieve phase in order to also consider plans which satisfy a "similarity" criterion. Our main intention is to retrieve plans whose goals are represented by predicates which are semantically connected to the new one. Once a similarity is recognized we also need a pre-adaptation phase to perform a substitution between similar actions and predicates before applying the PRIAR's algorithm.

For the sake of space our description is very succinct. A more detailed explanation can be found in (Cesta and Romano 1992).

2 ABSTRACTION-BASED SIMILARITY

Our definition of similarity is strictly connected with the concept of abstraction. In particular we define abstraction hierarchies among predicates and actions. To this aim we define predicates as follows:

Defpredicate predicate-name
   :Arguments (*{parameter}*)
   :Constraints (*{constraint}*)
   :More-general-predicate predicate-name
   :More-specific-predicates (*{predicate-name}*)

---

[1] Also affiliated with the Dipartimento di Informatica e Sistemistica, University of Rome "La Sapienza".

The *Constraints* property contains restrictions regarding the *Arguments'* type. Figure 1 shows an example of hierarchy. In particular, three specializations of the *Copied* predicate are shown in boldface and the related constraints in italics. *Text* and *Graphic* are elementary predicates because their constraint fields are empty. Moreover they are specializations of a generic predicate denoting the domain objects which are directly manipulable.

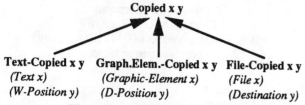

Copied x y

Text-Copied x y	**Graph.Elem.-Copied x y**	**File-Copied x y**
(Text x)	*(Graphic-Element x)*	*(File x)*
(W-Position y)	*(D-Position y)*	*(Destination y)*

Figure 1: A Hierarchy of Predicates

The definition of similarity between complex predicates is derived from the similarity between simpler predicates:

> *Definition 1* - Two predicates are *similar* when they have the same more general predicate and their constraints are either empty or similar to each other.

A possible implementation of a function that would check similarity between two predicates is the following:

```
Function SIMILAR (pred-1 pred-2)
  (And (Equal    (Generalization-of pred-1)
                 (Generalization-of pred-2)))
       (Or (And  (Null (Constraints-of pred-1)
                 (Null (Constraints-of pred-2)))
       (For each constr-1 in (Constraints-of pred-1)
       there-is constr-2 in (Constraints-of pred-2)
       such that (SIMILAR    (Pred-of constr-1)
                             (Pred-of constr-2]
```

Both Definition 1 and the related implementation catch the similarity between *Graphic-Element-Copied* and *Text-Copied* predicates. They neglect the similarity between *Graphic-Element-Copied* and *File-Copied* because *File* and *Graphic-Element* are not specializations of the same concept.

The similarity among predicates induces a notion of similarity among actions according to the following definition:

> *Definition 2* - Two actions are *similar* when they are specializations of the same action and when their filter conditions, preconditions and effects are also similar.

A procedure for checking similarity among actions easily derives from the similarity among predicates.

Our retrieve algorithm is composed of three steps, in which the previous definitions are used:

- *Retrieve plausible candidates*: this step selects the plans that have at least one goal similar or equal to the new problem. When similar predicates exist, the function also returns the mapping between them. The analysis of predicates allows for the construction of such a mapping.
- *Select the best candidate*: the step is based on the analysis of the *g-features*, *f-features* and *pc-features*. First it selects the plans supporting most goals of the

new problem; then it selects the plans having most filter-conditions verified in the new initial state and finally the same mechanism is applied to the preconditions; if more than one candidate is selected, then the first one is chosen. The selection procedure takes the mapping between predicates into account. For example, when a precondition of the old plan is mapped into another relation, its verification is carried out on the new relation.

- *Pre-adapt the plan*: the last step substitutes the similar parts for the old ones in order to allow the application of the *annotation verification procedure*. Without this step the subsequent procedure would eliminate all the parts containing similar predicates.

Applying the algorithm to the previous problem results in a plan which directly solves the problem without any other modification. In the more general case, the pre-adapted candidate is given as input to the standard PRIAR's *annotation verification procedure*.

In summary, our approach divides the solving process into two phases: a heuristic phase which selects the most promising solution and an analytical phase which verifies its correctness and provides the appropriate modifications. The heuristic phase is important because it allows a reduction of the search process. A local search is performed in order to find out how to substitute for a step or to achieve a new producer of a condition. The similarity of the two situations enables the system to utilize the old plan as a scheme to tackle the new problem, instead of starting from scratch. Moreover, our similarity definition is able to discriminate among various predicates with the same generalization by selecting the more useful analogies. As a consequence the search process is shortened.

Acknowledgements

This work has been partially supported by "Progetto Finalizzato Sistemi Informatici e Calcolo Parallelo" of CNR under grant n.104385/69/9107197. Amedeo Cesta was partially supported by CNR Special Project on Planning. Giovanni Romano carried out his work in the framework of the agreement between the Italian PT Administration and the Fondazione Ugo Bordoni.

References

A. Cesta, and G. Romano (1989). Planning structures for an intelligent help system. *Proceedings of the Third International Conference on Human-Computer Interaction*, 767-774, Boston, MA.

A. Cesta, and G. Romano (1992). Using Abstraction-based Similarity to Retrieve Reuse Candidates. (forthcoming).

S. Kambhampati (1989). Flexible reuse and modification in hierarchical planning: a validation structure based approach. Ph.D. Dissertation, CS-TR-2334, University of Maryland.

A. Tate (1977). Generating project networks. *Proceedings of 5th IJCAI*, 888-893, Cambridge, MA.

The Planning of Actions in the Basal Ganglia

Christopher I. Connolly
Computer Science Department
University of Massachusetts at Amherst
Amherst, MA 01003

J. Brian Burns
Computer Science Department
University of Massachusetts at Amherst
Amherst, MA 01003

In this abstract, a new theory is put forth on the mechanisms of the planning of goal-oriented and obstacle-avoiding behavior in biological systems. It is argued here that the basal ganglia may be an important locus for aspects of these activities. Furthermore, the mechanisms for its function may in part be characterized as the computation and storage of harmonic functions in parameter spaces associated with the positions and movements of various body parts, and possibly additional representations of action and intention. This abstract is intended primarily to offer a theory for aspects of biological motor planning, which has been motivated by recent research in robotics. An expanded discussion of the material found here, with citations, can be found in Connolly and Burns [4].

Several approaches have been taken for solving the robot path planning problem (see Connolly and Grupen [1] for references). Recent work in robot path planning by Connolly, et al. revolves around the use of harmonic functions for complete robot path planning. Harmonic functions are solutions to Laplace's Equation. This equation describes several physical phenomena, one of which was exploited by Tarassenko and Blake [3] for a hardware implementation of harmonic function planning. This consists of an array of transistors which are used as a programmable resistive grid. Since Kirchhoff's Law is a discrete form of Laplace's Equation, such a grid is able to compute harmonic functions very rapidly. This grid may have a biological analogue.

The model presented here is primarily concerned with two nuclei of the basal ganglia: the putamen and to a lesser extent, the caudate nucleus (collectively termed the neostriatum). The putamen receives projections specifically from the primary motor cortex, the supplementary motor area, the premotor cortex, and the somatosensory cortex [5]. In particular, premotor cortex ablations are known to affect obstacle avoidance in reaching behavior. The origin of the cortico-striatal projections is consistent with experiments showing the involvement of the putamen in motor function. Moreover, these projections are somatotopic, and divide the putamen into contiguous regions corresponding (in primates) to the arms, legs, face, and hands.

Several researchers have reported that subjects with damaged basal ganglia have significant deficits in the ablity to localize and orient themselves with respect to environmental stimuli or maps representing the environment. Patients with Parkinson's disease, an affliction strongly associated with the basal ganglia, have difficulty using maps to walk through a course. Rats with lesions in the basal ganglia perform poorly in maze traversal. In general, the nature of basal ganglia input and output, and the cellular response timing during sensorimotor tasks seems appropriate for a planning role, as well as other aspects of motor control.

Our model suggests that the basal ganglia are an integral part of the brain's planning machinery. We do not wish to suggest that planning is the *exclusive* domain of the basal ganglia, only that the basal ganglia can perform many planning functions. In contrast to models which suggest selection of a motor program, we propose that the basal ganglia actually create (or plan) the program by performing a gradient descent on a harmonic function, in effect generating a trajectory which describes the successive state changes needed to reach the desired state. The harmonic function is produced by a relaxation process on the membrane potentials within cells in the neostriatum. This relaxation process results from two factors: a) cortically "programmed" high and low membrane potentials at different regions within the neostriatum and b) electrical coupling of the cells via gap junctions.

1 Biological Background

The cells in the neostriatum have been divided into three groups [6]: giant aspiny, medium aspiny, and medium spiny. Although the aspiny cells play an important role, they do not form the main input-output path through the striatum. Their function appears to be regulatory in nature. Medium spiny cells are the primary cells of the neostriatum and comprise 70-

90% of that tissue in mammals. They receive direct excitatory cortical input, and are the primary output neurons for the neostriatum. Several researchers have shown clearly that medium spiny neurons fire in direct relation to passive and active joint movement.

The neurotransmitter glutamate is supplied by the cortex, and medium spiny cells produce the neurotransmitter GABA. The neurotransmitter dopamine is supplied to the neostriatum by another body, the substantia nigra. Heinonen et al. have shown that glutamate elevates membrane potentials in medium spiny cells. Glutamate typically drives membrane potentials toward 0 mV. Glutamate can also induce the release of GABA in medium spiny cells. Recent studies support the notion that GABA can serve to "clamp" medium spiny membrane potentials at the −50 mV level. Williams and Millar show that dopamine at low concentrations apparently induces cell firing, while higher dopamine concentrations prevents firing.

Dye-coupling experiments suggest that gap junction coupling may exist between medium spiny cells. Gap junctions allow a cytoplasmic, hence electrical connection between cells. It is known that dopamine modulates such coupling within the visual system and cardial cells. Recent dye-coupling experiments suggest that this is also true in the neostriatum. If electrotonic communication is occurring among the medium spiny cells of the neostriatum, then these cells are effectively behaving as programmable resistors.

2   The Model

We propose that medium spiny neurons effectively form a resistive network which is programmable via cortical input. Somatotopic projections exist from the cortex into contiguous, non-overlapping regions within the putamen. This suggests that the putamen can be divided into functional units corresponding to the limbs and face. We propose that each of these units is map of the state space (e.g., joint space) of the corresponding limb. Cortical input sets up the potential function by directly depolarizing certain medium spiny cells using glutamate, and indirectly clamping other medium spiny cells via dendritically-released GABA. The difference in potentials thus produced is propagated among the remainder of neostriatal medium spiny neurons, whose membrane potentials are left to relax to the mean values.

We propose that resistive coupling is responsible for actually computing the potential function. The membrane potential of each medium spiny cell corresponds to the function value. Higher (glutamate-induced) potentials could represent repelling states, while low (GABA-induced) potentials indicate goal states. It has also been shown that the spines on medium spiny neurons act as a low-pass filter (Wilson, in [6]). This greatly diminishes the effect of an action potential on membrane potentials at the dendrites. Such a filtering effect would serve to protect the integrity of the potential function being computed. Local, high-frequency, temporary changes to a cell's potential would therefore have a minimal effect on the potential function. Such a system would result in very few neurons actually firing at any given time, since the vast majority of neurons would be computing the function passively via gap-junctions (and indeed, medium spiny cells are normally rather quiet).

Once computed, the function can be used to drive state changes within the organism. We propose that at any one time during the execution of movement, only a small cluster of medium spiny cells will fire within the neostriatum. We postulate that dopamine is acting as a thresholding mechanism to induce these selected cells to fire. One can make an analogy of this cluster to a ball rolling down the potential surface. The cluster of firing cells changes as movement progresses, but tends to migrate in a continuous fashion toward those cells which represent the organism's goal state. Once the organism has reached the desired state, the process terminates.

References

[1] C. I. Connolly and R. Grupen. Applications of harmonic functions to robotics. Technical Report 92-12, COINS Department, University of Massachusetts, February 1992.

[2] C. I. Connolly, J. B. Burns, and R. Weiss. Path planning using Laplace's Equation. In *Proceedings of the 1990 IEEE International Conference on Robotics and Automation*, pages 2102–2106, May 1990.

[3] L. Tarassenko and A. Blake. Analogue computation of collision-free paths. In *Proceedings of the 1991 IEEE International Conference on Robotics and Automation*, pages 540–545. IEEE, April 1991.

[4] Christopher I. Connolly and J. Brian Burns. The basal ganglia and the planning of actions. Technical Report 92-18, COINS Department, University of Massachusetts, February 1992.

[5] Eric R. Kandel, James H. Schwartz, and Thomas M. Jessell, editors. *Principles of Neural Science*. Elsevier Science Publishing Co., 1991.

[6] Gordon M. Shepherd, editor. *The Synaptic Organization of the Brain*. Oxford University Press, New York, 1990.

Probabilistic Network Representations of Continuous-Time Stochastic Processes for Applications in Planning and Control

Thomas Dean   Jak Kirman
Department of Computer Science
Brown University, Box 1910
Providence, RI 02912

Keiji Kanazawa
Department of Computer Science
University of British Columbia
Vancouver, B.C., Canada V6T 1Z2

Discrete Markov processes provide the basis for a variety of powerful techniques in decision theory [5] and stochastic control [2]. In previous work [4, 6], we have demonstrated how to represent discrete Markov processes compactly using probabilistic networks. In keeping with standard approaches in artificial intelligence, our methods allow the system modeler to decompose the state space into a set of propositions (or state variables) and represent the causal dependencies between state variables at consecutive time points using conditional probability tables.

While discrete Markov models provide useful approximations for a wide variety of problems in planning, scheduling, and optimal stochastic control, obtaining the required accuracy in modeling can result in a considerable cost in terms of the number of state variables or the number of discrete time points necessary to model a fixed planning horizon. Here, we consider methods for representing dynamical systems in which the time separating state transitions can vary continuously. In particular, we show how semi-Markov processes and variable duration actions can be modeled using compact probabilistic networks.

We assume that the reader is familiar with Bayesian networks and influence diagrams [10].

1 Representing Stochastic Processes

Markov processes provide a simple, well-understood method of representing change. To represent Markov processes, we introduce a special case of probabilistic networks [4]. Given a set of *state* variables, $\mathcal{X}$, and a finite ordered set of states or time points, $\mathcal{T}$, we construct a set of chance nodes, $\mathcal{C} = \mathcal{X} \times \mathcal{T}$, where each element of $\mathcal{C}$ corresponds to the value of some particular $X \in \mathcal{X}$ at some $T \in \mathcal{T}$. Let C_T correspond to the subset of $\mathcal{C}$ restricted to T. A process model is said to be k-Markov for $k \in \mathbf{Z}$ just in case,

$$\Pr(C_T | C_{T-1}, C_{T-2}, \ldots) = \Pr(C_T | C_{T-1}, \ldots, C_{T-k}).$$

Figure 1.i shows a simple Markov chain with $\mathcal{T} = \{T_1, T_2, T_3, T_4\}$ and $\mathcal{X} = \{X_1, X_2, X_3, X_4\}$. Although

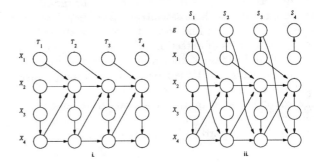

Figure 1: Networks representing stochastic processes

two time points are enough to represent the Markov chain, we are generally interested in computing a sequence of state changes at the discrete times in $\mathcal{T}$.

An expressive limitation of this approach to representing change concerns the need for there being a next state separated from the previous state by an interval of fixed duration. We can overcome the fixed-duration limitation by introducing continuous random variables to represent the delay between state changes. A *semi-Markov* (or Markov renewal) process changes from state, i, to state, j, according to a Markov chain with probability, $P_{i,j}$. The duration of the interval of time spent in state i given that the next state is j is determined by a distribution function, $F_{i,j}$, so that all durations are independent when conditioned on the sequence of states [8].

In representing a semi-Markov process using a probabilistic network, we introduce a real-valued duration variable, E, representing the time between state transitions. The state transition probabilities, $P_{i,j}$ and the distribution governing duration, $F_{i,j}$, are encoded as dependencies between the state and duration variables. A subset of the state variables are dependent on the duration variable for the previous state, and the duration variable is dependent upon some subset of the state variables, often including the action variable, for the corresponding state. Figure 1.ii depicts the probabilistic network for a semi-Markov process.

We use the notation S_i rather than T_i to emphasize that the columns correspond to state transitions and not specific times. The specific time of a particular state transition can be estimated from our knowledge of the current time and the duration of the time between state transitions.

2   An Example

We are applying this framework to the *Fixed Target Reconnaissance* problem. In this problem, a robot is given a task involving covert search and survey; the robot is sent out to find and report on the location of some set of fixed targets, while at the same time avoiding detection by some set of either fixed or mobile observers, referred to here as sentries. Avoiding detection involves preventing line-of-sight contact with sentries. Potential threats of detection might be determined beforehand in the case of known intervals coinciding with satellites being positioned overhead or ground-based sentries on periodic inspection tours. Alternatively, the robot might employ fixed-location sensors or deploy relocatable sensors to detect and supply advance warning with regard to less predictable sentries.

3   Conclusions

The semi-Markov process generalizes the discrete Markov process. In [7], we show a derivative of semi-Markov processes that generalizes the types of stochastic processes represented by *networks of dates* [3]. A network of dates represents a *point process*, where random variables correspond to the time of occurrence of events. In certain cases, the network of dates is a more expressive representation than the discrete Markov process, as it can represent the duration of facts.

The emphasis in this paper is on using probabilistic networks to represent stochastic processes for sequential decision problems. Our methods are designed to be used in conjunction with standard techniques from decision analysis and stochastic control [11, 1]. As mentioned earlier, in the worst case, our network models require time and space exponential in the number of state variables and linear in the number of states considered. In practice, however, we have been able to build systems for applications in mobile robotics with quite modest space requirements and response times on the order of a few seconds [9].

Acknowledgements

This work was supported in part by a National Science Foundation Presidential Young Investigator Award IRI-8957601, by the Air Force and the Advanced Research Projects Agency of the Department of Defense under Contract No. F30602-91-C-0041, and by the National Science foundation in conjunction with the Advanced Research Projects Agency of the Department of Defense under Contract No. IRI-8905436.

Also supported by the Institute for Robotics and Intelligent Systems Group B5 and Natural Sciences and Engineering Research Council of Canada Operating Grant OGP0009281 awarded to Alan Mackworth.

References

[1] Bertsekas, Dimitri P., *Dynamic Programming*, (Prentice-Hall, Englewood Cliffs, N.J., 1987).

[2] Bertsekas, Dimitri P. and Shreve, Steven E., *Stochastic Optimal Control: The Discrete Time Case*, volume 139 of *Mathematics in Science and Engineering*, (Academic Press, New York, 1978).

[3] Berzuini, Carlo, A Probabilistic Framework for Temporal Reasoning, *Artificial Intelligence*, (to appear).

[4] Dean, Thomas and Kanazawa, Keiji, A Model for Reasoning About Persistence and Causation, *Computational Intelligence*, **5**(3) (1989) 142–150.

[5] Howard, Ronald A., *Dynamic Programming and Markov Processes*, (MIT Press, Cambridge, Massachusetts, 1960).

[6] Kanazawa, Keiji and Dean, Thomas, A Model for Projection and Action, *Proceedings IJCAI 11, Detroit, Michigan*, IJCAII, 1989, 985–990.

[7] Kanazawa, Keiji, Dean, Thomas, and Kirman, Jak, Representation Issues for Modeling Change under Uncertainty, In preparation, 1992.

[8] Karlin, Samuel and Taylor, Howard M., *A First Course in Stochastic Processes (Second Edition)*, (Academic Press, New York, 1975).

[9] Kirman, Jak, Basye, Kenneth, and Dean, Thomas, Sensor Abstractions for Control of Navigation, *Proceedings of the IEEE International Conference on Robotics and Automation, Sacramento, California*, 1991, 2812–2817.

[10] Pearl, Judea, *Probabilistic Reasoning in Intelligent Systems: Networks of Plausible Inference*, (Morgan-Kaufmann, Los Altos, California, 1988).

[11] Tatman, Joseph A. and Shachter, Ross D., Dynamic Programming and Influence Diagrams, *IEEE Transactions on Systems, Man, and Cybernetics*, **20**(2) (1990) 365–379.

A Completable Approach to Integrating Planning and Scheduling

Melinda T. Gervasio and **Gerald F. DeJong**
The Beckman Institute for Advanced Science and Technology
University of Illinois at Urbana–Champaign
405 N. Mathews Ave., Urbana, IL 61801
gervasio@cs.uiuc.edu dejong@cs.uiuc.edu

Extended Abstract

The need to integrate planning and scheduling becomes more apparent as more complex real–world problems are addressed by researchers in planning and scheduling. Consider the problem of manufacturing a particular part from a block of raw material. Solving this problem involves determining some sequence of operations to be performed on the block to achieve the desired features, as well as actually selecting the machines and the tools to carry out the operations. Planning research has concentrated on the problem of determining an ordered sequence of actions to achieve the goal, while scheduling research has concentrated on the problem of assigning tasks or operations to resources to meet some performance criterion. Realistically, however, the planning problem cannot be treated independently of the scheduling problem. The value of decisions such as which operation to use to achieve a specific part feature, or the order in which to perform a set of operations, depends not only on a priori information such as process capabilities but also on runtime information such as machine availability. The classical approach of first doing planning and then scheduling may result in overcommitted plans which needlessly constrain the scheduler in its search for task–to–resource assignments. Early scheduling research showed that flexible machine selection and operation sequence process routing improves performance.[1] More recently, reactive methods have been developed for incorporating runtime information in scheduling decisions to facilitate scheduling in dynamic domains [Ow88, Prosser89, Zweben90].

The completable approach to integrating planning and scheduling grew out of our previous work on completable planning [Gervasio90a, Gervasio90b, Gervasio91]. A completable planner consists of a classical (deliberative) element augmented with the ability to defer achievable goals to a reactive element. A goal is *achievable* if the reactive element is guaranteed to find a plan to achieve the goal.[2] This integration permits a system to adapt to unpredictable situations and utilize runtime information in its planning while retaining the goal–directedness afforded by projection. In contrast to other integrated approaches—which compile projection into reactive rules [Drummond90, Kaelbling88, Mitchell90, Schoppers87] or defer planning until certain information is available [Firby87, Olawsky90]—our approach maintains a distinction between deliberative and reactive goals and defers only achievable goals.

Completable planning was designed for domains in which the expected situations and effects of actions could be characterized fairly well but imperfectly. Process planning is just such a domain. Given a part to manufacture, process planning involves determining a set of operations (tasks) to achieve the part and the assignment of these tasks to a set of machines (resources). For a particular feature, there are often many alternative operations, and for each operation, many alternative machines. Resources generally behave as expected—i.e. they are usually available and succeed in processing a task as expected. However, they are also subject to some unpredictable events, such as sudden unavailability due to breakdown or preemption, which may in turn render particular operations unexecutable or less desirable. By deferring goals until execution time, a completable system can use runtime information to complete and correct its imperfect a priori information about a domain. The use of runtime information to provide additional constraints is particularly important in scheduling, where underconstrained problems are the norm and the focus is on finding a *good* solution.[3] A system which utilizes all the available information in making its decisions is thus likely to do better than one which relies only on a priori information.

The completable approach to planning and scheduling permits the deliberative element to defer goals involving operator choice and operator ordering.[4] A completable system defers the decision of which operation to use to service a particular task if there are multiple methods for achieving the task and the a priori information does not enable the system to isolate one. If different methods are applicable in different situations, the deferred goal is considered achievable if the situations corresponding to the different conditions

---

1. See [Conway67], pp. 239–243, for a summary.
2. See [Gervasio90a,b] for examples of achievability proofs.
3. In contrast to planning, where the focus is on finding *a* solution.
4. A third type, parameter instantiation, is discussed in [Gervasio90a,b].

sufficiently covers the space of possible situations. In the case of multiple applicable actions, the question is more one of optimality than achievability, and while the completable approach does not directly solve the problem of finding an optimal solution, it may facilitate the search for one through the utilization of additional runtime information. A completable system defers ordering decisions if a priori planning yields no ordering constraints between the tasks—i.e. each task neither establishes nor denies the preconditions of the other tasks. In this case, the additional constraints provided by runtime information may be useful in determining preferred orderings. Because of the achievability criterion, the choice of deferred goals is highly dependent on the available a priori information and the kinds of information the system knows it is capable of obtaining during execution.

Deferred operator choices and ordering decisions are addressed during execution by conditionals and dispatchers. The form of a conditional is $\{COND\ c_1 \rightarrow a_1; \ldots; c_n \rightarrow a_n\}$, where each c_i is a set of conditions and a_i, an applicable action. To execute a conditional, a system evaluates the different condition–action rules to determine an appropriate action. In the case of multiple conditions being satisfied, the system uses some given performance metric to evaluate the proposed actions and choose the best candidate. A dispatcher may be viewed as a repeat loop over a conditional on the unordered set of tasks, with the set of tasks becoming smaller with every loop, and the exit condition being that all the tasks are serviced. While a completable system may employ the same heuristics as a reactive system for choosing between multiple applicable alternatives, its a priori planning will generally result in a smaller space of alternatives to be searched by the reactive element, and its achievability proofs guarantee that a completion will be found.

The performance of a completable system in a simple job–shop scheduling domain was compared to that of a classical (purely deliberative) system and a purely reactive system. The basic problem was to determine a plan/schedule which successfully serviced a given set of tasks in the least time possible. Uncertainty entered the system via the possibility of sudden resource unavailability (e.g. breakdown, preemption) during execution. Plans/schedules were evaluated on two aspects: ability to successfully service a set of tasks, and when successful, the cost incurred in servicing the tasks. The results supported our hypotheses: 1) completable plans equal or outperform classical plans, 2) the performance improvement of completable plans over classical plans is increases as uncertainty increases, 3) completable plans are more successful than reactive plans, and 4) the success rate of reactive plans is decreased by greater task interactions.[5]

The completable approach achieves a well–founded integra-

tion of planning and scheduling based on the achievability criterion, which enables a completable system to gain the benefits of reactivity without losing the benefits provided by a priori planning. However, other scheduling concerns, such as deadlines, resource utilization, and resource contention, remain to be addressed in the completable approach.. Further experimentation is also needed to more exhaustively test the approach and to develop a framework for understanding the various factors which influence the relative merits of the different approaches.

Acknowledgments

This research was supported by the Office of Naval Research under grant N–00014–91–J–1563. We also thank Michael Shaw and Steve Chien for many useful discussions.

References

[Conway67] R. Conway, W. Maxwell and L. Miller, *Theory of Scheduling*, Addison–Wesley, Reading, MA, 1967.
[Drummond90] M. Drummond and J. Bresina, "Anytime Synthetic Projection: Maximizing the Probability of Goal Satisfaction," *Proceedings of the Eighth National Conference on Artificial Intelligence*, Boston, MA, Aug. 1990.
[Firby87] R. J. Firby, "An Investigation into Reactive Planning in Complex Domains," *Proceedings of the National Conference on Artificial Intelligence*, Seattle, WA, July 1987.
[Gervasio90a] M. T. Gervasio, "Learning Completable Reactive Plans Through Achievability Proofs," Technical Report UIUCDCS–R–90–1605, Department of Computer Science, University of Illinois, Urbana, IL, May 1990.
[Gervasio90b] M. T. Gervasio, "Learning General Completable Reactive Plans," *Proceedings of the Eighth National Conference on Artificial Intelligence*, Boston, MA, Aug. 1990.
[Gervasio91] M. T. Gervasio and G. F. DeJong, "Learning Probably Completable Plans," Technical Report UIUCDCS–R–91–1686, Department of Computer Science, University of Illinois, Urbana, IL, Apr. 1991.
[Gervasio92] M. T. Gervasio and G. F. DeJong, "A Completable Approach to Integrating Planning and Scheduling," Technical Report UIUCDCS–R–92–1733, Department of Computer Science, University of Illinois, Urbana, IL, Mar. 1992.
[Kaelbling88] L. P. Kaelbling, "Goals as Parallel Program Specifications," *Proceedings of The Seventh National Conference on Artificial Intelligence*, Saint Paul, MN, Aug. 1988.
[Mitchell90] T. M. Mitchell, "Becoming Increasingly Reactive," *Proceedings of the Eighth National Conference on Artificial Intelligence*, Boston, MA, Aug. 1990.
[Olawsky90] D. Olawsky and M. Gini, "Deferred Planning and Sensor Use," *Proceedings of the Workshop on Innovative Approaches to Planning, Scheduling and Control*, San Diego, CA, Nov. 1990.
[Ow88] P. S. Ow, S. Smith and A. Thiriez, "Reactive Plan Revision," *Proceedings of the Seventh National Conference on Artificial Intelligence*, St. Paul, MN, Aug. 1988.
[Prosser89] P. Prosser, "A Reactive Scheduling Agent," *Proceedings of the Eleventh International Joint Conference on Artificial Intelligence*, Detroit, MI, Aug. 1989.
[Schoppers87] M. J. Schoppers, "Universal Plans for Reactive Robots in Unpredictable Environments," *Proceedings of the Tenth International Joint Conference on Artificial Intelligence*, Milan, Italy, Aug. 1987.
[Zweben90] M. Zweben, M. Deale and R. Gargan, "Anytime Rescheduling," *Proceedings of the Workshop on Innovative Approaches to Planning, Scheduling and Control*, San Diego, CA, Nov. 1990.

---

5. [Gervasio92] provides a more detailed description of the experiments, as well as a more extensive discussion of the completable approach.

Isolating Dependencies on Failure by Analyzing Execution Traces

Adele E. Howe   **Paul R. Cohen**
Experimental Knowledge Systems Laboratory
Department of Computer Science
University of Massachusetts
Amherst, MA 01003
Net: howe@cs.umass.edu, cohen@cs.umass.edu

1 Introduction

Failures due to flaws in a planner's reasoning or knowledge can be hard to track down – planners may interleave plans for independent goals, world state information may be disregarded or not collected, sensors and effectors may be inaccurate. In this paper, we present an approach to determining how a planner's actions may lead to failure: analyzing execution traces of the planner's failure recovery for significant dependencies between actions and subsequent failures.

2 Analyzing Execution Traces

An *execution trace* is an abstracted view of the interactions between the planner and its environment. For example, we can view the operation of a planner in its environment as a series of effector actions on the planner's part followed by assessments of the state of the environment, as in the following trace:

$$A_b \rightarrow E_f \rightarrow A_a \rightarrow E_e \rightarrow A_b \rightarrow E_g \rightarrow A_a \rightarrow E_e$$

where E's are environment states and A's are actions. The subscripts indicate individuals from a set, so A_a means action of type a. It appears from this short trace that event E_e is always preceded by action A_a and that the preceding event does not matter, but without more examples we cannot be confident of the relationship. Because we are interested in how failure recovery might lead to failure, the execution traces for our analysis include plan failures (as the aspect of the environment of interest) and recovery actions.

2.1 Isolating Dependencies

Given execution traces, we can ask how a planner's actions influence failure and how a failure influences subsequent failures, or stated more generally, whether a failure *depends* on the planner's action and/or the failure that precedes it. We call the disproportionately high co-occurrence between failures and particular predecessors *dependencies*. The example execution trace suggests a $[A_a, E_e]$ dependency.

Dependencies can be isolated by statistically analyzing execution traces for differences between the incidence of some environment state following a particular precursor (action and/or environment state) and the same environment state following any other precursor. For example, to determine whether E_e is related to A_a, we compare the incidence of E_e after A_a to E_e after any action other than A_a. To test the significance of the difference between the incidences, we apply a statistical test (the G-Test which is similar to the χ^2 test) to a 2x2 contingency table of the counts of E_e after A_a, states other than E_e after A_a, E_e after actions other than A_a, and environment states other than E_e after actions other than A_a. We collect these frequencies from many execution traces and arrange them in a contingency table as follows:

	E_e	$E_{\overline{e}}$
A_a	42	21
$A_{\overline{a}}$	250	655

In this case we see a strong dependency between the precursor, A_a, and the failure, E_e. A G-Test on this table will detect a dependency between the failure and its precursor; in this case, $G = 41.4, p < .001$, which means that the contingency table is extremely unlikely to have arisen by chance if A_a and E_e are independent.

We can test dependencies between some failure and any precursor. For our analysis, we have chosen three precursors: recovery actions (A), failures (E) or pairs of a failure and the recovery action that repaired it (EA). If we test for dependencies in all three types of precursors, we shall find cases of overlap: we observe dependencies involving both a particular action itself (e.g., A_a) and the action in combination with some failure (e.g., $E_f A_a$). To distinguish whether the action itself or the combination best describe the relationship, we can apply a variant of the G-test to determine the contribution of each combination to the effect of the action itself. In this way, we can reduce a large set of overlapping dependencies to a smaller set of mutually exclusive dependencies.

2.2 Isolating Failure Dependencies in Recovery Traces

We developed these techniques to help us understand how a planner might influence its own failures. Prior experience with failure recovery in the Phoenix system showed that seemingly minor changes to the design of Phoenix's failure recovery component, such as adding two new recovery actions with limited applicability, changed system performance much more than expected; in particular, different sets of recovery actions resulted in changes in the type and frequency of failures [Howe and Cohen, 1991]. Analyses of dependencies determine whether the actions taken to recover from one failure might precipitate another, suggesting that the recovery actions themselves are flawed; or the failures co-occur regardless of the recovery action, suggesting that the underlying plan is flawed. By isolating dependencies, we hope to discover how the observed changes in performance were produced.

3   Assets and Liabilities

Debugging failures involves isolating the actions and environment states that precipitated the failure and explaining how they caused the failure. Isolating dependencies is the first step in debugging failures. Dependencies do not prove that some action or failure *causes* a particular failure, but knowing a dependency can direct the search for the underlying cause.

Analyzing execution traces for dependencies does not require a model of the environment or the planner itself. Thus, if either model is buggy, the technique can help determine how. Complementary to more knowledge intensive and comprehensive approaches (e.g., [Hammond, 1986] and [Simmons, 1988]), ours is most appropriate when a rich domain model is not available or when the existing model may be incorrect or buggy, as when the system is under development.

Any execution trace can be analyzed for dependencies between any factors of interest. The algorithm for computing dependencies is indifferent to the nature of the precursors or environment states of interest.

To gain this degree of generality, the technique examines many possible combinations and requires a lot of execution data. The algorithm for discovering the dependencies is combinatorial: as the number of factors increases and the number of values for the factors increases, so does the number of potential dependencies. However, this complexity is mitigated by the sparseness of possible relationships in the data (e.g., not all actions are applied successfully to all failures), by the reduction gained by removing overlapping dependencies, and by the automation of the analysis. Of 2697 possible dependencies in the failure recovery data for Phoenix, 632 were observed in the data; G-tests identified 190 as significant and testing for overlapping

effects dropped the total number to 101. Gathering these data required running the Phoenix planner for about a week, but analyzing the data required about ten minutes.

While the combinatorial nature of dependencies implies dramatic increases in the data requirements, the consequence of a lack of data is less dramatic: occasional intermittent failures will be more difficult to find with fewer data, but more frequent dependencies can still be identified. In other words, our technique does not promise to find all possible dependencies; but, if our results from Phoenix are representative, we can still expect to find many of them.

4   Conclusion

We have analyzed the failure recovery performance data for dependencies between failures, recovery actions and the failures that immediately follow repairs. Dependencies in failure recovery execution traces tell us what led up to particular failures, but do not tell us why particular precursors tend to precede particular failures. Given our original goal, debugging planning failures, this analysis seems limited. In fact, debugging failures requires considerably more work. The analysis described here is only the first step of a procedure called *failure recovery analysis* which uses dependencies to focus the search for flaws in the planner and failure recovery [Howe, 1992].

Acknowledgments

This research was supported by a DARPA-AFOSR contract F49620-89-C-00113, the National Science Foundation under an Issues in Real-Time Computing grant, CDA-8922572, and a grant from the Texas Instruments Corporation.

References

Hammond, K.J. 1986. Learning to anticipate and avoid planning problems through the explanation of failure. In *Proceedings of the Fifth National Conference on Artificial Intelligence*, Philadelphia, PA. 556–560.

Howe, Adele E. and Cohen, Paul R. 1991. Failure recovery: A model and experiments. In *Proceedings of the Ninth National Conference on Artificial Intelligence*, Anaheim, CA. 801–808.

Howe, Adele E. 1992. Analyzing failure recovery to improve planner design. To Appear in *Proceedings of the Tenth National Conference on Artificial Intelligence*.

Simmons, Reid G. 1988. A theory of debugging plans and interpretations. In *Proceedings of the Seventh National Conference on Artificial Intelligence*, Minneapolis, Minnesota. 94–99.

Posture Planning For Agent Animation

Moon R. Jung
Dept. of Computer and Information Science
University of Pennsylvania
Philadelphia PA 19104-6389

Norman I. Badler
Dept. of Computer and Information Science
University of Pennsylvania
Philadelphia PA 19104-6389

Abstract

A human motion planning method called *posture planning* is described that addresses how an agent controls and coordinates body parts to achieve a given task in the Cartesian task space.

1   THE PROBLEM

Animating human bodies with respect to designed workspaces helps designers evaluate their design decisions. Motion planning is needed to generate motions to be animated. As an example, consider an agent who stands in front of a table (Figure 1) and is given a goal of *picking up* the block (Figure 2), which is under the table. Our goal is to find a motion plan by which the agent approaches the table, grasps the block, and lifts it up.

The fundamental problem of motor control is the problem of *degrees of freedom*, that is, how the body controls the massively redundant degrees of freedom of the body joints. The body postures can be uniquely represented in terms of joint angles directly. But there are 88 joint degrees of freedom in our body model (not counting fingers) and we do not know how the body actually controls massively redundant degrees of freedom.

The degrees of freedom problem is solved by sufficiently constraining the joint degrees of freedom by means of constraints imposed on the body. The body constraints are obtained from three sources: (i) the structural and physical properties of the body, (ii) the environment (e.g., obstacles), and (iii) the goals of the agent. Posture planning is a process to identify and solve these body constraints that are changing over time.

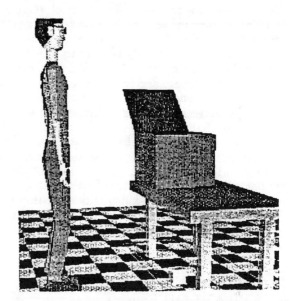

Figure 1: The Agent In Front Of The Table. A Small Block Is Under The Table.

Figure 2: Reaching and Grasping The Block Under The Table.

2   TASK-SPACE CONTROL PARAMETERS

To control the redundant degrees of freedom of the joints, we represent body constraints in terms of higher-level control parameters called *task-space control parameters*. Three kinds of task-space control parameters are posited: *control points*, *control vectors*, and *pivot joints*. *Control points* are important points on the body, e.g., the feet, the pelvis, the head, and the hands. *Control vectors* are important vectors defined on the body to control orientation of the body. For example, the torso upward vector is a control vector for controlling the bending orientation of the upper body. The control vectors include *pelvis-forward-vector*, *righthand-palm-upvector*, *rightfoot-forward-vector*, and *head-view-vector*. *Pivot joints* are joints on the body relative to which control points/vectors are moved. At a given moment, only some of the task-space degrees of freedom are relevant, which are determined by a set of primitive motions selected to achieve given goals. The posture is viewed as a process that modifies *postural states* of the body using given motion strategies. Postural states of the body are defined by the values of the task-space control parameters identified above. Given values of the control parameters, a body posture that satisfies them is found by a robust inverse-kinematics algorithm (Zhao and Badler 1989) that formulates the body positioning problem as nonlinear optimization over the joint space of the body.

3   POSTURE PLANNING STRATEGIES

Motion strategies are obtained using gross-level structural properties of the body. Examples of them are as follows:

(1) A hand can be stretched to the ground by bending the upper body, while the pelvis is lowered.
(2) To reach an object, the agent tends to stretch his arm as much as possible while bending the pelvis as little as possible.
(3) When stretching a hand to reach the ground from the standing posture, the agent bends the upper body at the pelvis rather than lowering the pelvis (by bending the knee).
(4) When orienting the body along the vertical axis, stepping is triggered to avoid twisting of knee joints.

Using the motion strategies, the planner selects a partial sequence of primitive motions of control parts/vectors using a standard planning method (Chapman 1987). A motion of a control point or vec-

tor is primitive if it has a single moving or rotation direction, respectively. Selected primitive motions are mentally simulated to determine whether selected motions would satisfy the collision avoidance constraints. When a stepping motion is planned, the bounding box of the whole body is used to test collision between the body and obstacles. When other motions are considered, collision of the end effector (a hand), the head, and the torso is tested. That is, collision of the elbow is not considered at planning stage. The assumption is that a workspace for the end effector is designed so that it may provide enough free space for the elbow if it provides the free space for the end effector. Collision is determined by checking if the polyhedral sweeping volumes generated by the end effector, the head, the torso intersect obstacles. If a planned motion causes the end effector, the head, or the torso to collide with an object, the face of that object that is in the way of the sweeping volume is identified. Then the motion is modified so that the sweeping volume would pass by the boundary of that face. The majority of robot motion planning methods (Lozano-Perez 1987, Ching and Badler 1992) use the *joint-space* motion reasoning. That is, they assume that the goal configuration of the body is given in terms of a sequence of joint angles and constructs the *free joint-space* (the set of joint angles at which the body does not touch obstacles) to find a collision-free path of the body. The posture planner complements the robot motion planner by providing a feasible macro-level path and by finding a goal posture of the body using heuristic motion strategies.

Acknowledgements

This research is partially supported by Lockheed Engineering and Management Services (NASA Johnson Space Center), MOCO Inc., NSF CISE Grant CDA88-22719, and ARO Grant DAAL03-89-C-0031 including participation by the U.S. Army Human Engineering Laboratory, Natick Laboratory, TACOM, and NASA Ames Research Center.

References

Chapman, D. Planning for Conjunctive Goals. *Artificial Intelligence*, 1987, 32:333-377.

Ching, W. and N. Badler. Collision-free Path and Motion Planning for Anthropometric Figures. Submitted to the *SIGGRAPH*, 1992.

Lozano-Perez, T. A Simple Motion-Planning Algorithm for General Robot Manipulators. *IEEE Journal of Robotics and Automation*, Vol RA-3, No. 3, June 1987.

Zhao, J., & N. I. Badler. *Real Time Inverse Kinematics with Spatial Constraints and Joint Limits*. Technical Report MS-CIS-89-09, Computer and Information Science, University of Pennsylvania, PA, 1989.

Tradeoffs in the Utility of Learned Knowledge

Smadar T. Kedar and Kathleen B. McKusick
Sterling Software, Inc.
NASA Ames Research Center
AI Research Branch, Mail Stop 269-2
Moffett Field, CA 94035
kedar@ptolemy.arc.nasa.gov, mckusick@ptolemy.arc.nasa.gov

Abstract

Planning systems which make use of domain theories can produce more accurate plans and achieve more goals as the quality of their domain knowledge improves. MTR, a multi-strategy learning system, was designed to learn from system failures and improve domain knowledge used in planning. However, augmented domain knowledge can decrease planning efficiency. We describe how improved knowledge that becomes expensive to use can be approximated to yield calculated tradeoffs in accuracy and efficiency.

1 INTRODUCTION

Successful planning and control systems in realistic domains depend on the ability to improve with experience. One characteristic of such systems is the ability to recover gracefully from failures, and avoid similar failures in the future. The long term objective of our machine learning research (Kedar et al., 1991) is to improve planning and control systems by autonomously and systematically detecting failures, and refining domain knowledge to correct them.

Adding knowledge to a system via machine learning methods is not without consequent cost to the system making use of this knowledge. Recent research in machine learning has begun to address this cost in addition to considering system performance improvement which results from the added knowledge. The notion of a *utility problem* was first presented in (Minton, 1988), to refer to the degradation of system performance by machine learning (specifically Explanation-Based Learning). Holder (1988) generalized this idea to other learning paradigms and performance metrics.

Most approaches to utility analysis focus on a single performance system, a single learning paradigm, and a single measure of utility (e.g. *efficiency* in Minton, 1988; Tambe 1990; or *accuracy* in Holder, 1991). The utility of learned knowledge in more complex integrated systems needs to be measured along several dimensions at once. In this paper, we present a case study of a multi-strategy machine learning system, *mutual theory refinement*, which refines knowledge for an integrated reactive system, the Entropy Reduction Engine (Drummond, et al., 1991). We describe a method for trading off two conflicting utility metrics, system accuracy and system efficiency, in order to achieve particular global performance objectives.

2 LEARNING IMPROVES PLAN ACCURACY

Our case study is cast within the Entropy Reduction Engine (ERE), a system which integrates planning and scheduling with reaction. ERE uses *operators* to model actions, and *domain constraints* to model physical laws (e.g., "the agent cannot be in two locations at once"). The operators and constraints are only approximate models, and therefore may not always correctly predict the results of actions. Prediction failures drive the learning system, *mutual theory refinement* (MTR) (Kedar et. al., 1991), to refine these two world models.

MTR distinguishes itself from other analytic theory refinement methods (e.g. Hammond, 1986; Chien, 1989) in the ability to use an approximate model, rather than a fully correct and complete one, to refine other approximate models. MTR is also unique in its ability to switch from analytic to inductive refinement when the approximate models are insufficient. While reducing prediction failures, the ultimate aim of MTR is to improve the overall performance of the associated system (e.g. ERE). We have demonstrated experimentally that MTR increases the accuracy of the associated ERE system, but does so while degrading its efficiency (Kedar & McKusick, 1992) . That is, overall performance involves an accuracy/efficiency tradeoff.

3 APPROXIMATION IMPROVES PLANNING EFFICIENCY

Learning in an integrated system needs to promote some global performance objectives, e.g. a certain level

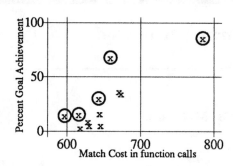

Figure 1: Tradeoffs in Efficiency and Accuracy While Approximating Operator Preconditions.

of system goal achievement given an efficiency constraint. Unfortunately, an augmented domain theory may be too inefficient to use given such a constraint. Our objective here is to show that by approximating the refined theory in an informed manner, we can improve system efficiency while maintaining an acceptable level of accuracy. Through experimentation, we can anticipate how effective a particular approximation is likely to be with respect to the global accuracy and efficiency objectives.

We illustrate this process using data from our case study. We use two methods of approximating our theory: first, to improve efficiency in operator match cost once missing preconditions have been learned, the system approximates certain preconditions by truifying or nullifying them (as in Keller, 1987). Second, to improve efficiency in planning search once multiple outcomes have been learned, the system approximates the operator model by pruning some of the outcomes.

Figure 1 shows accuracy and efficiency results, averaged for a set of 100 test problems, for all the approximate theories generated using the first approximation method. The horizontal axis plots efficiency, as measured in match cost. The vertical axis plots accuracy in terms of percent goal achievement. Each point on the scatter plot represents the average tradeoff yielded by a particular approximated theory. Boundary points, also known as *pareto-optimal* points (Ellman, 1988), are circled. Each point represents a version of the refined knowledge that cannot be improved in one dimension without degradation in the other dimension. A system can attain global objectives if a pareto-optimal point exists which meets or exceeds these objectives.

For example, consider global objectives where desired accuracy on a set of problems is at least 60% goal achievement, with match cost below 700 function calls. We find the pareto-optimal point which best satisfies the global objectives at 67% goal achievement. By explicitly measuring and plotting the tradeoffs for particular approximations, the system is able to identify one yielding a tradeoff that is likely to achieve the performance objectives on new tasks.

4   CONCLUDING REMARKS

The goal of approximating refined knowledge is to achieve improvement in one utility dimension without unacceptably degrading another. In different situations different approximations of the same knowledge may be appropriate to satisfy particular performance objectives. We are currently implementing an ERE/MTR performance system monitor that will enable the performance system to *dynamically* approximate the knowledge, sensitive to various performance measures and performance system components. Such an approach could lead to a more flexible system which achieves goals efficiently without having to limit or destructively modify its store of learned knowledge.

References

Chien, S. (1989). Using and refining simplifications: Explanation-based learning of plans in intractable domains. *Proc. of the Eleventh IJCAI* (pp. 590–595). Detroit: Morgan Kaufmann.

Drummond, M., Bresina, J., and Kedar, S. (1991). The entropy reduction engine: integrating planning, scheduling, and control. *AAAI Spring Symp. on Integrated Intelligent Architectures* (pp. 48–53). Palo Alto, CA.

Ellman, T. (1988). Approximate theory formation: An explanation-based approach. *Proc. of the Seventh Natl. Conf. on AI* (pp. 570–574). St. Paul, MN: AAAI Press.

Hammond, K. (1986). Learning to anticipate and avoid planning problems through the explanation of failures. *Proc. of the Fifth AAAI Conf.* (pp. 556–560). Philadelphia: Morgan Kaufmann.

Holder, L. B. (1988). *Maintaining the utility of learned knowledge using model-based adaptive control.* Master's thesis, Dept. of Comp. Sci., University of Illinois, Urbana.

Holder, L. B. (1991). Selection of learning methods using an adaptive model of knowledge utility. *Proc. of the First Internatl. Workshop on Multistrategy Learning.* (pp. 247–254). Princeton, NJ.

Kedar, S., Bresina, J., and Dent, L. (1991). The blind leading the blind: Mutual refinement of approximate theories. *Eighth Internatl. Workshop in Machine Learning* (pp. 308–312). Evanston, IL: Morgan Kaufmann.

Kedar, S. and McKusick, K. (1992). There is No Free Lunch: Tradeoffs in the Utility of Learned Knowledge. (Tech Rep FIA-92-04): NASA Ames Research Center.

Keller, R. (1987). Defining operationality of explanation-based learning. *Proc. of the Sixth Natl. Conf. on AI* (pp. 482–487). Seattle, WA: AAAI Press.

Minton, S. (1988). Quantitative results concerning the utility of explanation-based learning. *Proc. of the Seventh Natl. Conf. on AI* (pp. 564–569). St. Paul, MN: Morgan Kaufmann.

Tambe, M. and Rosenbloom, P. (1990). A framework for investigating production system formulation with polynomially bounded match. *AAAI Spring Symp. on Case-Based Reasoning* (pp. 693–700). Palo Alto, CA.

Reaction and Reflection in Tetris

David Kirsh   Paul Maglio
Cognitive Science Department, 0515
University of California, San Diego
La Jolla, CA 92093

Abstract

To discover how to couple reflection with re-action we have been studying how people play the computer game Tetris. Our basic intuition is that the job of the reasoner is to monitor the environment and the agent's behavior over time to discover trends or deviations from the agent's normative policy, and tune the priorities of the attentional system accordingly.

Introduction

How can a high level planner interact with a reactive system? The question is of interest because it is likely that a system able to cope in real-time with the complexities characteristic of many human activities will require an architecture with both reactive and reasoning components. The question is hard because truly reactive systems tend to be immune to top-down interference.

In mobot architectures, for instance, activity control systems are linked together in a layered fashion that permits communication only at lines of input or output (Brooks, 1990). Input to a layer may be suppressed, output inhibited or augmented. But the processes occurring inside each activity layer are well-insulated and modular, sealed off from the computations occuring in other layers. Cross talk can occur only at the periphery.

A similar information encapsulation is thought to obtain for human subjects during skilled behavior. After extensive training, typists learn to carry out long sequences of movements with little attention and seem unable to interrupt particular chunks of their behavior on cue (Gentner, 1988). Apparently subjects cannot directly control automatic processing. The computation is data driven, fast, displays little temporal variability, and is probably parallel (Schneider, 1985). In short, practiced behavior seems the product of specific highly dedicated procedures, often parallel, which are insensitive to outside information.

To discover how humans integrate planning, or rather reflection, with reaction we have been studying subjects at different levels of skill playing the interactive video game Tetris. In Tetris players must choose from three actions: rotate, translate or drop. Tetrazoids enter from the upper boundary of a rectangular playing field at a fixed speed. As the game proceeds the pieces drop faster, leaving the player with less and less time to make the decision as to the column and orientation to place a zoid. We have implemented a computational laboratory that lets us record keystrokes and game situations, and allows us to dynamically create situations. Our goal is to tease apart the contributions a rational reflective component makes to performance from the contributions a highly automatic reactive component makes, and then to explain how these components interact.

Skill-Based Systems

In the literature on human process control it is widely claimed that one consequence of practice is that an agent begins (unconsciously) to form a model of the statistical structure of the inputs it confronts and the effects of the actions it takes (Moray, 1986). These models allow (imperfect) predictions of future inputs and the actions required to compensate for those future inputs. Typically process control theorists study domains that are slowly varying dynamic systems such as steel making, or control of a bakery oven, where non-linearities and discontinuities occur, but which in general can be expected to vary smoothly. They have noted that by attending to locally detectable error signals, practiced technicians are able to select appropriate control actions to minimize a smooth cost function.

We can exploit this idea to define, to a first approximation, a skill as an error reducing control mechanism built on a statistical model of the environment. From our viewpoint it is an implementation detail whether the agent's model is explicit and declarative or implicit in the structure and success conditions of its procedures, though we assume the model is implicit.

Central to this notion of skill is the idea that behavior is *perceptually driven*—since errors are perceptually discernable—and *goal specific*—since the goal of reducing differences is intrinsic to a skill. Thus skills do not set goals, they adaptively carry them out. They rely on their perceptual representation of the current situation and their implicit model of the domain to respond adaptively. Activity layers in mobots qualify as skills according to this definition.

RoboTetris

We have implemented a simple skill-based system that plays Tetris. Although in principle there are 17×2^{270} possible Tetris states, our system represents a board situation by a vector of six features: number of holes present, total board height, mountain height, covered holes, filled rows, and local fitness. This particular feature set is based on experts' verbal protocols and performance data. RoboTetris computes the overall goodness of a possible placement as a weighted sum of the features. All possible placements are considered and the best one is selected.

Though RoboTetris' weights can be adjusted to outperform any human expert, it does not play like a person. For example, it is much less consistent than intermediate players, even though it performs above experts; that is, the standard deviation of its scores is unnaturally high. Similarly, RoboTetris has a bizarre highest peak/lowest valley profile. Of course, these unnatural characteristics may disappear with better weighting functions, better qualitative feature sets, and the addition of specific case knowledge. But at present we take its inability to achieve thoroughly reliable behavior as an indication of limitations of the skill-based approach.

It is in keeping with this view that verbal protocols of players become significant. Experts report that they have a high level strategy which shows itself as a *set of concerns*. They claim to monitor ongoing activity mindful of these concerns. If the protocols are to be taken at face value, these concerns serve to focus attention on certain regions of the board or onto certain board properties. In particular, flatness seems to be a crucial topic of concern.

Exactly what an expert means by flatness, however, is not apparent. We assume that the concept must be perceptually identifiable: that in principle it is a geometric or topological notion that can be applied on the basis of current perceptual input. Hence, in principle, it might be added as a new feature to the feature set of the skill module. But again judging from protocols it would seem that an expert's concern with flatness varies in the course of a game, often with one's current estimation of abilities at the time. If flatness, or rather one's degree of concern with flatness, varies with

the internal state of the agent, it cannot be reducible to currently perceivable properties. Pending new evidence to the contrary, we take the varying nature of concern with flatness to be a key empirical indicator of higher level control.

Integrating Reflection and Reaction

We believe that reflective concerns can improve performance. But what is the mechanism by which high level reflection can interact with lower level skills? Most existing accounts of architectures coupling planners to reactive systems begin with the assumption that planners are able, if necessary, to *override* the output of reactive systems, or to *suppress* the input to particular activity layers. Little effort is paid to actively redirecting the sensors of the system to *bias* the input stream.

We are just in the process of implementing a model which works by controlling *input* in a sophisticated manner, sensitive to what we call *concerns* and *policies*. A *policy* is a set of norms, specified in a high level language reflecting a global perspective on the game. Policies identify how things ought to go in the course of a game. The job of the planner is to monitor for signigficant differences between how things ought to be and how things are. These significant differences are concerns—high level descriptions of respects in which the reactive agency is falling short of implementing the system's policies. Once concerns are identified they are translated into directives for changing the focus of attention. Changes in attention, in turn, affect the feature vector presented to the skill module and hence indirectly affects behavior. Accordingly, reasoning affects attention, which has the effect of biasing the perception of certain board regions, or increasing the precision of values being returned by visual routines and the like, which in turn tends to change the behavior with predictable effect over several moves.

References

Brooks, R. (1990). Intelligence without representation. *Artificial Intelligence*, *47*, 139–160.

Gentner, D. (1988). Expertise in typewriting. In Chi, M., Glaser, R., & Farr, M. (Eds.), *The Nature of Expertise*, pages 23–70. Hillsdale, NJ: Lawrence Erlbaum Inc.

Moray, N. (1986). Monitoring behavior and supervisory control. In *Handbook of Perception and Human Performance, Vol II: Cognitive Processes and Performance*, chapter 40. New York, NY: John Wiley & Sons.

Schneider, W. (1985). Toward a model of attention and the development of automatic processing. In Posner, M. & Marin, O. (Eds.), *Attention and Performance XI*, pages 475–492. Hillsdale, NJ: Lawrence Erlbaum Inc.

Towards a Logical Treatment of Plan Reuse

Jana Koehler
German Research Center for Artificial Intelligence (DFKI)
Stuhlsatzenhausweg 3
D-6600 Saarbrücken 11

Abstract

We discuss a deductive approach to plan reuse that integrates planning from second principles into a deductive planner. The logical formalism is reflected in a theorem proving approach in which the reuse component tries to prove a new plan specification using one of the generalized plan specifications stored in a plan library. If the proof succeeds the old plan can be used to satisfy even the new specification. If it fails the information for successfully modifying the old plan can be extracted from the failed proof.

1 Plan Reuse in a Deductive Planning Environment

Planning in complex domains is normally a resource and time consuming process when it is purely based on first principles. Once a plan is generated it represents problem solving knowledge which is generally lost in classical planning systems after the plan has been successfully executed. If such a planner has to solve the same problem again, it will spend the same planning effort and is not capable of "learning" from its "experience." Methods of *planning from second principles* try to reuse former problem solutions in order to make planning more efficient and flexible.

Besides planning from first principles as it is performed by the deductive planner [Biundo/Dengler], we integrate planning from second principles by incorporating a plan reuse component into it. As with plan generation we ground this plan reuse component on a deductive formalism [Biundo/Dengler/Koehler].

Planning and plan reuse interact in the following way: A formal plan specification (provided to the planner) is forwarded to the reuse component. If the reuse component succeeds in hunting up a plan from the library that (perhaps after minor modifications) can be reused to solve it the *plan modification* process starts. This process implements planning from second principles: It takes an existing plan together with its generation process (which in our case is a proof) out of the plan library. If the plan has to be modified, for example, by inserting additional actions, a formal subplan specification is generated and passed to the planner. The planner generates a subplan, which then is used to extend the already existing plan in such a way that it satisfies even the current specification. If no reuse "candidate" can be found the deductive planner has to generate a completely new plan out of the given specification.

1.1 A Four Phase Model of Plan Reuse

To formalize planning from second principles we have developed a four phase model of plan reuse reflecting the different tasks that have to be addressed [Koehler]:

1. In the phase of *Plan Determination* a plan specification formula Φ is retrieved from the plan library to solve a new planning problem given as a plan specification formula Ψ. We presuppose that the plan library does not contain (user-)predefined plan entries, but is built up using information provided by the deductive planner, e.g., the specification formula, the generated plan, and the proof tree for the plan.

2. In the phase of *Plan Interpretation* the formula Φ has to be interpreted in the current planning situation by investigating whether Φ can be instantiated to Φ_{inst} such that Ψ is obtained.

3. In the *Plan Refitting* phase the instantiated plan specification Φ_{inst} is compared with Ψ and necessary refitting tasks for the planner are derived. Planner and plan reuse component interact in such a way that the reuse component generates subplan specifications for which the planner is activated to generate the subplans which have to be deleted from or incorporated into the plan to be reused.

4. The reuse process finishes with a *Plan Library Update* in which the plan specification formula Ψ

is generalized and compared with already stored plans. If Ψ is "worth" storing it is added to the plan library.

In the following we shortly describe how plan interpretation and refitting, summarized as *plan modification* are realized deductively.

2 A Deductive Approach to Plan Modification

The deductive formalism is worked out using the framework provided by an interval-based temporal modal logic, the so-called Logical Language for Planning LLP that is used by the planner the reuse component is interacting with [Biundo/Dengler].

We assume that plan specification formulas given in LLP [Plan$_\psi \to \psi$] are of form [Plan$_\psi \to [\psi_i \to \psi_g]$], where the subformulas ψ_i and ψ_g describe the facts holding before executing the plan and the facts that have to be reached by it, respectively. Suppose, given a plan specification [Plan$_\psi \to \psi$] the plan determination process succeeds in finding an appropriate entry in the plan library and comes up with a specification formula [Plan$_\phi \to \phi$] and a plan formula P_ϕ that had been generated from this specification to replace the metavariable Plan$_\phi$. To find out whether P_ϕ can be reused as a solution even for Plan$_\psi$ in order to satisfy the current specification we try to prove the formula:

$$[\phi \to \psi]$$

This step is justified by the fact that [$P_\phi \to \psi$] if [$\phi \to \psi$], provided [$P_\phi \to \phi$] holds.

If the proof of [$\phi \to \psi$] succeeds the "old" plan P_ϕ can be reused without any modifications. But in general, the proof of $\phi \to \psi$ will fail since the old plan will not be applicable without any modification to solve the new planning task. Therefore, we conduct the proof attempt in such a way, that from the failed proof sufficient information can be extracted to modify P_ϕ successfully.

[$\phi \to \psi$] is attempted to be proved using a matrix calculus for the modal logic LLP based on results by [Bibel, Wallen]. The proof attempt consists of two steps: First the matrix corresponding to that formula has to be built and paths in the matrix are determined for which *simultaneously complementary literals* under an *admissible substitution* (meeting several criteria posed by the underlying logic) can be constructed. The result of the *plan interpretation phase*, i.e., the desired instantiation for Φ is provided by the substitution under which the number of these paths has a maximum.

Secondly, to formalize the *plan refitting phase* we analyze the remaining paths in the matrix. The formula

described by the set of these paths represents refitting information from which we derive logical specification formulae representing the necessary refitting tasks for the planner. This unique characterization of refitting tasks allows to reduce the problem of plan refitting to *one* basic refitting strategy resolving the two possible plan failures, viz. *plan reduction* and *plan expansion* that have to be distinguished.

It finally has to be verified that the modification of P_ϕ leads to a correct, i.e., executable plan.

3 Conclusion

In this paper we discussed the ideas of a logical and domain-independent approach to the problem of plan reuse inside of deductive planning. The main idea is to base it on a theorem proving approach to provide the logical framework for a completely automated solution to the problem of plan modification. The developed modification method is purely based on information arising in the deductive planning process and does not require additional information supplied by a user.

Current investigations are related to the characterization of the proof attempt as a kind of subsumption test to provide the framework for further theoretical investigations of such important aspects as decidability of the test procedure, soundness, i.e., the modified plan is indeed a solution for the current goal and completeness, i.e., in general every plan can be modified to obtain a solution.

Acknowledgements

I want to thank Prof. Wolfgang Wahlster for his advice and support and Dr. Susanne Biundo, Jochen Heinsohn, and Claus Sengler for valuable comments on earlier versions of this paper.

References

W. Bibel (1982). *Automated Theorem Proving.* Vieweg, Braunschweig - Wiesbaden.

S. Biundo and D. Dengler (1992). An interval-based temporal logic for planning. Research report, German Research Center for Artificial Intelligence.

S. Biundo, D. Dengler, and J. Koehler (1992). Deductive planning and plan reuse in a command language environment. Research report, German Research Center for Artificial Intelligence.

J. Koehler (1991). Approaches to the reuse of plan schemata in planning formalisms. Technical Memo TM-91-01, German Research Center for Artificial Intelligence.

L. A. Wallen (1989). *Automated Deduction in Nonclassical Logics.* MIT-Press, Cambridge, London.

Abstracting Operators for Hierarchical Planning

Martin Kramer, Claus Unger
Praktische Informatik II
FernUniversität Hagen
Postfach 940
D-5800 Hagen 1, Germany

In problem domains with a big number of operators, conventional planning methods must fail. With a non-hierarchical planning method, when attempting to achieve a (sub)goal it would consume by far to much time to merely check all operators for appropriateness. On the other hand, hierarchical planning methods are undue as well. Methods following ABSTRIPS [Sacerdoti 1974] even diminish the number of preconditions to be considered simultaneously, but not the number of operators to be checked. Hierarchical planning methods using conventional operator abstraction (e.g. NOAH [Sacerdoti 1975], NONLIN [Tate 1977] or SIPE [Wilkins 1984]) diminish the number of operators to be checked, but in domains with hundreds of operators (e.g. operating systems like UNIX) they suffer from the fact, that either too many different sets of concrete operators have to be abstracted, or that only few particular action combinations are preferred at all. Moreover, the definition of abstract operators 'by hand' is hard and error prone. Thus, we developed an algorithm which supports the designer of the problem domain's knowledge base by automatically deriving a hierarchy of abstract operators from a given set of concrete ones. The operator hierarchy produced by the algorithm is a *type hierarchy*, i.e. the abstract operators are not merely macro operators representing a fixed, possibly still unordered set of concrete operators, but in fact are new operator types subsuming all possible (partial) combinations of their constituting more concrete ones. Our approach significantly diminishes the number of operators from abstraction level to abstraction level, this method allows a much more flexible refinement and, therefore, is independent from the designers view of possible actions in the domain. So, it provides a better access to commonsense planning in extensive domains.

Additionally, a set of rules is provided how to *formally* derive preconditions, postconditions as well as so-called *capabilities* of an abstract operator from the corresponding conditions of the constituting more concrete operators. The formalism and the algorithms were successfully used in a planning system for UNIX.

The basis of the abstraction algorithm are *purpose descriptions* describing the effect of an operator on a very abstract level. They can be automatically derived from the pre- and postcondition of an operator. In the following we assume:

- Each operator refers to a single main object called its *central object*.
- All operations an operator may perform on its central object can be grouped into the *purpose types* create, destroy, modify, and info (= retrieve information).

Depending on its type, an operator *purpose* is specified by one of the following schemes:

- create <*class*> [<*inputclass*>]: create a <*class*> object, possibly using an input object.
- destroy <*class*>: destroy a <*class*> object.
- modify <*class*> <*set-of-attr-names*>: change attributes of an object.
- info <*class*> <*set-of-attr-names*>: retrieve information about attributes of an object.

A purpose description may include several purposes. For instance, an editor has the purpose description:

```
((create text-file)
 (modify text-file {contents})
 (info text-file {content}))
```

Purpose descriptions are used to define similarities between operators. In this context, object classes are regarded as *comparable* ($\approx$), if they belong to the same class hierarchy.

Let $op_1,...,op_n$ be operators with purpose descriptions $purp_1,...,purp_n$, $p_i \in purp_i$ be a purpose of operator op_i, and $p = (p_1,...,p_n)$.

$op_1,...,op_n$ are *type-i-similar-with-regard-to-p* ($\overset{i}{\sim}$), i=1,...,4:

$$\overset{1}{\sim}(op_1,...,op_n)(p) :\Leftrightarrow \exists\, p_1 \in purp_1 ,..., p_n \in purp_n :$$
$$p_1 = ... = p_n$$
$$\overset{2}{\sim}(op_1,...,op_n)(p) :\Leftrightarrow \exists\, p_1 \in purp_1 ,..., p_n \in purp_n :$$
$$type(p_1) = ... = type(p_n) \wedge class(p_1) = ... = class(p_n)$$
$$\overset{3}{\sim}(op_1,...,op_n)(p) :\Leftrightarrow \exists\, p_1 \in purp_1 ,..., p_n \in purp_n :$$
$$type(p_1) = ... = type(p_n) \wedge class(p_1) \approx ... \approx class(p_n)$$
$$\overset{4}{\sim}(op_1,...,op_n)(p) :\Leftrightarrow \exists\, p_1 \in purp_1 ,..., p_n \in purp_n :$$
$$class(p_1) \approx ... \approx class(p_n)$$

Operators are *similar*, if they are type-i-similar, i=1,...,4.

The following algorithm creates a hierarchy of concrete and abstract operators linked by the relationship *abstracted-from*.

Step 1:

```
Let OP contain all operators.
for all op_i,op_j ∈ OP do
    if op_i 'subsumes' op_j then
        make op_i an abstract operator op, abstracted
        from op_j;
        remove op_i,op_j from OP;
        add op to OP
    fi
rof
```

Step 2:

```
for all OP' ⊆ OP : op_i,op_j ∈ OP' ⇒
purpose(op_1)=purpose(op_2) do
    create a new abstract operator op, using all
    op_i ∈ OP';
    remove OP' from OP;
    add op to OP
rof
```

Step 3:

```
repeat OP_old:=OP
    for i=1,...,4 do
        for all OP'=(op_1',...,op_n') ⊆ OP :
                ~OP'(p_1',...,p_n') do
            create new abstract operator
            for all op_i' ∈ OP' do
                purpose(op_i')−p_i'
                if purpose(op_i')=() then
                    remove op_i from OP
            rof
        rof
    rof
until OP=OP_old
```

When applied to a subset of UNIX commands, the algorithm sketched above resulted in the following operator hierarchy:

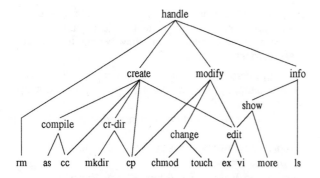

When refining plans, an abstract operator has to be replaced by one or more of its constituting more concrete ones. Using our type-oriented operator abstraction, the replacement does seldom contain all of these operators. Thus, if the precondition of the abstract operator was sim-

ply the conjunction of the preconditions of its constituting operators, it would mostly include requirements which do not have to be fulfilled to solve the actual problem. In the worst case, the planning could fail, although the problem is solvable in principle. Thus, the precondition of an abstract operator should be constructed in such a way, that only those preconditions are included which are required in every possible refinement. This idea leads to an abstract precondition being a kind of disjunction of all its constituting preconditions. Thus, an additional abstraction in the sense of ABSTRIPS is provided.

The postcondition of a concrete operator describes which post-states can be caused by the operator if it is applied to a pre-state which meets the corresponding precondition. With regard to abstract operators, and their use in a planning system, postconditions serve two purposes. They have to describe post-state conditions

- which are inevitably caused whatever refinement by the constituting more concrete operators will be chosen,

- which are able to be caused by one or several appropriate more concrete operators.

While in case of a concrete operator both purposes are met by the same postcondition, in case of abstract operators the purposes conflict. The first purpose is achieved by defining the postcondition of an abstract operator op as an abstract intersection of the postconditions of its constituting operators op_i (similar to preconditions).

To achieve the second purpose, we introduce another kind of postcondition, called capability:
If an operator op is abstracted from operators op_i, i = 1,...,n, its *capability* is an abstract union of the capabilities of its constituting operators. The capability of a concrete operator is its postcondition.

For more information, especially about operator search and refinement, see [Kramer, Unger 1992].

References

M. Kramer, C. Unger (1992). *Algorithms for Operator Abstraction and Operator Selection in Hierarchical Planning Systems*, Research Report, University of Hagen.

E.D. Sacerdoti (1974). Planning in a hierarchy of abstraction spaces. *Artificial Intelligence*, 5:115-135.

E.D. Sacerdoti (1975). The nonlinear nature of plans. In *Proc. 4th International Joint Conference on Artificial Intelligence*, 206-214.

A. Tate (1977). Generating project networks. In *Proc. 5th International Joint Conference on Artificial Intelligence*, 888-893.

D.E. Wilkins (1984). Domain-independent planning: Representation and plan generation. *Artificial Intelligence*, 22:269-301.

Planning for soft goals

Bruce Krulwich
Northwestern University
The Institute for the Learning Sciences
1890 Maple Avenue
Evanston, IL 60201
Electronic mail: `krulwich@ils.nwu.edu`

1 Hard and soft goals

All of the following are goals for which an agent may wish to construct plans:

1. Put block 1 on block 2 and block 3 on the table
2. Build a tower of blocks as high as possible
3. Project the ball exactly 40 feet
4. Project the ball as high in the air as possible
5. Move a pawn to the square in front of the queen
6. Construct a line of pawns for defense
7. Minimize the number of vulnerable chess pieces
8. Catch a train as early as possible, given that the last express leaves at 9:41am

These are all goals that an intelligent agent may wish to achieve. There are, however, important differences between the goals. Goals 1, 3, and 5 are the types of goals that planners have classically handled: they have the characteristic of being either fully achieved or not achieved in any world state. We shall call goals such as these *hard goals*. We call the other goals in the list above *soft goals*, because the degree to which they are achieved can vary along a range of satisfaction, being more or less satisfied as well as unsatisfied [Haddawy and Hanks, 1990].

2 Planning for hard and soft goals

The purpose of an agent's reasoning about its goals is, of course, to construct plans to achieve them. Many approaches to planning have been developed, including such methods as means-ends analysis [Newell and Simon, 1963], linear planning [Fikes and Nilsson, 1971], and non-linear planning [Sacerdoti, 1977; Chapman, 1987]. These *classical planning* methods reason about the effects of possible sequences of actions (plans) on the world, and attempt to construct plans that will achieve the goals.

Most planning methods can be classified into one of two categories: goal-regression planners and forward-directed planners. *Goal-regression planners* construct plans by starting from the goal descriptions and working backwards. Constructing a plan in this way requires that the planner regress the goal description backwards through the system's operators (or macro-operators, or schemata, or whatever) to determine what must be done or already true before the execution of the operator. *Forward-directed planners,* on the other hand, start at the agent's initial state, and search forward towards the goal.

How can these planning methods be used to generate plans for soft goals?

Previous discussions of planning for soft goals have been in the context of agents which attempt to maximize the expected utility of their decisions [Feldman and Sproull, 1977; Haddawy and Hanks, 1990; Hansson *et al.*, 1990]. In such an approach, symbolic goals are replaced by utility functions, and plans are generated in a forward-directed fashion in such a way as to maximize the utility of the expected outcome of the plan. For example, goal number 8 in our list of goals, catching the earliest train possible, would be handled by constructing a utility function which has a higher value the earlier the agent got to the train station. The agent would then search through the possible sequences of actions it could perform to get to the station, and choose the plan which maximizes the utility. This is a fairly straightforward application of forward-directed planning to soft goals.

In some situations a straightforward form of goal-regression can be used for soft goals. Consider goal number 4 above, the goal to project the ball as high in the air as possible. If the planner has an operator that says: *to achieve the goal of projecting the ball to a certain height, first figure out with what strength to throw the ball, and then throw the ball with the specified strength,* a goal-regression planner could start with the goal, retrieve the operator, and determine that the goal would be achieved if the ball were thrown with the maximum strength. Such a goal-regression process can determine that in order for the height of the ball to

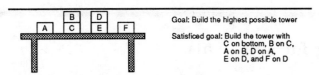

Figure 1: Soft goal planning: Building a tall tower

be maximized by the throwing operator, the planner should maximize the value of the throwing strength which is used by the throwing action. In general, the planner can take a soft goal to maximize (or otherwise optimize) the value of a given variable, and regress it back over an operator in which the variable being maximized is explicitly referenced. We will call goals for which this can be achieved *regressable soft goals.* Unfortunately, the parameters of the actions an agent can execute are most often discrete values such as routes for travel, locations, other agents, tools, etc. Because of this, the *regressability criterion* is very difficult to achieve in practice.

To use goal-regression planning for non-regressable soft goals, we use the idea of *satisficing* [Simon, 1981]. In this context, satisficing involves transforming the soft goal into a hard goal that, if achieved, will achieve a sufficient value for the soft goal. This hard goal can then be used directly for goal-regression planning.[1]

As an example of satisficing a soft goal, consider goal number 2, shown in figure 1. This goal, building a tower of blocks as high as possible, is not regressable (within the standard implementations of blocks world) because the planner's operators do not relate to the height of towers. To plan for this goal using goal-regression, the planner must transform the goal into a hard goal to build a particular tower. The tower given in the hard goal would be close to the tallest tower which can be built in the current situation, or at least would be tall enough for the planner's purposes.

The satisficing process requires information about the soft goals the planner can handle and how the different ways they can be satisfied relate to the planner's initial situation. In the example in figure 1 the planner has to know that towers are constructs consisting of chains of blocks on top of each other, and that maximizing the height of a tower means including as many blocks as possible. It can then examine the current situation and determine what that hard goal should look like.

3   Summary

We have discussed the distinction between *hard goals* and *soft goals,* and discussed how soft goals can be handled by a planning system. They may be

---

[1] We discuss this process in more detail in the full paper, which is available from the author.

regressable, in which case they can be planned for by standard goal-regression techniques. Alternatively, they may be *non-regressable,* in which case the planner must either generate plans in a forward-directed fashion, or *satisfice* the goal to make a corresponding hard goal that can then be handled normally. Future research is necessary to elaborate many aspects of the issues we have raised.

Acknowledgements: Thanks to Larry Birnbaum, Gregg Collins, Matt Brand, Mike Freed, Eric Jones, and Louise Pryor for discussions on this paper and on the research presented. This work was supported in part by the Air Force Office of Scientific Research under grant number AFOSR-91-0341-DEF, and by the Defense Advanced Research Projects Agency, monitored by the Office of Naval Research under contract N-00014-91-J-4092. The Institute for the Learning Sciences was established in 1989 with the support of Andersen Consulting, part of The Arthur Andersen Worldwide Organization. The Institute receives additional support from Ameritech, an Institute Partner, and from IBM.

References

[Chapman, 1987] D. Chapman. Planning for conjunctive goals. *Artificial Intelligence*, 32(3):333–374, July 1987.

[Feldman and Sproull, 1977] J.A. Feldman and R.F. Sproull. Decision theory and artificial intelligence II: The hungry monkey. *Cognitive Science*, 1(2):158–192, 1977.

[Fikes and Nilsson, 1971] R.E Fikes and N.J Nilsson. Strips: a new approach to the application of theorem proving to problem solving. *Artificial Intelligence*, 2:189–208, 1971.

[Haddawy and Hanks, 1990] P. Haddawy and S. Hanks. Issues in decision-theoretic planning: Symbolic goals and numeric utilities. In *Proceedings of the Workshop on Innovative Approaches to Planning, Scheduling, and Control*, pages 48–58, San Diego, CA, 1990.

[Hansson *et al.*, 1990] O. Hansson, A. Mayer, and S. Russell. Decision-theoretic planning in bps. In *Working Notes of the Spring Symposium on Planning in Uncertain, Unpredictable, or Changing Environments*, pages 44–48, Palo Alto, CA, 1990.

[Krulwich, 1991] B. Krulwich. Determining what to learn in a multi-component planning system. In *Proceedings of the Thirteenth Annual Conference of The Cognitive Science Society*, pages 102–107, Chicago, IL, 1991.

[Newell and Simon, 1963] A. Newell and H. A. Simon. GPS, a program that simulates human thought. In *Computers and Thought*, pages 279–293. McGraw-Hill, New York, 1963.

[Sacerdoti, 1977] E.D. Sacerdoti. *A Structure for Plans and Behavior.* North-Holland/American Elsevier, New York, 1977. Phd thesis, 1975. Also Tech. Note 109, SRI.

[Simon, 1981] H.A. Simon. *The Sciences of the Artificial.* Massachusetts Institute Technology Press, Cambridge, MA, 1981. (Second Edition).

Representing Conflicts in Parallel Planning

Alfredo Milani
Dipartimento di Matematica
Università di Perugia
via Vanvitelli, 1
06100 Perugia, ITALY

Maurizio Terragnolo
Istituto di Linguistica
Computazionale - C.N.R.
Via della Faggiola 32
56100Pisa, ITALY

Abstract

The notion of Affected and Protected clause extends classical action models to enable a more reliable composition of parallel nonatomic actions. A notion of legal action description is given. On the basis of the given model conditions are stated in order to allow analysis of conflicts in parallel and nonlinear planning.

REPRESENTING CONFLICTS

Many models of actions aim to represent not only what happens outside the action (as an effect of its execution) but some internal states of nonatomic actions execution, (the *during* clause introduced by (Georgeff 1983) describe some aspects of those internal states), in order to allow conflict checking.

In order to extend a classical Strips-like plan model as Chapman's to deal with parallel execution of actions, we adopt the definitions of (Morgensten 1987), which require for two actions to be parallelized that they must be:
a) resources compatible;
b) mutual conflicts free;
c) effects compatible;

The first two requirements correspond to the **satisfied preconditions** and **conflicts free** requirements in non-linear planning.

The last constraint has the purpose of ruling out the problem of computing the resulting effects of simultaneous application of the two actions when they are not consistent.

We say that an action **a** is an *active* actor in a conflict with *passive* actor action **b** if **a** produces some resources which damage **b** execution, (i.e **a** negates some preconditions of **b** before it, or **a** negates some condition which are to be maintained during **b**).

A nonlinear plan can be analyzed in order to find possible parallelization of its actions, the above conditions for parallel execution cannot be checked only on the basis of precondition/effect informations, but additional information about actions are needed.

AN ACTION MODEL

Definition 1 Action Description

An action A is described by an **initial instant** $i(A)$, a **final instant** $f(A)$, (between $i(A)$ and $f(A)$ the default temporal relation $i(A) > f(A)$ holds), and a tuple (Preconditions, Protected, Affected, Effects) with the following meanings:

Preconditions: is a list of facts which are required to be true at instant $i(A)$ in order the action to be executable;

Effects: is a list of facts which are guaranteed to be true at instant $f(A)$ is action A is executed;

Protected: is a list of facts which cannot be asserted or negated (affected) by any other action *during* execution of A, (after $i(A)$ and before $f(A)$);

Affected: is a list of facts which are asserted or negated at some instants *during* execution of A.

Definition 2 WF-Action Description

An action description is say to be well-formed if:
i) Preconditions are consistent;
ii) Effects are consistent;
iii) all variable of facts in the description are instantiated when all variable in Preconditions are instantiated;
iv) Effects in the Effects clause represents the state generated by executing the action in its minimal initial state (the minimal initial state of an action is the initial state where the preconditions of the action and only them are true).

Definition 3 NonLinear/Parallel Plan

A *nonlinear/parallel plan description* P is a partial order relation $(TI(A),>)$, where A is a set of actions instances and

$TI(A) = \{j$ such that: $(j=i(X)$ **or** $j=f(X)$) **and** $X \in A\}$

The additional requirements of well-formation restrict the allowed action descriptions, while many existing models does not give a semantic for certain cases (i.e. execution of actions with uninstantiated effects).

The following are some of the most significant relations between well-formed actions which can be given, in the frame of temporal logic (Allen 1983). It is important to note that feasible free of conflict plan executions requires conditions on actions clauses.

JustBefore: Action a can be executed JustBefore b in plan P, if there is a completion in the partial order relation of P where a > b, and not other action c is a>c>b and: Preconditions(b) are consistent with Effects(a)

AnyOrder: Action a can be executed in AnyOrder with respect to action b, if it is possible:
a JustBefore b and b JustBefore a

Parallel: Action a can be executed in Parallel with respect to action b if they can be executed in AnyOrder and moreover if the following two conditions hold:
Effect(a) and Protected(a) are consistent with each Affected(b)
Effect(b) and Protected(b) are consistent with each Affected(a)

INTERNAL STATE OF ACTION

Consider the following Strips-like action description "paint_a_room" and a possible well-formed description of "paint_a_room" action in our model:

Name: paint_a_room
Preconditions: have_color, have_brush, hand_empty
Effects: not(have_color), painted(room), have_brush

Name: paint_a_room   Time: I,F
Preconditions: have_color, have_brush, hand_empty
Protected: have_color, have_brush, hand_empty
Affected: on(fresh_paint,wall), hand_empty
            not(on(fresh_paint,wall),
            not(hand_empty)∪ Effects
Effects: not(have_color), painted(room),
            painted(wall), not(on(fresh_paint,wall),
            have_brush, hand_empty

Note that the first one is not well-formed (*hand_empty* is in its the minimal initial state while is not in the effects), *Preconditions* (*Effects*) contains all the informations needed to make conflicts checking in a not-parallel scheme, in order to recognize if the action has *passive* (*active*) role in conflicts of type JustBefore and AnyOrder.

Coordinating the parallel execution of actions needs to take into account that: actions can *affect* some properties and *consume* it *during* their execution (i.e. hand_empty, on(fresh_paint, wall)); actions needs that some conditions are to be *guaranteed during* action execution (i.e. have_color, have_brush), note that a condition *p* and the same negated *not(p)* can be necessary in different intervals during the same action execution, finally actions must be *synchronized* with other actions which affect or require the same "internal" properties (i.e. the conditions for *Parallel* fail on actions *hang_a_picture* and *paint_a_room*).

The internal state of an action is represented in Affected and Protected clauses without regard of its temporal details.

Affected and Protected clause are used in order to prevent an action from being respectively the *active* and the *passive* actor of a conflict (failure of Parallel relation) in the execution time interval (I,F).

In a traditional non-parallel model, informations about the internal state are not necessary, because actions have linear executions, and temporary properties (like on(fresh_paint, wall)) which does not persist until the end of the action, do not appear at all.

The notion of well-formed action guarantee that all the relevant informations are explicitated.

Acknowledgements

This work has been supported by Progetto Speciale Pianificazione Automatica - Consiglio Nazionale delle Ricerche, Italy.

References

J.F. Allen "Maintaining KNowledge about Temporal Intervals", Comm. ACM 26 (11) 1983a

G.Brewka, J.Hertzberg, "How to do things with worlds: on formalizing actions and plans"- Tech.Tasso-Report n.11, November 1990, GMD Institut - Bonn Germany

D.Chapman, "Planning for conjunctive goal", Artific. Intell. n.32 (1987)

M.P.Georgeff, "Communication and Interaction in Multi-agent planning" in Proceedings of AAAI-83

L.Morgensten, "Knowledge Preconditions for Actions and Plans" in Proceeding of IJCAI 1987

R.E.Fikes, N.J.Nilsson "STRIPS : A New Approach to the Application of Theorem Proving to Problem-solving", Artificial Intelligence 2, 1971

D.E.Wilkins, "Representation in a Domain-Indipendent Planner",SRI International Technical Note n.266, May 1983

Protograms

Eyal Mozes and **Yoav Shoham**
Computer Science Department
Stanford University
Stanford, CA 94305

Abstract

Motivated largely by tasks that require control of complex processes in a dynamic environment, we introduce a new computational construct called a *protogram*. A protogram is a program specifying an abstract course of action, a course that allows for a range of specific actions, from which a choice is made through interaction with other protograms. We demonstrate the protogram framework through an example, which we have implemented as a simulation, of a robot navigating and exploring a set of corridors and using several considerations to determine its path.

1   What are protograms?

Protograms reflect the intuition that most activities are determined by several influences, which refine, reinforce, complement, and often contradict one another. This is true of our everyday behavior. We use a car to get to work because walking would take too long, and furthermore we use our spouse's car because ours is low on gas. We drive to the city fast, in order to make the concert, but not too fast, to avoid accidents and speeding tickets. When we learn how to ski we try to lean forward as instructed, but fear of falling tends to make us lean back.

These multiple influences exist also in programming. We sort the list of employees alphabetically, but place the manager, Zbigniew Zablowski, at the head of the list; we drive the robot towards the goal, but veer it away from obstacles. The standard view of programs requires the programmer to resolve these various influences and produce a single course of action. This is often feasible. In complex tasks, however, it can be very difficult.

Protograms allow the programmer to specify only the individual influences — each represented by an abstraction of an action, allowing for a (continuous or discrete) range of concrete actions, and relative preferences within that range — as well as information about the relative importance of the influences. The protogram interpreter then uses that information to produce an unambiguous action description, which satisfies, to various degrees, the requirements of the individual protograms. The advantage to the programmer, besides exemption from the need to specify one global behavior, is modularity and incrementality: influences may be added and removed without having to write the program from scratch each time. The price is that the behaviour of the system in specific cases is less easily predictable.

Specification of a system of protograms consists of three parts:

1. For each protogram, a range of actions and preferences among them, as a function of the input.

2. For each protogram its relative "urgency" or "priority," again as a function of the input.

3. An arbitration procedure for trading off the deviations from the various ideals given the relative priorities.

The arbitration procedure is the most interesting component, the heart of the protogram approach. The complexity of the system is, in effect, pushed into this component, allowing other components to each handle an isolated part of the problem.

We do not regard protograms as a general panacea for the problems of AI, and in particular do not intend it to replace classical search and planning. In some applications of protograms, the individual protograms and the arbitration procedure will be simple; in others (such as the example discussed below), the arbitration procedure will need to be a sophisticated procedure using classical search and planning techniques (though the use of protograms will still reduce the complexity of the task of programming the system).

2 Application: robot navigation and exploration

To experiment with the use of protograms, we have developed a protogram interpreter, which accepts a collection of protograms, and automatically handles the interaction between them.

Dean and Wellman [1991] discuss several robotic applications of decision theory. One application, which seems particularly suitable for implementation as protograms, is their example of robot navigation and exploration (Dean and Wellman, sec. 7.7). We have chosen this example as the main focus of our experimentation with protograms, and have developed a simulation of this problem using the protogram interpreter.

The robot moves around in a building, which can be represented as a grid. For every vertical or horizontal arc in the grid, there may or may not be a corresponding corridor in the building. The robot starts out without any knowledge of which corridors exist in the building. Whenever it is physically located at any point, its sensors discover which of the four possible corridors actually exist, and it then adds that information to its internal map of the building.

The robot is continually given tasks, which require it to get to given destinations on the grid, and needs to decide on a path from its current location to its destination. The robot prefers the path that will take the least amount of time. The robot's expectations, regarding how long a path will take, are influenced by two considerations (each of which can be represented as a protogram):

1. The length of the path (the shorter, the better).

2. The number of grid-points in the path that are still unmapped (the more there are, the greater the risk that the path is actually impossible, so a robot starting out on this path will have to make a detour or backtrack; therefore, the robot will prefer a path with less unmapped points).

A third consideration, which the robot should take into account (and can be an additional protogram), is:

3. The chance to augment its map during the trip. The more complete the robot's map becomes, the greater its ability to perform subsequent tasks. This protogram will generally act contrary to 2, in that it will lead the robot to prefer paths containing *more* unmapped points.

Dean and Wellman treat the example as a problem of decision-theoretic *single-attribute utility with uncertainty* (the robot's only consideration is the expected time it will spend on all tasks, including the current one and subsequent ones). However, I believe that the above analysis as protograms (which correspond

to decision-theoretic *multi-attribute utility with certainty*) allows for a more natural implementation.

Computing the benefit of passing through unmapped points, according to Dean and Wellman, "boils down to a simple value of information calculation, where we compare the increase in immediate cost ... against the decrease in expected future costs". This calculation, however, is not simple at all; it requires the robot to compute a probability distribution over its future tasks, and then compute the expected effect of the information over the performance of these tasks; performing such a calculation directly, if possible at all, would be tremendously complicated and time-consuming. A much more natural approach is to have the amount of exploration (i.e. the number of corridors which the robot can add to the map during the trip, perhaps weighted by their estimated chance of being useful for future tasks) as a separate consideration, represented by protogram 3.

The priorities of the protograms can depend on several influences. The more complete the map, the smaller the importance of augmenting it, and so the smaller the priority of 3. The priorities of 1 and 2 are determined by the urgency of the current task, and the priority of 2 relative to 1 will represent the robot's degree of risk-averseness. Generally, as the deadline for the current task comes closer, the priority of 2 will increase, since the robot will not want to risk being late. However, in some cases, if the deadline is very close, or if the robot is already late, that may increase the priority of 1, representing the robot's willingness to gamble on the chance of reducing its lateness by discovering a shortcut.

Additional protograms, representing additional considerations in choosing the path, can now be naturally added. Some of the corridors may be "rough", causing more wear and tear on the robot's wheels, so we may have a protogram for having as few such corridors as possible; there may be some cost to changes of direction, so there may be a protogram for having as few changes in direction as possible; some specific corridor or point may contain some danger, so there may be a protogram for avoiding it; etc.

The modularity of the protograms approach, when used in this program, makes it possible to represent a large number of considerations to affect the choice of path, and to easily make changes such as removing some of the considerations, adding new considerations, or changing their relative importance.

References

[Dean and Wellman, 1991] T. Dean and M. Wellman. *Planning and Control*. Morgan Kaufmann Publishers, 1991.

Planning in Intelligent Sensor Fusion

Robin R. Murphy
College of Computing
Georgia Institute of Technology
Atlanta, GA 30332-0280

1 Introduction

Our research focuses on intelligent sensor fusion for autonomous mobile robots. Sensor fusion has been typically viewed as the process by which multiple sensors provide observations of the world which are then combined into a single measure of the evidence for a sensing objective (an object, place, or event). Sensor fusion is expected to supply a mobile robot with more reliable perception than can be generated by current single sensor systems.

The dominant trend in robotics research is to treat the sensor fusion process solely as the ability to achieve prespecified sensing objectives with multiple sensors. This ability places sensor fusion at the first of three levels of autonomy [7]. However, this view of sensor fusion does not address how the fusion process functions in a completely autonomous robot where it must 1) be able construct a sensing plan for achieving the sensing objectives and 2) be able to adapt that plan to sensor malfunctions and sudden changes in the environment. A sensor fusion process which includes these abilities is referred to as intelligent sensor fusion.

Previous work summarized below has demonstrated a system which can perform autonomous execution and limited adaptation to failures. Work in progress is considering how to add the ability to autonomously construct a sensing plan.

2 Summary of Our Research in Intelligent Sensor Fusion

Our approach to the problem of intelligent sensor fusion has been to develop the foundations of a computational theory using the action-oriented perception paradigm. This paradigm emphasizes that the sensing process should be tailored to the *perceptual context* which exists at the time of the execution of the process. The perceptual context consists of the sensing objectives and any constraints on how to achieve those objectives, the availability of sensing resources on the robot, and the impact of environmental conditions on the robot's sensing capabilities.

The computational theory describes the operations involved in a perceptual process which has been instantiated to accomplish the sensing objectives of a particular robotic motor behavior. The perceptual process begins in an investigatory phase where it first predicts a family of symbolic descriptions which should provide sufficient evidence of the sensing objective. The symbolic descriptions are represented by a context-free perceptual grammar. After prediction, the process then constructs a sensing plan which specifies how the available sensors and algorithms will be used to observe each of the descriptions. Once the sensing plan is complete, the perceptual process begins the execution sequence, where it collects observations from the sensors and algorithms, preprocesses them, and fuses them into a final measure of evidence for the objective. The perceptual process repeats the execution sequence until either the perception is no longer required or an error occurs. Errors may result from an exception to an assumption made during the construction of the sensing plan– a sensor is now malfunctioning, the environment has changed, or the needs of the motor behavior are unreasonable. The process transfers control to an exception handling activity which attempts to repair the sensing plan and resume the execution sequence.

The execution sequence and exception handling portions of this computational theory have been implemented on our Denning DRV-1 mobile robot and tested using a variety of sensors in a cluttered office setting. The sensing plan for observing the relevant descriptions of three areas in the office was manually generated. The robot was able to determine that significant changes had occurred in different areas of the office using simple 2D features observed by a Hi8 color camera, a Pulnix black and white camera, an Inframetrics true infra-red thermal camera, and Polaroid ultrasonic transducers. The exception handling module was able to use a Hamamatsu UV light camera to determine if a visible light camera was malfunctioning and should be replaced or if the lights had been turned off in the room and the visible light cameras should be eliminated from the sensing plan. Details of the action-oriented perception paradigm and this implementation are given in [4,5].

3   A Sensing Planner for Intelligent Sensor Fusion

Our current work concerns how the sensor fusion process should autonomously construct a *sensing plan*. This plan reflects the resolution of strategic issues such as the projection of the perceptual context for the expected duration of the perceptual process (essentially the *temporal projection* problem [3]) and the allocation of sensing resources between concurrent perceptual processes. The sensing plan must also specify the tactical configuration: the selection of sensors and sensing algorithms, the ordering of these algorithms, and interactions between sensors (e.g., focus-of-attention, feedback). Since robots function in an open world where the assumptions may be invalidated during execution, the sensing plan must lend itself to being repaired in response to an exception condition. The plan must be constructed in a bounded time, and it should be optimized over some parameter (minimal total uncertainty, computational cost of the sensing, etc.).

The planning activity can be viewed as transforming symbolic descriptions of a sensing objective into an ordering of sensors and algorithms to observe each symbolic feature in the description. Since the relationships between the component features of a symbolic description are expressed as a context-free grammar, a description is represented as a top-down directed, acyclic graph (DAG). The resulting sensing plan is a bottom-up DAG which has one or more "virtual sensor" nodes associated with each feature node in the description DAG. The links of the sensor plan DAG specify the ordering of the execution of the algorithms and any interactions between sensors.

The ideal sensor fusion planner shares characteristics with many planning paradigms. Like classical planners, a sensor fusion planner must produce a complete sensing plan or else the perceptual process cannot proceed. In some sense, the planner should produce a universal plan [6] which permits the interleaving of active perception and opportunistic perception within the sensing plan. The sensor fusion planner shares similarities with a RAP planner [1], since the sensing plan allows the perceptual process to autonomously pursue a sensing objective. Further, we expect an implementation of a sensor fusion planner to include some, if not all, of the structures found in a procedural reasoning system [2]. However, no existent planner seems to capture all of the desired attributes, and more research is called for.

4   Summary

The first step toward implementing an architecture for intelligent sensor fusion for autonomous mobile robots has been made: a system with the ability to both achieve sensing objectives and to recover from a variety of failures has been demonstrated with sensor data acquired from a mobile robot. The next step is to add the capability to autonomously construct the sensing plan. The resulting planner must exhibit attributes of both classical and reactive planners in order to produce a complete plan for autonomous execution which resolves both strategic and tactical sensing issues.

Acknowledgements

This work has been supported in part by a Rockwell Doctoral Fellowship and the Georgia Tech CIMS Program.

References

[1] Firby, R.J., "An Investigation into Reactive Planning in Complex Domains", proceedings of *AAAI 87*, vol. 1, July 13-17,1987, pp. 202-206.

[2] Georgeff, M.P., and Lansky, A.L., "Reactive Reasoning and Planning", proceedings of *AAAI 87*, vol. 2, July 13-17,1987, pp. 677-682.

[3] Hanks, S., "Practical Temporal Projection", proceedings of *AAAI 90*, vol. 1, July 29-Aug 3,1990, pp. 158–163.

[4] Murphy, R.R., "SFX: An Architecture for Action-Oriented Sensor Fusion", to appear in proceedings of *IROS 92*, July 7-10, 1992.

[5] Murphy, R.R., "State Based Sensor Fusion for Surveillance", to appear in *Proceedings SPIE Sensor Fusion IV*, Boston, MA, Nov. 1991.

[6] Schoppers, M.J., "Universal Plans for Reactive Robots in Unpredictable Environments", proceedings of *IJCAI 87*, vol. 2, August 23-28, 1987, pp. 1039-1046.

[7] Zeigler, B.P., and Chi, S.D., "Model-Based Architecture Concepts For Autonomous Systems", proceedings of *5th IEEE International Symposium on Intelligent Control*, vol. 1, Sept 5-7, 1990, pp. 27-32.

An Introduction to Planning and Meta-Decision-Making with Uncertain Nondeterministic Actions using 2nd-Order Probabilities

John K. Myers

ATR Interpreting Telephony Research Laboratories

Sanpeidani, Inuidani, Seika-cho, Soraku-gun, Kyoto 619-02, Japan

myers@atr-la.atr.co.jp

When a limited autonomous agent is interacting with the world, ie planning with uncertain actions, there are many requirements. It needs a method for explicitly **representing uncertainties** in a precise manner; for **initializing**, **updating** (*learning*), and **computing** with those uncertainties; for **representing uncertain actions**, outcome situations, and plans composed of such actions; for **constructing plans**; for **deciding** between competing plans; and for **meta-deciding** whether it should embark on a course of action, or investigate the situation further. All these must be well-grounded in philosophy/mathematics.

This paper briefly introduces a system of theories and implementations that support such behavior. An agent models a nondeterministic action by listing its n known possible outcome situations $A_1, .., A_n$ (possibly with values $V_1, ..., V_n$ comprising $\vec{V}$). These form a *partition* A of the space of possible outcomes. The current theory assumes that the number n and types of the situations are known. Uncertainty is explicitly **represented** using two types of second-order probability: *partition*, and *event* distributions. Each outcome situation forms a possible world; a partition plus a *valid* ($\Sigma p(A_i) = 1$) assignment of probability measures to all outcomes forms a *universe*. Given repeated trials of the same action in the same universe, different possible worlds will result as outcomes with the given probabilities. The "real universe" exists and has fixed probabilities (stationary processes); however, these are generally unknowable. An agent models the real universe by considering the space of all possible (valid) probability assignments to the partition, $\vec{p}$, then measuring this with a function $q_A(\vec{p})$ that represents the believed probability (confidence) that a given set of probability assignments (likelihoods) to the partition is real. This function maps an n-dimensional vector space to a scalar, and is the *partition distribution*. For invalid assignments $q = 0$. The partition distribution measures the entire partition at once. If this distribution is projected down onto one outcome event axis, it measures the cumulative believed probability (confidence) that the event will occur with a given probability (likelihood). This function maps a scalar to a scalar, and is the *event distribution* $q_{A_i}(p)$. It only measures one outcome, ignoring the rest. Partition distributions carry full information but seem to require a symbolic integration package. Event distributions are easy to work with, but lose some information. The *expected probability* assignment of a (partition or event) distribution, giving the best probability estimate, is found by taking its center of mass.

Normative distributions are what people *should* believe; *doxastic* distributions are what people *actually* believe. A normative distribution is <u>initialized</u> using the method of maximum entropy on the space of all possible probability assignments (see equations (2) and (3), which assume that the number of outcomes and nothing else is known about the action (a good approximation)). If the action is performed m times and the outcomes $A_1, .., A_n$ are certainly observed to have occurred $k_1, .., k_n$ times respectively, then the distributions can be normatively <u>updated</u> using Bayes's theorem (equations (4) and (5)). These are combined in closed form for event distributions in (6). Importantly, the methods work quite well for low sample counts. A significant result is that (7) is the optimal expected probability estimate for the described problem. **Computing** here consists of the *union, conditional, expectation distribution, EVPI*, and *EVI* operators discussed later. Uncertain NonDeterministic Actions (UNDAs) are <u>represented</u> using the B-SURE (Believed Situation and UNDA Representation Environment) system that models state, situation, and nonmonotonic action types and instances in multiple possible temporal action worlds. <u>Plan construction</u> is not significant and a favorite method can be used; the implementation uses a simple case-based planning method. Issues in uncertain planning include: (1) Plans form reactive *trees* of *contingency plans*; (2) Alternate *sets* of scored goals are searched for; (3) Planning is neither purely predictive nor reactive but *interactive*; (4) Nondeterministic decompositions become problematical; (5) A history mechanism distinguishes past from future actions; (6) Practical systems require implementing *recognition demons* that can infer and certify when a given outcome has occurred [Mye91]. <u>Deciding</u> which plan to use is based on decision-theoretic "averaging-out and folding-back" techniques, using the second-order computations. Actions are chosen based on the maximum expected value strategy[1]. Actions are "folded back" by taking the refinement of a partition using **conditionals** (partition:$q_{A'}(p_{A_1}, .., p_{A_{n-1}}, p_{A_n B_1}, .., p_{A_n B_m}) = q_A(p_{A_1}, .., p_{A_n}) q_B(p_{B_1}, .., p_{B_m})$

event:$q_{A_i B_j}(p_{ij}) = \int_{p_{ij}}^1 \frac{1}{|s|} q_{A_i}(s) q_{B_j|A_i}(\frac{p_{ij}}{s}) ds$), which effectively splits an outcome event up into sub-events representing subsequent outcomes. Actions are "averaged out"

---

[1]Other significant strategies besides m.e.v. include min risk, max possible gain, max thrill, and max learning. Max utility subsumes all these and is too subtle for casual use.

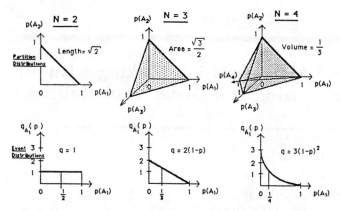

Figure 1: Initial 2nd-Order Partition and Event Probability Distributions.

by using the **union** operator (Taking the union $A_{i+j} = A_i \vee A_j$ of disjoint events A_i and A_j in $\mathcal{A}$ forms a new partition $\mathcal{A}'$ having $(n-1)$ elements. Without loss of generality let $i = n-1$ and $j = n$. Then: $q_{newA}(...p_{A_{n-2}}, p_{A_{i \vee j}}) = \int_0^{p_{A_i \vee j}} \sqrt{2} \, q_A(...p_{A_{n-2}}, (s), (p_{A_{i \vee j}} - s)) \, ds$). In general, *there is not enough information to determine the second-order event distribution of the union from the event distributions of A_i and A_j.* The **expectation** operator determines the range of possible expected values for an action (plan branch): The expected value of a given point $\vec{p}$ in the probability space is the dot product $E(\vec{p}) = (\vec{p} \cdot \vec{V})$, a function of $\vec{p}$. E is a random variable, and the confidence that this particular E is correct is the partition distribution $q_A(\vec{p})$. The probability distribution $q_{E(A)}(E)$, representing the likelihood that any particular scalar E is the actual expectation of $\mathcal{A}$, is found by integrating over the probability points where E holds:

$$q_{E(A)}(E) = \int_{\vec{p}} q_A(\vec{p}) \; \Delta(E - \vec{p} \cdot \vec{V}) \, d\vec{p} \qquad (1)$$

where $\Delta(0) = 1$, $\Delta(x \neq 0) = 0$. In general, *there is insufficient information to determine an accurate expectation distribution from the n event distributions $q_{A_i}(p)$.* Rough heuristic approximations are available.

The *decision* problem is the task of choosing between a known set of known but uncertain *alternatives* each comprising a tree of actions with a set of ultimate outcome situations, their values, and the likelihoods of reaching them. However, the current believed decision problem may not represent the best model of the real decision problem–and if more information is added (by performing *information-gathering actions* such as thinking, testing, or acting), the model *may change* to a *new* decision problem. Deciding whether to decide and act with the current decision problem, or whether to attempt to change the current problem by performing an information-gathering action, is a *meta-decision problem.*[2] **Meta-decision problems** involving likelihood estimates are properly answered using *confidence*

---

[2]Other meta-decision alternatives besides *observing/interacting* include *do nothing*, *wait* for a possible change, *waffle* by trying to take two or more alternatives, *consult* experts, *relegate* the problem to a human superior, *delegate* an inferior or sibling agent to make the decision, *react* randomly, *respond* in a habitual/reflexive manner, or *transcend* the problem.

measures. If the agent has high confidence in its believed estimates of likelihoods, with known values, alternative sets and outcome sets, then it believes that *learning more information will probably not change the decision problem in a significant manner.* With low confidence, *learning may significantly change the believed decision problem model, and is therefore valuable. Second-order probability distributions* represent confidence and should be used to solve meta-decision problems involving clarification of likelihood estimates.

Initialization of Partition and Event Distributions.

$$q_A(\vec{p}) = \frac{(n-1)!}{\sqrt{n}} \text{ (if } \Sigma p_i = 1, \; p_i \geq 0; \text{ else } q_A = 0) \quad (2)$$

$$q_{A_i}(p_i) = (n-1)(1-p_i)^{n-2} \qquad (3)$$

Note $q_{A_i}(0) = (n-1)$ and the expected $p(A_i) = \frac{1}{n}$.

Updating of Partition and Event Distributions.

$$q_{newA}(\vec{p}) = \frac{p_1^{(k_1)}...p_n^{(k_n)} \; q_{oldA}(\vec{p})}{\left(\int_{\vec{p}} p_1^{(k_1)}...p_n^{(k_n)} \; q_{oldA}(\vec{p}) \, d\vec{p}\right)} \qquad (4)$$

$$q_{newA_i}(p_i) = \frac{p_i^{(k_i)}(1-p_i)^{(m-k_i)} \; q_{oldA_i}(p_i)}{\left(\int_0^1 p_i^{(k_i)}(1-p_i)^{(m-k_i)} q_{oldA_i}(p_i) dp_i\right)} \qquad (5)$$

Closed Form for Event Distributions.

$$q_{newA_i}(p_i) = \frac{(m+n-1)!}{k_i!((m+n-2)-k_i)!} p_i^{(k_i)}(1-p_i)^{((m+n-2)-k_i)} \qquad (6)$$

Expected Probability for Event Distributions.

$$p(A_i) = \frac{k_i + 1}{m + n} \qquad (7)$$

not $\frac{k_i}{m}$, as is customarily taught.

Expected Value of Perfect Information $\vec{p}^*_{a_{alt}}$.

$$EVPI(\vec{p}^*_{a_{alt}}) = \int_{E(a_{max})}^{\infty} (gain(\text{info})) q_{E(A)}(E_{a_{alt}}) dE_{a_{alt}} - cost(\text{info}) \qquad (8)$$

where $(gain())$ is typically $(E_{a_{alt}} - E(a_{max}))$. This equation concerns reducing uncertain confidence to perfect confidence and is one of the main results of this paper. In effect, it computes and uses $q(E_{a_{alt}} \geq E(a_{max}))$, the possibility that the variable expectation of the new alternative action *could be* greater than the scalar current best action's average expectation, which is a second-order result. Note that if first-order probabilities are used, $E(a_{alt})$ is a constant, not a random variable, and $E(a_{alt}) \geq E(a_{max})$ is either true or not. Event expectation distributions are insufficient.

Value of Testing Action Once.

$$EVI(test) = \sum_{i=1}^{n} gain(q_{newA}(\vec{p}) \mid A_i \text{observed}) p(A_i) \qquad (9)$$

This equation apparently offers a closed-form optimal solution to the "two-armed bandit" problem for k arms with n_k known outcomes apiece.

References

[Dea91]   Thomas Dean. Decision-theoretic control of inference for time-critical applications. International Journal of Intelligent Systems, 6:417–441, 1991.

[Mye91]   John K. Myers. Plan inference with probabilistic-outcome actions. In Conf. Proc. Information Processing Society of Japan, volume 3, pages 168–169, Tokyo, Japan, March 1991.

[Pap84]   Athanasios Papoulis. Probability, Random Variables, and Stochastic Processes. McGraw-Hill Book Company, New York, NY, 1984. First edition 1965.

A Hierarchical Approach to Strategic Planning with Non-Cooperating Agents under Conditions of Uncertainty *

Stephen Joseph Smith   **Dana S. Nau**[†]
sjsmith@cs.umd.edu   nau@cs.umd.edu
Computer Science Department
University of Maryland
College Park, MD 20742

Tom Throop

Great Game Products
8804 Chalon Drive
Bethesda, MD 20817

1   Problem Statement

Much of the difficulty of planning is due to the large number of alternatives that must be examined and discarded. This is especially true of strategic planning with non-cooperating agents. To develop a complete strategy that takes into account all of the possible actions of the other agents, a planner must generate and evaluate an immense number of alternative plans.

In previous work on strategic planning with non-cooperating agents, planning has generally been done by searching a game tree (Biermann, 1978; Charniak & McDermott, 1985, p. 281; Pearl, 1984). Since the planner does not know what moves the opponent will make, a *strategy* is not just one path through the game tree, but is instead a subtree containing *one* arc from each node where it is the planner's move, and *all* arcs from each node where it is the opponent's move. Game-tree searching works well when the planner has complete knowledge about the state of the world, the possible actions, and their effects. However, if some of this knowledge is uncertain, then the branching factor of the game tree can be very large, making the tree so immense that game-tree searching is completely infeasible. For example, the game tree for bridge contains approximately 1.56×10^{46} leaf nodes.

2   Our Approach

To address the problem described above, we propose searching a tree whose branches are determined not by the number of actions that an agent can perform, but instead by the number of different tactical and strategic schemes that the agent can employ. As a case study, we have implemented this approach for the game of bridge, in a planning system called Tignum.

Our approach has three parts. First, we define a multi-agent task network (see below). Second, from the multi-agent task network, the planner generates a set of plans. Finally, the planner uses a search to pick the plan with the greatest utility.

A multi-agent task network (MATN) is similar to the task decompositions used in hierarchical single-agent planning systems such as Nonlin (Tate, 1977) and NOAH (Sacerdoti, 1977), but extended to include nodes that represent the possible actions of agents other than the planner. In addition to the task decompositions that ordinarily appear in task networks, a MATN contains a new kind of decomposition called an external-agent node (EAN). Each link from the EAN represenetes some class of possible actions that some external agent may perfrom. Associated with each link is a *validity condition*, which determines whether or not the external agent is capable of performing the given type of action. A validity condition is similar to a filter condition, in the following sense: since it governs the planner's beliefs about what the other agent might do rather than what the planner might do, if it is not satisfied the planner will not try to achieve it.

The links emanating from an EAN do not necessarily represent all the possible actions that the external agent can perform. Instead, they represent only those actions that are deemed "worth considering". Thus, if we know in advance that a certain action is extermely unlikely, we can prevent the planner from considering it by omitting it from the EAN. Essentially, we trade a little bit of accuracy for a lot of efficiency.

Given a multi-agent task network, our planner generates all possible strategies from the initial state, producing an AND/OR tree. The planner then searches this tree to produce a single strategy for execution. This strategy is then executed until it proves invalid (at which point the planner re-plans), or until the strategy runs to completion. If at each node, the number of applicable schemes is smaller than the number of possible actions, this will produce a smaller branching factor, and a much smaller search tree.

*Supported in part by Maryland Industrial Partnerships (MIPS) grant 501.15, Great Game Products, NSF grants IRI-8907890 and NSFD CDR-88-003012, and an AT&T graduate fellowship to S. J. Smith.

[†]Also in the Systems Research Center and the Institute for Advanced Computer Studies.

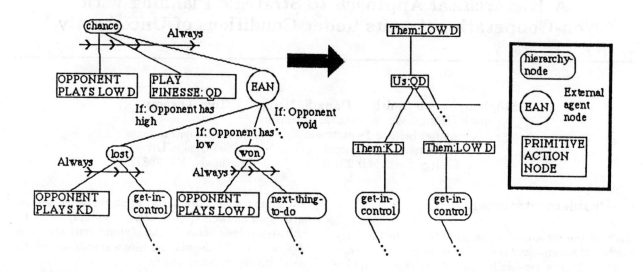

Figure 1: Producing an AND/OR tree from a portion of our scheme for finessing.

As an example, consider the tactic of finessing in the game of bridge. Here we want to get rid of a *loser* (a card which would otherwise be lost). For example, suppose that in some suit, we have the Queen and Ace, but lack the King. Then the Queen would be a loser, suggesting a finesse against the King. Since one opponent can usually be forced to play before we play the Queen, we take the chance that that opponent has the King, and we try to win a trick with the Queen.

Thus our tactical scheme has several parts: getting to the appropriate hand, playing a low card, waiting for the left-hand opponent's play, and (if the opponent has made the play we expect), playing the finesse card—in this case the Queen. Finally, the crucial opponent plays, either winning the trick with the King—in which case the finesse fails—or playing low to the trick—in which case we win the trick with the Queen and the finesse succeeds. Fig. 1 shows our planner instantiating a portion of this tactical finesse scheme, thus producing part of an AND/OR tree.

3   Conclusions

Empirical studies with Tignum indicate that even in the worst case, Tignum generates search trees containing no more than about 1300 nodes, a number small enough that Tignum can generate and evaluate alternative plans by searching the entire tree. It is about $1/10^{43}$ of the number of nodes that would be generated by a brute-force game tree search. Thus, we have transformed an effectively impossible search problem into a reasonably efficient planning problem.

Preliminary tests of Tignum suggest that this approach has the potential to yield bridge-playing programs much better than existing ones. We further anticipate that this approach will be useful in a variety of multi-agent and adversarial planning situations.

References

H. J. Berliner, G. Goetsch, M. S. Campbell, and C. Ebeling. Measuring the performance potential of chess programs. *Artificial Intelligence* **43**:7–20, 1990.

A. W. Biermann. Theoretical issues related to computer game playing programs. *Personal Computing*, September 1978:86-88.

E. Charniak and D. V. McDermott. *Artificial Intelligence*. Reading, Mass.: Addison-Wesley, 1985.

D. E. Knuth and R. W. Moore. An analysis of alpha-beta pruning. *Artificial Intelligence*, 6:293-326, 1975.

I. H. Lavalle. *Fundamentals of Decision Analysis*. New York: Holt, Rinehart and Winston, 1978.

J. Pearl. *Heuristics: Intelligent Search Strategies for Computer Problem Solving*. Reading, Massachusetts: Addison-Wesley, 1984.

E. D. Sacerdoti. *A Structure for Plans and Behavior*. New York: American Elsevier, 1977.

A. Tate. Generating project networks. In *IJCAI-5*:888–893, 1977.

An Architecture Supporting Multiple Organizations for Cooperative Mobile Robots

Fabrice R. Noreils
Alcatel Alsthom Recherche
Route de Nozay
91460 Marcoussis - France
email: noreils@aar.alcatel-alsthom.fr

1 Motivations

Cooperation occurs when several vehicles have to work together in order to fulfill a task which is not achievable by one robot only. Cooperation consists in a team of robots provided either with different skills, referred to as *heteregeneous robots*, or with the same skills, referred to as *homogeneous robots*.

Despite the fact that cooperation faces a lot of problems, one major benefit resides in the *robustness* of the team with respect to contingencies. Indeed, a team composed of homogeneous robots capitalizes on robustness, *i.e.*, if one robot fails, others are still available to fulfill the task.

All potential applications (mining, construction, warehousing, space exploration) involve heterogeneous robots because (1) we do not know how to make a polyvalent and versatile robot yet and (2) we have to use the existing material.

Robustness in an heterogeneous team of robots becomes a much more complex challenge than for homogeneous robots. If robots are provided with different and independent skills and one of them fails, it may jeopardize the success of the overall team. One possibility to overcome this drawback is to force robots to share some skills. When one robot may be replaced by other(s) if it fails, we call this *redundancy* in terms of skills. Therefore, we have to manage this redundancy so as to recover any failure that may occur. It means that in order to cope with the current situation, the team is *dynamically re-organized*.

We argue that an architecture for multiple mobile robots should support different organizations and some control mechanisms to switch from one to another.

The organization answers the two following questions:

[1.] How is the behavior of a robot *controlled* so as to coordinate its activity with other robots?

[2.] How are *data* broadcast among robots?

Basically, we can list three types of organization in terms of control and data: (1) local is the behavior of a robot based on orders and data provided by robots in its vicinity. Data contain local information; (2) distributed is the same as local organization but the orders and/or data contain information on the global task of the cooperation; and (3) centralized is characterized by one robot either taking decisions and giving orders to a set of robots or centralizing the information. Moreover, it is possible to mix these organizations in order to develop new ones.

The goal of this paper is to show that an organization of robots is not static but is dynamically modified. An architecture for cooperative mobile robots should be able to switch from an organization to another according to the context. We think that an efficient cooperation should be based on this ability because it improves:

• The robustness of a heterogeneous team of robots with respect to contingencies. If there is a centralized organization and that the leader fails, robots may switch to a local one so as to ensure their safety the time to find a new leader and then come back to the former organization. In the worst case, robots may switch to a completely local organization where they are loosely coupled but still capable of doing useful actions. Therefore, robots are never idle and there is a graceful degradation of the performances of the team.

• The adaptability of the team facing the dynamics of the world. The organization may change according to the state of the world. A typical example consists in roaming robots (local organization) looking for a large flat surface where they can build something. At this moment they switch to a more structured organization that can support the interactions necessary in the construction process.

2 An Architecture for Cooperation Between Robots

The architecture (described in more details in (Noreils 1992a) can be decomposed in three layers:

1. The *cooperation layer* that manages the collaboration between robots and the local planning. This system decomposes a task into subtasks and allocates

them to a network of robots. The allocation is based on the contract net protocol (Davis and Smith 1983). The leader sends a *call-for-participation* where it defines the task and the skills necessary to fulfill it. If some robots are able to achieve it, they apply for and issue a *proposal* that contains their skills and other information useful for the leader to take a decision. The leader sends a *final-response* to accept or not a specific robot in a team.

2. The *coordination layer* that manages *coordinated protocols*, which are programmed using a specific language. Coordinated protocols model the cooperative (or social) behaviors between robots and are described in details in (Noreils 1992b).

3. The robot layer composed of (1) a set of modules that provide for basic processing functions (perception and data processing, action and motion computation, and closed-loop processes) and event detection and programmable reactivity, and (2) a control system that executes tasks (expressed in a language we have designed).

After a task given to a robot at the planning layer, is decomposed into subtasks and assigned to a set of robots, the subtask becomes for these robots either a goal for the local planner that generates a local plan or a task that can be decomposed again into subtasks through a set of new robots, and so on. A local plan is composed of primitive operators that call either missions (executed by the robot layer) or CMRmissions (executed by the coordination layer). As the planning is local, local planners communicate among each other to detect and solve conflicts.

This cooperation is based on a specific organization (centralized, local, etc). The concept of *skeletal-task* permits different organizations to be supported by the architecture. A *skeletal-task* is a frame composed of slots containing different information relevant to the task to be performed, its decomposition into subtasks (only for the robot that did the decomposition), the construction of a team (skills required, number of robots, ...), dependencies between robots (leader, supervisor, worker, ...), and the sequence of actions to be performed.

3   Application: From a Local Organization to a Centralized one and Back

Consider an area where some blocks are scattered (blocks are either isolated or in piles). The tasks of robots is to clean up this area. The task is fulfilled by a set of heterogeneous robots whose capabilities are given Table 1. All robots are able to create and manage a team.

At the beginning, cooperation consists of a set of robots wandering until they detect an object. Each robot is provided with the same skeletal-task, which contains the same task and the same sequence of actions: detect and remove blocks. The organization is purely local. If a robot detects other robots in its vicinity (robots send regularly their position), they are avoided using a local collision avoidance algorithm.

Robots	Dump robot	Pickup Robot	Push robot
Skills	Carry objts	Pick up objts	Push objt
		Detect objects	
		Carry one object	

Table 1: List of robots with their skills.

If a robot detects a pile of blocks, it will organize a team in order to clean up this area in an efficient and fast way – this robot is referred to as the leader. The former skeletal-task is pushed in a stack and a new one is created. This skeletal-task contains a new goal (clean-up a pile) and asks for the creation of a team of robots provided with specific skills: pick-up robots and/or dump-robots (the number of robots depending on the size of the pile). The leader issues a call-for-participation (cfp) in order to create a team corresponding to the specifications contained into the skeletal-task. If robots are available, they send a proposal, and join the team if they are accepted by the leader – these robots are referred to as workers. Notice that workers created a new skeletal-task corresponding to the cfp sent by the leader. At this moment, the organization is centralized and supervised by the leader. When robots cooperate to clean up the pile, tight coordinations occur. Only one robot at a time can take off a block (the pile is an exclusive resource) and thus, robots must coordinate their activity to avoid conflicts. When a pick-up robot wants to leave the block it carries into the dump of a dump robot, it moves towards it. Meantime, it asks the dump robot whether it can servo its movements with respect to the dump (in order to leave the block in it) or it has to wait (because another robot is already near the dump robot). All these behaviors are programmed with coordinated protocols. When the pile is cleaned up, robots switch back to a local organization by poping the skeletal-task that was into the stack. See (Noreils 1992c) for a more detailed description of the ideas presented in this paper.

Davis R. and Reid G. S. 1983 Negotiation as a metaphor for distributed problem solving. *Artificial Intelligence*, pp 63 – 109.

Noreils F. R. 1992a. An architecture for autonomous and cooperative mobile robots. To appear in *IEEE Intl Conf. on Robotics and Automation*.

Noreils F. R. 1992b. Coordinated protocols: An approach to formalize coordination between mobile robots. To appear in *IEEE/RSJ International Conference on Robots and Systems*.

Noreils F. R. 1992c. Dynamic re-organization for cooperative mobile robots. Forthcoming.

SEPIA: A Resource-Bounded Adaptive Agent

Alberto M. Segre
Department of Computer Science
Cornell University
Ithaca, NY 14853-7501

Jennifer S. Turney
Department of Computer Science
Cornell University
Ithaca, NY 14853-7501

Abstract

This extended abstract presents a new architecture, called SEPIA, for planning, learning, and executing effective behavior in a dynamic environment. It combines a reactive executive with a classical planner based on a formalism for generating and reasoning about approximate plans, and incorporates multiple speedup learning techniques in order to improve its performance with experience.

1. INTRODUCTION

The goal of the SEPIA project is to build a scalable, pseudo real-time, learning apprentice system operating in a dynamic environment. The design of our SEPIA intelligent agent architecture (Segre & Turney, 1992) builds on our previous work in both learning and planning (Segre, 1988). It is neither a classical planner nor a reactive system; instead, it is a hybrid of techniques from both traditions. While others have proposed hybrid agent architectures before, SEPIA differs from those proposals in at least four important respects. First, the SEPIA planner relies on a formalism for incrementally generating and reasoning about *approximate plans*. Second, the planner is based on an adaptive theorem-proving system that incorporates multiple speedup learning techniques. Third, the SEPIA executive is guided by approximate plans produced by the planner. Finally, the SEPIA agent is intended to operate as a *learning apprentice system*, and thus can learn either from its own planning performance or by analyzing a human agent's problem-solving behavior.

This abstract presents an overview of the SEPIA system and the speedup techniques used within the planning component. The current SEPIA implementation is applied to a video game domain called GOLDDIG. GOLDDIG is played by maneuvering the player through successive levels of a maze, all the while collecting goldpieces and avoiding hostile badguys (see Figure 1). Each level begins with a certain number of goldpieces and badguys. A level is completed when all of the goldpieces have been collected. The game is won when all the levels are complete; the game is lost when the player is killed by a badguy or by environmental hazards. Each successive level introduces new aspects of the GOLDDIG world, generally becoming more and more difficult to complete.

The GOLDDIG domain embodies both complex constraints and an element of unpredictability. These characteristics imply that neither purely local approaches (*e.g.*, gradient descent in the player's sensory space) or purely deliberative approaches (*e.g.*, search through the space defined by the current level and the GOLDDIG physics) are likely to be sufficient. The SEPIA agent architecture combines both approaches.

2. THE SEPIA AGENT ARCHITECTURE

The SEPIA architecture consists of two components, a *planner* and a reactive *executive*, managed by a third component, the *control module*. A *control policy*, explicitly encoded within the control module, determines when to interrupt one component and transfer control to the other. The planner and executive exchange information via a propositional truth maintenance system (or TMS), which is also consulted by the control module.

The job of the executive is to assimilate sensor and plan information in order to decide what action should be taken by the player in the current time step. The executive has no memory; instead, it makes its decision based on a prespecified heuristic strategy and local conditions as reported by a fixed set of *sensors*. Inspired by Brooks (1985), we have implemented a software tool to support the design of different heuristic execution

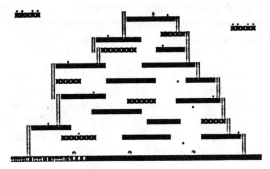

Figure 1: GOLDDIG Level 1

strategies. Each heuristic strategy is composed of smaller software modules embodying particular GOLDDIG behaviors. Each module consists of a collection of forward-firing production rules expressed in a simple language where the rule antecedents are either partial descriptors of *sensor events* or simple relations between such descriptors. Each rule consequent votes for or against one of the eight available primitive player actions. Each *sense-fire-arbitrate-act cycle*, votes are summed and the highest scoring action is taken; ties are broken according to a pre-specified strategy (*e.g.*, randomly).

Since the number of sensor events per cycle is both small and bounded, any executive constructed within this framework can be assumed to operate in real time given a fast enough computer. The SEPIA executive is performing gradient descent in a space defined by current sensor events; nevertheless it is able to survive and collect goldpieces for short periods of time in simple domains. Building an executive that operates effectively in more complex GOLDDIG levels would probably require extensive changes to the executive design, *e.g.*, the addition of memory to the agent.

The SEPIA architecture eschews adding more structure to the executive; instead, we propose the use of an adaptive planning component to advise the executive. The SEPIA planner is a first-principles classical planner based on the PERFLOG situation-calculus-based planning formalism (Elkan, 1990). The planner is both *approximative* and *incremental*, and is therefore able to generate plausible candidate plans quickly, refining these plans when allotted more computation time.

We describe the physics of the GOLDDIG world as a logical theory. We express the eight primitive player actions as SEPIA operators (similar to STRIPS operators), which are automatically compiled into the PERFLOG calculus. To complete this theory, we add SEPIA operators describing the goal structure of a GOLDDIG level; *i.e.*, that collecting goldpieces is desirable behavior, that once all goldpieces in the current level are exhausted it is appropriate to advance to the next level via a portal, that sharing a space with a badguy terminates the game, etc. This logical theory, when combined with a theorem-proving engine, will in principle compute a solution to any GOLDDIG level which is adequately described by the theory.

Clearly, this kind of exponential search is unacceptable. Thus at the core of our implementation lies an adaptive theorem-proving system whose performance characteristics improve with experience (Segre *et al*, 1992). This speed up is obtained via a combination of several different mechanisms, including an integrated *explanation-based learning* component, bounded-overhead success and failure caches, heuristic antecedent reordering strategies, and a dynamic abstraction mechanism. The theorem prover, when provided with the GOLDDIG theory, quickly produces an approximate plan that incorporates explicit assumptions. The assumptions underlying can later be verified if additional resources should become available.

The approximate plan produced by the planner is used to constrain the behavior of the executive. If no plan is available, the SEPIA executive is simply free to react to its environment. However, if an approximate plan is available, we extract an operational description of the plan and interface it with the executive via an additional sensor event. This additional sensor information is folded into the executive's behavior via the inclusion of a special module which needn't preempt other behaviors embodied in the executive.

3. CONCLUSION

This short abstract has described the SEPIA intelligent agent architecture, a learning apprentice system operating in a dynamic planning domain. We have described the ongoing application of our ideas to the GOLDDIG dynamic planning domain. While there are in fact many as yet unresolved research issues that remain to be studied, we feel SEPIA represents a novel framework for the integration of planning and reactive improvisation along with a host of speedup learning methods.

Acknowledgements

Support for this work was provided by the United States Office of Naval Research grant N00014-90-J-1542. Thanks to Alex Siegel for making his GOLDDIG implementation available for use in SEPIA.

References

A.M. Segre and J. Turney, "Planning, Acting, and Learning in a Dynamic Domain," in *Machine Learning Methods for Planning and Scheduling*, S. Minton (editor), Morgan Kaufmann Publishers, San Mateo, CA, To appear, 1992.

A.M. Segre, *Machine Learning of Robot Assembly Plans*, Kluwer Academic Publishers, Hingham, MA, Mar. 1988.

R. A. Brooks, "A Robust Layered Control System for A Mobile Robot," AI Memo 864, MIT AI Laboratory, Cambridge, MA, Sept. 1985.

C. Elkan, "Incremental, Approximate Planning," *Proc. of the Natl. Conf. on AI*, Boston, MA, July 1990, pp. 145-150.

A.M. Segre, C. Elkan, D. Scharstein, G. Gordon and A. Russell, "Adaptive Inference," in *Machine Learning: Induction, Analogy, and Discovery*, S. Chipman and A. Meyrowitz (editors), Kluwer Academic Publishers, Hingham, MA, To appear, 1992.

Multi-Agent Planning and Collaboration in Dynamic Resource Allocation

Uttam Sengupta and Nicholas V. Findler
Dept. of Computer Science and AI Laboratory
Arizona State University, Tempe, AZ 85287-5406

Abstract

We discuss some innovative concepts for distributed resource allocation, such as *Dynamic Scoping, constrained lattice-like structures*, for message routing, and prioritizing the rule base of expert systems for medium-level time-critical task environments.

1 INTRODUCTION

We have been concerned with modeling the behavior of a set of semi-autonomous intelligent agents in medium time-criticality domains. We have built a Distributed Planning and Problem Solving (DPPS) testbed for testing and evaluating different forms of inter-agent cooperation and communication, organizational structures, planning strategies, and task distribution techniques. The hierarchical planning mechanism utilizes a rule-based system with a time-critical inference mechanism.

2 THE SENTINEL SYSTEM

A large programming system, SENTINEL (Sengupta, 1991), models the environment of a hierarchy of decision making entities or nodes. A node has a certain area of jurisdiction and controls a given set of resources which are in various states of readiness and availability. The tasks are non-stationary and can migrate across the boundaries of several jurisdictions. There is a need for interaction and resource sharing among the nodes. The environment is characterized by resource attributes, dynamic environmental effects, legal, fiscal, organizational and other constraints. The capabilities of dynamic simulation models and distributed decision-support systems are combined. SENTINEL has similar goals to those of the PHOENIX project (Cohen, *et al.*, 1989); however, unlike the latter, we use *truly* distributed planning agents.

Concerning *inter-agent cooperation*, let us suppose that a task of a given priority and complexity occurs within the jurisdiction of a particular node (agent) that does not have the resources of the appropriate type and in sufficient number to take care of the task within the desired time period. *Dynamic Scoping* permits the node to contact its adjacent nodes, giving them the specification of the task at hand. The following cases may arise: (1) An adjacent node has the needed resources in an "idle" condition. (2) The node has the resources but they are engaged in tasks of lower priority than the task at hand. These resources are pre-empted. (3) The adjacent nodes jointly cannot provide the needed resources. They must then communicate with *their* adjacent nodes and ask for their help. This process goes on iteratively until either all needed resources have been acquired or a so-called *envelope of effectiveness* has been reached. The latter is defined by the constraint that the time and expense necessary for reaching from it the task can no longer be justified by the benefit obtained from the accomplished objective. Such soliciting of cooperation from neighboring nodes is similar to CNet (Davis & Smith, 1981). However, Dynamic Scoping does not use a "free-for-all" bidding process, requests are based on geographical proximity, and the requesting node resolves any conflicts and overcommitment of resources.

Agents have to *communicate* with each other at different levels. In a Command, Control and Communication (C^3) environment, usually there is a strict hierarchical structure of decision making entities, determining the flow of information and control (King, 1983). The notion of *constrained lattice-like* organizational structures permits direct communication and coordination between functionally related decision making agents at any level. The 'constraints' refer to domain specific requirements the routing strategy must abide by. This flexible structure can enhance cooperative problem solving and reduce plan generation time.

Planning (and the related scheduling) is *time-critical* when the time scale of satisfying various constraints is commeasurable with the time requirements of the planning process itself. The time available varies due to changes in the environment, and unexpected events may occur and generate a need for replanning in a limited time. Our approach, *iterative constraint satisfaction*, allows the proper ordering of operating attributes and constraints used in decision making. In the measure

```
PRIORITY = IMPORTANCE * URGENCY
```

IMPORTANCE describes the relative *static* value of an attribute in the decision making process, and URGENCY characterizes its gradually *increasing* relative criticality on the time scale. The program module, *Time-Criticality Supervisor*, oversees, interrupts if necessary, and coordinates any part of the planning process, communicates with the changing task environment, updates the relevant part of the knowledge base and, in general, tries to make sure that the plan execution is near-optimal while the prioritized constraints are satisfied as well as time has permitted "so far" (Dean & Boddy, 1988).

3   EXPERIMENTAL RESULTS AND CONCLUSIONS

To test the SENTINEL system, we chose the C^3 operations of the U.S. Coast Guard (USCG)[1]. Their main responsibilities are to perform Search and Rescue (SAR) and the Enforcement of Laws and Treaties (ELT) missions. Its maritime jurisdiction are divided into a hierarchically organized set of subdivisions called areas, districts and groups and stations. SAR and ELT cases represent unscheduled tasks of medium-to-high priority and require *reactive* resource planning. The decision makers determine how to allocate the resources under their jurisdiction so that all tasks are attended to as soon as possible and in the order of their merit.

The goal of SENTINEL is to produce the best plan of action for the tasks in the simulated world, given the constraints, restrictions and regulations under which the USCG operates. A *plan* consists of a resource-mix selection and an ordered set of mission steps (e.g., boarding, searching, etc.) to be carried out at designated locations. The primary performance metric is the interdiction rate for the total suspect traffic generated over a time period.

In Figure 1, Level-1 means that a Station (agent) may ask and get resources from the two adjacent ones "on loan", and Level-2 indicates that two additional farther Stations' resources may also be involved in the Dynamic Scoping process. Results are aggregated over 100 simulated days.

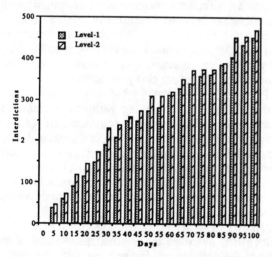

Figure 1: Interdiction Rates with Dynamic Scoping.

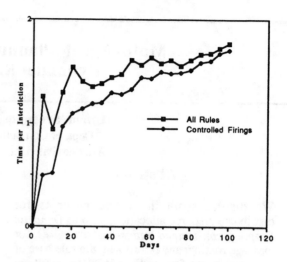

Figure 2: Average Interdiction Times.

Concerning *time-critical planning*, we have ordered the rules in the knowledge-base of an expert system whose task is resource selection for given tasks. Different subsets of rules are considered for tasks of different priorities. Figure 2 shows a comparison of the average times taken for an interdiction in the two sets of experiments.

The number of interdictions went up when Dynamic Scoping was extended from Level-1 to Level-2 expansion. The lattice-like message routing strategy fared better than the strictly hierarchical arrangement. The studies on time-critical planning indicate the effectiveness of the prioritized rule base and the controlled inference mechanism.

References

Cohen, P. R., Greenberg, M. L., Hart, D. M., & Howe, A. (1989). Trial by Fire: Understanding the Design Requirements for Agents in Complex Environments. *AI Magazine*, Fall, pp. 32–48.

Davis, R., and Smith. R. G. (1983). Negotiation as a Metaphor for Distributed Problem Solving. *Artificial Intelligence*, 20(1). pp. 63–109.

Dean, T. & Boddy, M. (1988). An Analysis of Time-Dependent Planning. In *Proc. of the National Conf. on Artificial Intelligence*, pp. 49–54 .

King, J. L. (1983). Centralized versus Decentralized Computing: Organizational Considerations and Management Options. *ACM Computing Surveys*, Vol. 15, No. 4. pp. 319–349.

Sengupta, U. K (1991). A Distributed Planning System for Dynamic Resource Allocation.*Unpublished Ph.D. Dissertation*, Dept. of Computer Science and Engineering, Arizona State University.

---

[1] The opinions or assertions contained herein are those of the authors and do not necessarily reflect the views of the U. S. Coast Guard.

A Critical Look at Knoblock's Hierarchy Mechanism

David E. Smith
Rockwell International
444 High St.
Palo Alto, CA 94301
de2smith@rpal.rockwell.com

Mark A. Peot
Rockwell International
444 High St.
Palo Alto, CA 94301
peot@rpal.rockwell.com

Abstract

Recently, Knoblock has advocated a mechanism for automatically constructing planning hierarchies. We show that Knoblock's method, and more generally, the principle of ordered monotonicity, can produce hierarchies that perform arbitrarily poorly. The reason is that Knoblock's technique addresses only one of two important factors in ordering clauses. We propose a technique for the other based on evaluating the number of potential solutions to different possible subgoals in a plan.

1 Knoblock's Method

Recently Knoblock [1, 2] has advocated a mechanism for automatically constructing fixed hierarchies to control planning search. The technique involves constructing a directed graph of potential conflicts between operators relevant to a goal. The graph is then broken into components and sorted to give the resulting hierarchy.

To illustrate Knoblock's approach consider a simplified machine shop example with the following operators for shaping, drilling, and painting an object:

Operator	Shape(x)
Precs:	Object(x)
Effects:	Shaped(x), ¬Drilled(x), ¬Painted(x)
Operator	Drill(x)
Precs:	Object(x)
Effects:	Drilled(x), ¬Painted(x)
Operator	Paint(x)
Precs:	Object(x), Steel(x)
Effects:	Painted(x)

Suppose that the goal is

$$\text{Shaped}(x) \wedge \text{Drilled}(x) \wedge \text{Painted}(x)$$

The graph that Knoblock would construct for this problem is:

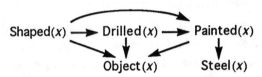

According to Knoblock's technique, the planner should work on Shaped(x) before Drilled(x) or Painted(x). After expanding Shaped(x), the planner should work on Object(x) (because it is unaffected by any operators). It should then work on Drilled(x) before Painted(x), and so on.

2 The Problem

Suppose that the initial conditions are such that there are 100 pieces of stock in the machine shop, but only one of them is made of steel. In this case, Knoblock's approach would have the planner hunt through and build partial plans for many pieces of stock before finding one that is steel, and hence amenable to painting. In contrast, if the planner were to start work on Painted(x) followed by Steel(x), very little search would be required.

As this example illustrates, Knoblock's technique can perform arbitrarily poorly in comparison to the optimal fixed hierarchy for a problem. More generally, *Ordered Monotonic* (OM) hierarchies [1, 3] have this unpleasant characteristic.

The problem is that there are two different reasons why a conjunctive goal may be more difficult to solve than the two conjuncts taken independently:

1. Action interference,
2. Variable binding conflicts.

Knoblock's technique and OM attempt to address the first of these; they order clauses to minimize interference between actions. In fact, Knoblock's technique imposes more ordering constraints than necessary to accomplish this task. In the example above, all possible operator conflicts can be resolved by simple temporal ordering constraints among the actions in the plan. These ordering constraints are detected and resolved by a non-linear planning system. This is discussed further in [6].

3 Evaluating Clause Difficulty

In our machine shop example, the primary difficulty is related to variable binding conflicts; i.e. finding a variable binding for x that allows a solution to all three goal clauses. Knoblock's technique and OM have nothing to say about this.

One approach to this problem is to estimate the number of possible solutions to each clause and order the clauses to minimize the size of the resulting search space. For the example above, it is relatively easy to see how this might be accomplished. For the clause Shaped(x), there is only one possible operator that applies and its precondition Object(x) has 100 different solutions. As a result, there are 100 possible solutions to Shaped(x). Similarly, Drilled(x) has 100 possible solutions. For the clause Painted(x), only one possible operator applies, which has two preconditions Object(x) and Steel(x). Object(x) has 100 solutions, but Steel(x) has only one, so the conjunction has at most one solution. This means that Painted(x) has at most one solution.

The clause Painted(x) therefore has the fewest possible solutions. If the planner starts with that clause only one solution will be considered for the other two clauses and a minimal amount of search is done.

The possibility of recursion among the operators, adds additional complexity to the problem of calculating the number of solutions for clauses. Techniques for dealing with this are described in [6].

4 Conclusion

To control search in planning, we need a much better means of estimating the difficulty of solving the goals and subgoals in a planning problem. Knoblock's technique and OM attempt to address one aspect of this problem; estimating action interference between subgoals. However, these techniques impose unnecessary and sometimes detrimental ordering constraints.

A second, and equally important aspect of problem difficulty is recognizing possible variable binding conflicts between goal clauses. Ordering clauses to minimize the size of the search space is a key to minimizing such conflicts. Doing this requires the ability to estimate the number of solutions possible for each different goal clause. We have given a hint as to how this might be accomplished and are currently implementing and evaluating this technique (see [6]).

Acknowledgments

Thanks to Craig Knoblock, Steve Minton, Qiang Yang and anonymous reviewers for comments and discussion. This work is supported by DARPA contract F30602-91-C-0031.

References

1. Knoblock, C., *Automatically Generating Abstractions for Problem Solving*, Report CMU-CS-91-120, Carnegie Mellon University, 1991.

2. Knoblock, C., Learning abstraction hierarchies for problem solving. In *Proc. 8th NCAI*, pages 923–928, Boston, MA, 1990.

3. Knoblock, C., Tenenberg, J., and Yang, C., Characterizing abstraction hierarchies for planning. In *Proc. 9th NCAI*, pages 692–697, Anaheim, CA, 1991.

4. Smith, D., Controlling Backward Inference, *Artificial Intelligence* 39(2):145–208, 1989.

5. Smith, D., *A Decision Theoretic Approach to the Control of Planning Search*, Report LOGIC-87-11, Department of Computer Science, Stanford University, 1988.

6. Smith, D., and Peot, M., *Ordering Clauses in Nonlinear Planning*, Technical Report, Rockwell International, Palo Alto Laboratory, 1992.

On Traffic Laws for Mobile Robots
(Extended Abstract)

Yoav Shoham and Moshe Tennenholtz
Robotics Lab
Department of Computer Science
Stanford University
Stanford, CA 94305

1. Introduction

The motivation underlying the work described in this abstract is a theory of social laws in a computational environment, laws which guarantee successful coexistence of multiple programs and programmers in a shared environment.

To illustrate the issues that come up when designing a society, consider the domain of mobile robots. Although still relatively simple, state-of-the-art mobile robots are able to perform several sorts of tasks. However, when we consider gathering several robots in a shared environment, a host of new problems arises. The activities of the robots might interfere with one another, and robots may require the assistance of other robots to carry out their task.

How is one to deal with these phenomena? There are two extreme answers, neither of which is in general acceptable. One is to assume a single designer, whose job it is to program all the robots. This answer is unsatisfactory for many reasons: It is unreasonable to expect that a single individual will control all agents, the set of agents can be expected to change over time and one would hardly want to have to reprogram all agents upon each addition or deletion of an agent, etc.

An alternative extreme answer is to admit that agents will be programmed individually in an unconstrained fashion, and to equip the agents with the means for handling these interactions during execution. These means may take various forms. For example, one approach is to merely detect the interactions as they occur, and appeal to a central supervisor for resolution. An alternative method for handling interactions is to equip the agents with communication capabilities, and program them to engage in series of communications to resolve interactions. Again, using the domain of mobile robots for illustration, when two robots note that they are on a collision course with one another, they may either appeal to some central traffic controller for coordination advice, or alternatively they might engage in a negotiation resulting (say) in each robot moving slightly to its right. Nonetheless, there are limitations to this second approach as well. By placing no constraints in advance, the number of interactions may be prohibitive; either the central arbiter may be deluged by pleas, or else agents will have to enter into negotiations at every step. While we certainly do not argue against the utility of either a central coordinator or a negotiation mechanism, we do argue that it is essential to add a mechanism that will minimize the need for either. Again, we draw on the domain of mobile robots for intuition. Suppose robots navigate along marked paths, much like cars do along streets. Why not adopt a convention, or, as we'd like to think of it, a social law, according to which each robot keeps to the right of the path? If each robot obeys the convention, we will have avoided all head-on collisions without any need for either a central arbiter or negotiation.

This then is the image we have. The society will adopt a set of laws; each programmer will obey these laws, and will be able to assume that all others will as well. These laws will on the one hand constrain the plans available to the programmer, but on the other hand will guarantee certain behaviors on the part of other agents. In an accompanied paper[1] we develop an abstract theory of computational societies, augmenting some universal computational framework with additional ingredients which capture the societal aspects. In this abstract we illustrate the society metaphor in a particular domain of application. Our full paper includes many additional details and extensions.

2. The multi-robot grid system

The domain we investigate will be called the *multi-robot grid system*. It consists of an $n \times n$ grid, and

---

[1] "On the synthesis of useful social laws for artificial agents societies", to appear in the proceedings of AAAI-92.

a set of m robots. At each point in time each robot is located at some grid coordinate. The fact that several robots occupy the same coordinate denotes a collision among them; part of our goal as designers of the system will be to ensure that collisions are avoided. We assume that each robot has the capability at each stage to move to one of its neighbor coordinates or stay in place. Each such operation lasts a certain amount of time and consumes a certain amount of energy. We assume that movement to a neighbor coordinate takes one time unit and consumes one energy unit, unless this motion follows a stop (that is, taken from a resting position). In the latter case we assume that movement to a neighbor coordinate takes c time units and consumes c energy units, where $c > 1$. Remaining motionless wastes no energy. In the following we assume that each robot in the multi-robot grid system is able to perceive robots that are at a distance of one coordinate away from it (including robots that are at a distance of one on both rows and columns).

At random times robots are given target locations, and their goal is to reach those destinations, minimizing either time, or energy consumption.

The job of the programmer of the individual robots will be to implement an efficient path-planning program. Our job as designers of this small social system will be to impose on it traffic laws which will guarantee that no collisions will occur – provided that all programmers abide by the law. We will be interested in traffic laws that allow robots to reach their destinations without collision in a reasonably efficient manner.

3. An efficient traffic law

The basic idea is to adopt familiar traffic laws such as giving way to a robot arriving from the right. However, naive laws of this kind quickly give rise to deadlocks and related problems, and so we will craft a somewhat more sophisticated law. The law is as follows:

1. Superimpose on the original grid a coarser one. The squares of the coarser grid will be sub-grids of size $2m \times 2m$ of the original grid. A sketch of the "multi-grid" created appears in figure 1.

2. In odd rows of the coarse grid robots will be required to move only right, while in even rows of it they will be required to move only left. In odd columns of the coarse grid robots will be required to move only down while in even columns of it they will be required to move only up. In junctions of the coarse grid, priority will be given on the basis of "first in first out."

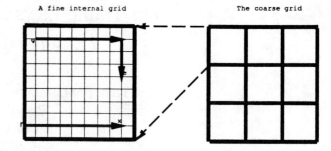

Figure 1: A coarse grid imposed on the fine grid

3. While a robot is moving along the coarse grid then it is allowed to change its movement direction (from "along a row" to "along a column" and vice versa) only k times before leaving the coarse grid.

4. Inside each $2m \times 2m$ grid each robot will move in the following way (see figure 1): The entrance point to the grid will be from the leftmost coordinate of the row denoted by r. The robot will then be required to move along the row r to the coordinate denoted by x. During the movement along r, if the robot perceives the existence of a robot in the coordinate in front of it or finds that it reached x then it has to stop and wait for $2n + cmk$ time units. Then, it has to continue (if still necessary) along r to x. After reaching that coordinate (x) and waiting there (if still necessary) for the above mentioned period, the robot has to reach the coordinate denoted by g in exactly $4m - 2$ steps without entering any of the areas appearing in thick lines in figure 1. Afterwards, the robot will be required to move from g to the coordinate denoted by e along the path appearing in thick lines in figure 1, and leave that grid from there.

5. Robots are not allowed to stop moving unless the robot in front of them does not move or when they are required otherwise by the social law.

6. The points of return from an $2m \times 2m$ grid to the coarse grid will be considered as additional junctions of the coarse grid.

Assuming that there are $m = O(\sqrt{n})$ robots in the $n \times n$ multi-robot grid system, we can show:

Theorem: The above traffic law guarantees that no collisions occur, and that given a goal which can be achieved in isolation in t time and energy units, there exists a plan that achieves it in $t + 2n + o(n)$ time units, and (for t satisfying $m = o(t)$) in $t + o(t)$ energy units.

The above traffic law guarantees close to optimal energy consumption. If c is relatively small, then a minor modification of the above traffic law guarantees close to optimal time consumption also.

When Goals Aren't Good Enough

Christopher N. Toomey
Stanford University
Lockheed AI Center
O/96-20 B/254F, 3251 Hanover St.
Palo Alto, CA 94304
toomey@laic.lockheed.com

Abstract

This paper discusses the limitations of goals in expressing one's planning objectives and presents the decision-theoretic *value function* as an attractive alternative. An approach for planning to maximize value rather than to satisfy goals is then discussed.

1 INTRODUCTION

Most work in AI planning has addressed *how* to achieve a set of goals that are assumed to adequately represent *what* one is trying to achieve. Unfortunately, the fact that goals are an extremely impoverished representation of objectives has only recently begun to be addressed in the planning community [Wellman, 1988, Haddawy and Hanks, 1990, Wellman and Doyle, 1991]. Goals can only discriminate between two large classes of outcomes: those in which all of the goals are satisfied (the "good" outcomes) and those in which at least one goal is unsatisfied (the "bad" outcomes). The implication is that all "good" outcomes are equally desirable and all "bad" outcomes are equally undesirable.

Most of the time, however, one can discriminate further between the outcomes in each of these broad classes. For example, an outcome in which 90% of the goals are satisfied would likely be more desirable than one in which only 10% were. Another basis for discrimination could be the degree to which the various individual goals are satisfied. When a set of goals is distilled and handed off to the planner, however, all of this preference information is lost. The selection of goals thus becomes a critical decision: setting them too low leads to underachievement, while setting them too high leads to empty-handedness after the planner fails.

Consider a production planning problem wherein a set of parts is to be manufactured by specified due dates. Ideally, one would give a planner the set of parts and their deadlines as goals and receive back a plan that manufactures all the parts by their deadlines. If the shop is realistic and thereby constrained by limited resources, however, it's very likely that all of the deadlines could not be met and the planner would thus fail. One could guess at how to sufficiently slip the deadlines to make them achievable and try the planner again, but this would become quite tiresome after a few iterations.

A more appealing solution would be to circumvent the goal-setting procedure altogether by giving the planner a richer description of one's preferences and allowing it to achieve the best outcome that it can. The remainder of this paper describes an approach for realizing such a solution.

2 VALUE FUNCTIONS

One can turn to decision theory for a principled and expressive means of representing preferences [Henrion *et al.*, 1988, Keeney and Raiffa, 1976]. If one subscribes to its simple axioms governing normative thought, then one must have a weak preference ordering over any possible set of outcomes. That is, for any two outcomes o_1 and o_2, one must either prefer o_1 to o_2, prefer o_2 to o_1, or be indifferent between the two. The fact that such an ordering exists implies that there must also exist a scalar-valued *value function* $v(o)$ such that $v(o_1) > v(o_2)$ if and only if o_1 is preferable to o_2.

Thus one can completely capture one's preferences over the possible outcomes of a situation via a value function. The usual procedure for constructing a value function is to identify the set of attributes that are relevant when valuating outcomes and then to define the value function in terms of those attributes. In the production problem above, for example, assume that the shop was trying to minimize the maximum tardiness of the scheduled parts. Then the attributes would be the tardiness T_i of each part and the value function $v(T_1, T_2, \ldots, T_n) = -max(T_1, T_2, \ldots, T_n)$.

3 VALUE-BASED PLANNING

How is one to find a plan that maximizes value rather than one that satisfies a set of goals? Our approach to this value-based planning problem is to decompose it into two separate but interacting subproblems. The first subproblem addresses *what* to achieve and thus explores points in the outcome space over which the value function is defined. The second subproblem addresses *how* to achieve a particular outcome deemed to be worth achieving. An outcome selected during the *what* phase is passed to the *how* phase, which returns either a plan that achieves the outcome or an indication that the outcome is unachievable.

Once a particular outcome is selected during the *what* phase, a set of goals can be fashioned from the attribute settings defining the outcome. Thus we can use existing goal-based (GB) planning technology to tackle the *how* subproblem.

The *what* subproblem is to find the highest-valued achievable outcome and return the plan that achieves it. Our basic approach is to perform a best-first search over the outcome space, which is represented as an n-dimensional grid (where n is the number of attributes defined for the value function). The search begins at the outcome corresponding to the initial state and moves to neighboring points in the grid. During this search the GB planner is periodically invoked to achieve selected outcomes, and when a user-defined termination criterion is met the plan achieving the highest-valued outcome visited is returned.

While the basic idea is straightforward, there are several key issues that have to be addressed in order to build a practical system. The first issue is when to invoke the GB planner during the search through the outcome space. We are evaluating several strategies, ranging from a simplistic approach that invokes the planner every time an outcome better than the best achievable outcome so far is visited to an approach that delays plan construction until a locally maximal outcome is reached. The latter approach is complicated by the need for a backtracking strategy to be employed when the local maximum turns out to be unachievable.

The second key issue is what to do upon reaching an unachievable outcome. This can be detected not only from the failure of the GB planner to find a plan, but also via a user-supplied `unachievable` function provided as a means for conveying *a priori* domain knowledge about unachievable outcomes. Although this issue is interrelated to the previous one, we see two general strategies. One is to be optimistic about the extent of the unachievable region (or lack thereof) and continue the search in the same neighborhood. The other is to be pessimistic and seek out a new region to explore via a randomization technique.

The last key issue is how to combat the potential high-dimensionality of the outcome space. In such cases escaping from local maxima via best-first search can become intractable. Randomization techniques have proven to be effective against high-dimensional configuration spaces explored by a potential-field path planner [Barraquand *et al.*, 1989], however, so we are encouraged about the prospects of similar techniques for this problem.

4 CONCLUSION

Goals have too coarse a granularity for adequately expressing one's objectives in many situations. A much more expressive representation is provided by the decision-theoretic *value function*. This paper has outlined an approach for planning to maximize value rather than planning to achieve goals and has discussed some of the key issues in realizing such an approach. Work is continuing on the further development and implementation of the ideas presented here.

Acknowledgements

Thanks to my advisor at Stanford, Jean-Claude Latombe, and to Raj Doshi, Rich Pelavin, and David Hinkle of the Lockheed AI Center for useful discussions.

References

[Barraquand *et al.*, 1989] J. Barraquand, B. Langlois, and J. C. Latombe. Numerical potential field techniques for robot path planning. Technical Report STAN-CS-89-1257, Department of Computer Science, Stanford University, 1989.

[Haddawy and Hanks, 1990] Peter Haddawy and Steve Hanks. Issues in decision-theoretic planning: Symbolic goals and numeric utilities. In *Proceedings of the Workshop on Innovative Approaches to Planning, Scheduling, and Control*, 1990.

[Henrion *et al.*, 1988] Max Henrion, John S. Breese, and Eric J. Horvitz. Decision theory in expert systems and artificial intelligence. *International Journal of Approximate Reasoning*, 2:247–302, 1988.

[Keeney and Raiffa, 1976] Ralph L. Keeney and Howard Raiffa. *Decisions with Multiple Objectives: Preferences and Value Tradeoffs*. John Wiley & Sons, New York, 1976.

[Wellman and Doyle, 1991] Michael P. Wellman and Jon Doyle. Preferential semantics for goals. In *Proceedings of AAAI-91*, 1991.

[Wellman, 1988] Michael P. Wellman. Formulation of tradeoffs in planning under uncertainty. Technical Report TR-427, MIT Laboratory for Computer Science, August 1988.

Efficient Temporal Reasoning for Plan Projection

Mike Williamson & Steve Hanks
Dept. of CS and Eng., Univ. of Washington, Seattle, WA 98195
mikew@cs.washington.edu, hanks@cs.washington.edu

Abstract

Efficient and expressive temporal reasoning
can only be achieved by taking advantage of
regularities within the structure of the domain. We present a novel temporal reasoning
system which demonstrates this approach,
applied to the task of temporal projection.

1 Introduction

We take *temporal reasoning* to be the problem of maintaining a set of constraints between time points and/or
intervals, and responding to queries about the temporal separation between those individuals. Formal
investigations of this constraint-satisfaction problem
have yielded clear tradeoffs between the expressive
power of the constraint language and the time required
to answer queries. A simple constraint language admits an algorithm cubic in the number of temporal
individuals, whereas allowing unrestricted disjunctive
constraints makes the algorithm exponential [Vilain
et al. 1989,Dechter and others 1991]. [Dean and
McDermott 1987], and [Kautz and Ladkin 1991] report on implementations of these domain-independent
algorithms. These formal results about temporal-
reasoning algorithms are troublesome. The problem
is that many applications of temporal reasoning, *e.g.*
plan projection, need both disjunctive constraints and
an algorithm *much* faster than $O(n^3)$. It is significant,
however, that the nature of the constraints added by
and the queries posed by an application tend to be
structured and predictable. Our solution to the problem is to exploit the structure of the application domain to provide fast responses to typical queries.

2 The Plan Projection Problem

We demonstrate our approach by considering a particular application domain for temporal reasoning, plan
projection under uncertainty [Hanks 1990]. The projector is given a plan and a partial description of the

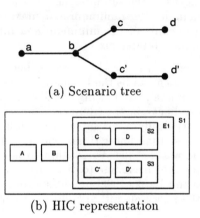

(a) Scenario tree

(b) HIC representation

Figure 1: Projection Example

world, and builds a *scenario tree*, which is a temporal trace of the plan's execution. Each path through
the tree is one possible course of execution. Our plan
language consists of *simple actions*, each of which may
have many possible *outcomes*, depending on the conditions that hold when it is executed, and *complex actions*, which represent sequential, parallel, conditional,
and iterative execution of simple actions.

The projector will create a branch in the scenario tree
whenever there is uncertainty about the outcome of
an action. For example, consider projecting a plan
such as (**sequence** *a b c d*). Suppose that the projector can identify a single outcome for each action
except *c*, which has two possible outcomes, depending
on the truth value of some proposition which is currently unknown. Figure 1(a) shows what the scenario
tree would look like. The nodes in the tree represent
the outcomes of the primitive actions in the plan. The
projector has to answer temporal queries like "how
long will the plan take to execute?" and "will this
segment of the plan take more than 15 minutes?" We
will next describe the Hierarchical Interval Constraint
structure, which is an attempt to mimic the sorts of
temporal structures generated by the projector.

3 Hierarchical Interval Constraints

A hierarchical interval constraint (HIC) represents an interval of time, which may comprise one or more sub-intervals. The HIC's duration depends on the durations of its subintervals and on its *type*. HIC types represent various temporal reasoning situations, some of which cannot be represented as simple temporal constraint graphs. Interval types *simple, sequence, selection,* and *parallel* support the projection task. A *simple* HIC corresponds to a simple action. It has no sub-intervals, and its temporal length must be specified explicitly by the application. Durations for the other types, known as *complex* HICs, are calculated from the lengths of the sub-intervals. For a *sequence* HIC, for example, the minimum and maximum duration are the sums of the minimum and maximum durations of its sub-intervals.

Temporal queries ask for the distance between two time points, which can be the beginning or end of any hierarchical interval. Computing this distance requires time at most linear in the number of intervals, but queries that typically occur in practice often require significantly less than linear time. The HIC structure effectively allows the query algorithm to ignore constraints which are irrelevant to the particular query. [Williamson and Hanks 1992] provides a complete discussion of the query algorithm and its computational complexity.

Figure 1(b) shows the interval structure produced by projecting the plan in Figure 1(a). The smallest boxes are *simple* intervals that represent the outcomes of each action. E1 is a *selection* interval that represents the fork in the scenario tree. It represents the fact that exactly one of the branches will be traversed at execution time. S1, S2 and S3 are *sequence* intervals. S1 represents the temporal interval over which the entire plan is carried out. Queries could be made about the temporal distance separating the beginning or end of any pair of intervals in the structure.

4 Empirical Results

We implemented our projector on top of three different temporal reasoning modules: our own HIC system, the Metric/Allen Time System (MATS) of Kautz and Ladkin [1991], and the temporal reasoning component of Dean's [1987] TMM. For each we projected plans that generated scenario trees of various sizes, then performed 100 random temporal queries. Table 1 shows the time (in msec) required for projection and query processing.

Note that the query time required by the MATS system is cubic in the size of the scenario tree, making it infeasible for larger problems. TMM's temporal reasoning mechanism required linear time to answer

Scenario Size	HIC		TMM		MATS	
	Project	Query	Project	Query	Project	Query
25	33	366	834	11984	133	4583
51	134	1033	3101	27067	350	34133
101	200	1050	12633	64983	1050	256250
201	434	1233	61717	173584	—	—

Table 1: Time for projection and 100 temporal queries

queries, but seemed to require quadratic time to construct the original constraint graph. Our HIC system required only linear time for projection and performed queries in sublinear time, suggesting that our system is capable of handling projection problems several orders of magnitude larger than either of the others.

5 Conclusion

Our paper has shown how to build an efficient temporal reasoning module by exploiting regularities both in the constraints added by the application and in the queries posed. A temporal projector using our module dramatically outperformed current domain-independent systems. It is clear that if a temporal-reasoning system is to be of practical value to a realistic implementation, it will have to have *some* model of its applications' behavior. Identifying a set of HIC-like structures offers a promising means of providing functionality midway between truly domain-independent temporal reasoning and problem-specific programs.

Acknowledgements

This work was supported in part by NSF grant IRI–9008670 and by an NSF Graduate Fellowship.

References

[Dean and McDermott 1987] T. Dean and D. McDermott. Temporal data base management. *Artificial Intelligence*, 32(1), April 1987.

[Dechter *et al.* 1991] R. Dechter, I. Meiri, and J. Pearl. Temporal Constraint Networks. *Artificial Intelligence*, 49, May 1991.

[Hanks 1990] S. Hanks. Practical Temporal Projection. In *Proceedings of AAAI-90*, August 1990.

[Kautz and Ladkin 1991] H. A. Kautz and P. B. Ladkin. Integrating Metric and Qualitative Temporal Reasoning. In *Proceedings of AAAI-91*, July 1991.

[Vilain *et al.* 1989] M. Vilain, H. Kautz, and P. van Beek. Constraint propagation Algorithms for Temporal reasoning: A Revised Report. In *Readings in Qualitative Reasoning about Physical Systems*. Morgan Kaufmann, San Mateo, CA, 1989.

[Williamson and Hanks 1992] Mike Williamson and Steve Hanks. Informed temporal reasoning. Technical report, University of Washington, Department of Computer Science, 1992. Forthcoming.

Author Index